D1610904

KING ALFRED'S COLLEGE
WINCHESTER

To be returned on or before the day marked
below :—

29. MAR 1..?/		
15. FEB. 1983		
2 1 JAN 2008	WITHDRAWN FROM THE LIBRARY UNIVERSITY OF WINCHESTER	

PLEASE ENTER ON ISSUE SLIP:

AUTHOR $\underline{DOYLE}$

TITLE $\underline{Parlement \ of \ Bordeaux}$

ACCESSION No. $\underline{47760}$

THE PARLEMENT
OF BORDEAUX AND THE END
OF THE OLD REGIME
1771-1790

THE PARLEMENT
OF BORDEAUX AND
THE END
OF THE OLD
REGIME 1771-1790

WILLIAM DOYLE

ERNEST BENN LIMITED
LONDON & TONBRIDGE

First published 1974 by Ernest Benn Limited
25 New Street Square, Fleet Street, London EC4A 3JA
& Sovereign Way, Tonbridge, Kent TN9 1RW

Distributed in Canada by
The General Publishing Company Limited, Toronto

© *William Doyle 1974*

ISBN 0 510–26210–4

Printed in Great Britain

To

my mother

and to the memory of my father

Stanley Joseph Doyle

(1910-1973)

Preface

IN THE ENDLESS debate on the French Revolution more and more attention has recently been focussed on the problem of its origins. Historians seem increasingly agreed that the ultimate meaning of the Revolution cannot be understood without more analysis of how and why it came about. The present work was undertaken in the belief that the most important questions about the Revolution are questions about the old régime.

In the collapse of the old régime, a crucial and spectacular role was played by the parlements. This problem too, after years of fossilization in the most rigid of orthodox interpretations, is now attracting renewed attention. François Bluche, Jean Meyer, and Robert Forster, for example, have all studied the social and economic importance of noblemen and magistrates in extensive and very rewarding detail. In compiling Part I of this work, I have been guided throughout by the model studies of such formidable pioneers. Similarly, scholars like Jean Egret and J. H. Shennan have re-examined the political attitudes and public role of parlements, with illuminating results which show how undeserved is the current neglect of the old régime's political history. Their example encouraged me in the writing of Part II.

So if this book has any originality, it does not lie either in the problems it examines, or in the methods used. It seems rather to reside in the attempt to combine social and political history in roughly equal proportions. Social historians (and those who have studied the parlements among them) too readily assume that political behaviour is automatically conditioned and explained by social and economic circumstances, and therefore that it needs little further examination. Political historians often neglect or take for granted the social circumstances of those whom they study. Neither attitude seems very healthy. Part I of this book began, in the form of an Oxford D.Phil. thesis, as an exclusively social study. But in the course of researching for this, I became convinced that such a narrow approach left too many important questions without satisfactory answers; especially when even the basic outlines of the parlement of Bordeaux's political history in these years were largely unknown. So Part II evolved; in which I hope, by setting the story of the last public years of the parlement alongside a description of its members' private circumstances, to show just how much, and how little, the politics of the parlement reflected those circumstances, and were explained by them. The result, indeed, remains far from clear; but it is at least certain that the link between social standing and political action was far more baffling and complex than conventional assumptions tend to allow.

I hope, too, that this book will help to fill a number of gaps. It adds Bordeaux to the growing list of parlements whose members or whose political activities have been studied in detail in this period. In this way it should contribute to a more complete general picture. Equally, it is a contribution to the history of a city better known and studied in the 18th century for its merchants. The history of Bordeaux is currently being completely renovated by a brilliant group of local scholars. One enters with trepidation into such a company. Even so, the social and economic structure of the 18th-century parlement has never been analysed in any depth before, nor has anything substantial been written on its political history for almost a century. If it has been left to a foreigner to attempt these tasks, he hopes that native experts will view his labours as a compliment to the fascinations of their city and its history.

Important defects undoubtedly remain. Areas of great significance, notably the parlement's role as a law court, and its social attitudes as revealed in its judicial decisions, are not treated. This is perhaps a serious flaw at a time when criminality as a social phenomenon is attracting increasing attention from historians. But although the relevant records exist in abundance, as yet they are unclassified, so I leave this problem for others to explore. And I certainly hope that this work as it stands does not suffer irreparably from such omissions. After all, the distinctive character of parlements was that they were far more than simply courts of law; it is this that made them historically so important.

Purists will not excuse the inconsistencies of the text. It is in English, but the quotations are in French. This is because I assume that most potential readers, though English-speakers, will be at least French-readers. It also helps to preserve the inimitable flavour of the originals, impossible to convey into another language. In all cases the original spelling and punctuation have been preserved, including the quite random distribution of accents practised by most 18th-century Frenchmen. On the other hand, I have tried wherever possible to translate all technical terms and titles which occur in the text into English, in order not to interrupt the flow with too many italics. Only those terms which appear to be beyond convenient and obvious translation have been left in French, and those whose meaning might not be self-evident are followed, the first time they appear, by a translation in brackets. The only exceptions are the terms *arrêt* and *arrêté*, and it might avoid a certain confusion if their meanings, and the differences between them, are explained here. An *arrêt* was a public decision of a court of law; an *arrêté* was a resolution concerning a court's internal procedures. It should be clear at once how difficult a direct and precise English translation would be.

No work like this would have been possible without the aid of grants. It was begun with a state-studentship; it was continued with the help of the University of York and the Twenty-Seven Foundation. To these bodies I am extremely grateful. Nor could any book have been produced without the kind help I received at the various archives and libraries in which I needed to work. Most of the groundwork by far was done in the extremely congenial surroundings of the Archives Départementales de la Gironde, whose staff I remember with particular affection and gratitude. Most of the writing has been done at York, where the friendly atmosphere and generous arrangements of the History Department have contributed much to the pleasure and speed with which the work was accomplished.

Otherwise my greatest debts are to individuals. Some of them may have forgotten the help they gave, but I have not. My attention was first drawn to Bordeaux by Professor Robert Forster, and his original advice was invaluable. I hope that he will regard my petty disagreements with some of his conclusions as a tribute to their pioneer quality. Among Frenchmen whose help and suggestions I have found invaluable at one stage or another, I should like to thank M. Piquard, *conservateur en chef des bibliothèques de l'Université de Paris*, M. le Proviseur of the Lycée Louis-le-Grand, the late marquis Du Paty de Clam, Comte Emmanuel Du Paty de Clam, the late M. Alain d'Anglade, Professor J. Godechot, Professor Michel Antoine, M. A. Gazier, M. Marc Perrichet, M. Paul Butel, M. Daniel Roche, M. Dominique Julia, M. J.-P. Avisseau, M. P. de Peguilhan de Larboust, and Mlle M. T. Bouyssy. Above all I have benefited enormously in Bordeaux from discussions and contacts with my good friend Jean-Pierre Poussou, whose work on Bordelais society promises one day to humble us all.

Among fellow-foreigners, I found correspondence with Perry Viles and frequent discussions with Robert B. Wheaton of great help. Dr Robert Shackleton and Professor J. S. Bromley, in their capacity as examiners, also made me aware of many possible improvements. Professor Bromley's kind interest since that time has played a major part in bringing the book to publication. Dr John M. Roberts supervised my researches as a graduate student, and his encouragement and advice have been a constant benefit. Similarly, this would have been a very different, and a much inferior, book without the frequent discussions which I enjoyed over three years with John Rogister, whose knowledge of French 18th-century politics is unrivalled. Need I add that any flaws or defects were achieved without the help of anybody?

Finally I must thank Christine. Though untrained as either, she has patiently played the secretary and the historical critic during the preparation of this book. This has involved her in the follies and exasperations of the Bordeaux magistrates to an extent that I would wish upon nobody but myself. I hope she does not feel that, in marriage to an 18th-century historian, the spirit of the *corvée* lives on.

York   W.D.
December 1973

Contents

Abbreviations

Maps

Bordeaux and its Parlement

'Bourdeaux', wrote an English traveller in 1775,

> yields to very few cities in point of beauty; for it appears to have all that opulence which an extensive commerce can confer. It is finely situated on the banks of the *Garonne*, . . . The quay which is extended on a straight line, for more than two miles, with a range of regular buildings, cannot fail of striking the eye with admiration; which is encreased by the noble appearance of an immense rapid river, and the multitude of ships and vessels which trade here.[1]

Arthur Young, passing through 12 years later, agreed. Indeed he was almost carried away by the sight. 'Much as I had read and heard of the commerce, wealth, and magnificence of this city', he declared, 'they greatly surpassed my expectations. Paris did not answer at all, for it is not to be compared to London; but we must not name Liverpool in competition with Bordeaux'. The new streets of white stone houses were 'truly magnificent', and improvements still projected, 'splendid'; the great new theatre was 'by far the most magnificent in France. I have seen nothing that approaches it'. And as he was ferried across the still-unbridged river to continue his journey, Young observed that: 'The view of the Garonne is very fine, appearing to the eye twice as broad as the Thames at London, and the number of large ships lying in it, makes it, I suppose, the *richest* water-view that France has to boast'.[2]

For it was wealth, prodigious and unashamed, that attracted the curious to Bordeaux; whether it was the Emperor Joseph II, or princes of the French Blood Royal, or any of a host of important if less distinguished visitors. Bordeaux was expanding and renovating itself in sumptuous style. There were sites everywhere, and the peace of the town was frequently disturbed by riotous bands of stone-masons.[3] Around the walls of the old town now ran spacious boulevards lined with graceful new houses, and punctuated by handsome squares.[4] Even larger schemes were now in contemplation; there was a plan to build a canal round the city, and in 1785 it was decided to demolish and level the *Château Trompette*, a fortress built by Louis XIV in less placid days to control the roadstead and dominate the restive city. The plan was to replace it with an immense and grandiose *Place Ludovise*, comprising 1,800 houses and 13 converging streets. 'It would, if executed, be one of the most splendid additions to a city', wrote Young, 'that is to be seen in Europe'.[5]

The city's amenities were equal to their setting. The hotels were the most comfortable in the south of France, and the cabs were better than those of Paris.[6] The theatres could afford Parisian performers at Parisian prices, and offered a wide range of dramatic and musical entertainment day and night throughout the week.[7] There was a public park, a pleasure garden, and many fashionable gaming houses.[8] Cagliostro made a comfortable living for many months in the early 1780s from introducing rich and credulous citizens to his mystic health cures,[9] and indeed there was no novelty which the fashionable world of the town overlooked. In the hectic atmosphere of money-making and money spending, less transient values had perhaps been neglected, and the corruption and irreligion for which the city was notorious were not diminished by the activities of a sleepy university and an exclusive, self-regarding academy. But nothing was beyond improvement, and in the 1780s friends of mankind endowed a Philanthropic Society to channel the profits of trade into benevolence; while those with a taste for serious subjects, literary or practical, combined to form the *musée*.[10]

Bordeaux under Louis XVI was at the height of a prosperity and European fame unequalled in its history. First impressions are not always faithful, but in this case they were. From the first thing all visitors from the north saw, the road-stead of the 'port of the moon' thronged with ships from all parts of Europe and America, it was clear that trade was the source of the city's wealth, and that the expansion of the 18th century was a veritable boom. In 1715 the population of the city was only slightly more than twice what it had been three centuries before.[11] Immigrants, attracted by the apparently limitless opportunities for employment and enrichment that the city seemed to offer, had doubled it to nearly 110,000 by 1790.[12] Old men in 1774 could still remember the quieter days of Louis XIV, when the Bordelais had made their money by exporting their wines to Holland and the lands of the North. This still went on, and wine exports on the eve of the Revolution were 56 per cent higher than in the early decades of the century.[13] Bordeaux exported rather less than one-half of its product, whereas for the whole of France the proportion was only something like 10 per cent.[14] However, the really spectacular growth was in the colonial trade, the provisioning of the French West Indies, and the re-export of their precious sugar and coffee to the whole of Europe. If wine exports rose by a half, the commerce of Bordeaux as a whole rose almost 20 times in value, from 13m. livres to almost 250m. livres between 1717 and 1787,[15] and its share of French commerce rose from 11 per cent to one-quarter.[16] This staggering rise was almost entirely the result of the growth of the colonial trade. The colonies were the source of the fabled wealth of the merchant princes of Bordeaux, which they displayed with such ostentation in their huge houses, sumptuous furnishings, and expensive pleasures. 'The mode of living that takes place here among merchants is highly luxurious', wrote Young.

> Their houses and establishments are on expensive scales. Great entertain-ments, and many served on plate. High play is a much worse thing; and the scandalous chronicle speaks of merchants keeping the dancing and singing girls of the theatre at salaries which ought to import no good to their credit.[17]

John Adams, fresh from the pure air of America in 1778, was shocked by the brazen behaviour of the ladies of fashion, and reflected that the French were not made of the stern stuff which founded republics.[18] It was as if the Bordelais, living for the pleasures of the moment, realized that their soaring prosperity was not as stable as it was spectacular. The profits to be made from arming ships for the Indies were certainly immense, but the outlay was also very high, and the risks of a voyage of 6,000 miles or more very great. When the perils of war with England were added, as they were four times during the century, to other more normal hazards, the long-distance trade of Bordeaux might collapse catastrophically, as it did in 1744 and 1758–59.[19] Indeed, even in times of peace,[20] violent year-to-year fluctuations were normal, and bankruptcy was as common as luxury.[21] To exploit the boom was to indulge in speculation on a grand scale, and the excitement and uncertainty which this bred was the dominant atmosphere in the city.

The decisive factor in Bordeaux's emergence as the European capital of the French West Indies seems to have been its rich agricultural hinterland. From here came surpluses of food for provisioning the precious islands, whose inhabitants preferred to devote every square foot to the lucrative sugar and coffee.[22] Even the expansion experienced by wine exports was mainly caused by the growth of the colonial market.[23] Most of the Bordelais, admittedly, was infertile. The *landes* began almost at the city's western gates and stretched all the way to the sea in the west, and southwards to the foothills of the Pyrenees, a semi-desert of marsh and heathland. Very thinly populated, they supported mostly large flocks of sheep and cattle, producing in addition resin, wax, and honey;[24] but their part in the economy of the Bordelais was small. Most of the agricultural wealth of the area was concentrated narrowly along the rivers, particularly the Garonne. From Toulouse down to Langon the river flowed through fertile cornlands, the source of most of the flour sent to the Indies, and much that went to other parts of France, too. The only really fertile land nearer to Bordeaux itself consisted of the narrow strips of the *alluvions* or *palus*, along the river banks, and at the Bec d'Ambès, where Garonne and Dordogne meet. These alone were suitable for any crop. Between the rivers and the *landes*, stretching over a hundred miles between Langon and the pointe de la Grave, was a gravelly strip, only a few miles wide, and hardly more fertile than the *landes* themselves. But it was perfect for growing vines. Not only was the soil unsuitable for anything else; the climate, with its wet springs, hot summers, and long dry autumns was also favourable. The situation of the port in the middle of the producing area made marketing easier, and facility of export stimulated production for something more than a local market. The result of centuries of development was that by the 18th century wine-growing in the Bordelais had reached an advanced level of sophistication. The area offered an unparalleled variety of wines, both in type and quality, within easy reach of the foreign buyer. By the mid-18th century the great *crus* were internationally known.[25] The markets for wines of this quality were hardly affected by the crisis of overproduction which affected French wine-growing in the later 18th century,[26] and even the production of coarser wines was sustained by the colonial market.[27] So the wine-growers were an economic group comparable in importance to the colonial merchants, and in fact the two overlapped considerably. They opposed all attempts to restrict the wine privilege of Bordeaux, under which local producers were given preference in the export of wine from the port, and they welcomed the commercial treaty of 1786 with England because of the favourable terms it offered for the sale of French wine in an opulent northern market.[28] In this, their interest in the port's prosperity, and that of the merchants who carried their products, was similar. On the other hand, their attachment to the land of the Bordelais was more than a mere investment; it was a way of life they had practised for centuries, rooted in a business where tradition and long experience were at a premium. Wine-growing was dominated by the Bordelais; but trade, the boom, was mainly in the hands of outsiders.[29] The true Bordelais was not a merchant, but an owner of vineyards who depended on others to distribute his product.

So the economic tentacles of Bordeaux stretched far. The West Indies looked to her as their European capital; northern Europe looked to her for fine wines and the products of the Isles; and the whole Garonne valley, and to a lesser extent that of the Dordogne too, saw the port as a natural outlet and a natural market. At the focus of many trade routes, economically speaking Bordeaux was a metropolis. This very fact made it a social metropolis, too, a magnet to fortune-hunters from the whole south-west, and the place which set the tone even for West Indian society. And long before America had even been heard of, the city had been an ecclesiastical, administrative, and political capital. The prosperity of the 18th century only made these arrangements more obvious, as the intendants channelled colonial wealth into grandiose projects of embellishment, which both flattered the citizens and proclaimed the king's majesty.

The oldest-established authority in the city was the archbishop. Presiding over a province with nine suffragans, and a city whose clerical population approached twelve hundred,[30] he was one of the most powerful men in Guienne. The fact that he was always a courtier, who owed his position to his interest at Versailles, only underlined his political importance, and he was frequently employed as an agent of the government, both locally and nationally. At the accession of Louis XVI the archbishop was the prince de Rohan,[31] and it was he who transformed the old archiepiscopal residence, 'a large, old, irregular structure, tho' not without some good Apartments',[32] into the sumptuous and regular palace which still faces the Cathedral of St André. By the time Champion de Cicé[33] became archbishop in 1781, this lavish edifice was complete. If its lines did not win the universal approval which greeted those of the grand theatre, it could hardly be ignored, and formed a fitting residence—when he chose to occupy it—for the Primate of Aquitaine.[34]

The supreme agent of the government in the area, in theory at least, was the governor of the province of Guienne, and his seat was also at Bordeaux. Louis XIV had reduced the power of governors but they still remained more important than was apparent. In the mid-18th century they were increasingly called upon to overawe recalcitrant provincial parlements with the panoply of military sessions, for which the prestige of a peer of France was usually essential. Since 1755 the governor of Guienne had been the marshal duc de Richelieu,[35] intimate friend of Louis XV. He held the office until his death in 1788. After the accession of Louis XVI, he was not allowed to revisit his province, but in his heyday, between 1758 and 1774, he had come regularly to Bordeaux, and ruled Guienne like a viceroy. Even after that he often intervened from Paris in local affairs, sometimes at the government's request; but the most active part of the governor's role was performed between 1775 and 1786 by his lieutenant-general, the marshal duc de Mouchy.[36] On the occasion of Mouchy's almost annual visits under Louis XVI, the governor's mansion, though not comparable in size and luxury to the new archbishop's palace, became the social as well as the political centre of the city and the whole province.

The permanent resident representative of the government was the intendant. The intendant headed the everyday administration of France's largest generality, with wide powers whose vagueness was a subject of much disquiet among other local authorities. Justice, police, finances, economic development, public works, charity—all these fields were, to a greater or lesser extent, within the intendant's competence. The great age of the intendancy of Bordeaux was the administration of Tourny in the middle decades of the century.[37] A vigorous and imaginative administrator, it was mainly he who reshaped the topography of Bordeaux on the spacious scale that can still be seen. Yet his administration was dogged by conflicts with the city government, and above all with the parlement, and his departure went unlamented in Bordeaux. Subsequent intendants were transient figures, and until 1774 were completely overshadowed in local politics by Richelieu. Only in 1776, with the arrival of Dupré de Saint-Maur,[38] did Bordeaux acquire another intendant of comparable imagination and vigour—and these qualities only brought down on him the same hostility as Tourny had encountered.

The city of Bordeaux was governed by the *jurade*, a council of six *jurats*—two noblemen, two advocates, and two merchants.[39] At the head was a mayor who was usually a great nobleman and did not take much part in municipal affairs. The *jurats* were chosen for a two-year term by the king from a short list of candidates presented to him by a 24-member elected council of notables. The largest council of the city, the *cent-trente*, met only seldom on important occasions, so the *jurats* were the only effective day-to-day government of the city and a sizeable district all around; in the watch (*guet*) they commanded the only armed force allowed within the city boundaries. The parlement and the intendant vied with each other in asserting a right of supervision over them, and they of course tried wherever possible to play the one off against the other.

The *jurade* also constituted a law court of first instance for all crimes committed in the city and its district, for Bordeaux was, like all 18th-century political and administrative capitals, a judicial centre. There were three financial courts—in ascending order of competence, the election, the office of finances, and the sovereign jurisdiction of the court of aids. There were commercial and maritime courts and a seneschalcy, the judicial court of second instance for the whole of Guienne. The intendant, too, had judicial functions. The legal profession, or 'people of the robe', must have numbered several thousands, if we add the swarm of advocates, procurators, and clerks which congregated around courts. At the top of the scale socially, and at the apex of the judicial pyramid, legally, was the Sovereign Court of Parlement.

Citizens of Bordeaux in the 18th century always maintained that their parlement went back to 1451. By article 20 of the Capitulation of Guienne, of 20 June, Charles VII conceded to conquered Bordeaux:

> ... Justice souveraine pour connaître, discuter et déterminer définitivement de toutes causes d'appel qui se feront en iceluy païs, sans pour iceux appeaux par simple querelle ou autrement être traité hors de ladite cité.

This made the parlement of Bordeaux the third oldest in France, after Paris and Toulouse, for it preceded Grenoble by a good two years. Grenoble, however, never accepted such claims, and until the Revolution this point of honour impeded friendly relations between the two companies. For a year after the capitulation, Bordeaux revolted and called back the English, the treaty was forgotten, and there is no evidence that the king of France ever had time to set up sovereign justice. Moreover, the question never arose after the second subjugation of Bordeaux in 1453. Sovereign justice over Guienne was attributed to the parlement of Paris. It was only in 1462 that Louis XI created a parlement at Bordeaux, and it was only from that date that it could trace a continuous history.[40]

The parlement of Bordeaux was the supreme court of appeal for a jurisdiction of over 2 million souls.[41] Throughout most of the three centuries of its existence the parlement had entertained final appeals from 30 seneschalcy courts, and hundreds of royal and seignorial courts of first instance, covering Guienne, Gascony the *landes*, Agenais, Labourt, Limousin, Périgord, Bazadais, and Saintonge.[42] The law by which this vast jurisdiction, the fourth largest in France, regulated its affairs, was Roman law for the most part, its force modified in certain districts by a series of local customs, such as that of Bordeaux itself. The parlement was the supreme authority on them all.

The court was divided into five chambers. The grand chamber, composed of senior magistrates, was the highest, and heard pleas in the most important civil cases. The two chambers of inquests, equal in attributions, dealt in writing with all others. Criminal cases were heard by the *tournelle*, a chamber recruited half from the grand chamber and half from the two chambers of inquests. Finally, there was a small chamber of requests, whose exclusive concern was with the privilege of *committimus*, which conferred upon noblemen and certain others direct access to a sovereign court for all suits. Its decisions were subject to appeal to the grand chamber, so its justice was not really sovereign at all, a fact reflected in the chamber's low prestige.[43]

At first the parlement had been made up of one president and seven counsellors. By the time of Louis XVI it had a complement of 115 officers enjoying the full privileges and status of members of the parlement. There was a first president, and nine presidents à *mortier* who were qualified to preside over the court in the absence of its head. Four of them always sat in the *tournelle*, the others in the grand chamber. The grand chamber itself had 30 counsellors, headed by the longest-serving among them, the dean. In this number were two clerical counsellors, and in addition there were two knights of honour, who had no functions other than to adorn the court with the dignity of their birth.[44] Each of the chambers of inquests had 30 members, including two clerical counsellors and two presidents each. The chamber of requests was made up of two presidents and eight counsellors. In addition the parlement had a procurator-general, the legal voice of the crown, assisted by two advocates-general and one or more 'substitutes'. Finally there were two chief-clerks, who kept the records, and whose signatures validated all legal documents.

These men were the true members of the parlement. Around them clustered a host of inferior officers, all exercising some judicial function—numerous clerks and ushers, the whole staff of the chancery, the advocates, the procurators, their clerks, and so on. But only the magistrates had a vote in the decisions of the court, only they were the parlement proper. Even ex-magistrates, with the rank of honorary president or counsellor, and who could deliver opinions during the court's deliberations, might not vote, and therefore had no part in making the policy of the court.

It may seem curious to attribute 'policies' to a court of law; but no parlement had ever been simply that. A parlement possessed a distinctive mixture of judicial and administrative powers which could hardly be separated, and which together gave it its peculiar character. Not only did it pronounce on cases brought before it; it also had an autonomous legislative function within its own jurisdiction. It could promulgate *arrêts de règlement*, binding on all those living in the area, which constituted a sort of corpus of bye-laws of local and often transitory relevance and application. They were an important part of government as the frequent co-operation of intendants in their issue shows. Above all, parlements had the right of remonstrance. Laws emanating from the king took effect as soon as they were transcribed on to the registers of the courts which were to administer them. It was a form of promulgation. When they registered new laws, however, the king's sovereign courts had the right, in remonstrances, to point out defects in them, and suggest improvements. It was the exercise of these legislative and remonstrative powers, normally wielded by all the chambers assembled together, which gave the parlements political importance. Throughout the 18th century they had used them to delay, attack, and sometimes countermand royal legislation. Although the activities of provincial parlements seldom altered the general course of government policy, as those of Paris sometimes did, they could still obstruct its application for long periods in their own provinces. The parlement of Bordeaux was particularly well placed to employ such tactics, supreme in a province without the rival power of estates, and with a jurisdiction wider than that of any single intendant or governor.

And in fact the parlement had a long tradition of independence and resistance to the government. Henry IV regarded it as the worst of a worthless collection of courts.[45] In the Fronde it seemed to bear him out, for it levied an army against the king and raised Bordeaux in open revolt. In 1675, under the great king himself, it led a revolt against increases in royal taxation, and on its defeat was exiled for 15 years to a series of small towns up river—La Réole, Condom, Marmande. Only by such draconian measures was it subdued. Even then, the intendant was writing in 1698 that:

> Le parlement est à présent soumis aux ordres du Roy; personne ne songe à s'écarter de l'obéissance, mais il y a si peu d'union parmi les officiers de cette Compagnie et il y a tant de jalousie entre eux qu'il n'est pas possible de pouvoir se flatter de leur faire prendre aucun party dans des temps difficiles; il paroit tous les jours tant de vivacité et de l'inquiétude dans les affaires particulières de la Compagnie qu'il est très à craindre que le même esprit ne régnât dans des affaires générales si le temps changeoit, d'autant plus qu'ils ne croyent pas qu'il puisse y avoir d'autre autorité que celle du Parlement, qu'ils veulent tous les jours étendre jusques dans les plus petites choses qui ne les regardent pas et qui sont fort au dessous d'eux.[46]

It was an accurate prophecy. After the death of Louis XIV, the parlement of Bordeaux threw itself into the religious and financial conflicts of the reign of

Louis XV with a passion equal to that of any provincial parlement. The climax of its activity came in the 1750s, when it resolutely set its face against the government's new taxes, and all but drove out the intendant Tourny. The sour pages of d'Argenson's journal for these years are full of references to the outrageous behaviour of the Bordelais magistrates: 'des gens fermes, chauds, ignorants et fort intéressés . . . le parlement de Bordeaux est une des mauvaises jugeries du royaume'.[47] And if, in the 1760s, the parlements of Toulouse, Pau, Besançon, and above all Rennes, found new levels of extreme behaviour, that of Bordeaux was hardly less strident in defence of the interests of its province, especially over taxation. Nor was it deterred by exiles or forced registrations from emphasizing its views with strikes, deputations, and suspensions of legislation; for the magistrates felt sure of their local support. 'Ici', noted d'Argenson, 'le parlement ne parle pas pour ses droits et pour ses hautaines prérogatives, mais pour le peuple qui gémit de la misère et des impôts'.[48]

It was against this background that the parlement of Bordeaux entered the final, crisis-ridden years of the old régime, years which culminated in its own destruction, along with all the other parlements. What part did it play in the crisis of the old régime? What were its motives and preoccupations in the events which finally plunged France into a Revolution? These are the problems confronting this study, public problems, concerning the march of events. But the men who make and act out public events are creatures of multifarious private circumstances. We can know little of the parlement of Bordeaux, unless we first acquaint ourselves with the magistrates who made it up.

NOTES

1. [Palmer], *A Four Months Tour through France* (Dublin, 1776), 230, 234. Bordeaux, 19 July 1775.
2. C. Maxwell (ed.), Arthur Young, *Travels in France during the years 1787, 1788, and 1789* (Cambridge, 1929), 58–61, 26–28 August 1787.
3. J. Cavignac, 'Le compagnonnage dans les luttes ouvrières du XVIIIe siècle: l'exemple de Bordeaux', *Bibliothèque de l'Ecole des Chartes* (Juillet–Décembre 1968), *passim*.
4. The fullest modern appreciation of these works is that by F. G. Pariset in F. G. Pariset (ed.), *Bordeaux au XVIIIe siècle* (Bordeaux, 1968), 591–647.
5. loc. cit., 59.
6. Meaudre de Lapouyade, 'Impressions d'une Allemande à Bordeaux en 1785', *R. Hist. Bx.* (1911), 178.
7. Young, loc. cit., 59–60; see also P. Courteault, *La Révolution et les théâtres de Bordeaux d'après des documents inédits* (Paris, 1926), *passim*, and M. Fuchs, 'Le théâtre à Bordeaux de 1772 à 1790, d'après le "Manuscrit Lecouvreur" ', *R. Hist. Bx.* (1940).
8. J. Bencazar, 'Les jeux du hasard à Bordeaux, 1701–89', *R. Philomat. Bx.* (1905).
9. E. Lanoire, 'Cagliostro à Bordeaux', *R. Philomat. Bx.* (1932).
10. R. Céleste, 'La Société Philomatique de Bordeaux de 1783 à 1808', *R. Philomat. Bx.* (1897–98).
11. R. Boutruche (ed.), *Bordeaux de 1453 à 1715* (Bordeaux, 1966), 527, and Y. Renouard (ed.), *Bordeaux sous les rois d'Angleterre* (Bordeaux, 1965), 434.
12. J. P. Poussou in *Bordeaux au XVIIIe siècle*, 325–7.
13. ibid., 246. F. Crouzet's chapters on the Bordelais economy in this volume, although authoritative, may now be supplemented in greater detail by P. Butel, 'La croissance commerciale bordelaise dans la seconde moitié du XVIIIe siècle' (unpublished doctoral thesis of the University of Paris, I, 1973), 2 v., which was not available when the present work was written. I am grateful to M. Butel for placing a copy of his thesis at my disposal during final revisions.

14. Crouzet, op. cit., 249.
15. ibid., 195–6.
16. ibid., 197.
17. Young, loc. cit., 60.
18. L. H. Butterfield (ed.), *The Adams Papers: Series I*, IV, *Autobiography* (Cambridge, Mass., 1961), 37.
19. Crouzet, op. cit., 60.
20. ibid., 302–4.
21. J. Marchand (ed.), *Voyages en France de François de la Rochefoucauld (1781–1783)* (Paris, 1938), II, 120. See also Butel, op. cit., I, 653–7, II, 904–16.
22. See Crouzet, op. cit., 298–300. Butel, I, 103–14.
23. Crouzet, op. cit., 250.
24. AD C3159, 'Mémoire concernant l'élection de Bordeaux', 1756, for a lucid analysis of the economy of the *landes*.
25. R. Pijassou in *Bordeaux au XVIIIe siècle*, 165–6.
26. C. E. Labrousse, *La Crise de l'économie française à la fin de l'Ancien Régime et au début de la Révolution* (Paris, 1944), 513.
27. Crouzet, op. cit., 250.
28. Young, loc. cit., 61.
29. See A. Leroux, *Etude critique sur le XVIIIe siècle à Bordeaux* (Bordeaux, 1921), 170.
30. A. Nicolaï, *Essai statistique sur le Clergé, les Communautés Religieuses, la Noblesse, la Magistrature, la Bourgeoisie, les Corporations et le Mouvement de la Population à Bordeaux au XVIIIe siècle, 1700–1800* (Paris and Bordeaux, 1909), ch. 1; L. Desgraves and J. P. Poussou in *Bordeaux au XVIIIe siècle*, 121–5.
31. Ferdinand-Maximilien-Mériadec de Rohan, prince de Rohan-Guéménée (1738–1813). Grand Provost of the Church of Strasbourg; archbishop of Bordeaux, 1769–81; archbishop of Cambrai, 1789–91; emigrated; subsequently first almoner to the Empress Josephine.
32. J. Breval, *Remarks on Several Parts of Europe . . . in several tours since the year 1723* (London, 1737), II, 246.
33. Jérôme-Marie Champion de Cicé (1735–1810). General Agent of the Clergy, 1765; bishop of Rodez, 1770; archbishop of Bordeaux, 1781; Keeper of the Seals, 1789–90; emigrated, returning 1802; archbishop of Aix, 1802–10.
34. On the palace, see Pariset in *Bordeaux au XVIIIe siècle*, 616–24.
35. Louis-François-Armand du Plessis, duc de Richelieu (1696–1788). Peer of France, 1721; King's Lieutenant in Languedoc, 1738; First Gentleman of the Bedchamber, 1744; governor of Guienne and Gascony, 1755.
36. Philippe de Noailles (1715–94). Known until 1775 as comte de Noailles; Grandee of Spain, 1741; Marshal of France and duc de Mouchy, lieutenant-general and commander-in-chief in Guienne, 1775; resigned, 1786; notable, 1787; executed, 1794.
37. Louis-Urbain Aubert, marquis de Tourny (1695–1760). Counsellor at the Châtelet, 1714; counsellor at the grand council and master of requests, 1719; intendant of Limoges, 1730; intendant of Bordeaux, 1743–58; councillor of state, 1755. On his administration, which touched all aspects of Bordeaux life in the mid-18th century, see M. Lhéritier, *Tourny* (Paris, 1920), 2 v.
38. Nicolas Dupré de Saint-Maur (17 ?–9?). Counsellor at the parlement of Paris 1751; master of requests, 1755; intendant of Bourges, 1764; intendant of Bordeaux, 1776–85; councillor of state, 1785.
39. H. Barckhausen, 'Essai sur l'administration municipale de Bordeaux sous l'Ancien Régime', Introduction to *Inventaire-sommaire des archives municipales de Bordeaux*, II, *Livre des privilèges* (Bordeaux, 1787), pp. vii–xxxv.
40. This well-known passage is quoted in C. B. F. Boscheron des Portes, *Histoire du Parlement de Bordeaux, depuis sa création jusqu'à sa suppression (1451–1790)* (Bordeaux, 1878), I, 6. A recently discovered warrant of 1452, in favour of 'nostre juge ordinaire des appeaulx de Bourdeloys et de Gascogne' (B.N. MSS fr. 25712, no. 296) suggests that after all sovereign justice was established after the first capitulation. I owe this information to the kindness of my colleague Dr M. G. A. Vale.
41. Leroux, op. cit., 91; E. Semichon, *Les Réforms sous Louis XVI, Assemblées Provinciales*

et Parlements (Paris, 1876), gives Paris 10 million subjects to its jurisdiction, Toulouse 3 million, Rennes 2,300,000, Bordeaux 2,200,000, and the rest, less.

42. *Etrennes Bordeloises ou Calendrier Raisonné du Palais, Année 1776* (Bordeaux, 1776), introduction, 76–7.
43. Cf. the parlement of Rennes: A. Le Moy, *Le Parlement de Bretagne et le pouvoir royal au XVIIIe siècle* (Paris and Angers, 1909), 7; see also below, pp. 20, 28, 42–3.
44. This office had been created in 1702 as a financial expedient.
45. Boscheron des Portes, op. cit., I, 352.
46. Memoir of Bazin de Bezons, 1698. Quoted in Nicolaï, op. cit., 75.
47. E. J. B. Rathéry (ed.), *Journal et Mémoires du Marquis d'Argenson* (Paris, 1859–68), IX, 410, 12 March 1749.
48. ibid.

PART ONE

No Judge, Sir, can give his whole attention to his office; and it is very proper that he should employ what time he has to himself, to his own advantage, in the most profitable manner . . . No, Sir, there is no profession to which a man gives a very great proportion of his time. It is wonderful when a calculation is made, how little the mind is actually employed in the discharge of any profession. No man would be a Judge, upon the condition of being totally a Judge.

(Samuel Johnson, 1775)

CHAPTER 1

The Recruitment of the Parlement

A member of the parlement of Bordeaux was a person of undoubted prestige. Yet most of them would have been men of consequence even if they had never undertaken a legal career. Members of the parlement came only from certain areas, were born into certain narrow groups, married within the same groups, and shared a similar personal status. Who, then, were these provincial 'senators'?

The vast majority of them were natives of the city of Bordeaux or its immediate neighbourhood. The prestige of the parlement had indeed always attracted some recruits from much further off, like president Dupaty from La Rochelle, counsellor Moreau de Montcheuil from Poitiers, or counsellor Darblade de Séailles from Perpignan. But most outsiders still originated from the province of Guienne or its near neighbours. They looked and came to Bordeaux as a regional capital, with its august supreme court as the summit of provincial ambition. President de Bienassis from Agen, counsellors Perez d'Artassan from Mont-de-Marsan, Jaucen de Poissac and Lafagerdie de Saint-Germain from Tulle, Chanceaulme de Fonroze from Bergerac, de Malet from Périgueux, Reculès de Poulouzat from Limoges, and de Mothes from Albret, had all pulled up their roots to come to Bordeaux. Many of them were ambitious sons of local magistrates, who could climb no higher in the society of the little towns where they lived. It was the same for colonials, like counsellors Thilorier, de Lamolère, and P. L. de Raymond from Saint-Domingue, or counsellor Pocquet and the Pelet or Prunes families from Martinique. For them too Bordeaux was a capital, however distant. No doubt most of the ancestors of members of the parlement had also come from outside Bordeaux. Yet at any given time outsiders remained a minority.[1] The common local origin of the majority underlay many of the court's public attitudes. Even the West Indians came from an area with special links with Bordeaux. All this bred a certain solidarity of interest in the face of the outside world, and especially the government.

Not only were most of the magistrates drawn from local families; most of them came from the even narrower world of Bordeaux legal families. Once a family had a representative in the parlement, heredity of offices, the local prestige attached to them, and the fact that, outside Paris, membership of a parlement was the highest attainable social distinction, all combined to create a tradition. 'L'espoir le plus flateur des magistrats', wrote a group of them in 1778, 'qui ont vieilli dans le penible exercice de leurs fonctions, est de Transmettre à leur postérité, le rang qn'ils ont occupés dans la Société . . .'[2] Or as the unmarried president de Gascq wrote in favour of a cousin: 'Il est assez naturel que je desire Laisser quelqu'un après moy dans une Compagnie ou nous sommes depuis 250 ans . . .'[3] Out of 153 magistrates[4] in the parlement between 1774 and 1790, 71 (or 46·4 per cent) were sons of magistrates in the parlement. During the same short period, no less than 21 families had representatives of two successive generations in the court. This had been the pattern for generations; 46 of the magistrates, representing 33 families, could boast paternal grandfathers in the court before them, and 29, representing 19 families, could boast great-grandfathers. Around 14[5] could lay claim to more than four generations in the parlement. Among these were the presidential families of Le Berthon, Gascq, Gourgue, Lavie, and Verthamon, for meteoric rises to the presidential bench were not normal, as president Dupaty found to his cost.[6] High rank was only attained usually by long association with the court, and even this was hardly enough without the money to buy presidencies and maintain the appropriate state. Thus the Cursol, Castelnau, Leblanc de Mauvezin, and Laboyrie families, all with traditions in the parlement, longer than those of presidential families like the Casaux and de Lancres, never provided more than counsellors. The Filhot family, one of the largest and oldest in the parlement, only produced a president for the first time in 1789.

Magistrates were usually eldest sons. As its future head, it was natural that the eldest son should be destined for the highest dignity in the family. As always, there were exceptions, such as clerical counsellors; the law of inheritance led families to exert strong pressure against eldest sons going into the church. Exceptions too were younger brothers who succeeded elder ones dying without issue: this was the case with president J. C. Daugeard, counsellor de Lagubat, and the chief-clerk Lafargue. Counsellor Laroze de Fonbrune succeeded his father in the family office because his elder brother had made the mistake of entering legal life in the Maupeou parlement, and the restored parlement after 1775 could not be persuaded to receive him.[7] The classic pattern was for sons to succeed to their fathers' offices. Yet the 21 families with representatives of two generations in the court after 1775 suggest that fathers were no longer so inclined to resign in favour of their sons. And in fact, out of the 71 who were sons of magistrates, only 25 had succeeded to their fathers' offices. Two succeeded grandfathers, three succeeded fathers-in-law, and one, a brother-in-law. To succeed a father in fact was no longer necessary in most cases to the further end of family ennoblement, as it had once been.[8] No longer did fathers exercise their offices for 20 years in order to obtain their letters of honour, and then pass on their offices to their sons; they now bought them separate offices as soon as they were old enough, but remained in place themselves. Eldest sons usually had little choice about their career. 'Je n'ai pris ma charge que pour plaire a mes parens', wrote counsellor de Castelnau in 1772, 'n'ayant jamais eu de goult pour mon état que j'aurois quitté si j'en eusse été le maitre il y a bien long tems'.[9] Counsellor Drouilhet de Sigalas even wrote (without success) to the chancellor the same year for a *lettre de cachet* to compel his eldest son to join the parlement.[10]

It was exceptional to find two members of the same generation of a family together in the parlement. Between 1775 and 1790, only seven sets of brothers served together. Of these, the Daugeards, Gourgues, Fégers, and Pelets were extremely rich. Their families could afford the heavy capital investment represented by two offices. The Meslon brothers both inherited their offices, one from their father, another from an uncle. With the Filhot brothers, the matter was decided by their father's will of 1770.[11] The eldest son was already a counsellor. As to the younger:

> ... ne sachant encore quel etat il embrassera, voyant la difficulté de le placer avantageusement au service, je veux d'aportionner de façon a luy donner le moyen d'entrer dans le parlement et d'y prendre charge de Conseiller, dans le cas ou il se trouvera porté pour cet etat, et avoir les dispositions, talents et volonté necessaires pour en remplir dignement les penibles fonctions ...

To this end he left him 50,000 l. to buy an office of counsellor, and enough property to maintain an appropriate state. If he chose not to enter the court, then the legacy was to be considerably reduced, and he was to lose the 50,000 l. It is hardly surprising to find that this son joined the parlement in 1779, the year after his father's death.

If, however, nearly half the magistrates had a parlementaire tradition behind them, slightly over half had not. The majority came from families relatively new to the court, and most had not been notable when the century began. This too was natural as old dynasties died out. Some families passed out of legal circles to form military traditions. Still more became naturally extinct. Under Louis XVI the parlement no longer contained representatives of the families of Ségur, Lecomte de Latresne, Dalesme, Pontac, Lalanne, Pichon, Bacalan, Guyonnet, or Secondat de Montesquieu, although all of them had provided distinguished magistrates in the first half of the century or earlier. Their place had been taken by members of the newer presidential families like the Pichards, and this in turn left room for totally new families to begin traditions of their own. And so relative newcomers were always in a majority. Yet even newcomers often came from legal families. Eleven were sons of members of the court of aids, and others were grandsons. Nineteen in all had ancestors there on the paternal side, for, as the malicious Bernadau[12] put it: 'C'est là où vont se décrasser de roture et d'ignorance ceux qui veulent faire entrer leurs enfants au sénat'.[13] Another nine were sons of treasurers of France,[14] and nine, sons of officers in lower courts. The fathers of 11 more had moved on the periphery of legal society as king's secretaries in the chanceries of sovereign courts, while a further five were sons of simple advocates. Clearly most magistrates, whether their families had previous links with the parlement or not, would have lived in a legal atmosphere from their earliest childhood.

Another significant field of recruitment was among families of what might be called local notables. The Bergeron, Biré, Boucaud, Brach, Demons, Degères, Lamouroux, Lasalle, Ragueneau, and Raymond families were of a gentle and leisured character, without important legal traditions. Not all were settled in the immediate neighbourhood of Bordeaux, but their names were distinguished and looked upon by the magistracy as an adornment to the parlement. Often their traditions were military, and among the fathers were at least six knights of St-Louis and even a camp-marshal who had served the elector of Bavaria.[15] The fathers of five magistrates had also served as *jurats* of Bordeaux. This office, though a mark of distinction, was not considered the equal of an office in the parlement, and when L. J. Demons, an honorary counsellor at the parlement, accepted office in the *jurade* in 1781, his former colleagues considered that he had demeaned himself.[16] On the social ladder, the *jurade* came before and below the 'senate'.

Such a pattern of recruitment was very similar to that of other parlements.[17] At Bordeaux, however, a significant minority did not originate in legal or noble circles, but from the merchant community, which for a parlement was hardly typical. At first sight, indeed, it appears very small. Only seven magistrates had fathers who admitted to being merchants and two of these were not from Bordeaux.[18] But most of the king's secretaries were in fact merchants in disguise. Of the 11 with sons in the parlement, most can be classed as merchants. The office was a sinecure, conferred immediate complete nobility, and sold very dear.[19] It was perfect for the rich, socially-ambitious businessman; like G. J. Saige, father of an advocate-general, the city's richest merchant.[20] Jean Pellet, father of the two Pellet brothers, was in the same class.[21] The counsellors Dubergier de Favars, father and son, were son and grandson of a king's secretary, but members of the great mercantile Dubergier family, which played a leading role in the commerce of Bordeaux throughout the century.[22] So in reality at least 15 magistrates and possibly more had fathers in trade; a proportion of nearly 10 per cent which, though not large, was probably the largest of any parlement in France.[23]

The evidence of marriages reinforces the conclusion that the world of the parlement and that of the merchants were closely linked. We are concerned with 162 persons. Of these, nothing is known about 20, not even whether they married or not. The wives of eight more are simply names. Of the rest, we may discount ten genuine clerical counsellors. Another 11 remained bachelors, at least while they were magistrates. Possibly some of the unknowns, especially the young ones, did so too. What happened to them after the dissolution of the parlement does not directly concern us, although it is certain that at least two of the 1790 bachelors married subsequently. This leaves at least 123 first marriages and 14 second marriages.

Intermarriage among parlementaire families was one of the oldest and most dominant characteristics of the society that revolved around the parlement. Strictly, royal ordinances forbade magistrates to serve in the parlement alongside relatives within certain degrees;[24] but royal dispensations were easily obtainable. The mothers of at least 50 of the magistrates were themselves from parlementaire families,[25] and 33 of the 162 married daughters of magistrates, the last generation of an old tradition. The result, stretching over several generations, was to bind the magistrates very closely together in a web of cousinhood. Few of them did not have some relative, however distant, in the parlement with them. The longer their family had been providing members, the more relatives there would be, and the more likelihood of actually marrying one. The family of Verthamon is an extreme example. It provided two presidents under Louis XVI, who both had wives of parlementaire extraction. Of four daughters in the last generation of magistrates, three married magistrates, and all the Verthamons were descended from J. M. de Verthamon, counsellor 1715–67, and his wife Catherine de Verthamon, who was also his aunt,[26] and the daughter of a magistrate in the Paris parlement. Counsellors Dalphonse, Degères de Loupes, de Raymond de Lalande, and P. L. de Raymond all married wives from their own families. In the last case, counsellor de Lamontaigne noted that:

Ce monsieur de Raymond, originaire de l'Amérique, est frère de la femme de M. le comte de Raymond, seigneur baron de Ryons, frère de M. de Sallegourde et oncle de la nouvelle mariée. Ainsi le nouvel époux est beau-frère et neveu de M. le comte de Raymond et sa femme se trouve aujourd'hui sa nièce et sa belle-soeur.[27]

What was more, both her father and her new husband were magistrates. In the parlement as a whole under Louis XVI, 15 magistrates could count between one and three sons-in-law in the court. No less than 57, over one-third of the court, had brothers-in-law among their colleagues. One had four, five had three, and ten had two. This was merely one generation; the cousinhoods which resulted from such conditions over a long period stretched so far and were so complex that it is impossible to give any precise idea of them. The social composition of the parlement, as of others,[28] was therefore dominated by dynasties, to which it was of great prestige to become attached. Dynasties of course rise and fall. The reign of Louis XVI saw the extinction of that of Gascq, and the more ancient ones of Pontac, Dalesme, and Caupos represented only by females marrying into more flourishing families. At the moment of its dissolution, the parlement's greatest dynasties were those of Verthamon, Darche, Marbotin, Filhot, and Castelnau.

Marriage into the 'robe' outside the parlement was rarer. President J. B. M. de Verthamon married the daughter of a president of the parlement of Pau; president Dupaty married the daughter of a counsellor at the chamber of accounts of Paris, the sister of the famous Parisian magistrate Fréteau de Saint-Just. Nearer home, five magistrates married daughters of members of the court of aids of Bordeaux; and three married daughters of treasurers of France. Counsellor de Minvielle and counsellor de Taffard went even lower in the local judicial hierarchy. Most magistrates who sought wives from the legal world, however, generally did not look outside the ambit of the ennobling courts of Bordeaux.

The largest number of wives were not daughters of magistrates at all, but of other noblemen and notables. If 33 were magistrates' daughters, 45 had fathers ranging from marquis, camp-marshals, or *jurats* of Bordeaux, to simple *écuyers*, often of very recent extraction. Even so, nine of the 45 came from families which had recently provided members of the parlement, so that in extraction noble wives were fairly evenly divided between 'robe' and 'non-robe'. In social terms there was no rift between 'robe' and 'sword'. They intermarried freely, as they did all over France in the 18th century.[29] Yet there were no marriages with the greatest families of the area, the Richelieus, the D'Aiguillons, the Lesparres, the Duras, the Latour du Pins. Such families moved in the Versailles circle, which members of the parlement did not. Magistrates drew their wives from the nobility of the second rank, the resident nobility; matches were between equals in esteem. The result over several generations was that, whereas not all magistrates might be related to other local noblemen, nearly all the latter were related to magistrates, since at any time the parlement constituted about one-third of the nobility of Bordeaux.[30] Such tight links were of inestimable importance when the nobility came, in the last years of the old régime, to concert its action.

A fair number of magistrates, the third largest group, sought wives in the world of commerce, including the king's secretaries. So 25 magistrates had fathers-in-law in commerce, of whom 12 were king's secretaries. This, one-fifth of the known marriages, is a strikingly high proportion and only adds to the evidence of strong links between the world of commerce and that of the parlement. Nor were such matches always in the literary tradition of poor noblemen marrying 'to regild their arms'. More often magistrates of relatively short lineage linked themselves to families of similar age or only one step behind on the social ladder. The older a family, the less likely it was to seek a match in the world of commerce. Yet rules are hard to make, as the spectacular example of the Saige family shows. G. J. Saige, king's secretary, married his daughter to president P. E. de Casaux, and his eldest son the advocate-general to a Verthamon daughter. Her sister married the son of the first president. Another married counsellor Demons. So the Saige family linked itself in a few years to some of the greatest families in the parlement. The same happened when Jean Pellet, king's secretary, married his two sons, both counsellors, to noble wives. One of them as a result linked himself at once to the family of the first president.[31] One of the most important results of close intermarriage between parlementaire families was therefore that when an outside match was made, the outsider was at once accepted and absorbed because he acquired not just a wife, but a host of relatives in the parlement. The world of the parlement was not closed to outsiders because it was inbred. This inbreeding actually had the effect of making it easier to enter and be accepted.

Most wives were of local origin. Members of the parlement seldom sought far for a wife. The greatest exception to this rule is that of the heiresses from the colonies. In 1757 Mme Duroy wrote to Lamontaigne:

> M. Roland se marie, du moins on me l'a dit, avec cent mille francs et mlle tilaurier, vous ne la connoisses peutetre pas c'est une grande demoiselle née au de la du tropique bien élevée ... ce ... vent de sudouest nous doit amener au moins 45 vaisseaux de retour de la martinique chacun de 400,000 l. voules vous qu'on vous arrete quelqu'une de ces cargaisons a condition d'epouser non pas le vaisseau mais quelqu'une de ces demoiselles qui s'ennuyent de rester filles aux isles.[32]

No less than 14 of the magistrates serving Louis XVI adopted this course, and married colonial heiresses sent to France by their fathers for an education and a husband. Particularly successful in this respect were the Godet Dubrois, a legal family from Guadeloupe. Of five daughters in this generation, two married members of the parlement of Bordeaux, and a third found a nobleman who was both son and brother of members of the parlement.[33] Even so, magistrates who married colonial wives, such as counsellors de Lamolère, Prunes, or Thilorier, were often of colonial stock themselves.

In a sense even these marriages were not to outsiders. The abundance of colonial heiresses was peculiar to Bordeaux. Wives from Paris itself were more foreign and therefore far less common. Both president de Pichard's wives were from the capital, but both matches were quite exceptional. Exceptional too were the Irish wives of president Lavie and counsellor de Basterot. Counsellors Chaperon de Terrefort and de Laliman married daughters of John Collingwood, an English merchant; but Collingwood had naturalized himself and even bought an office of king's secretary.[34] Wives not from the Bordelais were still normally found in Bordeaux as a result of the special circumstances of the place. Similarly there were few exceptions to the rule that wives were noble, and even fewer to the rule that they were rich. Such examples, like that of the eventual Mme de Richon,[35] were scandalous, and outraged the magistrates' sense both of propriety and social solidarity.

The parlement was by no means therefore a closed world. As in the parlements generally,[36] over half the members were new men. Less than half of them married into parlementaire families. Admittedly, most were not new to legal society, or venal office, and to that extent there was a certain degree of homogeneity in families of extraction. But the legal world covered a wide range of society; there was little in common between a counsellor at the parlement and, say, a clerk in the election of Guienne.[37] Marriages and recruitment from outside these circles, notably from trade, were significant too. In any case, 'closed' implies a conscious effort to exclude new men, and even in other parlements where recruitment followed a similar pattern to Bordeaux,[38] the existence of such an effort has only been inferred, not proved. Narrow would be a more appropriate word. Most members of society had not the combination of money, prestige, and ambition to aspire to the parlement; but none of these prerequisites were of the magistrates' deliberate making. Nor was the fact that the biggest group in a position to attain to the parlement was that of the magistrates themselves. The parlement was open to all who could reasonably aspire to membership. The only indispensable requirement was money. Everything else followed from this.

There is, however, another way in which a conscious effort to exclude was noticed among the parlements. This was in the sphere of nobility. Office in the parlements had always carried personal nobility on the principle, derived from the right of every man to be tried only by his peers, that judges who might have to try noblemen should be noble themselves. Office in the parlement of Bordeaux conferred gradual nobility: it only became hereditary either after two generations of 20 years or death in office. However, throughout France in the 18th century this provision became increasingly superfluous as more and more magistrates enjoyed nobility independently of their offices. It could hardly be otherwise when so many were sons of magistrates or holders of other ennobling offices. Yet several parlements took matters a stage further by laying down nobility as an essential prerequisite for membership, which was to make the courts closed in a very real sense. It began with Rennes in the 17th century; Grenoble followed in 1762, Aix in 1769; Nancy and Toulouse also made such provisions.[39] On 16 February 1780, immediately after the first rejection of Dupaty's attempt to become a president à mortier, the parlement of Bordeaux did the same.[40] A set of commissioners was nominated to examine the proofs of new candidates. ('Chose absurde', remarked Mme Duplessy,[41] 'car ses charges donnent la Noblesse à qui ne l'a pas'.) The arrogance of the commissioners created a very bad impression, especially as some of their own credentials as noblemen were not distinguished.[42] But did this commission outlive the Dupaty storm which had given it birth? There is no evidence of its activity after August 1780. Did the arrêté in fact remain a dead letter? What were the noble credentials of the magistrates?

Those of the presidential families were almost uniformly unimpeachable. The Le Berthon, Gascq, Gourgue, Daugeard, Pichard, de Lancre, and Lavie families went back in nobility to the 16th century or beyond. The Casaux and the

Verthamons went back to the 17th century. Several had provided Knights of Malta, which presupposed a distinguished extraction. The exception among them was Dupaty, who had occasioned the *arrêté* of 1780. Although it was not the real objection against him, low birth was urged as pretext for refusing him. In fact, he did possess 3rd-degree nobility, both his father and grandfather having been counsellors on the sovereign council of Cap Français (Saint-Domingue) and treasurers of France at La Rochelle. 'Elle n'est pas éclatante, sans doute, mais elle n'est pas vile', he protested, but it was humble enough to be used against him. 'La noblesse du mérite est la seule que les places exigent', he declared, but nowhere was this less true than on the presidential bench of a parlement.[43]

As a group, our 162 magistrates can be broken down into 127 families. On the nobility of five of these, no information has come to light.[44] Genealogy is in any case a treacherous jungle. Among other things we must distinguish between what a family's descent actually was, and what it thought it was. The Brivazacs, for example, were only definitively ennobled by office in the early 18th century, but treasured a filiation back to one 'Leonardus Brivazaca' in the 12th century.[45] The Domenge de Pic de Blais, in fact ennobled by letters of 1722, claimed descent from no less a person than Pico della Mirandola.[46] The Pellets dropped an 'l' from their name and spent two generations trying to prove a link with the old Languedoc house of Narbonne-Pelet.[47] Strange names too could be usefully embroidered: the Marbotins, of Agenais origin, claimed that they were a branch of a medieval Florentine family, the *Marbottini*.[48] The *Spens* in the name of Spens d'Estignols de Lancre was held to be Scottish in origin. Safest of all were the Lynches, whose Irish origin was beyond doubt, but who took the opportunity of foreign descent to extract letters from the Jacobite Athlone Herald, declaring them to be of the oldest stock, and so giving them automatic noble status in France. They could hardly help it, they pleaded, if their proofs had been destroyed in 1689 by marauding English protestants.[49] In reality, only four out of 127 families had nobility that was certainly older than the 16th century—Pichard, Piis, Degères, and Raymond de Sallegourde. Of these, the last two only entered the parlement in the 18th century, which incidentally underlines the meaningless-ness of any division between 'robe' and 'sword' in 18th-century Bordeaux. As long ago as 1698 the intendant had written:

> Il y a peu de noblesse établie à Bordeaux hors ceux qui tirent leur origine des officiers du Parlement parce qu'il n'y a pas un Conseiller qui ne se croye fort au dessus de tous les gentilshommes qui ne sont pas titrés . . .[50]

In 1775 the nobility on the capitation roll numbered 225; at any given time, ex-magistrates and relatives of magistrates would number about one-third of this total; and this is to ignore the magistrates themselves,who were taxed separately.[51] So there were very few noblemen of non-robe origin; only a small minority of their families had never had a representative in the parlement.

Twenty-four families in the parlement under Louis XVI had nobility going back to the 16th century. With some of these it may have gone further. Most of them had been ennobled by office, and it is among them that we find most of the presidential ones. These old families had huge prestige, were much sought as alliances, and their members could afford a certain amount of contempt for the origins of their colleagues. It was always useful to fall back on when under attack on political grounds: the dean Dussault, in 1775, was much reviled for his role under Maupeou by counsellor Duluc. Perhaps his robe had been stained, he admitted, but at least it had not been stained with flour—a reference to Duluc's grandfather who had been a flour merchant.[52] With noble ancestors in the 16th century, Dussault could afford to jibe.

The rest of the parlement, the vast majority, was evenly divided. Forty-six families could trace their nobility to the 17th century; 48, not back beyond 1700. To put it another way, 38·5 per cent of families in the parlement had acquired nobility within living memory, in the 18th century. Of these, the nobility of two families was 4th degree,[53] ten, 3rd degree; twenty-one, 2nd degree. Three are represented by two generations, and passed in our period from 2nd to 3rd degree. Only 13 were commoners on entry, and had purely personal nobility. So the parlement was an aristocratic body which hardly needed to restrict its recruitment. Well over half of its members had several generations of nobility going back at least to 1700. It is true that the nobility of a large minority was quite recent, and it was possible for commoners to join the court. Nevertheless, of the 13 commoners, only three were ordinary counsellors, and one of those had begun in the very inferior chamber of requests.[54] Two were clerical counsellors.[55] Four were in the chamber of requests throughout their careers, although one was a president there,[56] and the other four were all chief-clerks. Clearly commoner entrants seldom aspired to the full dignity of the parlement, and seldom attained it.

Hardly any non-nobles even considered the parlement as a career. Between 1775 and 1790, 53 magistrates were received for the first time; 37 are recorded as proving their nobility so as to avoid paying the gold mark of nobility, a fee payable by those who were ennobled by accession to office, and so theoretically by aspirants to membership of a parlement.[57] But the records are not complete, and we are safe in assuming that more people were dispensed from paying this fee than are recorded.[58] The only commoners to be received after the *arrêté* of 1780, even if this was sheer coincidence, were chief-clerks.[59] Even so, it is tempting to wonder how far in normal times the magistrates thought of such matters. In 1787 the parlement conferred a signal honour on one of its members. It was unprecedented. The court became, by unanimous consent, collective godfather to a magistrate's son. And it was to the same magistrate, four years later, that it confided its last *arrêté* of loyalty to the king, before its final dissolution. The magistrate was not a president, not the son of a magistrate, and not even the son of a nobleman, but Gabriel Bouquier, who had begun in the requests, and whose father was a simple advocate.[60] This suggests once again that however narrow the recruitment of the parlement was, the narrowness resulted more from the complex combinations of circumstance than any conscious and deliberate policy on the part of its members.

NOTES

1. On the members of the parlement in the 17th century, see F. Giteau in *Bordeaux de 1453 à 1715*, 482ff.
2. AAE MD France, 1589, f.31, remainers to Vergennes, 27 June 1778.
3. BVC [Richelieu papers, Maréchal de] Richelieu XVI, f.48, Gascq to Maupeou, 2 May 1772.
4. I have no information on the background of nine others.

5. The uncertainty of this figure stems from the uncertainty of the genealogical information. I have relied heavily here upon P. Meller, *Armorial du Bordelais, Sénéchaussées de Bordeaux, Bazas et Libourne* (Paris, 1906), 3 v., but even this work is far from detailed and some of its information seems, *prima facie*, suspect. The figures I give, therefore, are always what seems a reliable minimum, although I do not think that more complete information would alter them, or their significance, dramatically.

6. See below, ch. 12.

7. AD F MS 46, 'Copie d'une lettre d'un magistrat à un magistrat', 29 Oct. 1775; also AAE MD France, 1588, f.252, petition of Laroze, 27 Oct. 1775. The elder brother joined the army and eventually took a presidency in the court of aids of Bordeaux.

8. See below, p. 124.

9. BVC Richelieu XVI, f.26, Castelnau to Richelieu, 16 March 1772.

10. ibid., f.75, Maupeou to Richelieu, 2 July 1772; f.86, same to same, 18 July 1772.

11. AD 3E 5.594 no. 904 (Duprat). Sealed 1770, opened 14 Sept. 1778.

12. Pierre Bernadau (1762–1852). Advocate, publicist, polygraph, historian of Bordeaux, published over his lifetime many works on local topics. His 'Tablettes' are a prime source for the years 1787–89 and beyond. The information they contain is of varying reliability, and the judgements often malevolent, but used with caution, they are a valuable source.

13. BVBx MS 713 (sér. I), V, 'Tablettes' of Bernadau, 338. 2 Oct. 1788.

14. Three of these not of Bordeaux.

15. J. M. de La Colonie (*c.*1670–1759). Father of the dean J. F. A. M. de La Colonie.

16. BVBx MS 1201 (Duplessy Correspondence), IX, 20 Aug. 1780.

17. For Paris, see F. Bluche, *Les Magistrats du Parlement de Paris au XVIIIe siècle (1715–1771)* (Paris, 1960), sect. I, ch. 5; Dijon, A. Colombet, *Les Parlementaires Bourguignons à la fin du XVIIIe siècle (1775–90)* (Lyon, 1936), 42; Rennes, J. Meyer, *La Noblesse Bretonne au XVIIIe siècle* (Paris, 1966), II, 956; Toulouse, P. de Peguilhan de Larboust, 'Les Magistrats du Parlement de Toulouse à la fin de l'Ancien Régime (1775–90)' (mémoire de diplôme de la Faculté des Lettres de Toulouse, 1965), 33–6. This last was kindly lent to me by Professor J. Godechot.

18. The seven families were: Barbeguière, Darblade de Séailles, Féger, Lafargue, Laporte-Pauillac, Perez d'Artassan, Roche de Lamothe. Of these, Darblade came from Perpignan, Perez from Mont-de-Marsan.

19. See W. Doyle, 'Le prix des charges anoblissantes à Bordeaux au XVIIIe siècle', *Annales du Midi* (1968), 75–6. Butel, op. cit., II, 1055–9. Also below, graph, p. 28.

20. A Grellet-Dumazeau, *La Société Bordelaise sous Louis XV et le salon de Mme Duplessy* (Bordeaux and Paris, 1879), 298.

21. J. Cavignac, *Jean Pellet, Commerçant de Gros, 1694–1772: contribution à l'étude d Négoce Bordelais au XVIIIe siècle* (Paris, 1967), 315.

22. M. V. Labraque-Bordenave, 'Histoire des Députés de Bordeaux au conseil de com merce, au comité national, et à l'agence commerciale à Paris, 1700–1793', *Actes l'Académie Nationale des Sciences, Belles-Lettres et Arts de Bordeaux*, 3e série, 5 année (1889), 351.

23. Certainly larger than Paris, Toulouse, Dijon, Rennes, Rouen, and Grenoble.

24. *Bordeaux de 1453 à 1715*, 484ff. For Toulouse, see J. C. Paulhet, 'Les parlementair Toulousains à la fin du XVIIe siècle', *Annales du Midi* (1964), 195; for Dijon, t implication is in G. Roupnel, *La Ville et la campagne au XVIIe siècle: étude sur populations du Pays Dijonnais* (2nd ed., Paris, 1955), sect. II, ch. 3, *passim*; for Pa see Bluche, loc. cit., ch. 5, *passim*.

25. The imprecision of this figure derives from the scanty information, often merel name, which is available on the mothers of the magistrates. One or two I suspect the basis of name alone to be of parlementaire family. It seems likely too that sev more mothers whose names, even, are not recorded, were also from such familie

26. G. O'Gilvy, *Nobiliaire de Guienne* (Bordeaux, 1856–83), II, 'Verthamon'. O'Gilv full of errors, but this entry, insofar as it is used here, seems accurate.

27. P. Courteault (ed.), *Chronique Bordelaise, 1757–1784, de François de Lamont* (Bordeaux, 1926). The contract, of 7 Feb. 1783, before Chalu, notary, is in the rec of Me Jondrau, cours de Verdun, Bordeaux. He was kind enough to let me see it.

28. For Paris, Bluche, loc. cit., ch. 5, *passim*; for Dijon, Colombet ,op. cit., 58; for Rer

Meyer, loc. cit., II, 955–6; for Toulouse, Larboust, op. cit., 38.

29. See F. L. Ford, *Robe and Sword: the regrouping of the French aristocracy after Louis XIV* (Cambridge, Mass., 1953), 143.
30. See below, pp. 18–20.
31. Cavignac, op. cit., 284–5. For a fuller discussion of marriages between mercantile and noble families, see Butel, op. cit., II, 1059–73.
32. BVBx MS 1696 (Fonds Lamontaigne), II, no. 3. Letter undated, but the marriage referred to took place in 1757.
33. See below, pp. 116–17.
34. Information on him and his family in the private collection of notes by A. D'Anglade, 'Recherches sur la Compagnie des Conseillers Secrétaires du Roi Maison et Couronne de France à Bordeaux (XVIIᵉ–XVIIIᵉ siècles)', f.99. M. D'Anglade, sub-archivist at the Departmental Archives of the Gironde, was kind enough to put these notes at my disposal.
35. See below, p. 117.
36. J. Egret, 'L'aristocratie parlementaire française à la fin de l'ancien régime', *Revue Historique* (1952), *passim*.
37. Office occupied by the father of counsellor J. S. de Laroze.
38. e.g., at Dijon, 45 families out of 120—Colombet, op. cit., 42; at Toulouse, 38 per cent parlementaire families—Larboust, op. cit., 35.
39. Egret, op. cit., 7.
40. [Bachaumont], *Mémoires secrets pour servir à l'histoire de la République des Lettres*, XV, 61, 28 Feb. 1780. See also below, p. 180.
41. Jeanne Marie Françoise Duplessy, *née* Chazot (*c*.1702–82). Married counsellor Claude Duplessy, 1724, widowed 1736. As a young widow, she kept the most notable *salon* in mid-century Bordeaux, and was all her life extremely well connected in parlementaire circles. Her letters to her daughter (BVBx MSS 1201) are a major source of Bordelais history, 1768–82, and a useful guide to respectable opinion in the city. She is the heroine of Grellet-Dumazeau's *La Société Bordelaise sous Louis XV*.
42. BVBx MS 1201, IX, 31 Aug. and 26 Sept. 1780.
43. AN K708 no. 60. Speech at the assembled chambers, 23 Feb. 1780. See also W. Doyle, 'Aux origines de l'affaire Dupaty', *R. Hist. Bx.* (1969), *passim*, and below, pp. 177–80.
44. Dubarry, Lorman, Monforton, Reculès de Poulouzat, Minvielle.
45. P. Meller, *Essais généalogiques—Famille de Brivazac* (n.d.); O'Gilvy, op. cit., I, 387.
46. BVBx MS 1696, II, no. 20. Copy of supposed letters of Henry IV recognizing this, in the hand of Lamontaigne. There was also a Breton family of Pic, represented in the parlement of Rennes, which added this title to its name. Meyer, op. cit., I, 158, 162.
47. Cavignac, op. cit., 326–31.
48. L. de Baillenx, *Notice généalogique sur la famille de Marbotin du Parlement de Bordeaux avec des notes sur les familles alliées* (Bordeaux, 1960).
49. Letters patent of March 1755. Printed in *AHDG*, XXIV, 474.
50. Quoted in Nicolaï, *Essai statistique*, 73.
51. ibid., 73–4; R. Forster, 'The noble wine producers of the Bordelais in the eighteenth century', *Econ.HR*, second series, XIV (1961–62), 21, misinterprets this, and so actually underestimates the numbers of the 'robe'.
52. BVBx MS 1201, IV, 6 March 1775.
53. i.e., fourth generation from ennoblement.
54. J. S. de Laroze, G. Bouquier, and F. Perez d'Artassan. Bouquier had begun in the chamber of requests.
55. H. L. Barbeguière and J. Féger.
56. President J. E. Bienassis; counsellors E. J. Chanceaulme de Fonroze, P. N. Cajus, and B. Roche de Lamothe.
57. A de Roton, *Les Arrêts du Grand Conseil portant dispense de marc d'or de noblesse* (Paris, 1951). The article by J. Egret (cited above, n.36) is based upon the information contained in this collection.
58. e.g., Dupaty on becoming a president received such a dispensation, despite Egret, op. cit., 5 n.6, although it is not printed in Roton's collection. The original is in the papers of the marquis Du Paty de Clam, who was kind enough to show it to me.
59. 1783, A. Delpech; 1787, L. A. Lafargue.
60. AN BB⁵ 74, Bouquier to Keeper of the Seals, 27 Nov. 1820.

CHAPTER 2

Entry into the Parlement

A large proportion of the magistrates were destined for office in the parlement almost from the moment of their birth. It was important, therefore, to give them an appropriate education. The will of counsellor Louis Desmoulins de Maspérier left very precise instructions about the education of his only son René by his grandmother:

> Je demande de sa pieté de saisir Les premiers temps qu'il sera susceptible de quelque connoissance pour luy faire connoitre dieu Et ses premieres obligations Envers Luy, laissant à Sa Sagesse d'augmenter La force De ses instructions à mesure que celles de L'esprit paroitroient le permettre; je la prie de Luy donner Ces petites Leçons En forme d'amusement Et avec toute la Douceur que peut Luy inspirer sa bonté naturelle quand il aura atteint l'age de sept ans, ma mere aura La bonté de Luy donner un gouverneur d'un mérite reconnu; de moeurs sur touttes choses irréprochables d'un caractère Doux, et qui aye des lumieres . . .[1]

After such a grounding, around the age of 12 the future magistrate would be sent off to some school.

Until 1762 the two main schools in Bordeaux were the municipal college of Guienne, and the college of the Madeleine, run by the Jesuits. The former was much decayed in the 18th century, but the Jesuits appear to have maintained their standards. Perhaps the majority of the older magistrates, those who were over 20 in 1762, received their education from the Bordeaux Jesuits. At least 11 are known for certain,[2] among them the first president Le Berthon, the two successive deans Dussault and La Colonie, and several notable counsellors like Laroze, Cursol, and J. A. Leblanc de Mauvezin. It seems certain that others too were educated at this college, as the names of several of their brothers and fathers appear on the lists. After 1762, however, when the court (ironically enough) expelled the Jesuits from its jurisdiction, like other parlements, the college of the Madeleine was no longer available.

Even early in the century, by no means all future Bordeaux magistrates were educated in Bordeaux. Several families had a tradition of sending their sons to the Oratorian college of Juilly, near Paris, among them that of Montesquieu. The archives of Juilly reveal at least 32 families connected with the parlement who sent sons there between 1705 and the middle of the century. At least nine or ten magistrates serving between 1770 and 1790 were among them.[3] Others were educated, like many Parisian magistrates,[4] at the great college of Louis-le-Grand, still then under the Jesuits, and more, probably, were scattered among other Parisian institutions; like Dupaty, at the college of Beauvais.[5] So the majority of the older magistrates, those over 40 in 1790, were educated by the Jesuits. The parlement which expelled the Society, as in Paris, Grenoble, Rennes, and doubt-less elsewhere, was predominantly educated by the Society.

From school the future magistrates proceeded to the law faculty of a university. Some magistrates like Dupaty had studied law and become advocates at Paris. Others had studied at some great provincial centre, like F. Perez d'Artassan at Toulouse. Most, however, graduated from the university of Bordeaux; all advo-cates had to have legal degrees on paper at least, and all magistrates had to be qualified advocates. The required degree of Licenciate in Laws necessitated in theory three years of study, and the passing of two examinations. However, it is clear from the very youth of some of the entrants to the parlement that they could not have had three years of study. One of the most famous of Bordeaux advocates at the end of the old régime, Vergniaud, spent about two, and he intended to be a serious advocate and had no parlementaire ambitions. Even so, he took his two examinations in the space of three months.[6] Pierre Bernadau bought his degrees in the space of four months, noting:

> Pour mon argent, je prend le Grade de Licentie es Lois, ce qui suppose une connaissance assez étendue de la Jurisprudence pour exercer l'honorable et delicate fonction d'Avocat. Je suis etonné de me trouver sitot un habile Homme . . .[7]

It seems that the university's degree meant very little. Practice was the test of an advocate's worth and knowledge. But all that was asked from candidates for the magistracy was a certificate from the body of advocates that they were members.[8] The only exceptions to this rule of a poor and superficial university education were certain clerical counsellors, who sometimes held doctorates in theology; but they, of course, were very special cases, who often came to the parlement late in life.

A career in the parlement usually began early in life, and the court encouraged this. As counsellor de Lamontaigne put it:

> Si l'on venoit à refuser aux jeunes gens l'entrée de ces charges, l'on pourroit bientôt manquer de sujets pour les remplir, parce qu'à un certain age on se détermine difficilement à entrer dans une carrière aussi penible.[9]

Legally, candidates were required to be at least 25. In practice, there was nothing easier than to obtain a royal dispensation from this requirement, and 76 out of the 162 magistrates who sat between 1775 and 1790 had been received under age. One of the edicts promulgated at the re-establishment of the parlement in 1775 stipulated that no more dispensations should be granted, but was a dead letter from the start. Of the 53 magistrates received between 1775 and 1790, 24 were under age. Of the rest, 10 were in their late twenties, 17 in their thirties, one was 45 and another, 55. Out of the whole 162, only 12 were over 40 on reception.

Nevertheless, at any given time few magistrates were under the statutory age for their rank. At the dissolution in 1790 there were only four. Moreover, age dispensations invariably denied the right to vote in the courts' proceedings until the statutory age was attained. The overall average age of the court in 1790 was 47;[10] that of the grand chamber was 58, the first inquests, 44; the second inquests, 36; the requests, 49. There were only 22 magistrates under 35. It was never possible, therefore, for young to outvote old at an assembly of chambers. Whatever the case elsewhere, there was no correlation at Bordeaux between the turbulence of the parlement and the youth of the majority of its members. Few parlements had a more troubled history than that of Bordeaux under Louis XVI, yet it was predominantly a body of middle-aged men.[11]

Some members of the parlement had not begun their careers there. Clerical counsellors, for example, were by definition priests before magistrates, even though six out of nine were still under 30 on reception. However, most magistrates had followed some sort of legal career. Only president Daugeard de Virazel had served in another parlement, at Toulouse, between 1760 and 1769; but counsellors de Garat and de Gobineau had been counsellors at the court of aids of Bordeaux. Counsellor de Laroze had been, and remained, lieutenant-general at the seneschalcy court of Guienne. Counsellor Roche was, and president de Verthamon the younger had been, king's advocate at the same court. Counsellor de Poissac had been lieutenant-general at the seneschalcy of Tulle, and counsellor de Mothes, at that of Albret. President Dupaty had been treasurer of France at the office of finances of La Rochelle. Counsellor de Lascombes was king's procurator at the court of admiralty of Guienne. Some of them obtained letters of compatibility, which enabled them to keep their positions even while serving in the parlement. Of those few whose careers had not been legal throughout, only one had been in trade; and this was the chief-clerk Lafargue de Laroque, who was 55 when he took the office, left to him by his brother. All the others, nine in all, had been soldiers. Several had seen active service in the Seven Years' War, and one had been decorated. But such cases constituted a very heterogeneous group of younger sons, colonials, and others outside the usual parlementaire tradition. Four were sons of magistrates in the court, but two of these were younger sons. Two were sons of members of the court of aids. Two came from Martinique, but for them office in the parlement was more a source of personal prestige at home than a career.

Aspirants to office in the parlement began by informally sounding out their contacts. 'M de Jacobet s'est Enfin décidé à achetter une Charge de conseiller au parlement pour son fils ainé', wrote M. de Mazières from Ste-Livrade to his nephew, counsellor de Filhot de Chimbaud in 1786.

tous ses autres Enfans sont placés, et il est bien juste qu'il donne un etat à celuy-la. il me fit prier de passer chés luy pour conférer de cette affaire. il fut arrété que Je vous Ecrirois pour Scavoir I⁰ S'il n'y auroit pas une Charge à vendre 2⁰ quel en seroit Le prix 3⁰ quels termes pour les payemens ou combien d'argent compté on Exigeroit 4⁰ Combien il en Couteroit pour Les provisions et la Reception. nous avons besoin d'Etre fixes sur tous ces objets afin de Ramasser l'argent qui sera nécessaire pour Consommer cette affaire Le plus promptement possible. M de Jacobet per [sic], seroit bien aise aussi, que vous en parleassies à M de Loyac à qui il a L'avantage d'appartenir. il a été instruit dans un autre tems d'un pareil projet, il eut meme la bonté de se donner des soins; aujourd'huy on Espére qu'il voudra bien les continuer . . .[12]

For somebody like young Jacobet, with only distant links in the parlement, such preliminaries were essential. However, his interest was sizeable as this letter shows; only two counsellors were approached directly, but Filhot could invoke his uncle counsellor de Brane, his cousin counsellor de Basquiat, and doubtless his two Filhot cousins. Counsellor de Loyac was also Brane's cousin; his brother-in-law was counsellor de Raignac, and so on. It was not through lack of supporters that Jacobet never entered the parlement, but through disagreements over payments for the office he wished to buy.[13]

No doubt less preparation was needed for the sons of members of the court, whose candidacy was taken for granted. Yet the formalities had to be observed, and the first of these was for the candidate or his father to visit the first president to seek his approval and ask him to propose the candidacy to the assembled chambers. Parlements enjoyed the right to accept or refuse candidates for membership. Even Maupeou did not dare to abolish this old-established right completely.[14] 'Le roy s'en remet sur le choix des sujets aux Cours', Miromesnil, Keeper of the Seals, told counsellor de Laroze, when the latter protested at the exclusion of his son, 'tachés de mériter par votre Conduite et que votre fils mérite par ses talens d'obtenir un jour l'agrément de la compagnie'.[15] These circumstances were doubtless frustrating to those who suffered by them, but magistrates on the spot were perhaps better qualified than the government to know whether candidates were well qualified; and the right of co-optation was a useful counterweight to the effects of the venality of offices.

At the same time as approaches were made to the first president, the presidents of the inquests were also approached to secure the consent of their respective chambers to the candidacy.[16] Once consent was secured, the proposal was formally put to the assembled chambers.[17] At this stage, substantial objections were seldom raised, and the candidate (or his father) could feel free to conclude the purchase of the office. At the same time he wrote to the Keeper of the Seals asking for provisions and producing his title to them—a *procuratio ad resignandum*, or legal act designating him successor, signed by the previous owner at the time of the sale of the office. The first president would write at the same time to confirm all this, and formally recommend the candidate. After such formalities, the crown never exercised its right to refuse to issue provisions.

On receipt of his provisions, the candidate made a round of visits to present them, in the company of a sponsor, to all the magistrates in order of precedence. He then remitted them to the dean, the senior counsellor, for examination. The dean's task was to see that they were in order, and that due dispensations and legal degrees had been obtained. Subsequently the chambers were again assembled, the dean delivered his report, and there was a deliberation followed by a vote. If the candidate survived this, he was subjected to an inquiry into life and morals, to verify that he was of Roman religion and good morality. The latter was a nebulous rubric under which hostile commissioners of inquiry could bring any objection to the candidate. For new men, unknown to the court, this inquiry took a month. For those who were magistrates already, it was a summary affair of three days. When it was complete, the candidate made a second round of visits, the chambers were assembled again, and the two commissioners made their report. Another vote followed, at which the candidate needed a two-thirds majority. Successful here, he passed to the examination. Kneeling before the first president in the assembled chambers, he was given a text from the Roman law Code, opened at random. He was then given several days to prepare an exposition on it, which he delivered at another assembly. After a few formal questions he was then normally admitted in the same session.[18]

Behind the formalities lay the fact that candidates had certain essential qualifications. A closer analysis of these shows exactly what was required of aspirants to membership of the parlement.

Above all, candidates must be owners of an office, for magistrates were officeholders by definition. Pieces of real property, offices could be bought, sold, bequeathed, even leased, at will. In capital value, at least, a magistrate's office was usually a substantial item in his fortune.

There were two exceptions to the venality rule. The first president and the procurator-general were chosen by the king and did not buy their offices. Yet even they had usually to pay a sum, arbitrarily fixed by the king, to their predecessors. At the same time he usually granted to the new occupant of the office a credit note (*brevet de retenue*), usually for the same sum, payable to him by his successor. When F. B. Le Berthon became first president in 1735, he had to pay to the heirs of Gillet de Lacaze 150,000 l., and in return he only got a note for 75,000 l. at first.[19] But after protesting he was granted a 'gratification' of the other 75,000 l. payable on the port dues of Bordeaux. When P. J. Dudon became procurator-general in 1763, he had to pay 50,000 l. to his predecessor's family, but was at once granted a note for the same sum.[20] So in fact the only thing which distinguished these offices from truly venal ones was a guarantee against money loss when they were resigned. By the end of the 18th century, they were even tending to become hereditary. Neither the elder Le Berthon nor Dudon was ever paid for his note, since both were succeeded by their sons; and the same thing was happening all over France.[21]

The higher the rank in the court, the more offices cost.[22] The most important and expensive were those of president à *mortier*. The average selling price for these offices between 1739 and 1778 was, to the nearest thousand, 123,000 l.[23] They ranged between 135,000 l. paid by president de Gourgue in 1753 to 114,000 l. paid by president de Lavie in 1768.[24] The overall trend seems to have been downwards. Admittedly, they had risen since the end of the 17th century, when an office of president à *mortier* sold for as little as 72,000 l.,[25] but the peak for prices came in the 1730s, and after that they slowly declined. '... Un notaire est venu me parler pour ma charge', wrote Gascq in 1765. 'Jay dit 45 mille écus. Si on veut m'en doner 40, je seray fort tente de la doner. celle du p Lalane na ettee vendue que 114 mille francs et je suis moins que luy, en estat d'attendre . . .'[26] Most of these offices were passed on from father to son at the end of the old régime.

Next in price came the two offices of advocate-general. In 1760 N. P. de Pichard sold his to F. A. Saige for 84,000 l., and Dudon sold his to Dupaty in 1767 for the same sum. Both acquirers made profits when they sold these offices in 1778. E. L. Dufaure de Lajarte paid Saige 91,200 l. and P. de Raymond de Lalande, buying Dupaty's office for his son, paid 92,400 l. The prices for the two

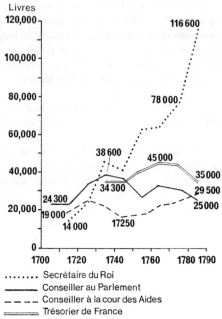

Fluctuations in the price of ennobling offices in Bordeaux over the
eighteenth century. Average prices per decade

offices of chief-clerk were similarly rising. While they were to be had in 1728 for
65,000 l., by 1777 one sold at 80,000 l., and prices had mounted steadily in
between those years.[27] Finally, in the higher ranges, the two purely honorific
functions of knight of honour were to be had at between 75,000 l. (1738) and
48,000 l. (1748).[28]

Much cheaper were presidencies of lower chambers. Presidencies in the
inquests rose up to 35,000 l. in the early 1720s, and stayed absolutely level
throughout the century. In 1789 G. R. B. de Filhot could still pay 36,000 l. On
the other hand, these offices could not be held by themselves; in theory they were
commissions conferred on counsellors, so each president of the inquests had to
hold the office of counsellor too.[29] But presidencies of the requests did not fetch
more than those of full counsellor at the parlement, at 30,000 l.[30]

Three classes of office prices corresponded to the three sorts of counsellor.
Cheapest were those of offices in the requests, very inferior magistrates. The
average was about 16,500 l. From a high of 25,000 l. in the mid-1720s, the overall
trend was down. When B. Roche was approached for his office by Jacobet in
1786, he asked 18,500 l.; the buyers, though willing to pay it, considered the
price 'exorbitant', and the deal was never concluded.[31] The clerical counsellors
also formed a special group. Because the candidates were normally limited to
clerics in major orders, the field of competition was reduced both on the score of
age and qualifications. Priests who became clerical counsellors also tended to be
younger brothers, whose meagre fortunes did not run to the purchase of very
expensive offices. 'Ma fortune est mince', protested the abbé A. de Meslon in

1771, when his office, suppressed by Maupeou, was not compensated at once. 'Ma légitime est presque entierement absorbée par le prix de mon office supprimé et des provisions et frais de reception. Jai été pourvu depuis peu d'un Canonicat dans une Collegialle dont les revenus sont mediocres'.[32] Such factors are reflected in the price of offices, whose average was about the same as those in the chamber of requests, or a little less. Once more there was a shallow century-long decline, from 20,000 l. in 1725, to 16,000 l. in 1787.

The prices for the most numerous offices, those of full counsellor at the parlement, were normally a good deal above this. In Paris between 1682 and 1771 office prices in the parlement, though in general slowly falling, were subject to substantial year-to-year fluctuations.[33] Fluctuations also occurred at Bordeaux, but the average price per decade over the 18th century actually rose until the decade 1730–39, when it was just under 39,000 l. From there indeed it did fall off during the two central decades of the century, but there was a notable recovery in the decade 1760–69, by the end of which some offices were selling at 40,000 l. Then from 1770 there was a steady overall decline until the Revolution. The magistrates were aware of these fluctuations and their possible causes. In a letter of 1758 Lamontaigne wrote:

> Le prix auquel les dernières charges ont été vendues, n'est pas bien brillant; elles l'ont été à 26000 ou 27000 l. mais vu les malheurs du tems, on peut n'en être pas surpris. elles augmenteront, sans doute, si la paix venoit rouvrir le commerce et l'aisance . . .[34]

He seems to have been right. Until 1770, the curve of prices for the office of counsellor followed closely enough the fortunes of Bordeaux's 18th-century boom. When the British fleet made the seas unsafe, the prosperity of Bordeaux suffered, and there was not so much capital for investment in offices. The same downward curve in prices is strongly registered in the 1740s for that most typical of merchant offices, that of king's secretary.[35] As in perhaps most things, war curbed investment by all those, whether merchants or wine-growers, who depended on the freedom of the seas for their prosperity.

The decline from 1770 was more complex. There was another war; yet it was far less harmful to Bordeaux trade since the British control of the sea was broken. And prices for the office of king's secretary continued to shoot up, so that by the 1780s these offices were worth as much as those of president *à mortier* in the parlement. Prices for the office of counsellor at the court of aids continued the steady rise that they had registered since the 1740s, and by the 1780s actually surpassed those of counsellor at the parlement. One reason for this remarkable circumstance may be that all the other ennobling offices involved less work for the privileges that they conferred than office in the parlement.[36] Yet this does not fully explain the fall in the case of the parlement. In 1776 the average price for the office of counsellor was buoyant at 30,700 l. in a year of peace and a brisk market. But this burst of selling in 1776 significantly followed the Maupeou revolution, with its suppression and tardy compensation of all parlementaire offices. It seems likely that the 3½-year suppression of the old parlement was a blow to confidence in the safety and reliability of parlementaire office from which prices never recovered. Those of the court of aids, which underwent no such suppression, underwent no such decline. The endless internal quarrels and strikes which dominated the last years of the parlement probably also deterred potential buyers. The reason most often suggested for the fairly general fall in the price of offices in the sovereign courts over the 18th century, is that increasingly stringent requirements of nobility restricted the market. The fewer the applicants qualified to bid, the less vigorous the bidding. Yet at Toulouse, after Rennes perhaps the most aristocratic parlement in the kingdom, following a slump in the 1760s, prices recovered after 1775, and stayed far above those paid at Bordeaux until 1789, even though commoners were excluded, and there were equally bitter internal quarrels. On the other hand, at Toulouse a number of offices in the parlement were suppressed in 1775, and there were fewer ennobling offices to be had outside it.[37] The reason for the decline at Bordeaux after 1775 seems therefore not to have been the parlement's exclusiveness, but rather a combination of the blow to confidence represented by the Maupeou revolution and all its ramifications—including its aftermath of bitterness—and the coincidence of a growing local demand for painless and quick ennoblement with the large number of alternative ennobling offices on the local market.

Whatever the reasons, this decline was an important fact in the lives of all magistrates, for the current price of office represented an important portion of their capital assets. For counsellors at least, the value of this portion was clearly falling from the 1730s onwards, after a long-sustained rise. This meant an even more marked decline in real value owing to the general rise in prices over the century.[38] Those who succeeded to their fathers' offices and subsequently sold them must inevitably have lost. More counsellors made a net loss over their lifetime than made a profit. In the 1780s most offices were selling at prices which Lamontaigne had considered 'pas bien brillant' in 1758. By 1781, the fall had become notorious, and although Mme Duplessy dismissed the idea, claiming that 'on oroit toujours trouvé des gens prets à les prendre à aussi Bas prix, ne fussent [sic] que pour en faire Comerce',[39] the fact remains that in 1782 one office of counsellor sold for as little as 20,000 l.; and president de Lavie, who put his office of president à mortier on sale in 1782, had still not managed to sell it in 1789.[40]

Such was the depressing situation of capital sunk into parlementaire office. The returns on the investment were equally uninspiring, as we shall see.[41] But of course office was not just the monetary investment, it was a status in society, a job, and the key to a certain sort of power. And these intangibles far outweighed the financial disadvantages, as is shown by the fact that candidates and buyers were seldom lacking, right up until 1789. Long vacancies there certainly were, some of five or six years, but when an office was not filled, it was usually a sign that it was being kept by its owner for a young relative. Certainly this reflects a reluctance to go outside for a buyer, but it does not mean that an office was unsaleable. Lavie's case is special, because of the large sums required. Another reason for long vacancies of several years (since the transfer of an office, from sale to reception, normally took about a year) was that certain people went through all the formalities of obtaining provisions only to be rejected in the end; which meant that somebody else had to start again from the beginning. Why then was such a poor and declining investment so constantly sought after? The fact is that a magistrate's office was not usually his only or even his major investment in cash terms. The bulk of his capital was usually more safely anchored elsewhere. Investment was never the prime motive for buying an office. Far less tangible social considerations were the decisive thing, and there is no evidence that they were declining in their appeal.

The cost of entering the parlement did not end with the purchase of the office. There were still heavy fees attached to the granting of provisions. There was the right of *survivance*, which gave to the owner free disposal of the office. There was the gold mark, one-fortieth of the official market price of the office. This was the actual fee for the letters of provision. Finally, from 1771, those who were not already noble had to pay the additional gold mark of nobility on gaining the ennobling office of magistrate. On top of this there were various legal fees involved in applying for provisions, and if the candidate was related to other magistrates, or under age, the cost rose yet further, for the gold mark was payable on letters of dispensation. When Dupaty became a president in 1780, his provisions cost him a total of 12,809 l. 19s, including an age dispensation.[42] The father of counsellor Duval had to pay 3,328 l. 12s 3d in all for the provisions of his son's office of counsellor in 1786.[43] Nobody could expect to pay much less. In addition there were certain donations, running in all to over 1,000 l., payable to the common fund of the court, to certain officers in particular, and to the lawyers' brotherhood of St-Yves.[44] Compared to the ability to pay the price, the other qualifications demanded of a candidate were small indeed, and he could be dispensed from most of them by the king.

He must be 25 to be a counsellor, 30 to be one of the crown lawyers, and 40 with ten years' experience to be a president. Since nearly half the magistrates entered the court under 25, they must have obtained age dispensations. Six out of seven crown lawyers were under 30 on reception as such. Seventeen out of 22 presidents were under 40 on becoming presidents, though because of early entry, nine had ten years or more of experience.

Candidates must not have close relatives in the parlement. Close relatives were defined as, father, son, brother, uncle, nephew, father-in-law, son-in-law, and brother-in-law. This too was a dead letter. The magistrates were deeply interrelated. *Dispenses de parenté* (for new entrants) or *d'alliance* (for those making subsequent marriages within the prohibited degrees) were therefore extremely common.

Candidates must not occupy other offices. However, letters of compatibility dispensed from this provision. Counsellor de Navarre, lieutenant-general at the admiralty, counsellor de Lascombes, king's procurator at the same court, and J. S. de Laroze, lieutenant-general at the seneschalcy, among others, all held concurrent offices with royal approval. The last was one of the most important single offices in Bordeaux, and because of this, even letters did not assure Laroze an unopposed entry into the court. Some members protested that it was 'moralement impossible de pouvoir exactement remplir ces deux charges à la fois', but the majority were untroubled by this.[45] Sometimes, however, the letters stipulated that the officer must sell one of his offices within a certain time, as when in 1760, Poissac, lieutenant-general at the seneschalcy of Tulle, entered the court.[46]

Candidates must be qualified lawyers, and hold the grade of advocate, but that in itself meant little, and dispensations from studies were available. The legal examination, the last stage of the process of entry, was very perfunctory. Those who were magistrates of some sort already were usually excused it,[47] which at least proves that it did normally take place. The secret registers corroborate this up to 1767. But did the examinations ever make the difference between reception and rejection? It seems doubtful. In September 1765 A. J. de Minvielle and J. J. de Boucaud had passed all the stages of the procedure except the examination and already a contest had arisen between them as to who should have precedence in the court. They acted as if the result of the examination was a foregone conclusion. So did the first president in putting the question before the court. He said it ought to be decided before the court proceeded 'to the examination and the reception'.[48] Clearly the two were inseparable, and in fact they always took place on the same day. Everything indicates that the examination was no more serious obstacle at Bordeaux than it was elsewhere in France.[49]

If the examination was supposed to test professional competence, the inquiry into the life and morals was supposed to test professional aptitude. The commissioners normally contented themselves with taking a deposition from two witnesses as to a candidate's moral worth. It was not normally an exhaustive inquiry, and the court had a number of magistrates whose continence, at least, was not all it might be. Only twice, however, did the morality of a candidate put his admission in doubt. It was alleged in 1816 that the first application of counsellor A. de Lajaunye had been rejected on the grounds that he was 'mauvais fils, mauvais mari mauvais Citoyen et homme dépourvu de lumières', although there may have been an element of personal enmity in this charge, hard to verify after 34 years and a revolution.[50] Enmity there certainly was in the case of Dudon the younger when he obtained provisions as second procurator-general in 1783.[51] Nevertheless, his case was special. Normally the life and morals of a candidate were of little importance in themselves, but were a useful field in which to find objections to those who were not acceptable for other reasons.

What, then, was the rate of rejection of candidates? It varied according to time and the candidates presenting themselves. In 1758 counsellor de Lamontaigne informed a fellow-counsellor that for two candidates recently received, three had been rejected:

> si ce n'est pas le moyen que les places se remplissent, c'en est un pour qu'elles se remplissent par des sujets qui puissent faire honneur a la Compagnie. je crois que vous ne trouverés point cette attention déplacée.[52]

Contested receptions, let alone rejections, remained exceptional however. A few contested the entry of Laroze in 1756. The abbé de Malromé stood out against Saige's candidacy to be advocate-general in 1760, Saige 'étant encore fort jeune, n'ayant point suivi le barreau assidument, n'ayant donné aucune preuve de ses talens, n'ayant passé par aucune autre charge qui eût pû le former'.[53] The office of advocate-general was too important to be treated in this way, he said; but he remained in a minority of one. Then after 1775 there were the contested admissions of P. J. Domenge (1775–81) and J. G. de Lorman (1782), both sons of Maupeouan counsellors, and of course that of Dudon, the Maupeou 'intruder', the biggest admission crisis of them all. Of the seven non-parlementaires who had sat in the Maupeou parlement, only Dudon was ever received into the restored court. Indeed he was the only intruder in the whole of France to achieve such a reception.[54]

There is some evidence of further rejections. Counsellors Montforton, de Garat, de Lamolère, Durand de Naujac, Duval, de Malet, Maignol, and Maurice de

Sentout the younger, the last four all in the 1780s, were second candidates for the offices they held. Others had been nominated to succeed before them, and apparently rejected.[55] Only one of these intermediate choices was of parlementaire family, which may be significant.[56] Another may have been related to a Maupeou 'intruder'.[57] Also nominated, by president de Verthamon the younger to succeed to his late father as president in the inquests, in 1788, was J. Duranteau, an eminent advocate. But in his case it may have been the advent of the Revolution rather than opposition which was responsible for his never being received.[58]

To enter the parlement of Bordeaux in the 18th century, therefore, all that was absolutely essential was to be Catholic and rich. Money bought office, bought nobility for the few without it, bought provisions, and bought dispensations from the legal qualifications. It was helpful to be a nobleman. It was useful to have relatives in the parlement and essential to have friends there, but here too money might create an interest. It was not essential to be experienced or learned in the law, of mature age, or of stainless character; but after 1775 it was crucial to have been on the right side in 1771, and this was a new element. After 1775 those who had been exiled in 1771 formed a majority. They kept the memory of Maupeou's revolution alive, sporadically, right up to the eve of the greater Revolution of 1789, by rejecting or persecuting those who, personally or through their families, had links with the Maupeou parlement—that negation of all that the old magistracy stood for.

NOTES

1. AD 3E 17.596 (Perrens). Sealed 14 June 1765, opened 4 Nov. 1776. His wife, née de Nort, had committed suicide in 1765.
2. AD H (fonds non classés) 'Registres des Jesuites', no. 2. 'Liber status Classium Collegii Burdigalensis Societatis Jesu ab an 1644'; covering the years down to 1730–31; AM GG 986 (fonds ancien), 'Collège de la Madeleine', festival programme, 1745.
3. R. Shackleton, *Montesquieu: a critical biography* (Oxford, 1961), 5; AD 3J E35. Bill for academic half, 1764–65; AD 3E 5.594. Will cited above, p. 14; all these are fragmentary Bordeaux sources. I was unable to consult the archives of Juilly, but I am grateful to M. Dominique Julia, of the University of Paris, who kindly sent me a list of Bordeaux pupils at Juilly taken from the registers.
4. Bluche, op. cit., 254.
5. Lycée Louis-le-Grand, Archives. Fichier Dupont-Ferrier, boxes 1 and 2, which contain at least four certain names; R. Delayant, 'Les Dupaty', *Annales de l'Académie de La Rochelle* (1856), 30.
6. C. Vatel, *Vergniaud, Manuscrits, Lettres et Papiers* (Paris, 1873), I, 27 n.14.
7. BVBx, 'Tablettes' of Bernadau, 12 May 1787.
8. AD 2E 1089 (tit. fam. Duval) 'Etat des frais de lettres de provision et de dispense d'âge' of J. L. J. Duval.
9. BVBx MS 1696, VI, no. 8.
10. At Toulouse, for example, it was 48. Larboust, op. cit., 33.
11. cf. Egret, op. cit., 11–13.
12. AD 2E 1213[5] (tit. fam. Filhot de Chimbaud), 5 Feb. 1786.
13. That of counsellor Roche de Lamothe. ibid., other letters.
14. See below, p. 149. Under Maupeou, the court designated the candidates, and the king made the final choice.
15. AD F MS 46, 'Lettre d'un magistrat à un magistrat', 1775. See also below, p. 170.
16. BVBx MS 1696, VI.

17. The secret registers (AM MS 758–809) record many such proposals. I have used principally MS 808 (1765–67), in which are recorded the receptions of several of those who sat between 1775 and 1790.
18. ibid. e.g., reception of Thilorier. AM MS 808, 24. 24 July 1765.
19. AD C3783. Protest of 16 May 1747.
20. *AHDG*, XVIII (1878), no. *CCCXXI* Maupeou the elder to Dudon, 29 Dec. 1763.
21. Egret, op. cit., 4.
22. See in general W. Doyle, 'Le prix des charges anoblissantes à Bordeaux au XVIIIᵉ siècle', *passim*. Figures given here, but not in the article, are mostly taken from the same source, the *répertoire numérique* no. 100 at the AD. 'Cessions d'Offices: Minutes Notariales retirées des fonds en exécution du décret de brumaire An II, portant suppression des offices: Inventaire alphabétique par noms de personnes et de lieux suivi d'une table de matières', 2 v.
23. Based on nine transactions.
24. Ford, op. cit., 50, gives 70,000 l. to 100,000 l. as typical for the provinces between 1715 and 1748, well below these figures.
25. See Doyle, 'Le prix des charges . . .', 65, 68.
26. BVC Richelieu XXXVIII, f.37, Gascq to Richelieu, 7 Dec. 1765.
27. There were only four transactions in all, however.
28. The only two figures available.
29. This may account for the discrepancy between these prices and those given as typical of the provinces by Ford, loc. cit. His prices would be the equivalent of the two added together.
30. The only figure available.
31. AD 2E 1213⁵. Correspondence cited above, n. 12.
32. AD 2E 2056 (tit. fam. Meslon), Meslon to intendant, 18 Jan. 1772.
33. Bluche, op. cit., 167.
34. BVBx MS 1696, II, no. 90. 28 Nov. 1758.
35. See graph, above p. 28, reproduced from Doyle, 'La prix des charges', 70.
36. ibid., *passim*.
37. Larboust, op. cit., 61–6, is the source of all this information on Toulouse. 43,000 l. was the average price for an office of counsellor, 1775–90.
38. One corollary of this is to make the rise in court of aids price look less important. Their real value must have been merely keeping level. But no argument of this sort will explain the rise in prices for the office of king's secretary.
39. BVBx MS 1201, X, 16 March 1781.
40. AN B III 34, p. 925, Pichard to Keeper of the Seals, 11 April 1789.
41. See below, pp. 40–2.
42. A minute in the family papers of the marquis Du Paty de Clam.
43. AD 2E 1089, loc. cit. above, n. 8. l. stands for *livres*, s for *sols*, d for *deniers*. There were 12 *deniers* to the *sol* and 20 *sols* to the *livre*.
44. Du Paty de Clam papers. Minute of 1768.
45. BVBx MS 1696, VI, no. 2.
46. AD C871, request of 1763.
47. e.g., Laroze in 1756; Dupaty in 1768.
48. AM MS 808, p. 106.
49. For Paris, Bluche, op. cit., 61–2; for Grenoble, J. Egret, *Le Parlement de Dauphiné et les affaires publiques dans la deuxième moitié du XVIIIᵉ siècle* (Paris, 1942), I, 20; for Rennes, A. Le Moy, op. cit., 20; for Dijon, Colombet, op. cit., 55; for Toulouse, however, Larboust, op. cit., 42, suggests that the examination was serious.
50. AN BB⁶ 56, Rateau, procurator-general of the royal court of Bordeaux, in a report on the personnel of the court to the Keeper of the Seals. Lajaunye certainly claimed later that these stories were put about by his enemies; ibid., Lajaunye to Keeper of the Seals, 18 April 1831.
51. See below, ch. 12.
52. BVBx MS 1696, II, no. 90. Undispatched letter of 28 Nov. 1758.
53. ibid., VI, 'chronique', 11 June 1760.
54. AAE MD France, 1589, f.241, Mouchy to Vergennes, 16 Aug. 1783.
55. To be found in various registers in AD IB (registres du parlement).

56. J. J. de Loyac, brother of Laurent, who sold his office to G. Montforton in 1750. Since he made a loss of 12,000 l., it hardly seems likely that he was speculating.
57. P. Duvergier, first choice to succeed in the office of J. L. J. Duval. One G. Duvergier was substitute procurator-general in the Maupeou parlement.
58. AD 3E 21.603 (Nauville). Act of 14 Feb. 1788.

CHAPTER 3

The Parlement as a Career

High over the old heart of Bordeaux, towered the turrets of the *Ombrière*, the medieval palace of the king-dukes of Guienne which had been the seat of the parlement since its foundation in 1462. By the 18th century it had become a general judicial centre.

> on y a Non seulement Etabli la Grande Chambre, Celle de Enquettes, Requettes et Greffe du parlement, Mais Encore le Senechal, les Eaux et forest, Lamirauté, La Table de Marbre, la prévôté, la Chancellerie, les archives du parlement &c dans les Rez de Chaussees et Souterains toutes les prisons, Cachots, logements de Concierge Relatif a ces differentes Jurisdictions.[1]

The dilapidated fabric was very expensive to maintain, and the extent of decay usually ran far beyond the resources available to repair it.[2] Nothing was ever done about the filthy and insanitary prisons in the cellars, where epidemics and riots among the inmates were regular.[3] Amid the frantic architectural activity of 18th-century Bordeaux, however, the king's courts were not forgotten. In 1772 a plan was drawn up to bring together all the various courts of the city on a new site. After the expulsion of the Jesuits, in 1762, their college of the Madeleine lay empty for several years, and the proposal was to use these buildings as the basis for a new palace of justice. The project was authorized by letters patent of March 1773.[4] In 1774 conversion work began, but when the old parlement was restored a year later, work was stopped, on the complaint of Le Berthon. The prisons were too near to the rear of his house. Several years of wrangling followed, before the building was resumed, and none of the courts left the *Ombrière* before 1790. The parlement finished its days in the palace where it had begun them, and it was against this crumbling background that the magistrates passed their working lives.

The judicial year began at Martinmas. The opening session on 12 November was marked by a Mass, attended by the magistrates in their scarlet robes, in the palace chapel. This was followed by hortatory speeches from the crown lawyers on judicial topics, and the promulgation of the service roll for the year. The year ended on 7 September, eve of *Notre Dame*, when the magistrates, except those serving in the vacation chamber (for urgent cases),[5] dispersed to their estates for the vintage. In reality the vacation lasted longer than the official two months, for the judicial year only began in earnest after Epiphany. Most magistrates, especially when the harvests were bad and money lacking, were in the country from early September to early January or beyond. In addition, the court did not sit between Maundy Thursday and Low Sunday, and on 36 religious feastdays throughout the year. The working judicial year was therefore just over six months long.[6]

In fact it was frequently even shorter than this, owing to haphazard attendance or deliberate strikes. Very little ordinary judicial business was done, for example, in 1780–81, when most of the parlement was on strike over issues arising from the Dupaty case. Nor was anything done in the year 1787–88, when the parlement was in exile at Libourne, and publicly refused to transact any business. When magistrates who had served under Maupeou, nearly half the parlement, ceased attendance from March to July 1775, this too must have retarded business. Individual absenteeism was also not uncommon. Some, like counsellors de Piis, de Cursol, Desnanots, and Maignol, never returned to the parlement after 1775 and sold their offices as soon as they could. President de Gascq, ex-head of the Maupeou parlement, retired to Paris on a pension. Judicial pluralists like Laroze and Navarre gave a large part of their time to their non-parlementaire work, especially when their record of co-operation with Maupeou made life in the parlement uncomfortable, after 1775. For health reasons, counsellor de Boucaud did not appear for nearly the whole of the decade of the 1780s.[7] President de Lavie ceased attendance in 1781, during the Dupaty troubles, and did not return.[8] There was more check on those wishing to leave Bordeaux, in that the permission of the company and of the Keeper of the Seals was needed, but neither was hard to obtain. Counsellor de Basterot was allowed to spend the years 1778–81 in England.[9] President Dupaty had permission in 1785 to spend six months in Italy, and on his return was dispensed from rejoining the company. Throughout the century, too, the 'Americans', with lands in the West Indies, were allowed to visit their estates on business from time to time, as the two Prunes brothers did in the 1760s. Counsellor Pocquet de Lillette de Puilhéry, who came from Martinique, only appeared once in 19 years of membership of the parlement— on the day of his reception.[10]

In those who lacked a legal vocation, this absenteeism is easily understood, for conscientious attendance at the parlement was indeed exacting. Sittings began at dawn, and went on until the middle of the day. In the afternoon, complex cases were dealt with by sets of commissioners drawn from among senior magistrates. The higher their rank, the greater was the responsibility and the harder the work. The inquests and requests, who dealt with cases in writing, only held morning sessions twice a week. The grand chamber, where pleas were heard, met on Mondays, Tuesdays, Thursdays, and Saturdays in the morning. All chambers met to deal with more complex cases on Mondays, Wednesdays, Thursdays, and Saturdays in the afternoons. From Epiphany to the Assumption the grand chamber also met on Friday afternoons.[11] Perhaps it was not so much the youth of the members of the inquests which gave them their lively interest in public affairs, but the fact that they had less routine judicial business to occupy their minds.

But even in normal times, the ordinary course of judicial business did not go forward uninterrupted. Hearings were constantly being cut short by summonses

to meetings of the assembled chambers. The procurator-general, or the representatives of any chamber, could call for an immediate assembly, which the first
president was usually obliged to grant. One of the objects of new regulations
promulgated at the restoration of 1775 was to place procedural restrictions on calls
for such assemblies, by confining them strictly to specific times, and giving the
first president and procurator-general more discretionary and delaying powers in
granting them; but it is uncertain how far this improved matters.[12] At the
assembled chambers the crown lawyers presented royal acts for registration, they
were discussed, and, if appropriate, remonstrances were decided upon. The
assembled chambers also discussed any matter of public or even internal business
laid before them by members or whole chambers of the court. This practice was
not abusive in itself, for it was an integral part of the parlement's function; but
it could of course be abused for trivial reasons. Another object of the 1775 regulations was to prevent such abuses. But even without abuse, a week seldom passed
without at least two assemblies of the chambers.

From the point of view of litigants, the uncertainty of the parlement's justice
must have been maddening, with strikes, holidays, assemblies of chambers,
judges not appearing, and so on. Vergniaud wrote in 1784 that:

> L'hyver, sans être bien rude à Bordeaux, a tellement glacé le zèle de MM du
> Parlement que les audiences se montent apres 11 heures pour finir à midi ...
> les jeunes avocats, qui n'ont pas de pain cuit, commencent à trouver le tems
> un peu long. Ce sont eux qui temoignent le plus de zèle pour que la justice
> soit bien administrée.[13]

In sum: 'La justice du parlement de Bordeaux n'a ni de bras ni jambes; et quand
on est ainsi estropié, on agit bien lentement'.[14] The fact is, that justice at the
parlement was costly, slow, and uncertain. One thing which helped the Maupeou
parlement to establish itself was the seeming promise that this state of affairs
would alter, a promise not entirely unfulfilled. The first months of his parlement
were ones of unprecedented judicial activity, even with half the number of magistrates, and there were fewer assemblies of chambers, no strikes, and an unparalleled regularity of attendance. But 1775 proved to be a restoration in every sense.
Not only did the strike of the remainers slow business down; the refusal of the
'returners' to give proper recognition to decisions of the Maupeou parlement
created additional annoyance and delay for litigants unfortunate enough to have
cases borne upon by such decisions.[15]

The legal competence of the magistrates was equally uncertain. They entered
the court young, their legal degrees meant next to nothing. To be sure, there were
some mitigating circumstances. Well over half, coming as they did from legal
families, must have grown up with the law, and grown up, whether they liked it
or not, for the law. This circumstance must have produced misfits, but equally it
must have given others a degree of preparation. Young entrants to the court were
also denied a vote in decisions until they were 25; between their reception and
that age they merely sat and listened. This constituted a sort of training. Furthermore, counsellors began their careers in the inquests, where sessions were not
public and where cases were judged in writing on the report of a single magistrate
on whose opinion his colleagues sat like a jury. There was thus plenty of opportunity for informal debate and discussion, during which the young magistrate

could not fail to equip himself better for the solemn hearings of the grand chamber later in his life.

Some magistrates were extremely learned in the law. The elder president de Verthamon reconstituted in 52 volumes the secret registers of the parlement from its origins to 1767.[16] Counsellor de Poissac published in 1776 a collection of notable decisions of the parlement.[17] The procurator-general Dudon, when still advocate-general, had had his account of the constitutions of the Jesuits published,[18] and left an unpublished manuscript of 'Conférences sur la Coutume de Bordeaux'. Counsellor de Lamontaigne collected remonstrances, and kept a detailed journal of the parlement's affairs in the late 1750s and early 1760s. He was extremely well informed on everything that concerned the parlement, and corresponded with Boucher d'Argis, who wrote many of the legal articles of the *Encyclopaedia*.[19] Richelieu and Gascq, when they were recruiting the Maupeou parlement, took special pains to enlist eminent judges like counsellors de Cursol, Fonteneil, and Lamontaigne; or Lascombes, known for his 'science profonde en matiere de droit ecrit'.[20] Any reading of the remonstrances of the parlement reveals the skill, intelligence, and legal knowledge of the commissioners who drew them up; yet few magistrates consigned their learning to print, and it was left to the brothers Lamothe, advocates, and L. F. de Salviat, counsellor at the seneschalcy of Brive, to write the most reliable modern commentaries on the law which was the parlement's everyday business.[21]

A special case was president Dupaty, who devoted much of his life to the reform of the criminal law. In 1782 he proposed to Miromesnil that a royal commission on the criminal law be established, with the ultimate object of reforming and codifying it.[22] Unsuccessful in this, the next year he persuaded the government to authorize a tour of Europe to collect materials for a comparative study of criminal law.[23] His famous *Lettres sur l'Italie*, which contain many reflections on it, were the result. In 1786, on his return, he published anonymously his *Lettres sur la Procédure Criminelle en France*, and undertook the defence of the famous *trois roués de Chaumont*. By 1788 he was a national authority on the criminal law, and was appointed by the Keeper of the Seals Lamoignon to his commission on legal reform. Nevertheless, his conflict with the parlement gave him little scope for the exercise of his judicial talents in Bordeaux, and the impact he made on the parlement's jurisprudence, after he resigned as advocate-general in 1780, was minimal.

Magistrates' libraries were rich in legal books, often representing the accumulation of several generations in the magistracy, a useful kernel of works of reference. All had, as was natural, editions of the custom of Bordeaux. The customs of Saintonge and other districts of the jurisdiction were also to be found, along with collections of decisions of the parlement. Several families had copies of secret registers of the parlement. Most had copies of and commentaries on the great ordinances of Louis XIV, and the Roman law collections of Justinian. The dictionaries and repertories of Ferrière, Bourdot de Richebourg, and Guyot were often found too.[24]

Clearly there was a nucleus of learned and assiduous magistrates. Assiduity alone must have led before long to a certain amount of knowledge and experience. Probably the majority were unexceptional one way or the other in knowledge of the law; doubtless there was a fair number without vocation or interest. Justice,

however, is not only a question of law, but equity. Were they impartial? The
common practice was to solicit judges. There are several examples in the 1780s in
the correspondence of the young counsellor Filhot de Chimbaud.[25] His uncle
M. de Mazières wrote in 1786, on behalf of a cousin in litigation:

> Mon parent desireroit que je Luy envoyasse quelques Lettres pour Mes-
> sieurs ses juges de ma connaissance. Je scay que ces Lettres ne font pas . . .
> de sensation . . ., cependant il est des circonstances où l'on ne peut guère se
> Refuser d'Ecrire . . . ainsi j'Ecrirai à Messieurs de gobineau, biré Marans et
> chalup, à moins que ma belle-soeur ne me promette de solliciter ces
> Messieurs.

Filhot himself often received such letters:

> Mon gendre . . . me mande quil a le bonheur de vous avoir pour juge, dans
> un procés, au rapport de M de gobineau, permettez-vous, Monsieur, que je
> vous supplie de vouloir bien donner toute vôtre attention ordinaire à cette
> affaire.[26]

It is almost impossible to say what effect such letters had. It is equally difficult to
decide how much influence magistrates could exert in cases in which they had a
personal interest. A group as litigious as they undoubtedly were was certainly not
afraid of going to law. But the first president was outraged when it was suggested
in 1776 that cases to which his colleagues were parties were being decided in the
parlement on political grounds, and he gave examples to prove the contrary.[27]
Yet in a court where, contrary to all the ordinances, it was possible for a magistrate to be named reporter to the court on his own case,[28] it seems open to doubt
how impartially justice was administered.

The financial rewards of office were modest. Magistrates received no salary
from the crown. They were paid with the interest on the purchasing price of their
offices (gages), and by the fees of justice paid by litigants (épices). Gages did not
represent interest on the actual price paid by the officeholder to his predecessor,
but only that paid by the original purchaser to the crown. For these purposes it
was assumed that prices were uniform for each grade. Gages, therefore, in no way
reflected the price paid for an office, but only its rank. Moreover, they never came
to the magistrates in full, for the capitation tax of magistrates was deducted from
them, and in addition they were subject to a standard deduction of a tenth:

Annual Gages 1775–90[29]

Grade	Before deductions	After
First president	2,212 l. 10s	191 l. 5s
President à mortier	1,425 l.	742 l. 10s
Presidents: inquests and requests	750 l.	225 l.[30]
Knight of honour	2,000 l.	1,510 l.
Clerical counsellor	310 l. 13s 9d	9 l. 12s 5d
Counsellor	375 l.	67 l. 10s
Counsellor, requests	375 l.	67 l. 10s
Crown lawyers	956 l.	590 l. 12s 6d
Chief-clerk	181 l.	167 l. 7s[31]

THE PARLEMENT AS A CAREER

Even if we discount the capitation deduction as representing a sum that would have to be paid anyway, the *gages* in no case represented a return of more than 2 per cent on prices actually paid for office, and sometimes far less than that. Other payments from the government augmented them a little. Magistrates who served annually in the vacation chamber received small sums,[32] and so did those counsellors of the grand chamber and the inquests who served in the *tournelle*.[33] More substantial were the pensions paid to all the more important officers in the court. Like the *gages*, they were subject to a deduction of one-tenth, which shows how routine they were. That deducted, the first president received 3,206 l. 5s; each president *à mortier*, 405 l.; the dean of the counsellors, 450 l.; and the crown lawyers, 945 l. each.

Certain favoured magistrates also held pensions on the Royal Treasury. Except for a standard payment of 4,050 l. net enjoyed by the first president, and small domains which he and the procurator-general had by virtue of their offices near Blaye, all these payments were purely personal. However, first presidents and procurators-general seldom failed to obtain them; they were too important in the dispatching of government business to risk the loss of their goodwill.[34] From 1767, the year after his succession, Le Berthon received 6,000 l. p.a. Dudon in 1789 had 3,360 l. dating from 1751, when he was advocate-general, and another 3,000 l. from 1767. Until his death in 1781 Gascq, as ex-first president of the Maupeou parlement, enjoyed 10,000 l. a year. Pichard through assiduous time-serving enjoyed a gross total annual pension of 9,600 l. (8,662 l. after deductions) from 1771 to 1790.[35] President de Loret, another regular government correspondent, received 1,200 l. p.a. from 1773. Laroze had 1,200 l. p.a. from 1778, which was quickly stopped in 1788 when he refused to participate in the Lamoignon reforms and preside over the projected grand *baillage* of Bordeaux.[36] Clearly the government regarded personal pensions as rewards for services rendered, or as safeguards against disservices. They were not given to unimportant people: only one simple counsellor, J. R. de Cursol, enjoyed a pension, from 1767 onwards,[37] and he had exceptional prestige and influence in the company.

Epices—judicial fees—generated a great deal of heat in France, although foreign observers like Adam Smith saw much to commend in them.[38] Paid by litigants on a time basis, assessed by the president of the chamber, they were obviously prone to abuse by unscrupulous or greedy judges. As a source of income, *épices* varied greatly according to the amount of judicial business done in a year. 1778–79,[39] for instance, was a quiet year. The post-Maupeou schism was being forgotten, and the storm over Dupaty had not yet broken. *Epices* totalled 26,295 l. 1780–81, on the other hand, was a year when the company was bitterly divided, and factional strikes interrupted the course of justice almost daily; *épices* fell to 13,638 l. In 1786–87, at the moment of exile to Libourne, they had yielded over a peaceful year 33,777 l., but they did not rise higher because at Libourne the whole court went on strike. This strike continued throughout the year 1787–88 and no more *épices* were levied until November 1788.[40] These fees were paid to an officer, the payer of *épices*, who deducted the standard tenth, and then towards the end of the judicial year paid them out to the magistrates. Most always went to presidents, senior counsellors, and the reporters of cases; but when we consider that there were nearly 120 magistrates to share them among, it seems unlikely that anybody could have had as much as 1,000 l. a year from them.

There were other fees. Complicated cases, those with five or more heads of demand, were judged in the afternoons, by a set of commissioners made up of senior magistrates. They levied *après dinées* at 38 l. 10s a time.[41] Called outside the palace to sit in judgement, a magistrate could also exact *vacations*, on a time basis. Finally, those magistrates who were pluralists, like Laroze, Navarre, and Roche, could add to their earnings in the parlement the *gages* and *épices* of these other offices too. These and the presidents must have profited from the legal profession to the tune of several thousand livres a year.[42] But the average counsellor could not have brought in from all legal sources much more than 1,000 l. at the most.

Magistrates could, of course, be as busy as they wished to be and earn accordingly. Only the first president, crown lawyers, and presidents in the inquests had certain minimum obligations. There was always a need for reporters, and there were always in being a number of standing committees and commissions, for drawing up remonstrances or conducting judicial inquiries. There were also occasional deputations to the government or to visiting dignitaries. But the financial return was hardly worth the effort. For the work involved, remuneration was extremely modest. And the financial privileges of the magistracy were negligible, except for exemption from the *taille*, which nearly all the families which provided magistrates already enjoyed in any case. The *gabelle* did not operate fully in Guienne, and so the privilege of *franc-salé* was of little value. If we view all judicial payments—*gages*, *épices*, and others—together with the other financial advantages of judicial office, as a return on the capital laid out on the purchase of office, they never could have represented a return of more than 5 per cent at the most.

A career in the parlement of Bordeaux had other limitations, too. 'Vous le Scavés, Monsieur le Comte', wrote the procurator-general Dudon to Vergennes, minister of the province, in 1782, 'en aspirant a la magistrature dans les Parlements de province, C'est en quelque sorte tourner le dos a la fortune pour sacrifier a L'honneur et au devoir'.[43] There was no paradox here. The parlement was certainly the most august body in the province, a local senate indeed, the summit of provincial aspiration. But whereas in Paris, membership of the parlement could be the first step on a ladder which led to intendancies, the council of state, and perhaps even the king's council itself,[44] membership of a provincial parlement seldom led to greater things on a wider stage. Nor were promotion prospects good within the company to compensate for the lack of opportunities outside.

The level at which a magistrate entered the parlement depended upon his fortune, his extraction, and the range of offices then on the market. The cheapest, but the humblest, level, was in the chamber of requests. Age and length of service in the requests gave no precedence in the parlement as a whole, except in ceremonies. A counsellor in the requests had six years in which to buy an office of full counsellor at the parlement. If by that time he had not done so, he lost all claim to precedence over full counsellors received after him.[45] Of the six full counsellors between 1775 and 1790 who had begun in the requests, none had stayed there long enough to lose their seniority in the parlement. But most of those who joined the requests stayed there, probably because they could not afford to buy a more dignified office. Two counsellors, de Leydet and de Lorman, were actually of the second generation of their families in that chamber. Its presidents were drawn from among its members too; although presidencies here cost as much as full offices of counsellor, they found it preferable to stay in this lowly chamber and be able to speak of themselves and sign 'Le président Maurice' or 'Le président Bienassis', as neither failed to do.

Another special case were the six clerical counsellors, whose offices could even be held by laymen with letters of dispensation. In 1725 no less than four of them had been held by dispensed laymen. A declaration of that year said that in future no such dispensations would be granted,[46] but it was not strictly observed.[47] They usually had a time limit, however, and under Louis XVI all the offices of clerical counsellor were in fact occupied by priests. It was a limited office. Though ascending normally through the court in order of reception, a clerical counsellor could never become dean, however old he was.[48] Nor could he be a president, or serve in the *tournelle*, although these restrictions did not necessarily deprive clerical counsellors of influence in assemblies of the chambers.

New entrants as ordinary lay counsellors were always added to the bottom of the list of one of the two chambers of inquests. On entry sons of parlementaires, followed by sons of members of the court of aids, had precedence over others joining the parlement at the same time. Members rose in seniority as others came in below them and their seniors moved up to the grand chamber. It could be many years before a magistrate arrived in the grand chamber. Only the two presidents of each chamber did not move up. Strictly, presidencies in the inquests were not offices but commissions and presidents had to hold the rank of counsellor as well. They were not entitled to preside outside their chambers. But because they did not move upwards, these presidents were often much older than the members of their chambers, and could in theory exercise a moderating influence. In practice constant contact with extreme junior counsellors often kept them less moderate than the members of the grand chamber. They fought all attempts by the grand chamber to override its juniors, and in the assembled chambers the opinions of such presidents as Verthamon, Loret, or Gourgue carried great weight, for they were senior in age and experience to most of the presidents à mortier. Verthamon and Gourgue were intractables, who were exiled under Maupeou. Loret had stayed, for he had always been and always was a government man, and often wrote unsolicited reports of secret proceedings to the minister of the province and the governor.[49] President Lynch, though much younger, was also very influential, for he was the son-in-law of the first president, went everywhere with him, and followed his line on all issues. But even mere counsellors in the inquests were not always less powerful for being junior. Each chamber could demand a convocation of the assembled chambers, where the inquests formed a numerical majority. The militant leaders of extremist opinion in the parlement, like counsellors de Poissac or de Loyac, were often found in the inquests, too, but militants were militants whatever their age, and sooner or later they carried their extremism up into the grand chamber itself.

The grand chamber was the heart of the parlement, and all counsellors reached it if they lived long enough. Here sat the first president and the chief-clerk of the parlement; here one of the advocates-general was always in attendance. The longest serving counsellor was the dean. He sat on the right hand of the first president and never served in the *tournelle*. He presided when no presidents were present. He examined the provisions of all candidates for membership, and received a special pension. It was an office of great prestige and ceremonial importance and was naturally coveted, but most counsellors retired before the age when deans normally attained their dignity. Retirement, if it was after 20 years' service, brought letters of honour, which conferred nobility on those who did not already enjoy it. For those who did, there was the status of honorary counsellor, which gave the right to attend the parlement at all its meetings and ceremonies, though not to vote in its decisions. This status was all a counsellor could confidently expect after a career in the parlement.

If the inquests were chambers of young men presided over by old, the grand chamber was one of old men presided over by young, at least by the 1780s. But the presidents à mortier were steeped in parlementaire tradition. All except Dupaty were of distinguished lineage, sons of parlementaires, and ten were themselves sons of presidents à mortier. They occupied by far the most expensive offices in the court, which also demanded that the holders keep the most impressive state. 'Mr de Pati de Rayet', wrote Mme Duplessy in 1775,

> est à Paris, et en marche avec . . . M de Gasq, pour sa charge de Pt à Mortier et . . . il en veut 40 mille livres contant et dix mille livres de Rente viagere. Je doute que Nôtre Ami Pati, soit en Etat de faire un pareil marché, et de Soutenir cet Etat . . .[50]

She was right. The beginnings of the Dupaty affair[51] suggest indeed that the presidential bench was not beyond the aspirations of outstanding talents coupled with a generous fortune, irrespective of birth, nobility, and connections. But not all ambitious men were so fortunately endowed. The parlement was, in fact, a very narrow field for the ambitious to operate in. Above the rank of counsellor, in a court of 115 officers, there were only 14 presidencies (excluding the requests) and the three offices of the crown lawyers.[52]

The two offices of advocate-general were acceptable alternatives to presidencies, and less expensive. It was an office for the young, energetic, and inexperienced. Of the six magistrates sitting between 1775 and 1790 who held or had held the office,[53] the eldest (Saige) was only 26 on reception. Four of them had never served as counsellors at the time of their reception, and the other two had only served in each case for a year. On the other hand, it was an office that could lead more quickly to fame than most others, for an advocate-general was on his feet, pleading before the court, on most days. It was in this capacity that Dupaty made his reputation as an orator. So it often led to higher things: Pichard and Dupaty passed to the bench of presidents, and P. J. Dudon became procurator-general.

After the first president, the procurator-general was the most important man in the parlement and its jurisdiction. He was also the hardest worked. The crown's permanent counsel in the court, he served the king and the company. When the company asked for conclusions, or the king ordered delivery of conclusions with the presentation of edicts, a date was usually fixed, and when it came, the conclusions had to be ready. In addition, the procurator-general had to keep up a day-to-day supervisory correspondence with all the inferior courts of the jurisdiction, report regularly to the government, and concert the public policies of the parlement with the first president. This was particularly difficult when the two were enemies, as were Dudon and Le Berthon for many of the last years of the parlement. Even with his secretary, two advocates-general, and several substitutes to help him, the procurator-general still found little leisure, for his office lay at the very heart of the legal functioning of the whole jurisdiction. The office was not venal; its functions were too important for the king to run the risk of its being obtained by an unco-operative magistrate. Dudon, who held the office throughout the reign of Louis XVI, was in general a loyal government man. He had been a crown lawyer for nearly 25 years when he was appointed. Immediately the office fell vacant, the intendant Boutin[54] wrote to the government that Dudon was the obvious successor:

> peut estre ses concurrents proffiteront-ils pour l'écarter, de quelques circonstances delicates dans lesquelles il a donné des preuves d'un role qui a paru outré. Mais l'age et l'experience ont Calmé cette vivacite je puis au moins vous assurer Mr qu'il jouit d'une tres Grande probite, Beaucoup d'esprit et de talent pour son etat, je crois pouvoir y joindre un meritte plus rare encore et dont peutestre on ne fait pas asses de Cas les moeurs les plus purs, et les plus exemplaires je suis Mr fort peu lié avec Mr Dudon, et c'est uniquement le bien du service qui me pousse a vous écrire en sa faveur, mais j'ai eprouvé s[ouve]nt comment il étoit avantageux pour ceux qui ont quelque p[art] à l'administration d'avoir a traitter avec des personnes capables de discutter les affaires, de sentir la force des raisons qu'on peut leur oposer, et sur la pro[bit]é desquels on puisse compter.[55]

The choice was a wise one, for Dudon never forsook for long the government line. In 1771 he stayed to become procurator-general of the Maupeou parlement. In 1775 he outfaced all the intrigues which were raised against him by the returned exiles. He supported the candidacy of Dupaty. And although at first he was one of the leaders of the parlement's opposition in August 1787 to the provincial assemblies, by December he was at the head of a minority government party. Yet such conduct took its toll of his reputation inside and outside the parlement, and his role under Maupeou was never forgotten. His obtaining of the succession to his office for his son confirmed his reputation as an audacious intriguer. This succession was indeed not unprecedented. Dudon's predecessor Duvigier had succeeded his father. But this did not console the ambitious magistrates, such as Poissac,[56] who had eagerly awaited his retirement.

Without doubt the most important member of the company was its head. The first president had immense responsibilities. As the chief magistrate of the jurisdiction, his administrative role was equal to that of the intendant, and greater in the sense that the jurisdiction covered several generalities. He was the chief representative of the parlement in all affairs to which it was a party. He was the government's man in the parlement, and the parlement's man with the government. He had, too, more influence than anybody else over admissions to the court. It would be difficult to overestimate his power; and his responsibilities were commensurate. Within the company he had to keep harmony, which demanded endless expensive entertaining, negotiation, and manoeuvres. It demanded his presence at all the crucial sessions. At the same time he had to maintain contact between the company and the government through a correspondence with Versailles, and constant conferences with the governor (or his representative) and the intendant. Ceremonial duties, inside and outside the parlement, took up a great deal of time, but the day-to-day judicial work came on top of this.

This office too was in the gift of the crown alone. The succession of 1735 illustrates the attributes required of a first president.[57] When Gillet de Lacaze died there were nine rumoured candidates to succeed him, including four presidents, an advocate-general, a counsellor, the first president of the parlement of Metz, and two intendants.[58] The decision took several months to make. The first question was, should it be a Bordelais or an outsider? The government feared that each local contender had his party in the parlement, and that, whoever succeeded, the others would combine to make his life impossible.[59] As soon as it was satisfied that this would not be the case, however, the final choice lay between local men. Such a policy was pursued in most parlements throughout the century, and has been characterized as 'worrying' or 'astonishing',[60] on the grounds that the king's man should be an outsider, without local bonds. This is to misunderstand the nature of provincial parlements. Intensely local, suspicious of outsiders, a local man was normally essential to persuade them to follow the king's policies. It was impossible to be the king's man and not the company's man, or the company's man and not the king's man. A first president needed the confidence of both. The successful candidate in 1735, president F. B. Le Berthon, certainly had it. He was of ancient family, with a long parlementaire tradition. He was the son of a president, had served for 13 years as a counsellor, and 18 as a president himself. Naturally he was of mature age, well known and esteemed in the court, and with no enemies there. His public reputation was that of an equitable and learned judge. To add to this he had powerful protectors at Court: the archbishop of Bordeaux, the duc de Duras, and the maréchal de Belleisle.[61] His moral life was unimpeachable. Moreover, he was very rich, perhaps the most constantly important consideration of all. The processes of negotiation and conciliation which were the daily business of a first president, revolved around entertaining, both of colleagues and other local powers, and the head of a great company had to keep an estate worthy of it. The remuneration of the office, though greater than that of any other, was still not enough to cover such expenses completely. So the first president was always one of the richest of magistrates. Such a combination of requirements clearly limited the field.

Le Berthon's son, however, was born to preside. Grandson of a president, son of a first president, his career had an inevitable air: counsellor in 1732, president in the inquests by 1736, president à mortier by 1748, first president in 1766. But in 1766 there was no contending, for in 1753 he had already obtained the survivance of his father's office, and had it registered by the court. For 13 years he was the official heir apparent.

This was not entirely popular. As the parlement recalled at the time of the Dudon crisis, 31 years later:

> Lorsque votre auguste ayeul accorda la survivance au premier président de votre parlement de Bordeaux, Le Corps entier aplaudit à ce choix; et il s'en félicite encore: mais quelles en furent les suites? Des magistrats recommandables aspiroient à cette place; ils en furent exclus, sans qu'on eût examiné leurs prétentions: ils crurent que c'étoit une injustice, et ne pouvant le suporter, ils abandonnèrent leurs fonctions. Si Sa Majesté eut renvoyé ce

choix à la vacance de cette place, la délicatesse des autres Magistrats n'en eut pas été blessée, Il est facheux pour l'amour propre d'être vaincu dans la carrière; mais il est humiliant de ne pas être jugé digne d'y entrer.[62]

The main contender, and a very learned and worthy one, was president de Gascq, who by 1766 was the senior president à mortier. He seems despite the survivance not to have given up hope until the moment it became operative, and when he was not successful, obtained a royal pension of 4,000 l. in compensation.[63] He had the talents, age, experience, and connections in the court and at Versailles. But quite apart from Le Berthon's survivance, Gascq had two severe disadvantages. His lechery was proverbial, both in Bordeaux and Paris; and even more important, he had no money. With a theoretical capital fortune of over half a million (half the size, or less, of Le Berthon's) he was deep in debt, and repayments ate up most of his annual revenues. Such drawbacks were decisive. It is true that in 1771 he became first president of the Maupeou parlement, whose fortune he guided with immense skill. But he had to be buttressed with a large salary and a huge additional pension even then.

The recruitment of the Maupeou parlement is closely bound up with the ambitions of magistrates. President de Pichard, most ambitious of men, jumped from low on the list to the office of second president and heir presumptive to Gascq. Counsellors Duroy, Bacalan, Dussault, Rolland, and Lascombes became presidents. Venality disappeared, the members of high appointive offices rose from two to ten[64] while the number of candidates fell from 113 to 41. The result was the promise of much more scope for the ambitious within the parlement. In 1775, however, the old system returned. Hence the furore over the reception of Dudon the younger. Among other things it was the outcry of thwarted reversionary interests, for far more had hoped to succeed the procurator-general than ever could think of becoming first president. Not that Le Berthon's son, though a president from 1779, ever received the right to succeed to his father's office; a feckless character, it is doubtful if he ever sought it. The resulting open succession kept hope alive in others, and in particular, Pichard. Late in 1774 or early in 1775, when it was clear that there would be a restoration of the old parlement, he asked outright to be granted Le Berthon's succession[65] or a first presidency or equal dignity elsewhere. Nothing happened, but he continued to press his claims. By 1781 he was the senior president à mortier. He had refused to compromise himself by striking with the other 'remainers' in 1775. He took the government's line over Dupaty and Dudon, and was always its assiduous correspondent. At 56 years of age he must have seemed Le Berthon's most likely successor before the dissolution of the parlement.

For the ordinary counsellor, all these circumstances were not encouraging. There was little hope of a presidency and hardly any of the first presidency. It is hardly surprising, therefore, that several also made a career outside the parlement, either concurrently, or after passing through the court. Some were judicial pluralists, like Laroze, lieutenant-general at the seneschalcy, and Navarre, lieutenant-general at the admiralty. Usually, however, it was necessary to leave the parlement in order to progress. Some transferred to higher office in the court of aids. In 1775, counsellor Maignol de Mataplane resigned his office in the parlement to become procurator-general at the court of aids in succession to his father.

Here family tradition, ambition, and the desire to escape from post-Maupeou recriminations coincided; although in the event he had a difficult reception on account of his recent past.[66] So did counsellor Duroy, son of a first president of the court of aids, when in 1778 he succeeded his brother-in-law, P. J. Pascal, in that office. But for those with national ambitions it was essential to leave not just the parlement, but Bordeaux itself. The surest way to success in politics was through the higher offices of the magistracy in Paris. The lowest rung on this ladder was the expensive office of master of requests, and one or two Bordeaux magistrates bought one. Before 1775 counsellors Giac and Bacalan are examples. After 1775 we find J. B. Taffard (1777) and J. Thilorier (1778) doing so. Neither of them achieved any eminence by their expensive gamble. The office might indeed lead to an intendancy and a place on the council of state, but might equally, without talent or connections, prove a dead end, as it did in these cases. In 1782 the dignity of councillor of state was conferred on Laroze, but far from entering the highest ranks of the government, he remained in Bordeaux. It seems to have been an appointment à brevet, a purely personal honour without duties, conferred perhaps to compensate him and his family for the discomfiture they had undergone as a result of their co-operation with Maupeou.[67]

Beyond these modest achievements, none of the magistrates rose to high rank outside Bordeaux. Undoubtedly the best-known member of the parlement under Louis XVI was Dupaty, but his fame was derived from his literary achievements and his conflicts with law courts, rather than his success in them. Besides, to leave Bordeaux for Paris was a risk, and the scale of expense which such a move would incur was out of all proportion to the likelihood of success in the capital. A great fortune in Bordeaux was a mediocre one in Paris. Local eminence was metropolitan obscurity. 'Le P. de Montesquieu', wrote Malesherbes, 'estoit homme de condition, connu pour tel dans sa province, mais tres peu à la Cour et à Paris, ou la qualité de président ne prévient pas favorablement sur la naissance'.[68] Montesquieu's fame had owed little to his prestige in the Bordelais. Few had the talent, wealth, or courage, to take the risk of uprooting themselves. Ambitious men, therefore, had to make their marks within the parlement itself.

Few fields could have been less promising. Doubtless for many it was enough to have joined, and so consummated for their families generations of social ascent. Even if wealth was the key to entry, that wealth still had to be acquired, and to have acquired enough was a real achievement. But for at least half and probably more of the magistrates, the sense of achievement must have been slight. They were born to it; they had been destined for this career from an early age. There was nothing very attractive for them, either in rewards or prospects. As Gascq confided to Richelieu in a moment of depression:

> Prunes ... ne veut plus aller au palais ny moi aussi il n'y a rien a gagner dans ce metier la que du travail de lenuy et des occasions de deplaire ainsi il faut prendre son palty surtout quand on na pas la fortune necessaire.[69]

A place in the parlement was a reward in itself, but it seldom led to further rewards. It was a dignified dead end.

Even the prospects of promotion within the court were dim. The few offices that were the reward of talent alone seemed to be acquiring hereditary character. Presidencies and other dignities required a conjunction of money, opportunity, and influence which few experienced. The result was a particular virulence in personal quarrels over the succession to the higher offices. They tore the court apart in a way that public issues never did. But the absence of wider opportunities had a result on the discussion of public issues all the same. It helped to eliminate the consideration of wider interests than those of Bordeaux and Guienne. Without the prospect of going on to deal with national affairs, a magistrate had little incentive to take the national view of government policies; he was only interested in their local effect. Though not new, such attitudes remained part of the essential background to the parlement's activities under Louis XVI. Career prospects and conditions of service were not unimportant in public actions. As cardinal de Bernis put it:[70]

> Un conseiller au Parlement qui a du mérite, et qui sent qu'il en a, ne peut rien espérer de la fortune: son sort est fixé à jamais. La crainte ni l'espérance ne peuvent agir sur lui; il est à couvert sous l'égide du Parlement qui est son seul juge, qui le protège dans la disgrâce et la réclame dans l'exil. Sa charge l'assujetit à une vie dure, laborieuse et retirée; aucun salaire, aucune distinction n'est attaché à ses travaux: il doit chercher nécessairement à se dédommager par la réputation de ce qu'il ne peut espérer de la fortune; et cette réputation n'a jamais plus d'éclat que lorsqu'il détermine sa compagnie à résister à la cour, dans des moments qui intéressent la religion ou le bien-être des peuples. Par conséquent, tout magistrat qui a du génie doit être dans le parti de l'opposition . . .

In these circumstances lies much of the explanation for the public turbulence of the provincial parlements.

NOTES

1. AD C3666. Memoir on the palace, 1768.
2. AD C1982.
3. AD C97. Memoir on the projected new palace, 1778.
4. AD IB 52, ff.185 vo.—187.
5. Called in Bordeaux the *chambre de retenue*.
6. *Etrennes Bordeloises ou Calendrier Raisonné du Palais* for 1776, 74–5.
7. AN BB⁵ 73, Boucaud to minister of justice, 2 July 1811.
8. AN B III 34, p. 925. Pichard to Keeper of the Seals, 11 April 1789.
9. BVC Richelieu XXXVII, f.169. Anon. account of the session of 7 March 1781.
10. E. Hayot, 'Les officiers du conseil souverain de la Martinique et leurs successeurs les Conseillers à la Cour d'Appel 1675–1830', *Mémoires de la Société d'Histoire de la Martinique*, I (1964), 218.
11. *Etrennes Bordeloises*, etc., for 1776, 78–83.
12. AD IB 56, ff.10 vo.—14 vo. 'Edit portant ordonnance pour le Parlement de Bordeaux (Versailles, Feb. 1775), arts. 8–19.
13. Vatel, op. cit., I, 93. 7 Feb. 1784.
14. ibid., I, 94. 16 Feb. 1784.
15. See below, pp. 168–9.
16. Collection now in AM MS 758–809.
17. *Arrêts Notables rendus en la Première Chambre des Enquêtes du Parlement de Bordeaux pour fixer la jurisprudence de cette cour* (Bordeaux, 1776).
18. Bordeaux, 1762.
19. Journal in BVBx MS 1696, IV. Letters of Boucher d'Argis to Lamontaigne, ibid., II, nos. 83, 86, 88, 91, 92.

Antoine Gaspard Boucher d 'Argis (1708–91). Advocate, 1727; member of sovereign council of Dombes, 1753; *échevin* of Paris, 1767–68; member of sovereign council of Bouillon. Wrote articles on judicial matters for the *Encyclopedia*, and numerous works of legal commentary.

20. BVC Richelieu XXXVIII, f.138, Gascq to Richelieu, 25 Feb. 1772.
21. A. and D. Lamothe, *Coûtumes du ressort du Parlement de Guienne; avec un commentaire pour l'intelligence du texte; & les Arrêts rendus en interprétation* (Bordeaux, 1768), 2 v.; L. F. de Salviat, *La Jurisprudence du Parlement de Bordeaux, avec un recueil de questions importantes agitées en cette Cour & les arrêts qui les ont décidées* (Paris, 1787).
22. AN K874 (marked K873 no. 9), 'Mémoire à Monseigneur de Miroménil, . . . ou Coup d'oeuil sur la nécessité de réformer incessamment en France la Législation Criminelle, et sur la manière de procéder à cette réformation'.
23. ibid., pièce 10. Another copy, marginally different, in AAE MD France, 1395,ff.231–2, along with correspondence on the subject between Dupaty and Vergennes. See also below, pp. 189–90.
24. The booklists consulted are those of *émigrés* and *condamnés* in the town library at Bordeaux. Cited, with references, below, pp. 136–8, 141.
25. AD 2E 1213[5] (tit. fam. Filhot de Chimbaud), Mazières to Filhot, 21 May 1786.
26. ibid., de Faget to Filhot, 6 July 1785.
27. AN O[1] 352 no. 438. Reply to charge in AAE MD France, 1588, ff.316–19, Remainers to Vergennes, 3 Sept. 1776.
28. Pichard was so appointed in 1777. AD 2E 2285 (tit. fam. Pichard de Saucats). 'Instructions pour mettre le Ministère public en état de procéder a l'instruction du procès criminel contre Girodeau', 6–7. See also below, pp. 97–8, 171.
29. AD C4014, 4016. 'Etats du Roi, 1776–88'.
30. In addition, presidents in the inquests received 375 l. for the office of counsellor which they were obliged to hold concurrently.
31. Capitation was not deducted for the clerks, since their *gages* were too small.
32. AD C4014, 4016: 14 counsellors received 60 l. 18s 9d each, 3 crown lawyers 243 l. 15s each.
33. AD 8J 481 (Fonds Bigot). Account books of Dumas de Fonbrauge: 33 l. 15s each. The figures noted by this counsellor confirm the official figures used in the table.
34. So, at the end of 1787, only the first presidents of Grenoble, Nancy, Rouen, and Toulouse had no personal pension, and only the procurators-general of Douai and Toulouse. AN BB[20] 62.
35. Letter in AN BB[30] 58; also *Etat Nominatif des Pensions sur le Trésor Royal, imprimé par ordre de l'Assemblée Nationale* (Paris, 1789–90), I, 90.
36. All these figures are from *Etat Nominatif*. The Laroze story from AN B III 34, pp. 984–7, Laroze to Keeper of the Seals, 14 April 1789.
37. AN O[1] 265, f.43 vo.
38. *Wealth of Nations*, Bk. V, ch. 1, pt. *II*.
39. These are judicial years, from November to November.
40. These sums are calculated from the *épices* written by the president at the foot of each *arrêt*: AD B (Arrêts du Parlement). Grellet-Dumazeau, *La Société Bordelaise sous Louis XV*, 296, gave a total of about 40,000 l. for 1770. R. Forster, *The Nobility of Toulouse in the Eighteenth Century* (Baltimore, 1960), 105, states that a year's *épices* for the whole court at Bordeaux came to 2,051 l. I have examined the source that he cites, and it is clear that he has misread it. These are the *épices* of one man, the payer of the *gages*.
41. BVBx MS 1486. 'Journal et Formulaire du Parlement de Bordeaux' of Mathieu de Lamontaigne (d. 1737).
42. The office of lieutenant-general at the admiralty was especially lucrative during this period of intense commercial activity at Bordeaux. It has been estimated that it yielded 25,000–35,000 l. p.a. See M. Gouron, *L'Amirauté de Guienne, depuis le premier amiral anglais en Guienne jusqu'à la Révolution* (Paris, 1938), 270.
43. AAE MD France, 1589, ff.194–5, Dudon to Vergennes, 30 Sept. 1782.
44. See Bluche, op. cit., 52–3. Also V. Gruder, *The Royal Provincial Intendants: a governing élite in eighteenth-century France* (Ithaca, New York, 1968), chs. 2 and 3, *passim*.
45. BVBx MS 1696, VI, pièce 5. This stipulation followed a rule of 1686.

46. AN AD XVI 13B. Déclaration du Roy, 10 April 1725.
47. In 1742, for example, P. F. J. de Spens d'Estignols de Lancre, a layman, became a clerical counsellor by royal dispensation. J. A. Brutails, *Inventaire-sommaire des archives départementales de la Gironde, Série IB, 1 à 58* (Bordeaux, 1925), 184.
48. Boscheron des Portes, *Histoire du Parlement de Bordeaux*, II, 425.
49. For example, AAE MD France, 1386, f.2. Reports to Vergennes of discussions in the spring of 1778. 'Vous voudrés bien, monseigneur, laisser ignorer à toute personne, sans exception d'où vous vient l'avis'. Loret to Vergennes, 17 Jan. 1778.
50. BVBx MS 1201, IV, 2 May 1775.
51. See below, pp. 177–8.
52. We can ignore the two offices of knight of honour, which functioning magistrates never occupied.
53. P. J. Dudon, 1739–64; N. P. de Pichard, 1755–60; F. A. Saige, 1760–78; C. J. B. M. Mercier Dupaty, 1768–80; E. L. Dufaure de Lajarte, 1779–90; P. de Raymond de Lalande, 1780–90.
54. Charles Robert Boutin (17? –1749). Master of requests; intendant of Bordeaux, 1760–66; councillor of state, 1766; commissioner for the administration of the generality of Bordeaux, 1784–85.
55. AD C3623, Boutin to Laverdy, 24 Dec. 1763. Rough draft.
56. BVBx MS 1201, IV, 28 Aug. 1775.
57. It is chronicled in letters between Le Berthon and H. de Ségur in the Ségur papers in AD 2E. Most of them are printed in A. Communay, *Le Parlement de Bordeaux: notes biographiques sur ses principaux officiers* (Bordeaux, 1887), 142–6.
58. ibid., 142. One of the intendants was Tourny, of Limoges, who subsequently became intendant of Bordeaux in 1742.
59. ibid., 146, Intendant Boucher to Le Berthon, 12 July 1735.
60. Egret, 'L'aristocratie parlementaire', 3–4.
61. Communay, op. cit., 142.
62. AM Fonds Delpit 167 (Parlement). Remonstrances of 3 March 1784.
63. AN F¹ 1956. Request of Dec. 1766.
64. Seven presidencies, including the first; three crown lawyers.
65. AN K708 no. 83. Undated and unsigned memoir in Pichard's unmistakable hand. The date can easily be deduced from the content. See below, p. 161.
66. BVBx MS 1201, IV, 7 March 1775. See also below p. 166.
67. On this distinction, see *Encyclopédie Méthodique: Finances* (Paris, 1784–87), I, 359. The appointment of Laroze is reported in BVBx MS 1201, X, 19 July 1782.
68. P. Grosclaude, *Malesherbes: nouveaux documents inédits* (Paris, 1964), 55. Malesherbes to Sarsfield, 28 Nov. 1766.
69. BVC Richelieu XXXVIII, f.37, Gascq to Richelieu, 7 Dec. 1765.
70. F. Masson (ed.), *Mémoires et lettres de François Joachim de Pierre Cardinal de Bernis (1715–1758)* (Paris, 1878), I, 347–8.

CHAPTER 4

The Wealth of Magistrates

Among all the preconditions for office in the parlement, one outweighed all the others: wealth. French 18th-century society was not strewn with impassable social barriers; there were no substantial barriers to rich men. Money, not privilege, was the key to social success, for, as Malesherbes observed, a rich commoner was more highly regarded in high society than a poor nobleman.[1] No better example of this state of affairs could be found than the society of Bordeaux. The parlement, summit of social aspiration for a whole province, was recruited from groups whose only common feature, apart from Catholicism, was their ability to buy an office. Offices, as we have seen, were substantial investments, but their financial rewards were for the most part meagre. This meant that magistrates needed considerable independent resources, and we must now turn to consideration of what these resources were, and how they were acquired. First of all, it would be useful to form some general idea of the scale of parlementaire wealth. It is far from easy to be exact about income except in isolated cases; only with the rough figures obtainable from tax-rolls can we put together larger samples. All these suffer from one defect or another. Nevertheless, they can be made to yield certain information about the income of some of the magistrates, relative both to that of their colleagues, and that of the other inhabitants of Bordeaux.

The best and most detailed tax-roll of the century before 1789, as far as the members of the parlement are concerned, is the schedule for revising the twentieth of 1755.[2] It gives in detail the estimated gross agricultural revenue from landed estates of 68 robe families. It gives nothing on urban real estate, or other sources of income; and even in respect of rural revenues, it probably underestimates the 'feudal' element. Nevertheless, an analysis is well worth reproducing as a guide to the relative income of magistrates from their most important source—agriculture.

Distribution of Gross Landed Income among 68 Robe Families in 1755

40,000 l. or above	1 (42,340 l.)
30,000 l. to 39,999 l.	2
20,000 l. to 29,999 l.	9
15,000 l. to 19,999 l.	8
10,000 l. to 14,999 l.	17

7,000 l. to 9,999 l.	13	
5,000 l. to 6,999 l.	10	
3,000 l. to 4,999 l.	7	
1,000 l. to 2,999 l.	0	
0 l. to 999 l.	1 (905 l.)	
	68	

After this, we find no more rolls with enough detail or reliability for calculating income until the Revolution. The decree of 6 October 1789 authorized the levy of a 'Patriotic Contribution' of at least one-quarter of net annual revenue for all citizens with over 400 l. a year,[3] and in 1790 local authorities were given the power to verify declarations. A comparison of the assessments for this tax with those for the forced loan of the Year II indicates that most of the sums declared were fairly accurate. The following table indicates sums declared, income thereby presumed, the number of people in Bordeaux in each class, and the number of parlementaires in each class.[4]

Patriotic Contribution of ¼ net revenue, 1790–91. 66 Robe Families

Assessment	Income	Subject in Bordeaux	Parlementaires
Over 20,000 l.	80,000 l.	1	0
15,000 l.	60,000 l.	2	0
13,000 l.	52,000 l.	4	0
12,000 l.	48,000 l.	1	0
10,000 l.	40,000 l.	2	1
9,000 l.	36,000 l.	4	1
8,000 l.	32,000 l.	5	0
7,000 l.	28,000 l.	3	1
6,000 l.	24,000 l.	23	6
4,000 l.	16,000 l.	45	20
2,000 l.	8,000 l.	176	14
1,500 l.	6,000 l.	111	6
1,200 l.	4,800 l.	75	3
1,000 l.	4,000 l.	151	11
600 l.	2,400 l.	295	2
500 l.	2,000 l.	154	0
300 l.	1,200 l.	543	1
200 l.	800 l.	369	0
100 l.	400 l.	767	0
			66

But however near to the truth these estimates come, the figures are always curiously round. For greater precision, we must turn to the accounts of the forced loan of the Year II. This was a tax on wealth. A year's net revenue was to be taxed on a sliding scale up to 9,000 l., when one-half was taken. Anything above that, was to be taken in full. So somebody with, for example, 100,000 l. revenue was expected to contribute 95,500 l.[5] Moreover, the terror conditions of the

Year II ensured that declarations were fairly precise and accurate. Only three full detailed statements of ex-magistrates have been found,[6] but from the totals levied on 51 ex-members of the parlement it is possible to work out their full declarations.[7] Even these figures, precise as they are, must be subject to certain reservations as a guide to old régime income. There was no more income from office, from the colonies, or from 'feudal' rights. Moreover, some magistrates under revolutionary conditions changed their source of income completely. Another disadvantage is that assessments were sometimes affected by the numbers of dependants. Above all, there was the depreciated value of the *assignats*. Yet the loan appears not to have been levied at *assignat* real values. Comparison of individual assessments with those for the patriotic contribution bears this out. With these reservations, the declarations for the forced loan can be regarded as the most precise information we have.

Forced Loan of the Year II—51 parlementaire assessments[8]

Assessment	Income	Subject in Parlementaires Bordeaux	
Over 100,000 l.	Over 104,500 l.	6	0
50,000 l.–100,000 l.	54,500 l.–104,500 l.	5	1
20,000 l.– 50,000 l.	24,500 l.– 54,500 l.	59	5
10,000 l.– 20,000 l.	c. 9,500 l.– 24,500 l.	104	6
5,000 l.– 10,000 l.	c. 9,500 l.	122	8
1,000 l.– 5,000 l.	c. 5,500 l.–c. 9,500 l.	811	15
500 l.– 1,000 l.	c. 4,000 l.–c. 5,500 l.	340	7
100 l.– 500 l.	1,000 l.–c. 4,000 l.	880	5
50 l.– 100 l.	Under 1,000 l.	360	3
1 l.– 50 l.	Under 500 l.	374	1
			51

An examination of these tables reveals certain common features. First, in all three, only a small minority of magistrates had incomes of less than about 4,000 l. a year, whereas the majority of citizens had incomes falling below this figure. Most parlementaires had incomes between 4,000 l. and 20,000 l., which put them among the richer inhabitants of Bordeaux. A few were even in the ranks of the richest of all. At the top was Saige; after him in 1790 came the first president, who declared by inference an income of about 40,000 l. a year; and president J. B. M. Verthamon who declared about 36,000 l. in 1790 and 44,452 l. 7s in 1793. The biggest annual incomes usually belonged to presidents. Of the ex-members of the grand bench taxed in 1793, four had less than 20,000 l., but one of these was Pichard, who would have had much more had it not been for extraordinary debt service; and another was Daugeard de Virazel, who was a younger son. The procurator-general Dudon, counsellor de Lassalle, and the widow of counsellor Dalphonse had over 30,000 l. Incomes like these underpinned the magistrates' pretensions to lead local society.

Almost equally striking, however, is the fact that the majority of magistrates enjoyed incomes that were unremarkable for Bordeaux. In 1790–91, 37 out of 66 declared 8,000 l. or under, along with 2,632 other inhabitants; in 1793, 31 out of 51 declared up to 9,500 l. along with 2,734 others. This does not mean that they were poor; simply that there were relatively large numbers in Bordeaux who were comfortably off.[9] Another feature was the immense range of incomes within the parlement itself, which makes the magistrates hardly appear a homogeneous group. Yet none were poor in absolute terms, and they were bound together by a common and prestigious career, family links, and similar economic interests. In forming group solidarity, these circumstances far outweighed the wide disparity in the fortunes of individuals; and it was on all these grounds, rather than wealth alone, that the magistrates based their social pretensions.

Compared to the incomes of Parisian parlementaires, those of Bordeaux do not seem much. 40,000 l. a year was not enough to sustain the estate of a president à mortier in Paris,[10] whereas only two or three Bordeaux magistrates ever had such an income. Similarly, in Paris a counsellor needed about 25,000 l. to be respectable.[11] But Parisian incomes had to cover Parisian expenses, which were always higher than those of the provinces. There is no doubt that the Bordeaux parlementaires 'came near the top of the revenue scale in provincial France'.[12] Possibly their revenues were not as great as those of the parlementaires of Rennes,[13] but they were comparable to those of Toulouse,[14] and certainly greater than those of Dijon.[15] But far more significant than their place in the magistracy as a whole was the parlementaires' place in local society, for it was upon this that their real power and influence was based. And here its financial base, while not exclusive, was still extremely secure.

Revenues are only one way of assessing wealth. What sort of capital values did they represent and derive from? Here accurate information is much harder to find. It abounds on individual items of fortune, but only with inventories after death and family divisions is comprehensiveness possible, and these are rare because families preferred to avoid the expense of such legal processes.[16] Thus we only find them when there were family disputes, or when a succession was overwhelmingly complicated. Of course inventories and estimates of goods confiscated during the Revolution are very detailed, and of incomparable value for information about estates. But the estimates of value, though strictly supposed to reflect the values of 1790, were usually made some years after that, and their reliability is often dubious. So, in the following list, only those estimates have been used which the historians of the confiscations in the Bordelais consider most full and reliable—that is, those for the goods of relatives of émigrés.[17] Reliable capital values that have come to light from other sources are also included.

Gross Capital Value of some Parlementaire Fortunes

Name	Date	Amount
B. de Basterot, counsellor	1788	2,528,000 l.[18]
J. C. Daugeard, president à mortier	1789	2,414,320 l.[19]
L. G. de Brivazac, counsellor	1782 (contested)	1,798,807 l. or 1,925,404 l.[20]
Presidente de Gourgue	1753	1,023,544 l. 16s 5d[21]
P. J. Dudon, procurator-general	1789	at least 720,360 l.[22]
P. de Ragueneau, counsellor	1778	571,258 l.[23]
J. A. H. Daugeard, president à mortier	1789	at least 460,474 l.[24]
A. A. de Gascq, president à mortier	1781	430,000 l.[25]

J. B. Maignol, procurator-general		
court of aids	1774	401,585 l. 8s 7d[26]
J. de Castelnau, counsellor	1774	396,343 l. 7s 8d[27]
J. B. Féger, chief-clerk	1777	208,869 l. 19s 7d[28]
J. B. L. Dufaure de Lajarte,		
honorary counsellor	1781	180,500 l.[29]
L. J. Demons, counsellor	1789	at least 149,813 l.[30]
J. B. L. Barret, chief-clerk	1787 (d. 1781)	135,000 l.[31]
J. de Filhot de Chimbaud,		
counsellor	1789	136,930 l. 10s[32]

The rough size of several other fortunes is known or can be guessed at. Saige in 1793 was supposed to be worth 10 million, which seems not incredible.[33] Pelet d'Anglade at the same time was said to be worth four.[34] The first president, presidents de Pichard, de Lavie, and de Verthamon, were all millionaires, perhaps more than once, in terms of capital. Many of the colonial proprietors also must have been theoretically at least millionaires, in view of inflated colonial land values; and unvalued holding in Martinique, for example, would probably put the total value of the Dudon fortune in the millionaire class. Counsellors de Brane, de Laboyrie, J. A. Leblanc de Mauvezin, Chaperon de Terrefort, Dalphonse, and de Lassalle all probably had more than half a million. So, probably, did the advocate-general de Lalande, and the knight of honour de Brach.[35] Perhaps most parlementaire fortunes, however, amounted to between 100,000 l. and 400,000 l.; a wide range, but not meaningless for all that. Those within it, while they cannot be considered among the very opulent few, were nevertheless very comfortably endowed. A fortune below 100,000 l. might sustain the state of a single magistrate, but hardly that of a married one.

In terms of capital, as in terms of income, the magistrates of Bordeaux did not match those of Paris. In Paris there were more millionaires;[36] a fortune of 150,000 l. to 400,000 l. was mediocre,[37] and anything much below that inadequate. At Bordeaux, the line of inadequacy could perhaps be set around 80,000 l. At Toulouse, in a sample of 51, or just under half the members of the parlement, there were only three millionaires; half fell into the class between around 160,000 l. and 400,000 l., and only just over 2 per cent fell below 63,000 l.[38] These ranges were much the same as those of Bordeaux, although at Toulouse there seem to have been fewer millionaires. At Rouen, a poorer parlement, two-thirds[39] of the magistrates had less than 200,000 l.; and at Dijon, poorer still, there were no millionaires, and a large proportion with under 100,000 l.[40] The great majority of the members of the parlement of Rennes, on the other hand, were worth over half a million, with several millionaires.[41] The great difference was that elsewhere, the members of provincial parlements were by far the richest group of citizens. But at Bordeaux, there were many millionaire merchants,[42] which made the richest magistrates altogether more commonplace and the poorer ones quite unremarkable, in their local context. Because of the business world of the port, the high robe of Bordeaux could never enjoy the absolute economic predominance which other parlementaires added to their social prestige in their towns. What is striking is the extent to which, despite everything, they overcame this disadvantage.

A true picture of wealth must also take into account the level of debts. This was an item in the balance of fortunes which could be considerable:

Assets against Debts—Four Examples

Name	Assets	Debts	Difference
Castelnau	396,343 l. 7s 8d	140,947 l. 17s 10d	255,396 l. 9s 6d
Ragueneau	571,258 l.	91,337 l. 14s 2s	479,920 l. 5s 10d
Féger	208,869 l. 19s 7d	33,000 l.	175,869 l. 19s 7d
Maignol	401,585 l. 8s 7d	92,757 l. 3s 6d	308,828 l. 5s 1d

The assets of the magistrates, in fact, were burdened with considerable debts. The main charges on their wealth were threefold—family debts, personal debts, and taxes.

Family debts were both the heaviest and most common; they consisted of dowries and portions to daughters and sons, *légitimes* to be paid to brothers and sisters, and so on. They were payable out of patrimonies theoretically at least capable of bearing the burden. Nevertheless, it could be very heavy and not easily or quickly lightened; the saving feature was that creditors in the family were seldom pressing. Dowries, normally the heaviest part of such liabilities, were paid over long periods, and could usually be recouped by other dowries coming into the family when sons married.[43]

The level of personal debts was not always negligible, either. During the Revolution, the creditors of condemned men and *émigrés*, whose goods had been forfeit to the state, were invited to lodge their claims with the office of national domains.[44] From these we can draw up a list of the debts of some magistrates at the moment of confiscation.

Some Parlementaire Debts in the Year II

	Personal	Family[45]
Basterot, counsellor	527,320 l. 4s 3d	
Pichard, president *à mortier*	154,923 l. 18s 11d	
Leblanc de Mauvezin, counsellor	111,712 l. 10s 4d	70,000 l.
Laporte-Paulliac, counsellor	111,654 l. 2s 3d	174,000 l.
Chaperon de Terrefort, counsellor	90,518 l. 4s 8d	
Dussault, counsellor	76,333 l. 8s 3d	
Prunes Duvivier, counsellor	74,086 l. 17s 10d	
Paty du Rayet, counsellor	65,784 l. 18s 9d	89,000 l.
Dufaure de Lajarte, advocate-general	52,000 l.	
Lamolère, counsellor	47,098 l. 7s 8d	
Montsec de Reignac, counsellor	41,413 l. 12s 10d	9,000 l.
Dudon (younger), procurator-general	41,289 l. 1s 8d	
Rolland, president	37,164 l. 18s	
Loyac, counsellor	31,130 l.	
Baritault, counsellor	30,482 l. 18s 6d	
Meslon, counsellor	25,109 l. 2s 4d	
Dumas de Laroque, counsellor	20,857 l. 15s	13,000 l.
Filhot, president	20,000 l.	
Raignac, counsellor	18,565 l. 17s	

Maurice de Sentout, president	14,000 l.
Daugeard, president *à mortier*	7,652 l. 7s 6d
Lalande, advocate-general	5,894 l. 1s
Dumas de Fonbrauge, counsellor	1,555 l.
Pelet d'Anglade, counsellor	1,509 l. 9s 9d
Fauquier, counsellor	1,453 l. 11s 6d

For complex reasons, debts registered in 1793 probably exceeded the level normal under the old régime, and therefore they only reinforce the impression that the debts of magistrates were not overwhelming. Most totals were under 50,000 l., and only five exceeded 100,000 l. An average magistrate could easily cover such sums with the value of his estates. Some could have wiped out their debts with one or two years' income.

Bankruptcies were therefore rare. Nevertheless, some magistrates only just escaped. In the 1760s president de Gascq needed capital so badly that he resolved to sell his office:

> il faut songer a faire honeur à ses affaires et a vivre honettement le reste de ses jours; c'est a quoy je ne puis parvenir sans vendre, car linteret de ce que je dois absorbe le revenu tres incertain de mes fonds, et il ne me reste que la plus valeur qui diminue chaque jour . . .[46]

This was a man whose estates sold in 1785 for over half a million![47] In the 1760s, his day-to-day financial situation was only improved by a timely bequest and a series of royal pensions. Death saved Jacques Delpy, honorary counsellor, and father of counsellor J. L. H. Delpy de la Roche. At his death he left an overall deficit of 487,264 l. 16s 10d,[48] his succession was declared bankrupt, and the result was a series of lawsuits. Counsellor de Basterot, who heads our list with debts of over half a million, was saved by the Revolution. Early in 1789 he invited all his creditors, and those of his father who had died the previous year, to send in their claims.[49] Through no fault of his own, he was unable to call in his assets. He had huge credits in Saint-Domingue from his second wife's dowry which he was unable to realize. His first wife had been Irish, again with a large dowry which was difficult to obtain. Attempts to raise capital in the 1780s by the selling of life annuities (claims for which are included in the Year II total of his debts) did not alleviate his difficulties. By December 1790 he was bankrupt, and a council of his creditors was established to run his estates until he was discharged.[50] It was with their permission that in 1791 he went to Dublin to institute proceedings for recovery of his first wife's dowry. He won his case, but understandably did not return to France until the restoration. By then his debts were forgotten.

Basterot is striking because he was an exception. Although most magistrates had extensive debts, they were in nature inevitable, and in amount not unmanageable. They were partially the result of the composition of fortunes, in which there was a clear predominance of real estate over moveables and cash. In Paris, fortunes were more diversified,[51] but at Rennes and Rouen, real estate predominated,[52] as it did at Toulouse.[53] The result was that assets were difficult to realize quickly, and ready cash was short. Hence loans, or that legal fiction, the selling of *rentes*, were necessary. Often the magistrates borrowed from each other, but if colleagues or relatives could not oblige, there was always the large community of Jews. The rich merchant family of Gradis was particularly obliging: in 1789 they were owed 60,893 l. by the first president, 38,159 l. by one of the Daugeards, and 93,125 l. by the procurator-general.[54] In 1793, president de Pichard had 340,000 l. worth of debts, of which 102,000 l. was owed to Jews.[55] The same year, when the widow Rodriguez declared her income, her late husband emerged as the creditor of several ex-magistrates, five of whom she labelled bad debtors.[56] And of course there must have been some, like Pelet d'Anglade, who paid by court order in 1791 one debt of nearly 2,000 l. which had been outstanding since 1768.[57] But parlementaire debts were not the result of inability to manage affairs, nor were they in general overwhelming. They were part of the normal financial structure of society; and they indicated, if anything, that wealth was safely invested in the most reliable and solid, though least realizable, of all propositions—real estate.

How far was this wealth tapped by that most inexorable of creditors, the state? How far were these noble magistrates exempt from common fiscal burdens? Was the weight of taxation as crushing for them personally, as they constantly claimed it was for those over whom they had jurisdiction?

The least onerous tax paid by the magistrates was the capitation, for which the parlement was taxed on a special roll, comprising practising advocates as well as the magistrates themselves. A lump sum was fixed by the government, but the parlement was allowed to apportion it among its members as it saw fit.[58] It was actually paid by the deduction of each year's amount from the *gages* of the magistrates. The sums were not large, and hardly varied for decades on end.

Capitation of the Parlement, 1790[59]

First president	1,800 l.
President *à mortier*	540 l.
Chamber president	450 l.
Others	270 l.

Plainly the capitation did not fall heavily on them, and under Maupeou, presumably as an additional inducement to join the court, it was reduced to almost nothing. In 1775 the total sum levied on the parlement was 40,318 l., whereas in 1774 it had been only 9,512 l.[60] Admittedly the Maupeou parlement was only half the size of the old one, but the reduction was still disproportionate. Counsellor de Filhot de Chimbaud, who sat in the Maupeou parlement, paid 279 l. in 1770, but only 80 l. in 1773.[61] On the other hand, the capitation paid by the magistrates whom Maupeou had exiled was raised to a normal rate now they were deprived of the special favour that membership of the parlement conveyed. Le Berthon's complaints were unavailing.[62] The magistrates also paid capitation on behalf of their servants, although with the exception of presidents most members of the parlement did not pay over 20 l.[63] The sum for the whole company only came to 1,519 l. in 1777.[64] Nevertheless, it was an occasion for conflict: between 1775 and 1778 only 17 magistrates paid any capitation on their servants, the rest objecting that it was not levied by deduction from *gages*.[65] The court of aids and the office of finances followed the example; and not until 1781 did the government, by agreeing to deduction, persuade them to resume payments.

Without doubt the most important tax paid by the magistrates was the twentieth. In Bordeaux there were seven rolls altogether, and members of the parlement normally appeared on several all at once—those of the lands of the nobility, of town houses, and sometimes the *bourgeois de Bordeaux*.[66] Originating in 1749, within the living memory of most magistrates, the twentieth was basically a land tax of one twentieth of net annual yield. Throughout the years 1775–90, in fact, two twentieths were levied, along with 4 *sols pour livre* on the first twentieth. Between 1781 and 1786, indeed, three twentieths per year were levied, as they had been between 1760 and 1763. At these times, the government laid claim to about one-quarter of a man's net annual income. Such claims made the French nobility, in theory at least, one of the most highly taxed in Europe.[67]

In practice, however, assessments seldom came to one twentieth, so that the amounts levied were seldom as much as they could or should have been. The most detailed and precise twentieth roll of the century, as far as the parlementaires of Bordeaux were concerned, was that of 1755.[68] It gave estimates of income and assessments for tax, which, even taking into account that the estimates were for gross and not net income, can seldom have amounted to one twentieth. Only when more than one was in operation was a true twentieth likely to be levied. As the intendant wrote to Turgot in 1775:

> Il est certain . . . que le produit actuel de cette imposition n'est pas forcé dans cette généralité; et que les grands propriétaires surtout sont singuliere- ment menagés, ainsi en repartissant avec Egallité a proportion dans toutte la province, le montant actuel de l'imposition, il en resulteroit un soulagement considerable pour la pluspart des contribuables . . . Mais L'embaras est d'etablir cette proportion . . . l'on ne peut en effet espérer de parvenir a une juste repartition qu'en obligeant a de nouvelles Declarations et en ordonnant que ces Declarations seront verifiées par les Controlleurs. Cette double operation ne se peut faire sans porter l'allarme parmi tous les propriétaires, et sans exciter des plaintes et des murmures.[69]

Nor was this all. For the 3,000 or so parishes of the generality, there were only ten comptrollers. Since leases at fixed annual sums were rare in the Bordelais, estate incomes were very hard to assess, all the more so when the basis of the income was a crop as unpredictable as wine. Tourny himself had taken up the magistrates' case on the occasion of a poor vintage in 1744, when the govern- ment had ordered the raising of the assessment for the tenth.[70]

The remedy for any injustice resulting from such causes was a discharge. Each year, the government fixed for each generality a sum out of which the intendant might remit to hard cases a proportion of their tax debt. Even so, Dupré de Saint-Maur, not one to favour any unjustified tax-evasion, could complain that:

> La somme que je puis y appliquer est si modique pour une Province aussy Vaste, qu'au lieu de vous proposer d'y faire aucun retranchement, J'aurois pour en solliciter L'augmentation, Les raisons les plus fortes par les Vicis- situdes auxquelles Les Contribuables sont Exposés dans un Pays dont le Commerce at les Recoltes de vins font les principales ressources.[71]

Members of the parlement regularly solicited, and obtained, partial or total discharges. They were accorded particularly frequently in the lean years of the late 1760s and the early '70s, and after the wine-growing disaster year of 1778 when some magistrates obtained several years' complete discharge. For the twentieth was a tax on net income, and it was only necessary to show extraordinary losses to qualify for a reduction.

Nor was the twentieth on town houses any more onerous. Assessments did not rise throughout the last 30 years of the old régime, although on Arthur Young's testimony rents were rising. None of the assessments, except possibly on newly built houses, came anywhere near one twentieth; yet it was only necessary to prove that property had been vacant to obtain an alleviation of the tax. Theoretically the value of property should have been easy to assess by reference to lease agreements in the public notarial records, but most leaseholds were consigned to private agreements. Perhaps tax-evasion was the reason for this.

Nevertheless, the government's indulgence was not limitless. Its processes were slow, but those of the taxpayers were often slower. In the last resort, it could confiscate the goods of slow payers. In 1777, after two warnings, the fruits of the Brivazac estates at Birac (Agenais) were impounded until the counsellor's twentieths were paid. His protests that he was awaiting the outcome of a case at the court of aids, to determine whether his lands were noble or not, were ignored.[72] In 1780 some of president de Pichard's goods were seized at Salles and Belin: he owed his servants' capitation since 1775, the twentieth on his town house since 1776, and the twentieth on his estates since 1777. Affronted, he wrote to the receiver:

> Au reste, Monsieur, moins par rapport à ma Personne qu'en Consideration de mon titre de President à Mortier et de Doyen du grand banc du Parlement de Bordeaux, je me serois flaté que vous auriés eu l'honneteté de m'ecrire avant d'en venir à cette Rigueur . . . je ne veux rien faire perdre au Roi . . .[73]

Necker commented drily to the intendent:

> Les Magistrats doivent L'exemple de l'exactitude à contribuer aux charges de l'Etat, et cet exemple est d'autant plus necessaire, de leur part, dans votre Generalité, que le Recouvrement y est tres arrieré.[74]

The capitation and the twentieth were the only taxes to which all the magistrates were subject. Certain of them did pay the *taille*, that supremely non-noble tax, because some of them owned lands in the one part of the generality of Bordeaux which was an area of *taille réele*, the elections of Agen and Condom. Here the *taille* was assessed on a landed, not a personal, basis. There were still exemptions, but they were attached to nobility of land, not of person. Among those with non-noble lands in these districts were president Daugeard de Virazel, and counsellors Marbotin, Laliman, and Drouilhet de Sigalas.[75]

Of the other tax-exemptions enjoyed all over France by members of parlements, the *franc-salé*, which limited the obligations to buy salt from the government monopoly, was of little use to the Bordelais. Guienne was a *pays rédimé*,[76] where the weight of the monopoly was light, and so privileged status was unimportant. The only burden of any weight, which the magistrates escaped entirely and without exception was the *corvée*, or forced labour. It is perhaps not a coincidence that it was on this issue that the parlement took one of its most extreme stands under Louis XVI.

The members of the parlement, therefore, did benefit from fiscal privileges, but by no means escaped entirely from taxation. Yet, owing to the inability of collectors to produce anything like accurate assessments, they certainly paid far less than they ought to have done—probably no more than a twentieth of their income even when taxes were at their heaviest. This compares very favourably with the burden borne by peasants. But the letter of the law was still extortionate, and it was this which took the taxpayers' attention. So it is not surprising that, extremely moderate though their tax burden was, the magistrates considered themselves overtaxed. Many of them could remember a time when there had been no twentieth, yet they lived to see not one, but two and sometimes three imposed, as well as a raising of attendant surtaxes. Where would it all end? Few doubted that the seemingly limitless growth in taxation would bring about their ruin, through the destruction of the country's greatest resource—agriculture. This conviction lay behind the magistrates' hostility to new taxes, for agriculture was the main source of their own wealth, too.

NOTES

1. P. Grosclaude, *Malesherbes*, 47, Malesherbes to Sarsfield, 28 Nov. 1766.
2. AD C3018. 'Etat du vingtième des biens fonds des officiers du Parlement', printed by A. Nicolaï as 'Documents sur la fortune privée au XVIIIᵉ siècle', in *AHDG*, XLIV (1909), 355ff. Analysed into a table by R. Forster. 'The noble wine producers', 21, although under an erroneous reference. See also below, pp. 86–7.
3. See R. Brouillard, *Des impositions extraordinaires sur le revenu pendant la Révolution (Contribution Patriotique—Emprunts Forcés) et de leur application dans la commune de Bordeaux* (Bordeaux, 1910), 14–16. For supplementary information, and for statistics on groups outside the parlement, I have drawn heavily on this work. The evidence of these revolutionary tax rolls is examined and analysed for the merchant community by Butel, op. cit., II, 978–83.
4. ibid., 44. 'Bilan de la contribution patriotique', for the general figures. The parlementaire figures have been taken from the rolls themselves in AD 4L 113 and AM fonds révolutionnaire G 27. When it came to the verification of the figures, 31 parlementaire declarations were raised: then, on petition, some were lowered again, though seldom to the original figure. The complexity of tabulating these changes would be so great that here only the original declarations have been taken; in any case, the original difference was seldom more than 2,000 l., and the final one, usually less.
5. Brouillard, op. cit., 78.
6. AD 14L 10. Commission militaire: Chaperon (Chaperon de Terrefort); AM fonds révolutionnaire G 16: emprunt forcé (J. B. M. de Verthamon); AN W 400 (927): tribunal révolutionnaire (Pichard).
7. AD 4L 117. Emprunt forcé de l'An II.
8. Brouillard, op. cit., 92, 'Bilan de l'emprunt forcé'; AD 4L 117.
9. Butel, op. cit., II, 980, notes that 14 merchants were, according to the revolutionary declarations, enjoying incomes equalling or surpassing that of the richest magistrate. He concludes that the merchant community was cornering an ever-growing proportion of Bordelais wealth, following J. P. Poussou in *Bordeaux au XVIIIᵉ siècle*, 352.
10. Bluche, op. cit., 150.
11. ibid., 234.
12. Forster, op. cit., 22.
13. Meyer, *Noblesse Bretonne*, II, 979. Meyer, however, gives no direct information on revenues.

14. Forster, *Nobility of Toulouse*, 119, estimates the average annual income of a Toulousan aristocrat at 5–6,000 l., whereas the average gross landed income of the Bordeaux magistrates was 12,691 l. ('Noble wine producers', 21). The Toulousan parlementaires were richer than their aristocratic brothers, so it seems likely that their level of income was the same as at Bordeaux. See J. Sentou, *Fortunes et groupes sociaux à Toulouse sous la Révolution* (Toulouse, 1969), 82ff. This work has no details on revenues, however, only capital.

15. Colombet, *Les Parlementaires Bourguignons*, 71–2. This evidence is admittedly rather fragmented.

16. Sentou, op. cit., bases his extensive conclusions on the archives of *enregistrement*—declarations of successions authorized under the law of 5 December 1790 and that of 22 Frimaire, Year VII. Doubtless, some information resides in these records for Bordeaux; but it would confine itself to those few magistrates who died in Bordeaux after 1790, and would not reflect all their old régime investments. In any case, I was unable while in Bordeaux to devote the extensive time required to pursuing this elusive information.

17. M. Marion, J. Bencazar, and J. Caudrillier, *Documents relatifs à la vente des biens nationaux: Département de la Gironde* (Bordeaux, 1911), I, introduction.

18. Cte de Basterot, *Souvenirs d'enfance et de jeunesse—notes biographiques et ethnographiques* (Paris, 1896), 13.

19. Marion, Bencazar, Caudrillier, op. cit., I, 117. Butel, op. cit., II, 1037 and footnotes, 230, notes that the estate of the parents of the Daugeard brothers, who died respectively in 1738 and 1767, was estimated at its division between the heirs in 1770 at well over 2 million.

20. Factum in AM. 'Tableau d'une partie de la succession de feu M. de Brivazac'. The amount was disputed between the parties to the case.

21. AD 2E 1405 (tit. fam. Gourgue); the mother of the Gourgue brothers.

22. Marion, Bencazar, Caudrillier, op. cit., I, 176.

23. AD 3E 5.591 (Duprat), 1778 no. 539.

24. Butel, loc. cit. above, n. 19.

25. AM Fonds Alain d'Anglade, dossier 35.

26. AD 2E 1933 (tit. fam. Maignol). Inventory, 22 April 1776.

27. AD 2E 565 (tit. fam. Castelnau).

28. AD 3E 13.262 (Guy *père*). *Partage*, 6 Jan. 1777.

29. AD 3E 15.491 (Morin). Agreement, 9 June 1781.

30. Marion, Bencazar, Caudrillier, op. cit., I, 177.

31. *Partage*, 24 July 1787, before Morin. AD Q $\frac{Bx}{q}$ I. 'Tableau alphabétique des partages'.

32. AD 2E 1213[1] (tit. fam. Filhot de Chimbaud).

33. Boscheron des Portes, *Histoire du Parlement de Bordeaux*, II, 452.

34. Cavignac, *Jean Pellet*, 297.

35. These estimates are mostly based on information in Marion, Bencazar, Caudrillier, op. cit.

36. Bluche, op. cit., 150–1.

37. ibid., 152.

38. Sentou, op. cit., 86. Larboust sets out 64 capital fortunes, but Sentou considers some of his figures suspect. Larboust finds ten millionaires, but only five magistrates with under 100,000 l., op. cit., 85–6. Both sets of figures indicate the same broad conclusions.

39. Summary of P. Robinne, 'Les Magistrats du Parlement de Normandie à la fin du XVIIIe siècle (1774–1790)' (Thèse de l'école des Chartes, 1967), *Annales de Normandie* (1967), 267.

40. Colombet, op. cit., 71–2.

41. Meyer, *Noblesse Bretonne*, II, 979.

42. P. de Joinville, *La Commerce de Bordeaux au XVIIIe siècle* (Paris, 1908), 161, suggests as many as 60. This claim is not substantiated by examples; and the more exhaustive recent work of P. Butel, op. cit., II, 1036–7 suggests without directly contradicting Joinville that millionaires were relatively few, and that the apparent capital wealth of most of them was tied up in credits that were uncertain or difficult to realize. A large

and growing proportion of Bordelais merchants' assets were not tied up in real property, which Butel contrasts unfavourably with the landed solidity of parlementaire fortunes.

43. See below, pp. 119–22 for a fuller discussion of the mechanics and implications of marriage.
44. Registers in AD Q1296–1300, drawn up under the law of 9 Ventôse, Year II.
45. These claims are mostly those of the widows of executed magistrates, reclaiming their *cas dotaux*. For their rights, see below, p. 119. The relative size of these family debts should be noted.
46. BVC Richelieu XXXVIII, f.50, Gascq to Richelieu, 3 Jan. 1766.
47. D. Petit and A. D'Anglade, *La Seigneurie de Castres, Portets, et Arbanats* (Hossegor, 1934), 36.
48. AM factums: open shelves B 6/14 ff.152–205. Two factums of 1768.
49. BVBx MS 713 (V), 'Tablettes' of Bernadau, I, 504, 4 Feb. 1789.
50. AM Fonds Delpit 23 (Basterot). 'Registre des Délibérations du Bureau de Direction, nommé par le traitté passé entre Mr. Barthélemi Basterot et ses créanciers en date du 24 Xbre 1790'.
51. Bluche, op. cit., 153–5.
52. Meyer, op. cit., II, 969–76; Robinne, loc. cit.
53. Sentou, op. cit., 84 stresses far more than Larboust, op. cit., 93 the major role played by movables in the fortunes of Toulousan magistrates—often nearly half. The richer a magistrate, the greater the proportion of movables in his fortune.
54. Butel, op. cit., II, 1022. See also below, p. 103, for the acquisition by Gradis of the Prunes family's plantation in Martinique in lieu of debts outstanding.
55. AN W400 (927). Forced loan declaration.
56. AM fonds révolutionnaire G 16 f.43. Forced loan declaration.
57. AD 2E 2221 (tit. fam. Pelet d'Anglade).
58. Edict of 12 March 1701.
59. AM fonds révolutionnaire G 14 (presumed 1790).
60. AD C2737.
61. AD 2E 1213¹³ (tit. fam. Filhot de Chimbaud). Tax receipts.
62. AD 2E 1089 (tit. fam. Duval), Le Berthon to Duval, 12 July 1773; 2E 1091 (idem), Same to same, 11 Oct. 1772.
63. AD C2696 (1775 and 1777); AM loc. cit. above, n. 59 (1790).
64. AD C96.
65. AD C3171, C3759, C96 for details of this affair.
66. See M. Marion, *Les Impôts directs sous l'Ancien Régime, principalement au XVIIIᵉ siècle* (Paris, 1909), 69, n. 1.
67. See, in this context, the excellent and provocative article by B. Behrens, 'Nobles, privileges, and taxes in France at the end of the Ancien Régime', *Econ. H.R.*, second series, XV (1963).
68. AD C3018. For a critical appraisal and analysis, see pp. 52–3.
69. AD C74, intendant to Turgot, 11 Sept. 1775.
70. AD C3214, Tourny to Orry, 27 March 1744. Quoted in A. Nicolaï, *Au bon vieux temps: chronique économique du XVIIIᵉ siècle pour Bordeaux et la Guienne* (Bordeaux, 1906), 7–9.
71. AD C253, intendant to Necker, 12 Feb. 1780.
72. AD C302, Brivazac to intendant, 23 Dec. 1778.
73. AD C302, Pichard to Mel de Fontenay, 1 Jan. 1780.
74. ibid., Necker to intendant, 6 Jan. 1780.
75. AD C2981, C3006, C3007. 'Dispenses du vingtième taillable, 1766–70'.
76. Leroux, *Etude critique*, 106.

CHAPTER 5

Magistrates as Landowners

The kernel of a magistrate's fortune was land. In nearly every case it was the largest capital item, and the largest source of revenue too. But it was more than simply a form of wealth; it was the foundation of social standing. No doubt it was land that Montesquieu had in mind when he wrote that fortune was a status, not a possession.[1] Parlementaires were aristocrats; and aristocrats, almost by definition, were landowners.

The strict rule was, no title without land. In the parlement under Louis XVI were five marquis, four comtes, four vicomtes, one *captal*, and 28 barons.[2] It was normal for magistrates not to use their titles,[3] but this does not mean that they did not prize them. President M. F. de Verthamon, for instance, already in the 1780s the possessor of two *vicomtés* and three *baronnies*, proudly reached the top of the noble scale for a magistrate by having his domain of Tercis near Dax elevated into a *marquisat*.[4] Counsellor de Paty, baron du Rayet, began on the strength of his estates in 1775 to style himself comte de Beaumont without authorization, and ended up as a result in a lawsuit.[5] Counsellor Pelet d'Anglade had tried in 1758–59 to erect his land of Maisonneuve into a *vicomté* bearing his name, but the intendant advised the government that it was far too recent to deserve the honour.[6] It was much simpler, if possible, to buy title-bearing land, and Saige, advocate-general, was baron de Beautiran et Laprade thanks to his father's purchases. Similarly, counsellor Raymond de Lalande bought the land and *marquisat* of Castelmoron in 1769. Even the first president, vicomte de Castillon, owed this title to one of his father's purchases in 1739. Landless titles did in fact exist, but they carried little prestige. Lands were even essential ornaments of the untitled nobility. In legal acts where the full name was required, they never failed to list their *seigneuries*, the next best thing to a title. Feudal lordship seldom went without ownership of at least part of the land in question. Ownership of land was the safest way of making a living, and in a society ruled by aristocrats, the most honourable way. All magistrates therefore owned some.

Their estates were most densely grouped in the immediate neighbourhood of Bordeaux, reflecting the origin of family fortunes. Most families began their rise to prominence in the city, and bought their first domains nearby. The time when they had first invested their wealth in the countryside was still quite recent for

65

some families, and the Saiges and the Pelets are 18th-century exemplars of a process which had occurred at one time or another in the history of most of the families in the parlement. When they wanted to enter the robe, besides contracting marriages in its ranks, they fortified themselves with lands near to Bordeaux: as did the Pelets at Izon in the Entre-deux-Mers, or the Saiges at Beautiran and Laprade to the south, and Mérignac to the west. 'Si la Paroisse de Mérignac est peuplée et cultivée', wrote the abbé Baurein[7] in the 1780s,

> ce n'est pas à la bonté de son terroir qu'elle en est redevable . . . C'est . . . uniquement à sa proximité de la Ville de Bordeaux qu'elle doit sa bonne culture. Un Négotiant, un particulier, qui a quelque faculté, est bien aise d'avoir une maison de campagne, où il puisse aller le matin et s'en retourner le soir ou même y passer quelques jours pour se récréer; mais cela suppose une certaine aisance . . .[8]

Perhaps he had Saige, or his merchant father, in mind. At any rate, this sort of process had established most of the families who were in the parlement as landowners near to Bordeaux.

The lands of the magistrates were most closely distributed in two main areas. The first was the western bank of the Gironde and Garonne from Lesparre to Langon, the long narrow strip of good wine-land flanked by the river on one side and the wild *landes* on the other. The city stands about half-way down this strip. It is hardly an exaggeration to say that it would have been possible to travel from north of Lesparre to south of Langon without passing through a single parish where there was no land owned by a member of the parlement.[9] When counsellor Chanceaulme de Fonroze bought the domain of Monplaisir, at Bègles, in 1784, he found that it adjoined the land of no less than seven magistral families— Chaperon, Raymond, Féger, Barbeguière, Dalon, Saige, and Castelnau.[10] The reasons for the concentration of estates along this narrow strip are clear. These were the best, indeed the only economically viable, lands in the region of the city. The *landes* were of very limited value. The communications into the broken uplands of the Entre-deux-Mers were in general very bad. Only the triangle of alluvial land, made between the two rivers and a line from La Bastide, opposite Bordeaux, to Vayres was comparable, and it was in this second area that most of the other magistrates had their estates.[11]

Some estates were indeed more widely scattered. The families of Ruat (La Teste), Marbotin (Lège), Verthamon (Lacanau), and Pichard (Salles, Belin, and Beliet) owned huge stretches of the *landes*, to the west and south of Bordeaux. Others had property far up the river valleys of the Dordogne and the Garonne. Some distant estates belonged to those who had made the family fortune in the outlying towns of the province. They were obviously near the towns where they had first prospered. Thus, the main Poissac estates were at Poissac near Tulle. Those of the Dumas de Fonbrauge family were around Saint-Emilion, near Libourne. Those of the Mothes family were at Villefranche, near Casteljaloux, and those of the Bienassis family were at Port Ste-Marie sur Garonne, in the Agenais. Lands with which they had buttressed their local position remained in their hands, serving their new dignity. Occasionally, outlying estates belonged to those well-established families of nobility of race who came to the capital to join the 'senate'. Such was the case with the Piis family, whose main lands were near

Map 1   The south-west, showing the main places mentioned

Puybarban, in the Bazadais. Most frequently of all, families accumulated distant properties through dowries and bequests. President J. A. H. Daugeard's domain at Virazel in the Agenais was brought to the family by his mother, Catherine Belrieu de Virazel. President L. M. A. de Gourgue's estate at Lanquais and St-Aigne, up river from Bergerac, came from the succession of his mother, Marie de Mons, who had bought it in her own right in 1732.[12] M. F. de Verthamon had the estate of Ambloy, in Poitou, through his mother, Catherine de Verthamon.[13] J. J. de Boucaud was left the estate of Longchamps, around Grezac in Saintonge, by his uncle.[14] J. de R. de Lalande received lands in the Ile d'Oléron through his marriage to Honorine Etiennette D'Alesme;[15] and so we could go on.

In fact estates seldom consisted of one compact block. They tended to be fragmented, even in the Bordelais, and even those of the least well-endowed magistrates. B. Roche, counsellor in the requests, had only two properties, but one was in Labrède, to the south of the city, and the other was in the village of St-Paul near Blaye, far to the north across the Gironde.[16] The first president had extensive lands around Castillon, on the Dordogne, and others at Virelade, on the Garonne, south of Bordeaux. When L. G. de Brivazac, honorary counsellor, died in 1782, he left lands in Montferrand (Entre-deux-Mers), Pessac to the west of Bordeaux, Birac in the Agenais, and La Salle in the Blayais, as well as several others.[17] The richer a family was, the more scattered its estates would tend to be. President de Pichard, one of the richest, had vast tracts in the *landes*, vineyards in Médoc, the Graves, the Sauternais, and the Bazadais.[18] The Verthamon lands, equally rich, were similarly scattered.[19] So were those of the newcomer Saige family.[20] Some of this fragmentation resulted from dowries, but perhaps equally important was a rational desire to diversify, if not the crop, at least the quality of its product. As Montesquieu had pointed out earlier in the century:

> Les étrangers tirent plus de vingt sortes de vins de la Guyenne pour différentes destinations . . . Or le goût des étrangers varie continuellement, et à tel point qu'il n'y a pas une seule espèce de vin qui fut à la mode il y a vingt ans qui le soit encore aujourd'hui; au lieu que les vins qui étaient pour lors au rebut sont à présent très estimés. Il faut donc suivre ce goût inconstant . . .[21]

Scattered estates were an insurance against loss in such cases.

It remains true that one favoured estate was often bigger than the rest, and here the magistrate would have his favourite *château*, to which he would retire each September for the vintage, and to which his main title was often attached, if he had one. His other lands he saw far less often, and probably regarded only as a source of revenue. Many magistrates, so extensive were their domains, had several *châteaux*. Pichard had six. The Gourgues had three. The Le Berthons, Bergerons, and Duroys had two each. So did Daugeard de Virazel, and so did Saige.[22] Many more had country houses which did not quite merit the name of *château*, for of course each estate needed a minimum of buildings to assure facilities for its exploitation, and a residence for the landlord if he should choose to visit.

The estates of parlementaires, then, though diverse were overwhelmingly concentrated in the small area of the Bordelais. As a result the interests of the magistrates were overridingly local, and overridingly uniform, owing to the very limited variety of the Bordelais agricultural economy. At the same time, the position they occupied in the parlement, a legal avenue of complaint to the throne, made them in a real sense the voice of all the large landowners of the Bordelais.

Landownership was not a steady state. Holdings fluctuated considerably from generation to generation. One aspect of this process was the extension and consolidation of estates. Among 15 noble families whose domain-building activities have been studied in the later 18th century, ten had members in the parlement; all of them enlarged certain of their properties between 1755 and 1790.[23] Other sources illustrate other families about the same business. Between 1771 and 1791, counsellor G. R. B. de Filhot enlarged his domains at Sauternes in 21 exchanges and purchases at prices between 20 l. and 3,860 l.[24] Similarly on his estate at Merignac Saige spent 25,055 l. between 1769 and 1790 in 20 transactions legally registered at Bordeaux, at prices between 95 l. and 6,000 l., but mostly below 500 l.[25] Between 1768 and his death in 1780, counsellor P. F. I. de Laibat de Savignac concluded 26 transactions, obviously with the intention of consolidating his estates situated mainly in the parishes of Bruges and Le Bouscat. Of these, 11 were purchases, 11 were sales, and four, exchanges.[26] At Le Taillan, and in the neighbouring parishes of Blanquefort, Eyzines, and Le Vigean, president de Lavie passed 50 acts before Berninet, notary, between 1774 and 1790, whose combined value was over 288,504 l. 2s 0d.[27] This, admittedly, included 61,200 l. for the purchase of three mills, and other sizeable sums for large properties, but most of the transactions were sales or exchanges of small slices of land, often less than a *journal* in area,[28] for a few hundred *livres*. He was also prepared to sell to consolidate his domain, if he could not do it by exchange, but all his exchanges and alienations in this period, to the number of 14, only amounted in value to 2,724 l. It is clear in whose direction the ownership of land was tending in this district.

But Lavie's landlordly vigour nearly cost him his head in later times. In the Year II he found himself under arrest when 13 peasants of the commune of Le Taillan came forward and made a statement to the Military Commission at Bordeaux about his activities in the previous decade. They claimed that he had closed roads in the district and dug ditches across them, appropriated 7 *journaux* of common land, exchanged or purchased peasant lands without adequate recompense, refused to draw up legal deeds for these transactions, allowed a *métairie* which had once yielded 60 *boisseaux* of corn to go to scrub, pulled up fruitful vines, and consistently refused to show his titles. At once, however, 13 other peasants came forward and declared that they were completely satisfied in their dealings with him. The commission, happily for Lavie, noted that he had an enlightened and philosophic reputation, and decided that these crimes, if crimes they were, were cognizable in the civil courts, and he was acquitted.[29]

This case raises the whole question of the methods which the magistrates used to extend their domains, and that of the provenance of their new acquisitions. Notarial acts show that most of the small acquisitions came from peasants. It would be interesting to know how much duress on the part of the landlords lay behind these acquisitions, but it is almost impossible to say. Miranda, passing through Bordeaux in the spring of 1789, was told of a Médoc peasant who had had his crops destroyed for refusing to exchange a portion of land with a president of the parlement; but this may have been one of those rumours born of unsettled times.[30] On the face of it, the exchanges made by Lavie seem equitable enough, and he often gave away more land than he took; but the quality of the land exchanged is the really important question. How many sales too were foreclosures on accumulated arrears of 'feudal' dues? Nothing suggests that this was often the case, and it seems somewhat incredible that magistrates should out of deliberate policy allow dues to mount up for decades in order to take tiny morsels off peasants who could not pay.[31] Arrears certainly did mount up, they certainly were suddenly called in, and lands certainly were confiscated when peasants could not pay. But this was rather a routine part of the process of reconstructing the terriers, than a devious way of domain-building.[32] It has also been suggested that the acquisition of peasant land by *retrait féodal* was 'frequent',[33] yet president de Lavie used the right only once, for a patch worth only 60 l., between 1774 and 1790.[34] Counsellor de Loyac performed one *retrait* for 17 purchases and exchanges in Cameyrac between 1750 and 1790.[35] Far more often the piecemeal acquisition of peasant properties was done by outright purchase or exchange.

Sometimes, too, the magistrates bought whole new domains. There was no special pattern among those from whom they bought—sometimes they were non-robe noblemen, sometimes merchants or other Bordeaux notables, and quite often other members of the parlement. The more recent a family's arrival on the scene, the more vigorous its buying activities. The estate of Mérignac, which Saige was consolidating with acquisitions from peasants, had only been acquired by him in 1768, at the cost of 170,000 l.[36] By the time of the Revolution, he had spent nearly 100,000 l. more on extending it. Large tracts were acquired from the archbishop, and also from the Brivazac family, fellow-magistrates. In 1768 too he had bought an estate for 100,000 l. from another such family, the Desmoulins de Maspérier.[37] In 1771 he spent 161,000 l. at Ambarès; in 1782, 90,000 l. at Mont-ferrand. In 1783 he spent in all 128,000 l. on land in Blanquefort, much of which, admittedly, he resold in 1787 to president de Lavie,[38] but which he largely re-placed straight afterwards for 85,720 l. Only in scale and range was such activity exceptional; for most magistrates were buying land. It would be impossible to cite all the large-scale purchases made by them even in the 15 years before the Revolution. The most famous was the purchase by Pichard of Château Lafitte, probably for over a million livres.[39] Almost as impressive must have been the purchase by the Brane family of the nearby domain of Mouton. Chanceaulme de Fonroze paid 130,000 l. in 1784 when he bought the domain of Monplaisir, south of Bordeaux.[40] G. B. R. de Filhot bought the domain of Coutet, Barsac, in 1791 for 240,000 l.[41] These were some of the biggest. The commonest transactions were usually below 20,000 l., admittedly, yet although 20,000 l. was not much where *grands crus* were concerned, there were not many of these, and a great deal of useful land could be obtained for that amount. It was rare in fact for magis-trates to buy whole domains, however small. More often they bought single farms, *métairies*, or smaller pieces to extend existing holdings.

However, purchase and extension was only one side of the land market, and one which has perhaps been overemphasized. The magistrates also sold a good deal of land. They sold as many estates as they bought in the later 18th century. In 1771 president M. J. de Gourgue sold his estate at Talence for 184,800 l.[42] In 1770 P. F. I. Labat de Savignac sold his estate at Caudéran for 40,000 l.[43] In 1776 J. C. Dubergier de Favars sold the estate from which he derived his title for

97,000 l.[44] In 1775 J. B. R. de Navarre sold the 'noble house' of Camponnac (Pessac) for 45,000 l. In 1778 J. S. de Laroze sold an estate at Le Taillan for 78,600 l. J. A. P. de Carrière sold his estate at Aoudat in 1785 for 69,550 l.: and so on. These sales, again, are only the most spectacular of their sort. Sometimes they were resales for profit, as often in the case of Saige. Pichard made 60,000 l. profit when he resold the estate of Coutet to Filhot, after only seven years. But most were sales of necessity, to liquidate successions, or pay other debts, for the law was so narrow on these matters that few families could hope to retain their domains intact for long. The vigour shown by the magistrates in extending their lands by small purchases can be explained partly at least in terms of the reparation of large alienations. The same circumstances suggest that there was no clear growth in parlementaire holdings over the later 18th century. Purchases and sales probably cancelled each other out.

Purchase, exchange, and *retrait* were not the only means of extending and consolidating estates. In the later 18th century the government, increasingly concerned to extend land under cultivation, promoted the clearing of waste by offering clearers 15 years' exemption from all taxes on the land cleared.[45] In the generality of Bordeaux from 1768 this policy was supplemented with money prizes, distributed jointly by the intendant and the first president to enterprising small proprietors,[46] but only in the election of Bordeaux, bordering on the *landes*, was there much land of value not already under cultivation.[47] Between 1775 and 1790, 20 magistrates declared clearings for exemption, mostly in Médoc, but mostly in batches below 20 *journaux*.[48] This suggests that members of the parlement were not great clearers; or, if they were, they did not bother to declare their work for tax benefits.

Magistrates apparently found it more attractive to seek large-scale concessions. To obtain 'vacant' land, or a stretch of the abundant marsh of the Bordelais, from the king at a nominal 'feudal' payment, was by far preferable to buying. Notorious in this sort of activity was counsellor J. A. Leblanc de Mauvezin, whose name will recur as 'un homme extrêmement entêté de ses idées; homme à systemes; frondeur impitoyable du genre humain; croyant tout savoir, et savoir mieux que les autres . . .'[49] In 1761 he asked for the concession of the marsh of Arcins, and gained at Versailles the support of the duc de Choiseul.[50] In 1762 he demanded the concession of the island of Patiras, in the Gironde opposite Pauillac, offering to grow corn on it, at an annual payment to the crown of a gold piece worth 30 l. Unfortunately he did not mention that the island already belonged to his colleague president de Casaux.[51] The same year he also sought the concession from the crown of the marsh of Montferrand, which he offered to drain, claiming it was 'vacant'. In fact, part of it was owned by the communities of Ambès and Montferrand, and the rest by individuals, most of them Mauvezin's own colleagues. Montferrand had perhaps more parlementaire estates than any other parish in the Bordelais. Those of Mauvezin himself were across the river and 15 miles away. 'M de Mauvezin scait la sensation que sa seule demande a formé a Bordeaux et combien elle a revolté tous ceux qui en ont eu connoissance, et plusieurs de ses confrères',[52] noted the intendant. By 1763 all these bold schemes had been abandoned.

Wherever land was vacant, magistrates were often inordinately quick to assume that it was crown land, and ask for the concession. Islands, formed of fertile

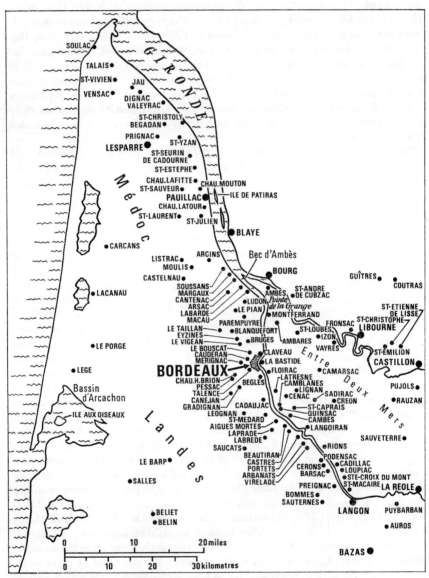

Map 2 The Bordelais, showing the main places mentioned

alluvium, were popular objects. In 1758 counsellor J. F. de Marbotin, baron de Lège, asked for and received the concession of the Ile aux Oiseaux in the Bassin d'Arcachon. It was partly formed, he pointed out, from soil washed away from his mainland domains.[53] In 1785 five claimants sought the concession of the island of Le Grand Faignard, of 90–100 *journaux*, in the Gironde. Among these were counsellors Laporte-Paulliac and Leblanc de Mauvezin junior.[54] In 1789 counsellor de Chalup solicited a small island in the Garonne opposite the village of Podensac, in compensation for loss of port dues owing to him because it blocked the channel.[55]

On the question of dividing up the common lands, the magistrates were not unanimous. Here was obviously another way of enlarging a domain: but we can discern three attitudes. Some magistrates, in asking for vacant land, seem not to have realized that it was common. Thus Leblanc de Mauvezin with the marsh of Montferrand, and thus president de Lancre, who from 1757 was claiming vacant land at Sainte-Croix du Mont. He was opposed by the community of that parish, who claimed the 700–800 *journaux* as common and wished to divide it, and also by the *jurade* of Saint-Macaire who claimed it as their common, and did not wish to divide it. In 1762 counsellor J. L. Darche met a similar problem when he solicited 500–600 *journaux* elsewhere in the jurisdiction of Saint-Macaire; he had trouble in convincing the *jurade* that it was not the same land.[56] Other magistrates knew perfectly well that they were claiming commons, and, being often the largest proprietors of their areas, stood to gain in certain ways by the division. Counsellor Pelet d'Anglade from the early 1770s was attacking alleged common rights on 1,500–1,600 *journaux* in the neighbourhood of Izon. The leaders of a bitter opposition were his own colleagues, counsellors Loyac and Gobineau, also large local landowners. Loyac had 40 head of cattle which he pastured on the commons, and so had several other notables in the area. Division would cut down their effective pasture.[57] This in fact was the third attitude—opposition to any division or concession of commons. At Montferrand, no sooner had Mauvezin's attempts been diverted, than others were made. From 1780 to 1783 various projectors sought the concession of the same marsh, and were opposed by 'la communauté de ces deux paroisses Composée de tout ce qu'il y a de plus considérable à Bordeaux dans la noblesse et dans le parlement',[58] led by counsellors de Richon and de Brivazac. The question here was not one of division, but of total loss; but it is surely significant that nobody ever proposed division as an alternative step, among all the magistrates who lived around these 400 *journaux* of marsh.

Standing somewhat apart from all these activities, but worthy of mention if only because of their ambitious scale, were attempts to bring the *landes* into cultivation. Most of the *landes* of the area around Bordeaux were owned by four members of the parlement, Ruat, Verthamon, Marbotin, and Pichard. Marbotin's barony of Lège consisted of over 11,000 *journaux*. 3,000 of these, he estimated, could be turned into ploughland if cleared, and certain other terrain could be put under vines. The main problem was that the area was constantly being diminished by the advance of coastal dunes, which it had been found impossible to fix.[59] It was the same with the Ruat lands. Counsellor de Ruat, as *capital* of Buch, was the largest landowner of all, and throughout the century his family had sought to make their vast possessions more lucrative. These vast virgin lands caught the imagination of 18th-century projectors. In 1766 F. A. Amanieu de Ruat, honorary counsellor, conceded 40,000 *journaux* south of La Teste to a Parisian company headed by a Swiss speculator named Nézer. They paid Ruat 77,500 l., and recognized his lordship of all the land thus alienated.[60] The aim was to clear these huge stretches of waste, and plant them with vines and corn, or turn them into meadows; and not until this was done, was Nézer's company to become the full owner of the lands. This concession had been previously authroized by an *arrêt* of the council of 21 January 1766. The parlement also confirmed the contract by registering the letters patent which authorized it. When Chassaing, syndic of the community of La Teste, brought a case opposing this registration before the court, on the grounds that the Nézer contract was detrimental to common rights, it was dismissed with costs.[61] Unfortunately for optimists, within a very short time Nézer went bankrupt, and all his schemes lapsed.

The main activity of this *captal* and his son, counsellor F. A. de Ruat, after that was devoted to planting and so fixing the dunes around La Teste. Between 1772 and 1787 they constantly met opposition in this from the community of La Teste, who refused to be excluded from their common rights even for a limited period while the trees were still growing. In 1782 at last the community's protests were overridden, and planting began.[62] The fixing of the dunes was essential if the government's great project of a canal linking the Adour and the Bassin d'Arcachon was ever to be effected. But it was not until 1787 that Brémontier, chief engineer of bridges and roads,[63] began really successful planting on the dunes. All Ruat's attempts came to very little; but president de Verthamon, vicomte de Biscarosse, was so impressed by Brémontier's success that, on the eve of the Revolution, he began planting his own dunes.[64] The *landes* themselves remained uncleared.

The salient feature of the land market among the magistrates is its briskness. They were buying a great deal, and also selling a great deal, often among themselves. Their overall holdings neither grew nor declined significantly. The vigorous market was a manifestation of the wealth that was general in 18th-century Bordeaux.[65] Land always found a ready market, and members of the parlement participated with the others. However, their activity is not so much evidence of expansion, as of constant rationalization. Every generation had to rationalize its domains afresh, indeed often rebuild them, after the havoc wrought each generation by an egalitarian succession law. Under these circumstances, a steady expansion of domains was almost impossible; the first thing was to refurbish losses made to younger brothers. Only those with huge incomes could afford domain-building for its own sake—the Pichards, the Lavies, the Saiges. The rest spent most of their time keeping holdings at a more or less constant level.

This also explains concession-seeking. It was domain-building without initial expense, a disadvantage which even tax-free clearings laboured under. The governmental atmosphere also could not have been more favourable. But there was a paradox here. Throughout their history, and especially in the 18th century, the parlements spent much time opposing and condemning the judicial pretensions of the intendants, and evocations to the council. However, when it was a matter of concessions, individual magistrates were very quick to resort to these authorities. Concession-seeking involved establishing that the land in question was royal domain, and then applying to the department of the domain, whose ultimate head was the comptroller-general. Such applications went through the intendant. Leblanc de Mauvezin, in his project for the marsh of Ambarès and Montferrand, even specifically asked that contests over his proposed concession should be cognizable only by the intendant, with appeal to the council.[66] Similarly in contested cases, the magistrates did not scruple to appeal straight to the council if they thought their case would be better received than in their own strife-torn parlement. With the administration, it was sufficient to invoke the public good in order to bypass the law. 'S'il est des cas où il soit nécessaire de s'écarter des règles exactes, c'est lorsqu'il s'agit de faire un bien aussi considérable que celui qui resulterait du projet que M de Ruat propose', wrote the intendant in 1773.[67] So it was that land hunger often led individual magistrates to try to evade that law whose sanctity they often extolled and claimed to defend, collectively, on the benches of the Ombrière.

In pre-revolutionary France two systems of property prevailed, not side by side so much as one on top of the other. Ownership in the modern sense was already the pre-eminent property right; yet lordship in the medieval sense, as a complex of rights, survived. The forms that such obligations or rights took, in personal service, fees, or payments in kind, were endowed with the full status of property. Moreover, because of their association with a noble or chivalric past, these rights were valued by all those who possessed or sought nobility, as symbols or as confirmation of their status. The vast majority, if not all, of the magistrates were themselves not only landowners, but also *seigneurs*.

Lordship and ownership were seldom totally divorced. The head of a *seigneurie* was usually an estate of which the acquirer was both lord and owner. All carried two sorts of rights—honorific and useful. The first were symbols of prestige, and the second, while they carried prestige too, were also sources of income.

It is very difficult to go beyond this in generalization. In the face of 'feudalism', statistical methods break down. 'Feudal' rights were prescriptive, customary rights, whose origins went back beyond the limits of reliable memory. Their variety was almost inexhaustible, both in quality and in quantity; there is nothing harder about which to make confident general statements. But most magistrates had them, and they provided a proportion of the income of those who did. These proportions fluctuated wildly from lord to lord.

Honorific rights included the right to keep a crenellated castle such as those of president de Gourgue at Lanquais,[68] the first president at Aiguilhe, counsellor Dumas de Laroque at St-Germain de Fronsac,[69] or counsellor Sauvat de Pommiers at Agassac. This honour at least was less and less coveted in the 18th century, savouring as it did of Gothic darkness. So early in the century, the Ruat family had abandoned their castle at La Teste to move to a newer one at Le Teich.[70] Similarly the Piis family in the course of the century moved into a modern house alongside their old feudal stronghold at Puybarban.[71] However, other honorific distinctions were jealously maintained, for example the seignorial pew in the parish church. Le Berthon occupied this on the rare occasions when he visited his *vicomté* of Castillon.[72] P. F. de Brach, knight of honour, enjoyed similar rights at Montussan.[73] The right to a tomb in the parish church was also enjoyed by the Brach family, as it was by the Ragueneau family at St-Loubès.[74] Sometimes these rights in the parish church even went as far as the nomination of the parish priest. For instance counsellor de Raignac, baron de Frespech, was lay impropriator of the living of St-Jean de Bourdeils, in the jurisdiction of Frespech, and paid the priest a *portion congrue*.[75] Le Berthon did the same with the living of St-Philippe d'Aiguilhe.[76]

Seignorial justice was another right of great prestige. High justice strictly carried the power to condemn to death in the seignorial court, and cognizance of all cases, civil and criminal, which the king had not reserved.[77] But seignorial courts did not condemn to death in the 18th century. This right and its manifestations —the *fourches patibulaires* or gallows at the entrance to the village—were maintained now merely for prestige, although as late as 1784 counsellor de Poissac, lord high justiciar of Poissac, secured letters patent permitting him to erect 'fourches patibulaires à quatre piliers' there.[78] Middle and low justice covered civil cases over small sums, and especially cases fo the violation of the lord's rights by the peasants. For these purposes the *seigneurie* would have a court, presided over by a judge nominated by the lord. In 1758 the *feudiste* of president L. M. A. de Gourgue recorded that at Lanquais:

> Le Seigneur a droit de creer un juge, un Lieutenant, un procureur fiscal, des procureurs postulans, notaires, et Bailes ou Sergens. La justice de Lanquais est actuellement composé d'officiers de toutes ces especes, et le Seigneur est en possession d'en nommer depuis longtems.[79]

It is not unreasonable to doubt the impartiality of these courts when the lord was a party. The judge did as he was told, or he suffered. As Pichard, lord high justiciar of Salles, wrote to his steward Giraudeau, about his judge:

> Informez vous qui pourroit remplacer Pascal, je me propose de le casser; dites-lui que s'il n'amplie pas le prisonnier, il aura à faire à moi, car j'ai de grandes preuves contre lui et contre son fils. Informez-vous si à Bellin ou Belliet, il y a quelque paysan en état de savoir écrire, & remplacer les anciens Officiers, que je veux tous casser, afin d'être maître de ma Justice.[80]

Quite often, however, a lord did not have justice over all the land he owned, so complicated was the geography of lordship in the 18th century.

> La haute justice ne comprend pas toute la terre mais elle est dans ce qu'il y a de mieux, neuf gros villages qui entourent le château y sont compris. La moyenne et Basse s'etend sur toute la terre . . .[81]

In the parish of Le Taillan, most of which was owned by president de Lavie, he only had justice in the eastern half.[82] President de Verthamon shared the justice of Lacanau with the duc de Duras.[83] Doubtless the right of justice could be turned to profit, though not perhaps in the sense of a direct and regular source of income. However, it had its obligations too, like the maintaining of prisons, and the care of abandoned children, which could prove expensive.

Where towns or larger communities fell within a lord's jurisdiction, he often had rights in choosing its officers. At Castillon, Le Berthon cast the first vote in the election of the mayor and the two *jurats* and he had the right to confirm or reject the result.[84] At Castelmoron the marquis, counsellor Raymond de Lalande, chose four *consuls* from a list of eight candidates submitted to him annually.[85] However, when counsellor Paty du Rayet claimed the right of nominating the town council of Beaumont, in Périgord, his claim was rejected by the government.[86] Throughout the 1770s Paty tried to increase his powers over Beaumont. In 1776 the harassed mayor begged the intendant to intervene:

> C'est alors que nous n'aurions plus a craindre la profanation trop Commune du Sanctuaire de Themis, surtout lorsqu'il y est question de sacrifier l'ambition quoiqu' intollerable de ses ministres[87]

—a reference to an *arrêt* of the parlement upholding Paty's claims.

Certainly the magistrates were in a position of incomparable power and influence for enforcing their seignorial claims, as members of the supreme court of the province. Yet as influential lords, they were able to benefit their communities as well. During hard conditions in the spring of 1765, president de Gourgue wrote directly to the comptroller-general on behalf of the inhabitants of Lanquais, to ask for a free distribution of grain.[88] During his exile under Maupeou, Le Berthon ordered improvements to the quayside of Castillon, at his own cost.[89] In 1758 president de Pichard was authorized to hold a weekly market at Saucats.[90] In 1760 president de Gascq secured a similar authorization for the community of Portets.[91] It is possible, however, that such markets were also seen as devices for levying dues. Le Berthon at Castillon, and Lalande at Castelmoron, each owned the market hall, and perhaps levied tolls for its use.[92]

Tolls were a common source of revenues. Some maintained river ferries and naturally charged for their use. So Le Berthon on the Dordogne, again at Castillon.[93] Counsellor J. F. de Marbotin kept a ferry at Meilhan on the Garonne which he leased at 250 l. a year, though he assured the intendant that it cost about 270 l. a year to maintain.[94] Rights over the river at this point also included fishing. At Castelmoron Lalande had a fishing monopoly of the Lot throughout his jurisdiction.[95] On the Ciron, which runs from the *landes* into the Garonne near Barsac, several lords constructed water mills and charged dues on each raft of pine-logs floated down from the *landes* which passed them. In 1780, there were ten such mills, all charging dues, one belonging to J. Duroy, ex-counsellor and first president of the court of aids, and another to counsellor de Ruat. They each charged 10 *sols* per raft. In 1779 these charges were abolished by *arrêt* of the council, as 'un péage onéreux au commerce'; but the next year they were re-established, though at a slightly lower rate, to compensate for the digging of by-pass canals.[96]

Banalités were a species of monopoly levied on the inhabitants of *seigneuries*. Under such rights, a lord could force all dwellers within his jurisdiction to bake their bread, or mill their corn, or press their grapes, at his oven, mill, or press. He could then charge monopoly prices, and in addition sometimes levied a right consisting of a proportion of all goods brought there. At Castelmoron, Lalande had *banal* ovens and *banal* wine-presses. He was entitled to one-fifth of all the red wine pressed there.[97] At Lanquais, president de Gourgue had *banal* ovens and *banal* mills. A 16s fine was levied each time the inhabitants failed to bring their corn there to be ground.[98] Similarly, some lords enjoyed the monopoly of butchering in their *seigneuries*, like president de Gascq, in his barony of Portets. This monopoly was farmed by his successors in 1789 at 800 l. a year.[99]

Several magistrates still had the right to *corvées*, or forced labour by their feudatories. But it was seldom heavy. At Portets, they owed two days' *corvée* a year, with cart and animal, or, if they had none, with a spade.[100] At Lanquais,

three days a year, or a commutation into a 12d tax, was the rule.[101] At Longchamp, the estate of counsellor J. J. de Boucaud in Saintonge, each owed four
days of *corvée* a year.[102]

The key to 'feudalism' was the *cens*, a payment by each feudatory on land held,
which was the sign of feudal tenure. The total of the *cens*, even for huge *seigneuries*,
was often so derisory that at first sight it would seem to have been more trouble
than it was worth to collect. The *cens* for all the six villages of the *marquisat* of
Castelmoron in 1770, came in all only to 263 l. 11s 3d annually.[103] Those of the
Montsec de Reignac family in 1763 from the noble house of Reignac (450
journaux) came to 29 l. 16s 3d.[104] But *cens* were not always so small and not always
levied in cash. The *rentes* or *cens* of Boucaud's Longchamp *seigneurie* came to
125½ *boisseaux* of wheat, 7 *boisseaux* of barley and 73 of oats, 308 capons, 65 hens,
and 140 l. in cash.[105] If nothing else was collected, the *cens* was, because it was the
key to everything else, the essential sign, however small, of a feudal obligation.
In the Bordelais, it was almost always accompanied by the *exporle*, another money
payment, also very small, payable at each change of lord or tenant. But neither of
these payments was usually more than one livre, and often much less. Their
importance was purely symbolic, though not less for that.

The really lucrative feudal rights were far less common. The most important
were the *agrières*, annual payments in kind of a proportion of crops to the lord.
At Longchamp they were leviable on 1,523 *journaux* at the rate of one-eighth
except for 223 *journaux* where one-ninth was the rate. In an average year they
produced 60 sacks of corn, 60–80 sacks of 'spanish corn', and 100–120 *barriques*
of wine.[106] In 1793 J. de Raymond de Lalande claimed that under the old régime
he had had *agrières* in the Ile d'Oléron whose annual yield was 150 *tonneaux* of
white wine, 50 of red, 300 *boisseaux* of corn, 500 *boisseaux* of barley, and other
corn.[107] To this must be added 226 *boisseaux* of corn, 80 of oats, and 163 of barley
from Castelmoron.[108] This represented a substantial amount of money. In 1789
the *agrières* of the late Gascq *seigneurie* of Portets were estimated to be worth
4,600 l. a year.[109]

Lucrative also, in a degree dependent largely upon the size and value of the
land in question, were the *lods et ventes*, leviable each time that property changed
hands. The rate was one-twelfth of the price in the Agenais, one-tenth in the
Condomois and the Bazadais, one-eighth in the Bordelais, and one-sixth in
Périgord.[110] They could not have a constant annual value, but since *lods et ventes*
were a due so universal in application, most magistrates must have benefited from
them sometimes. At Portets in 1789 their average annual yield was estimated at
1,500 l.[111] After two years of growing neglect by his steward, Pichard estimated in
1773 that he was owed 14,000 l. in arrears of *rentes*, *agrières*, and *lods et ventes* in
Salles, Belin, and Beliet, and Le Barp.[112]

'Feudal' revenues could therefore be quite considerable. What is often forgotten is that most landowners paid out dues as well as collecting them. Many
magistrates were each other's lords. Counsellor Filhot de Chimbaud, with extensive estates along the right bank of the Garonne, had lands at Floirac in the
lordship of counsellor de Lamolère, lord of Feuillas.[113] At Izon, counsellor
Pelet d'Anglade was lord of part of the land owned by counsellor de Gobineau,
though how much, was a point of dispute between the two magistrates which they
took to the parlement to settle between 1775 and 1779.[114] Even more magistrates

had non-parlementaire lords; all those with land in the area of Villenave d'Ornon paid dues to the *jurade* of Bordeaux, the collective comte d'Ornon. When in 1781 Bordeaux received a new archbishop, and *exporles* were levied on all the land in his lordship, 18 members of the parlement were among those paying.[115] *Exporles* were negligible, but *lods et ventes* could fall very heavily on large buyers. When Saige bought the mill of Plassan, at Blanquefort, from the duc de Duras in 1785, its lord demanded 8,000 l. *lods et ventes* from him, on the price of 36,000 l.,[116] and collected another 8,000 l. from president de Lavie when he bought the mill from Saige in 1787.[117] When in 1778 counsellor Chaperon de Terrefort bought the fief and barony of Calamiac and Tustal from the *captal* of Latresne, for 240,000 l., several lords demanded *lods et ventes* from him, including the royal domain, which asked alone for 89,925 l.[118] In the light of such figures it is debatable whether large landowners did not have more to lose than to gain from the system of *lods et ventes*.

But that magistrates profited, often substantially, from the 'feudal' structure of property seems beyond dispute;[119] so is the fact that they valued their rights highly. True, president de Verthamon agreed with the traveller Guibert in 1775 that seignorial rights were an 'abuse' which the government ought to end, but only over a long period and only by buying them out in full.[120] Doubtless such opinions were seen as eccentric. The activity of other magistrates in revising their terriers shows how worthwhile they considered up-to-date records to be. Most of the examples already cited come from contemporary reassessments of the value of feudal rights. In 1758 president de Gourgue went to Lanquais mainly to see if there were grounds for making a new terrier. 'On a discouru', wrote the *feudiste* he took with him,

> beaucoup sur le renouvellement des terriers. M de Monbrun y est opposé, M Boivert le croit necessaire mais il excepte La parroisse de Varenne, M le Curé ne voudroit pas que L'on fit des frais aux tenanciers, mas il convient des embaras qu'il y a dans La Levée des rentes. Le juge et lui voudroient que L'on s'en tint a un arpentement.[121]

A few days later, however, it was decided to proceed, even though some thought the chosen *arpenteur* 'ignorant, et homme a rançonner les habitans pour les arpentemens et le renouvellement du terrier'. The agreement was made on 25 June 1759, when for 1,000 l. the *feudiste* promised to have the new terrier completed by 1762. In 1765 counsellor Pelet d'Anglade commissioned a similar terrier at Izon; but the work was still not finished in 1772.[122] Fragments of many other new paper terriers made for magistrates also survive. In the 1760s and 1770s counsellor Leblanc de Mauvezin was making one for his Médoc fiefs.[123] From 1764 J. de Gombault de Rasac, knight of honour, was having a new terrier made for his barony of Pujols.[124] In the same decade counsellor de Spens d'Estignols de Lancre was continuing the work of terrier revising at Ste-Croix du Mont which his ancestors had begun earlier in the century.[125] At Floirac, coun-sellor de Lamolère had a new terrier made between 1777 and 1789, but he too was continuing his predecessor's work.[126] The same thing was happening on the Filhot de Chimbaud fiefs, in the same district,[127] and on the fiefs of the Brane family, around Pauillac, in Médoc.[128] The indefatigable Pichard also employed a *feudiste* to revise his terriers in the *landes* at Salles and at Beliet, where the yield of feudal dues was high.[129] When counsellor Raymond de Lalande, from whom Pichard had bought the *seigneuries* of Beliet and Le Barp in 1764, had acquired them himself a few years earlier at a cost of 25,000 l., their main value was said to be in justice and feudal *rentes*.[130]

The precision with which the magistrates were determined to exact their dues is striking; and the results could often be brutal, as in the case of sudden foreclosures on accumulated arrears, which enabled men like Castelnau d'Essenault to confiscate peasant lands in lieu of payment.[131] But as suggested earlier, such foreclosures were not a deliberate policy aimed at obtaining land cheaply; they were rather the result of a renewed precision in collecting, after a generation of changes in ownership. Such changes would in time make previous terriers almost useless for the levying of dues, and so bring collection to a stop. It is curious and significant that few dues reimposed in new terriers seem to have lapsed more than a generation—25 or 30 years—beforehand. This, the limit of legal memory, is also exactly the interval at which we might expect lordships to change hands, and new lords find old terriers inadequate. But none of this was new. So it seems unlikely that any of this activity, spread as it was over much of the century, amounted to some peculiarly fierce feudal or seignorial 'reaction' in the old régime's closing decades.[132] The only 'reaction' was that which occurred in every well-run *seigneurie* every generation, to bring it up to date. Nor is there any evidence to show that the lords of the Bordelais were actually raising the levels of their dues in the 18th century—another facet of the so-called 'reaction'.[133] If the burden on feudatories increased, it was the result of lords exploiting to the full the assets they had, at a time when prices were rising. Rising prices made dues in kind, like the *agrières*, more lucrative to the lord and more onerous to the payer. The legal cost of new terriers and *arpentements*, always partly borne by the feudatories themselves, were an irksome additional charge. In these senses, the feudal burden increased in the 18th century, but it was not through the raising of dues and not through any unprecedented precision in levying them.

Many 'feudal' rights enjoyed by magistrates have not been mentioned, indeed they were so diverse that it would be impossible to mention them all. We have seen that on occasion the *retrait féodal*, the right to pre-empt a feudatory in the land market, was employed. Those lords who wished to expand their property at the expense of the common lands often had their eyes on the right of *triage*, under which the lord was entitled to a third, or some similar proportion, of the common land enclosed on his *seigneurie*. At Belin in the *landes*, two successive parlementaire lords, Lalande and Pichard, sought division of the commons against the wishes of the community:

> Pourquoi . . . le S dela Lande . . . resistet-il à la demande de la Communauté? son objet est sensible: c'est qu'il veut se conserver cette magnifique portion de Landes en toute proprieté . . . et en outre, disposer du surplus par des affieffemens à cens et rentes qu'il en fait Journellement.[134]

In a division, he would have been entitled to one-quarter. In 1793 the *feudiste* Graves claimed that Dudon the younger owed him 150 l. for drawing up *triages* in the parish of Bruges, where the main Dudon estates were.[135] The Gascq family for 200 years fought to secure full lordship over Portets en Comtau, an island of allodial tenure in the middle of the *seigneurie* of Portets. When in 1777 president de Gascq at last received confirmation of this claim, the right of *triage* was specifically assured to him. This last unsuccessful lawsuit on behalf of the inhabitants of the *comtau* cost them 24,000 l. over 20 years.[136]

How shall we sum up the value of feudal dues to the magistrates? Not exclusively in terms of money, certainly. The prestige of lordship had an intangible value of its own. Yet in pure cash terms, feudal dues often brought an enviable return. The larger a *seigneurie*, the more likely this was. On the Gascq *seigneurie* of Portets, sold for 517,660 l. in 1785, dues brought in all told 7,810 l. in 1789.[137] The seignorial revenues of Le Berthon nearby in Virelade, were farmed in 1773 at 2,000 l.;[138] and to this must be added the unknown yield of his *vicomté* of Castillon. In 1783 it was estimated that the seignorial rights of the *marquisat* of Dunes, near Valence d'Agen, owned by counsellor Demons de Saint-Pauly, were worth 6,000 l. a year.[139] Most of these, admittedly, were large and compact *seigneuries*. Magistrates without such assets doubtless had much more meagre returns. Nevertheless, the size of the figures which we have makes it perfectly understandable why the magistrates in the *alluvions* case were almost as concerned over threatened lordship as over threatened ownership; why their libraries boasted such contemporary handbooks as Guyot's *Dictionnaire des Fiefs*, or Boutaric's *Traité des Droits Seigneuriaux*; and why they were always prepared to undertake lengthy and expensive litigation on feudal matters. And this is why, too, certain of them tried to take the National Assembly at its word in 1789 when, after the heady renunciations of the night of 4 August, it hedged them about with provisos for the continued payment of dues until they were bought out. Between 7 and 15 October 1789, president de Pichard and counsellor de Brane, as joint owners of several *agrières au sixième* near Pauillac, issued eight summonses to a total of 30 defaulting feudatories. Pichard even drew up a list, as in the old days at Salles, of:

> Noms des tenanciers . . . qui n'ont pas payé l'agriere et aux quels Mr de Pichard a fait faire une sommation . . . Ceux qui sont distingués par une croix sont les plus Riches tenanciers et ceux qu'il faudra faire assigner.[140]

Clearly they had forgotten, or were ignoring, the provisions of the law and were refusing to pay. There is no evidence that they ever did. For by now feudal dues were doomed, and, at this late stage, the parlement had lost all power to sustain those who wished to levy them.

NOTES

1. *Pensée* 72 in the *L'Intégrale* edition of the complete works (Paris, 1964), 859.
2. Families represented by two generations are only counted once, but in the case of families with more than one title, each one is counted separately.
3. An exception was E. F. C. Jaucen de Poissac, created baron de Poissac in 1770, who always signed thus.
4. Correspondence in AD C352.
5. BvBx MS 1201, IV, 17 March 1775.
6. AD C2369, quoted in Cavignac, *Jean Pellet*, 330.
7. Jacques Baurein (1713–90). Priest, antiquarian, topographer. Member of academy of Bordeaux, 1761; archivist to the chapter of the cathedral of St-André, 1771; published in six volumes, 1784–86, *Variétés Bordeloises ou Essai historique et critique sur la*

topographie ancienne et moderne du diocèse de Bordeaux, a major source on the country-side of the Bordelais in the 18th century.

8. ibid., re-edition of 1876, IV, 409.

9. For example we find, among others, in the lower Médoc the names of Verthamon (Vensac, St-Yzan, Prignac), Daugeard (Bégadan, Prignac), Basterot (Jau, Prignac), Bergeron (Vensac), Degères (Saint-Sauveur), and Maignol (Lesparre). In upper Médoc, Leblanc de Mauvezin (Moulis), Sauvat de Pommiers (Agassac, Ludon), Lamouroux (Parempuyre), Pichard (Pauillac), Brane (Pauillac), Casaux (Macau), Lavie (Le Taillan), Dupaty (Blanquefort), Dudon (Bruges), Labat de Savignac (Le Bouscat), and many more. In the Graves, we meet the names of Saige (Mérignac, Beautiran, Laprade), Roche (Labrède), Pichard (Saucats), Gascq (Portets), Le Berthon (Virelade), and so on down to the Sauternais where the estates of many more magistral families were concentrated.

10. Now Château Pontac-Monplaisir. AD 3E 24.282 (Collignan). Sale of 20 Feb. 1784.

11. e.g., the holdings of such families as Brach, Brivazac, Barret, Baritault, Chauvet, Darche, Degères, Domenge, Duroy, Filhot, Gombault, Laboyrie, Lagubat, Loyac, Maurice de Sentout, Paty, Saige, Gobineau, and Pelet.

12. AD 2E 1405 (tit. fam. Gourgue).

13. She was a cousin of his father. See above, p. 15.

14. AM MS 653, 'La Terre et Seigneurie de Longchamp'.

15. AD 3E 21.716 (Rauzan). Marriage contract, 13 April 1782.

16. AD C23. Request for alleviation of the twentieth, 1773.

17. Printed brief of 1789, AM factums; will in AD 3E 13.071 (Cheyron). Sealed 20 July 1774, opened 5 Oct. 1782.

18. M. Marion, J. Bencazar, and J. Caudrillier, *Documents relatifs à la vente des biens nationaux: Département de la Gironde*, I, 144. See also AD Q1009.

19. Marion, Bencazar, Caudrillier, op. cit., I, 187.

20. ibid., 160.

21. *L'Intégrale* edition, 190. 'Mémoire contre l'arrêt du Conseil du 27 février 1725 portant défense de faire des plantations &c.'.

22. Many are recorded in E. Guillon, *Les Châteaux historiques et vinicoles de la Gironde* (Bordeaux, 1866–69), 4 v. See also below, pp. 128–9.

23. R. Forster, 'The noble wine producers', 31. His table is based on a comparison between the twentieth rolls of 1755 (AD C3018) and documents in Marion, Bencazar, Caudrillier, *Biens nationaux*. The families concerned were Gourgue, Laboyrie, Gombault, Carrière, Castelnau, Brivazac, Le Berthon, Pelet d'Anglade, Dudon, and Baritault.

24. AD Q1009. Inventory after emigration of the Filhot papers.

25. Calculated from AD Q, 'Tableaux des acquéreurs et vendeurs'.
$$\frac{Bx\ 2}{M\ \&\ N}\ 2\ (1769\text{--}80),\ \frac{Bx\ \frac{1}{2}}{M\ \&\ N}\ 1\ (1781\text{--}84),\ \frac{Bx\ \frac{1}{2}}{M\ \&\ N}\ 2\ (1784\text{--}88),\ \frac{Bx\ \frac{1}{2}}{M\ \&\ N}\ 3\ (1788\text{--}91).$$
In fact between 1768 and 1780 Saige passed all told 64 acts, AD Q1012.

26. ibid., see also J. P. Poussou, 'Les structures foncières et sociales des vignobles de Caudéran et du Bouscat en 1771', in *Vignobles et vins d'Aquitaine: histoire, économie, art* (Bordeaux, 1970), 222, 234–5.

27. Berninet's archives for these years are in AD 3E 28.260–28.275.

28. 0·8 of an acre.

29. AD 14 L 25. Commission Militaire: dossier Lavie.

30. O. Baulny, 'Miranda et Bordeaux', R. Hist. Bx. (1966), 137. The Miranda concerned is of course the South American liberator.

31. Here I contradict Forster, loc. cit., 30.

32. See below, p. 80. Forster, ibid., cites various foreclosures by counsellor L. A. de Castelnau. AD Q1009 records two transactions by counsellor de Filhot, of 3 Sept. 1772 and 3 Jan. 1783, as *déguerpissements*, which seem to be foreclosures of this sort.

33. R. Forster, 'The provincial noble: a reappraisal', American H.R., LXVIII (1963), 685. Colombet, *Les Parlementaires Bourguignons*, 154–8, shows that this right was used by the magistrates of the parlement of Dijon.

34. AD 3E 28.261 (Berninet), 23 Jan. 1776.

35. AD Q1010. Inventory after emigration of Loyac's papers.

36. AD Q1012. Inventory after condemnation of Saige's papers.
37. Resold for 112,400 l. before Rauzan, notary, 5 April 1771.
38. AD 3E 15.037 (Baron), 19 Nov. 1787.
39. Forster, 'Noble wine producers', 31 n. I have been unable by other means to verify or date this transaction. Probably it was passed *sous seing privé*, and possibly in Paris. In the Year IV the value of the property was estimated at 1,715,474 l., according to Marion, Bencazar, Caudrillier, op. cit., I, 144.
40. AD 3E 24.282 (Collignan), 20 Feb. 1784.
41. AD Q1009. Inventory after emigration of Filhot's papers.
42. AD 3E 5.563 (Duprat), 8 Feb. 1771.
43. AD Q 'Tableaux des acquéreurs et vendeurs', cited above, n. 25, are the source for all the figures that follow, unless shown otherwise.
44. AD 3E 21.705 (Rauzan), 16 July 1776.
45. Royal declaration of 13 Aug. 1766, Isambert, Jourdan, and Crusy, *Recueil général des anciennes lois Françaises* (Paris, 1822–33), XXII, 461.
46. AD C1332. Here I contradict Forster, 'Noble wine producers', 32.
47. ibid., see also P. Butel, 'Défrîchements en Guyenne au XVIIIe siècle', *Annales du Midi* (1965), 179.
48. Based on AD C4709–4911. Registers of declarations under the royal declaration of 13 Aug. 1766.
49. BVBx MS 1696, VI, pièce 8. 'Chronique' de Lamontaigne, 21 May 1760. See the comments also of president de Gascq, below, p. 154.
50. AAE MD France, 1587, f.351, Choiseul to Boutin, 28 July 1761.
51. AD C2352.
52. AD C3675 has most of the pieces on this affair. The quotation is a paragraph crossed out in an undated letter draft.
53. AD C2352. Letter of Tourny, 16 May 1758.
54. AD C2357.
55. AD C3734.
56. AD C1336. Forster, 'Noble wine producers', 33, mentions these two cases, but gets them badly confused.
57. AD C1357. See also A. Cobban, *The Social Interpretation of the French Revolution* (Cambridge, 1964), 114, for a rather extreme statement about such circumstances.
58. AD C3675, comptroller-general to intendant, 3 June 1782. The parishes concerned with Montferrand and Ambarès. This whole issue was subsequently submerged in the *alluvions* affair, below, ch. 16.
59. AD C3671, 'Mémoire de la terre et Baronie de Lège en Buch'; undated, but after 1765.
60. AD 2E 37 (tit. fam. Amanieu de Ruat) contains a printed copy of the contract, dated 5 Feb. 1766. Information also in D. Petit, *Le Captalat de Buch pendant la Révolution Française (1789–1804)* (Bordeaux, 1909), 28ff.; and A. Ferradou, *Mémoire sur la propriété des dunes de La Teste* (Bordeaux, 1930), 62ff.
61. *Arrêt* of 1 Aug. 1766.
62. Ferradou, op. cit., 78, *arrêt* of the council, 21 May 1782.
63. Nicolas-Thomas Brémontier (1738–1809). Successively sub-engineer at Caen, Périgueux, and Bordeaux. Chief engineer of bridges and roads of the generality of Bordeaux, 1784, a post he held, *mutatis mutandis*, throughout the Revolution until his death. The first effective fixer of the dunes.
64. Ferradou, op. cit., 98–9.
65. See the conclusions of J. P. Poussou, *Vignobles et vins d'Aquitaine*, 234–5.
66. AD C3675.
67. Quoted in Ferradou, op. cit., 66.
68. AD 2E 1408 (tit. fam. Gourgue), 'Titres historiques de la maison de Lanquais'.
69. Guillon, *Les Châteaux historiques*, IV, 186.
70. ibid., 449.
71. P. Meller, 'Une rupture de mariage en 1758', *R. Hist. Bx.* (1909), 334; W. Doyle, 'Deux parlementaires bazadais du XVIIIe siècle', *Les Cahiers du Bazadais*, XVI (1969), 25.
72. F. Guignard, *Histoire de Castillon-sur-Dordogne (l'une des filleules de Bordeaux) et de la région Castillonaise depuis les origines jusqu'à nos jours* (Paris, 1912), 361.

73. Guillon, op. cit., III, 147.
74. AD 3E 24.268 (Lavau). Will of counsellor J. J. de Ragueneau, sealed 27 May 1672; opened 12 Dec. 1771.
75. AD 2E 2421 (tit. fam. Reignac), notarial acts of 1–4 Jan. 1772.
76. Guignard, *Histoire de Castillon*, 360.
77. J. B. Denisart, *Collection de décisions nouvelles et de notions relatives à la jurisprudence actuelle* (7th ed., Paris, 1771), III, 79.
78. AD IB 57 (registers of the parlement), f.10. Letters patent of May 1784.
79. AD 2E 1408.
80. AD 2E 2285 (tit. fam. Pichard). Printed in *Réponses aux observations préliminaires et au mémoire de M. le Président de Pichard. Pour le Sieur Giraudeau, notaire à Salles*, 8. Pichard to Giraudeau, 20 July 1771.
81. AM MS 653. The estate in question was that of Longchamp, belonging to counsellor J. J. de Boucaud.
82. Baurein, *Variétés Bordeloises* (1876), II, 417.
83. ibid., 55.
84. Guignard, op. cit., 283.
85. AD C4192. 'Aveu et dénombrement de la Terre et Seigneurie de Castelmoron', 25 March 1770.
86. AD C891.
87. AD C453, Montsec to intendant, 28 Nov. 1776.
88. AN 109 AP (16), Gourgue family papers. Laverdy to L. M. A. de Gourgue, 22 May 1765.
89. AD 8J 67 (Fonds Bigot: parlement), *Récit de ce qui s'est passé dans le voyage que M. LEBERTHON, Premier Président du Parlement de Bordeaux, a fait d'Aiguille à Virelade* (Bordeaux, 1775).
90. Baurein, *Variétés Bordeloises* (1876), III, 32.
91. AD IB 50, f.57, Feb. 1760.
92. Guignard, op. cit., 407; AD C4192.
93. Guignard, op. cit., 213.
94. AD 2E 1968 (tit. fam. Marbotin). 'Titres relatifs aux droits de passage & de pêche sur la rivière de Garonne en la juridiction de Meilhan'.
95. AD C4192.
96. AD C1952. *Arrêts* of the Council, 27 Nov. 1779 and 24 Sept. 1780.
97. AD C4192.
98. AD 2E 1408.
99. D. Petit and A. D'Anglade, *La Seigneurie de Castres, Portets, et Arbanats*, 122.
100. ibid., 74.
101. AD 2E 1408.
102. AM MS 653.
103. AD C4192.
104. AD C4769. 'Aveu et dénombrement de la Maison Noble de Reignac', 17 Jan. 1763.
105. AM MS 653.
106. ibid.
107. AD 4L 116, Contribution patriotique: discharge request, Feb. 1793.
108. AD C4192.
109. Petit and D'Anglade, loc. cit.
110. AD C2295, cited in Marion, 'Etat des classes rurales au XVIIIᵉ siècle dans la généralité de Bordeaux', *Revue des études historiques* (1902), 65.
111. Petit and D'Anglade, op. cit., 122.
112. AD 2E 2285, *Réponses aux observations*, 23, 7 March 1773. See also below, pp. 97–8.
113. AD 1J 324, Terrier of Feuillas, f.53, 5 May 1780.
114. AM MS 638, Izon—mélanges.
115. AD 3E 5.633 (Duprat), Répertoire, 1783–86. Duprat was clearly the archbishop's notary.
116. AD C4785, sale of 30 Jan. 1785, before Bouan, notary.
117. AD 3E 15.037 (Baron), 19 Nov. 1787.
118. AD C4785, sale of 26 Feb. 1778.
119. Another point of disagreement with Forster, 'Noble wine producers', 23.

120. *Voyages de Guibert, dans diverses parties de la France et en Suisse, faits en 1775, 1778, 1784, et 1785 . . . ouvrage posthume, publié par sa veuve* (Paris, 1806), 15, 22 June 1775.
121. AD 2E 1405, 'Journal de voyage et de nos opérations', 23 Sept. 1758.
122. AD 2E 2221 (tit. fam. Pelet d'Anglade), letters and contracts.
123. AD E (terriers) 577.
124. AD E (terriers) 960. Dated 1766.
125. AD 3E 14.784 contains nearly 120 feudal recognizances, 1724–56, along with evidence too of a *feudiste* at work in 1768.
126. AD 1J 324.
127. AD 2E 1213[7] (tit. fam. Filhot de Chimbaud).
128. AD E (terriers) 618.
129. AD 2E 2285, recognizances of 22 Aug. 1785 and 8 Sept. 1787.
130. AD C3018.
131. Forster, 'Noble wine producers', 29–30. See also above, p. 70.
132. See W. Doyle, 'Was there an aristocratic reaction in pre-revolutionary France', *Past and Present*, 57 (1972), 114–20.
133. I have found no such evidence among the papers of the parlementaires, and Marion, not a man to understate such evidence if he found it, found none in 1902. See his 'Etat des classes rurales', 74–6. A. Colombet, *Les Parlementaires Bourguignons*, 170–1, found no evidence of it, either, among the Dijon magistrates in these years.
134. AD C952, undated 'Mémoire de la Communauté de Belin'.
135. AD Q1296. Register of the debts of *émigrés* and *condamnés*.
136. Petit and D'Anglade, op. cit., 26–33.
137. ibid., 36, 122.
138. AD Q $\frac{9}{S}$ I. 'Bureau de Cadillac: baux de toute nature de biens appartenans aux Laics—table alphabétique (1756–An X)'.
139. Marion, Etat des classes rurales', 64. In AD Q402 there is a 'Livre pour la levée des rentes seigneuriales de la terre de Dunes', of 1790, detailing sizeable *agrières* in corn.
140. AD E (terriers) 930.

CHAPTER 6

Magistrates as Cultivators

In the opinion of the government, the agriculture of the province of Guienne was not well-balanced. For most of the 18th century the government's notion of a well-balanced economy was one which was self-sufficient in corn, which Guienne was not. This is why the government was always so eager to sponsor projects for clearing the *landes*. But what aggravated matters was the constant extension of vines, a crop which seemed likely soon to take up all the fertile land there was. Early in the century the intendant Boucher[1] complained of the 'planting fury' which seemed to grip the Bordelais,[2] and by an *arrêt* of the council of 27 February 1725, reiterated on 5 June 1731, the government forbade all further plantings on pain of a fine and the tearing-up of the offending vines. It was against the first of these that Montesquieu wrote his famous memoir,[3] in which he argued that the proprietor was the best judge of his own interests, and that the situation of Bordeaux as a port would always afford easy access to emergency supplies of grain. The Bordelais, he declared, enjoyed the advantages of a concentrated yet diversified production, and easy disposal—advantages whose solidity was demonstrated by the profits to be made. And in fact planting continued to outstrip all the intendants' efforts to control it. By mid-century the *arrêts* against further planting were clearly dead letters.[4] The policy of encouraging clearing, which the government adopted in the 1760s, was designed above all to increase ploughland, but there seems little doubt that the area under vines was extended by this process, too.[5]

The magistrates of the parlement, like Montesquieu himself, were in the forefront of these developments. Their estates were concentrated on the gravels of the Médoc, the Graves, and the Sauternais, and in the *palus* along the river banks. On the gravels the obvious, indeed the only really profitable, cash crop was wine; the colonial taste for *vins de palu* was a powerful incentive to turn over the fertile river banks to vines too. The members of the parlement dominated the group of large-scale, high-quality wine-producers who were the mainstay of the traditional economy of the Bordelais. Men like counsellor de Brane, at Mouton, counsellor de Laroze, at St-Julien, president de Casaux, at Margaux, or counsellor Duroy, at Preignac, grew vines on some of the best soil in the world. Even their less fortunate colleagues often produced wine of very respectable quality. In 1755, on average, 73 per cent of the gross landed income of 68 families of the parlement came from wine.[6] One-quarter of the yield came from the Médoc, 18 per cent

86

from the Graves, and 11 per cent from the *palus* of the Bec d'Ambès, areas where well over half the parlementaire vineyards were situated.[7] Overall, the members of the parlement had over 10,000 *journaux* under vines, and their products amounted to about 7 per cent of the wine exports of the port.[8] This percentage does no justice to their cash value, since they included most of the best-quality wines from the famous *crus*.

Immense profits could be made from quite small patches of land in good areas. A *journal* in a normal year would yield 700–750 bottles, Thomas Jefferson was told in 1787,[9] and the next year he discovered that the comte de Fumel was asking 6 l. per bottle of Haut Brion 1784.[10] At Château Lafitte, owned by president de Pichard and already known by name throughout Europe, there were in the 1790s 169 *journaux* under vines, their net annual yield between 30,000 l. and 40,000 l.,[11] even after deducting the heavy costs of cultivation. Jefferson heard that in the 1780s Pichard got 175 *tonneaux*[12] a year from Lafitte, selling at between 1,500 l. and 2,400 l. each. He also owned Château Coutet at Barsac, in the Sauternais, with 48 *journaux* of vines which normally yielded him 150 *tonneaux* at 280 l. new and 600 l. mature.[13] Pichard's estates were of course exceptional in the uniquely high quality of their product, but they are only an extreme example of that incomparably high yield per unit of surface area that underlay the 18th-century 'planting fury'.

The example of Pichard is unfortunately peculiar in other respects too; it is a scrap of useful information amid a more general lack. The absence of evidence is the greatest obstacle to studying the Bordeaux wine trade in the 18th century.[14] Nevertheless, certain things are clear. First of all the quality and therefore the price of wine largely depended on the area it came from. Only a handful of individual vineyards and great *crus* were famous by name in the 18th century, such as Lafitte, Latour, or Haut Brion, but the importance of the area of provenance was clearly understood. A list drawn up in 1767 shows the immense variations in the price per *tonneau*, according to district: hardly any of the parishes mentioned were totally without some parlementaire property, as can be seen.[15] Proportions of the magistrates' product represented by each area in 1755 are indicated.[16]

REDS	GRAVES (18·3%)	
1ers *crus*	Pessac *crus* de Pontac	1,500–2,500 l.
	„ others	800–1,200 l.
	(Saige, Brivazac)	
	Mérignac	400–800 l.
	(Saige)	
2es *crus*	Talence, Léognan	300–400 l.
	Gradignan, Caudéran	200–300 l.
	(Mauvezin)	
	Bègles	200 l.
	(Montsec de Reignac)	
3es *crus*	Poudensac, Virelade, Portets, Castres,	150 l.
	Arbanats, Beautiran, Aiguesmortes, Eyrans,	
	Cadaujac, Le Bouscat, Canéjan, Eysines	
	(Gascq, Le Berthon, Saige, Raymond,	
	Dufaure de Lajarte)	

MEDOC (24·6%)

1ers crus	Pauillac, Margaux (Pichard, Brane, Casaux)	1,500–1,800 l.
	St-Mambert, Cantenac, St-Seurin de Cadourne, St-Julien (Laroze)	800–1,200 l.
2es crus	Soussans, Labarde (Sauvat)	600 l.
	Agassac, Arcins, Arsac	400–500 l.
	Listrac, Moulis, St-Laurent, St-Estèphe, Le Pian, Macau, Ludon, Le Taillan (Lavie, Saige, Casaux)	300–400 l.
Others		120–150 l.

PALUS (9·3%)

1ers crus	Queyries	300–400 l.
	Montferrand, La Souys, Ambès (Baritault, Dufaure de Lajarte, Dussault, Loyac, Saige, Peyronnet)	200–300 l.
2es crus	Fronsadais, Vayres, Quinsac, Ile St-Georges, Cadaujac, Bègles, palu de Bordeaux, Parempuyre, St-Macaire, Macau, Ludon (Lamolère, Filhot de Chimbaud, Saige, Baritault, Montsec de Reignac, Lamouroux, Sauvat)	150–200 l.

WHITES   SAUTERNES (8·9%)

1ers crus	Barsac, Preignac, Langon, Ste-Croix du Mont, Sauternes, Cérons, Bommes, Pujols (Dudon, Pichard, Filhot, Darche, Castelnau d'Auros, Delpy, Marbotin, Lasalle, de Spens, Duroy, Basquiat, Montalier)	300 l.

ENTRE-DEUX-MERS (23·1%)

2es crus	All[17]	180–240 l.

Against high profits must be set high capital outlay on the costs of cultivation. The vine is a delicate plant at the best of times; but when planted to produce a high-quality crop it needs constant attention throughout the year, in pruning, propping, digging several times round the roots, and ensuring good drainage. The actual process of pressing and storage after the harvest was an equally skilled business. Labour costs therefore were very high. The gross product of Château Lafitte in 1792 was 75,713 l. 9s, but 39,851 l. 15s had to be deducted for costs of cultivation.[18] It is a measure of the declining value of money that this was twice as much as the marquis de Ségur had paid out for cultivation of the same estate in the 1730s and 1740s.[19] More typical, however, were the returns of counsellor Dumas de Fonbrauge in 1779–80. He had two main properties: just over 35 *journaux* at Château Claveau just north of Bordeaux, and the domain of Fon-brauge, 302 *journaux* in the parishes of St-Christophe and St-Sulpice, near to St-Emilion.[20] For Claveau the gross receipts of 1779–80 were 6,549 l. 10s, of which 5,860 l. came from wine.[21] Costs of cultivation were about 3,000 l. For Fonbrauge the gross receipts were 16,270 l. 1s 6d, of which 11,050 l. came from 42½ *tonneaux* of red wine at 260 l. each, and 2,415 l. from another 10 *tonneaux* of inferior wine at 230 l. each. Costs of cultivation came to about 4,000 l., of which the biggest item was 1,600 l. for 16 dozen new *barriques*. He also sold 83 *boisseaux* of grain from Fonbrauge, but this only brought in 952 l. 7s 6d in all.

The only surviving account book which yields a long series of figures is that of counsellor J. L. Darche over the years 1760 to 1780.[22] His domain at Sauternes was of 109½ *journaux*, 72 of which were under vines. The accounts of the latter have already been tabulated and published.[23] Those of a less lucrative domain at Langon have not. They may be found both together in graph form on the next page, with gross and net receipts shown. The most striking feature about them is the great fluctuation in income from year to year. While costs of cultivation remained uniformly high—on average 4,760 l. p.a. at Sauternes and 2,153 l. p.a. at Langon—receipts varied immensely, from the handsome profits of 1764 to the deficits or near deficits of 1777, which was a disaster year for wine all over France.[24] Making a profit depended on an immense number of variables.

One was the weather. The climate of Bordeaux is usually mild in winter, but some frosts do occur, and if vines are not well drained, frost can kill their product. The Bordelais is also prone to sudden and violent hailstorms which destroy the vines utterly, breaking off the shoots. Even so, in good *crus* a certain rarity of the wine might even force the price above that of abundant years. Equally, an abundant harvest was not always a lucrative one. As Le Berthon wrote in 1780, from Virelade:

> Il me manque icy Le quart du vin rouge, et le cinquième du blanc que je vendis l'an passé. Mais j'ay tout lieu de croire que l'une et l'autre qualité seront infiniment moins basses, et peut-être vendront-elles davantage vu la dizette dont on se plaint . . . partout.[25]

Similarly there was no effective way of ensuring good quality even to undamaged harvests, which were dependent on rain at the right time of the year, as well as sunshine, to determine the value of the wine which they produced.

The market was almost as fickle as the weather. Most of the wine produced in the Bordelais was exported. Changing foreign fashions, as Montesquieu pointed out in his 1726 memoir, could destroy or boost the value of a vineyard. Early in the century the Sauternais had been the most spectacularly successful part of the Bordelais, but by mid-century fashions in Holland, where most Sauternes had been sold, had changed, and the export and price of Sauternes had fallen. By the late 18th century the most coveted wines were those of Médoc.[26] Wine-growers were also at the mercy of the merchants who bought and exported their products.[27] Only the handful of *crus* which were known by name—such as Pichard's Lafitte, the only one in parlementaire hands on the eve of the Revolution—could be certain to sell in any year. Even their prices fluctuated enormously.

Worst of all the imponderables was war with England, because it made the seas unsafe. The mere rumour of war was enough to deter many merchants from buying

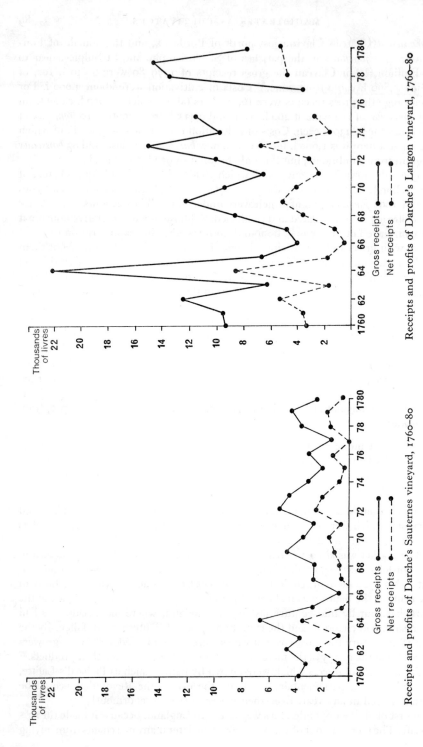

Thousands of livres

Receipts and profits of Darche's Langon vineyard, 1760–80

Gross receipts ●────●
Net receipts ●- - - -●

Thousands of livres

Receipts and profits of Darche's Sauternes vineyard, 1760–80

Gross receipts ●────●
Net receipts ●- - - -●

wine, and slow down commercial activity in general. Admittedly the effect of
the American war was far less severe than that of its two predecessors.[28] In 1744
Tourny had eloquently pleaded with the comptroller-general to accord the magistrates of the parlement tax-concessions in view of the danger of war, and the bad
quality of recent wine harvests, since wine sales accounted for four-fifths of the
magistrates' 'natural faculties'.[29] Two years later an English traveller noted that
'The nobility of Bordeaux have suffered more by the war than the merchants as
they have no fund of ready money and live by the sale of their wines'.[30] No
wonder that the wine-growers welcomed the commercial treaty of 1786 with
England,[31] for not only did it open that hitherto restricted market, it also reduced
the danger from hostilities. Nevertheless, the wine trade was not without its
fluctuations in the late 1770s; the American war may have affected it little, but
1776 was mediocre and 1777 was a disaster year for the wine harvest all over
France, with late frosts and summer drought. As the accounts of Darche vividly
reflect,[32] the Bordelais was hit as badly as anywhere. 1778 was therefore a year of
meagre or non-existent revenues, and it took more than the good-quality harvest
of 1779[33] to facilitate a full recovery; indeed, the overproduction of the early
1780s had effects almost as disastrous on the prices obtained by small producers.[34]

To offset the risks, however, the large growers enjoyed certain important
advantages. First was the mere size and scale of their operations. With territories
scattered all over the Bordelais, they were in a better position than the small
grower to avoid the full consequences of local disasters like hailstorms, or changes
in foreign fashions. Even their individual vineyards tended to be among the most
extensive in an area, on which they would spend large amounts in the hope of
larger returns. This meant that they were usually better equipped than their
smaller neighbours to sustain temporary losses or delays in marketing. The latter
had neither the money to invest in presses, vats, or barrels, nor had they the storage
space to keep superfluous stocks. And so the large producers tended to dominate
the market by buying up, pressing, and selling the wine of their tenants, vassals,
and neighbours, as well as their own.[35] In any case, to build up stocks was a normal
part of the business of high-quality wine production, since the best vintages took
several years to mature. Those of Lafitte, Jefferson was informed, needed three
years, and those of Latour, Margaux, and Haut Brion needed four. White wines
would keep up to 15 or 20 years.[36]

For this reason the magistrates seem to have suffered less than others from the
crisis of overproduction which afflicted the whole French wine industry in the
1780s, including that of the Bordelais.[37] Admittedly the sales of second-class
wines which all high-quality producers inevitably marketed anonymously as
unworthy of their reputation, must have suffered from the fall in prices. Le
Berthon reported in December 1783 that he could not find a market for his wines
—'je ne crois pas qu'on se souvienne de pareil Evenement'.[38] The steward of
counsellor Filhot de Chimbaud complained in August 1786 that his wines were
selling poorly because there were too many on the market. He advised him to
accept a low offer since better ones were not to be expected.[39] At least, however,
large-scale producers could cushion the blow by stockpiling their products
against leaner times, such as those of the late 1780s.[40] Wines of such *crus* as
Lafitte even increased in value; the 1786 vintage which sold at 1,500 l. per
tonneau in that year, was already bringing 1,800 l. in 1787.[41] If the wines of

Guienne were glutted in 1786,[42] the best wines of the magistrates, at least, were almost certainly not among them.

Magistrates enjoyed a special advantage when there was too much cheap wine on the market. They enjoyed the privilege of *Bourgeoisie de Bordeaux*, one facet of an extensive network of privileges in the wine trade enjoyed by Bordeaux and its inhabitants, which had their origins in the 13th century.[43] *Bourgeoisie* had nothing directly to do with social status: it was a hereditary privilege enjoyed by a number of notable families, some noble, some not, under which they were allowed to bring their wine into the city free of duty, and had the monopoly of retail sale within its precincts. The register of such families, the *Livre des Bourgeois*, was revised several times in the early 17th century, and again in 1762.[44] Several parlementaire families had been admitted in the 17th century, others had done so in the meantime, and most merely acted as if they had. The revision of 1762 evoked an *arrêt* by which the parlement declared that henceforth all its members and their families were to enjoy automatically the privilege of *bourgeoisie* whether they had been registered or not:

> La dignité dont ils sont revêtus comprend la plénitude de tous les privilèges du droit de cité et ... il seroit contre l'ordre des choses que MM de la Cour, fixés par état à Bordeaux et y ayant leur domicile de droit, et juges nés des différens qui arrivent au sujet du droit de bourgeoisie et de l'état des personnes revêtues de la première et plus suprême magistrature de la ville, fussent privés de l'exemption bourgeoise . . .[45]

Magistrates could therefore sell their inferior wine retail within the city, without the expense of a middleman.

As inhabitants of the seneschalcy of Bordeaux, members of the parlement benefited too from the more general aspects of the wine privilege. Only wine from the seneschalcy, comprising 350 parishes, might be sold within the city, or freely introduced there. Wine for export from up river, and generally outside the seneschalcy, had to be stored in a specially designated part of the Chartrons quarter. Wine from the more remote parts of the Entre-deux-Mers was only half privileged, and paid on passing through the town the duty of the *demy marque*, 2s 6d per *tonneau*. Wine from beyond paid the *double marque* of 5s per *tonneau*.[46] The former was not allowed down the Garonne till Martinmas; that is, until the vintage in the Bordelais was over and the crop sold. The latter was not allowed down until after Christmas; and all non-Bordelais wine had to be out of the port by 8 September each year, on pain of confiscation and conversion into brandy. The overall effect of the privilege was to increase the price of non-Bordelais wine when it reached the port, and to exclude it altogether during the crucial period of the vintage. It gave the Bordelais an immense advantage.

After their work in the parlement, therefore, wine-growing was the major activity of the magistrates, as it was of most of the notables of Bordeaux who owned lands. This gave them a certain unity of interests. 'Il faut avouer', wrote Mouchy in 1781,

> que le temps des vendanges pour ce pais ci ne ressemble a rien de ce qu'on voit ailleurs; tout le monde ne parle, n'entend et ne voit autre chose, les affaires les plus serieuses et les plus essentielles sont abandonnées pour cet objet.[47]

It would be easy to conclude that this was a one-crop economy, as the government tended to do. But matters never quite reached these proportions. The high yield per surface area of vines meant that only a small proportion of a sizeable estate in a good area need be under vines to bring it its largest item of revenue. Besides, it would have been impossible, with vineyards that were too large, to give the vine the amount of detailed attention that it needed. Individual vineyards were often quite small; most were well below 100 *journaux*. Significant proportions, and sometimes the greatest part, of each holding were under other forms of cultivation—corn, meadow, or woodland, especially in the alluvial *palus*, where the soil was rich. Even up on the gravels, wine was not completely dominant. The richest wine-grower of the middle of the century, president de Ségur, whose inventory after death was drawn up in 1755, had a very significant part of his domains, even on the precious soil of the Médoc, in ploughland, pinewoods, and sheep-runs.[48] Only a small proportion of the overall holdings of those with property in the *landes* was under vines; but Pichard's thousands of *journaux* at Salles, Belin, and Beliet, only yielded him each year a fraction of what he got for the product of his 169 *journaux* of vines at Lafitte. He estimated in 1793 that the net yield of Lafitte and dependencies in the previous year had been in all 33,135 l. 18s 11d, whilst that from his immense properties in the *landes* only came to 5,128 l. 18s 2d.[49] Thus, more of the magistrates' domains were under other forms of cultivation than the proportion of income deriving from them might suggest.

Arthur Young believed that only meadows in France yielded anything approaching the value per acre of vines.[50] However, meadows did not form a very large proportion of magistrates' domains. In mid-century in the Bordelais they yielded between 1½ and 4 cartloads of hay per *journal*.[51] Most domains contained small meadows, often under 10 *journaux* and hardly ever over 20. This was because of intense competition from other crops; for most of the meadows were in the *palus* which were also under pressure from the vine owing to the colonial taste for the sturdy, easy-travelling wines which grew there. What expansion the wine exports of Bordeaux saw over the century was mainly accounted for by the colonies.[52] Outside the *palus*, except in a few marshy parishes like Blanquefort, the land was ill suited to meadows. Meadows certainly were extended as the century went on. The nationalized lands which had been owned by members of the parlement up to the Revolution often contained far larger portions of meadow than are indicated in the twentieth roll of 1755; many were above 50 *journaux*. This rise is much more spectacular than that in vineyards. Hay was apparently becoming a cash crop, rather than a commodity grown on small patches for domestic consumption.

Forage was certainly necessary, for in addition to the universal oxen[53] for ploughing and drawing, magistrates often reared considerable numbers of livestock. The 1770s were a bad decade for cattle and sheep. A number of plagues, spreading from Spain, swept the south of France, notably the *epizoötie*, which appeared in 1771, and reached its height in the years 1774–75. In 1774 counsellor Durand de Naujac lost nine head of cattle. In 1775 counsellor Demons lost 63 head. In these same two years, president Daugeard de Virazel lost 200 head.[54] Losses on this scale represented a considerable capital value. Counsellor Dumas de Fonbrauge estimated his losses on livestock in these years at 5,164 l.[55] Not surprisingly the parlement co-operated vigorously with the intendant to stop all fairs where the disease might be spread.[56] Smaller herds of cattle at any rate were not kept so much for meat or milk as for manure, which, being rare but important in an area so intensely cultivated as the Garonne valley, sold well.[57] Sheep were kept for wool and meat as well as manure. In the Médoc and in the *landes* there were many flocks. The Basterot family kept a famous flock at Les Granges d'Or.[58] In 1787 president de Verthamon had 282 rams and 92 ewes on his domain at Loudenne.[59] In 1793 president de Pichard had 3,085 head in the *landes*,[60] which were ideal for free-rein pasture, and could support such large flocks all the year round.

In addition, the *landes* were known for a number of specialized products. There was honey and wax: at Saucats and Belin, Pichard had 220 beehives;[61] at Mérignac president de Casaux had 52.[62] Also they grew pinewoods and their by-products. The pines were not as extensive in Guienne as they are now, but Young believed that 'Improvements on the heaths of Bordeaux are not . . . obvious, because on immense tracks the *proprietor* receives as much perhaps at present from pines as he would receive were the whole in cultivation'.[63] Resin, for instance, could be very lucrative when thousands of *journaux* of trees were tapped for it. At Salles in the 1780s there were 24 resin ovens.[64] In 1777 president de Verthamon's agent at La Teste sold 40,000 pounds of resin at 98 l. the thousand, and still had another 116,076 pounds left in storage the next year.[65] Then there was the wood itself. The pines produced resin up to their 20th year. After that, they could always be cut and sold. In 1793 in Pichard's estate yard at Salles, 9,000 bundles of faggots were found, and 10,000 cut pine-logs.[66] Wood sold very well in the Bordelais. Wine-growing required large amounts, in effect a prop for every vine; also there was the wood for casks and wine vessels. For the latter, and for the best wines, only imported hardwood was good enough. However, for more ordinary wines, local hardwood was used, and, being scarce, it sold well. There was oak in the *landes*, and many estates outside them had patches of woodland in unkempt coppices. There is little evidence of systematic use of woodlands for income, except in the *landes*. The saplings demanded by magistrates from the royal nurseries were mostly fruit trees or ornamental ones like poplars.[67] However, every few years the sale of a *coupe* could bring in a useful rise in income. In 1783 counsellor Degères de Loupes practically cleared his domains for 24,000 l.,[68] although such a step seems to indicate an overriding need for money. But many had patches of woodland which they profitably cut every few years.

All this seemed to leave little room for corn. Yet many estates had patches of ploughland, often more extensive than those of vines. On the first president's estate at Virelade and Arbanats, early in the Revolution, 296 *journaux* were described as ploughlands, and only 79 *journaux* were under vines.[69] On counsellor P. L. de Raymond's estate at St-Médard d'Eyrans in 1792, 96 *journaux* were under the plough, and 93 under vines.[70] On the precious soil of Pauillac, adjoining Château Lafitte, Pichard's domain of Lorte was divided into woods, meadows, and ploughland, with no vines at all.[71] Nevertheless, only in a few cases was corn the main source of revenue. In terms of profit its yield was mediocre compared to wine. Moreover, the stony gravels of Bordeaux, perfect for vines, only produced poor or indifferent grain. So it was only a handful of magistrates, those with estates up river in the fertile Agenais, such as presidents Daugeard de

Virazel or Bienassis, who made most of their money from grain.[72] The magistrates were not therefore one-crop cultivators, even though one crop did dominate their operations. They never gambled on turning their whole property over to vines, and this reveals men more cautious than reports of monoculture and planting fury would lead us to expect. Caution, conservatism, and precision were their watchwords when it came to the management of their estates.

Methods of estate management depended on the distance from Bordeaux, size, and the quality of the crop involved. Distant estates were almost invariably farmed out. Thus president de Gourgue farmed Lanquais at 13,000 l. p.a. in the middle of the century.[73] The Lalande family farmed its estates at Castelmoron for 10,000 l. a year;[74] president de Lavie farmed his domain of Laroque at St-Etienne de Lisse near St-Emilion, at 13,000 l. a year.[75] The Verthamons even farmed various small properties that they owned close to the city.[76] But as the intendant, musing on the difficulties of just taxation, wrote to the comptroller-general in 1775:

> Il n'en est pas de cette province, comme de celles ou presque tous les domaines sont affermés . . . la plupart des domaines de la guienne sont exploités pour le compte des propriétaires, soit par des valets a gages, soit par des métayers, les vignes particulièrement ne sont affermés nulle part, les propriétaires les font cultiver et faconner à prix d'argent, et retirent pour leur compte la totalité du produit . . .[77]

Day-labourers (*valets à gages*) were employed for the most valuable vineyards, and this method of cultivation was one which spread throughout the century.[78] Of all methods, it cost the grower least, especially since, though prices rose throughout the century, the wages of day-labourers in the vineyards did not.[79] 'The vineyards of first quality are all worked by their proprietors', reported Jefferson.[80]

> Those of 2d rent for 300 l. the journal: those of the 3d at 200 l. They employ a kind of overseer[81] at four or five hundred livres a year, finding him lodging and drink; but he feeds himself. He superintends and directs, but is expected to work but little. If the proprietor has a garden the overseer tends that. They never hire labourers by the year. The day wages of a man are 30 sous, a woman's 15 sous, feeding themselves. The women make the bundles of sarment, weed, pull off the snails, tie the vines, gather the grapes. During the vintage they are paid high and fed well.

Sharecropping, in the vineyards at least, was diminishing in most areas. The relatively even annual outlay of such a system, in provisions for the sharecropper, was too high for a return as variable as that from wine. It persisted in the Sauternais, and perhaps this was as much responsible as the change in foreign fashions for the relative decline of that area. At any rate, in most of the Bordelais, by the late 18th century, sharecropping was only common for crops other than the vine.[82]

The Filhot de Chimbaud estates are a typical example of a parlementaire domain in the Bordelais.[83] In 1790 the total real estate of counsellor J. de Filhot de Chimbaud was estimated to be worth 136,930 l. 10s. Of this, 94,232 l. 10s 6d was in country estates. The smallest was a tiny patch of land at Blazimont, deep in the Entre-deux-Mers, estimated at 814 l. 16s 4d, and farmed out at 150 l. a year. Filhot also owned three *métairies* in the marsh of Blaye, one of which was farmed at 2,800 l. a year. However, his most important estates were in the Entre-deux-Mers in the string of villages stretching between Floirac, opposite Bordeaux, and Cambes. At Floirac he had three separate domains, totalling 91 *journaux*; at Camblanes, 4½ *journaux* of vines; at Cénac, 104 *journaux* of wood-land, at Lignan, 113 *journaux*; and at Quinsac, three domains, of which one was a *métairie* of 187 *journaux*. The latter was partly under corn, being in the *palu*, but there were vines too. Filhot provided 12 *boisseaux*[84] of seed a year for the corn, and the product was shared. The vines, however, were cultivated *à prix fait*. The *prix-faiteur* undertook to prune and tend the vines, and dig around their roots three times a year. In addition he provided the owner with two cartloads of vine prunings (*sarment*), and in return received 150 l. a year.[85] Similar arrange-ments prevailed on the other 11 domains, varying in area from 16 to 113 *journaux*, into which the estates were divided. If grain was grown, as it was on four of them, Filhot gave a proportion of the seed; for the vines, he paid between 300 l. and 500 l. a year for three workings and general care,[86] in return receiving between 1½ and 4 cartloads of prunings from each. On the domain of Montagne, 54 *jour-naux*, at Floirac, there was a flock of 43 sheep and a ram. There the contractor also paid one-third of the price of manure whenever any was bought, and pro-vided the landlord with 24 chickens and 100 eggs a year. Meadows around Sadirac were farmed out at 134 l. a year. The produce of the woods at Cénac was sold to a contractor who guaranteed to take it all for a number of years. Finally, at Quinsac there were water-mills, farmed respectively at 600 l. and 800 l. a year, plus a certain number of chickens, eggs, and other produce.

The economy of the estates was then very diversified, as were their methods of management. The main crop was certainly the grape; the wine of Floirac brought 120 l. a *tonneau* in 1755, when 16 *journaux* had yielded Filhot's grandfather 12 *tonneaux* a year; that of Quinsac brought similar prices for first quality, and 80 l. a *tonneau* for second.[87] But there was also a good deal of corn, wood, and cattle. Counsellor Filhot was not in fact totally dependent on the wine crop, though it still represented by far the largest portion of his income. In addition to his revenues from other crops, he had a guaranteed return from his more distant, farmed lands. His case was typical. No magistrate put himself totally at the mercy of the unpredictable vintage.

Caution in diversity; conservatism in cultivation. Magistrates were not pre-pared to make agricultural experiments. The wine trade was so much built upon foundations of immemorial confidence among its consumers, that innovation was positively discouraged, and this attitude of mind was infectious. Indeed, there was a general lack of interest in agricultural theory in the whole Bordelais. Attempts in 1761 and 1772, at the instigation of the central government, to form a local society of agriculture, came to nothing. In 1761 the attempt was actually thwarted by the parlement, allegedly because certain magistrates, being also members of the Academy of Bordeaux, feared that such a society might be a competitor.[88] The Academy's occasional discussion of agricultural questions was the sole manifestation of any abstract interest in agricultural principles.

However, account books, their number, and the care with which they were kept, show a precise attention to the details of cultivation. It is our misfortune that so few of these books have survived, but the inventories of the papers of the *émigrés* attest their existence in considerable numbers. In the Basquiat papers, 15 such books were found for the years 1735–92;[89] in the Filhot papers, eight for 1733–91;[90] in the Pelet papers, 22 for 1738–91, and so on.[91] Those of Filhot de Chimbaud, Dumas de Fonbrauge, and Darche have already been mentioned. There also survives a very illuminating set of letters from president de Pichard to his steward of Salles and Belin in the years 1769–73.[92] Written over a period when the steward, Giraudeau, was slowly losing control of the running of the estates, they show the absent Pichard growing increasingly frantic at Giraudeau's inefficiency. It is clear that the president's knowledge of his possessions was detailed and intimate.

> Je viens d'apprendre qu'on n'avoit trouvé à Bellin que trois charretées de foin, quoiqu'il dut y en avoir neuf charretées . . .[93]

Or:

> Vous ne m'écrivez que par monosyllabes, j'aime les détails & l'exactitude dans le promesses.[94]

He certainly liked a rigorous exactitude in the recovery of what his peasants owed him:

> Je vous charge de m'envoyer l'état des arrérages qui me sont encore dûs, je veux faire assigner tous mes débiteurs.[95]

And later:

> Je vous ordonne de faire assigner, dans ce moment-ci, tous mes débiteurs; prenez garde à l'inexécution de ces ordres: le moment de la récolte est le moment décisif pour le payement.[96]

He even directed speculation in corn:

> Si le bled est dans ce moment-ci trop cher, il faut attendre qu'il soit dépiqué; mais du moment qu'il baissera, il faut prendre le moment favorable pour en acheter cent boisseaux au plus bas prix, mais pas au dessus de 9 l. 10s.[97]

Then, seven months later:

> Le bled augmente à chaque instant; ainsi, si vous n'avez pas vendu les cent-cinquante boisseaux de bled, n'en vendez que cent boisseaux, à raison de 12 liv. ou de 12 liv. 5 sols, mais argent compté . . .[98]

Giraudeau, through malice or incapacity, eventually brought about the near-ruin of Pichard's estates in the *landes*, to his employer's fury:

> Vous êtes, Monsieur, un frippon, qui ne meritez aucune protection ni faveur. Il faut que vous soyez bien hardi d'accumuler mensonge sur mensonge, en soutenant des faits dont j'ai la preuve contraire. Oui, Monsieur, je vous poursuivrai avec la plus grande rigueur . . . je ne vous ferai nulle grace, et je vous poursuivrai rigoureusement par les voies de la Justice.[99]

And so he did. Giraudeau was condemned for misappropriation of his employer's goods by the seneschalcy court. He appealed in 1775 to the restored *parlement*, and the returners took up the case in order to spite Pichard. But the publication of the letters did the president little harm:

Elles ne prouvoient que la hauteur, et la Dureté de Caractere, d'un homme irrité, Contre un homme d'affaire dont il Etoit mécontent.[100]

Such was the opinion of Mme Duplessy. They were certainly not enough by themselves to lose him a case at the parlement, or even secure Giraudeau a hearing, had Pichard not also served under Maupeou. Unthrifty stewards were the nightmare of all landowners. Yet this was a vivid example of what could happen when landlords relaxed their personal hold on the administration of their domains. It is easy to see why so few did so. Care alone could assure good returns from agriculture, especially when the largest earning crop had such a fluctuating value. As president de Casaux put it, 'L'exactitude et la précision ne sont jamais de trop dans les affaires'.[101] It was the same spirit that animated the magistrates' attitude to their 'feudal' assets.

But no attempt, other than this exactitude, was made to increase the security or the returns of agriculture. There was no interest in experiment. Precision, far from the sign of a vigorous market-seeking attitude to production, was the result of a deep conservatism. The high-quality of wine trade accentuated it. On the one hand, failed experiments could be costly, and ruin a vineyard's reputation for good. Besides, a generation of vines lasted 80 years—a long time for an experiment.[102] On the other hand, wine-producing was a highly speculative venture, demanding a constant high outlay for extremely variable returns. In this it had more in common with commercial speculation in the colonial trade than might at first appear. If the magistrates had an agricultural policy, it was the simple one of increasing the area under cultivation, and maintaining a certain diversity of crops; but there was nothing extraordinary and progressive about this. And what was the point of innovation? Existing methods worked, in their precarious way. Besides, most magistrates also had the insurance of other, non-agricultural sources of income.

NOTES

1. Claude Boucher (1673–1752). Counsellor at the court of aids, 1693; president, 1699; intendant of Auvergne, 1717; intendant of Bordeaux, 1720; resigned, 1743. On Boucher in general, see L. Desgraves, 'L'intendant Claude Boucher, 1720–1743', R. Hist. Bx. (1952).
2. R. Pijassou in Bordeaux au XVIIIᵉ siècle, 155–9.
3. Cited above, p. 68.
4. Pijassou, loc. cit., 157; Lhéritier, Tourny, I, 384–7.
5. Forster, 'Noble wine producers', 32–3, implies that the clearings were primarily for vineyards. Pijassou, loc. cit., 159, is more cautious, but they agree on the general extension of vineyards throughout the century. Pijassou's remarkable map, 160, shows vividly the predominance of the vine in local agriculture.
6. Forster, 'Noble wine producers', 21, 23. The source is the tax roll in AD C3018, which also serves as the basis for many of the conclusions of Pijassou, op. cit., 170–4. For another use of the roll, see above, pp. 52–3.
7. Pijassou, loc. cit., 172–3.
8. ibid., 173–4.

9. J. P. Boyd (ed.), *The Papers of Thomas Jefferson* (New Haven, 1950–), XI, 455, Jefferson's Journal of a tour through southern France, 24 May 1787.
10. ibid., XIV, 336, Bondfield to Jefferson, 6 Dec. 1788.
11. AN W400 (927).
12. 1 *tonneau* = 42 cubic feet. J. A. Brutails, *Recherches sur l'équivalence des anciennes mesures de la Gironde* (Bordeaux, 1912).
13. *Jefferson Papers*, XI, 456.
14. See the lamentations of E. Labrousse, *La Crise de l'économie française à la fin de l'Ancien Régime et au début de la Révolution* (Paris, 1944), 255–7. Not only are there few series of figures pointing to general conclusions; evidence of individual activities, such as account books, has also disappeared. In these circumstances we can only advance the most tentative general conclusions about their activities in this sphere.
15. Printed in C. T. Malvezin, *Histoire du commerce de Bordeaux* (Bordeaux, 1892), III, 277–8. Details on situation of estates from Marion, Bencazar, Caudrillier, *Documents*, and selected other sources.
16. Pijassou, loc. cit., 173. The classifications are not identical. The Entre-deux-Mers figure, for instance, includes several of Pijassou's classifications.
17. Individually listed in the original.
18. AN W400 (927).
19. Nicolaï, *Au bon vieux temps*, II. On Ségur and Lafitte, see also Pijassou, op. cit., 174–5.
20. Marion, Bencazar, Caudrillier, op. cit., I, 154; AD 8J 481 (Fonds Bigot), Dumas de Fonbrauge family papers.
21. AD 3E 23.308, account book of Dumas de Fonbrauge; unfortunately only three years are documented.
22. AD 2E 63 (tit. fam. Darche), 'Livre pour les biens de Sauternes et de Langon commencé en 1760'.
23. Forster, 'Noble wine producers', 27.
24. Labrousse, *La Crise*, part II, chs. 2 and 3.
25. AD 2E 1089 (tit. fam. Duval), Le Berthon to Duval, 27 Oct. 1780.
26. AD C3159, anonymous memoir on the election of Bordeaux.
27. Butel, op. cit., II, 457–63, emphasizes how complete the merchants' control over the growers' outlets was.
28. Crouzet in *Bordeaux au XVIIIe siècle*, 315–16.
29. Quoted in Nicolaï, *Au bon vieux temps*, from AD C3214, 27 March 1744.
30. Quoted in R. Shackleton, *Montesquieu*, 206.
31. Young, *Travels*, 61.
32. The fullest evidence for the disaster is of course that presented by Labrousse, *La Crise*, 273–5.
33. *Jefferson Papers*, XI, 456–7.
34. Labrousse, op. cit., part II, chs. 2–5.
35. Forster, loc. cit., 27.
36. *Jefferson Papers*, loc. cit.
37. Labrousse, op. cit., 294, 341–7, 357–9.
38. AD 2E 1810 (tit. fam. Leberthon), Le Berthon to Duval (?), 28 Dec. 1783.
39. AD 2E 1213^5 (tit. fam. Filhot de Chimbaud), Boudin to Filhot, 19 Aug. 1786.
40. Labrousse, op. cit., 376, 512–18.
41. *Jefferson Papers*, loc. cit.
42. I allude to the pamphlet *Engorgement de vins de la généralité de Guienne. Moyens d'y rémédier* (Bordeaux, 1786), which is much used by Labrousse (e.g., 342, 358), and is certainly evidence that the mercantile community was conscious of overproduction in the 1780s. Unfortunately I have been unable to find a copy of this pamphlet.
43. See J. P. Trabut-Cussac in Y. Renouard (ed.), *Bordeaux sous les rois d'Angleterre* (Bordeaux, 1965), 54–6; and H. Kehrig, *Le Privilège des vins à Bordeaux jusqu'en 1789* (Paris and Bordeaux, 1886), *passim*.
44. The 1762 revision is printed in *AHDG*, XXXIII (1898). In it are the names of 45 families represented in the parlement under Louis XVI.
45. *Arrêt* of the parlement, 18 Aug. 1762. Printed in *AHDG*, XXVI (1891), 205.
46. Kehrig, op. cit., 37–42.

47. AAE MD France, 1589, f.77, Mouchy to Vergennes, 11 Sept. 1781.
48. P. Butel, 'Grands propriétaires et production des vins du Médoc au XVIIIe siècle', *R. Hist. Bx.* (1963), 129–41, *passim*.
49. AN W400 (927).
50. *Travels*, 294.
51. Conclusion drawn from perusal of the tax roll in AD C3018.
52. Crouzet, op. cit., 250–1. Butel, 'La croissance', I, 110–14.
53. *Jefferson Papers*, XI, 454.
54. AD C3195, 'Etat des décharges sur les Vingtièmes', 1775–76.
55. ibid. This probably means that he lost perhaps 50 head. He was selling young cows in 1780 at around 100 l. each—AD 3E 23.308 (account book of Dumas de Fonbrauge).
56. AD C1551. *Arrêt* of the parlement, 20 Aug. 1774.
57. In the Graves and Médoc, Jefferson observed, wine-growers struck a nice balance between fertilizing and keeping the flavour of the grapes pure. *Papers*, XI, 455.
58. Malvezin, *Histoire du commerce*, III, 101.
59. AD 1J 312, 'Actes concernant le Médoc'.
60. AD Q934. Inventory after condemnation of Pichard's goods.
61. ibid.
62. AD Q908. Inventory after confiscation of Casaux's goods.
63. Young, *Travels*, 281, 289.
64. Baurein, *Variétés Bordeloises* (1876), III, 368.
65. AD 3J—E35 (tit. fam. Verthamon), letter of 17 Feb. 1778.
66. AD Q934.
67. AD C1509, 'Pépinière royale de Bordeaux, 1778'.
68. AD 2E 1359 (tit. fam. Degères). Contract of 27 Oct. 1783. The contractors provided all the labour, as was customary in the Toulouse region also. Forster, *Nobility of Toulouse*, 88–94.
69. Marion, Bencazar, Caudrillier, *Documents*, I, 140.
70. AD Q936, inventory after confiscation of Raymond's goods.
71. Marion, Bencazar, Caudrillier, loc. cit., 144.
72. AD 7B 1564 (fonds des négociants), contains various letters of 1783 from Bienassis to his corn-broker.
73. AD 2E 1405 (tit. fam. Gourgue), *Bail à ferme*, 9 June 1753.
74. AD 3E 15.414 (Dugarry), *Bail à ferme*, 3 Oct. 1779.
75. AD C3171, intendant to subdelegate of Libourne, 5 March 1782.
76. e.g., at Cadaujac, 3,200 l. p.a. AD 3E 13.065 (Cheyron), 18 May 1765; *palu* de Bordeaux, I, 900 l. p.a., ibid., 3 July 1765; Blaye, 1,100 l. p.a. AD 3E 13.067 (Cheyron), 8 July 1776.
77. AD C74, intendant to comptroller-general, 11 Nov. 1775. See also Forster, 'Noble wine producers', 25–6.
78. AD C3195, cited above, n 54.
79. Forster, loc. cit.; Marion, 'Etat des classes rurales', 108.
80. *Jefferson Papers*, XI, 455.
81. Known in the Bordelais as *prix-faiteurs*, which is usefully translated by Forster, loc. cit., 26, as 'contract-labourers'.
82. The methods of management of counsellor Darche, whose returns are tabulated above, p. 90, were not therefore typical, since both his vineyards were exploited through sharecroppers. Here I am at variance with Forster, op. cit., 27–8.
83. All that follows is taken from the family papers in AD 1213[1] (déclarations du centième denier, 1776 & 1790), AD 1213[11] (livre de raison, 1788–90), and Marion, Bencazar, Caudrillier, *Documents*, I, 153.
84. 1 *boisseau de Bordeaux* = 78·808 litres. Brutails, *Recherches . . . mesures*.
85. A good deal less than Jefferson was told was typical. Cf. above, p. 95.
86. Nearer to Jefferson's estimate.
87. AD C3018, Twentieth roll of 1755.
88. *AHDG*, I (1859), 247, Esmangart to Bertin, 18 July 1772; AN H[1] 1503, Bertin to Esmangart, 4 July 1772. See also below, p. 132.
89. AD Q1008.
90. AD Q1009.

91. AD Q1011.
92. AD 2E 2285 (tit. fam. Pichard). Printed in *Réponses aux observations préliminaires et au mémoire de M. le Président de Pichard. Pour le Sieur Giraudeau, Notaire à Salles.*
93. ibid., p. 2, 16 April 1770.
94. ibid., p. 15, 1 Feb. 1772.
95. ibid., p. 4, 2 Feb. 1771.
96. ibid., p. 18, 4 July 1772.
97. ibid., p. 8, 19 July 1771.
98. ibid., p. 15, 1 Feb. 1772.
99. ibid., p. 28, 3 Oct. 1773.
100. BVBx MS 1201, V, 16 July 1776. See also below, p. 171, for this affair in another context.
101. AD 7B 2013 (fonds des négociants), Casaux to Servenier, 1 March 1773.
102. *Jefferson Papers*, XI, 455.

CHAPTER 7

Subsidiary Investments

The Bordeaux boom of the 18th century was many-sided. Its basis was the colonial trade, but around this core other industries flourished too—shipbuilding, refining, and even building to accommodate the expanding population. All this meant that Bordeaux offered a broader field for speculative investment than most French provincial towns. Magistrates who relied on wine for most of their income were no strangers to speculation, and many of them were involved in the boom in one way or another too.

A considerable number were involved in the colonial trade itself. A few had been born in the colonies, others were of colonial extraction, and colonial heiresses brought colonial links to 15 more. Magistrates from mercantile families, such as Saige, Féger, and Dubergier, moved in circles where the colonial interest was paramount. Some magistrates visited the colonies; earlier in the century special provisions had even been made for members of the parlement of Bordeaux on visits to take a seat on the sovereign council of Guadeloupe.[1] Later, counsellors de Lamolère and de Raymond certainly made visits to the colonies, as did several members of the Prunes family. Counsellor Pocquet actually spent most of his life in Martinique.[2] So it is not surprising that the parlement took an active interest in the structure of the colonial trade, as for example in its letter to the king of January 1785.[3] When in 1789 an 'American Society resident at Bordeaux' was founded to concert action in defending colonial interests with the Parisian Massiac Club, several members of the parlement joined. Counsellor de Basterot was on the steering committee.[4] For the links these magistrates had with the colonies were the strongest possible—links of property.

In Saint-Domingue, for example, the Dupaty family was one of the most extensive owners.[5] The father of the president had a sugar plantation in the parish of Acul, which ultimately he inherited; he also had the expectation of the goods of his mother, consisting of a sugar plantation at Quartier Morin. The wife of counsellor P. de Raymond de Lalande shared with her brother the ownership of a sugar plantation in Quartier Morin and a coffee estate at Grande Rivière. P. L. de Raymond, counsellor, had a coffee plantation and hereditary rights in a sugar plantation at Petit-Trou. Counsellor de Lamolère had a sugar estate in Quartier Morin. Counsellor de Basterot ran the sugar estate of his wife in Le Terrier Rouge. Among the other Saint-Domingue proprietors were counsellor J.

Thilorier in Ounaminthe, and president J. J. Maurice de Sentout in Port-au-Prince. The most detailed available information concerns the habitations of the Dupuy sisters.[6] Jean-Patrice Dupuy, treasurer of France in the office of finances of Bordeaux, had two daughters. The elder married Pierre Dutasta, by whom she had one son before he died. In 1769 she married counsellor de Poissac, and by the 1770s Poissac and his father-in-law were jointly administering from Bordeaux in their wives' names three coffee plantations in the parish of Dondon, Saint-Domingue, employing between them 400 negro slaves. They estimated the movables on these estates alone to be worth over 1,200,000 l. In 1788 the other daughter married counsellor R. J. A. Dubergier de Favars, and, her father being dead, as a dowry was promised half of her mother's lands in Saint-Domingue, whose estimated value was 60–80,000 l. a year. The children of this marriage estimated in the 1820s the capital value of the three properties in 1789 to have been 1,204,350 l. The revenue from coffee in 1788 had been 177,646 l., and in 1789, 223,805 l. Another estimate of 1830 gave slightly lower figures, but none below 190,000 l.

The value of colonial property was in fact astronomical. The theoretical annual net value of a single estate administered by counsellor de Basterot in Le Terrier Rouge, Saint-Domingue, was 50,000 l.[7] The Prunes brothers sold their habitation at Basse-Pointe, Martinique, to the Jewish merchant house of Gradis, by contracts of 1767 and 1775, for a total of 611,330 l. 16s 5d.[8] It employed 120 slaves, and brought in an estimated revenue of 55,000 l. a year.[9] Before we conclude, however, that to marry an 'American' heiress was the key to fabulous riches, it is worth reflecting that the sale of the Prunes brothers' habitation was a foreclosure by the Gradis on insuperable debts. When the first half was sold to them, the price fixed was 128,236 l. 19s 4d, out of a value of 311,330 l. 16s 5d. The difference was debts. When the other half was sold in 1775, the Gradis kept 200,000 l. of the 300,000 l. price, again for debts. For debt was the bane of colonial proprietors, and a burden that was almost inevitable sooner or later. The peril of hurricanes, the passage of the Atlantic, and the hazards of the English blockade in wartime, along with the constant high outlay on cultivation, gave West Indian agriculture a character superficially similar to viticulture, but with stakes and risks that were far higher. Moreover, normally trade with the islands was carried out on a basis of goods for goods, with little money changing hands. This made it extremely hard for proprietors ever to lay hands on liquid assets, often forcing the planter at the same time to live on credit. War, when it came, aggravated these disadvantages, especially for producers of goods of great bulk and relatively low value, like coffee:[10] 'Le bas prix du caffé . . .', complained Poissac during the American war,

> paroit chaque Jour devoir Diminué, soit à raison des impots Excessifs portes sur cette denrée tant dans les colonies que Dans la metropolle, soit Encor a raison des Embarguo mis par les puissances du nord . . . En telle sorte que tout le produit des plus immenses habitations se trouve Devoré par le frais de culture, Le fisc, Et le fret Exhorbitant qu'exige Le commerce pour le Transport de Ces Denrées.

He hoped to compensate himself by securing concessionary land on which to enter the more stable and lucrative sugar market.[11]

When the proprietor was also an absentee, the difficulties were almost insuperable. Yet most of the magistrates had never been to the islands and never intended
to go. Credits were hard to call in at 3,000 miles distance, when letters took months
to arrive, and when resident managers resented their subjection to distant, unknown, and uncomprehending masters.[12] Colonial law courts were staffed by
residents with little sympathy for the metropolitan creditor, whether merchant or
proprietor. In 1783, counsellor de Basterot complained to the secretary of the
navy that he had:

> une multitude de débiteurs au cap St domingue, depuis plusieurs années ils
> me retiennent, Monseigneur, des sommes tres considerables dont ils ne me
> payent pas même les interêts et avec une fortunne brillante pour mon etat,
> je me vois par leur inexactitude dans une gènne cruelle. Il en est surtout qui
> me doit près de cent mille ecus et à raison de la faveur que lui accorde le
> procureur général du Cap je n'ai pû encore Monseigneur, parvenir depuis
> deux ans à lui faire rendre son compte de tutelle j'ai offert de recevoir mon
> payement en fonds, en negres, et bestiaux, de faire même des sacrifices s'il
> le faloit et malgre cett excès de complaisance je suis traité avec le plus parfait
> dédain.[13]

The minister promised to help, and wrote to the sovereign council, but there is
no evidence that Basterot obtained satisfaction. Indeed, by 1790, he was bankrupt,
the result of living at a level commensurate with a large income which remained
purely notional, since he was unable to realize his assets.[14] Doubtless this was also
why the Gradis foreclosed on the Prunes brothers. Even when the proprietor was
resident, sooner or later he would probably become indebted to shippers; when
he was an absentee, too, these debts still accumulated, but out of sight. They
affected him in the form of deficient revenues, which in turn led to debts in
France. Many colonial proprietors, therefore, enjoyed only the illusion of great
riches, and many an heiress-hunter among the magistrates must have been un-
pleasantly surprised at the precarious and uncertain nature of the immense
wealth which she had seemed to promise. Even so, colonial revenues must have
paid at least in part for the new mansions of men like Lamolère and Poissac, for
they were both men whose French estates were not big enough to support such
unreturning capital expenditure. Part of the secret, perhaps, was to be shipper
and planter at the same time. The question of debts, and reciprocal suspicions of
monopoly, made the relationship between planters and merchants notoriously
hostile, as each side clamoured for the preservation of its own monopoly, and the
abolition of the other's.[15] Poissac, however, avoided the unpleasantness and disadvantages. In 1770 and 1771 we find him, sharing the capital outlay with his
father-in-law, financing consignments of very diverse goods—cloth, hats, axes,
sealing wax, paper, and so on—for Saint-Domingue.[16] Counsellor Dumas de
Fonbrauge also traded directly with Guadeloupe through the agency of his first
wife's family who were important planters there.[17]

Traditionally, of course, magistrates were noblemen, and noblemen could not
indulge in trade on pain of loss of status (*dérogeance*). This prohibition did not
apply to wholesale trade, from which the greatest mercantile fortunes were made
in 18th-century Bordeaux, yet few of the magistrates tried to take advantage of
this. Admittedly there were exceptions, like the two cases already cited. There

was also the ubiquitous Saige, himself the son of a great merchant. In 1783 he took one-quarter share in financing the building of a ship, *Le Saige*, which cost in all 86,329 l. 5s 6d. Its first voyage to the isles brought in a net profit of 67,135 l., of which he got one-quarter. Its second in 1786 made 51,100 l.; its third in 1786–87 made 94,550 l., of which Saige got five-eighths. His five-eighths on the fourth voyage of 1787–88 alone amounted to 77,677 l.[18] These were the sort of returns that the great merchants of Bordeaux realized in the 18th century, and which only exceptional vineyards could match. But Saige had already retired from the parlement when he went into this business. Trade was full-time work; this alone was enough to prevent magistrates, who had a profession, from entering it. Not all of them would have felt inclined to; the law of *dérogeance* was merely the legal expression of a social prejudice powerful in its own right. Yet the magistracy as a whole was too closely linked to the mercantile world to harbour this prejudice in its fullest form. Too many of its members had merchant fathers, grandfathers, or brothers; too many had married mercantile heiresses; one or two had traded before entering the court. Most of them were dependent on the merchants for the sale of their wine,[19] and also met them regularly in social life. Relations between the court and the mercantile community were on the whole good. The fact that few magistrates actually participated in trade simply indicates that their time was occupied in other things, and their money sunk in less obviously hazardous and demanding investments.

Shipbuilding and sugar-refining, boom industries in and around Bordeaux, attracted none of the magistrates' capital; although the Daugeard family's glass-works at Bourg doubtless permitted them to exploit the growing demand for wine-bottles while maintaining their noble honour in an industry traditionally open to nobles.[20] Even the traditional annuities (*rentes*) did not seem as attractive as they once had. Among Parisian magistrates, life annuities often constituted a major item in their fortunes.[21] They were common at Toulouse, too, although lower in value.[22] At Bordeaux, without the central institutions of confidence of Paris, and without the loan-raising estates of Languedoc, they were always rarer, and most magistrates had only a few contracts. In 1768 the government requested the surrender of all titles to annuities for examination, and a register of them gives us some idea of the holdings of certain magistrates.[23]

Annuities of some magistrates

Name	Return p.a.	Capital	No. of contracts
Brivazac, counsellor	609 l. 10s 6d	24,201 l.	3
Loyac, counsellor	362 l. 11s	14,502 l.	2
Conilh, counsellor	295 l. 7s 6d	11,275 l.	4
Verthamon, president	533 l.	10,660 l.	9
Piis, counsellor	208 l. 5s	8,330 l.	1
Le Berthon, first president	124 l. 9s	4,978 l.	3
de Spens, counsellor	74 l. 19s 11d	2,506 l. 18s 11d	2
Filhot de Chimbaud, counsellor	16 l. 9s	658 l.	1

All these titles were old ones, mostly dating back to the 1720s, and all had been reduced in 1766. This, along with the partial bankruptcy operated by Terray in

1770 and 1771, may help to explain why annuities were so rare among the magistrates in the last decades of the 18th century. They seemed no more secure in value than any other form of investment, never went up, and even, in violation of all good faith, went down. So holdings of them were not only rare, but also diminishing. Counsellor Pelet d'Anglade was quite exceptional with his 7,900 l. a year on a capital of 96,000 l.; even these assets were inherited from his father.[24]

Much more attractive in a city where capital was always in demand, was the *rente constituée* or private loan.[25] Not that such loans were uncommon among noblemen and magistrates in other parts of France;[26] everywhere they tended to lend surplus capital to friends and colleagues. In Bordeaux most such loans were well below 20,000 l. in principal and only yielded at most a few hundreds per year; the normal interest rate was 5 per cent. They went mostly to those who had family settlements to make, or needed ready cash for some reason. Specie in large amounts was rare; most business was transacted in negotiable paper, and magistrates like everybody else found it hard to realize their assets quickly. Cash, as soon as it came in, was at once reinvested, often itself in the form of loans. And so a structure of mutual obligation was built up, which is reflected in the number of small contracts inventoried after the death or emigration of magistrates. Some magistrates carried their financial operations beyond this routine level. Saige speculated on the exchange rate between *livres tournois* and Spanish piastres, although the returns on this transaction were somewhat disappointing.[27] He also preferred to sell annuities as a means of raising capital, for although his father had been one of the richest men in the city, when he died the usufruct of his vast fortune remained, in accordance with the custom of Bordeaux, in the hands of his widow, who lived to be over 90 and survived her son. So Saige never disposed freely of his family's vast capital, and not even his marriage portion of 400,000 l. was payable until after his mother's death.[28] All that was strictly his, was a pension of 10,000 l. a year. Yet by selling annuities he was able to raise plenty of capital. When his papers were inventoried in 1793, records of no less than 48 were found, all but two of them still payable. They represented an annual outlay of at least 42,258 l., but a capital value of well over 300,000 l.[29] In the 1780s counsellor de Basterot also attempted to raise capital by selling annuities; they constituted bridging loans to cope with his debts until he could call in his vast colonial assets.[30] They did not save him from eventual bankruptcy. Saige, however, prospered and the capital provided by his loans was the basis of diverse projects in land, trade, finance, and housing.

Apart from acquiring land in the colonies or trading with them, the easiest way to tap the expanding wealth of Bordeaux was to invest in urban property. 'The new houses that are building in all quarters of the town', wrote Arthur Young,

> mark, too clearly to be misunderstood, the prosperity of the place. The skirts are everywhere composed of new streets; with still newer ones marked out, and partly built. These houses are in general small, or on a middling scale, for inferior tradesmen. They are all of white stone, and add, as they are finished, much to the beauty of the city. I inquired into the date of these new streets, and found that four or five years were in general the period . . .[31]

Saige was certainly in the van of this movement. When president de Gascq died in 1781, his property eventually went to his presumed bastard son, A. N. Valdec de Lessart, master of requests,[32] including a house and garden on the outskirts of the town near the church of St-Seurin. This Valdec sold in 1787 to Saige, for 56,560 l.[33] Gascq himself had viewed investment in real estate in this quarter as unpromising: 'A mesure qu'on batira du cotté du jardin public les maisons de ce quartier diminueront toujours de prix'.[34] Saige clearly did not agree. In 1789 he began to sell off the old Gascq estate, the first batch going for 9,680 l.[35] When his goods were confiscated in 1793, they included several houses in the area,[36] on land which had merely been described as a plot (*emplacement*) in 1787. He was obviously speculating on the expansion of the city.

Other magistrates were doing the same. President J. C. Daugeard owned land in the parish of Sainte-Croix, in the extreme south of the city.[37] In the 15 years preceding the Revolution he enfeoffed 37 small plots to tradesmen and craftsmen, while retaining overlordship. The entry fines levied were so heavy that these transactions amounted to straight sales. Altogether Daugeard made 14,984 l. 16s 8d from entry fines between 1775 and 1789. He also made eight outright sales over the same period, at prices ranging from 192 l. to 5,000 l. Another example was E. L. Dufaure de Lajarte, advocate-general. When in 1781 he came to divide with his sister the successions of their father and brothers, who had both died intestate, he deliberately chose for his portion of the succession three town houses and the portion of the family estate at Sablonna, on the southern fringe of expanding Bordeaux, which was nearest to the city. He left their large country estate at La Sauve, worth 90,000 l., to his sister. Obviously he intended to make his money from urban property.[38] Sure enough, in June 1782 he began to sell plots of land in Sablonna and in the adjacent suburb of Sainte-Eulalie, the fastest expanding quarter of the town. He even created a street and gave it his name, along which he sold plots. In ten years Dufaure de Lajarte made 47,909 l. 15s 2d from such sales. At his father's death this estate was valued at 6,000 l., yet by selling it piecemeal he made eight times that sum. N. M. Moreau de Montcheuil, counsellor, had the good fortune to own extensive lands around the public garden, a quarter that was becoming fashionable by the 1780s.[39] Moreau made the most of this, and from 1774 began to sell small plots of land behind the garden. As with Dufaure de Lajarte, this was no haphazard business; by the 1780s we find that these plots are along the 'rue Moreau' or the 'rue Montcheuil', which suggests that he had some co-ordinated plan of development. Between 1774 and 1790 he sold no less than 66 plots of land behind the public garden, though retaining his feudal overlordship in each case. The overall sum he received was 144,491 l. 15s 0d, one of the largest capital gains to come to any of the magistrates at the end of the old régime. Apart from Saige, few magistrates actually bought suburban land in order to exploit the building boom, but clearly those who were fortunate enough to possess or inherit such land did not hesitate to profit from it.

The profit from city centre properties was not so clear, although, according to Young,

The rent of houses and lodging rises every day, as it has done since the Peace considerably, at the same time that so many new houses have been and are erecting, unites with the advance in prices of everything. They complain that the expenses of living have risen in ten years full 30 per cent.[40]

A general idea of the stake of the magistrates in urban property can be obtained

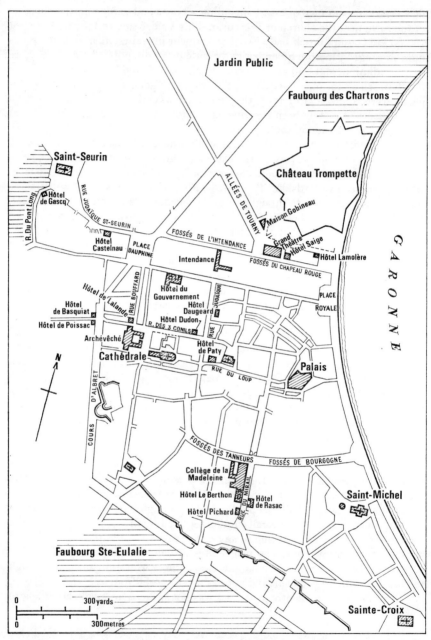

Bordeaux under Louis XVI, showing the main buildings and districts mentioned

from the urban twentieth rolls of 1777 and 1790.[11] The assessments were never a twentieth of the value of the properties, and were not changed substantially between 1760 and 1790, but they do give a proportional picture of the extent of the magistrates' urban property:

Members of the Parlement paying the twentieth on houses, 1790

Assessment	No. of families
Over 500 l. p.a.	3
400–500 l.	1
300–400 l.	4
200–300 l.	10
100–200 l.	22
50–100 l.	24
Under 50 l.	26
	90

Apparently, some families owned no urban property at all, not even their own dwellings. Only between 90 and 100[42] out of 130 or so families are mentioned. Many of the younger magistrates lived with their parents, which must explain the absence of some names. And as at Toulouse,[43] some magistrates lived in leased apartments, such as counsellor Roche,[44] president J. C. Daugeard before he bought his mansion,[45] or president M. J. de Gourgue, who paid rent on a seven-year lease to his own brother for part of the family house from 1779.[46] But obviously most families had some real estate within the city. Thirty of them in the lower groups of assessment owned only one property, presumably living in it. Even so, they were not prevented from leasing out part of it. Counsellor de Laliman, a bachelor, lived in one furnished room of his own house.[47] Saige and Gobineau leased off substantial sections of their huge mansions.[48] The remaining families, representing about half the parlement, owned more than one property and therefore derived urban income from outside their own domicile.

At the top of the list, inevitably, came Saige. He and his mother were assessed for 12 properties, including his new mansion and houses adjoining it next to the grand theatre, the ex-Gascq holdings, and several others. Even in 1777, when the more striking of these properties were as yet unacquired, he still headed the list. It is impossible to set a precise capital value on the Saige properties, but it does not seem excessive to place it between half a million and a million livres. It must have yielded tens of thousands annually in rent. Second on the 1790 roll was the Brivazac family. When L. G. de Brivazac, honorary counsellor, died in 1782 he left a fortune approaching 2 million. About one-third of this was made up of 23 houses worth at least 677,000 l. in capital value.[49] But between 1770 and 1790 five houses were sold, and only two modest properties acquired. The Brivazacs were clearly running down their urban investments rather than expanding them; and perhaps this contrast suggests a wider pattern. Six of the first eight parlementaire families on the 1790 roll were relatively new both to nobility and the parlement.[50] They had been ennobled since 1700, and their appearance in the parlement was still within living memory. Great fortunes in city properties seemed to be new fortunes. Indeed, it was natural that those whose fortunes had been made in an urban context should make their initial investments in town property, before turning their attention to more prestigious rural property. Only in the suburbs, where town and country met, were the rewards of property speculation so attractive as to be irresistible. Otherwise activity by the magistrates on the urban property market in no way compared to their vigour on the rural one.

It is very difficult to assess the return on urban property. Tax-rolls are unreliable, and leases are elusive. Moreover, no account books of urban income have survived. However, the few records of leases which do survive[51] suggest that terms tended to be short; none over nine years and most under five. This suggests that rack-renting may well have been taking place. It is clear that the tenant bore all the burden in terms of repairs, while at the same time being forbidden to sub-let. Nothing more solid survives to confirm or negate Young's reports on the rapid rise in rents, but there are some static figures. In 1794 counsellor Pelet d'Anglade had 12 houses, all leased out except for the one he occupied. His annual rental was estimated at 17,605 l.[52] The counsellors Basquiat de Mugriet, father and son, after they had emigrated were reckoned to own between them 17 houses and shops, estimated in capital value at 521,000 l., on which the rental, to judge by the leases of a few items, must have been higher than Pelet's.[53] The return on property depended on what it was and where it was. Apart from mansions in the middle or in fashionable areas of the town, the most valuable property was in Chartrons, the business and trading quarter, especially on the quayside. Wine sheds (chais) in particular were in great demand, since under the wine privilege of Bordeaux, it was only in Chartrons that up-country wine might be stored during its permitted period in Bordeaux. In 1777 about 20 parlementaire families had property in Chartrons; their holdings included 21 wine sheds and five cellars.[54] In the city proper, where most holdings were, rents were derived not only from whole dwelling houses, but from parts leased off piecemeal, especially ground floors, which were frequently leased as shops.

The mansions of magistrates were far more than sources of revenue or speculative investments. They were at once a witness to their wealth, their social importance, and their taste. The crown itself was well aware of the importance of a fitting residence for its magistrates, and when in 1741 the first president's house was burnt down, the king built him a new one at public expense running to 100,000 l.[55] But by the end of the century a mania for monumental building had far outdistanced the scale of this solid and old-fashioned mansion. Owners and architects, as if in competition with each other, conceived ever more vast projects. The culmination came with 'Bonnaffé's Island', a huge block built in the 1780s for the great colonial merchant by Laclotte, with the deliberate intention of overwhelming Victor Louis's grand theatre across the road.[56] Not only merchants built on such a colossal scale. In 1775 Saige acquired several plots of land behind the still rising theatre for a total of 186,020 l. 2s 2d.[57] On some of these he built houses whose usufruct for life he managed to sell off to eager customers even before they were built,[58] but he reserved the main plot for himself, and there he commissioned Victor Louis, architect of the theatre, to build him a massive residence.[59] Some fragments give a rough idea of the cost; every few weeks Louis drew up a list of expenses, and two of these survive. Between 9 and 21 October 1775 the bill was 3,652 l. 3s 2d, and between 22 April and 4 May 1776 it ran to 5,008 l. 14s 9d.[60] This house took over five years to complete; the cost at this sort of rate must have been staggering. Louis also worked for counsellors de Lamolère and de Gobineau. On a plot which cost him 27,000 l. in 1774, not far from Saige's house and overlooking the roadstead, Lamolère had built a corner house scarcely smaller.[61] Gobineau's house was the only part ever built of Louis's grandiose project to replace the *Château Trompette* with a huge piazza dedicated to Louis XVI.[62] Plots of building land were on sale in 1787 and Gobineau bought the first for about 40,000 l. By 1789 the great, triangular house was inhabited, having cost about 200,000 l. to build. By itself it was enough to put Gobineau third on the 1790 list of assessments for the twentieth. Partially leased out, it was assessed, probably not unjustly, at 440 l.

Less spectacular, but perhaps more tasteful, were the houses built by Lhôte for several of the magistrates. In the mid-1770s he worked for counsellor de Basquiat de Mugriet. His house on the cours d'Albret opposite the new archbishop's palace cost 14,190 l. 4s 9d.[63] Next door counsellor de Poissac had a very similar house constructed. Lhôte was also responsible for the high-roofed, light, and handsome house of counsellor J. de Raymond de Lalande in the rue Bouffard.[64] Counsellor de Castelnau d'Auros and his brother did not employ one of the better-known architects; nevertheless, in 1785 they began to build themselves a large house in the rue Judaïque Saint-Seurin, which they sold in 1790 for 125,000 l.[65]

Not all magistrates, of course, needed to build new houses. Newcomers like Saige, Lamolère, or Poissac needed to establish themselves, but others were stylishly accommodated already. The Dudons in the rue des Trois Conils, the Pichards and Gombaults in the rue du Mirail, the Casaux in the rue Judaïque, the Gourgues in the street which bore their name—all these families had ancestral houses which bore witness to their deep local roots. From time to time somebody felt that their position merited more exalted quarters. In 1770 L. de Paty du Rayet, counsellor, sold his house in the rue Leyterie for 42,000 l., and the proceeds went towards buying a handsome 17th-century residence in the rue du Loup, which had once belonged to the first president Gillet de Lacaze. This cost him 65,000 l.[66] President J. C. Daugeard felt even more undignified in 1783. He found himself, a comfortable millionaire, renting a house. For 136,000 l. he ended this situation by the purchase of a house more suited to his dignity, that of the former president de Latresne, rue Judaïque, itself only built in mid-century.[67] Nearly half of the magistrates had not been noble and had not been established in the parlement when the century began; many were still consolidating and improving their social position, and to change the style and scale of life was one way of doing this. Out of our 162 magistrates, 85 had only one address from 1775 to 1790 or the time when they left the court. The rest changed their residence, most once, some twice, and several three or four times.[68] It is to be presumed that they were moving, in most cases, to more acceptable surroundings. There was indeed no parlementaire quarter, as there was for instance at Toulouse.[69] Magistrates did not live in the parish of Sainte-Croix, or in the southernmost parts of that of St-Michel, an artisan quarter of the town; although some might have substantial and lucrative holdings in the area, like president Daugeard. Nevertheless, it was next to the street where, for its length, more magistrates lived than in any other, the rue du Mirail.[70] Neither did magistrates live on the north side of the *Château Trompette*. Chartrons was infested with foreigners and merchants, and although it was acceptable and, as we have seen, not uncommon to own and lease out property in Chartrons, one did not live there. Beyond this there was no pattern. Many lived in the congested, evil-smelling centre of the town, in the tangle of streets around the palace. Many former parlementaire mansions to this day line the central rue Castillon, then called rue Judaïque. Others, like Gascq and Castelnau, lived in the more salubrious suburbs. Ostentatious newcomers often took or built spectacular residences on the Fossés du Chapeau Rouge or the Allées de Tourny.[71] What is certain is that the average magistrate's house yielded in nothing, in point of style or scale, to that of the colonial merchant. Their tastes were similar, they employed the same architects. Both lived on a spacious, comfortable scale, behind discreet screens and coach-gates, in houses liberally endowed with salons, libraries, and well-appointed amenities. Here again there was less to divide them than might be thought.[72] Nevertheless, such style meant different things in different cases. With merchants, if not the taste for sheer luxury, it was the expression of social pretensions and cultural ambitions. With the magistrate, it was *noblesse oblige*; a member of the parlement felt that his position in the world dictated a certain style of life. Houses were a major part of this, transcending the peculiar circumstances of the boom. They could never be regarded purely as investments. They symbolized that their owners were men of consequence in the world. The return was to be recognized as such.

Apart from the striking houses in which they lived, the investment of magistrates in urban property has been neglected.[73] Although, even at Bordeaux, such property formed a subsidiary segment of the fortune of magistrates, this segment was not always small or without importance. The same could be said of investments in the colonies, trade, and finance. They represented a certain diversification of sources of income, so that the magistrates were never totally dependent on the wildly fluctuating returns of viticulture. We should not be surprised that some of the members of the parlement, however conservative, should have been attracted by the very wide opportunities for speculative investment that 18th-century Bordeaux offered. Yet nor should we be surprised that none based their whole financial position on such ventures. To do that would require more time than magistrates could spare. So they dabbled where the opportunity arose, and profited from the boom. They never allowed themselves to become totally dependent on it.

And such diversity as there was in their fortunes remained strictly local. National or central fields of investment attracted little or none of their capital. The boom was as peculiar to Bordeaux as was the wine trade. Nothing in their economic circumstances, therefore, led them to take a more than local view of affairs, and this fact underlay the provincialism which characterized so many of their public attitudes.

NOTES

1. AN Colonies F^3 224 (Collection Moreau de Saint-Méry), p. 180, ordres du Roy, 31 Dec. 1726 and 27 Aug. 1728.
2. AN Colonies F 5^B 39–42, 'Embarquements à Bordeaux pour les Isles, 1749–90'; AFOM, papiers Hulot de Collart, notes on the Pocquet family; AD 3E 6.220 (François), marriage contract Prunes/Thilorier, 21 Feb. 1746; Hayot, 'Les officiers du conseil souverain de la Martinique', 218.

3. See below, pp. 210–13.
4. G. Debien, *Les Colons de Saint-Domingue et la Révolution: essai sur le Club Massiac* (*Août 1789–Août 1792*) (Paris, 1953), 105–6.
5. *Ministère des Finances—Etat détaillé des liquidations opérées par la commission chargée de repartir l'indemnité attribuée aux anciens colons de Saint-Domingue en exécution de la loi du 30 avril 1826* (Paris, 1828–33), 6 v. No areas or useful values are given, but the information can be supplemented from certain pieces in AFOM, fonds de l'indemnité.
6. Information collated from AFOM, fonds de l'indemnité, 'Dupuy', adjudication of 10 Feb. 1827, and letter of R. A. Dubergier de Favars to minister, 5 Sept. 1830; AD 2E 2325 (tit. fam. Poissac); AD 3E 20.391 (Gatellet), marriage contract Dubergier/ Dupuy, 9 July 1788; AM Fonds Delpit 83.
7. Cte de Basterot, *Souvenirs d'enfance et de jeunesse*, 13.
8. AD 3E 17.593 (Perrens), 23 July 1773; and AD 3E 15.025 (Cheyron), 20 April 1775. See also Butel, 'La croissance', I, 815, II, 1021, 1082.
9. This information was kindly sent to me by M. Emile Hayot, secertary of the *Société d'Histoire de la Martinique*.
10. R. Pares, *War and Trade in the West Indies, 1739–1763* (Oxford, 1936), 326–43, lucidly analyses these conditions. So does Butel, 'La croissance', I, 769–817.
11. AD 2E 2325 (tit. fam. Poissac), undated memoir. Probably he meant white sugar, since brown was subjected to the same disadvantages as coffee. Pares, loc. cit., 330.
12. Debien, op. cit., 40–1, discusses this problem and its consequences.
13. AN Colonies E^{18} (dossiers personnels: Basterot), Basterot to secretary of the navy, 13 Dec. 1783.
14. See above, pp. 57–8.
15. Pares, loc. cit., 326; Debien, op. cit., 50–2; Butel, 'La croissance', I, 801–17. For the parlement's attitude on these questions, see below, pp. 210–13.
16. AD 2E 2325, accounts of consignments, Nov. 1770 and May 1771.
17. AD 8J 480 (Fonds Bigot), correspondance Dumas de Fonbrauge.
18. AD Q1012, inventory after execution of Saige's papers.
19. Butel, 'La croissance', II, 1155, 1160, places great emphasis on the integration of the world of the parlement and that of the great merchants. Economically speaking, he considers that the merchants dominated the partnership by controlling the wine-growing magistrates' outlets, although he concedes that the parlement retained its pre-eminent social prestige.
20. Butel, 'La croissance', II, footnotes, 230, n. 31 to V^e section, ch. 1.
21. Bluche, *Les Magistrats du Parlement*, 212–16.
22. Forster, *Nobility of Toulouse*, 110–16.
23. AD C2473, 'Registre des rentes sur les tailles, 1767–71'. There are others, too, but for them the information is less clear.
24. AD Q1011, inventory after execution of Pelet's papers. For merchant investment in *rentes*, see Butel, 'La croissance', II, 1024–7.
25. Loans at interest were of course illegal in Catholic France; to avoid committing usury, lenders had to perform the legal fiction of buying an annuity outright. For a clear exposition of the legal status of *rentes*, see Forster, *Nobility of Toulouse*, 106–10.
26. e.g., at Toulouse, Forster, op. cit., 117–19, Larboust, 'Les Magistrats du Parlement de Toulouse', 127; and Dijon, Colombet, *Les Parlementaires Bourgignons*, 76.
27. AD 2E 2537 (tit. fam. Saige).
28. AD 3E 5.511 (Duprat) no. 997, Marriage contract, 12 May 1764.
29. AD Q1012, inventory. The figures are minimum, since not all values are specified.
30. This emerges from the claims of his creditors after he went bankrupt. See above, pp. 57–8.
31. *Travels*, 60–1, 26 Aug. 1787.
32. Antoine-Nicolas Valdec de Lessart (1744–92). Master of requests, 1768; close collaborator of Necker in both his ministries; comptroller-general, Dec. 1790; minister of the interior, Jan. 1791; minister of foreign affairs, Nov. 1791; indicted for treason and removed, March 1792; massacred at Versailles, 9 Sept. 1792.

Gascq's will is in AN (minutier central), étude LIII, liasse 374. It was sealed 15 Sept. 1761, and opened 27 March 1781. There is a copy in AM Fonds Alain D'Anglade, dossier 35.

33. Contract of 4 Aug. 1787 (Troupenat).
34. BVC Richelieu XXXVIII, f.7, Gascq to Richelieu, 1 Oct. 1765.
35. Sale of 1 June 1789 (Séjourné).
36. Marion, Bencazar, Caudrillier, *Biens nationaux*, I, 160.
37. Most of the information in this section comes from the *tableaux des acquéreurs et vendeurs* in AD série Q. The precise references are given above, p. 82, n. 25. On mercantile involvement in speculative building, see Butel, 'La croissance', II, 1100–6.
38. AD 3E 15.491 (Morin), division of 9 June 1781.
39. Several magistrates moved there, e.g., J. B. D. Desananots, 1776, P. J. de Laboyrie, 1799, J. L. Peyronnet, 1783; M. F. de Verthamon, 1780, and E. L. Dufaure de Lajarte, 1781.
40. *Travels*, loc. cit.
41. AD C4572, 'Minute du Rolle du Vingtième des Maisons de Bordeaux pour l'année 1777'; AD 4L 109 (one half) and 4L 111 (the other half), 'Role des sommes réparties au marc la livre, des impositions ordinaires & des vingtièmes, pour la présente année 1790, sur tous les propriétaires et contribuables de la municipalité de Bordeaux pour le remplacement des differents droits supprimés par l'Assemblée Nationale'. This is not a *vingtième* roll at all, strictly, but it contains assessments for that tax.
42. Only names which are obviously those of parlementaire families have been included.
43. Forster, *Nobility of Toulouse*, 170.
44. AD C3732, Roche to intendant, 21 Nov. 1779.
45. Lamontaigne, *Chronique*, 138.
46. AD 2E 1405 (tit. fam. Gourgue). The elder brother died in June 1779, however, and the younger inherited the whole house.
47. AD Q925, inventory.
48. Saige: AD Q1012, inventory of his papers, 1793. Gobineau: G. Ducannès-Duval, *Inventaire-sommaire des archives municipales: période révolutionnaire (1789–An VIII)* (Bordeaux, 1929), IV, 541, Gobineau to Lhôte, 15 messidor, An II.
49. AM factum I $\frac{8}{23}$ 'Tableau d'une partie de la succession de feu M. de Brivazac'. The vagueness of certain terms here is owing to the fact that these assessments were disputed. Brivazac's daughter claimed that they ought to be higher.
50. The six were Saige, Gobineau, Dufaure de Lajarte, Peyronnet, Domenge, and Pelet.
51. I have recovered about 30 leases by magistrates.
52. AD Q933, an undated list, which I place after his execution.
53. AD Q1309, 'Biens des émigrés à Bordeaux; Basquiat'.
54. AD C4572.
55. *AHDG*, LV (1923–24), no. LV. 'Chronique Bordelaise redigée de 1735 à 1759 par un personnage anonyme au collège des Jésuites de Bordeaux . . . &c'. This house still exists in the rue du Mirail. It is now a bank. When Gascq succeeded Le Berthon as first president in 1771, he had no such imposing residence. The plans for the new palace therefore included yet another house for the first president.
56. F. G. Pariset in *Bordeaux au XVIIIe siècle*, 639–40. Butel, 'La croissance', II, 1085, 1098.
57. C. Marionneau, *Victor Louis, sa vie, ses travaux, 1731–1800* (Bordeaux, 1881), 440.
58. AD 3E 15.026 (Baron), contract of 18 April 1776. Butel, 'La croissance', II, 1091–2, speculates that this was a sign that Saige lacked the money to complete his great house; but I do not believe that these alienations of usufruct relate to the mansion itself.
59. Now the prefecture of the Gironde. See Pariset, op. cit., 630.
60. AD 2E 2537 (tit. fam. Saige).
61. Still standing, too. Marionneau, op. cit., 441; Pariset, op. cit., 631.
62. ibid., 633–5.
63. AD 2E 168² (tit. fam. Basquiat). This house is now the residence of the rector of the university. See Pariset, op. cit., 641.
64. ibid. This house is now the Museum of the Decorative Arts.
65. AD C4236, and 3E 21.732 (Rauzan), sale of 17 Feb. 1790.
66. P. Meller, *Généalogie de Paty* (Bordeaux, undated, only five printed). This house now contains the municipal archives.
67. Figures from the 'Tableaux des acquéreurs, &c', 7 April 1783.

68. Based on a year-to-year analysis of addresses given in the *Etrennes Bordeloises* . . ., 1775–90.
69. Forster, *Nobility of Toulouse*, 19; Larboust, op. cit., 154.
70. Names include Le Berthon, Pichard, Darche, Gombault, Lancre, and Voisin.
71. The families of Féger, Gautier de Latouche, and Prunes, all of recent mercantile origin, had residences in the Allées de Tourny.
72. A conclusion confirmed by Butel, 'La croissance', II, 1083–1100.
73. For this question in Paris, see Bluche, op. cit., part II, ch. 3; for Dijon, see Colombet, op. cit., ch. 2, section 1; there is also a brief general picture in Ford, *Robe and Sword*, ch. 8, section 3, which is, however, confined to the topic of residences.

CHAPTER 8

Marriage and the Transmission
of Property

The central act in the life of a man of property was his marriage contract. In combination with his father's contract, and will if he left one, it regulated his share in the family succession. It also laid down, in greater or less detail, how he was to transmit his share to his own children. He might supplement it later in life with a will, but from the moment of marriage the unborn children acquired certain minimum rights on his estate which could not be abrogated. Thus the contract of marriage, while it limited the individual in the disposal of his property, guaranteed it to the family as a whole; in this way the social position of the family and its members was secured against the personal aberrations of its head. Of course any law of inheritance which gave all children guaranteed rights in their parents' succession must ultimately lead to the decimation of the family property. What prevented this was dowries: in each generation new property entered the family through marriages, and the effect was to prevent or at least retard the steady diminution of the eldest son's portion from generation to generation. The choice of a wife was therefore mainly important for the family fortune.

We have already examined the social groups among which the magistrates sought their wives. Marriage being primarily a business arrangement, wives were sought and marriages were arranged by shrewd and often hard bargaining. Nor did negotiations once begun always lead to the conclusion of a contract. 'J'avois été très affligé, Monsieur', wrote Richelieu to counsellor J. B. Dalphonse, 'lorsque j'avois vu échouer la négociation du mariage de Mademoiselle votre fille avec son cousin, toute les apparences et convenances paroissant convenir au succès de cest evenement'.[1] He advised the counsellor to accept another suitor who not only had character, birth, and possessions but also was prepared to accept a bride without a dowry. The duke hoped that Dalphonse was sufficiently master in his own house to ignore any objections that his wife might raise.

Magdeleine de Godet Dubrois, whose father was a rich planter in Guadeloupe, was sent to Bordeaux by her father in 1770 to find a husband. Her sister, by then dead, had married counsellor Dumas de Fonbrauge, who advised her throughout the negotiations while she took up residence in a convent. Her father's instructions were to marry neither a merchant nor a fiscal officer, but preferably a member of the parlement. On these grounds, Dumas advised her to reject one suitor who refused to buy an office in the parlement. In any event, she should never see any suitor too often, in case negotiations fell through:

> jusques là tu t'exposes à la position facheuse de rompre avec quelqu'un que tu auras peut être gouté; ou a te priver des avantages que l'on auroit pu te ménager; Independamment de ce que le public en pensera . . . observes tes demarches dans une affaire qui, une fois consommée, sera sans retour. méfies toi de l'Impatience que te donne le sejour du couvent, Il arrive trop souvent que ce motif prepare des repentirs . . .[2]

She was courted by two magistrates from the parlement and three relatives of parlementaires in the space of a month, before deciding to give her hand to counsellor de Lamolère, who offered the best terms.

She was luckier than most brides in that she at least had some freedom to choose. Most were married off with very little reference to their own wishes. When in 1776 the eldest daughter of counsellor de Marbotin was married to the younger Dudon she boldly declared, though only 15, that she did not wish to marry him if it meant living with the procurator-general, and this expression of opinion caused a sensation.[3] Nor was the marriage a success; in 1787 the couple separated on the grounds that they could not stand each other.[4] Mistaken marriages were as much a hazard of arranged matches as affairs of passion. In 1773 the irascible counsellor Leblanc de Mauvezin worked off the frustrations of exile to his estates by beating his wife, a mild creature who, not being exiled herself, took refuge in Bordeaux.[5] When in 1788 counsellor Dumas de Laroque had his second wife wife locked up as mad, observers concluded that her infidelity was a more likely reason.[6] It was also suggested that the beautiful wife of counsellor Thilorier (who later married the famous Duval d'Eprémesnil) bought him his office in the parlement by selling her favours.[7]

Not that the magistrates themselves were without their sexual adventures. Counsellor de Loménie in 1782 was involved in a scandal with a prostitute so remarkable that the story even reached Paris.[8] President de Gascq, though he never married, was like his friend Richelieu notorious for loose living, and was reputed to be the father of the master of requests A. N. Valdec de Lessart. His bequests to Valdec, and the close interest he took in his career, make the rumours seem probable.[9] Counsellor de Basterot had an illegitimate daughter after the death of his first wife, in the late 1770s.[10] In 1784 P. de Richon, honorary counsellor and 61 years old, married 'une dem.ˡˡᵉ. Seignoret, du Chartron, de basse extraction, sans agrément et sans fortune'.[11] What counsellor de Lamontaigne, who primly reported this incident, perhaps did not know, was that she had already borne Richon two illegitimate children. Yet another was born after the marriage took place.[12]

Such marriages were of course quite exceptional. Even so, by modern standards magistrates were often quite old when they married. Only one was under 20. Thirty-five were in their twenties, 47 were in their thirties, and ten were over 40. Wives tended to be younger, although few were as young as the bride of counsellor P. L. de Raymond, who was only 12½, and who bore a child at 14.[13] Most first wives who lived locally seem to have been under 20 at the time of marriage. Raymond was 12 or 13 years older than his wife. Counsellor L. J. Demons, whose second marriage was to a Verthamon daughter, was 21 years older than his.[14]

Such a gap, however, was more to be expected in a second marriage than in a first, and at least 16 of the magistrates had first wives who died young, and married again.

The frequency of second marriages bore witness to the fact that magistrates never lost sight of the main purpose of marriage—to beget heirs. The uncertainty of life also dictated that families should not be too small. The size of families is an elusive subject, and evidence is fragmentary.[15] Nevertheless, it has been possible to put together fairly reliable figures for 94 marriages. At least 13 more were childless. Because of the Revolution, many magistrates never had the opportunity to live out a normal life span. We cannot tell how many of those young married members of the parlement who were executed, or fled during the Revolution, might have had children in other circumstances, or might merely have had more. It seems reasonable to assume, however, that most older magistrates, those who were dead or over 50 in 1790, had had such children as they were going to have by then. There were 65 of these, of whom seven were childless. The distribution of children was as follows:

Children of 65 parlementaire families

Number of children	*Number of families*
10	0
9	2
8	5
7	3
6	2
5	8
4	12
3	11
2	5
1	10
0	7
	——
	65

The average magistrate who married, then, had four children. Among the nobility of Toulouse, whose 'average family' in the decades 1760–90 has been estimated at 3·33 children, the size decreased over the century;[16] it would not be surprising if this happened at Bordeaux too. Not all survived. Still births, sickly children, or deaths from disease at tender ages were not uncommon, and were looked upon with a lightness which seems at first surprising. 'Nous avons appris', counsellor Duroy wrote to his friend Lamontaigne, 'que M et Mde de Basterot venoient de perdre le seul garcon qu'ils eussent: c'est un mal qui n'est pas, pour eux, sans remède . . .'[17] Much worse was for the wife to die in childbirth, like the first wives of both Pichard and Basterot. Nevertheless, when all hazards and exceptional circumstances had been taken into account, a normal parlementaire family could expect to have three or four children to provide for and, ultimately, to perpetuate itself. Depending on what sex they were, whether they married or not, whom they married, and whether they were the children of first or second marriages, the succession settlement would be more or less complicated.

The fundamental act regulating successions was not the will. All men of property who married had contracts, but many did not make wills. Partly this reflected reluctance to face the unpleasant prospect of death before it seemed necessary. Most wills seem to have been made on the deathbed, and magistrates who died suddenly did not even have this opportunity. Also, for the present purpose the number of possible wills restricts itself to the number of deaths occurring between 1775 and 1790, which is not the case with marriage contracts. So, against 81 marriage contracts we have only 14 wills, although 36 magistrates died during this period. However, the fundamental reason for the paucity of wills remains the relative unimportance of the will in successions.

Successions were regulated by the custom of Bordeaux, certain royal ordinances and, in the rare instances where the custom and the ordinances were both silent, by Roman law. Nearly all magistrates married under the custom, on which their own court was the supreme authority. Only three of their contracts admitted the custom of Paris, the most widespread in the kingdom, and two of these were actually signed in Paris. The custom of Bordeaux classed marriage as a *société d'acquêts*—that is, an arrangement whereby all goods acquired during the marriage were held equally and in common, and entailed upon the children to be born of the marriage, if any.[18] All contracts except one stipulated such a *société*, and the exception specifically renounced it.[19] Marriage as a legal contract was still subject to a *régime dotal*, by which extensive rights were assured to the partners over their personal goods acquired outside the marriage. Most important, the dowry of the wife was adjudged inalienable; treated, whatever its form, as real estate; and guaranteed by the husband on all his goods. If the husband predeceased the wife, she had the usufruct of all his goods until she had assured herself the complete repayment of her dowry; this was known as the *droit de rétention*.[20] The custom of Bordeaux went to extreme lengths to protect the wife in the event of the husband's premature death. She was assured her *bagues et joyaux*—her jewels, everyday clothes, and mourning attire. Some *agencement* or *gain de noces* was nearly always stipulated; this was a lump sum accruing to the surviving partner on the death of the other, entailed upon the children. Finally, contracts sometimes (though by no means always) stipulated a *douaire*, usually an annual payment for life to a widow out of her husband's estate. All these things represented *cas dotaux*, so all were subject to the *droit de rétention*. Add to this the right of the wife, if widowed, to the usufruct of the totality of the *acquêts* of the marriage, and we see that a widow had a complete stranglehold on the goods of the family into which she had married, and it was usually impossible for her children to touch more than a proportion of them until after her death. The most spectacular example of this was Saige and his 90-year-old mother.[21]

At the drawing-up of the contract, both parties were endowed by their parents, or their representatives. If they were over 25, they sometimes endowed themselves, especially if their parents were dead. The *apports* (goods brought to the marriage) of women were all considered dotal, unless, as sometimes happened, a certain proportion of them were set specifically aside as paraphernal.[22] Generally the value of their dowries was specifically stated in cash, if only to take the fullest advantage of the legal protection they were entitled to.

Dowries of 81 parlementaire wives[23]

Unascertainable	20
Under 20,000 l.	0
Under 30,000 l.	1
Under 40,000 l.	3
40,000–60,000 l.	8
60,000–80,000 l.	14
80,000–100,000 l.	11
100,000–125,000 l.	13
125,000–150,000 l.	1
150,000–175,000 l.	4
175,000–200,000 l.	1
200,000–400,000 l.	5
	81

The majority fell between 40,000 l. and 125,000 l. Such figures, alongside those for the wealth of magistrates (recalling that most fortunes seem to have ranged between 100,000 l. and 400,000 l.),[24] show what a heavy burden the dotal claims of a widow might impose on a family estate. Nor was her dowry all that she could claim. As a widow she was entitled to her *agencement*, and only five contracts out of 81 were without provision for one. In 39 cases it amounted to 6,000 l., and in 19 cases to more, although never more than 12,000 l. in contracts signed in Bordeaux. As a general rule, the bigger the dowry, the bigger the *agencement*. Moreover, husbands usually added at the time of marriage a lump sum, equivalent in value to the *agencement*, to their wife's *bagues et joyaux*, though these ornaments themselves were seldom assessed. Finally, in 48 out of 81 cases, there was a *douaire* to pay the widow annually, though it was only over 2,000 l. p.a. in ten cases.

Occasionally women, especially if they were without brothers, were merely named their parents' heirs, and no cash value was set upon their expectations. This happened in the majority of cases with men. Most magistrates were eldest sons, and the most popular way among parents of endowing them was either to give them the expectation of a fixed proportion of their goods, or to make them their general heirs, that is to say, heirs to all that was not specifically or automatically left to others, known as the particular heirs. This happened in 50 per cent of the cases, and it is impossible to set a value on the man's *apports* in them. In 24 there is not so much as a mention of *apports* on the man's side, though we cannot doubt that there were some. Often there was simply no means, except by an arbitrary estimate, of assessing the value of a man's expectations until they actually came into his hands, after the deduction of his brothers' and sisters' portions, on the death of his parents. Nearly all male endowments were for the future, even those on which a sum was set. They represented a sort of entail, as is shown by the fact that in certain cases parents reserved to themselves free disposal of goods up to a specified amount, as well as the life usufruct of the whole donation. However, there were only four cases of the long entail (*substitution*) by which specific properties were assigned in advance over several generations to specific future persons. Male portions clearly defined in cash terms were usually the large ones. The largest was that of counsellor F. J. Chaperon de Terrefort, at 450,000 l.[25] Close behind came those of the Pelet brothers,[26] and Saige, all at 400,000 l.[27] Most of the others were between 100,000 l. and 200,000 l.

In addition to the constitutions received by both sides, young couples normally went to lodge with the parents of one or the other for the first years of married life, and the parents usually assured them a small pension of a few thousand livres for their expenses. All this was usually spelt out in the contract and provisions were always made for raising the value of the pension if or when the couple chose to leave or set up house on their own. Such arrangements were inevitable when constitutions were hardly ever paid over at once in their entirety. Usually a small portion was paid in cash, and often not to the new husband but to his father. Periods were agreed in the contract for the payment of the rest, and only rarely was full payment envisaged before the death of the parents. This was the origin of the most important sort of debt under which magistrates laboured.[28]

Marriage constitutions represented the apportionment of a total heredity, and most parlementaire property was in real estate, not cash or movables. Only with a guarantee of maintenance for life, and only usually at the charge of paying all debts, did parents sign all their property away to their children within their lifetime;[29] only, in fact, when circumstances were exceptional. In the case of daughters, the normal practice was to give some of the dowry in cash on account, at once or over a long specified period, and promise the real estate at death. Interest on the value of the expectation would be paid annually to the husband. Sometimes lodging and a pension were deemed interest. Only in the richer marriages were daughters given the usufruct of the real-estate portion of their dowry, when it did not represent the total of the parents' real estate. In the case of sons, the resignation of the usufruct of some real estate, along with the office they occupied in the parlement (usually bought by the father in the first instance), was more common; husbands in public office needed some estate to sustain themselves and their position, for owing to the fairly late age of marriage and the early age of entry into the parlement, most were already in office when they married. Even here parents retained life usufruct of most of their sons' portions. The result was that marriage portions, on both sides, were seldom paid off in the lifetime of the parents, and couples were normally well advanced in years before they enjoyed the full rights assured them by their contract of marriage.

Each parent endowed a child separately. Contracts setting a value on portions normally stipulated how much came from the father and how much from the mother. In most though not all cases, the father's contribution was larger. Similarly, when only mere proportions of goods were stipulated, those of the father and the mother were stated separately, and were often not the same. Marriage contracts often proved the occasion for childless relatives, maiden aunts, or those in religion, to dispose of their own property in favour of young nephews, nieces, or cousins. For example, P. L. de Raymond, a native of Saint-Domingue, owed all his property in the Bordelais to the dispositions of an aunt at the time of his marriage.[30] J. de Raymond de Lalande received 150,000 l. from his uncle alone, not to mention his parents' heredity.[31]

Such dispositions could be the source of great confusion when the moment of succession came; things became even more complicated, and strict accounting even more necessary, when there were second marriages. The law of succession in the Bordelais was the Roman law of inexorable division.[32] If there were four or less children, one-third of the parental goods had to be divided equally between them. If there were five or more children, the divisible proportion rose to a half. The portion owing from such a division was known as the *légitime*. Only after such provisions had been safeguarded were parents free to dispose at will the rest of their goods; but then the children had no automatic advantage in theory. In practice, marriage contracts entailed most property upon the children, and usually the eldest child, by creating him or her the general heir. There was no alternative if property, the basis of a family's social position, was to be maintained.

The rarity of wills raises the question of why they were made at all if the marriage contracts of children disposed so effectively of family property. There were circumstances which marriage contracts could not cover, however. Wills usually gave directions for the funeral, for Masses, pious works, and alms in memory. They usually stipulated also small bequests in lump sums or annuities to household servants. None of these things were in place in marriage contracts. When men did not marry or had no children for some other reason, a will also assumed a new importance in the transmission of property. Perhaps most important was the fact that sometimes there were unmarried children to deal with. If no will was made, the law took care of them automatically by assigning them *légitimes*. But frequently parents wished to augment *légitimes*. The most detailed wills were those made when children were below marriageable age, for they laid down different arrangements according to whether they subsequently married or not. Finally, a will was sometimes used to impose on certain properties a longer and more specific entail (*substitution*) than was provided for by the marriage contract. They were, in short, a vehicle for refining the broad principles of the law to suit specific cases, but they could not alter those broad principles. The most a testator could threaten, in the event of his or her will being contested, was the automatic reduction of the dissatisfied legatee to his or her 'légitime tell que de droit'.

After the signing of the marriage contract, therefore, the most crucial moment in the transferring of a family's property from one generation to the next was the death of the last surviving parent. Then, a generation's accounts were settled, and some sort of inventory was usually made. A useful example of this complex process is that of the Maignol family.[33] Jean-Baptiste Maignol (1694–1774), procurator-general of the court of aids, married Roze David. She died in 1754, but not before she had borne him four children—Etienne, Alexis-Etienne, René, and André. The first two became counsellors at the parlement, and the second of them died in 1772.[34] The father did not die until 1774, and when he did, an inventory of his goods was drawn up. It took two years to complete, and was divided into several different categories to facilitate the final division of property. First, the total estate at the time of the father's death had to be assessed; then the total of the *acquêts* of his marriage at the time of his wife's death, to be set against the debts of their *société d'acquêts*. By the eldest son's marriage contract of 8 September 1753,[35] one-third of the goods of both parents were entailed upon him, and these too had to be separately inventoried, in their 1753 state, burdens and all, so that this third could be apportioned. He emerged entitled to 52,121 l. 10s 3d on the maternal side, and 54,593 l. 7s 9d on the paternal. But this was not all: next, the extant goods of the father at the marriage of his second son, on 14 August 1757, had to be estimated. By this contract he had been left a quarter which came to 40,945 l. os 10d. In addition his mother left him one-third of the two-thirds of her goods not left to his elder brother. However, he predeceased his father, so these portions went straight to be divided on similar principles between his two surviving children. The two younger brothers simply received their *légitimes* in paternal goods, and one-third each of the undisposed two-thirds of their mother's goods. And so the estate was split up. The father left 401,585 l. 8s 7d in all; the eldest son, the embodiment of the family's tradition, was left after the division with 155,176 l. 18s, and the others with far less; such was the effect of a law of division. Yet the Maignol family was not necessarily fated to decline as its fortune was diminished, for the new head of the family had married Françoise Foucques who, as the daughter of a rich merchant, must have brought him a substantial dowry.[36] In this way, with properties in a constant flux, families maintained their position in the teeth of the law. Only childlessness was a total disaster—and it was this in fact which extinguished this senior branch of the Maignol family.

Of course childless marriages posed different problems. They could mean the extinction of a family name, or the passing of seniority to a collateral branch. In such cases, there was still a *légitime* of the obligatory third, which went to the nearest relatives,[37] but two-thirds of goods were disposable at will. J. M. de Montalier de Grissac owed his whole fortune, including his office in the parlement, to his distant cousin, counsellor P. de Montalier de Grissac, whose marriage had only borne one daughter who died young.[38] The reign of Louis XVI saw the extinction of the Ragueneaus. Counsellor P. de Ragueneau, who died in 1778, married but childless, had himself been heir to two-thirds of the goods of his brother, counsellor Jean-Joseph de Ragueneau, who died in 1771, also married but childless.[39] The family goods were divided, according to Pierre's will, among his wife's family, of which the knight of honour P. F. de Brach was head, and the families of his cousins, Desnanots, Dudon, and Guyonnet, all parlementaire families.[40] Hardly more fortunate were marriages which only bore daughters. Unless they were able to marry relatives, extinction of the family name was automatic. So, late in the 18th century, the Verthamon family absorbed the Caupos, the Lalande the Dalesme, the Le Berthon the Pontac, all through marriages. J. F. A. M. de La Colonie, the last dean of the parlement, had four daughters. The eldest, whom he constituted in his will his general heir, died a spinster. The other three he married off between 1773 and 1780, each with a portion of 50,000 l. So he divided up his patrimony, and his name and separate family disappeared with his death.

If division of property was the fundamental feature of the law of succession, division of actual units of property was not inevitable, and was regarded as one of the worst of evils. Rather than divide units, parents would distribute them unequally among theoretically equal heirs and impose a cash payment on the most favoured to his brothers and sisters, to compensate them for the disparity. If testators did not so provide, heirs often agreed on such a course when they divided goods after death. Occasionally, as in the marriage contracts of the two Pelet brothers, such an outcome was guaranteed by a *substitution*. But whatever happened, general heirs, who were in most cases eldest sons, were usually burdened in successions with heavy debts, for the general heir was usually the executor of an estate. The burden was on him to pay off both the ordinary debts incurred by his parents, and the family ones—what was still outstanding of his sisters' dowries and his brothers' *légitimes*. If his brothers and sisters were not satisfied with the way he did this, then they might sue him. To be sued for family debts was altogether more serious than to be sued for other sorts. The debts at law (especially the dotal ones) were more sacrosanct, and in amount were usually bigger than the others. Parlementaire families were very litigious, and their biggest cases were always over dowries and *légitimes*. Throughout the 1780s the granddaughter of counsellor L. G. de Brivazac was suing her uncle, counsellor J. B. G. de Brivazac, over his assessment of the estate of the deceased magistrate, and consequently the amount of her portion.[41] The same family was still engaged, in 1791, in a case with the family of Laville which had begun over a legacy in 1731.[42] In 1788 the Baritault family paid 100,000 l. to the Domenges to settle out of court a case over a 17th-century dowry payment which had been going on since 1710.[43] Such cases were complicated even further when there had been two marriages. After the father of the Pelet brothers eloped with and married his housekeeper in 1760, his sons sued him and obtained a division of all his goods as they were at the death of his first wife their mother.[44] Similarly in 1775–77 president de Lavie's two half-sisters, daughters of his father's first marriage, sued him over alleged sharp-practice with respect to their father's will.[45] Part of counsellor de Basterot's trouble, which led him down the road to bankruptcy, was his difficulty in obtaining payment of the large dowries of his two wives.[46]

None of this litigious passion should surprise us. To extract every penny legally due was a matter of the first importance to everyone. For younger brothers, *légitimes* alone stood between them and poverty. For heads of families, faced with the inevitable division of their wealth, the assurance of dowries, past, present, or future, was important to repair the loss and thus keep up the family's position. Above all, the general heir, the embodiment of the family's tradition, must be well endowed. Normally the eldest son, he would get the main fiefs and estates, and of course the family office. One function of wills was to make provisions for this. Pierre Lajaunye, dean of the court of aids, revoked all his children's legacies except *légitimes*, if the cost of succession seemed likely to impoverish his son Antoine, counsellor at the parlement:

> attendu qu'en ce dernier Cas il me seroit impossible de Leur donner au dela de Leurs Legitimes, Sans Réduire La fortune qu'il Est Nécessaire que Je Laisse à mon héritier . . . pour le mettre a meme de Soutenir avec décence La dignité de sa charge qui Est faite pour honorer La famille . . .[47]

For counsellor Montalier de Grissac, one object of leaving his fortune to his young relative was to equip him to enter the parlement.[48] President J. E. de Bienassis begged his wife to procure for his son 'mon état ou un état équivalent au mien'.[49] Counsellor L. G. de Brivazac entailed his fief of Lassalle upon his heirs who should take the robe,[50] and counsellor J. F. X. de Filhot, who wished his younger as well as his elder son to enter the parlement, actually stipulated a larger legacy if he did so.[51] For among the members of the parlement wealth and office were complementary. The first led to the second, the second dignified the first. And in a society where the physical manifestation of a family's wealth was, out of the nature of the law, constantly changing, representation in the parlement provided a visible focus of stability.

NOTES

1. *AHDG*, XVII (1888–89), no. LVI, 213, Richelieu to Dalphonse, 11 Jan. 1771. Other letters relating to this girl's marriage are in BVC Richelieu III, ff.237–40.
2. AD 8J 480 (Fonds Bigot), correspondance Dumas de Fonbrauge. Dumas to Mlle Godet, 23 July 1770.
3. BVBx MS 1201, V, 25 April 1776.
4. BVBx MS 713 (sér. I), V, 128, 29 Dec. 1787.
5. BVC Richelieu XVII, f.199, Gascq to Richelieu, 10 Aug. 1773.
6. BVBx MS 713 (sér. I), V, 166, 8 Feb. 1788.
7. Chamfort, *Maximes, pensées et anecdotes* (Paris, 1963), 162–3.
8. Bachaumont, XX, 153, 3 April 1782. They were discovered one night by the city guard, making love in the open air.
9. Gascq's letters to Richelieu in BVC are full of concern for the welfare of 'le petit Lessart'.
10. Basterot, *Souvenirs d'enfance*, 18.
11. Lamontaigne, *Chronique*, 147 (1784).
12. AD 4L 116, Contribution patriotique: demande en décharge, 1796.
13. Lamontaigne, *Chronique*, 137 (1783).
14. ibid., 126 (1770).
15. Long and painful labours in the *état civil* would doubtless produce more accurate information, but the time involved, for the significance of the result, makes this an almost impossible proposition for foreign scholars.
16. Forster, *Nobility of Toulouse*, 129–30.
17. BVBx MS 1696, II, no. 48, Duroy to Lamontaigne, 30 Jan. 1755.
18. E. Audubert, *Le Régime dotal d'après la coûtume et la jurisprudence du parlement de Bordeaux* (Paris, 1918), ch. 1.
19. AD 2E 2325 (tit. fam. Poissac), contract Poissac/Dupuy, 6 Sept. 1769.
20. Audubert, op. cit., 56; also article 52 of the custom of Bordeaux in Lamothe, *Coûtumes du ressort du Parlement de Guienne*, I, 309–13.
21. See above, p. 106.
22. e.g., the Poissac/Dupuy contract, where the wife reserved all such goods. Partial reservations were also made in the contracts Dumas de Laroque/Caila, AD 3E 24.996 (Brun), 1 Sept. 1779; Lalande/Dalesme, AD 3E 21.716 (Rauzan), 13 March 1782; Bienassis/Hacquet, AD 3E 21.579 (Barbarie), 18 Nov. 1769; and Darche/Deluxe, AD 3E 12.152 (Treyssac), 11 Sept. 1747.
23. It would be interesting and useful to compare these figures with those for Bordelais society as a whole. Unfortunately, the only attempt at an overall survey that has been made, E. Dravasa, 'Les classes sociales au XVIIIᵉ siècle à Bordeaux d'après les contrats de mariage', *Revue juridique et économique du Sud-Ouest—Série économique* (1963) no. IV, 961–1012, has been completely demolished in all its aspects by R. B. Wheaton, 'Notes critiques sur "Les classes sociales au XVIIIᵉ siècle à Bordeaux d'après les contrats de mariage" ', *Revue Historique* (1969), 99–114. The work of J. P. Poussou, tantalizingly foreshadowed in book II, ch. 5 of *Bordeaux au XVIIIᵉ siècle*, promises ultimately to replace Dravasa's conclusions. Meanwhile there are useful comparisons in Butel, 'La croissance', II, 983–6, and appendices, 143–4, which show that the dowries of nobles and great merchants were comparable both in scale and distribution over the group.
24. See above, p. 56.
25. AD 3E 17.577 (Perrens), 10 May 1764 (first marriage).
26. AD 3E 24.864 (Despiet), 7 June 1741 (J. J. Pelet); AD 3E 24.385 (Faugas), 14 March 1754 (J. Pelet d'Anglade).
27. AD 3E 5.551 (Duprat), no. 997, 2 May 1764, deposited 19 Dec. 1764.
28. See above, pp. 57–9.
29. e.g., in the case of the father of counsellor B. de Basterot. Contract in AD 3E 21.715 (Rauzan), 30 Oct. 1781 (second marriage).
30. Etude de Mᵉ Jondrau, Bordeaux (Chalu), 7 Feb. 1783.
31. AD 3E 21.716 (Rauzan), 13 April 1782.
32. Lamothe, *Coûtumes*, I, 354; Denisart, *Collection de décisions nouvelles*, III, 96–7.

33. AD 2E 1933 (tit. fam. Maignol), contains the inventory after death.
34. Details from O'Gilvy, *Nobiliaire de Guienne*, I, 45–7.
35. AD 3E 12.189 (Treyssac), 1753, no. 1142.
36. No details are given, however, in their marriage contract.
37. Lamothe, op. cit., I, 347.
38. Lamontaigne, *Chronique*, 127–8, Nov. 1770; will in AD 3E 5.562 (Duprat), sealed 3 Jan. 1772, opened 6 March 1778.
39. Will of Jean-Joseph in AD 3E 24.268 (Lavau), sealed 27 May 1762, opened 12 Dec. 1771; Pierre's is in AD 3E 21.290 (Petit, notary at Vayres), sealed 3 Jan. 1772, opened 6 March 1778.
40. AD 3E 5.591 (Duprat), no. 593. Partage de famille, 1778.
41. Factum in AM, cited above, p. 114, n. 49.
42. AD 2E 450 (tit. fam. Brivazac).
43. AD 2E 147 (tit. fam. Baritault).
44. Cavignac, *Jean Pellet*, 291–6.
45. AM factums B $\frac{6}{15}$ ff.292–345. Also BVBx MS 1201, IV, 2 April 1775.
46. See above, pp. 58 and 104.
47. AD 3E 24.455 (Troupenat), sealed 22 Feb. 1788, opened 21 Jan. 1789.
48. Will, cited above, n. 38.
49. AD 3E 26.622 (Banchereau), sealed 2 July 1789; opened by the author 7 Sept. 1965.
50. AD 3E 13.066 (Cheyron), codicil of 31 Dec. 1777.
51. See above, p. 14.

CHAPTER 9

The Quality of Life

The life of a magistrate, as the scale of their residences suggests, was usually felt to impose a minimum standard of outward display; and this was often matched by the taste and scale of internal surroundings which were not public. They lived spaciously. The corollary of space was servants. The capitation roll of 1767 enumerates 368 taxable servants maintained by members of the parlement, an average of between three and four each.[1] According to the same roll, the full complement of the court of aids only employed 81 servants altogether. The biggest household was that of the first president, who paid 54 l. a year for eight servants. By 1775 his assessment had gone up to 69 l.,[2] so we may assume that his domestic staff increased. In 1767 the procurator-general also employed eight servants, and his household too had grown by 1775. On the eve of his execution in 1793 the ex-advocate-general Saige was employing 12 domestics.[3] In this respect as in many others those with colonial links introduced an exotic note; four magistrates owned negro slaves in France.[4] Finally, not included on the rolls were secretaries, employed by most of the presidents and the crown lawyers. The most famous of these secretaries, viewed in retrospect, was Vergniaud, employed in the early 1780s by Dupaty. In the 1780s the secretaries of the first president and the procurator-general were locally notorious for their influence and corruption, a fact not neglected by anti-parlementaire pamphleteers in 1789.[5]

The magistrates' large, well-staffed houses were equally impressively furnished, as revolutionary and other inventories reveal. Expensive woods like walnut, cherry and mahogany were normal. Upholstery of chairs, ottomans, and *bergères* was invariably in silk or satin, often embroidered. Beds too were sumptuously decked. Dining rooms had large tables, for anything between 8 and 20 diners, and large ceramic stoves to serve as hotplates. Tapestries and mirrors were more common than pictures on the walls, but sets of small framed prints were not uncommon. Some had whole sets of family portraits. Le Berthon, Dudon, J. C. Daugeard, and Laroze all had their portraits painted under Louis XVI, three of them by the Fleming Lonsing, who spent several years in Bordeaux.[6] Saige was reputed to have several Vernets,[7] and he and several of his colleagues had copies of famous works of painting and sculpture; counsellor Dussault had what passed for a Raphael.[8] Figurines in *biscuit de Sèvres*, and elaborate and expensive clocks, agreeably completed the decoration of a room, but luxury did not end there.

Magistrates often, like the merchants described by Arthur Young, were in a position to dine off plate. The Brivazac silverware was estimated in the 1780s to be worth between 21,000 l. and 25,000 l.[9] That of the Castelnau family in 1774 was worth 6,900 l.,[10] that of the Gourgues in 1753 was estimated at nearly 17,000 l.[11] The Saige plate was famous throughout the town.[12] Such sums often surpassed the entire value of the rest of the furnishings. The Brivazac movables were estimated in the same inventory as their silver to be worth 26,021 l. The movables of the several Maignol properties in 1774 amounted to 28,083 l. 16s 6d.[13] Those of the three Ragueneau houses in 1778 came to 28,600 l.[14]

Admittedly in matters of dress traditions of magistral sobriety were far from dead. Black clothes predominated among those inventoried. But what they lacked in colour they made up in texture, and black suits in silk, satin, and velvet abounded. They all had some more colourful clothes, too. In Pichard's cabinet was found a pink suit embroidered in cloth of gold and silver and trimmed with pearls.[15] Travelling outside, the poorer among them normally had their own private sedan chairs; the richer had coaches. All the presidents had coaches. Saige had a berlin, a cabriolet, and a post chaise.[16] Counsellor Paty du Rayet had four carriages,[17] counsellor Loyac had two,[18] Pichard had two,[19] counsellor Dussault had a coach and a sedan chair,[20] and so on. Such carriages, and the scale on which they were decorated, were accounted symbols of great prestige and social superiority. President J. C. de Lavie, father of president P. M. A. de Lavie, was alleged to go everywhere on foot so as not to humiliate those without coaches.[21] On the other hand, they were a practical as well as a social necessity for gentlemen who divided their time so much between town and country.

Magistrates were city men who lived off the country. This was the most basic fact in their pattern of life. They divided their time between the town, where they worked and mingled in society, and the country, the storehouse of their fortune. The calendar of the judicial year strictly did not leave them much time to be in the country, but in practice the Martinmas commencement was usually ignored except for form's sake, and the vacation begun early in September normally lasted until Epiphany. A good third of the year at least was therefore spent out of town. If money was short owing to unfavourable circumstances in the wine trade, the period might be even longer. 'Jay été excessivement surpris', wrote Tourny in 1744, pleading against increased taxation for magistrates,

> de l'air mal aisé que j'ay vu cet hiver dans Bordeaux à tout ce qui n'est point commerçant, et cela en un temps où le gout du plaisir a coutume de déguiser le mauvais état de la fortune.
>
> L'Opéra quoique nouvellement établi et assez bon, a presque toujours été desert; point de jeux, point de bals, point d'assemblées, point de soupers . . .[22]

Most people, he said, stayed in the country until well into January.

Many magistrates built or rebuilt handsome country seats in the late 18th century. President J. A. H. Daugeard de Virazel from 1779 employed Victor Louis to build him a new house at Virazel in the Agenais, at the cost of 198,000 l.[23] A fine arts exhibition of 1787 included plans of the progress of works being done on the country estates of counsellors de Navarre, at Ambès, and de Lamolère, at Floirac.[24] The families of Piis, Lavie, Saige, Laboyrie, Conilh, Maurice de Sentout, Loyac, Ruat, all built new mansions or repaired old ones in the course of the 18th century,[25] in striking contrast with the nobility of Toulouse.[26] Few of them lived in gothic castles like that of Montesquieu at La Brède. Only that of counsellor Sauvat de Pommiers at Agassac came into this class. Most country houses dated back in substance to the 17th century.

Country houses were not so elaborately furnished as those in the town, even those favourite retreats to which magistrates returned again and again. There was less expensive wood, less silk and satin, fewer mirrors, more badly worn articles. Nevertheless, the difference was merely one of scale and not of style. The same sort of furnishings were to be found in country and town alike. The chief distinctive feature of country houses is that they often had their own chapels. If country movables were always estimated more highly than those of the town, it was because they included all the implements of agriculture; especially important in the Bordelais because of the size and value of the vessels, presses, and barrels used in wine-making.

The main rural activity, especially during the vintage of September and October, was estate supervision. However, everybody was in the country at the same time and each neighbourhood boasted, in vacation time, a small society and social round which recalled the town in miniature. There were *fêtes champêtres*, and masked balls which went on all night. In February 1755 the high society of the upper Bordelais converged on Bazas:

> Le bal commenca a 10 heures du soir et ne finit qu'a 5 du matin pendant tout ce tems, la sale fut pleine de masques de tout sexe, et tres proprement vetus. a 5 heures du matin le bal fut converti en un concert, dont les vois, les instrumens, et la musique ne laissoient rien a desirer dans ce genre . . .

The next day:

> les hommes allerent a la chasse, et les Dames se retirent chés elles pour s'occuper a relever par le secours de l'art les graces qu'elles tiennent de la nature, et se preparer a un ba [sic] qu'il y a eu cette nuit . . .[27]

Hunting was another popular country pastime, and the *landes* were particularly well suited for such pursuits. Parlementaire participation is well attested by the hunting coats and horns found among their belongings at the Revolution.

Such was the pattern of life of the majority of the magistrates, year in, year out. It was a comfortable scale of life, easily sustained by their resources. However, neither their resources nor their profession normally allowed them more luxurious pastimes such as travel. Only an occasional journey to the waters of Bagnères, or some other Pyrenean spa, varied their routine. These waters attracted visitors from all over France in the hot summer months. Apart from the medicinal value of such visits, they doubtless provided opportunities for meeting members of other parlements, from Pau, Toulouse, or further afield, and discussing mutual problems. When the old parlement of Pau was restored in November 1775, Bordeaux magistrates who were at the waters received a special invitation to go and watch the proceedings.[28] Clearly they had not returned to Bordeaux for their own commencement! Indeed, the attractions of the cool mountain spas took many magistrates off in August, before the judicial year ended. But only the richest members of the parlement frequently went as far afield as Paris. They formed a sort of élite, a group to which, in his day, Montesquieu had belonged. Most presidents came into this category. Gascq and Pichard went very regularly, the first president scarcely less often. Dupaty spent the last four years of his life there, and Gascq spent his last exiled years there with his friend Richelieu. Dupaty found his wife in Paris, Pichard found both his, and Gascq had at least one of his mistresses there. Dupaty alone aspired in Paris to the social and intellectual distinction that Montesquieu had enjoyed. Castelnau, who mooned about Versailles for years adoring the queen from afar, was clearly an eccentric.[29] Most of those who went to Paris did so on political business. Ambitious men liked to keep themselves in the government's eye. The government itself was hardly appreciative of such considerations; the professional place and the political value of the parlementaires was in their province, not at Versailles or in Paris. Many a time on arrival, magistrates were told brusquely to return. An entry in the letter book of Bertin, then minister of the province, reads for 1772:

> M de Pichard mande qe sa femme est guerie de son inoculation; qu'il ira faire sa cour au ministre à fontainebleau et prendre ses ordres.

To which Bertin drily

> a Repondu quil etoit bien aise de l'heureux succes de l'inoculation de sa femme; qu'il pouvoit se dispenser d'aller a font.bleau a moins qu'il n'y ait d'autres affaires.[30]

Paris and Versailles, or wherever the Court was, were magnets which the greater magistrates found it difficult to resist for long. Even so, their attitude to the centre of power was ambiguous. Pichard, a man of consequence at home, cannot have relished being brushed off by busy ministers at Court. President de Lavie was furious in 1781 when he heard that his wife, who had not been presented, had been unable to see certain galleries at Versailles until the king had left them, even though the king was taken out for the purpose by the queen herself.[31] The risk of such humiliations must have induced all but the most ambitious of the magistrates to stay in the province, where their social position was better established. When therefore in 1786 the parlement as a whole was convoked to Versailles in the *alluvions* case, for many magistrates it was the journey of a lifetime, and the punitive effect of the summons was limited. To give bite to the royal displeasure, the magistrates were also forbidden to visit Paris on the way. For as counsellor Filhot de Chimbaud's younger brother put it, 'en verite quand on a passé quinze jours a paris on peut en parler du moins pendant un an'.[32] A few magistrates travelled abroad, such as Basterot on a two-year visit to England, but that was only with special permission. Dupaty's trip to Italy in 1785 was partly at least government-sponsored, and Lavie's trip to Switzerland in 1776 'pour voir des hommes libres', and Voltaire into the bargain, was made during the vacation.[33] The education of magistrates seldom included a grand tour; so only a minority of them could ever have seen much of the world outside the province of Guienne.

Not that this province, and Bordeaux in particular, was without its variety. The city offered plenty of agreeable ways of passing the time, particularly of the lighter sort. Money was the only passport to acceptance in the city's extravagant high society. Merchants and magistrates not only sought the company of their fellows, but intermingled freely at all the centres of fashionable life. When John Adams arrived in Bordeaux in 1778, the American consul arranged a dinner for him at which merchants, sea-captains, government officers, and A. F. B. Le Berthon, son of the first president himself, were all present.[34] In August 1775 the merchants of the city entertained Mouchy to a great feast, and all the members of the parlement were invited.[35] The greatest centre of social mixing was Bardineau, a pleasure garden. Here all the richest and most distinguished citizens of Bordeaux were to be seen, and at the time of Maupeou it was regularly patronized even by the first president de Gascq and Richelieu himself. Here there was food, music, and above all, gambling. Moral harangues by Mouchy and raids on gaming houses by the *jurats* and the watch did little to restrict it.[36] The number of gaming tables inventoried in the parlementaire houses suggests that it was common enough among them at home, and so also probably in public places, where there was always the refuge of a mask. Gascq was reported to have made 80,000 l. at piquet in 1756.[37] The exile of the parlement to Libourne in 1787–88 increased the gambling activities of the magistrates because there was so little else to do.[38]

Victor Louis's grand theatre, opened in 1780, was the most magnificent in France, and maintained companies of comedy, tragedy, opera, comic opera, and a *corps de ballet*.[39] It could afford the most expensive Parisian performers. There was also the *Variétés Amusantes*, which though far less sumptuous was almost as popular. The idea of the grand theatre had been conceived in the extravagant days of Richelieu's governorship, and in 1760 he had formed a joint stock company to guide and profit from the project. Among its members were merchants, noblemen, and two presidents.[40] The theatrical tastes of the Bordelais were increasingly light—comedies and comic operas were far more frequently performed as the century went on than tragedies, sentimental dramas, or ballets. In this cultural atmosphere the magistrates must have participated, although Beaumarchais's *Le Mariage de Figaro* was banned in 1785 by the court 'comme une comédie contraire aux moeurs, aux loix, à la religion, & comme devant être proscrite de tout théâtre policé.[41] This ban lasted until March 1789, after which time it seemed unwise to try to stem the tide of 'patriotic' pieces which engulfed the theatres. *Le Barbier de Séville*, on the other hand, was acted untramelled 80 times in Bordeaux between 1775 and 1787,[42] several magistrates had works by Beaumarchais in their libraries, and some of them knew him personally from his stay in Bordeaux in the early 1780s. Naturally when, as on 20 October 1788 at its triumphal return, the theatre audience sang 'Vive Henri IV!' in the parlement's honour, it could only be flattered at the role that the theatre played in local life.[43]

Earlier in the century, *salons* and dining clubs had given the cultivated a place to meet and exchange polite conversation. Around 1760 Richelieu had organized *la cabane de Philémon*, where art and literature were discussed over dinner,[44] and where perhaps sometimes Gascq displayed the skill on the violin which was attested by Jean-Jacques Rousseau.[45] Earlier still, in the 1730s, various *salons* and conversational circles had flourished, where magistrates were the most assiduous attenders. Those of the parlementaire widow Mme Duplessy, and her rival Mme Desnanots had been the best known.[46] By the time of Louis XVI they had no successors, although informal dining and entertaining went on all the time. Then as now the world's important business was transacted over the dining table. Mme Duplessy picked up most of her fund of historically invaluable gossip at Pichard's where she was a frequent guest. In 1788 Bernadau noted the report that at Libourne, '*M de Pichard* tient tous les jours une table de 25 couverts pour ses confrères desquels il feint de se rapprocher'.[47] All presidents, and ambitious counsellors, must have spent much time entertaining. For the first president and the procurator-general it was a routine part of their business.

The more serious pleasures of the intellect were not so generally cultivated. The university was utterly undistinguished. 'Les Sciences en tout genre semblent fuir les villes de commerce et d'argent', Guibert sadly reflected.[48] There was the academy, a society of aspiring polymaths, a privileged, self-recruiting corporation guaranteed by royal letters patent registered by the parlement.[49] Nearly all its founder members in 1712 were magistrates of the parlement; Montesquieu himself was an early ornament. For the first 60 years of its existence the academy was an extremely exclusive body, with only 12 full members and a rather larger body of associates. Twenty-four out of the 48 full members before 1783 were or became members of the parlement, and up to 1750 the academy was recruited almost exclusively among magistrates. Only after that did its field of recruitment widen to include certain professional men.[50] However, this trend was a steady one, culminating in the reforms of 1781–83, when associate status was abolished and all academicians were put on an equal footing.[51] Yet despite numbers, the academy remained a body dominated by the aristocracy, and inroads made by outside groups were made by professional men rather than merchants.[52] Under Louis XVI nine members of the parlement were academicians: they included the procurator-general Dudon, Dupaty (who was also a member of the academy of La Rochelle), and the learned Lamontaigne, the academy's perpetual secretary. Its field of interest was nothing less than the advancement and exchange of knowledge; its members regarded themselves as qualified to deliberate on anything. On these grounds certain academicians persuaded the parlement to oppose the establishment of an agricultural society. However, as early as 1755 president de Loret had declared that the main concern of the academy should be with what was useful,[53] and the development of the subjects for prizes offered over the century shows a clear evolution towards subjects of utility—agriculture, the problem of the poor, health and sanitation[54]—in spite of the taste of many academicians for more traditionally construed subjects, like eulogies of Montesquieu.[55] Besides prize competitions, the academy sponsored a large public library. It also cherished from time to time the idea of sponsoring the publication of a great History of Guienne, although this never came to fruition. Such preoccupations reflect the strictly local recruitment of the 'ordinary' members (as opposed to associates and correspondents)[56] which made the academy, in the last analysis, a bastion of provincialism.

Until 1783 it was unchallenged as the forum where the intellectual élite of Bordeaux were to be found. In that year a rival institution made its appearance— the musée, a society of amateurs dedicated to organizing free public instruction in the sciences and the arts.[57] Since 1776 the idea had been current in Bordeaux, but it took the abbé Dupont de Jumeaux, who had lectured on mathematics at a Paris musée, to put life into it when he came to lecture in Bordeaux. In 1782 he circularized a large number of the notables of Bordeaux, in the worlds of the law, the professions, and commerce, and received many enthusiastic replies. The intendant placed a room at the disposal of the proposed society and on 10 April 1783 it held a preliminary meeting.[58] Among the members of the parlement whose participation was sought from the start were J. B. Chauvet (who was a member of the academy and already a corresponding member of the *musée* of Paris), Dupaty, Saige, Raignac, and Prunes-Duvivier.[59] The intendant was elected president, Dupaty vice-president, and Chauvet, one of the secretaries. The *musée* met thenceforth regularly until its suppression in 1793. It organized lectures, held public sessions at which the literary or scholarly offerings of its members were read, subscribed to most of the current journals,[60] gave concerts, and corresponded with other circles in Paris, Toulouse, and the Isles. The somnolent academy was somewhat eclipsed by it and the volume of support which it attracted. The membership consisted of 150 equal associates, very unlike the small circle of the academy. On the extant lists of those patronizing the *musée* are recorded 226 names, drawn from all sections of leisured society in Bordeaux. All the great merchants were there, and so were the famous advocates. Almost lost in this host of bourgeoisie were a few noblemen and members of the parlement.[61] At least 14 of them had their attendance recorded at one time or another, including Dupaty, Chauvet, Lamontaigne, and Poissac. Initially at least the *musée* represented, in the words of Vergniaud, 'ce qu'il y a de mieux dans la ville'.[62] Yet as time went on, and especially after 1785, noble attendance fell off, and the *musée* became in every way what it had been, numerically, from the start—a society dominated by advocates and above all merchants.

For tastes more practical still, a philanthropic society was set up in 1786.[63] Over 100 members were presided over by Le Berthon, the merchant Paul Nairac, and Dudon, 'presque tous nos Négotians & . . . quelques personnes de distinction'.[64] Its secretary, counsellor de Castelnau d'Auros, had published in 1786 a pamphlet outlining a plan of poor relief for large towns.[65] The society had three classes of associates in decreasing order of activity and amount subscribed, but they all committed themselves to the work of pensioning the old, the poor, and the widowed, through the medium of parish priests. It did not begin serious work until 1788, but by then it was rumoured to have funds totalling 17,000 l.[66] Here, members of the parlement were found co-operating once again with merchants and other notables, this time in projects directed towards the public good.

To estimate the importance of parlementaire participation in these bodies is not as straightforward as it may seem. Magistrates appeared dominant in the academy, weak in the *musée*; and yet more of them subscribed to the latter. Moreover, only a small minority of the parlement participated in any society at all, and it tended to be the same group in all of them. If anything bound them together, it was freemasonry. Philanthropy was a masonic ideal; the *musée* of Paris had found its original inspiration in masonry,[67] and clearly that of Bordeaux had masonic links, with its triangular badge and pregnant motto of 'Liberty, Equality'. Among the magistrates, known masons were the first to be circulated about the new project. Masonry was, in fact, very well established in Bordeaux. As early as 1742 the intendant had warned the government that:

> Il s'est introduit icy une espèce de société sous le titre de la confrairie des Francs-massons qui prend beaucoup de faveur . . . La nouveauté qui plaît infiniment en ce païs cy a déterminé nombre d'honêtes gens à entrer dans cette confrairie, meme des officiers du Parlement . . .[68]

It is uncertain how many masonic lodges there were in 18th-century Bordeaux.

Bernadau, a contemporary, gives 22 in 1788 'sans compter les affiliées, les partagées et les bâtardes'.[69] A later writer, with access to the archives of the Bordeaux Grand Orient lodges, found evidence of 16.[70] The earliest dated from 1732 and there were parlementaire freemasons from the start. Of those who were magistrates under Louis XVI, 23 belonged to lodges which were affiliated or became affiliated to the Grand Orient.[71] Of these, 17 belonged to the French lodge, four to the lodge of Harmony, and two to the lodge of Friendship. There were none outside these three, for after all, masonic equality was not opposed to the maintenance of social barriers. As the younger Dudon, *Vénérable* of the lodge of Friendship, wrote in 1785, opposing the formation of new lodges:

> . . . tous ces soi-disant maçons sont des Ouvriers, la pluspart aux gages des negotians de l'etat desquels ils se sont revetus.
> . . . ce seroit avilir, aneantir, ou au moins humilier L'art Royal, que d'admettre de pareils sujets dans le sein de maçonnerie, dont le privilege de l'Egalité deviendroit un abus bien dangereux, si sous ce pretexte on admettait indifferemment tous les etats.[72]

Masonry stood for equality, but equality between equals. And even then, certain lodges had more social prestige than others. The French lodge, to which most magistrates belonged, was the most aristocratic. In 1778 it had 67 members, including the first president and two presidents *à mortier* (Verthamon and Gourgue), one advocate-general (Dupaty), one president in the requests (Bienassis), and 13 counsellors. Also members were the duc de Duras, Victor Louis the architect, several officers of subordinate law courts, and 25 merchants.[73] Here was a further example of mixing between the nobility and the world of commerce. The lodge of Harmony was by contrast far smaller and almost exclusively legal. It had about 20 members, mostly advocates, also four members of the parlement, among whom was Poissac. Before coming to Bordeaux he had already been a freemason in Tulle.[74] The lodge of Friendship was large, mostly merchants and sea-captains, but with a sprinkling of other notables such as the comte de Fumel, two presidents at the court of aids, and Basterot and the younger Dudon from the parlement.[75] What importance can we attach to the fact that members of the parlement were freemasons? Doubtless masonry promoted a certain amount of social and professional mixing. At Bordeaux parlementaire participation was among the strongest of all parlements, after Toulouse and possibly Paris,[76] and it may have helped to link the magistrates more closely with the commercial world which, numerically, dominated the great lodges. It may also have helped to promote a certain amount of contact with other towns. The list of lodges in correspondence with the lodge of Harmony is long and impressive, but the real importance of such correspondence is hard to assess.[77] Freemasonry was surely at its most useful by affording travelling magistrates an entry into local society wherever they went, as with Poissac when he came to Bordeaux, or Dupaty, when he went to Paris. There he became prominent in the most famous lodge in France, the Nine Sisters, whose members supported his various legal crusades just before his death[78]—masonic philanthropy at work. But the clearest role played by Bordeaux masonry was political. The freemasons were responsible for organizing the triumphal welcome given to the returning exiles of the parlement in 1775.[79] They built triumphal arches, grandstands, and pavilions. They gave banquets and held *Te Deums*. The members of the French lodge made Le Berthon their perpetual *Vénérable* of honour. Possibly they also had a hand in the celebrations for the returns of 1786 and 1788. Masonic organization was obviously a powerful vehicle for promoting the popularity of the parlement.

Freemasonry was not the only mystical cult. In November 1783 Cagliostro arrived in Bordeaux, where he spent 11 months moving in the best society and selling his health cures. The freemasons fêted him and doubtless his mystic seances were attended by some magistrates.[80] Some of them were certainly affected by the craze for mesmerism which swept France in the early 1780s,[81] and in 1784 a branch of the societies of Harmony was set up in Bordeaux. In 1784 Duval d'Eprémesnil, counsellor at the parlement of Paris and freemason, attended eight sessions of the society and delivered various lectures.[82] He also collaborated in the publication of a list of cures effected in the Bordeaux region by the methods of Mesmer.[83] Among them were two by counsellor Prunes-Duvivier, who by 'magnetizing' sufferers in the area around his country estate, claimed to have brought about 'almost miraculous' recoveries.[84] Naturally he was a member of the society, and among its 59 other members—many doctors, some merchants, and some advocates—were five other members of the parlement.[85] The abbé de Poulouzat, clerical counsellor, was even Mesmer's *fondé de pouvoirs* in the society. These magistrates must have had a hand in persuading the parlement to revoke the ban on preaching imposed on the irrepressible father Hervier after he had sensationally broken off in mid-sermon to mesmerize one of his congregation.[86]

Orthodox religion tended to suffer eclipse in these days of para-religious and para-scientific wonders. Yet most magistrates had received a profoundly religious education, and throughout their lives most of them unostentatiously observed the conventions of the established church. There were no Protestants among them, by definition, although one or two had recent ancestors or relatives of Protestant extraction. Magistrates were pillars of their parish churches, both in town and country. They occupied the most honourable pews, they were syndics of the fabric, they made donations to parish funds.[87] Most of their wills began with endowments of requiem masses for their souls, and many left funds to be distributed, at the discretion of parish priests, to the poor of the various parishes with which the testator had connections. Most stipulated, in a spirit of Christian humility, the minimum of pomp at the funeral, although somebody like the first president A. F. B. Le Berthon, who died in 1766, can hardly seriously have expected the parlement not to give him all the honours normally received by one of its dead chiefs; it duly called out all the corporate bodies of the city to form his funeral procession.[88] The life of the parlement was full of masses, religious feasts and holidays, regular or occasional, in which the magistrates were expected to participate. There were too some genuine *dévots* in their ranks. None went so far as J. B. F. de Carrière, honorary counsellor from 1766, who, when a widower late in life, took Holy Orders.[89] But counsellors de Navarre and de Fauquier were considered so subservient to their confessors that when, along with the other 'remainers', they refused to return to the palace in 1775, Mouchy tried to bring them back by pressure exerted from this direction.[90] Others, while not susceptible to this sort of pressure, must have taken their religion as seriously. Yet it is remarkable how little evidence there is of concern with religious affairs in the parlement. The body which, in 1762, had joined the hue and cry against the Jesuits, and as recently as 1765 had censured the doctors of theology of the university for sustaining a thesis which contained excessively ultramontane opinions,[91] fell completely silent on religious issues after 1771. The ground of the great constitutional debate had clearly shifted decisively.

In the literary field, most magistrates seemed content simply to bask in the reflected glory of former members of the company. 'C'est, messieurs', declared counsellor de Lascombes, director of the academy in 1763, 'le glorieux destin de cette province d'avoir donné la naissance aux deux plus grands philosophes qui ayent paru depuis le renouvellement des lettres, Montaigne et M de Montesquieu'.[92] The only notable publications of the magistrates in the late 18th century were those of Dupaty, a poor third indeed. Nevertheless, from an early age he was used to having his works printed. With his flowery and emotional oratory he had taken the academies of La Rochelle and Bordeaux by storm. At La Rochelle in 1768 he founded a prize for the eulogy of Henry IV, and sent Voltaire an example of the medal he had had struck for the winner. The old man was enchanted. 'Mr. Du Paty . . . pétille d'esprit', he told Richelieu, '. . . il déteste cordialement les prêtres de Pluton. Il est idolâtre de la Tolérance . . .'[93] He predicted that his jeune socrate de Bordeaux'[94] would be one of the ornaments of the coming age.[95] Dupaty clearly hoped so too, and he devoted his years of exile under Maupeou to planning a great work on the reform of the criminal law. But it was not until 1786, when he had left Bordeaux, that he published his first book, or rather pamphlet, his *Lettres sur la procédure criminelle de la France*, in which he set out to show that:

> Jamais aucun peuple, excepté ceux qui ont le malheur de vivre sous le joug infame et odieux de l'inquisition, n'a eu des loix aussi dures et aussi tyranniques que les nôtres. Elles sont plutôt faites pour être la terreur des gens de bien que celle des méchants.[96]

Published anonymously, this pamphlet was timed to coincide with the appearance of the first printed briefs drawn up by Dupaty in favour of the *trois roués*. Then in 1788 he published his *Lettres sur l'Italie*, an account of his travels in 1785, whose appeal to the sensibility of the age is well attested by the 28 editions through which it passed over the next 40 years.[97] These letters describe Italian Institutions, especially judicial ones, but they also sentimentally evoke, in a way that was already becoming a cliché, the ruins and vanished glories of Rome, and the strange and romantic appeal of the catacombs and Vesuvius. It was indeed a work more fashionable than original, but doubtless it would have won Dupaty the 'immortal' chair to which he clearly aspired, if he had not died so soon after its publication.

Though producing nothing, however, many of the magistrates obviously shared the fashionable taste and opinions of their day. President de Lavie's friendship with Dupaty obviously flowered on shared opinions. President de Verthamon, the traveller Guibert noted, was a 'grand partisan des Economistes', lent him tracts on economic improvements, and discussed fiscal reform with him.[98] Perhaps the broadest indication of the tastes of the magistrates, however, is the content of their libraries.[99]

Revolutionary inventories survive for the libraries of several members of the parlement in our period.[100] They ranged in size from P. F. de Brach's 3,407 or Pichard's 1,003, to a few hundred volumes. All the others were well under one thousand, except possibly those of Dupaty and Lamontaigne. One or two had a pronounced bias, reflecting a clear preoccupation in their owners. For example, out of Poissac's 196 volumes, 175 were law books, and Poissac was the author of a work on the parlement's jurisprudence. Law books naturally figured prominently in many collections, although seldom as prominently as this. In those of Bouquier and Fauquier they made up over half. In those of Darche, Basterot, and Pelet d'Anglade they accounted for about one-quarter. Pichard's 122, though only just over 10 per cent of his library, were second in quantity only to those of Poissac. The kernels of all these collections were various editions of the custom of Bordeaux, Lapeyrère's local *Décisions Sommaires du Palais*, the *Code* and the *Digest*, collections of royal ordinances, various legal dictionaries, and of course numerous commentaries.

Theology, pious works, and sermons by Bossuet, Massillon, and Berruyer also figured prominently. Perhaps they accounted for half the library of Lamontaigne, though not as much as a quarter in all other cases. In four, the number of religious works did not reach double figures, and in most cases the dates of publication suggest that the books had often been in the family over a long period.

All the libraries were dominated by works on serious topics like law, theology, or history. Fiction and creative literature were always only a small segment. The basis of the literary section in them all was a collection of the classics, especially the Roman ones. None was without its Virgil, its Horace, or its Ovid. The representatives of stoical Roman virtue, like Cicero and Seneca, were often to be found. Roman historians, like Caesar, Livy, Tacitus, Suetonius, and Quintus Curtius were all prominent, but the only Greek author who recurred regularly was Homer. The greatest achievements of French classicism of the 17th century were usually to be found also—the plays of Corneille, Racine, and Molière; Boileau on poetry and Malherbe on the French language. Most magistrates possessed some representatives of 18th-century literature, like the works of Marivaux, Crébillon, J. B. Rousseau, the abbé Prévost, and Beaumarchais. Nearly all had Laclos's *Les Liaisons dangereuses*. Most had the poetical and dramatic works of Voltaire. Most had one or two translations of foreign works by such authors as Goethe, Richardson, or Sterne. Hardly any library was without a translation of Young's *Night Thoughts*. Stoicism and sensibility, those ill-matched twins so esteemed by the 18th century, were not therefore Dupaty's monopoly.

Utility, too: under this rubric natural science and philosophy went hand in hand. Admittedly scientific works were not outstanding in their number, but most libraries had copies of Buffon's *Histoire Naturelle*, and the *Spectacle de la Nature* and the *Histoire du Ciel* of the abbé Pluche. Pelet d'Anglade had a number of books of medicine and anatomy. Several had a handful on mathematics and geography. Saige,[101] Lamolère, Brach, Montsec de Reignac, Pelet d'Anglade, and Lamontaigne, had copies of the *Encyclopédie* in full or in part. Pichard, Filhot de Chimbaud, and Dupaty had abridgements or synopses of it. 'Philosophy' indeed was quite well represented. Nearly all had the complete works of Montesquieu, inevitably, but most also had some Voltaire, though most often his dramatic or historical works. Jean-Jacques Rousseau was better represented by his Dictionary of Music and *Emile*, than by the *Contrat Social*, although Pichard at least had a copy. The great seminal fathers of 18th-century thought, Bacon, Hobbes, Locke, and Bayle, all figured occasionally, and there were a few copies of works by Mably, D'Holbach, and D'Alembert. So the advanced thought of the age did not pass the magistrates by unnoticed. How far they subscribed to it of course is a different question. Many of these works, however, were prohibited in France, and published actually or in name abroad. The entry of illicit books into the port of Bordeaux was a constant source of worry to the intendant.[102] The libraries of most members of the parlement contained at least 10 per cent of books originating (supposedly or actually) abroad. Some of these had never been prohibited, but works by Voltaire, Raynal, and others certainly were. This suggests that their owners went to some trouble to get them, which in turn perhaps betrays a real wish to read them.

The factotum of the philosophic 18th century was history, that storehouse of example. The libraries of the magistrates were well stocked with historical works, not only on the ancient world and on France, though admittedly these fields were by far the best covered, but on England (here Hume was the teacher), eastern Europe (Voltaire on Charles XII and Peter the Great), and countries even further east. Such histories were supplemented by a certain scattering of accounts of travels to the East. Raynal on colonization occurred in most libraries, though we can only imagine what slave-owning magistrates thought of him. Collections of French history merged into current affairs, by way of memoirs and collections of anecdotes. The magistrates were well provided with works which touched them nearly in this field—the *Journal historique de la Révolution* (the Maupeou revolution of course) had its place in most libraries, as did certain other and rarer tracts of those times. The anonymous works of Le Paige were a point of reference for constitutional ideas. The works of Necker on the finances—('cet écrit administrera l'Europe', declared Dupaty)[103]—and Calonne's attacks on them, were also frequent. Several had treatises on the grain trade, that constant preoccupation of the parlement. When the greater Revolution came in 1789, some of the magistrates bought the more important pamphlets born of the ferment. Pichard and Pelet d'Anglade had Sieyès's *Qu'est-ce que le Tiers Etat?* and Pichard and Basterot had Saige's *Catéchisme du Citoyen*, a work which the parlement had had burned publicly when it first appeared in 1775.[104]

Finally, there was a significant local element. The magistrates had most of the contemporary works on the Bordelais. We have already noted the law commentaries, and especially that of the Lamothe brothers (1768).[105] When Dom Devienne[106] published his *Histoire de Bordeaux* in 1771, at least 46 parlementaire families subscribed to it in advance.[107] At least 25 subscribed in 1785 to Baurein's *Variétés Bordeloises*.[108] Perhaps local sentiment also encouraged the sale of the works of Montesquieu, or indeed those of Montaigne. These things again underline the deep local patriotism of the magistrates. They were proud of their province and its traditions. These traditions were of independence, and the parlement never ceased to vaunt the capitulation of 1451 as a sort of charter of provincial rights. It was to local history that they constantly appealed in the final crisis-ridden years of the parlement's life. One of the central themes of the early and 'pre'-revolution in France was the obvious desire of the provinces to reassert their local autonomy against the 'despotism' of the central government and the capital. The parlement of Bordeaux was an early leader of this movement, for everything in the circumstances of its members pushed it in this direction. On the other hand, the peculiarity of these circumstances was not new. They explain a lot, but not everything. The parlement's political role can only be finally explained in political terms. It is to a consideration of these that we must now turn.

NOTES

1. AD C278. The rolls certainly underestimate the true number.
2. AD C2696.
3. Brouillard, 'Le pillage de l'hôtel Saige', *R. Philomat. Bx.* (1937), 50.
4. AD C238, C3669, C4457. The magistrates in question were presidents Daugeard and Maurice de Sentout, and counsellors de Prunes and Lamolère.
5. BVBx MS 713 (sér. II), 'Spicilège' de Bernadau, t. 39. *Les Parlemens à tous les diables.* This anonymous pamphlet is attributed by Bernadau in a MS note to the advocate Marie de Saint-Georges. See below, pp. 303 and 314, n. 1.
6. Meaudre de Lapouyade, *Un Maitre flamand à Bordeaux—Lonsing 1739-99* (Paris, 1911), contains reproductions of the portraits of Le Berthon and Laroze. That of Dudon is lost.
7. Brouillard, op. cit., 53.
8. AD Q915.
9. Factum in AM, cited above, p. 114 n. 14 and p. 124.
10. AD 2E 565 (tit. fam. Castelnau).
11. AD 2E 1405 (tit. fam. Gourgue).
12. Brouillard, loc. cit., 52-3.
13. AD 2E 1933 (tit. fam. Maignol).
14. AD 3E 5.591.
15. AD Q934.
16. Brouillard, op. cit., 50.
17. AD Q932.
18. AD Q928.
19. AD Q934.
20. AD Q915.
21. Grellet-Dumazeau, *La Société Bordelaise sous Louis XV*, 249.
22. AD C3214. Quoted in A. Nicolaï, *Au bon vieux temps*, 8. Tourny to Orry, 27 March 1744.
23. Marionneau, *Victor Louis*, 437-8.
24. C. Marionneau, *Les Salons Bordelais ou expositions des beaux-arts à Bordeaux au XVIIIᵉ siècle (1771-1787)* (Bordeaux, 1883).
25. Guillon, *Les Châteaux historiques . . . de la Gironde*, 4 v., *passim*.
26. Forster, *Nobility of Toulouse*, 171.
27. BVBx MS 1696, II, no. 50, Duroy to Lamontaigne, 10 Feb. 1755.
28. Bachaumont, XVIII, 261-2, 22 Nov. 1775.
29. Mme Campan, *Mémoires sur la Vie de Marie Antoinette, reine de France et de Navarre* (ed. Nelson, n.d.). 173-5.
30. AN E3701. Bertin's letter book, 1772-73.
31. C. Nicoullaud (ed.), *Récits d'une tante—mémoires de la comtesse de Boigne, née d'Osmond, publiés d'après le manuscrit original* (Paris, 1907-08), I, 26. The story is also cited in H. Carré, *La Fin des Parlements, 1788-90* (Paris, 1912), 17.
32. AD 2E 1213⁵ (tit. fam. Filhot de Chimbaud), Edmê to Joseph Filhot de Chimbaud, 6 Aug. 1786.
33. T. Besterman (ed.), *Voltaire's Correspondence* (Geneva, 1953–), XCV, no. 19166, Dupaty to Voltaire, 20 Sept. 1776.
34. *The Adams Papers: Series I*, II, 294, 3 April 1778.
35. BVBx MS 1201, IV, 29 Aug. 1775.
36. J. Bencazar, 'Les jeux de hasard à Bordeaux', *passim*.
37. Leroux, *Etude critique*, 247. The reference is to a 'president de G****', which could only be Gascq, in the context.
38. BVBx MS 713 (sér. I), V, 123, 24 Dec. 1787.

39. See P. Courteault, *La Révolution et les théâtres à Bordeaux*, ch. 1, *passim*.
40. J. de Maupassant, 'Un grand armateur de Bordeaux: Abraham Gradis (1699–1780)', *R. Hist. Bx.* (1913–14), 152 n.
41. Bachaumont, XXIX, 155, 3 Aug. 1785; P. Bernadau, *Annales politiques littéraires et statistiques de Bordeaux* (Bordeaux, 1803), 253.
42. D. Mornet, *Les Origines intellectuelles de la Révolution française (1715–1787)* (Paris, 1933), 296.
43. Courteault, op. cit., 20.
44. Grellet-Dumazeau, *La Société Bordelaise*, 218.
45. *Confessions*, 1741.
46. Grellet-Dumazeau, op. cit., 160. Mme Duplessy and her activities form the main subject of this work.
47. BVBx MS 713 (sér. I), V, 177, 24 Feb. 1788.
48. *Voyages de Guibert*, 16, 22 June 1775.
49. On provincial academies in general, with Bordeaux as a specific example, see D. Roche, 'Milieux académiques provinciaux et société des lumières. Trois académies provinciales au XVIIIᵉ siècle: Bordeaux, Dijon, Châlons sur Marne', in G. Bollême *et al., Livre et Société dans la France du XVIIIᵉ siècle* (Paris—La Haye, 1965), 93–184. On that of Bordeaux in particular, P. Barrière, *L'Académie de Bordeaux centre de culture internationale au XVIIIᵉ siècle (1712–1792)* (Paris—Bordeaux, 1951).
50. ibid., 42–6; Roche, loc. cit., 114–20, 122–3.
51. Barrière, loc. cit., 23.
52. Roche, loc. cit., 130–1, disproves the assertions of R. M. Brace, *Bordeaux and the Gironde* (New York, 1948), 10.
53. Barrière, loc. cit., 86; see also Roche, loc. cit., 173–4.
54. Barrière, loc. cit., 131–4; Roche, loc. cit., 162–6.
55. ibid., 160–1.
56. ibid., 109.
57. Mornet, *Les Origines intellectuelles*, 284.
58. Many of these details come from R. Celeste, 'La Société Philomatique de Bordeaux de 1783 à 1808', 65–83.
59. BVBx MS 829 (I), Musée: correspondance, letters 12, 21, 33, 47, 59.
60. AM Fonds Delpit 202, 'Musée'.
61. Much of the following is taken from the notes of Mlle M.-Th. Bouyssy, who has written a *diplôme* for the *école normale supérieure* on the *Musée*. I have been unable to see a copy of this work, but the author kindly lent me her notes at an early stage in her researches. The source of most of the information are BVBx MS 829 (III), 'Tableaux du Musée'. The role and composition of this society is also analysed in P. Butel, 'La croissance', II, 1150–3. In 1788, he notes, 53 per cent of its members were merchants, and 36 per cent advocates. Out of 145 members in this year, only 11 were members of the parlement.
62. Vatel, *Vergniaud*, I, 76, Vergniaud to Allaud, 3 March 1783.
63. Leroux, *Etude critique*, 314.
64. BVBx MS 713 (sér. I), V, 92, 18 Oct. 1787.
65. ibid., 282, 11 Aug. 1788. See also W. Doyle, 'Deux parlementaires bazadais du XVIIIᵉ siècle', 27.
66. BVBx. loc. cit. above, n. 64, 93.
67. See F. G. Pariset in *Bordeaux au XVIIIᵉ siècle*, 654.
68. *AHDG*, XXVI (1888–89), no. XLVII, Boucher to Amelot, 23 July 1742.
69. BVBx MS 713 (sér. I), V, 240, 25 June 1788.
70. Abbé Brun, *L'Abbé J. P. Lapauze, vén.·. de la L.·. Ang.·., O.·. de Bordeaux, curé de Bonzac et Galgon, archiprêtre de Fronsac, au diocèse de Bordeaux* (Bordeaux, 1903), 82–3.
71. BN fonds FM. FM¹ 110, and FM² 170–8 contain the archives of the Grand Orient lodges of Bordeaux.
72. BN FM² 174, 'La Famille Unie des Bons Accords', letter of 1785.
73. BN FM² 174, 'Loge Française Elue Ecossaise'.
74. BN FM² 176, 'R.·. L.·. de l'Harmonie'; BVBx MS 847, 'R   Française, procès-verbal des séances, 1773–6'.

75. BN FM² 170, 'Loge de l'Amitié'.
76. L. Amiable, *La Franc-Maçonnerie et la magistrature en France à la veille de la Révolution* (Aix, 1894), 29–30.
77. BVBx MS 847.
78. Amiable, op. cit., 33ff.
79. See below, p. 163.
80. E. Lanoire, 'Cagliostro à Bordeaux', *R. Philomat. Bx.* (1931), 49–61.
81. R. Darnton, *Mesmerism and the End of the Enlightenment in France* (Cambridge, Mass., 1968), ch. 2.
82. Bernadau, *Annales de Bordeaux*, 254, Oct. 1785; Darnton, op. cit., 67 n. 13.
83. *Recueil d'observations et de faits relatifs au magnétisme animal, présenté à l'Auteur de cette découverte, & publié par la Société de Guienne* (Philadelphie, Paris, Bordeaux, 1785), 168 pp.
84. ibid., 45–8.
85. Darnton, op. cit., 74, is therefore wrong to find only two aristocrats in its membership.
86. Lanoire, loc. cit., 57; Darnton, op. cit., 55–8.
87. AN H93 bis contains two requests from Le Berthon and president de Verthamon for concessions to support or extend the fabric of their parish churches.
88. AM MS 808 (secret registers), p.385, 11 Aug. 1766.
89. Grellet-Dumazeau, op. cit., 160–1.
90. BVBx MS 1201, IV, 26 March 1775.
91. BVBx MS 713 (sér. II), *arrêt* of 14 Aug. 1765.
92. Barrière, *L'Académie de Bordeaux*, 62.
93. Besterman, *Voltaire's Correspondence*, LXV, no. 15301, Voltaire to Richelieu, 20 April 1770.
94. ibid., LXXVII, no. 15722, Voltaire to d'Alembert, 5 Nov. 1770.
95. ibid., LXXVI, no. 14573, Voltaire to Dupaty, 27 March 1769. There are several other flattering exchanges between the two in the *Correspondence*, as well as references by Voltaire in letters to others.
96. *Lettres sur la procédure criminelle*, 8.
97. P. Lelièvre, 'Un oublié: le Président Dupaty', *Annales de l'académie de La Rochelle* (1926–30).
98. *Voyages de Guibert*, 13–14.
99. For discussion of the methods and problems involved here, see D. Mornet, 'L'enseignement des biliothèques privées, 1750–1870', *Revue d'histoire littéraire de la France* (1910), and A. Dupront, 'Livre et culture dans la société française du 18ᵉ siècle: réflexion sur une enquête', in *Livre et société dans la France du XVIIIᵉ siècle*, especially 212–16.
100. Eleven in all. BVBx MS 849 (Basquiat, Bouquier), 850 (Poissac), 851 (Paty, Lamolère) 852 (Brach, Montsec de Reignac), 853 (Pelet d'Anglade, Fauquier, Filhot de Chimbaud), 854 (Pichard), 848–9 (Basterot). Inventories under the names of Demons, Dom Carrière, and Dufaure de Lajarte may also relate to members of the parlement, but this cannot be certain. Partial information also from AD 3J DI: 1808, *Catalogue des livres provenant de la bibliothèque de feu M. le Président Dupaty*; BVBx MS 1696, III, 'Pièces diverses relatives à la bibliothèque de Fr. de Lamontaigne'.
101. Brouillard, 'Le pillage', 58. Saige had a library of about 3,000 volumes.
102. See E. Brives-Cazes, *De la police des livres en Guyenne, 1713–85* (Bordeaux, 1883), *passim*, but especially 133.
103. *Lettres sur l'Italie*, no. XIX.
104. BVBx MS 1201, IV, 15 June 1775. On Saige, see C. W Garrett, 'The Moniteur of 1788', *French Historical Studies* (1968), *passim*.
105. Notably absent, however, was L. F. de Salviat's *Jurisprudence du Parlement de Bordeaux* (1787).
106. Charles Jean-Baptiste D'Aubigny Devienne (1728–92). Benedictine of the congregation of Saint-Maur, he worked 1754–71 at the abbey of Sainte-Croix, Bordeaux on his history of the city. He left after the first part, the only one to be published, received a hostile reception. In 1784 and 1787 he published a history of Artois.
107. *Histoire de Bordeaux*, 'Liste de souscripteurs'. Some names are uncertain.
108. *Variétés*, V, 'liste de souscripteurs'.

PART TWO

Il n'est pas vrai que l'intérêt personnel soit le mobile le plus puissant de la conduite des hommes; l'orgueil, l'amour-propre, la colère leur font très-aisément sacrifier cet intérêt.

(Mme de Staël, 1800)

CHAPTER 10

Dissolution: The Reforms of Maupeou

The royal Court was at Compiègne in August 1771, when Chancellor Maupeou sent an ominous note to the marshal de Richelieu: 'Les Succes de Benzancon et de Douay, Monsieur', he wrote, 'me font desirer de m'entretenir avec vous de ec qui regarde Bordeaux, ainsi je vous prie de me venir voir le plutôt que vous pourrés, car il n'y a pas de tems à perdre . . .'[1] In this way began the process by which the whole world of the magistrates of Bordeaux was turned upside down, the revolution which dominated their professional lives until they were overtaken by the greater upheaval which followed 18 years later. The parlement of Bordeaux had done nothing to incur the particular enmity of the Chancellor. Maupeou's quarrel was with the parlement of Paris, and in this the provincial magistracy were merely onlookers. But they could hardly be expected to stand by in silence when he attacked the first court in the kingdom, for the grounds on which he attacked were of equal concern to them all.

In the summer of 1770, therefore, after the king had suspended proceedings in the parlement of Paris in the case of the duc d'Aiguillon, the parlement of Bordeaux joined other provincial courts in protesting against the government's repeated refusal to reopen the case. On the motion of the advocate-general Dupaty, the protest of Bordeaux was couched in particularly blunt terms. Royal orders which contravened the law, it declared, 'ne peuvent être considérés que comme des actes passagers d'une volonté séduite et non comme les actes permanents d'une volonté raisonnée, libre et légale'.[2] There was nothing new in such ideas, but the language in which they were expressed was particularly pungent. Outraged that one of the crown lawyers should lead the opposition to its policies, the government quashed the *arrêt* and on 25 September, Dupaty was arrested and transferred to the fortress of Pierre-Encize, at Lyons, the Bastille of the south.[3] The parlement took up his case, but the arrest occurred in the depth of the vacation, and it was not until 16 January 1771 that it sent remonstrances to the king on his behalf.[4] By that time, he had been transferred to the more healthy atmosphere of nearby Roanne, and was finally released early in February.[5]

By this time, however, far more serious events were diverting the parlement's attention. By the famous edict of November 1770,[6] Maupeou had carried the conflict over the d'Aiguillon case to a new level; because although there was nothing in the letter of the edict with which the parlement of Paris could take issue, the insulting tone and innuendoes of the preamble constituted a provoking indictment of its conduct over several decades. It reacted by suspending its service, and when it resumed again early in January as a gesture of conciliation, the move was rebuffed. The strike was renewed, despite repeated royal injunctions, and it was in these circumstances that Maupeou forced the issue.[7] Asked to reply, yes or no, whether they would obey the king's orders without question, the Parisian magistrates at length almost unanimously answered no, with the result that by the end of January 1771, they were in exile.[8] In February, the jurisdiction of the parlement was divided up under a series of superior councils, competent to deal with all but the most important cases, staffed by non-venal magistrates, and dispensing justice freely, without *épices*. In April, the parlement was replaced by a new body, with the same title, but much smaller, composed and distributing justice on the same terms as the superior councils, and made up of ex-members of the court of aids, the grand council (now both suppressed), and various lower jurisdictions.[9] It was a revolution of the first magnitude, overthrowing principles on which the provincial judiciaries, quite as much as that of Paris, were based. Once again, they could hardly be expected not to protest.

The parlement of Bordeaux was in the van of the provincial protests. On 8 February it resolved to send remonstrances against the November edict, which, it declared, overthrew the fundamental laws of the realm, and which the parlement of Paris could not have registered without the calling of the Estates General.[10] This cry, originally raised by the parlement of Rouen at the end of January, was rapidly taken up by all the others in the weeks that followed.[11] The remonstrances, which also called for the return of the Paris exiles, were sent on 25 February. But by this time, the superior councils had been established. Clearly it was a question of permanent reforms, not simply disciplinary measures. A new wave of provincial protest therefore followed;[12] including new remonstrances from Bordeaux, decided upon on 26 March.[13] As before, however, the protest of Bordeaux came weeks after the first provincial outcry, and no sooner was it made than the establishment of the new parlement of Paris once more changed the ground for attack. Most parlements publicly dissociated themselves from the new body. Clearly the reforms would have to be extended if the judiciary was not to tear itself apart. As Maupeou later wrote, after the reformation of the parlement of Paris, it was impossible that the provincial parlements should not be subjected to the same operation.[14] Provincial magistrates suspected as much; and anticipating this, Bordeaux for once took an independent line. Maupeou's principle obviously was to suppress some courts in order to release magistrates for staffing others, newly-established. By an *arrêté* of 29 April 1771, the magistrates of Bordeaux now declared that:

> les obligations qu'ils ont contractées par leur serment ne leur permetront jamais d'accepter des places dans aucun des tribunaux formés ou qui pouroient l'être en remplacement des parlems toujours subsistans aux yeux de la loi . . .[15]

Other courts stopped short of such explicit declarations.[16] Yet behind this apparent intransigence the parlement was far from united, and trimmers were already mapping out their course. As early as 20 March, the procurator-general had written to Richelieu that:

nous sommes icy dans l'attente d'un prochain anéantissement: . . . Le bruit
est général à Bordeaux que vous allés incessament arriver pour exécuter sur
notre compagnie les ordres du Roy . . . j'ai toujours desiré la réforme de la
magistrature, mais je ne me preterai jamais a rien de ce qui peut tendre a sa
dégradation, ou à la diminution de sa dignité . . .[17]

On 11 May he wrote again to say that he had also been in contact with the
Chancellor:

. . . je ne luy laisse pas ignorer la façon de penser de tous nos magistrats en
cas de destruction. Il pourra dans ce cas chercher a faire une fondation
nouvelle, et composer un nouveau corps sur le protothype de Paris. on a
préféré la destruction a une réforme utile et necessaire . . .[18]

It was clear that Dudon for one would not be beyond approach in the case of a
remodelling, and letters from president de Pichard in July were equally ambiguous, disclaiming any wish to be involved, yet advising on how best to effect any
change. On 5 June the parlement condemned a pamphlet favourable to Maupeou
to be burned.[19] Richelieu was surprised that the friends of government had not
done more to prevent this: 'Il est sur', Pichard reassured him,

que ny le chef ny mr dupaty nont pas a l'exception des mineurs, et de quelques
esprits ardants baucoup de partisants dans la Compagnie; mais ils sont
partagés; on se lasse de Combattre, et dans la Conviction ou plusieurs
étoient d'une destruction ou refformation prochaine ils on evitté de se faire
des affaires particulières, imaginant que rien ne paroit l'empecher. les esprits
son ici occuppés et de la creation des Conseils superieurs, et de la refformation du parlement; avec les idées etablies et les moeurs de la nation, on ne
trouveroit dans ce parlement aucun sujet qui voulut entrer dans cette
nouvelle formation . . . et si par evenemant ce party prevaloit, je vous
demande avec le plus vive instance d'éviter qu'on ne songe a moy: la refformation du parlement presenttera bien des difficultés. La forme a prandre
est bien embarassantte. le choix des sujets quon feroit dans le cas d'une
suppression, et recreation seroit bien humiliante pour certaints; on naime
pas proffitter des depouilles de ses conffreres . . . et dans le Cas ou le malheur
que je prevois arrive, je me flate que vous eviterais qu'on ne me fait sacriffié
et que vous voudrais vous occuper et de ma fortune et du desir que j'ay de ne
rien faire qui puisse ettre blamé par mes concitoyens.[20]

Maupeou's note of 14 August can hardly have come as a surprise to the
governor. The remodellings at Besançon and Douai earlier that month announced
to the rest of the provincial parlements that the attack had begun, and that it was
only a matter of time for them all. *Lettres de cachet* of 23 August exiling the
leaders of the Bordeaux intransigents, the first president and Dupaty, announced
that the turn of Bordeaux was imminent,[21] and the parlement, certain now of
what was to follow, issued a solemn protest against all that might be done to it
after the manner of Paris, Besançon, and Douai, 'un traitement qu'elle ose croire
n'avoir jamais mérité'; it renewed the resolve of 29 April that no magistrats
would co-operate in any remodelling. This protestation was printed, and copies
circulated to the court on 2 September.[22] The next day, Richelieu arrived in the
Bordelais.

He acted swiftly. On 4 September, accompanied by the intendant Esmangart and a company of soldiers with fixed bayonets, and watched by apprehensive crowds, he went down to the *Ombrière*. On his orders, president de Gascq, presiding in the absence of Le Berthon, assembled the chambers. A move to terminate the session was stifled by the distribution of *lettres de cachet* forbidding magistrates either to leave the palace, or to inaugurate any deliberations, or to interrupt any of the proceedings. Letters patent were then registered, whose effect was to quash the *arrêtés* of 29 April and 23 August, after which new *lettres de cachet* were distributed, ordering all but five magistrates to return home at once, communicating with nobody, there to await further orders. Those who remained—Gascq, Dudon, the advocate-general Saige, and the two chief-clerks —were then apprised of an edict which suppressed all the offices in the parlement, and this was at once registered. The session over, the palace was locked.[23]

The parlement was not suppressed, but the offices which entitled their holders to sit in the court, were. The promise of compensation, also contained in the edict, showed that the government intended this suppression to be irrevocable. It was now free to nominate new personnel to the court, and new offices were established at a separate session on 7 September. The days between were spent by Richelieu in recruiting a full complement for the new court. On the night of the 4th, 35 magistrates were exiled, like Le Berthon and Dupaty, to their estates. Two women, president de Gourgue's wife and Le Berthon's sister-in-law, were also exiled.[24] These were the 'esprits ardants' to whom Pichard had referred two months before. Richelieu occupied the next two days in explanatory visits to those who remained. Not all were as amenable as he had hoped, and perhaps expected; and before the 7th, another 30 magistrates had been exiled. However, by that date, a mixture of bribes, threats, and promises had succeeded in persuading 47 others to co-operate. At least this was the number present at the second military session, for the registration of an edict creating new offices and new conditions of service in the parlement.[25] In place of the 115 offices in the old court, 53 new ones were now set up. The chamber of requests and one of the inquests were abolished. On the other hand, the provisions of new magistrates who had served in the old parlement were to remain valid. As in the superior councils and the new parlement of Paris, there were new regulations to ensure regular attendance, and payment by *épices* was abolished. Venality also disappeared. New magistrates were to be chosen by the court submitting a short-list of three candidates to the king, who would make the final choice. Letters patent registered at the same time fixed a new scale of *gages*. The session was concluded by the distribution of *lettres de cachet* to each of the magistrates of the new court, forbidding them to abandon their functions. The sittings of the parlement, due to end for the vacation on 7 September, were prolonged by letters patent to enable the new order to establish itself. Richelieu also made it clear that he would remain in Bordeaux for some time to ensure that matters went smoothly. He engineered an atmosphere of celebration by giving a lavish banquet on the night of the 7th, and ordering all the companies and corporations of the town to visit and congratulate the parlement, on the 8th. All these manoeuvres had the desired effect. The new parlement at once called for the release (but not the reintegration) of its exiled brothers, but this was a formality. There was no strike of the bar, which some had feared, nor were there any popular commotions in the town. Within a week Richelieu felt it safe to allow the vacation to begin, and letters patent to this effect were registered on 18 September.[26] The Martinmas commencement in November also passed off without trouble.[27] Nowhere, in fact, was the transition between the old order and the new more smoothly accomplished.

Undoubtedly the ease of the transition was mainly owing to the fact that so many of the old magistrates were prepared to serve under the new order. Only two of the new magistrates had not served in the parlement before. They were counsellor P. M. de Laroze, and the advocate-general J. B. P. J. Dudon, both sons of important magistrates who had consented to continue in the parlement. The only court which had bound itself not to co-operate in any remodelling, there-fore, co-operated in greater force than any of the others. Some certainly did so reluctantly, and the *lettres de cachet* which forbade the magistrates to abandon their functions were perhaps issued at their request, to permit them to claim that they had no choice but to co-operate.[28] At the head of the reconstituted parle-ment was president de Gascq, an old intimate of Richelieu, his close correspon-dent over a decade, and a skilful friend to the government. His co-operation came as no surprise. Nor did that of his cousin Pichard, or the procurator-general Dudon. Nevertheless, even these leaders did not give their services without con-ditions. Gascq requested to be relieved of his position after three years,[29] once matters had settled down, and accepted an annual 'gratification' of 20,000 l. over and above his *gages*, for as long as he remained in office.[30] In 1772 he also received a lump sum of 25,000 l. for establishing himself in due style.[31] Pichard was paid a lump sum of 6,000 l., which, after some solicitation, was made an annual pay-ment.[32] Dudon, in addition to the appointment of his son as advocate-general, was gratified with an annual payment of 6,000 l.,[33] and special concessions were also made to certain other favoured magistrates. But even without such special payments, the financial terms of service in the Maupeou parlement were very attractive. If *épices* were abolished, and the old *gages* disappeared with the sup-pression of the offices, a new, augmented scale of *gages* more than compensated:

Annual Gages, 1771–75[34]

First president	15,000 l.
President *à mortier*	6,000 l.
Counsellor-president	4,000 l.
Counsellor, grand chamber	3,000 l.
Counsellor, inquests	2,000 l.
Procurator-general	6,000 l.
Advocate-general	2,500 l.

In addition there were regular pensions of 1,500 l. for the dean, and 1,000 l. for the senior clerical counsellors. Even for those magistrates whose position in the new court was exactly the same as in the old, these sums were an improvement on previous emoluments. For those counsellors who now moved into higher cham-bers or became presidents the advantage was even clearer.[35] Such inducements help to explain the massive defection to the new order, although similar financial improvements occurred elsewhere without similar impressive results in the recruitment of personnel.

The key to Maupeou's reform did not lie in any restriction of the rights of registration or remonstrances, those twin bases of parlementaire power. They remained unchanged. It lay in the abolition of venality. When magistrates no longer had independent tenure of their offices, and when these offices were no longer hereditary, then the government might control them far more easily. Yet the government made little constructive use of this power. Indeed, it took pains to stress that magistrates remained theoretically irremovable. In appointing new candidates, it never went beyond those suggested to it by the parlement; and the parlement's short-lists were as narrow as its previous and subsequent recruitment. Of the six new magistrates replacing others[36] who had died or were promoted between 1772 and 1774, three were related to magistrates already sitting. Four of the six were certainly noble, two had legal backgrounds. They were in fact a fairly typical group, and none would have seemed out of place before 1771 or after 1775.

The most important characteristic of the new order, as far as litigants were concerned, was the abolition of *épices* and the establishment of free justice, which won for Maupeou the plaudits of Voltaire, Condorcet, and other advocates of judicial reform. However, this 'free' justice was deceptive. The new augmented *gages* of the magistrates, not to mention the sums in compensation for their suppressed offices, had to come from somewhere. So had the lavish new pensions and gratifications. The annual bill for the *gages* alone came to 206,500 l., and it was paid by an addition to the capitation. The new parlement, with less than half the numbers of the old, therefore, cost nearly twice as much.[37] The burden once borne by litigants alone was now borne by all the inhabitants of the jurisdiction on their capitation. The same shift of the burden, and a similar increase in the general cost of justice, occurred in the jurisdictions of Paris and Toulouse.[38] Not even then, however, were litigants spared their former costs. The declaration of 1 June 1771 increased the duties payable on stamped paper and fees at all stages of the judicial process. It was estimated that in the jurisdiction of Paris such payments went up by $2\frac{1}{2}$ times,[39] and in 1773 the parlement at Bordeaux protested that 'Les frais de justice excèdent de beaucoup ce qu'il en coûtoit auparavant, & avant la suppression des épices et vacations',[40] resolving to send remonstrances on the subject. So if some charges were abolished, others were raised, and removed much if not all the benefit to litigants. And nothing at all was done towards abolishing the *épices* levied by lower jurisdictions.

If justice was no cheaper under Maupeou at least it was probably more speedy. Under articles 9 and 10 of the edict establishing the new parlement, a register of attendance was to be kept by the clerk of each chamber, and *gages* were only to be paid according to attendance. The results were dramatic. Just before Christmas 1771 Gascq wrote to Richelieu that:

j'ay tenu cette aprez midy la Iere audiance de relevée, nous avons jugé plus d'une heure au flambeau ce qui n'étoit pas arrive il y a 15 ans. l'année dernière la Iere audiance de relevée fut tenue le 22 d'avril . . .[41]

'Je ne peux vous dissimuler', added Dudon a few weeks later,

L'insolence des propos que tiennent nos exilés; leur audace a considerablement augmenté depuis votre depart, et ils sont d'autant plus furieux, qu'ils ont appris qu'on avoit expédié beaucoup [plus] d'affaires depuis la rentrée du Parlement jusques a noël, qu'on n'en avoit expedié l'année dernière a lamy Caresme.[42]

And in April 1773, over a year later, it was reported that the grand chamber was still getting through far more business than in previous years.[43]

All this, as Dudon observed, was small comfort for the exiles, looking on from the country estates to which they had been banished. For Le Berthon, this meant the inhospitable fortress of Aiguilhe, near Castillon, a domain he never normally visited. '. . . je ne pourrai pas vivre ici longtemps', he complained, 'ma santé est altérée, au point qu'un peu de fievre s'en est melée depuis le moment que nous sommes arrivés . . .'[44] In 'ce maudit chateau', 'Je m' . . . ennuye à perir . . . et je m'y ennuyerai de plus en plus, jusqu'à ce que je sois mort . . .'[45]

Nevertheless, the decisiveness of the blow reduced the exiles to stunned silence, at least while Richelieu remained in Bordeaux. It was even rumoured that some of them were now prepared to serve in the new parlement.[46] However, once the governor had departed, and the Martinmas commencement had passed uneventfully, they became restless. By Christmas, the members of the remodelled court were worried because the exiles were referring to themselves as members of the *old* parlement, implying that what existed was a new one. '. . . ils se disent officiers de l'ancien Parlement', wrote Dudon,

> que cet ancien Parlement toujours subsistant est essentiellement opposé au nouveau, qui n'est composé que de Gueux et de Canaille: ce sont leur propos, c'est leur sistheme. Pour moy, je crois tres fort etre de l'ancien Parlement, et qu'ils n'en sont plus, que ce titre de President ou Conseiller de l'ancien Parlement meriteroit punition, et que si on dissimule on court risque de voir empirer le mal, et la contagion se glisser dans notre Compagnie . . .[47]

The exiles were encouraged by wavering within the ranks of the remodelled parlement. Within weeks of the remodelling the abbé Barbeguière was asking, with no success, to be excused.[48] By December counsellor de Castelnau was visibly dissatisfied too.[49] Gascq was unsure how to deal with requests to resign:

> . . . une reponse trop doulce auroit l'air de la foiblesse et seroit peu decente pour la place que j'occupe, si au contraire ma réponse est ferme on dira qu'elle est trop fort qu'on n'est pas des esclaves que quand quelqu'un veut s'en aller il faut luy ouvrir les portes &c . . .[50]

By the end of February Castelnau was creating such a bad impression, making only token appearances, refusing to vote, and hiding himself in the country, that Gascq advised the government to let him go.[51] But no sooner had he gone, than counsellor de Cursol, one of the most respected mainstays of the new order, began to talk of retirement after the government refused to compensate him in full for the loss of his office.[52] A delay in the payment of *gages*, in arrears since 1769, also created a more general discontent in the company.[53]

What made all these petty discontents serious, was that they coincided with the reception for registration by the parlement of a number of important but controversial government edicts. The most important was the edict of November

1771, which made the first twentieth in effect perpetual by making its revocation dependent on the state of the finances, prolonged the second twentieth until 1781, and imposed additional surcharges.[54] There was also, however, the edict of 2 June 1771 reforming the administration of mortgages, which had run into trouble with the parlement before the remodelling;[55] the declaration of 1 June under which the crown resumed various financial alienations;[56] and an edict supplementary to the suppression of offices in the parlement of 4 September which suppressed the two honorific positions of knight of honour.[57] The edict on the twentieths evoked remonstrances that winter from Paris, Toulouse, Grenoble, Aix, Dijon, and Rennes.[58] But nowhere was opposition carried so far as at Bordeaux. 'Il est bien malheureux, mon tres cher Seigneur', Gascq complained to Richelieu, 'qu'on ait ette oblige d'envoyer tant d'edits Bursaux à une compagnie ou il y a encor quelques esprits malades de la suppression du 7 7bre. Ils ont cauzé beaucoup d'humeur . . .'[59] 'Je feray de mon mieux', he warned, for there were

> d'excellentes raisons pour ne pas pousser les choses a l'extremité . . . mais le Qu'endiraton est souvent plus fort que tout cela . . . les exilez font courir toutes sortes de bruits tres desavantageux sur notre compte et entrautres qu'on verra bien que le parlement est enervé par l'enregistrement de la continuation du 20eme. Vous sentez mon tres cher Seigneur combien cela est fait pour transporter des gascons et les empecher de se preter aux circonstances.[60]

When the twentieth edict was submitted in January for registration, therefore, the parlement resolved to follow the general example and send remonstrances against it,[61] begging the king to withdraw the edict, and emphasizing how the tax burden had risen over the previous 30 years, and how the coming of peace in 1763 had hardly alleviated it. These arguments were supported, not only with the usual string of precedents, but with a detailed analysis of the effect of taxation on the wine trade, a subject that magistrates were well placed to explain.[62] While it waited for a reply, the parlement maintained itself in a state of outrage by subjecting the edict to suppress the knights of honour, and the edict on mortgages, to severe criticism.[63]

The king's reply to the remonstrances, dated 1 February, was conciliatory in tone, but he refused to withdraw or modify the edict.[64] 'Touts les propos', concluded Gascq,

> annoncent les dispositions les plus contraires à un enregistrement libre. les peuples sont surchargés d'impots, on veut les en accabler, qu'elles ressources emploiraton dans une guerre malheureuse? le roi est le maitre de faire ce qu'il voudra par voye d'authorité, nous ne pourrons en nottre honeur et conscience contribuer a un si grand mal. y consentir seroit nous perdre de reputation nous discrediter au point de ne pouvoir plus être utiles au roi en aucun genre. nous donerions beau jeu aux exilez qui disent et ont prevu que le parlement s'enerve, qu'il nest resté que des faquins qu'on paye pour sacriffier le peuple . . . on nous fait venir icy, dit on, pour dire librement nostre avis sans quoy il est fort inutile que nous y venions, pourquoy vouloir nous contraindre a dire ce que nous ne pensons pas? . . . la conservation des peuples est notre premier devoir, de quel oeuil pourraton regarder des magistrats qui auront voté pour la ruine de l'etat aprèz dix ans de paix? Si

on nous prend le dernier ecu qu'on nous laisse l'honeur. Voila mon tres cher
Seigneur ce que j'entends touts les jours au palais et dans la conversation ...
certains ajoutent mais on nous dit sans cessé qu'on n'a pas besoin de notre
enregistrement a la bone heure pourquoy donc le solliciter avec tant de
chaleur? qu'on envoye un porteur des ordres, quand on procedera par voye
d'authorité absolue. Nous protestons pour conserver l'image de la liberté à
nos descendants et nous ne serons point compromis parceque nous n'avons
point contribué à la perte de l'etat ... quand on parle a nos confrères des
exemples des austres parlements &c ils levent les épaules, c'est le moyen
presisement de leur faire prendre le party oppozé, ils se croyent d'un austre
aloy et desirent beaucoup le faire sentir au public. vous sçavez que l'opinion
est la reine du monde . . .[65]

He predicted a refusal to register all three fiscal edicts, and a new set of remonstrances were resolved upon and sent on 19 February;[66] separate ones were dispatched on each of the other two fiscal edicts.[67] The king remained, however,
unyielding, and this created uproar in the parlement. The inquests, led by the
abbé Barbeguière and counsellor de Montalier, immediately insisted on another
set of remonstrances,[68] but before they could be sent, the king dispatched formal
letters of *jussion* (2 March) ordering an end to the matter through immediate
registration.[69] They were ignored; on 18 March the new remonstrances were
sent, at the same time as a similar set on the same subject from the court of aids.
Clearly protest was spreading. President de Loret wrote to Bertin on 26 March
that new letters of *jussion* were necessary,[70] but Gascq held out little hope.
'. . . veritablement', he wrote, 'je ne crois pas qu'on registre un seul édit de finance
volontairement sur les lett. de jussion'.[71]

The resistance of the parlement had by this time acquired a more than local
significance. Other parlements had protested against the twentieths, but most
confined their protests to the limits laid down by the edict of November 1772.[72]
Having made their protest in remonstrances, they proceeded to register the edict
without further resistance. All this showed that Maupeou's system worked;
Louis XV by 1771 had decided that it was worth being called a despot if the tire-
some opposition of the parlements was broken once and for all. Maupeou's position in the government therefore depended upon his ability to ensure this. Equally,
the best hope for the Chancellor's rivals on the council lay in demonstrating to the
king that Maupeou had failed. In the case of Bordeaux, at least, by April 1771 it
began to look as if he had, and it became imperative for Maupeou to end the
attacks, and the grounds for them, by an act of authority. On 10 April the comte
de Fumel,[73] commandant of the *Château Trompette*, deputizing for Richelieu,
held a military session at the parlement at which he ordered the forcible registration of all four disputed measures. The moment the session was over, however,
the assembled chambers passed an *arrêté* of protest, which promised further
remonstrances.[74] There was nothing extraordinary about this *arrêté*. It was the
sort of protest that parlements usually made after forcible registrations; if anything, its language was more restrained than was usual in such cases. Gascq
expended much effort in making it sound as respectful as possible, and in ensuring that the parlement did not attempt to prevent the implementation of the
forcibly registered measures.[75] Nevertheless, it announced that the transcription

undermined legal forms, and that:

> les progrès, des Subsides, & cette manière de les introduire, ne laissent plus
> rien de stable dans les propriétés des Sujets dudit Seigneur Roi . . . ce genre
> d'exercice de son autorité accorde un libre cours à l'arbitraire & ne laisse
> plus aucun moyen d'arrêter les surprises qui pourroient être faits à sa
> Religion & a sa Justice . . .

It was not printed or published. It was, so Gascq protested, simply a testa-
ment to posterity on the parlement's true feelings.[76] And indeed in normal
times, even printed, such a carefully termed protest would have passed practically
unnoticed. But these were not normal times. This was only the second forced
registration in the whole of France since the remodelling, and the first such protest; moreover, whatever the parlement's precautions, its terms were soon known.
The king was furious at its language, and Maupeou's rivals encouraged his displeasure. The magistrates of Maupeou's own choice, said d'Aiguillon, were now
rebelling against him. If their protests were quashed, they would resign, yet the
court could not be dissolved as a reply without vitiating the principle of irre-
movability so loudly proclaimed the year before. Nor could a superior council be
put in its place without replacing other parlements, too; besides, the king had
already rejected such extreme courses, and Bertin and Terray now reiterated that
he had been right to do so, for the name of parlement bred public confidence.
Maupeou countered that such an apocalyptic analysis distorted the gravity of the
crisis out of all proportion. He was sure that it would be enough to quash the
offending *arrêt*. Others rallied to his side, and the king eventually agreed that it
should be condemned in strong terms.[77]

By now, however, rumours were circulating that the parlement of Bordeaux
was to be remodelled yet again, and that a superior council was to be set up at
Libourne. Most magistrates were horrified that their *arrêté* had had such results.
Dudon told Richelieu that he was 'in despair',[78] and Gascq very pessimistic:

> je vous diray avec verité que votre présence est fort necessaire icy pour la
> consolidation du parlem^t qui est votre ouvrage . . . si vous ne veniez dans le
> courant de may au plus tard a la fin, je crains qu'il n'arrive quelque sotise
> quelque division qui se trouvera excitée par les poliçons que vous savez . . .[79]

Meanwhile, the parlement hurried to repair the damage, and on 5 May it issued
another *arrêté* clarifying and glossing the first.[80] There was no immediate reply,
and the rumours continued to circulate, but during the second week in May the
government decided to send Richelieu. The *arrêté* of 5 May seems to have been
decisive in lowering the temperature, by showing that the magistrates were true
to Maupeou's principles after all. The decision to send Richelieu seems to have
been motivated by a desire to make their repentance permanent. But it remained
to decide what exactly the governor was to do. Gascq's idea was to give complete
satisfaction to the government, by supplementing the *arrêté* of 5 May with even
more explicit promises of obedience to be put in the remonstrances decided upon
on 10 April, but not yet sent. This would make any act of authority unnecessary,
and Richelieu's visit would merely serve to quell any continuing excitement. But
the government was determined to have the last word, and have it publicly, and
this meant some form of military session. The very thought horrified Gascq: he

was afraid that such measures would only prolong the trouble by provoking further protests, which might in their turn lead to the destruction of the parlement itself. His last letter to Richelieu before the marshal left Paris contained a threat to resign if the conflict was prolonged.[81]

Richelieu arrived in Bordeaux during the second week of June, and on the 17th he held a military session at the parlement where he forced the registration of a new set of letters patent.[82] A preamble recognized that the *arrêté* of 5 May had modified that of 10 April, and expressed royal satisfaction. The letters went on to stipulate that in future, during military sessions no magistrate was to leave his place or take any initiative until registration of the measures in question was complete, that such measures were to take effect as if freely registered, and that the parlement was to do nothing which would suspend or prevent them from taking effect; without prejudice, however, to the right of remonstrance. The point of these letters was simply to give the government the last word. The clause directing magistrates to remain in their places seemed to arise from the events of 4 September 1771 rather than 10 April 1772. The right of remonstrance was in no way restricted; the clause forbidding the parlement to hold up the execution of forcibly registered edicts, forbade it to do what it had not done in any case. So the remonstrances Gascq had spoken of never appeared. Richelieu was able, in concert with Gascq, Dudon, and the influential Cursol, to finish the affair once and for all, and on 27 June Maupeou wrote to congratulate him on his success.[83]

Since he was now in Bordeaux, Richelieu took the opportunity to clear up a number of minor matters. He held a military session at the court of aids, which, after having remonstrated over the twentieth edict, had only registered it on condition that the assessments for the tax were not raised in any way. These modifications were quashed.[84] He dismissed and exiled counsellor de Montalier, one of the leaders of resistance throughout the spring, who after the session of 10 April had insulted Gascq and asked to be allowed to resign.[85] Above all, his very presence, as Gascq had predicted, was enough to dissipate the excitement of the previous few months. After his departure early in August, matters continued to go smoothly, and the first year of the Maupeou parlement ended calmly after all.

It was a bitter blow for the hopes of the exiles. If the remodelled parlement was dissolved, it would almost certainly have to be replaced by a court made up of some of them at least. It was unlikely, in view of its attitude to the twentieths, that the court of aids would let itself be suppressed in order to replace a parlement dissolved for similar opposition, and certainly there were no other adequately qualified magistrates locally. So the exiles had attempted so far as they could to promote trouble in the parlement. Their attempts had seriously worried the magistrates who had remained, and who wavered between wishing for conciliation and severity. Gascq seems to have written at some point to Le Berthon offering to take some of the exiles who wished it back into the parlement,[86] and the abbé Barbeguière proposed that the process begin in replacing counsellor de Castelnau.[87] On the other hand, Gascq was upset when the terms of exile of certain of them were softened:

> come mauvesin par exemple qui est un fol, un menteur, un esprit de travers un Boutefeu et un insolent du premier ordre . . . les lavie, les poissac, les dupaty . . . ont esté traitez avec trop de menagement . . . Il y a de bones gens,

il y a des sots dans le nombre. Il suffit que ceux la ne soint pas a Bordx. il y a cinq ou six insensez et tres mauvais sujets qui ont manque au roi, ceux la doivent estre punis en touts sens et je ne seray jamais d'avis d'adoucir leur etat.[88]

In early summer their hopes were dashed all at once. Not only was the crisis resolved, but an edict was issued which gave them until 1 January 1773 to send in documents proving their right to compensation for their suppressed offices on pain of confiscation. But of course, to do this would be to recognize the legality of what had happened: '. . . eh bien qu'ils confisquent nos charges', wrote Dupaty, nous pouvons les laisser prendre, mais nous ne pouvons les donner . . . Si on liquide, tout est fini . . .'[89] 'Je ne liquideray pas', declared Le Berthon, on discovering that his tax assessments had been vindictively raised. 'L'honneur est au dessus des punitions pécuniaires'.[90]

This question rapidly replaced hopes for the destruction of the new parlement as the main topic of the exiles' speculation, and so it remained throughout the autumn. When 1 January came, Maupeou did not prolong the final date (as he did repeatedly for the Paris exiles) and those who had not liquidated, including Dupaty and Le Berthon, suffered confiscation of their offices without compensation.[91] Twenty-nine offices occupied by non-members of the Maupeou parlement were scheduled for liquidation under the declaration of 22 May 1773, in addition to 51 owned by magistrates who had co-operated. This means that some 35 magistrates had refused to liquidate, and seen their offices confiscated.[92] After January 1773 it must really have seemed, as Dupaty had predicted, as if all was over.

Nothing illustrates better than the history of Maupeou's ministry the fact that great events can depend on trivial causes. It arose out of a battle between ambitious individuals—Maupeou and Choiseul—for the favour of Louis XV. In the course of it, powerful men at Court and in the parlement of Paris took up extreme positions from which they were unable to extricate themselves; and so by a series of accidents and miscalculations on all sides a clash of personalities became a *coup d'état*. 'Quelles sont les causes de la pérsécution que nous éprouvons?', wrote president de Brosses, of Dijon.

> Des faits auxquels nous n'avons aucune espèce de part: une intrigue de Cour pour chasser un ministre, la vengeance qu'on vouloit prendre contre le Parlement de Paris. Pour donner à ceci d'autres apparences et quelque espèce de suite, on nous enveloppe dans cette étrange révolution . . .[93]

Provincial magistrates could not avoid involvement. The constitutional questions raised by Maupeou's act of authority affected them quite as much as their Parisian colleagues. If Maupeou could dissolve and reconstruct the parlement of Paris at will, he could and did do the same to the others. It was the ease with which these hallowed institutions were knocked down and remodelled which shocked constitutionally-minded men. Maupeou taught Frenchmen that there was nothing the king could not do, if he had a mind to it. He turned despotism from an academic point for the theorists into an urgent problem of practical politics. He thus set the tone of political discussion for the next two decades. It was no coincidence that the call for the Estates-General first became serious in 1771.

The real source of discontent was not so much the changes as the power by which they were made; and in Bordeaux at least the changes themselves were minimal. It kept its parlement; along with all the others it kept its rights of registration and remonstrance; the magistrates, although venality disappeared, remained theoretically irremovable. So if there was 'despotism', it was exercised with restraint and took care not to show itself too openly through institutions. Those who co-operated in Maupeou's reform soon convinced themselves, too, that it was a myth. But of course it was in their interests to do so. The real despotism lay elsewhere, in the treatment of their former colleagues. The exiles were confined to their estates by *lettre de cachet* for no crime and no cause shown; in fact for the sake of political convenience. Not only that, they were summarily deprived of the exercise of their profession, their status in the world, and their property and patrimony in the form of their offices. Political convenience was again the excuse. The offer of compensation did nothing to make the exiles and confiscations more legal or just.

Those who co-operated in the reforms, therefore, connived not simply at an administrative reorganization, but at their former colleagues' discomfiture. Those who opted to stay, though they could hardly have realized it, were making a wager on Louis XV's constancy and his continued good health. If they won, they earned more money, and maintained their social and professional positions. If they lost, they had compromised themselves for nothing. For nothing was more certain than that, whatever their constitutional principles, the exiles would never forgive them for a personal betrayal.

NOTES

1. BVC Richelieu XV, f.238, Maupeou to Richelieu, 14 Aug. 1771.
2. J. Flammermont, *Le Chancelier Maupeou et les Parlements* (Paris, 1883), 96–7; J. Egret, *Louis XV et l'opposition parlementaire* (Paris, 1970), 177.
3. Flammermont, loc. cit., 94–9.
4. BLR MS 1903, f.10, Dupaty to de Sèze, 1771 (precise date uncertain); remonstrances in AN K708, no. 51.
5. Du Paty de Clam papers. Letter of Maupeou, 1 Dec. 1770; Besterman, *Voltaire's Correspondence*, LXXIII, no. 16003, Voltaire to Servan, 22 Feb. 1771, shows he visited Ferney on his way home.
6. Text in Flammermont, op. cit., 116–20.
7. See ibid., chs. 4 and 5, *passim*, and Egret, op. cit., 177–9.
8. Edict of 23 Feb. 1771, Flammermont, op. cit., ch. 7. See also R. Villers, *L'Organisation du parlement de Paris et des conseils supérieurs d'après la réforme de Maupeou (1771–1774)* (Paris, 1937), *passim*.
9. Flammermont, op. cit., ch. 8; Egret, op. cit., 183–9.
10. BPR Le Paige 570, pièce 94, *arrêté* of the parlement, 8 Feb. 1771.
11. Flammermont, op. cit., 254–65.
12. ibid., 306–20.
13. BPR Le Paige 570, pièce 96, *arrêté* of the parlement, 26 March 1771.
14. 'Memoire au Roi', 1788. Printed in Flammermont, op. cit., 630.
15. BPR Le Paige 570, pièce 97, *arrêté* of the parlement, 29 April 1771. See also Boscheron des Portes, *Histoire du Parlement de Bordeaux*, II, 311–12, and Flammermont, op. cit., 393.
16. ibid., 386–93.
17. BVC Richelieu XV, f.188 vo., Dudon to Richelieu, 20 March 1771.
18. ibid., f.193, same to same, 11 May 1771.
19. BPR Le Paige 570, pièce 98, *arrêté* of the parlement, 5 June 1771.
20. BVC Richelieu XV, ff.205 vo.–206. Pichard to Richelieu, 1 July 1771.

21. Dupaty's *lettre de cachet* is in the Du Paty de Clam papers; C. Henri, *Correspondance inédite de Condorcet et de Turgot, 1770–1779* (Paris, 1882), 66. Condorcet to Turgot, 26 Aug. 1771.
22. BPR Le Paige 570, pièce 99, protestation of the parlement, 23 Aug. 1771. Ten magistrates, including Gascq, seem to have opposed this protestation. *Journal historique de la révolution opérée dans la constitution de la monarchie française par M. de Maupeou, chancelier de France* (Londres, 1775), II, 149–50.
23. Accounts of these proceedings are numerous. The official government *procès-verbal* is printed in *AHDG*, XXIV (1884–85), 432. There is also a copy in AD C3630. Other accounts are in BPR Le Paige 570, pièces 99 and 100, and *Journal historique*, II, 132–3, 139–40. There are secondary accounts in Flammermont, op. cit., 453–6, and Boscheron des Portes, op. cit., II, 313–14.
24. Flammermont, loc. cit., 456.
25. *Journal historique*, II, 149–50, 174–5; AD IB 52, ff.134–5, 'Edit portant création d'offices dans le parlement de Bordeaux (Compiègne, août 1771)'. See also Boscheron des Portes, op. cit., II, 314–15.
26. Flammermont, op. cit., 456–7; AD IB 52, f.137, letters patent of 13 Sept. 1771.
27. AD C48, intendant to chancellor, 16 Nov. 1771.
28. Boscheron des Portes, op. cit., II, 321; L. Desgraves in *Bordeaux au XVIIIe siècle*, 46; Flammermont, op. cit., 458; BVBx MS 1201, II, 8–9 Sept. 1771.
29. BVC Richelieu XVIII, Gascq to Richelieu, 27 Aug. 1774.
30. AD C3631, Maupeou to Richelieu, 13 Sept. 1771.
31. AN O¹266, 'Décisions du Roy, 1771–3', f.55, *bon* 23 Feb. 1772.
32. ibid., f.33, *bon* 29 Sept. 1771; AD C3631; BVC Richelieu XV, f.238, Pichard to Richelieu, 6 Oct. 1771.
33. AD C3631; AN H 91, dossier I.
34. AN H 91, dossier I. This broadly confirms the lists presented in Boscheron des Portes, op. cit., II, 314–15, and Grellet-Dumazeau, *La Société Bordelaise*, 332, although there are minor differences.
35. For previous and subsequent conditions, see above, pp. 40–9; also Appendix II, for a list of members of the Maupeou parlement.
36. See Appendix II.
37. In a Maupeou year, *gages* came to 206,500 l. for 53 magistrates. In 1779, *gages, épices*, and *aprèsdinées* from all sources came to 111,660 l. for 113 magistrates (chief-clerks excluded).
38. For Paris, see Villers, *L'Organisation du parlement de Paris*, 72–4; for Toulouse, see Flammermont, op. cit., 482–3, and *Essai historique sur la dernière révolution de l'ordre civil en France* (Londres, 1782), I, 150ff. Also Egret, op. cit., 197–8.
39. Villers, loc. cit., 73.
40. AM fonds ancien sér. FF 5ᵇ contains a copy of this, the *arrêt d'enregistrement*, 2 Aug. 1773, of the declaration which promulgated the arrangements for compensation of suppressed offices, 22 May 1773. Quoted also in Flammermont, loc. cit., 482.
41. BVC Richelieu XLI, no. 74, Gascq to Richelieu, undated, but the contents place it clearly before Christmas 1771.
42. ibid., XVI, f.134, Dudon to Richelieu, 9 Jan. 1772.
43. *Journal historique*, IV, 149.
44. AM Fonds Delpit 134 (papiers de famille, Le Berthon), Le Berthon to Roborel de Climens, 5 Sept. 1771.
45. ibid., same to same, 7 Sept. 1771.
46. BN MSS Fr. n.a. 4388, 'Journal de nouvelles' of d'Albertas, III, ff.1139–40, 12 Nov. 1771.
47. loc. cit. above, n. 42. The letters of Gascq around this date show a great preoccupation with this problem.
48. BN loc. cit. above, n. 46.
49. BVC loc. cit. above, n. 41.
50. ibid., XVII, f.110, Gascq to Richelieu, 28 Dec. 1771.
51. ibid. The Castelnau case is a constant theme in Gascq's letters to Richelieu throughout the spring. The letter of 29 Feb. 1772 (f.140) shows that by then it had been decided to let him go.

52. ibid., XVII, ff.121ff., same to same, 8 Feb. 1772.
53. ibid., XVI, f.19, Dudon to Richelieu, 10 March 1772.
54. Preamble in Isambert, Jourdan, Crusy, *Recueil générale*, XXII, 540. Analysis in M. Marion, *Histoire financière de la France depuis 1715* (Paris, 1914–28), I, 265–7.
55. Isambert, Jourdan, Crusy, op. cit., XXII, 530–7; Marion, op. cit., 261–2.
56. ibid., 263; not in Isambert.
57. The text of this edict (Dec. 1771), along with the others forcibly registered on 10 April 1772, is in AD IB 52, ff.140 vo.–174. A printed copy in AN AD XVI 13^B.
58. Flammermont, op. cit., 516–17; Egret, op. cit., 202–5.
59. BVC Richelieu XVII, f.104, Gascq to Richelieu, 13 Jan. 1772. (It is dated 1771, but clearly, from the content, this is a new-year slip.)
60. ibid., XVII, f.110, same to same, 28 Dec. 1771.
61. ibid., f.113, same to same, 11 Jan. 1772.
62. AN K708 no. 53, remonstrances of 18 Jan. 1772. For a fuller analysis, see below, pp. 209–10.
63. BVC Richelieu XVII, f.117, Gascq to Richelieu, 25 Jan. 1772.
64. ibid., f.119, copy of the reply, sent by Gascq to Richelieu, 8 Feb. 1772.
65. ibid., ff.121ff., Gascq to Richelieu, 8 Feb. 1772.
66. AN K708 no. 54.
67. BVC Richelieu XVII, f.136, Gascq to Richelieu, 18 Feb. 1772.
68. ibid., f.142, Gascq to Maupeou, 2 March 1772; remonstrances of 18 March 1772 in AN K708 no. 49. See also below, p. 224.
69. AN K708 no. 49.
70. AN E3701, letter-book of Bertin, 1772–73.
71. BVC Richelieu XVII, f.164, Gascq to Richelieu, 7 April 1772.
72. Rennes, Dijon, Besançon, and Grenoble held out longer. Flammermont, op. cit., 516.
73. Joseph de Fumel (1720–93). Comte de Fumel; governor of the *Château Trompette*, lieutenant-general, 1773; commander-in-chief in Guienne, 1786–87 and 1788–89; mayor of Bordeaux, 1789–91; executed 1793.
74. *Journal historique*, III, 112, 12 May 1772; BVC Richelieu XVI, f.39, Loret to Richelieu, 11 April 1772.
75. Text in BN Albertas, III, 1224; also *Journal historique*, III, 110–11, 12 May 1772.
76. BVC Richelieu XVII, f.146, Gascq to Richelieu, 14 April 1772.
77. Flammermont, op. cit., 517–18.
78. BVC Richelieu XVI, f.45, Dudon to Richelieu, 2 May 1772.
79. ibid., loc. cit. above, n. 76.
80. BN Albertas, III, 1240ff., 18 June 1772, and 1273ff., 1 Aug. 1772. I have been unable to discover the precise text of this *arrêté*, but its effect is clearly enough chronicled.
81. BVC Richelieu XVII, f.159, Gascq to Richelieu 26 May 1772.
82. AD IB 52, ff.174 vo.–177, letters patent of 31 May 1772. Text also in BN Albertas, III, 1273ff., 1 Aug. 1772.
83. BVC Richelieu XVI, f.70, Maupeou to Richelieu, 27 June 1772.
84. ibid., f.71, same to same, same date; f.72, same to same, 29 June 1772; f.83, same to same, 17 July 1772.
85. ibid., XVII, f.146, Gascq to Richelieu, 14 April 1772; XVI, f.86, Maupeou to Richelieu, 18 July 1772; BLR MS 1903, f.158, Dupaty to de Sèze, 22 April 1772; f. 202, same to same, 5 June 1772.
86. This seems to be the meaning of certain dark phrases in various letters—BVC Richelieu XLI, f.76, Gascq to Richelieu, 20 Jan. 1772; BLR MS 1903, f.158, Dupaty to de Sèze, 22 April 1772.
87. BVC Richelieu XVI, f.39, Loret to Richelieu, 11 April 1772.
88. ibid., XVII, f.140, Gascq to Richelieu, 29 Feb. 1772.
89. BLR MS 1903, f.178 vo., Dupaty to de Sèze (May 1772?).
90. AD 2E 1091 (tit. fam. Duval), Le Berthon to Duval, 11 Oct. 1772.
91. BLR MS 1903, f.244 vo., Dupaty to de Sèze (Jan. 1772?); and ff.248 vo.–249, same to same, 7 Jan. 1773. I have been unable to discover the exact number who 'liquidated'.
92. AM Fonds ancien FF 5^b, Declaration of 22 May 1773, schedule.
93. T. Foisset, *Le Président de Brosses: histoire des lettres et des parlements au XVIIIe siècle* (Paris, 1842), 319, de Brosses to marquise de Damas d'Antigny, undated.

CHAPTER 11

Recrimination: The Aftermath of Maupeou

In 1771 the parlement of Bordeaux was remodelled for reasons remote from its own activities. The same was true of its reintegration in 1775. The only difference was that the reintegration was, if anything, even more unexpected.

1773 was politically uneventful. The position of the Chancellor seemed firmer than ever. It was true that the parlement of Paris was being dragged through the dirt by the case of Beaumarchais versus Goezmann, that pamphlets bitterly hostile to Maupeou continued to be published, that most of the peers remained firm in their refusal to recognize the new parlement of Paris, and that the duc d'Aiguillon continued to seek ways of overthrowing Maupeou. There was even trouble with the parlements of Grenoble, Dijon, and Besançon.[1] Nevertheless, the king remained firm, for Maupeou had undoubtedly procured him a life quieter than he had had for years. From the ill-informed distance of the provinces, the permanence of the new order must have seemed certain. The release of most of the 1771 exiles in the course of 1772 and 1773 emphasized the government's confidence in its work. Gascq advised in August 1773 that all except Dupaty, Poissac, Loyac, and Mauvezin might safely be given their liberty.[2] In 1773 the parlement became involved in a major food crisis which afflicted the whole of the south-west, and when it was over, outspoken remonstrances were sent to the king, calling for the freeing of the corn trade.[3] But these events in no way affected the political standing of the parlement; if anything, the prompt action taken by Gascq to assure the grain supply increased public confidence in the new order. The magistrates could ignore the social discourtesies to which they were still occasionally subjected, and the malicious tongues of women of fashion,[4] confident in the ever-increasing security of their position.

Then, early in May 1774, everything was plunged back into uncertainty when the king died. The new king was young and unsure of himself; he recalled Maurepas from exile to advise him. All over France the opponents of the new order suddenly saw the unexpected possibility of its being reversed. The formalities of the accession required that all governors and intendants should proceed to their provinces,[5] and Richelieu arrived in Bordeaux on 22 June.[6] Gascq wrote in advance to warn him that the exiles proposed to visit him to convey their respects, and, doubtless, to sound him out on the possibilities of a restoration. To receive such avowed enemies of the government, he warned, would make the worst impression.[7] Richelieu's last sojourn in Bordeaux (for that is what it proved to be) was a drab affair compared to his previous visits. Mourning made the usual social round out of order, and as soon as the essential formalities of his stay were over, he made ready to depart,[8] although not before he had written to Maupeou to report rumours that the old parlement was to be restored, and say that the whole of Bordeaux was restless as a result.[9] By this time, however, Maupeou's own fate was in the balance, and on 24 August he and Terray were dismissed in the 'Ministers' St Bartholomew'. Popular jubilation, and the insults which were openly directed at the parlement of Paris in the days which followed, left no doubt of what public opinion took Maupeou's fall to mean. The matter took some weeks yet to be decided in the council, but as far as the world outside was concerned, the return of the parlements was a foregone conclusion.

Richelieu left Bordeaux on 10 August, and his departure was the signal for new disturbances. Gascq was sent an anonymous letter apparently threatening his life, and encountered hostility everywhere. He grumbled that the government was not behaving with due gratitude towards a parlement which had faithfully served its purposes.[10] He even pondered aloud to Richelieu on resignation, warning that he would take the whole company with him. By 26 August he was writing to ask Richelieu to permit him to go:

> ce n'est pas que je croye a la possibilité d'un changement dans les parlements de province mais tant de raisons reunies de santé, de fortune, de convenance et de désir de ma liberté demandent que je m'en aille . . .

He recalled that in 1771 he had not agreed to serve beyond September 1774.[11] The news from Paris on 27 August lent urgency to his claim. Clearly, if the parlement there was restored following the fall of Maupeou, then the provincial courts would be reintegrated too.[12] By the Martinmas commencement, the restoration of the parlements of Rouen and Paris, the Paris court of aids, and the grand council had been announced, leaving no doubt that his fears would be realized; but by this time he had left Bordeaux forever.[13]

Meanwhile, the exiles were jubilant. Although few were still confined to their estates, most had been forbidden to go to Bordeaux itself. Even these restrictions were now lifted.[14] In September Dupaty wrote cautiously:

> Si nous sommes retablis, j'ai resolu d'etre moderé, modeste, digne de la victoire. quel poids nos malheurs ont ajoutés à nos devoirs. il n'est pas aisé d'honorer la mauvaise fortune. jespere pourtant que je rapporterai dans le sanctuaire de la justice une ame libre, courage, le zele et l'amour des lois . . .[15]

But not all the exiles had made such generous resolves.

The Maupeou parlement had warning of what to expect in its quarrel with the company of advocates, which broke out in July 1774 and dragged on into the following spring. The timing hardly seemed a coincidence. Etienne de Polverel was a well-established advocate of 15 years' standing who in the course of a case insulted the court of *jurats*.[16] They complained to the parlement, which referred the matter to the procurator-general. At once the order of advocates protested that it had the right to discipline its own members, but the parlement insisted on judging the case. The advocates on 20 July demonstrated their disapproval by withdrawing from all sessions of the grand chamber and the *tournelle* until their rights should be recognized.[17] The hearing of all cases came to a standstill, and Polverel, rather than face charges before the parlement, left for Paris to lay his case before the council. The parlement thereupon fined him in his absence, and suspended him from the bar for three years; and so the breach widened yet further. It was not healed when the parlement dispersed for the vacation, and it persisted into the spring of 1775. The Maupeou parlement ended its brief career boycotted by the bar, in a way it had succeeded in avoiding when it began.

How had this confused and seemingly pointless affair come to such a pass? Basically, it was through the nervous oversensitivity of the magistrates. When Polverel was examined at an early stage in the proceedings, it was not his remarks about the *jurade* that the magistrates seized upon, but the fact that he had referred to members of the *tournelle* as *juges*, and their decision as a *jugement*.[18] Members of the parlement were senators, magistrates, but not mere judges. They gave their decisions in *arrêts* and *arrêtés*, but not mere judgements. Such technical points of terminology might have passed unnoticed in normal times, but in July 1774, when the legitimacy of the parlement as it stood was once more being called in question, they looked like an implicit attack on the court. Polverel was well known for his disapproval of the events of 1771,[19] and his remarks looked like part of the exiles' campaign of denigration. No wonder the parlement stood firm. But it was a mis-guided firmness. Events were moving against the existing order, and the boycott by the bar made the court an object of ridicule at a time when many people were satisfied to see it reviled. When in January 1775 the council suspended the sentence on Polverel pending its own examination of the case, it was seen as yet another sign that the Maupeou parlement's days were numbered.[20] Meanwhile Polverel was the toast of the restored parlement of Paris, before which he had begun to practise.[21]

By this time the magistrates themselves were trimming to the wind. The advocate-general Saige took the side of Polverel in the discussions over his case, well aware that in a short time this stand might put him in a more favourable light.[22] Late in February, Dudon the younger hurriedly sent in his resignation as advocate-general, to avoid the summary ejection which he realized was imminent.[23] Pichard had already sent two notes on his circumstances to the government.[24] Pointing out that he had been a faithful member of the Maupeou parlement and had presided over it during Gascq's lengthy absences he now asked for 'quelque dedomagement qui puisse le soutenir honorablement dans le parlement, ou l'en faire sortir d'une manière qui annonce que ses services sont agréables'. The second note was even more explicit:

> On ne doit pas se dissimuler, que d'abord apres que la reunion generale des officiers du parlement sera consommée, il y aura necessairement dans cette compagnie deux partis: l'un compose des magistrats anciens, et l'autre des magistrats actuels: donner trop de superiorité a un des deux partis, c'est accabler ou échauffer davantage l'autre; les traiter a peu pres egalement, c'est les aneantir et procurer par la meme le plus grand bien.

This would best be brought about by designating him, Pichard, as the ultimate successor to Le Berthon as first president. Such an announcement would both reassure those who had served under Maupeou and deter the returned exiles from vindictive reprisals. Above all, of course, it would get Pichard out of an awkward position. Failing this, he declared, only the headship of another parlement or a seat on the council of state could compensate him for the 'traits de l'envie et de la malignité' which he seemed likely soon to encounter. These views were ignored. But time proved him a better prophet than advocate.

All over France, throughout the winter of 1774–75, the return of the parlements was greeted with scenes of popular enthusiasm.[25] It was clear from the end of January 1775 that the restoration of the old parlement of Bordeaux too was imminent. On the 21st of that month the comte de Noailles was appointed commander-in-chief in Guienne, with the mission of restoring the parlement;[26] the last week in February he left Paris[27] accompanied by Bouvard de Fourqueux, councillor of state.[28] He arrived on the 27th to cries of 'vive l'ancien parlement!'[29] Meanwhile the exiles had received notice of the government's intentions. On 23 February Le Berthon received a *lettre de cachet* ordering him to be in Bordeaux at the king's orders on 1 March. The next day all other magistrates, exiled or otherwise, received similar instructions.[30] Among them were those counsellors, like Dussault the younger and Duroy, who had served as presidents in the Maupeou parlement; it was made clear that they were to return to their former status. Those magistrates who had taken office since 1771 were simply suspended.[31]

On 26 February Dupaty arrived in Bordeaux. As befitted the martyr of 1770 and 1771, he was given a hero's welcome,[32] but his reception was nothing to that received by Le Berthon two days later.[33] The first president had in fact already passed through Bordeaux once, on his way from his place of exile, to a nearer estate at Virelade, a few miles up river. This journey, unheralded as it was, was still interrupted by crowds and deputations. The official journey from Virelade on the 28th was again interrupted at several points along the way, as the coach advanced at the head of a great procession of between 200 and 500 carriages. Twelve procurators and 24 advocates were waiting at Le Bouscaut, where Me Garat delivered a speech of welcome,[34] but the real reception came at Le Bequet, just over two miles outside the city at 2 in the afternoon. Here the freemasons of the French lodge had erected a large and ornate triumphal arch surrounded by grandstands. Guns sounded and music played to greet Le Berthon's arrival and he was invited to descend from his coach to take refreshment at a table laid for a company of 40. Waiting for him was a group of his exiled colleagues, their womenfolk looking on from the grandstands. For three-quarters of an hour he was the object of harangues and addresses, serenaded, applauded, and crowned with civic laurels. He ate nothing, but shed polite tears, and so continued on in triumph escorted by hundreds of clerks and law students on horseback. Home at last, he found the courtyard packed with well-wishers, who sang and danced until the small hours, to the sound of fireworks. The windows of all polite society were illuminated that night. There were similar scenes of popular enthusiasm two days later, when Le Berthon drove at dawn to the palace for the ceremony of reintegration. Escorted by law students with drawn swords, he passed under six triumphal arches inscribed *vive Le Berthon, vive le Parlement*, and was even addressed and presented with a huge bouquet by a group of fishwives and flower-sellers. The restoration of the parlement was, in fact, the signal for a week of festivities throughout the city.

How genuine was this rejoicing? It was certainly more tumultuous and noisy than in some provincial centres.[35] The enthusiasm of most of the legal world could be taken for granted, right down to the clerks and the students who escorted Le Berthon on his triumph. He symbolized work and prosperity to them; the return of a more complex and spectacular legal order was also the return of a more lucrative one. Equally sincere must have been the enthusiasm of the local nobility, most of whom were related to the magistrates, and all of whom moved in the same social circle and shared many of the same privileges and prerogatives. No doubt their servants swelled the crowds. But many of the non-aristocratic, non-legal notables too shared in the celebrations. In short, all the leisured groups of Bordeaux fêted the returning parlement, all those who might have read and thought about the problem of despotism, or whose investments had directly experienced it at the hands of the abbé Terray. The French lodge of freemasons was prominent in the preparations; and even though the French lodge was the most exclusive, the mercantile community was better represented in it than the parlement.[36] Masonic money paid for triumphal arches, grandstands, cannon, and fireworks. For the populace which formed the bulk of the crowds, one spectacle was as exciting as another, especially on Shrove Tuesday, a public holiday, which happened to be the day of Le Berthon's return.[37] Perhaps this was no coincidence. But doubtless too some of the constitutional satisfaction that was so clearly animating their betters filtered down to such as the fishwives who harangued Le Berthon in their nasal Gascon; if the magistrates were the fathers of the people, this could only mean them. Visitors to Bordeaux were certainly impressed, at any rate, with the scale of Le Berthon's welcome and the numbers participating. Noailles himself observed wryly to Fourqueux as they left Le Berthon's hotel that this was the man nobody was supposed to want back.[38]

The session of reintegration took place at 8 o'clock on the morning of 2 March.[39] Present were 95 serving officers of the parlement, and ten honorary members. The occasion was marked with speeches from Noailles, Fourqueux, Le Berthon, and Dudon, all of them dwelling on the themes of reconciliation and unity under the orders of the king. But Le Berthon could not resist alluding to the recent judicial experiments, 'système destructeur des Loix de propriété, d'inamovibilité, de Liberté, Loix précieuses, sur lesquelles repose ... la tranquillité publique ...', before exhorting his colleagues to unity and vigilance in defence of the laws.

Three edicts were then registered on the express orders of the king. The first revoked all the remodelling measures of 1771 and reinstated all those who had then been dispossessed. All decisions and registrations of the Maupeou parlement were, however, to remain valid, and a rule of silence was imposed regarding them. The second, following the pattern of the disciplinary measure imposed on the parlement of Paris when it had been restored, contained a whole series of technical provisions to cut down a parlement's capacity for mischief. Their effect was to increase the predominance of the grand chamber in the parlement at the expense of its juniors, and to give the first president more discretion than before in assembling the chambers for public business. The right of remonstrance before registration was confirmed, but renewed remonstrances were only to follow registration. The old rules on age qualifications and residence were renewed, and strikes and mass resignations were forbidden on pain of forfeiture, to be pronounced by a new plenary court, composed of princes, peers, and royal councillors. The third edict diminished the judicial competence of the parlement, and

therefore the cost to litigants, by giving judgement in the last resort to the presidial courts over all cases concerning up to 2,000 l. Dudon at once voiced reservations on the new internal rules, and the increase in the powers of the presidial
courts. The parlement must reserve the right to remonstrate on both, if it saw fit,
he declared.[40] However, it was his duty to require their registration in the circumstances, and this he did. The session ended, at 10.30 a.m., to the sound of
applause, music, and cannon.

That night Noailles entertained the whole parlement to dinner, as the freemasons sponsored a huge firework display outside, and the whole town lit its
windows. Those who did not were apparently threatened.[41] In the streets, paper
lanterns were on sale, printed with the arms of Le Berthon;[42] doubtless already
the pamphlets from which we get so much information about this occasion were
available. The freemasons announced that they had endowed an annual mass at
the chapel of Le Bequet on 28 February, to celebrate forever the glorious memory
of the return of the parlement.[43] Only the Polverel problem remained to be resolved before the past could be buried. Not until it had been brought to a satisfactory conclusion could normal judicial service be resumed. By the very terms
of the edict of restoration, the sentence on Polverel still stood. Not until 10 March
did the assembled chambers of the parlement agree, on the motion of advocate-
general Saige, to revoke the sentence against Polverel and hand him over, for
what discipline seemed appropriate, to his colleagues.[44] They never took any
acton against him,[45] but they were satisfied, and on 10 March the advocates
appeared at the parlement in a body, and renewed their oaths.

This left the way clear for a ceremonial opening of hearings, which took place
on the 13th, in the presence of a large number of advocates.[46] Mᵉ Garat was once
agian their spokesman,[47] but this time the oratorical honours went to Dupaty,
whose duty it was, as advocate-general, formally to open the sessions of the
court.[48] France, he declared, had been rescued by Louis XVI from the universal
slide of all Europe into despotism and anarchy; in the new reign, property,
liberty, and justice would be sacred. He then proceeded to compliment Le
Berthon in lengthy and elaborate terms on his return.

> O, MESSIEURS! ce jour! ce beau jour! ce jour unique! cette fête à
> jamais mémorable, donnée par le coeur de cent mille Citoyens à la
> vertu! cette entrée triomphante d'Aristide dans la Capitale de cette grande
> Province! ...

And so on. The edict of re-establishment recognized above all:

> le principe précieux de l'inamovibilité des Offices; ... non une prérogative
> de la Magistrature, mais l'essence même d'une Magistrature, non un
> privilège des particuliers, mais un droit naturel et national ...

This principle was one of those fundamental laws which distinguish monarchy
from despotism, and as such it was graven into the human conscience, that
universal and imprescriptible charter of the rights of all humanity. There followed
sentimental eulogies of the king and all his new ministers, plucked by the royal
hand from the depths of misfortune and disgrace to restore public happiness.[49]
He also managed to include a condemnation of Terray's bankruptcies, and an
appeal for the thing nearest to his own heart, more humane criminal laws. He

concluded with an appeal to the magistrates themselves to honour the ideal of justice above all things.

> Ah! MESSIEURS, prenons-y garde; si nous ne sommes tous animés de l'amour de la concorde & de la paix, nous allons faire le mal dans le bien même, nous allons commettre l'iniquité en exercant la Justice . . . MESSIEURS, est-ce le Temple de la discorde que nous venons de rouvrir, ou celui de la paix? Sont-ce les flambeaux de la haine que nous venons de rallumer aujourd'hui, ou ceux de la justice? Est-ce le glaive de la vengeance que nous venons suspendre à ces voutes sacrées, ou celui des Loix?

The questions were pertinent. An appeal for unity and reconciliation was not superfluous. Dupaty had resolved to be just and moderate, but other returning exiles had no such feelings. Exile had been a martyrdom to true principles, as Le Berthon explained to John Adams in 1778:

> . . . he had long felt for me an Affection resembling that of a Brother. He had pitied me and trembled for me and was cordially rejoiced to see me. He could not avoid sympathising with every sincere friend of Liberty in the World . . . He had reason he said to feel for the Sufferers in the Cause of Liberty, because he had suffered many Years in that cause himself. He had been banished for cooperating with Mr. Malsherbs, and the other Courts and Parliaments of the Kingdom in the time of Louis the fifteenth, for their Remonstrances against the arbitrary Conduct and pernicious Edicts of the Court &c.[50]

Not all were prepared to forget their tribulations in such a cause. In July 1771 Pichard had warned Richelieu that any remodelling of the parlement would arouse hatreds and tear families apart.[51] But the hatreds raised by Maupeou's revolution were nothing to those which were to appear once it was reversed.

Trouble began even before the session of reintegration. When the remainers (*restants*), as they now became known, had paid courtesy visits to the released exiles or returners (*rentrés*) in the course of February, their reception had been cool.[52] When Pichard and Dudon paid a tactless public visit to Le Berthon on the evening of his return, the surging crowds greeted them in hostile silence. Later that night groups of youths sang requiems at the doors of remainers, and *Te Deums* at those of returners.[53] Remainers were jeered as they entered the palace on the morning of 2 March. When the session was over the catcalls and jostlings were so alarming that several refused to leave until late in the day.[54] Even then they were chased through the streets and pelted with mud.[55] These events were the culmination of weeks of insults. Never in 50 years on the bench, declared the dean Dussault, had he been so humiliated.[56] Others agreed, some suspecting that the turbulence had been organized by the returners themselves.[57]

At any rate, they felt that something must be done to salve their injured pride, and protested by absenting themselves in a body from the palace the next day, when the parlement was scheduled to organize itself for business. On 3 March, only four remainers braved renewed jeers and put in an appearance.[58] The rest made it clear that they would not return to their functions until some legal action was taken against the demonstrators of the previous day. So began a schism within the company that was to dominate the next three years, and echo right down to 1786.

The remainers took their stand on an awkward case. It is notoriously difficult to prosecute a crowd. Their position was hardly improved by the decision to demonstrate their grievances by striking. Quite apart from the difficulty of influencing an assembly they were boycotting, they were in contravention of the new disciplinary rules, registered on 2 March, which forbade strikes and mass resignations on pain of forfeiture. Above all the returners made up a majority of the court. This simple fact was to frustrate the remainers time and time again. But in any case, a conciliatory minority among the returners could have no effect on the parlement's decisions while the aggrieved magistrates stayed away. The strike left the returners free to invest any vindictive move virtually unopposed with the force and dignity of a decision of the parlement.

The full significance of this situation became clear as soon as the advocates' strike was brought to an end, and the prospect became imminent of sittings with only half the court present, and justice accordingly retarded. It now became urgent to end the remainers' strike.[59] Unfortunately, the very act of giving satisfaction to the advocates diminished the prospects, for it involved the reversal of the Maupeou parlement's decision against Polverel. The remainers chose to regard this as a deliberate insult to themselves. It began to seem to them that they were the object of some kind of vendetta on the part of their returned colleagues. Accordingly, they refused to abandon their strike.

Other evidence soon accumulated. A number of advocates who had begun to practise under the Maupeou parlement now began to come forward to renew their oaths, as if to imply that their original oaths had been invalid.[60] That the returners were prepared to administer these oaths showed the world that they shared this opinion. Discussions in the grand chamber on means of compensating lower magistrates who had resigned in 1771 in protest against Maupeou's revolution, had the same effect.[61] More insulting still was the returners' decision to draw up a *procès-verbal* of the registers of the parlement since 1771, to give them retrospective legal standing.[62] But worst of all were measures taken against personalities involved in Maupeou's revolution.

Among the remainers was counsellor E. Maignol, who in the spring of 1775 obtained provisions to his father's office of procurator-general at the court of aids. But as soon as the old parlement was restored, the court tried to block his appointment, alleging that Maignol was only using it as a refuge from obloquy in the parlement.[63] Noailles had to bring to bear all the influence at his disposal to persuade the court to return to its original approval.[64] Counsellor C. I. Drouilhet de Sigalas, another remainer, resigned his office in favour of his son during the course of March, but in 1772 he had procured this son an office in the Maupeou parlement; he was one of the eight 'intruders'.[65] It was certainly imprudent of Drouilhet to attempt to restore his son's position so soon after the reintegration of the court, and Le Berthon declared reasonably that it was hardly a suitable moment, asking him to wait.[66] Some returners, it seemed, had declared that they would never vote for relatives of remainers, and it would take time to cool such passions.[67] But the remainers interpreted Le Berthon's request, essentially a plea for moderation, as yet one more insult, and the most dangerous yet, since it threatened to set a precedent for proscribing half the families represented in the parlement. Drouilhet's became the test case; the remainers told Noailles that they would only return to the parlement if he guaranteed that young Drouilhet would be received.[68] But of course the comte was in no position to offer such a guarantee.

The attitude of the remainers won them little public sympathy. 'Tout est calme icy', wrote Mme Duplessy on 18 March,[69]

> il seroit seulement à souhaiter que les officiers du Parlement fussent mieux d'accort, et que tous les Restants eussent assez de fermeté pour se mettre au dessus des Mines des Revenus, Reprandre leurs fonctions avec dignité, ne pas paroistre faire attention aux Mauvais procedez, Remplir leurs devoirs avec Exactitude; on verrait bientôt tomber toutes les huées, toutes les grimaces &c Et, en se Respectant eux-meme, ils apprendroient aux autres à les Respecter, et ce procedé les feroit sans doute Reflechir a L'avilissement qui Retombera sur Eux, en dégradant la Magistrature; tous les gens sensez pensent ainsi, et l'on commence Beaucoup a approuver la Conduite du Pt Pichard, qui Entre tous les jours au Palais, qui fait teste à l'orage, et qui paroist mépriser tout ce qui afflige ses confreres . . .

She also felt that Noailles had not done all he might, and had shown himself too inclined to favour the returners. When he left Bordeaux on the 27th, in order to take the dignities of Marshal of France and duc de Mouchy at Versailles, she declared frankly that his mission had been a failure, owing to his lack of dignity, knowledge, and firmness.[70]

The remainers were certainly unimpressed by his attempts at impartiality, and on 25 March they sent the first of what became a whole series of memoranda to the king and his ministers, complaining of their treatment.[71] The commandant did not seem to appreciate, they said, the gravity of the insults of 2 March. They hoped that the king would not compel them to resume their duties until he had granted them 'par un acte public de sa justice et de sa protection une satisfaction convenable et proportionnelle aux humiliations et aux outrages que nous avons essuyés', and until he had ordered their colleagues in the most express terms to receive any of their relatives into any office they might acquire. The government did not reply, and the parlement remained immobilized.

By Easter the procurator-general had resumed his duties, but on 21 March he was refused permission to open a criminal inquiry into the events of 2 March.[72] This refusal probably prevented a general return to duty. Still, on 8 May counsellor Domenge followed Dudon's example. Perhaps he had already decided to resign in favour of his son, and did not wish this move to be blocked as that of Drouilhet had been.[73] The defections angered and alarmed the absentees and on 20 May, in a new memorandum to the king, they called for the sending of a judicial commission of the council to investigate the events of 2 March, and so vindicate them.[74] They asked the king to make a public declaration of satisfaction with their services since 1771, condemning the events of 2 March, confirming that the Maupeou parlement was legitimate, and forbidding all discrimination against its members or their relatives in admissions to the parlement. But this memorandum remained unanswered like its predecessor,[75] and the stalemate continued.

In the circumstances, it was easy for extremists among the returners bent on reprisals to induce moderates, distressed by the inactivity of the court, to help pass extreme resolutions. On 17 June, therefore, the assembled chamber of the parlement resolved that in future all the *arrêts* of the Maupeou parlement would be termed 'judgements of the intermediary commission',[76] a deliberate and calculated insult, evoking memories of the Polverel case. To describe the Maupeou parlement as a commission implied that it had not had irremovable officers, but mere commissioners with tenure at the king's pleasure—not magistrates at all in the fullest sense. Besides, this resolution contravened the edict of restoration, which expressly forbade any calling in question of the decisions of the Maupeou parlement. The remainers were quick to seize upon this, protesting vehemently on 20 June in a letter to Vergennes, minister of the province,[77] declaring that if the king did not do something soon, the differences between the sides would become irreparable. This at last stirred the government into some action. On 26 June, Miromesnil, Keeper of the Seals, sent a letter to each of the remainers, acknowledging their services since 1771, but reproving them for their persistent absence. The king's wish was, he said, that they should either resume their duties at once, or sell their offices.[78] This letter, which arrived on 1 July, was hardly the token of public support that they had clamoured for, but it did offer them the chance to extricate themselves from an otherwise impossible position. Although, a few days earlier, they had refused to attend a *Te Deum* for the royal coronation in company with the returners,[79] by 3 July they had resolved to make the best of the opportunity and return to their functions.[80]

However, by then circumstances had once more changed. Four deputies were sent to Le Berthon to inform him of the decision to resume, only to be told that, as a result of their refusal to attend the service for the coronation, on 26 June, the very day of Miromesnil's letter, the court had resolved to have no dealings or contact with the absentees, and not to count their opinions if they should return.[81] Shock as this was, it did not deter them, and on 6 July the absentees returned to their respective chambers. In all of them, however, after some tart exchanges, they and their votes were ostentatiously ignored by the presidents. Clearly they regarded the decision of 26 June as binding. There were similar scenes on the 7th. On the 8th, therefore, the remainers drew up *procès-verbaux* of all that had happened, and sent them off to Versailles along with another protestation,[82] declaring that: 'Il est inoui et sans exemple, que des magistrats s'attribuent Le pouvoir de dépouiller quarente magistrats du droit de sceance et de suffrage qui leur est donné par leurs provisions'. They would, they declared, continue to obey the royal orders and appear at the palace, but they would consign every act of discrimination against them to a *procès-verbal*, which they would send to Versailles. And so, dramatically, the parts were reversed. By their secret deliberation the returners found themselves obstructing the will of the king, while the remainers, previously recalcitrant, could congratulate themselves on an exemplary (if tardy) obedience, as in 1771.

For three weeks the pattern repeated itself. The returners made their entrance, were ignored or insulted, protested formally, and sent *procès-verbaux* off to Versailles.[83] Not much business was transacted otherwise. Outside opinion now condemned the returners for their extreme and 'despotic' behaviour, and Le Berthon for his weakness; people began to whisper that president de Gascq would not have followed his extreme colleagues so meekly, but would have reconciled all parties by this time.[84] It certainly looked from Versailles as though no ordinary measures would heal the schism; this meant that a military session would probably be necessary sooner or later. Mouchy arrived back in Bordeaux on 22 July, and on 2 August the magistrates all received *lettres de cachet* ordering them to be in attendance at the palace the next morning, to deliberate together.[85] For the moment, by this device, a military session was avoided. On 3 August there was merely an assembly of chambers where for the first time since the reintegration both sides voted in common. Yet this was not necessarily a great step forward, since the returnèrs had a permanent majority. The result of common voting was, in fact, simply to decide on a protest letter to the king, despite the objections of the remainers, and meanwhile to obey his orders only provisionally by prefacing all remarks with the phrase 'by the king's very express command'. All the remainers could do was send to Versailles new sets of *procès-verbaux* and memoranda.[86]

No reply to these renewed demands was received, however, before the letter decided upon by the returners' majority on 3 August was drafted and laid before the assembled chambers on 12 August.[87] There was a lively and acrimonious debate, but there was little the remainers could do in the face of their opponents' majority, and the letter was approved and sent in the name of them all.[88] It painted an innocent picture of their exemplary and conciliatory behaviour in March. Any measures they had ultimately taken against the absentees, they explained, were merely in obedience to the royal ordinances, which gave parlements the right and duty of disciplining their own members. It was, therefore, unjust to subject the parlement, which had shown nothing but zeal and remarkable tolerance, to such drastic and uncustomary instruments as *lettres de cachet*. On 14 August the helpless remainers sent a further protest to Versailles against the letter, this 'new outrage'.[89]

Meanwhile the daily clashes went on. Returners continued to preface all their remarks with the proviso that they opined by the king's very express command, and they continued to speak of the 'judgements of the commission'. The remainers for their part continued to draw up *procès-verbaux* and more memoranda to the government.[90] Every session of the parlement saw undignified squabbles and exchanges; 'cecy degenère en Opiniatre Enfantillage', declared Mme Duplessy,[91] '. . . quels Roles, pour des magistrats, tant d'un côté que de L'autre! et ne peut-on pas plaindre Ceux qui seront jugez dans ces temps cy? . . . il est bien a desirer pour le Bien public, que tout cecy finisse'. She had heard rumours that the king was very displeased, and that there was even talk of suppressing the parlement completely. But such rumours and opinions did not deter the magistrates; indeed the bitterness of their differences grew during the last weeks of August, as the returners resumed persecution of individuals in the opposite camp.

First of all they offered further mortification to the younger Drouilhet. Le Berthon refused once more to put forward his name so that he should have precedence over newcomers, on the grounds that he would be rejected. This inevitably evoked another protest to the king from the remainers.[92] Then certain of the returners attacked the procurator-general, alleging misconduct in three trivial cases;[93] he was ordered to deposit the relevant papers for examination. According to Mme Duplessy: 'Le dessous des Cartes qui anime les Revenants Contre le Pro[r] general, c'est que Mr. de Poissac Envie sa charge, et tout le monde dit, Dieu Nous garde qu'il le possede'.[94]

True or not, it was certain that Poissac was one of the more extreme leaders of the returners, who kept matters simmering much as Gascq had said he would.[95] He was, for example, also prominent in an attack on counsellor de Laroze for levying excessive fees. The chamber of which they were both members, the first inquests, condemned Laroze in the early days of September to make restitution of these monies, much to his mortification.[96] Similarly, on 2 September, Poissac trapped the younger Dussault into refusing to acknowledge the ruling that the decisions of the Maupeou parlement should be described as judgements. On 7 September the chamber placed him under a six-month suspension.[97] It was only after this that a letter from Miromesnil, which had arrived early the previous day, was read to the assembled chambers. It forbade the use of the proviso 'by the king's very express command' and at last the derogatory description of the *arrêts* of the Maupeou parlement. But by then it was too late, as the returners well knew, to save Dussault.[98] It was in a completely unrepentant atmosphere that the session drew to a close. 'Mrs du Parlement', wrote Mouchy to Richelieu on 9 September,[99]

> ont fini leurs sceances par une querelle forte dans une chambre, Mon cher oncle, vous croyez bien que cela m'a fort deplu. M. Dusault fils a mis de la hauteur, du sec, et de la roideur, mais ceux qui l'ont condamné a sabsenter ont eu plus de tord que lui. les voila Graces a Dieu separes et ne songeant plus qu'aux vendanges . . .

If it had been true, all might have been well. But in fact all the aggrieved parties saw the vacation simply as an opportunity to press their case with higher authority and Dudon, Laroze, Dussault, Poissac, and the first president himself, all made their way to Paris in the first few days of their release.[100] But there as was normal they spent weeks waiting to see Miromesnil, and when they did finally do so, they received little satisfaction. Dudon was told that so long as the charges against him were only charges, and not sentences, he had no grounds for appeal; he should return to Bordeaux and await the outcome of the case.[101] Dussault was told in similar vein that unless he could produce written evidence of his suspension, it had no legal standing and was not a cause for complaint.[102] Laroze was told that the parlement was within its rights to censure his conduct and that if he disagreed with the verdict, he should appeal to the council of state, not the government. The Keeper of the Seals added informally that however unreasonable the returners had been, in his view it was the remainers who bore the main responsibility for the troubles because of their intractable behaviour after 2 March.[103] So they returned home censured and empty-handed, not long before the end of the year.

Miromesnil might congratulate himself, as 1775 ended, upon calming the troubles in the parlement by inaction and the minimum of intervention, and he did not cease to do this throughout 1776.[104] However, troubles do not always go away for being ignored, and with the full resumption of judicial business in January, the ferment continued. When Dussault ignored Le Berthon's advice and reappeared in his chamber before his six months' suspension was up, he was refused admission.[105] When he protested to Miromesnil at this further mortification, he received a curt reply which condemned the hastiness of his conduct and ordered him not to trouble the king with it further. A final bitter protest evoked no reply.[106] Isolated instances also still occurred of derogatory references to the 'judgements' of the Maupeou parlement, instances which were never allowed to pass without *procès-verbaux* and renewed letters of protest.[107] But the division in the company continued to find its fullest expression in terms of personalities. The court refused to consider a new claim in February from the younger Drouilhet, and after an interview with Le Berthon, he conceded that his aspiration was hopeless as things stood.[108] Counsellor Domenge, however, thought that his son would have a better chance. Having paved the way for him by ostentatiously abandoning his remainer colleagues the previous May, he seems to have felt that the past was now distant enough for his son's candidacy to meet with no opposition. But he was wrong. His proposal was rejected. Later in the year he approached the first president in the hope that his support would change his colleagues' dispositions, only to receive another refusal, on the grounds that Le Berthon never proposed candidates whom he knew to be disagreeable to the majority of the company.[109] The remainers stressed repeatedly that they regarded such rejections as far worse than the petty irritations they continued daily to undergo, for they threatened to perpetuate the schism down the generations and destroy the social and professional standing of half the families in the parlement. As far as the returners were concerned one way to spite their unfortunate colleagues was much the same as another. Thus in July 1776 president de Loret became an object of attack on grounds of alleged misconduct in a case which had been concluded 20 years beforehand, despite the fact that he had never joined the remainers' strike, and had even ceased to attend their meetings when they persisted with it.[110] More substantial was the harassment of president de Pichard, another strike-breaker, in his case against his ex-steward Giraudeau.[111] A judgement of the seneschalcy court against Giraudeau was confirmed by the Maupeou parlement in January 1775, but on 7 March 1775, after the restoration, he appealed again. Members of the first inquests, that centre of returner activity, took up the case, and encouraged Giraudeau to print a memoir containing some 50 letters from Pichard which put him in a very unflattering light.[112] Pichard felt bound to reply in kind, which of course kept the affair going. At length, in 1780, Giraudeau was condemned to be exiled for ten years from Guienne. Again he appealed, on a legal technicality, and in 1782 the council of state transferred the case to the parlement of Paris; here, at last, the Bordeaux sentence was confirmed. 'Cest depuis 1774 et 1775 que cette affaire a eclatte. il y a jusques a present deux decisions et 4 arrets. il me semble qu'il seroit bien tems que cette affaire finit', wrote Pichard in June 1782, '. . . si je n'avais pas obei aux ordres du feu roy en 1771, Cette affaire qui trouble le reste de ma vie, n'auroit jamais pris naissance'.[113]

The judicial year 1775–76, therefore, was in its way as troubled as its predecessor. It is true that the sides now co-operated in the expedition of business, but it was with a very bad grace, and at least once some of the remainers serving in the *tournelle* found life so impossible that they boycotted its sessions.[114] It is a measure of how absorbed the magistrates were in their internal bickerings that they completely forgot to draw up the remonstrances they had decided to send on Turgot's edict of April 1776 which abolished the wine privilege of Bordeaux, a measure which touched them and their livelihood, as well as that of the whole Bordelais, deeply. When letters of *jussion* arrived, ordering the parlement to register the edict at once, the magistrates were taken by surprise.[115] They drew up hurried remonstrances only after a forcible registration by Mouchy at a military session. The judicial year ended with yet another protestation by 22 of the remainers, complaining of all the new insults that the year had brought, that 'on va scruter dans le sein des familles, dans la vie privée et Publique de chaque magistrat pour trouver des pretextes de vexation', and threatening to renew the strike if the government did not intervene in their favour.[116] The government of course did nothing, convinced that the worst of the troubles were now over.

Nevertheless, the year 1776–77 was full of echoes of the quarrels. When the comte de Provence visited Bordeaux in the early summer of 1777, and was pointedly polite to prominent remainers, they were overjoyed at what they regarded as the first mark of public esteem they had had from an official figure since the reintegration.[117] Yet they could not prevail upon their colleagues to relent in their policy of excluding the relatives of remainers and 'intruders', and every new candidate received reopened this wound. In the year 1777–78, Domenge made another attempt to secure the acceptance of his son, without success.[118] The remainers renewed their complaints, recalling that Drouilhet, too, remained unsatisfied. There were also the tribulations of counsellor Duroy in his attempt to secure reception as first president of the court of aids. Duroy's father had held this office, and his immediate predecessor was his brother-in-law. It seemed therefore natural that he should ultimately succeed to it. But like Maignol the procurator-general, he had served in the Maupeou parlement, and the court of aids, influenced by five or six extremists, refused to register his provisions.[119] The refusal came on top of three years of constant recalcitrance and obstruction of the intendant's administration.[120] By a declaration of 26 July 1778, therefore, the king transferred the sessions of the court to Casteljaloux, a little town on the middle Garonne, during his pleasure. This exile was enough to make the magistrates reflect, and by the end of September Duroy had been received. A declaration of 1 November transferred sittings back to Bordeaux, and after that Duroy encountered no more trouble.[121]

1778, in fact, saw the end of the worst quarrels, even though the younger Domenge did not secure reception until 1780, and Drouilhet never did. Certainly the old animosities reappeared a few years later, in the case of the younger Dudon,[122] but that was a very special case. Already in January 1778 president de Loret had the impression that the 'fire was almost out', although this judgement was rather premature, for intermittent talk of strikes continued.[123] Despite renewed protest letters in March, June, and September, the solidarity of the remainers was clearly crumbling, as their party was diminished by death, desertion, and resignation. These losses were replaced by newcomers with no personal involvement in the events of 1771. Their voices were added to those of moderates on both sides who regretted the divisions. By 1777 even the returners were falling apart. When in the summer of 1776 Le Berthon, still trying in his fashion to avoid the partisanship which divided his company, refused to convoke the chambers on the request of certain returners, they attempted to blackmail him by raising complaints of misconduct on the part of a distant cousin of his who was a magistrate in Saintes. They let it be known that only the surrender of his powers under the disciplinary rules of 1775, over the convocation of the chambers, would persuade them to drop the case. As a result the first president broke off all contact with them, and won general sympathy in so doing.[124] The extremists thus isolated themselves. The continuing scandals associated with the name of Poissac also kept moderate returners from associating too closely with him. Not only was there his open hostility to powerful figures like Richelieu; he was also accused of bias in handling a case concerning the duc d'Aiguillon, Richelieu's cousin,[125] and made himself a laughing-stock by complaining to the parlement about certain insulting innuendoes regarding him which had been pronounced in open court at Tulle, his home town.[126] All but the most extreme and hotheaded came to feel that it was not good policy to associate with Poissac, and this inevitably helped to weaken the returner front.

All these circumstances contributed to the subsidence of the post-Maupeou recriminations. They were strictly internal circumstances, however. Neither the intervention of the government, nor the pressure of a hostile and exasperated public opinion, had any noticeable effect in diminishing these bickerings. The magistrates remained totally self-absorbed, acknowledging no outside curb on their vendettas. And in fact the most important reason of all for the decline of the restoration quarrels, in and after 1778, was that a new internal issue now arose to divide the court along different lines—the Dupaty affair.

NOTES

1. Flammermont, *Le Chancelier Maupeou*, 513–16; Egret, *Louis XV et l'opposition parlementaire*, 207–8, 219–23.
2. BVC Richelieu XVIII, f.199, Gascq to Richelieu, 10 Aug. 1773.
3. See below, p. 206.
4. BVC Richelieu XVI, Pichard to Richelieu, 26 Feb. 1774.
5. *Journal historique*, VII, 32, 29 May 1774.
6. BVBx MS 1201, III, 23 June 1774.
7. BVC Richelieu XVIII, Gascq to Richelieu, 31 May 1774.
8. ibid., 12 July 1774.
9. BN Albertas, IV, ff.210–12, 29 July 1774.
10. BVC Richelieu XVIII, Gascq to Richelieu, 21 Aug. 1774.
11. ibid., Gascq to Richelieu, 26 Aug. 1774.
12. ibid., same to same, 27 Aug. 1774.
13. He was in Paris for the restoration of the parlement there in November. J. N. Moreau, *Mes Souvenirs* (Paris, 1898–1901), II, 109.
14. AN 109 AP (16) (Gourgue papers), Bertin to Michel-Joseph de Gourgue, 16 Nov. 1774.
15. BLR MS 1903, f.290, Dupaty to de Sèze, 8 Sept. 1774.
16. AD 2E 2328 (tit. fam. Polverel), printed petition to the council, 1774, *passim*.
17. ibid., *Mémoire apologetique pour le barreau de Bordeaux* (1774), 10.
18. Petition of Polverel, loc. cit., 56–8.
19. ibid., 2; *Journal historique*, VII, 49, 21 Jan. 1775.
20. ibid.
21. ibid., 116, 17 Feb. 1775.
22. BPR Le Paige 820, p. 13, speech of the advocate Garat, 18 March 1775, pp. 25–7.
23. BVBx MS 1201, IV, 24 Feb. 1775.
24. AN K708, nos. 83 and 83 ter. They mention that Pichard is 40, which places them, along with other circumstantial references, in 1774 or early 1775. Pichard's ambition seems to have been set on succeeding his cousin, so the restoration must have come to him as a cruel frustration. BVC Richelieu XVIII, f.204, Gascq to Richelieu, 4 Sept. 1773.
25. H. Carré, 'Les fêtes d'une réaction parlementaire, 1774–1775', *La Révolution Française*, XXIII (1892), *passim*.
26. *Journal historique*, VI, 73, 30 Jan. 1775.
27. ibid., 127 (20 Feb.), 142 (26 Feb.), 144 (27 Feb.).
28. Michel Bouvard de Fourqueux (1719–89). Counsellor at the parlement of Paris, 1738; procurator-general, chamber of accounts, 1743–69; councillor of state, 1769; comptroller-general, 9 April–3 May 1787.

29. *Journal historique*, VI, 216, 22 March 1775; E. de Biran, 'Lettre relative au rétablissement du parlement de Bordeaux, en 1775', *Bulletin de la société historique et archéologique du Périgord* (1908), 224–7.
30. *Journal historique*, VI, 216, 22 March 1775.
31. ibid.; Biran, loc. cit.; BVBx MS 1201, IV, 24 Feb. 1775.
32. *Journal historique*, VI, 216, 22 March 1775; AM fonds ancien FF 5ᵇ, *Lettre à M. le Comte de *** sur ce qui s'est passé à Bordeaux à la réintegration du parlement. Par M. de P.Y., Américain.*
33. Le Berthon's reception is very well documented. There are secondary accounts in Boscheron des Portes, *Histoire du Parlement de Bordeaux*, II, 331–3; H. Chauvot, *Histoire du barreau de Bordeaux, 1775–1815* (Paris, 1856), 12–13; and *Journal historique*, VI, 216, 22 March 1775. Primary accounts are to be found in Biran, loc. cit.; BVBx MS 1201, IV, 24 Feb. 1775; AM Fonds Delpit 134 'Leberthon', MS entitled 'Faits averes touchant les honneurs qui ont été rendus à Mr Le Pr Pt Le Berthon...[&c.]'; AM fonds ancien FF 5ᵇ, loc. cit. above, n. 32; and AD 8J 67 (Fonds Bigot), 'parlement', *Récit de ce qui s'est passé dans le voyage que* M LEBERTHON...*à fait d'Aiguille à Virelade*, which was clearly the main source used by Boscheron des Portes.
34. BPR Le Paige 820, p. 13.
35. Egret, *Parlement de Dauphiné*, II, 5–6, notes the tepidity at Grenoble.
36. See above, p. 134.
37. AM Fonds Delpit 134.
38. BVBx MS 1201, IV, 2 March 1775.
39. In addition to the sources cited above, see AD 8J 67 (Fonds Bigot), 'parlement', *Procès-verbal de la séance de M. le Comte de Noailles, Duc de Mouchy, au parlement de Bordeaux, accompagné de M. de Fourqueux, Conseiller d'Etat, Du jeudi deuxième mars mil sept cent soixante quinze;* and AD IB 56, ff.10 vo.–14 vo.
40. See below, p. 218.
41. AM Fonds Delpit 134.
42. BVBx MS 1201, IV, 3 March 1775.
43. AM fonds ancien FF 5ᵇ, loc. cit. above, n. 32.
44. BVBx MS 1201, IV, 5 March and 10 March 1775; *Journal historique*, VII, 232, 29 March 1775.
45. See Bachaumont, XXVIII, 79, 105–7, 112, 114, Feb. 1785, for Polverel's subsequent history.
46. BVBx MS 1201, IV, 14 March 1775.
47. BPR Le Paige 820, p. 13.
48. ibid., Le Paige 573, *Discours prononcé par M. Dupaty, Avocat-Général, le 13 Mars 1775, à la première Audience de Grand' Chambre, après le rétablissement du Parlement.*
49. Good Catholics, reported Bachaumont, were shocked to hear him link the names of Most Christian kings like Louis XII and (inevitably!) Henry IV with those of pagans like Marcus Aurelius and Titus, as candidates for the eternal glory due to friends of mankind. *Mémoires secrets*, VIII, 13, 12 April 1775.
50. *Adams Papers*; *Series I*, IV, 35, 2 April 1778. 'Mr. Bondfield had to interpret all this Effusion of Compliments', Adams added, 'and I thought it would never come to an End. But it did and I concluded upon the whole that there was a Fund of sincerity in it decorated and almost suffocated with French Compliments'.
51. BVC Richelieu XV, f.206, Pichard to Richelieu, 1 July 1771.
52. BVBx MS 1201, IV, 24 Feb. 1775.
53. ibid., 1 March 1775.
54. AM Fonds Delpit 134.
55. *Journal historique*, VII, 232, 29 March 1775; also Bachaumont, XXX, *Supplément*, 191, 31 March 1775.
56. *Journal historique*, VII, 232, 29 March 1775.
57. AAE MD France, 1588, ff.107–14, protestation of 25 March 1775. Here the demonstrators are described as 'une Cabale fomentée par des hommes Ennemis de la paix'.
58. Pichard, Loret, Saige, Marbotin, and Malromé. In BVBx MS 1201, IV, 3 March 1775, Mme Duplessy omits Saige, but from the way he co-operated with the returners a few days later over Polverel, it seems likely that he was there. She also notes on 15 June that counsellor de Lamontaigne had returned at the start. It was rumoured

that Pichard had been deputed by the absentees to keep a watch on events—BN Albertas, V, f.2165, 1 April 1775; *Journal historique*, VII, 232, 29 March 1775.

59. BVBx MS 1201, IV, 5 and 7 March 1775; and AAE MD France, 1588, f.196, memoir of remainers, sent to Vergennes 8 Aug. 1775, give accounts of earlier attempts at reconciliation.

60. ibid., ff.145–7, memoir sent on 8 July 1775; BVBx MS 1201, IV, 6 July 1775.

61. AAE MD France, 1588, ff.107–14, memoir of remainers sent to Vergennes on 25 March 1775.

62. ibid., ff.123–8, memoir of 20 May 1775. This *procès-verbal*, claimed in the memoir to be lost, is in fact in Bernadau's papers (BVBx MS 713, série I, XLVII, 329–82).

63. BVBx MS 1201, IV, 7 March 1775.

64. ibid., 15 March 1775; AAE loc. cit. above, n. 59.

65. The unfortunate son had not even wanted to take office under Maupeou.

66. AAE MD France, 1588, is full of references to the Drouilhet candidacy. The fullest account is in ff.282–90.

67. ibid., 23 March 1775.

68. ibid.; AAE MD France, 1588, memoir of 25 March.

69. ibid., 18 March 1775.

70. ibid., 23 and 29 March 1775.

71. ibid., ff.107–14.

72. BVBx MS 1201, IV, 21 March 1775.

73. ibid., 9 May 1775; Bachaumont, XXX, *Supplément*, 294, 25 July 1775. If this was his motive, his action was soon seen to be fruitless; see below pp. 171–2.

74. AAE MD France, 1588, ff.123–9; another copy AAE MD France, 1371, ff.19–24.

75. Mme Duplessy reported on 15 June that the magistrates had received orders to resume their duties or to sell their offices, but this was a groundless rumour. Miromesnil's letter to the absentees on 26 June states clearly that until that time the king had kept silent on the quarrels.

76. BVBx MS 1201, IV, 3 July 1775; BN Albertas, V, f.2206, 8 July 1775.

77. AAE MD France, 1588, ff.132–3. Signed by five leading remainers.

78. AAE MD France, 1588, f.134; Bachaumont, XXX, *Supplément*, 295, 25 July 1775.

79. ibid.

80. BVBx MS 1201, IV, 3 July 1775.

81. Bachaumont, loc. cit.; AAE MD France, 1588, ff.131–5, *procès-verbal* of 6 July 1775; BN Albertas, V, f.2209, 24 July 1775.

82. The documents are in AAE MD France, 1588, ff.131–57.

83. More of these documents ibid., ff.159–201.

84. BVBx MS 1201, IV, 3, 9, and 12 July 1775.

85. BVBx MS 1201, III, 3 Aug. (1775; this letter is mistakenly filed with those of 1774).

86. AAE MD France, 1588, ff.198–201, memoir of 8 Aug. 1775.

87. ibid., ff.212–13, *procès-verbal* sent by remainers.

88. AN O^{1}352, no. 439, for the text of this letter.

89. AAE MD France, 1588, ff.214–21.

90. ibid., ff.222–30, *procès-verbaux* of 18 and 22 Aug.; also AAE MD France, 1375, ff.242–3, letter of 18 Aug. 1775.

91. ibid., 21 Aug. 1775.

92. ibid., 21 and 26 Aug.; AAE MD France, 1588, ff.231–2 for the protest, signed by 24 magistrates, and dated 25 Aug. 1775.

93. These cases are fully documented in BN Albertas, V, ff.2221–31, where Dudon's defence is copied *in extenso*.

94. AAE MD France, 1588, 28 Aug. 1775.

95. See above, pp. 154–5, 159 BN Albertas, V, f.2239, gives a character sketch of Poissac, which seems to emanate from Richelieu. 'Cet homme est le plus vif, meme le plus violent qu'il y ait dans aucun Parlem^t, et d'autant plus dangereux qu'il est méthodique dans ses fureurs et froid en aparence'. He repeats (f.2233) a widespread rumour that Poissac had ruined a dinner party by attacking a plaster bust of Richelieu, crying: 'Je veux te traiter comme je voudrais traiter ton original', and thereupon cutting off its ears with a hunting knife. This story is also to be found in Moreau, *Mes Souvenirs*, II, 27 8–9.

96. AAE MD France, 1588, ff.239–40, 252–3, and 320–1, memoirs of Laroze giving details of the case, Sept. and Oct. 1775.
97. ibid., ff.239–48, *procès-verbaux* and memoirs sent by Dussault to Versailles, 2–15 Sept. 1775.
98. I have been unable to find the text of this letter, but it is alluded to in AAE MD France, 1588, f.259, remainers to Vergennes, 9 Sept. 1775, and f.293, same to same, 2 March 1776, where its contents are described. See also AN O^{1}352, no. 438, Le Berthon's response to the remainer letter of 3 Sept. 1775.
99. AAE MD France, 1399, f.172.
100. It was rumoured that they had been summoned to the capital by Miromesnil. Bachaumont, XXXII, *Supplément*, 322, 10 Oct. 1775; but all except Dupaty and Le Berthon had good personal reasons for being there.
101. BN Albertas, V, f.2284, 28 Nov. 1775; also f.2319, 21 Dec. 1775.
102. ibid.; also AD F MS 46, 'Copie d'une Lettre d'un magistrat à un magistrat, Le 29 8bre 1775'. This letter, from Poissac to an unidentified correspondent, gives an account of an informal meeting between Miromesnil, himself, and the remainers Dussault, Laroze, and Ruat.
103. ibid.
104. BN Albertas, V, f.2556, 3 Sept. 1776.
105. AAE MD France, 1588, ff.284–90 contains accounts of these events by Dussault, sent on 16 Feb. 1776.
106. ibid., f.291, Miromesnil to Dussault, 23 Feb. 1776, and ff.295–6, Dussault to Miromesnil, 1 March 1776.
107. e.g., ibid., ff.297–300, letters of 2 March and 6 April 1776, and *procès-verbaux* of 29 and 30 March 1776.
108. AN o^{1}352, no. 438; AAE MD France, 1588, ff.282–90, Drouilhet to Miromesnil, 11 Feb. 1776, and correspondence following.
109. AN O^{1}352, no. 438; Le Berthon's account.
110. BVBx MS 1201, V, 16 and 17 July, 1 and 11 Aug. 1776; also AAE MD France, 1386, ff.3–4, Loret to Vergennes, 17 Jan. 1778.
111. See above, pp. 97–8. The legal documents of this case are in AD 2E 2285 (tit. fam. Pichard de Saucats).
112. Some excerpts are printed above, loc. cit. Mme Duplessy, BVBx MS 1201, V, 16 and 31 July 1776, suggests that the returners furnished this memoir, forced a printer to run it off, distributed it, and even sent copies to Paris and Toulouse.
113. AAE MD France, 1589, ff.122–3, Pichard to Vergennes, 5 July 1782; ff.137–8, same to same, 28 June 1782.
114. AAE MD France, 1588, f.316, remainers to Vergennes, 3 Sept. 1776.
115. BVBx MS 1201, V, 5 Sept. 1776. For a fuller account of the parlement's reaction to this edict, see below, pp. 207–10.
116. AAE MD France, 1588, ff.317–18.
117. Moreau, *Mes Souvenirs*, II, 278; BVC Richelieu XVI, f.157, Pichard to Richelieu, 24 June 1777.
118. AAE MD France, 1589, f.11, remainers to Miromesnil, 18 April 1778; f.31, six remainers to Vergennes, 27 June 1778; ff.41–2, five remainers to Vergennes and Miromesnil, 1 Sept. 1778.
119. AD C3451, Duroy to intendant, 27 Sept. 1778; intendant to Keeper of the Seals, 8 Oct. 1778.
120. See below, pp. 233–4; also S. Quet, 'La Cour des Aides de Guienne: ses rapports avec le Parlement de Bordeaux', *R. Hist. Bx.* (1939–40), 1939, p. 182; AD C2473, intendant to comptroller-general, 28 Nov. 1778, and AN H92.
121. AN H92, Mouchy to Necker, 4 Dec. 1777 and 26 Feb. 1778; Declarations in AD C4865 (Registers of the Election); Mme Duplessy, BVBx MS 1201, VII, 14 Nov. 1778, notes the restoration of harmony.
122. See below, pp. 190–7.
123. AAE MD France, 1386, f.2, Loret to Vergennes, 17 Jan. 1778.
124. BVBx MS 1201, V, 20 Aug. and 5 Sept. 1776.
125. BN Albertas, V, f.2491, 30 July 1776; and f.2861, 28 April 1778.
126. BVBx MS 1201, VI, 14 Sept. 1777.

CHAPTER 12

Exclusion: Dupaty and Dudon 1778-86

There is no doubt that, if he had so wished, the advocate-general Dupaty could have played a major part in the recriminations after 1775. His record of opposition to 'despotism' in 1770 and 1771 made him a natural hero of the returner cause, yet throughout the divisions he remained true to his resolution of 1774 to be moderate and to preach reconciliation. He spent these years in conscientious discharge of his duties. But these duties were far from light, and Dupaty's health was poor. By 1777, he was feeling the strain unduly, and began to look around for some relief. Eventually, after prolonged negotiations, he bought Gascq's office of president à mortier for 126,000 l. in December 1778.[1] The same day he sold his own office to counsellor P. de Raymond de Lalande, who was acquiring it for his son. It is clear that Dupaty anticipated no trouble in transferring to the more leisured atmosphere of the presidential bench.

He had, after all, fulfilled the necessary preliminaries. At the time of his first approach to Gascq, he had cleared his action with Le Berthon, who encouraged him to proceed. This precaution had seemed all the more necessary in that Le Berthon clearly intended his son, who had been admitted to the parlement as a counsellor in 1777, to proceed to the presidential bench as soon as possible. Nothing seemed more natural, and Dupaty offered to concede precedence on the bench to him. When, early in December 1778, Dupaty wrote to inform Le Berthon that he was about to conclude a contract with Gascq, the first president replied:.

> Vous ne doutez pas assurement, Monsieur, des sentiments que je vous ai voués depuis le moment de notre connaissance. ils sont et seront toujours les memes. Je vous verrai avec grand plaisir pourvu de la charge que vous venez d'acquérir, et j'y prends d'autant plus d'intérêt que je crois la condition de votre santé attachée au nouvel état que vous embrassez, sans que le public perde vue de vos talents et de vos lumières. Je suis persuadé que le Parlement ne portera point d'obstacles à l'accomplissement de vos vues . . . il n'y aura, s'il vous plait Monsieur, dans vos provisions aucune clause qui vous soit étrangère et personnelle à mon fils, ne se trouvant point en concours avec vous, seul cas ou il pourroit reclamer le privilege de fils de Maitre pour la préseance, il seroit très déplacé qu'il passât avant vous en vertu d'une faveur qui a mon sens seroit une injustice. je m'en suis expliqué avec M. le Garde

177

des Sceaux il y a 18 mois, et je persiste dans cette opinion. Je n'en suis pas moins sensible à tout ce que vous voulez bien me témoigner d'obligeant pour mon fils et pour moi . . .[2]

The other presidents, also consulted at this time, replied in similar terms, as they had 18 months previously. Dupaty returned to Bordeaux in the early days of 1779, hoping for a speedy dispatch of the remaining formalities.

However, on his return he was shaken to learn that in making an approach to the presidents of the respective chambers before an assembly of the chambers, he had acted irregularly.[3] Alarmed, he at once sought to withdraw the approaches he had made. Le Berthon strongly advised against this course, but Dupaty insisted, and the presidents agreed not to proceed. What Le Berthon thought of being thus ignored is not certain, but certainly from this time onwards he began to drag his feet on Dupaty's candidacy, accusing him of undue haste. In March he had still not written the customary letter of recommendation to the Keeper of the Seals. Dupaty grew worried. On 17 March he asked president de Lavie to approach Le Berthon on his behalf.

Tu pourras lui dire de ma part que je suis pret, s'il l'exige, à faire les démarches dont il a fait dépendre, des le principe, son agrément personnel; démarches que probablement il continue à regarder comme nécessaires; je ne peuts croire qu'il y ait d'autre obstacle à la lettre que j'ai sollicitée de sa bienveillance et de sa justice. Ce seroit comme me l'a écrit M. le premier président lui-même *lui rendre trop peu de justice* que de craindre que les personnalités engagent un magistrat, dont l'integrité est irréprochable, à mettre des obstacles au succès de mes voeux si légitimes, si autorisés par lui il y a 18 mois, soit il y a 3 mois, et justifiés, j'ose le dire, par une approbation générale. Depuis la dernière visite que j'ai eu l'honneur de lui faire, où il m'avoit paru favorablement disposé; je ne conçois pas ce qui a pu changer, en apparence, ces bonnes dispositions.[4]

Soon afterwards, he left for Paris, where he secured an interview with the Keeper of the Seals on 31 March. It was then that he learnt of opposition to his candidacy within the parlement. Le Berthon had at last written, but only to say that Dupaty should not be accorded provisions since, first, his birth was too lowly, and secondly, he himself personally opposed it.[5]

Dupaty was mortified. Both objections took him completely by surprise. It was true that he only possessed third-degree nobility, small stuff compared to the lineage of the other presidents and many counsellors. But this objection had not prevented him from becoming advocate-general. The real obstacle was not birth at all, but Le Berthon's personal opposition. The key to this is to be found in Dupaty's letter to Mme Dillon, of April 1779, in which he declares that:

Le premier président qui, dit-on, est au désespoir, ne comptant plus ou bien faiblement sur la charge de M. de Lavie, de voir venir dans mes mains celle qui d'ici à longtemps pourra vacquer seule dans la compagnie, s'est démasqué tout à fait. Il veut s'opposer de toutes ses forces à ma réception, et, par une perfidie inouie, c'est lui qui seule forme et suppose un parti contre moi dans le Parlement.[6]

It seems that Lavie's office was also on the market and that Le Berthon intended to buy it for his son. Then for some reason Lavie decided to continue, thus ruining his hopes of an early promotion for his son, since Dupaty already had the only other available presidency. Lavie was a close friend of Dupaty, and perhaps Le Berthon saw this as no coincidence. Might they not have concerted a deception to assure Dupaty of Gascq's office without the competition of Le Berthon? If this is how it appeared to Le Berthon, his hostility, first aroused by the way Dupaty had ignored his advice in January, would be confirmed.

As it turned out, the younger Le Berthon did not have to wait long for his promotion after all. Early in June 1779, president L. M. A. de Gourgue died suddenly. He was a childless widower, and his heirs at once put his office on sale. On 16 July the first president's son received the succession to the office for the sum of 123,000 l.[7] On 13 November, at a thinly attended session, he was received president à mortier, without preliminary visits or inquiry into life and morals, an unprecedentedly simple reception. But the purchase of Gourgue's office for his son did not change Le Berthon's attitude towards Dupaty. It would have been remarkable if it had. By the end of March he had committed himself against the candidate to the Keeper of the Seals.He had also gathered a hostile party in the parlement around the issue of Dupaty's inadequate ancestry. He had to continue to oppose Dupaty in order to save his own face, and that of his supporters. So the parlement once more began to divide into parties, this time for and against Dupaty. When, on 10 November, Dupaty and his powerful friends and relatives in Paris[8] eventually persuaded the Keeper of the Seals to issue provisions without the recommendation of Le Berthon, the breach was complete. Dupaty's candidacy now represented the overriding of the privileges and customs of the company, and raised the issue of the king's power over judicial appointments. The origins of the affair became secondary as government intervention turned a personal quarrel into a matter of constitutional principle.

The division became public in February 1780 when on the 16th the chambers eventually assembled to consider Dupaty's case. By then it had already been carefully rumoured that Le Berthon would resign rather than see Dupaty received, and a number of his close friends and relatives, some of whom had not been inside the palace for years, were present.[9] At the mention of Dupaty's name, Le Berthon and his son ostentatiously withdrew. The procurator-general delivered conclusions favourable to the candidate, but when it came to the voting, several magistrates pronounced against Dupaty, and there were accusations of low birth, hostility to religion, and neglect of the customs and etiquette of the court. But counsellor J. L. Darche went to the heart of the matter:

> Il dit que puisqu'il sembloit qu'on désirait les motifs du refus qu'il faisoit de M. Dupaty, dont l'éloquence mensongère n'avoit séduit qu'un instant la Cour, il déclaroit que l'esprit de cabale et d'intrigue qu'il avoit montré, principalement contre le Chef de la Compagnie et dont les preuves étoient consignées, suffisoient pour le faire rejetter . . .[10]

In the face of such considerations, it was pointless for Lavie to declare that the only serious objections were those on grounds of birth and disrespect for the company, or to show how ill-founded even these were. For the really serious objection was the one he ignored—Le Berthon's personal hostility. That remained constant, and all else, including the voting, followed from that. At the end of the five-hour sitting, Dupaty's provisions were rejected, without an inquiry into life and morals, by 20 votes to 16.

Nor did his opponents leave matters there. They went on to carry a new ruling that in future nobody would be admitted to the presidential bench without proving nobility, or at least three generations in the magistracy.[11] Such a ruling was not unprecedented in the parlements[12] and this gave it the appearance of normality. Nevertheless, it was clearly the product of the extraordinary circumstances of the Dupaty case, a device to cover up its true motive and substitute another which was publicly more acceptable.

For Dupaty the rejection of his provisions ostensibly meant the end of his career. He had already sold his office of advocate-general to Lalande, who had by this time completed all the preliminaries, and was received into the office a few days after the session of the 16th. It only remained for Dupaty to say his farewells, which he did in a long and moving speech before the assembled chambers on the 23rd.[13] He had not come, he declared, to have the *arrêté* of the 16th reversed, but he had come to vindicate his honour. He then proceeded at some length to dissect the charges allegedly made against him—attacking religion, disrespect for the court, and low birth. He was not impious: his children were being educated by clerics. 'Moi impie, Messieurs! Ah, j'ai vu trop de malheureux et j'ai été trop malheureux moi-même pour être impie . . .' As to disrespect for the company in not seeking its approval before approaching the king for provisions, many magistrates had followed this course. Besides, was it useful that men of talent should only attain judicial office and promotion by their colleagues' jealous consent? The king should have total freedom in promoting men of talent. Similarly with nobility. He confessed that he could not trace his ancestry beyond his grandfather, and even though his family had been ennobled since then, merit was the only form of nobility that offices should demand.[14] The king's choice should not be restricted by extraneous considerations such as birth, a distinction

> humiliante à la constitution de l'Etat et au bien public, en rendant la Magistrature Aristocratique comme les Loix et en fermant au grand préjudice de la société à tant de conditions honnêtes une carrière qu'un sage politique a toujours tenu ouverte comme toutes les autres, à la bonne Education, aux moeurs honnêtes, aux Talens et aux vertus.

Blunt though such language was, it was not without effect. Several magistrates who had voted against Dupaty declared themselves convinced by his vindication, and on the strength of this Lavie moved that the motives for the rejection of the previous week should not appear on the registers, since Dupaty had clearly demolished them. This proposal was carried, leaving an unmotivated rejection, legally dubious, alone on the record.[15] Thus the ground was prepared for disputing the court's decision. A few days later Dupaty left for Paris to begin the process.

The affair was further complicated by the intervention of E. L. Dufaure de Lajarte, advocate-general. On 2 March Dufaure came before the grand chamber to deliver his maiden speech in this capacity; and, as was usual on such occasions, he spoke of late colleagues. The rejection of Dupaty, he inferred, was a public calamity: 'Les Gens de bien sont dans le Deuil, . . . les loix gémissent, et . . . c'est insulter à la douleur publique que d'emprunter un visage riant dans un temps de calamité'. If the functions of the crown lawyers were not in future to open the way to the presidential bench, then the court might find men unwilling to undertake them.[16] He implied that the king ought to reverse the court's decision, and this could hardly please the party of Le Berthon, any more than the suggestion that they had been the agents of a public disaster. Accordingly at an assembly of chambers the next day, it was resolved to punish Dufaure for his disrespect. He was called before the assembly, publicly reprimanded by the first president, suspended from his duties for three months, and directed to make a fitting apology at the end of that time before he resumed them. He was not allowed either to protest or defend himself.[17] Such high-handed behaviour on the court's part was unlikely to strengthen its position over Dupaty, and it had the immediate effect of uniting all three crown lawyers, led by Dudon himself, in protests to the government. They did not consider themselves, being the king's representatives, subject to the discipline of the parlement. Dufaure followed Dupaty's example by leaving at once for Paris to press his case with higher authority; meanwhile he took legal advice from the most celebrated, if notorious, advocate of the day, Linguet.[18]

In Bordeaux, divisions within the court widened and hardened. On 29 July Dupaty arrived back there accompanied by his eminent brother-in-law Fréteau de Saint-Just, whose prestige he doubtless hoped would influence his former colleagues.[19] At the same time the Keeper of the Seals went so far as to despatch a letter to the parlement, dated 24 July, recommending Dupaty, asking the court to reconsider his provisions, and at least permit an inquiry into life and morals, in response to his petition. The court was instructed to assemble on 11 August in order to do this.[20] This disconcerted Le Berthon's party, and there were two weeks of frenzied assemblies to discuss the next step. At length it was decided to give Dupaty a hearing, and he pleaded his petition in person according to all the fegular forms. But on 18 August once again it was rejected by a majority vote. On 19 August the parlement sent an explanatory letter to the king, requesting that in ruture no provisions be granted without the prior consent of the court and its first president.[21]

However, the government was ready for this eventuality. It had had enough trouble from the parlement that year, with delays in registering both the prolongation of the twentieths and new regulations on the competence of the presidial courts.[22] All this and now the cases of Dupaty and Dufaure were enough to justify strong measures, and on 29 August Mouchy arrived at the palace bringing letters patent dated 25 August to prolong the sittings of the court into the vacation. 'Lempressement naturele aux officiers de cette Cour', commented the intendant with evident satisfaction, 'pour se rendre dans cette saison à leurs campagnes peut infiniment contribuer à une soumission plus promte aux volontés de S.M.'.[23] This might well have been so, but the magistrates gave no sign of willingness to negotiate. They resolved to hear no cases during the prolongation,[24] and Mouchy eventually recommended that the outstanding issues should be settled by a military session.[25] Accordingly on 16 September the members of the parlement received *lettres de cachet* ordering them to be present at the palace on the 21st. This at least gave them time to protest, and on 20 September they consigned to their registers a formal dissociation from all that might happen the next day, declaring the proceedings in advance to be illegal.[26] Such dissociations were normal and for the record. They could not prevent compulsory registration and they did not do so on 21 September. That day Mouchy, in a long session, compelled the registration of the prolongation of the twentieth and the new rules for the presidial courts. Turning then to Dupaty, he produced letters patent to quash the decision against him of 16 February, letters of *jussion* ordering the registration of his provisions, and a dispensation from the inquiry into life and morals, on the ground that he had already passed such an inquiry on becoming advocate-general. All this was compulsorily registered, but even worse followed. Dupaty himself had been waiting in an anteroom while the session proceeded; Mouchy now sent for him and ordered Le Berthon to receive him into the parlement. The bitterness of this moment was only aggravated when Mouchy went on to force registration of letters quashing the sentence upon Dufaure de Lajarte. A vacation chamber was summarily appointed and the magistrates ordered to separate until Martinmas without further meeting, before the session ended.[27]

Evidently the government's hope was to clear up a large number of outstanding issues at once, and let heads cool over the vacation. The worst that could happen was that the very number and diversity of the issues might dissipate the strength of any protest that might yet be made, with the result that some at least would be settled without further trouble. And indeed, nothing more was heard on the nationally important questions—the twentieth and the presidial courts. The protest, when it came, concentrated entirely on Dupaty and Dufaure. At the Martinmas commencement the first thing the parlement did was to enter a formal protest, and at a subsequent deliberation it was decided not to recognize Dupaty as a member of the parlement, not to include his name on its list, and not to recognize his votes or opinions in deliberations.[28] This step followed the example of the parlement of Grenoble in refusing to accept the royally-imposed procurator-general de Moydieu, who had served under Maupeou. In that case, the government had finally yielded the point and perhaps the Bordeaux magistrates hoped for a similar result.[29] At any rate, when the roll was read, Dupaty's name did not occur and Gascq's still did. Whenever Dupaty appeared, Le Berthon and his party ostentatiously absented themselves and soon the court sent new remonstrances on the issue.[30] He behaved calmly in the face of these insults, but drew up *procès-verbaux* which he sent to Versailles. Meanwhile, he insisted on fulfilling his duties as a president and appeared regularly at the sessions of the *tournelle*, despite the walk-outs, which left the chamber understaffed and therefore unable to function. His supporters attempted to heal the threatening schism on 16 November by proposing that he should be given provisional recognition pending the royal reply to the remonstrances, but this motion was defeated by 36 votes to 16.[31] After that the court was clearly split and its sittings paralysed, a situation only intensified by the refusal of the majority at the commencement to recognize that Dufaure de Lajarte had purged his contempt. His remarks were pointedly ignored and his presence passed over.[32]

By this time the affair was beginning to echo outside the walls of the parlement. In Paris it was rumoured that an exile of the parlement was being considered by the government.[33] In Bordeaux, a pamphlet war had broken out.[34] One writer declared that the internal squabblings of the parlement had gone on long enough, and that the only solution would be the complete destruction of the court.[35] This went for all the other parlements too; they should be replaced by bodies of annu-ally elective magistrates. Even a more moderate pamphlet, which set out to dis-countenance these extreme proposals,[36] admitted that Dupaty was in the right and, eulogizing Gascq, gave implicit praise to the work of Maupeou. It was not surprising that, late in January 1781, the party of Le Berthon made moves to suppress these pamphlets.[37] Even so, hostile opinion could not be stifled. Mme Duplessy was scandalized that even the *tournelle*, 'cette chambre qui doit toujours travailler', was at a standstill;[38] and Vergniaud, who admittedly was biased in his new-found capacity as Dupaty's secretary, declared that:

> ce qu'il y a de sûr, c'est que le voeu public est absolument pour lui, et comment ne le seroient-ils pas? Jamais aucun malheureux n'est sorti de chez lui sans être consolé ou soulagé; c'est un coeur, une âme dont je ne saurois vous peindre la bonté.[39]

Fortunately, the parlement hardly ever transacted serious business until some time after Christmas, so that as yet the damage to judicial efficiency was slight. The government was evidently determined that this should remain the case, for on 23 December it sent new letters patent which quashed the deliberations of November against Dupaty, and a further set which overruled the decision which the court had also taken, to maintain the suspension of Dufaure de Lajarte pend-ing his apology.[40] These instruments were supplemented by *lettres de cachet* of 25 December sent to each magistrate, ordering them to perform their duties in the parlement without interruption.[41] By these means the government showed its determination to stand by Dupaty and forestall any general strike or boycott among the magistrates over the issues which he represented.

So after Epiphany sittings resumed; but the letters patent were only considered at a series of assemblies of chambers between 24 and 28 January, and the result of these was to defer registration pending yet more remonstrances, to be brought to the king personally, if he agreed, by a deputation of magistrates, who could explain the parlement's (or rather the Le Berthon party's) position more clearly.[42] This decision was bitterly and closely contested, but there was nothing a minority could do to obstruct it, and pending the king's reply to this proposal no business was transacted. The majority occupied the interim with instituting, on the recommendation of Le Berthon, a judicial inquiry into the pamphlets that had been circulating, in the hope that Dupaty was the author of one or more of them; if this could be proved, it would only serve to confirm his unsuitability for the presidential bench.[43] The commission of inquiry worked furiously and fast, interrogating a huge number of witnesses, but they unearthed nothing conclusive. By now the public, reported Mme Duplessy, had become indifferent.[44] In any case these activities were rapidly eclipsed by the king's acceptance of the pro-posal for a deputation. Only Dupaty's most virulent opponents were chosen to accompany Le Berthon to Versailles—president Lynch, the advocate-general Lalande, the abbé Féger, and counsellors Darche de Lassalle and Marbotin de Conteneuil. They regarded the king's acquiescence as a triumph,[45] and the deputation left Bordeaux during the second week in February, apparently con-fident in the success of their stand.

A shock awaited them. The deputation was received by the king on 21 February, and brusquely told that the remonstrances it had brought contained nothing to change the royal mind. The king ordered the crestfallen magistrates to return at once to Bordeaux, to register the letters patent, and to give Dupaty and Dufaure de Lajarte no more trouble.[46] These instructions were added in the king's own hand to Miromesnil's formal reply to the remonstrances, and Louis, who had not concealed his anger at the continued 'rebellion' of the parlement, told Le Berthon that he held him personally responsible for implementing his orders and setting an example of submission. So they were dismissed, leaving Versailles amid scenes of disapproving silence.[47] At the same time a messenger was sent to Bordeaux with *lettres de cachet* for each magistrate, enjoining them to be present at an assembly of chambers as soon as the deputies returned, to receive and implement the king's orders. He also brought further orders to suspend all investigations into the pamphlets published on the subject of the Dupaty affair.[48] The deputies arrived back in Bordeaux on 3 March.

On 7 March the chambers were assembled to receive the king's orders.[49] The deputies presented the royal orders and opened the discussion on them by bluntly declaring to a man that they were against obedience. Le Berthon declared that his honour prevented him from complying. 'Je suis bien curieux', mused Pichard maliciously in a letter to Richelieu,[50] 'de scavoir comment les ministres trouvent la conduitte qua tenu le 1er président, dans un gouvernement qui ne serait pas aussi doux, il devroit trembler'. However, despite this intransigence, Dupaty's opponents were divided on what course to take in the face of such clear orders from the king. Some proposed a mass resignation. Others favoured a strike. Dupaty himself said nothing. Eventually, after over five hours of heated discussions, the sides ranged themselves around the positions of a blank refusal to register, or a qualified registration. At the final vote, the intransigents were outvoted by 46 votes to 37. The qualifications in the registration, which provided for remonstrances,[51] were not material. The fundamental point—the acceptance of Dupaty—was carried, because enough magistrates who had hitherto been opposed or indifferent did not feel justified in flouting the king's explicit orders.[52]

With this decided, ancillary matters were soon cleared up. The next day another assembly of chambers considered the letters patent defending Dufaure de Lajarte, and the result was the registration of the letters by an even bigger majority than for those regarding Dupaty.[53] Finally there was the question of the pamphlets. In response to the king's orders quashing proceedings against them, Dudon had at once sent the evidence he held to Versailles. The assembly of chambers of 9 March could hardly dispute the orders; but an attempt was made to blame Dudon for implementing them without prior reference to the court, and only the intervention of Pichard, presiding, prevented a new storm.[54] The co-operation of the procurator-general with the government on yet another occasion, however, only increased the bitterness and perhaps the numbers of his enemies, as he was soon to realize.

By mid-March, however, everybody believed that the Dupaty affair and its ramifications were settled. It certainly looked that way from Paris, where the members of the parlement, doubtless stirred to interest by Fréteau, had viewed Dupaty's exclusion with concern.[55] And from Bordeaux, several magistrates wrote to Richelieu that the troubles were over. 'Enfin', declared Gobineau,[56] 'tout est dit, Laffaire est finie, Du moins je La Crois telle'. It seemed to Vergniaud that 'il est à croire que la paix va enfin revenir dans le Parlement'.[57] And Mme

Duplessy had heard rumours that matters would be concluded by offering Le Berthon the post of councillor of state and replacing him by Dudon.[58]

But if Le Berthon ever received such an offer, he refused it. He remained at the head of the parlement, and he remained a rallying-point for those not reconciled to Dupaty. After the letters patent had been registered, Dupaty made a round of visits to his colleagues, and was even received by some of his former opponents; but Le Berthon and his son refused him the door.[59] This was as much as to say that the struggle was still on. Dupaty's opponents simply changed their tactics.

The new approach emerged during the later weeks of March, when day after day it was found impossible in the grand chamber to assemble enough magistrates to transact judicial business. Dupaty's opponents seemed resolved to exclude him in practice by refusing to opine with him. Le Berthon fulfilled his own duties punctiliously, but few doubted that he looked with favour upon this undeclared strike. Even the *tournelle*, where Dupaty and his friends made a special effort to keep business going, was unable to work normally. The two senior chambers accomplished next to nothing in the three months following the March assemblies 'Les plaideurs se désespèrent', reported Vergniaud in May,

> et tout ce qui tient au Palais se trouve dans la consternation. Il n'y a pas eu une seule audience en nombre cette semaine. Il n'y a que la Tournelle qui fasse son service assez exactement; point d'audience et de relevée, et s'il n'arrive pas des ordres incessamment, on craint que le service ne cesse entièrement aux fêtes de la Pentecôte.[60]

Who were the dissidents? First of all they were the immediate circle of Le Berthon—his son and his Verthamon relatives, his son-in-law president Lynch, his neighbours Gombault and Marbotin, and his friend the abbé Féger. All the presidents *à mortier* except Pichard and Lavie, who each had special reasons for dissenting, also opposed Dupaty; as did intransigent defenders of the parlement's rights against royal encroachments, such as counsellors de Basterot and Fauquier. The supporters of the new president, on the other hand, were a curious combination of government men and enemies of Le Berthon, like Dudon and Pichard, and young liberals, typified by Lavie. It was remarkable, as the author of the *Mémoires Secrets* observed from Paris, how many old remainers supported the hero of the returners—'la malheureuse scission actuelle a fait disparoître l'ancienne'.[61] But the reversal was not as great or dramatic as it appeared; the tried friends to authority were simply rallying to a cause which authority had made its own.

Obviously the deadlock had not been broken, however. Early in June Mouchy arrived in Bordeaux on his eighth visit since becoming commander-in-chief. Each time, he complained, it had been troubles in the parlement which had brought him.[62] His homilies on the need for concord brought no more satisfactory result than usual.[63] The government therefore resorted to new measures of severity. On 20 July Dudon, at an assembly of chambers, handed Le Berthon a packet which turned out to be a *lettre de cachet* ordering him to be at Versailles by 8 August to report on how he had carried out the king's orders of February.[64] Hardly had the sensation died down, when Dudon produced a general *lettre de cachet*, dated 18 July, which ordered all magistrates to resume their services and dispense justice normally until the end of the session. But these orders had next to no effect. The next day, several of Le Berthon's friends ostentatiously left the palace with his obvious approval, so as to prevent any sitting in the grand chamber.[65] On the day before Le Berthon's departure, 1 August, Dupaty complained at an assembly of chambers that even the *tournelle* was soon likely to cease functioning, unless the parlement resolved upon a general resumption of duties. Le Berthon replied, carrying the majority with him, that since there had been no formal decision to cease service, there could be none to resume it. He would return, he announced, as he had left, that was to say, intransigent.[66]

Le Berthon's departure began a new phase in the struggle. Pichard now presided over the parlement, and encouraged Dupaty's party to profit from their enemy's absence with a renewed effort to hold sittings regularly. It was an uphill struggle, for even some of his strongest supporters, notably Lavie, had ceased to attend the court in sheer disgust. On 6 August, however, the grand chamber held its first sitting with a full complement for three months, a hopeful sign which was repeated several times during the next week. There was consternation in the Le Berthon party, for if it could be shown that his presence alone had impeded regular sittings, the government might try to settle matters by demanding his resignation. Several sessions during these weeks were spoiled not so much by a lack of magistrates as by the absence of advocates, who had been made to feel the danger of incurring the first president's displeasure by co-operating in sittings whose very occurrence discredited him. There was certainly no decline in bitterness. 'On était reduit au point', noted the pro-Dupaty counsellor de Lamontaigne, 'de désirer même une révolution, quelle qu'elle fut, pour le rétablissement de la paix et de l'ordre dans la compagnie'.[67] On 21 August came the news that Le Berthon, after a meeting with ministers on the 12th, had been exiled to Meaux.[68] In the same post arrived letters patent to prolong the sittings of the court into the vacation for the second year running,[69] *lettres de cachet* ordering each magistrate to attend all sessions assiduously until further notice,[70] further letters revoking all leaves-of-absence accorded to individual magistrates, and instructions by *lettre de cachet* to all presidents of chambers to send daily minutes of sessions with names of those present and details of cases judged. The exile of Le Berthon gave new life born of indignation to his party, however, and once more emphasized that the questions at issue concerned the rights and prerogatives of the parlement rather than Dupaty personally. As for the other orders, commented Vergniaud,

> Les officiers du Parlement sont tellement familiarisés avec les lettres de cachet, que celles-ci n'ont fait aucune impression. Il n'est pas entré un magistrat de plus qu'à l'ordinaire, et il y a à parier que les esprits encore plus aigris, n'en feront que plus mal leur devoir.[71]

The parlement registered the prolongation, by the king's very express command, on 23 August, but at once decided to draw up new representations against the ever-growing use of *lettres de cachet*, and the exile of Le Berthon. There were new clashes when Dupaty, as was his right as a president, appeared at Pichard's for the drawing-up of these remonstrances.[72] His enemies remained unreconciled, and so, in Meaux, did Le Berthon. 'Telle est ma constitution', he wrote to his friend Duval, 'que n'ayant point de reproches à me faire, je n'ay aucun remords qui m'inquiète et m'agite'.[73] Indeed, Meaux was so agreeable and so accessible to those who sympathized with him, that early in October he was ordered to move to more distant Châlons-sur-Marne.[74]

The parlement's protest was finally dispatched on 27 August, the heads of remonstrance having been fixed in an *arrêté* of the same day, which was soon being pirated and much sought after in Paris.[75] Clearly dictated by a majority sympathetic to Le Berthon, it rehearsed the grievances of the parlement since the beginning of the affair, emphasizing particularly the unflattering innuendoes of the December letters patent, the abundance of those pernicious and irregular instruments, the *lettres de cachet*, the exile of Le Berthon, the suspension of the inquiry into the pamphlets, and the prolongation of sittings. The parlement begged the king to listen to its pleas, and not dishonour it with his displeasure. Meanwhile, no more business was done during the compulsory sittings of September. Clearly the government's severity had failed, and it made it known towards the end of September that if the court would register the edict of August imposing a 10 per cent surcharge on all indirect taxes, the magistrates would be allowed to disperse. This it did, and the prolongation was lifted on 29 September; even though the parlement suspended the operation of the edict pending remonstrances, the magistrates were not detained.[76]

Two judicial years had now been ruined by the Dupaty affair, which had proved even more disruptive than the quarrels between remainers and returners. The public was bitter and exasperated, the government nonplussed on how to resolve the differences. However, the magistrates themselves were not entirely insensitive to the damage that the schism was doing to their position and reputation, and there were signs that the party of accommodation was growing.[77] It was certain, however, that nothing could be achieved so long as Le Berthon remained in exile. When sessions resumed in November, business was still immobilized,[78] and Dupaty was still persecuted, this time by the exclusion from sessions on the grounds of his involvement in the matters at issue. An *arrêté* of 23 November enumerated five new heads of remonstrance similar to those agreed in August,[79] and Pichard, who was in Paris, was instructed to return to Bordeaux to prevent new divisions.[80] On 22 December, finally, the government decided to risk the essential first step towards a solution—the release of Le Berthon from exile. The release came on 31 December, and by the second week in January he was back in Bordeaux, where he was received by his partisans with great festivity.[81]

It seemed at first that nothing had changed, that he had returned, as he said he would, intransigent as ever. He refused his door to the intendant, to Dufaure de Lajarte, and to two Dupaty supporters.[82] His partisans of the previous summer still boycotted most sittings, as did many advocates, afraid of his displeasure.[83] However, before leaving Châlons he had received the strictest orders from the king to promote harmony, and during the weeks up to 20 February, when the chambers reassembled, he had several meetings with Dudon, with whom he had been on bad terms for some years, and who of course was a leading Dupaty supporter.[84] This in itself was a good sign. At these meetings, the grounds for a settlement were prepared.

The royal policy emerged when a packet of orders was opened at the assembly on 20 February;[85] it was found to contain a letter,[86] dated 22 December 1781, in which ministers made the concession of agreeing to let the pamphlet investigation go ahead, on condition that it was put in the hands of the parlement of Toulouse.

This of course still consigned it to oblivion in practice, but it was a goodwill gesture towards Dupaty's opponents. The central problem now, the letter emphasized, was to bring about a general resumption of services. It went into some detail on the strikes and boycotts of the preceding months, emphasizing their malicious nature. Magistrates chose their profession freely, it pointed out, and therefore they freely undertook its obligations. Therefore:

> Si quelques-uns de vous, ce que nous ne pouvons présumer, étoient capables de refuser de se conformer à la volonté dans laquelle nous sommes de rétablir l'union & la paix entre tout [sic] les membres de notre parlement, & de faire rendre sans interruption bonne justice à nos sujets, nous leur permettons de renoncer à leurs fonctions, & nous leur ordonnons de la déclarer sur le registre, & avant de désemparer, dans la séance où cette lettre sera lue.

It was a bold gesture. To resign implied that a magistrate was an enemy of harmony and the administration of justice. Not to resign implied the intention to resume duties. The Le Berthon party were trapped, nor were they allowed time for deliberation. The first president himself, apparently mollified during his absence, suggested that the court write a letter to the king professing its intention to carry out its duties punctiliously in the future. In these circumstances his party collapsed, and nobody resigned. The proposal was carried unanimously, without even a vote.[87]

Admittedly the course adopted had a sting in the tail. The letter of obedience which was eventually dispatched to the king read more like a remonstrance, and was only agreed to after loud protests from the Dupaty party.[88] The court declared that, whatever the king thought, its own 'voeu le plus ardent, est de voir l'union & la paix régner dans son sein'.[89] It had never lost sight of the fact that its prime duty was to distribute justice, but the repeated blows (they were not specified) which had fallen on the parlement had left the magistrates no alternative but resignation, if the king had not by his letter of 22 December allowed them no way of doing it honourably. All the same, behind the waspishness, they were admitting that the king and Dupaty had won.

Events confirmed this. Slowly the court resumed its sittings. 'Le parlement va son train', reported Vergniaud in March,[90]

> les plus grands ennemis de M Du Paty montent regulièrement à l'audience, on ne parle plus de la procédure[91] et on espère que le tems remettra enfin la paix qui commence à rapprocher les membres les plus désunis.

In the course of the spring, moreover, the magistrates rallied behind Dudon to fire the first shots in the *alluvions* affair, which gave them other things to think about. There were also the events leading up to the forced registration on 27 May by the comte de Fumel of the August 1781 edict which increased various indirect taxes.[92] Letters of *jussion* had been dispatched on this question on 2 February. Such matters were soon diverting the attention of the magistrates, and so slowly the Dupaty controversy seemed to die down. It was not, however, forgotten. 'Ce qui vous surprendra le plus', Mouchy informed Vergennes in September 1783,[93] 'c'est que M Dupaty nest pas mieux au Parlement que quand je l'ai installé, on ne le regarde pas, on lui tourne l'epaule sur le banc des Presidents ...'

For Dupaty, in fact, 1783 was a year of troubles. In the spring, when the *tournelle* over which he presided fell into a jurisdictional dispute with Mouchy, his enemies convinced Mouchy that the blame for the *tournelle*'s behaviour lay with the president, even though he had been instrumental in modifying the chamber's position. Then in July he fell out almost simultaneously with the companies of procurators and advocates. Although some of the most prominent members of the bar were his close friends, perhaps the majority of the advocates, dependent as they were for cases on the patronage of the magistrates, preferred to associate themselves with the majority in the parlement. The procurators stood in much the same relation to the court. So it is not surprising to find them willing to seize upon small pretexts for embarrassing Dupaty. Accordingly, when the president publicly upbraided one procurator for not being present when a case which he was handling was called, the man in question complained to his order. The result was that the procurators as a body voted to boycott the *tournelle* until Dupaty apologized, which he was eventually forced to do.[94] The advocates took similar action when he dismissed one of their number from a court-room for appearing at the bar improperly dressed, and nothing Dupaty's friends in the company could do would persuade them to reverse their decision.[95] Throughout August, most of them boycotted all sessions at which Dupaty was present,[96] despite a letter of approval which he obtained from the Keeper of the Seals. Attempts made by president de Verthamon, a leading opponent of Dupaty, to oblige Vergniaud, then a promising young advocate and protégé of Dupaty, seem to confirm that a party among the magistrates were supporting and encouraging the advocates' action.[97] Perhaps the satirical songs and pamphlets against Dupaty[98] which were circulating at this time derived encouragement from the same source.

In any event, by the vacation he had had enough. The moment sittings ended, he left for Paris, and there delivered a brief memorandum on his position to the government:

> La position de M[r] le President Du Paty dans le Parlement de Bordeaux ne lui permet plus d'y continuer, ni avec sûrete, ni avec honneur, ni avec utilité pour le public, les fonctions que le Roi lui a confiées; du moins jusqu'a ce qu'une revolution malheureusement inattendue ait rétabli dans cette Compagnie, le calme, la discipline et le véritable esprit de la magistrature.[99]

His enemies, he declared, formed a majority in the parlement, and twisted or obstructed all he did. What then did he want? His proposal was to revive his project, first submitted to Miromesnil in 1782, for a survey of the criminal laws of Europe, with a view to the ultimate reform of those of France.[100] Miromesnil, while refusing to finance the travels that this would involve[101], did not frown on the project, and gave Dupaty permission to stay away from Bordeaux and travel abroad. 'Daignes, Monsieur le Comte', Dupaty begged Vergennes,[102]

> prendre mon projet sous votre protection. je ne vois pas ce qu'on peut opposer de solide contre une entreprise si avantageuse. considéres d'ailleurs que le Roi, en m'y employant, trouverait un moyen honorable pour moi et peu grêveux pour l'état, de m'éloigner pendant quelques années du plt de bordeaux, jusqu'a ce que la fermentation y fut Calmée.

Vergennes was agreeable; and so he was able in 1785 to make the tour of Italy which resulted in his well-known *Lettres sur l'Italie*. But as far as can be ascertained, he never saw Bordeaux again.

So Le Berthon and his party finally triumphed. They let Dupaty in only to drive him out. But the cost of this victory in terms of the loss to the parlement of public confidence, respect, and prestige, was out of all proportion to the satisfaction of the individuals who brought it about. The Dupaty affair made the parlement seem a bastion of militant aristocratic exclusivism; in which the magistrates did themselves less than justice. Perhaps more important still, it had prolonged the squabbling that followed Maupeou and confirmed the parlement's apparent disregard of its primary functions as a law court. Beside their personal vendettas, all other concerns seemed dwarfed in the magistrates' attention.

One set of quarrels blended imperceptibly into another. The Dupaty troubles did not so much eclipse the divisions between returners and remainers, as prolong them in new circumstances. 'Le parlement de Bordeaux', observed Miromesnil to Vergennes in October 1781,[103]

> . . . s'est divisé en 1771, et Cest Leffet de Cette division dont La Guerre subsiste Encor qui fait actuellement son malheur. Il est toujours pret a se diviser de nouveau, et nombre de mauvais Esprits veulent se servir de Loccasion presente pour satisfaire dans une autre forme Danciens ressentiments . . .

Indeed, no sooner had the court resumed more or less regular sittings in the spring of 1782, than new opportunities arose for reopening old wounds. It was true that early in the spring the son of counsellor Domenge, whose name had been repeatedly rejected ever since 1776, finally secured reception.[104] But when, a few months later, J. G. de Lorman took up the succession to his father's office of counsellor in the requests, he was opposed by a number of militants on the grounds that his father had served under Maupeou. It took a firm stand by Le Berthon, supported by Mouchy, to overcome these machinations.[105] At least, however, they *were* overcome, which might not have happened a few years before.

Some cases, of course, remained unforgivable. Gascq for instance never risked returning to Bordeaux, and lived in Paris from 1775 until his death in 1781 on a royal pension. Similarly most of the 'intruders', who vanished into prudent obscurity in 1775, remained there. One of Gascq's nephews won a certain notoriety as a pamphleteer later in the 1780s,[106] and he or his brother secured a royal gratification of 1,000 l. in 1784 on the strength of his services under Maupeou.[107] The eldest son of counsellor de Laroze eventually became a president at the court of aids; but those, like the younger Drouilhet, who aspired to sit in the restored parlemenr, were doomed to disappointment. Nowhere in France did Maupeouan intruders secure readmission to the parlemena in which they had sat; until, that is, the reception of J. B. P. J. Dudon as second procurator-general in the parlement of Bordeaux.

It was unfortunate that Dudon should have chosen the occasion of the Maupeou reform to introduce his son to the parlement. As advocate-general, at the restoration like all intruders he was summarily turned out.[108] Dudon was too experienced a magistrate to try at this stage to get him back into the court, and

expose him to the humiliations of the younger Drouilhet; but few other openings
arose in the late 1770s, and the continuing ferment in the parlement excluded any
possibility of his re-entry. Dudon therefore turned his attention to the *jurade*, and
in 1779, after some intrigue, he was one of the three candidates elected by the city
notables for nomination to the annually vacant post of *jurat gentilhomme*.[109]
Mouchy was of the opinion that he should receive the nomination, partly at least
to show that the government was not hostile to those who had co-operated with
Maupeou, and the government accepted this advice, despite much hostility in the
city.

> il est bon enfant, mais tres petit maistre et agreable et drole pour un magis-
> trat. vous croyez bien qu'il y a eu plus des deux tiers de Bordeaux contre . . .
> si m Bertin le veut, Il n'a qu'a me mander que le Roy L'a préféré par con-
> sidération pour les services de M le Procureur General et tout sera dit, le
> Roy etant le maistre de choisir sur les 3 proposés . . .[110]

Dudon's two years in the *jurade* were distinguished by a policy of subservience to
the government, and he widened his circle of enemies.[111] In 1781, apparently on
the request of the procurator-general, the government prolonged his term of
office for another two years despite the custom of Bordeaux which forbade successive terms.[112] Rapidly young Dudon came to share his father's reputation as a
willing tool of authority.

But Dudon knew that the king's enemies received no patronage. His hope was
that his son's services in the *jurade* might ultimately open his way to reception in
the parlement. In the summer of 1781 he had already made the first suggestion
of this to the Keeper of the Seals,[113] and in September 1782 he renewed it.
'Vous m'avés donné tant de marques de bonté et tant d'assurances de protection',
he wrote to Vergennes, at the same time,[114]

> que je ne balance pas de les réclamer de nouveau pour obtenir de M. le
> Garde des Sçeaux la Survivance de ma charge pour mon fils . . .
> . . . je ne sollicitois pour Luy la continuation de la jurade, que comme un
> moien honette de le tenir toujours en haleine, et de donner a M le Garde des
> Sçeaux le temps de retablir L'ordre dans notre compagnie.
> Aujourd'hui, Monsieur le Comte, le calme paroit avoir succédé à la
> tempete, et s'il y a encore quelques personnes remuans qui se plaisent dans
> le desordre, ce n'est heureusement que le plus petit nombre. Sur Le tout, il
> n'en est point d'un Procureur Général comme d'un autre officier qui est
> obligé de solliciter l'agrément de sa Compagnie, et d'avance je suis sur que
> mon fils seroit reçu avec satisfaction par le plus grand nombre des magistrats
> qui Luy ont accordé leur amitié et leur estime.
> il est temps, Monsieur le Comte, que je m'occupe de fixer son sort; il a
> près de trente trois ans, et je desire avec ardeur de Luy assurer ma place à
> titre de survivance et d'adjonction. C'est la seule récompense a laquelle je
> puisse pretendre après quarante deux ans de service le plus pénible et le plus
> laborieux dans le ministère public, il seroit bien cruel pour moy d'éprouver
> un refus, et de voir que l'on a accordé la mesme grace que je sollicite a tant
> d'autres qui n'avoint peut-être autant de raisons pour l'obtenir que moy.
> L'amour paternel, Monsieur le Comte, ne me fait point illusion, et je

> peux rendre témoignage à la droiture, L'intelligence, et les talens de mon fils, parceque je suis sur de celuy du public. Si L'on excepte quelques mal intentionés, quelques ennemis secrets qui n'oseroint se montrer, il n'est personne qui ne convienne qu'on n'avoit vu depuis longtemps a Bordeaux aucun jurat s'acquiter comme Luy des devoirs penibles de cette place, et je me garderois bien de Le proposer pour mon successeur si je croiois qu'en remettant mes fonctions dans ses mains, il put me faire tort.

Moreover, in case the ministry held these protestations suspect, Dudon invoked the aid of outside referees. Beaumarchais,[115] who was gun-running to America through Bordeaux at this time, sent the government a report on the parlement in October 1782, which it is impossible to believe was not concerted in advance with the procurator-general.[116] The government, he reported, had friends in the parlement whom it did not cultivate enough.

> A la tête de ces hommes essentiels est, selon moi, le procureur-general Dudon, vieilli dans un poste honorable avec l'estime universelle et sans aucune recompense de ses travaux. C'est une excellente race que ces Dudon; le père au Parlement, le fils aîné dans la Jurade, et tout cela bien ferme et bien vertueux; c'est ce qu'on peut appeler des magistrats de vieille roche. Il serait bien a désirer que le fils, élevé dans les principes du père, pût un jour lui succéder dans sa charge . . .

When Vergennes's reply, of 13 October, informed Dudon that he had the ministry's support, he was delighted. He only urged the ministry to make haste, so that his son could be received upon the expiry of his service in the *jurade* in September 1783.[117] He did not anticipate trouble in the parlement, but:

> il seroit bien triste pour moy Monsieur, que le succès de ma demande dependit de Mr Le Berthon, et je ne crois pas etre dans le Cas de L'attendre. personne n'honore plus que moy la vertu de ce magistrat, et j'ai ressenti plus vivement que Luy meme, tous les désagrémens qu'il a éprouvé [sic]. j'ose dire que s'il m'avoit rendu plus de justice, je luy aurois épargné bien des fautes. Aujourd'huy, Monsieur le Comte, je suis très bien avec luy. jay fait le sacrifice de mes justes ressentiments, j'ai été luy demander son amitié, nous nous sommes embrassés, et nous vivons bien ensemble . . .
>
> Néanmoins Mr Le P[er] Président a un fils, j'ignore s'il a sur luy les memes vues que j'ay sur le mien. je n'en dis pas davantage, mais j'en ai dit assés pour vous faire sentir que je ne dois pas etre livré à la discrétion de M. Le Berthon. je le crois trop honnette homme pour dire du mal de mon fils, il enregistreroit sans difficulté les provisions, mais je n'ai pas la même confiance dans sa reponce s'il est consulté, parceque j'ai toujours a craindre l'esprit de parti . . .

Such were the origins of the Dudon affair.[118] On 15 July 1783 young Dudon was issued with letters of provision as procurator-general designate, to take up his functions at once alongside his father. It was an unprecedented appointment, and the news struck Bordeaux like a thunderbolt. It meant that Dudon would remain one of the most powerful men in the city, and that he would be immune from the vengeance of any enemies that he had made while a *jurat*. It also spelled an end to the ambitions of Poissac, the young Le Berthon, the advocate-general de Lalande, or anybody else, to succeed to the powerful office of procurator-general. Naturally it met with bitter resistance.

Since it was hardly appropriate for Dudon to require his own son's admission to his own office, the provisions were put in the hands of Lalande, advocate-general. Here, trouble began. Perhaps Lalande had cherished the hope of succeeding Dudon. At any rate, he advised the grand chamber that the provisions were not in good order, and the question was referred to an assembly of chambers on 6 August.[119] At this assembly, Le Berthon ominously refused to preside, leaving the hapless Pichard with the unenviable duty. After this Lalande, who had been one of Le Berthon's allies against Dupaty, repeated his doubts concerning Dudon's moral probity, and made innuendoes about the public notoriety of his private life. He did not, he said, come to denounce or accuse, but merely to set out all the relevant material. But uproar followed, and the final decision was deferred until the 8th, when after five hours of discussion the majority voted by 30 votes to 22 to instruct Lalande at once to prepare conclusions. One or two declared that he was too biassed on the question to do so, but they were over-ridden. Lalande was ordered to deliver them on the 13th, after Dudon had made courtesy visits to his prospective colleagues. 'Je crois devoir vous Conffier', wrote Pichard to Vergennes after this session,[120]

> que quoique il se soit rettiré du palais avec son fils et son gendre jay tres bien remarqué et observe, que touts les magistrats sans exception qui ont des rapports avec m^r le 1er president ont touts etté davis de renvoyer mr dudon a huittaine affin qu'il obtint pendant cet inttervalle lagrement de la Compagnie. Ce qui ettablit de sa part une opposition decidee a sa reception mais comme ses demarches doivent ettre cachees il est tres possible quil ne soit pas le plus fort.

It certainly seems that, whatever preliminary steps the ministry had taken before issuing the provisions, they had offended Le Berthon, and Dudon's fears had been well grounded. It remained to be seen whether Le Berthon's opposition would be successful. To be received into the company, a candidate needed a two-thirds majority, and Pichard's fear was that Dudon's plurality would not be as great as that.[121] Mouchy, on his tenth trip to Bordeaux, pointed out to Vergennes that in abstaining with his son and son-in-law rather than voting openly against Dudon, Le Berthon had in fact increased Dudon's majority;[122] but it seemed likely that the candidate would not even then win the necessary two-thirds.

So it proved at the session of the 13th.[123] Lalande presented his conclusions, and it was debated whether Dudon should now be allowed to proceed to the final stage of admission, the examination. Twenty-nine voted in favour, 24 against, after a stormy session in which Dudon's opponents spoke quite openly against the intruders of 1771. There was, reported Mouchy, far more hostility than against Dupaty;[124] perhaps it was aggravated by the fact that Dupaty himself, hitherto no friend of the Dudon family, voted for admission,[125] one more step in the alignment of Dupaty with the remainers. It was undeniable, however, that Dudon had not received two-thirds of the votes, and his opponents claimed victory. In future, they declared, they would create no trouble for the remainers of 1771 and their children, but they would never admit an intruder:[126] 'Jai mandé a M le Garde des Sceaux', Mouchy wearily reported on 23 August, 'qu'il n'y auroit jamais que l'autorité du Roy . . . qui put faire recevoir M Dudon Procureur General en survivance et adjoint . . .'[127]

This advice was followed. On 26 August the king issued letters of *jussion* ordering the immediate registration of Dudon's provisions. Since the candidate had already served as advocate-general in the parlement, said the letters, incautiously, he should be dispensed from further inquiries and the examination which overrode the need for a two-thirds majority in his favour.[128] On 2 September Mouchy forced both the registration of the letters and the reception of Dudon.[129] Thus yet another prolongation into the vacation was avoided, but at the cost of extremely arbitrary conduct by the commandant. 'Je ne vous cacherai pas', Mouchy confessed to Vergennes, 'que je crains fort les suites, car il y a plus de la fermentation, c'est une espece de rage . . .'[130] The fury of his opponents was only increased when, the day after his reception, Dudon began to sign legal documents in his new capacity. 'Quand on a le malheur de deplaire a un certain nombre des Magistrats de sa compagnie', observed Pichard,[131] 'on ne gagne rien à les braver, et quand on est sûr de conserver sa place, il est quelque fois sage de s'abstenir d'user de tous les droits qui y sont attachés Lorsque cela n'est pas necessaire'. In any event, as soon as the session of 2 September was over, the court passed the usual protestations against its illegality, and ordered the drawing-up of remonstrances.[132]

Yet Dudon, far from diminishing his chances of final acceptance by signing documents the moment he had been received, had played a masterstroke. His signature raised the question of the legal standing of such documents, some of which concerned very valuable cases. To declare them invalid would delay the cases indefinitely. In these circumstances, the court was induced to resolve on 8 September that it would for the moment accept Dudon's ministrations, stressing that this in no way implied that it considered his position legitimate, or approved of his reception. Thus an internal quarrel was not allowed to impede the course of justice. A similar motion concerning Dupaty had been defeated in November 1780;[133] perhaps that of 1783 indicated a desire to avoid the worst excesses of the former troubles, and to present a more responsible impression to the world outside. Perhaps too, such a compromise suited Dudon's opponents because it wooed away some of those who had hitherto voted for him purely and simply, thus diminishing his support. Nevertheless, it still gave away the game, for it allowed Dudon to perform the functions of the office, so conceding those nine points of the law which are possession. Furthermore, no such compromise could satisfy the government in the long run, since it left Dudon's right incomplete. There was bound then to be further intervention on his behalf by the king, although for the moment everything was suspended by the end of the session.

Friends of the government always hoped that the vacation would cool tempers, but their hopes were seldom borne out. This occasion was no exception. When after the commencement on 13 November the clerk read out the official list for the forthcoming session, the mention of Dudon's name aroused protests from several magistrates. They demanded an immediate discussion as to whether his name should be included, and the result was a resolution that, as in the case of Dupaty, it should not.[134] So, throughout that judicial year, he continued to perform his functions without the court's official recognition. The rift was widened rather than narrowed when on 3 March 1784 the court at last despatched the remonstrances it had ordered the previous September. The very fact that they could be sent shows that Dudon's majority of August had been turned into a minority by the arbitrary way in which the government had imposed his reception. The strength of the feeling against him was demonstrated not only by shameful innuendoes about his private life, but by the fact that some of his more bitter opponents contrived to have these remonstrances printed and circulated throughout Europe in the *Gazette de Leyde*.[135] 'Les survivances sont un abus', they declared,

> que la sagesse de nos Roys a souvent proscrit, et que L'importunité et l'intrigue ont toujours fait renaître . . . Les survivances sont rarement le prix du merite et de la vertu . . . elles anéantissent l'emulation, elles font naître le decouragement; elles occasionnent la retraite de plusieurs sujets qui auroient été utilles.

Bad enough when candidates had merit, they were inexcusable when, like Dudon, they had none. Not only had he never been a magistrate, when the office of procurator-general was traditionally the reward of distinction on the bench; but he had served in the Maupeou parlement, and no such intruder had ever subsequently gained admission to a parlement.

> Le Sr Dudon et les autres intrus sont des usurpateurs, qui ont profité des malheurs publics, pour enlever l'etat et une partie de la fortune de leurs Concitoyens; que peuvent-ils donc avoir de commun avec des magistrats, en qui la nation entière a toujours reconnu un titre legal?

Even worse, Dudon's moral probity was in doubt:

> Le public a dit que la jeunesse du Sr Dudon fils, a été très orageuse, que dès son entrée dans le monde, il a eu les moeurs les plus dépravées; qu'elles ont toujours été et qu'elles sont encore un objet de scandale: il a dit que souvent le Sr Dudon pere a eu recours à la police, ou même a L'autorité pour faire renfermer les Compagnons des débauches de son fils; il a dit que, pendant que le Sr. Dudon a exercé la place de Jurat de Bordeaux, on l'a vu afficher la debauche, et proteger ces desordres, que sa place lui faisoit un devoir de punir.

The way to verify or dispel these rumours was to allow an unfettered inquiry into life and morals, which, however, the king's letters of *jussion* had curtailed. And so the remonstrances ended on the more familiar theme of free registration and an end to military sessions.

How true all these allegations were is uncertain. Perhaps Dudon did have a dubious past. Even Pichard, one of his most constant supporters, had admitted in August 1783 that: 'si les moeurs de mr dudon le fils eussent ette plus pures il ne reconttreroit pas tant de difficultes ou ce seroit un pretexte de moins pour ceux qui luy sont opposes'.[136] But the point is that they were a pretext. The real reasons for opposition remained his service under Maupeou, and the fact that his succession to the office of procurator-general thwarted the ambitions of a number of other magistrates. Nevertheless, despite everything he was exercising the office, and all attempts to reverse the effect of the provisional resolution of September 1783 were unavailing. The business of the court was thus never held up as it had been over Dupaty. It is true that there were dangerous moments. On 23 July 1784 the new procurator-general appeared for the first time at an assembly of chambers, and several magistrates declared that this could not be allowed to pass without a protest, lest it be implied that the court now accepted him, and a refutation of the March remonstrances which the government had inserted in the *Gazette de Leyde*.[137] So the parlement, by a majority of 40 to 7, renewed its protestations against his presence, while conceding as before that he should fulfil the functions pending the royal reply to the remonstrances.[138] The next month it was agreed by 32 votes to 12 that in future whenever Dudon appeared at an assembly of chambers, the protest of 23 July should be read to him, before business proceeded as usual.[139] So long as the king remained silent, therefore, this working settlement ensured that justice went forward uninterrupted while the parlement remained intransigent in principle.

Mouchy, however, felt that matters should be more clearly settled. 'Voila les vacances du Parlement le 8 de septembre', he wrote on 24 August 1784, 'si M le Garde des Sceaux ne prend pas des arrangemens prompts et solides pour M Dudon fils, il ne sera pas mis a la St Martin sur le tableau, et rien ne sera plus indecent pour L'autorité du Roy . . .'[140] The result of these counsels was the *arrêt* of the council of 2 November 1784 which, passing over and refuting the various decisions of the parlement regarding Dudon, as well as the remonstrances of 3 March 1784, ordered the parlement to inscribe his name on the court's official list for the forthcoming judicial year, dismissing the various charges in the March remonstrances.[141]

The *arrêt* and its covering letters patent were forcibly registered at a military session on 13 November, by the comte de Fumel, deputizing for Mouchy. Immediately afterwards there were the usual protestations of illegality, and on 19 November a letter expanding on this theme was sent to the king. Dudon's name did not appear, meanwhile, in the almanach for that year, and new obstacles were put in his way once sessions got under way in the spring. On 22 April 1785, after Dudon had appeared at the assembled chambers on the 8th, the parlement ordered that a protestation against his presence of that day, plus the similar protest of August 1784, were to be read by the clerk whenever he appeared in any chamber. On 27 April it was further decided that whenever Dudon's name appeared either on the registers of the parlement or on lists of its members, it should be noted that it occurred without the court's approval.[142] Such moves were enough to provoke hostile comment and at least one sensational anti-parlementaire pamphlet in the city,[143] but they did not substantially alter the working situation of the previous year. The only drawback was that the government remained unsatisfied by the court's continued prevarication.

This dissatisfaction emerged in a further *arrêt* of 8 November 1785,[144] which quashed at one blow all the protestations, *arrêtés*, and letters arising from this affair since August 1784. The king now formally bade the parlement place no more obstacles in the way of Dudon's exercise of his functions, and imposed a 'perpetual silence' regarding the whole affair. These instruments were forcibly registered at another military session, again conducted by Fumel, on 16 November. This time copies of a protesting *arrêté* passed immediately afterwards were sent to all the other parlements.[145] Dudon's name was at last inserted in the court's official list, and in the almanachs, but only with the proviso 'by the king's very express command'.

Nevertheless, it was the end of the affair. Most of the public time of that judicial year was taken up by the *alluvions* affair, in which the elder Dudon played a leading role on the parlement's side. Perhaps this induced his colleagues to look with more favour upon his son. At any rate, the magistrates raised no demur when, at the Versailles session in July 1786, the qualification against the younger Dudon's name was finally expunged from the record in the king's presence.[146]

So ended, at last, the recriminations over the Maupeou parlement, 11 years after they began. 'Les compagnies ne sont pas comme les particuliers', observed Beaumarchais in 1782,[147] 'dont le temps atténue les haines et dissipe les aigreurs; ici tout s'éternise et le peuple en souffre étrangement'. It was true. If the more rigid returners could have had their way, the conflict would have been carried on down the generations; and certainly some attempt was made to do precisely this, as the proscriptions against members of the Drouilhet, Laroze, Domenge, Lorman, and Dudon families show. Nevertheless, the passage of time did inevitably weaken the old animosities, and the younger Domenge, Lorman, and Laroze —the last the son of a remainer and brother of an intruder—were eventually received. The first two secured reception even before the Dudon affair began, which indicates that his appointment reanimated antagonisms that were already dying. They were revived partly because his case involved a new principle—the reception of intruders of 1771 whose offence was altogether greater than that of mere remainers. There is no doubt, however, that personal enemies of the procurator-general, and those who coveted his office, exploited this factor to the utmost for their own ends. The division of the magistrates into parties, originating for clear reasons in 1775, soon therefore came to be a vehicle for pursuing purely personal ends, and sometimes almost an end in itself.

At any rate, from 1775 to the mid-1780s the parlement was deeply divided into parties whose personnel did not greatly fluctuate. On the one side were the returners, most of the exiles of 1771, and the opponents of Dupaty and Dudon. They numbered in their ranks the most ambitious and turbulent characters in the parlement, such as Poissac and Loyac. These men had been the government's most determined opponents before 1771, and in the post-restoration quarrels they kept this role. Even so, their natural leader was Le Berthon, himself a returner, and although he was not a partisan in the restoration quarrels, he was completely open about opposition to Dupaty and Dudon. His conduct was indeed one of the main sources of trouble throughout these years. The immense power in the hands of a first president could do much to set the tone of a company, but Le Berthon used his in an entirely negative, passive way. Even during the post-restoration quarrels, he confined his role to not aggravating the situation; he did little positively to improve it. He led the opposition to Dupaty, and encouraged the opponents of Dudon by obvious demonstrations of sympathy. If the duty of a first president was to preserve peace and harmony within his company, then Le Berthon was a failure, and he was lucky to be treated as indulgently as he was by the government.

On the other side were the remainers, and, from 1780, Dupaty and his supporters. The natural head of this party was Dudon. The fact that he was a remainer, no friend to Le Berthon, and his son's father, all made this inevitable. Even so, the antagonism between the two factions never became totally personal;

it never became totally divorced from the deeper issues of principle raised by the events of 1771, and the line men took in that year was repeatedly reflected in their attitudes to the later crises. The party of resistance and the rights of the parlement in 1771 stood for the same principles in 1780 and 1783. Their opponents found themselves equally consistently on the side of authority and obedience, whether this meant co-operation with Maupeou, or support of the government's action in imposing Dupaty and Dudon on their reluctant colleagues. Some issues cut across these divisions, as we shall see; on these occasions the parlement took a fairly united stand on questions of general importance. But the persistence of the party quarrels is the most important single feature in the history of the parlement between 1775 and 1783. They absorbed and wasted far more time than anything else. If the amount of space here devoted to the tortuous story of these bickerings seems excessive, it merely reflects the amount of time and attention given to them by those involved.

The damage which the quarrels did to the parlement was incalculable. In Paris, the parlement of Bordeaux became a byword for faction and irresponsible neglect of the duties of the magistracy. In Guienne, it was the despair of all who had dealings with it, whether lawyers or litigants. The disgust and contempt with which onlookers were filled by the undignified scenes which occurred almost daily during some sessions, must have done much to damn the parlement and the judicial system of which it was a part. These memories were still fresh when the revolutionary crisis broke out. They must help to explain the mistrust of the parlements which was always so ready to show itself even when nothing but they stood between the nation and 'despotism'. Above all, memories of the conflicts and the standstill in justice must have contributed greatly to the indifference which greeted the eventual disappearance of the parlement of Bordeaux.

But there was, too, a more immediate way in which the quarrels harmed the parlement. They hampered its effectiveness in opposing or criticizing government policies. There is plenty of evidence that if the magistrates were called upon to choose between public and private demands on their attention, the private always took precedence. The best example of this is the way Turgot's edict lifting restrictions on the wine trade almost passed without demur because the returners and remainers were totally absorbed in their quarrel. The ease with which the tax legislation of 1780–82 passed may also have owed a good deal to the magistrates' absorption in other matters. A united court could have obstructed these policies far more effectively, as its success over the *corvées* and the *alluvions* suggests. The party strife between 1775 and 1785 therefore weakened the parlement's power as well as its reputation; and the work of Maupeou found a tardy and unexpected justification in the results of its own destruction.

NOTES

1. AD 3E 5.595 (Duprat), contract of 11 Dec. 1778.
2. W. Doyle, 'Aux origines de l'affaire Dupaty', *R. Hist. Bx.* (1968), 9; C. Fortier-Maire, *Dupaty (1746 à 1788)* (Bordeaux, 1874), 26; BVBx MS 1696, IV, pièce 90, anon. account of the Dupaty affair; AN K708 no. 60, speech of Dupaty, 23 Feb. 1780.
3. Much of what follows comes from Dupaty's own account in his speech of 23 Feb. 1780; see also Doyle, op. cit., 10.

4. Letter printed in *AHDG*, XXIV (1884–85), no. cxcvii. This and several other letters printed ibid., although sometimes inaccurately dated, constitute a major source for the Dupaty affair. See also Doyle, op. cit., 11.
5. Du Paty de Clam papers, Dupaty to Miromesnil, 1 April 1779; see also Doyle, op. cit., 11.
6. *AHDG*, XXIV, no. ccvii, dated *Avril? 1780*, but its content places it clearly in April 1779; see Doyle, op. cit., 12.
7. AD 3E 17.599 (Perrens), *procuratio ad resignandum*, 16 July 1779; Doyle, op. cit., 13.
8. His brother-in-law was the influential Fréteau de Saint-Just, counsellor at the parlement of Paris.
9. The fullest account of this session is in BVBx MS 1696, IV, pièce 87, 'Récit de ce qui s'est passé au parlement de bordx le 16 fevrier 1780 . . .'; see also Bachaumont, XV, 62, 28 Feb. 1780; and Doyle, op. cit., 14–15.
10. Bachaumont, loc. cit.
11. ibid.
12. See above, p. 18.
13. AN K708, no. 60.
14. See above, p. 19.
15. Bibliothèque Royale Albert Ier, Brussels, MS 15.709–25, f.170, 'Mémoire et Consultation pour Messire Elie-Louis Dufaure de la Jarte', by S. N. H. Linguet, 12 May 1780.
16. ibid., f.173 vo., for an extract of the speech; BVBx MS 1696, IV, pièce 89, for a copy of the whole speech; Bachaumont, XV, 98, 29 March 1780, for an analysis, and 99–101, 1 April 1780, for the full text.
17. Bib. Royale, Brussels, MS 15.709–25, ff.172–3, letter from crown lawyers to Keeper of the Seals, undated. See also Boscheron des Portes, *Histoire du Parlement de Bordeaux*, II, 391–3. The latter source is accurate enough on the course of this case, although the author is unaware of its connection with that of Dupaty.
18. Simon-Nicolas-Henri Linguet (1736–94). Journalist. Advocate, 1764; reputedly only lost two cases, but dismissed the bar following a quarrel with the parlement of Paris, 1775; imprisoned in the Bastille, 1780–82, after which he lived abroad until his return to France as an Austrian councillor of state in 1786; executed in Paris, 1794. Published *Journal de politique et littérature*, 1775–77, and *Annales politiques civiles et littéraires*, 1772–92; also *Théorie des loix civiles*, 1767, and *Mémoires de la Bastille*, 1789.
19. Bachaumont, XV, 246–7, 6 Aug. 1780.
20. AD IB 56, letter of Vergennes to the parlement, 16 Sept. 1780; Bachaumont, XV, 264, 20 Aug. 1780; AAE MD France, 1589, f.58, Mouchy to Vergennes, 27 July 1780.
21. AD IB 56; Bachaumont, XV, 286, 11 Sept. 1780.
22. See below, pp. 218, 225.
23. AD C3452, intendant to Keeper of the Seals, 30 Aug. 1780; also AAE MD France, 1388, ff.83–4, Mouchy to Richelieu, 2 Sept. 1780.
24. BVBx MS 1201, IX, 10 Sept. 1780.
25. AAE MD France, 1388, f.99, Mouchy to Richelieu, 18 Sept. 1780.
26. A. Communay, *Le Parlement de Bordeaux: notes biographiques sur ses principaux officiers*, 166–8, extensively prints the account by counsellor de Lamontaigne (BVBx MS 1696, IV, pièce 90) of the course of the Dupaty affair in the judicial year 1780–81. This and certain other details which follow come from that account.
27. AD IB 56, f.157, for the registers bearing all the transcripts of this session. An informal account in BVBx MS 1201, IX, 24 Sept. 1780, and in AAE MD France, 1388, f.102, Mouchy to Richelieu, 23 Sept. 1788.
28. Communay, loc. cit.
29. A. de Lescure (ed.), *Correspondance secrète sur Louis XVI* . . . (Paris, 1866), I, 359, 14 Jan. 1781; for the Moydieu affair, see Egret, *Parlement de Dauphiné*, II, 9–27.
30. Communay, loc. cit.; Bachaumont, XVI, 77, 27 Nov. 1780, and 81, 1 Dec. 1780; AD IB 56, f.157; BVBx MS 1201, IX, 24 Nov. 1780.
31. AD IB 56, f.157.
32. Bachaumont, XVII, 15, 7 Jan. 1781.
33. ibid., XVI, 77, 27 Nov. 1780.

34. AD C3604, for the correspondence between the intendant and the Keeper of the Seals, Oct.–Dec. 1780, and MS copy of one of the pamphlets.
35. *Observations sur l'affaire de M. Dupaty, ancien avocat-général, avec le Parlement de Bordeaux* (Bordeaux, 1780), alluded to in AD C3604.
36. *Question sur l'écrit intitulé Les Observations touchant l'affaire de M. Dupaty par un citoyen* (Bordeaux, 1780), MS copy in AD C3604.
37. AD série B, *arrêts du parlement*, 'extrait de registres', 1 Feb. 1781; Bachaumont, XVII, 105–6, 29 March 1781.
38. BVBx MS 1201, IX, 23 Dec. 1780.
39. Vatel, *Vergniaud*, I, 34, Vergniaud to Allaud, 13 Jan. 1781.
40. Communay, loc. cit.
41. AM MS 135³ no. 67, *lettre de cachet* of Fauquier.
42. Communay, loc. cit.; Vatel, op. cit., I, 40, Vergniaud to Allaud, 27 Jan. 1781; BVBx MS 1201, X, 28 Jan. 1781.
43. Communay, loc. cit.; BVBx MS 1201, X; Bachaumont, XVII, 105–6, 29 March 1781; Vatel, op. cit., I, 39, Vergniaud to Allaud, 24 Feb. 1781.
44. loc. cit., 5 Feb. 1781.
45. Vatel, op. cit., I, 36, Vergniaud to his father, Jan.(?) 1781.
46. Communay, loc. cit.; Bachaumont, XVII, 87, 4 March 1781; Vatel, op. cit., I, 42, undirected letter, 3 March 1781; AAE MD France, 1589, ff.68–9, Miromesnil to Vergennes, 18 and 20 Feb. 1781; AD 2E 1801 (tit. fam. Gourgue), letter of Le Berthon, 23 Feb. 1781.
47. BN Albertas, VII, f.3232, 22 Feb. 1781, and f.3233, 24 Feb. 1781.
48. Vatel, op. cit., I, 41, 3 March 1781; AM MS 135³ no. 68, Fauquier's *lettre de cachet*, dated 21 Feb. 1781.
49. BVC Richelieu XVI, f.166, Dudon to Richelieu, 9 March 1781. This volume contains various pieces describing the assemblies of chambers of March 1781. In addition to Dudon's, there are letters from Pichard (f.177, 10 March), counsellor de Gobineau (f.175, 10 March), and one Dupin (ff.179 and 181, 10 and 13 March), as well as a very full anon. account (ff.169–72). Further information in Vatel, op. cit., I, 43, Vergniaud to Allaud, 10 March 1781; BN Albertas, VII, f.3243, 17 March 1781; BVBx MS 1201, II, undated, but clearly March 1781, although filed under 1771.
50. loc. cit. above, n. 49.
51. These remonstrances were finally sent on 6 and 10 April. Fortier-Maire, *Dupaty*, 36.
52. e.g., president de Verthamon the elder refused to say anything at each round of opinion, save that the king must be obeyed. This obligation overrode all other considerations. Anon. account, f.170.
53. There is an account of this session, garbled where it is not simply erroneous, in Boscheron des Portes, *Histoire du Parlement de Bordeaux*, II, 393.
54. Dupin's account, 13 March; BVBx MS 1201, X, 16 March 1781.
55. BN Albertas, VII, f.3243, 17 March 1781.
56. loc. cit. above, n. 49.
57. Vatel, op. cit., I, 44, Vergniaud to Allaud, 10 March 1781.
58. BVBx MS 1201, X, 16 March 1781.
59. Dupin's account, 10 March 1781.
60. Vatel, op. cit., I, 46–7, 19 May 1781.
61. Bachaumont, XVII, 318, 6 July 1781.
62. Vatel, loc. cit., I, 47, 31 May 1781; AAE MD France, 1589, f.74, Mouchy to Vergennes, 14 July 1781.
63. BVBx MS 1201, X, 15 June 1781.
64. BVBx MS 1696, IV, pièce 90, continuation of Lamontaigne's account, the first part of which is printed in Communay, loc. cit.; Bachaumont, XVII, 310, 30 July 1781.
65. BVBx MS 1696, IV, pièce 90; Vatel, op. cit., I, 48, 7 July 1781, and 50, 25 July 1781.
66. BVBx MS 1696, IV, pièce 90.
67. ibid.; Vatel, op. cit., I, 51, Vergniaud to Allaud, 4 Aug. 1781.
68. ibid.; Bachaumont, XVII, 336, 17 Aug. 1781; BN Albertas, VII, f.3420, 17 Aug. 1781; Vatel, op. cit., I, 53, Vergniaud to his sister, 25 Aug. 1781.
69. AD C3630 for a copy of these letters, dated 14 Aug. 1781, forcibly registered on 23 Aug. 1781.

70. AM MS 135³ no. 69, Fauquier's *lettre de cachet.*
71. Vatel, loc. cit., I, 53, Vergniaud to his sister, 25 Aug. 1781.
72. BVBx MS 1696, IV, pièce 90; Bachaumont, XVIII, 10, 28 Aug. 1781; *AHDG,* XXIV, no. ccxii, Dupaty to Lavie, 25 Aug. 1781.
73. AD 2E 1810 (tit. fam. Leberthon), Le Berthon to Duval, Meaux, 10 Sept. 1781.
74. ibid., same to same, Châlons, 9 Oct. 1781; Bachaumont, XVIII, 23–4, 5 Sept. 1781, and 82, 11 Oct. 1781.
75. ibid., 44–8, 15–16 Sept. 1781.
76. AD IB 56, f.160 vo., *lettres de jussion* of 1 Feb. 1782, with details of previous exchanges; BN Albertas, VII, f.3452, 18 Oct. 1781; BVBx MS 1201, X, 9 Oct. 1781; AAE MD France, 1589, f.84, Miromesnil to Vergennes, 4 Oct. 1781; Vatel, op. cit., I, 55, 29 Sept. 1781; for details of the edict, see Marion, *Histoire financière,* I, 338–9.
77. AAE MD France, 1589, ff.82–3, Miromesnil to Vergennes, 2 Oct. 1781.
78. Vatel, op. cit., I, 56, 25 Nov. 1781.
79. Bachaumont, XX, 214, 1 May 1781.
80. AAE MD France, 1589, Pichard to Vergennes, 8 Dec. 1781.
81. Fortier-Maire, op. cit., 36; Bachaumont, XX, 40, 21 Jan. 1782.
82. ibid.
83. AAE MD France, 1589, ff.93–6, Pichard to Vergennes, 7 and 14 Jan. 1782; Vatel, op. cit., I, 60–3, 19 and 20 Jan., 2 Feb. 1782.
84. Bachaumont, XX, 125–6, 15 March 1782; Vatel, op. cit., I, 63–4, 2 and 16 Feb. 1782.
85. ibid., 64–6, 23 Feb. 1782; BVBx MS 1201, II, undated letter, wrongly filed, clearly referring to this session; Bachaumont, loc. cit. above, n. 84.
86. ibid., 214–18, 1 May 1782, for the text.
87. Vatel, loc. cit.
88. Vatel, loc. cit.; BVBx MS 1201, loc. cit. above, n. 85.
89. Bachaumont, XX, 218–19, for the text of this *arrêté.*
90. Vatel, op. cit., I, 67, Vergniaud to Allaud, 9 March 1782.
91. That is to say, the pamphlet investigation.
92. AD IB 56, f.160 vo.; AAE MD France, 1589, f.104 [Dupaty] to Keeper of the Seals, 16 March 1782; f.105, Mouchy to Vergennes, 17 March 1782. See also above, p. 187.
93. AAE MD France, 1589, f.246, Mouchy to Vergennes, 2 Sept. 1783.
94. BLR MS 683 'Dupaty, magistrat et auteur', p. 3, in an anon. late 18th-century collection of materials on Dupaty; Bachaumont, XXIII, 87, 4 Aug., and 90, 6 Aug. 1783.
95. ibid.
96. ibid., 129–30, 28 Aug. 1783.
97. Vatel, *Vergniaud,* I, 86, Vergniaud to Allaud, 22 Aug. 1783.
98. Bachaumont, XXIII, 152–3, 13 Sept. 1783; Boscheron des Portes, op. cit., II, 387.
99. Du Paty de Clam papers, undated memorandum, clearly of 1783.
100. AN K874 for the 1782 project; AAE MD France, 1395, ff.231–2 for the revised version of 1783. See above, p. 136.
101. Moreau, *Mes Souvenirs,* II, 366 n.
102. AAE MD France, 1395, f.230, Dupaty to Vergennes, 8 Nov. 1783.
103. AAE MD France, 1589, ff.82–3, Miromesnil to Vergennes, 2 Oct. 1781.
104. ibid., f.157; see also above, pp. 167, 171–2.
105. ibid., ff.157, 163, 164, Mouchy to Vergennes, 30 July, 10 Aug., 13 Aug. 1782; f.180, Pichard to Vergennes, 27 Aug. 1782.
106. *Jefferson Papers,* XI, 112–16, Gascq to Jefferson, 5 Feb. 1787.
107. AN O¹268, p. 68, request of 7 March 1784, *bon* of 28 March 1784.
108. AAE MD France, 1588, f.254, petition of Oct. 1775.
109. X. Védère (ed.), *Archives municipales de Bordeaux, tome treizième: inventaire-sommaire des registres de la jurade, 1520–1783,* VIII (Bordeaux, 1947), 390.
110. AAE MD France, 1388, f.222, Mouchy to Richelieu, 28 [Aug. 1779]; f.103, same to same, undated, but clearly August 1779.
111. AAE MD France, 1589, f.208, Mouchy to Vergennes, 16 Nov. 1782.
112. Védère, op. cit., 392, letters of 22 July 1781; Barckhausen, 'Essai sur l'administration municipale', xxvii.
113. AAE MD France, 1589, f.202, Dudon to Vergennes, 21 Oct. 1782: 'il y a quinze ou seze mois . . . que je me suis adressé a M. le Garde des Sceaux'.

114. ibid., f.194, Dudon to Vergennes, 30 Sept. 1782.
115. Pierre-Auguste Caron de Beaumarchais (1732–99). Playwright, author of *Le Barbier de Séville* (1775) and *Le Mariage de Figaro* (1784); periodic secret agent of the French government, notably during the American war.
116. AAE MD France, 1589, ff.198–9, 6 Oct. 1782. Printed in G. Labat, 'Beaumarchais à Bordeaux; octobre, novembre et décembre 1782', *Actes de l'Académie de Bordeaux* (1904), 78–82.
117. AAE MD France, 1589, ff.202–3, Dudon to Vergennes, 21 Oct. 1782.
118. General accounts in Courteault, *Chronique de Lamontaigne*, 140–1, and Boscheron des Portes, op. cit., II, 393–7.
119. AAE MD France, 1589, ff.234–7, Pichard to Miromesnil, 9 Aug. 1783, is the fullest account of these sessions. See also Bachaumont, XXIII, 130, 28 Aug. 1783.
120. AAE MD France, 1589, ff.232–3, Pichard to Vergennes, 9 Aug. 1783.
121. ibid., ff.236–7, Pichard to Miromesnil, 9 Aug. 1783.
122. ibid., Mouchy to Vergennes, 19 Aug. 1783.
123. Accounts ibid., f.241, Mouchy to Vergennes, 16 Aug. 1783; AD IB 56, f.173, preamble to letters of *jussion*, 26 Aug. 1783.
124. loc. cit. above, n. 123.
125. AAE MD France, 1589, f.242, same to same, 19 Aug. 1783. When the elder Dudon had become procurator-general, it had been Dupaty who had bought his previous office of advocate-general. During his exile after 1771 he had defaulted on the payments, however, and the result was an acrimonious lawsuit. BVC Richelieu XVI, f.19, Dudon to Richelieu, 10 March 1772.
126. AAE loc. cit. above, n. 122.
127. f.243, Mouchy to Vergennes, 23 Aug. 1783.
128. AD IB 56, f.173.
129. AAE MD France, 1589, ff.245–6, Mouchy to Vergennes, 30 Aug. and 2 Sept. 1783.
130. ibid., f.246.
131. ibid., f.249, Pichard to Miromesnil, 6 Sept. 1783.
132. ibid., f.248.
133. See above, p. 182.
134. AAE MD France, 1589, f.281, Mouchy to Vergennes, 20 Nov. 1783; AD IB 56, f.176.
135. Courteault, *Chronique de Lamontaigne*, 141; Bachaumont, XXV, 274, 5 May, and 277–9, 7 May 1784; XXVI, 133–4, 5 Aug. 1784. Extracts from the remonstrances in AM Fonds Delpit 167.
136. AAE MD France, 1589, f.233, Pichard to Vergennes, 9 Aug. 1783.
137. Bachaumont, XXVI, 133–4, 5 Aug. 1784.
138. ibid., 197–8, 16 Sept. 1784; AAE MD France, 1589, ff.321–2, Pichard to Vergennes, 24 July 1784.
139. ibid., ff.330–1, Pichard to Vergennes, 27 Aug. 1784.
140. ibid., MD France, 1589, f.329, Mouchy to Vergennes, 24 Aug. 1784.
141. AD IB 56, f.178.
142. ibid., f.188; Boscheron des Portes, op. cit., II, 396.
143. Bachaumont, XXIX, 67, 12 June 1785.
144. AD IB 56, ff.188–9.
145. Bachaumont, XXX, 110–11, 16 Dec. 1785.
146. See below, p. 259.
147. loc. cit. above, n. 116.

CHAPTER 13

Intervention I: Economic Issues

The issues about which the magistrates of the parlement felt most passionately in these years were personal ones. Yet it is remarkable, in view of the time they spent in attacking one another, how frequently and how unanimously they intervened in public affairs. Economic affairs constitute a good example. The government's preoccupation with them undoubtedly grew over the century; so accordingly did that of the parlements, who were after all part of the machinery of government.

The most burning economic issue in public debate in the later 18th century was the grain trade. All sides agreed that the proper object of policy was to foster wealth and comfort for the king's subjects. The issue was how best to do it. Physiocrats and advanced economists believed in the most complete freedom for the grain trade. Famine would be avoided since unrestricted supply would soon answer any demand; an uncontrolled or 'natural' price would be a high one, and the prospect of high returns would foster production by more efficient methods, which in its turn was bound to increase the wealth of the community. This policy would mean sweeping away the elaborate system of controls on external and internal export of grain which was the keystone of old-régime agricultural policy, and whose object seemed nothing higher than provincial self-sufficiency. In the 1760s, certain ministers were so impressed by these arguments that in 1763 free export between provinces was generally authorized, and the next year even export abroad was permitted below a certain price level.[1]

The conservative argument was more pragmatic. It revolved round such practical questions as getting relief to affected areas in time, at prices the afflicted could afford to pay. Export control meant reserves in hand; price control meant reserves within reach of the poorest. This view ignored the long term on the grounds that those who may starve cannot wait. It was also motivated by a concern for public order. A hungry populace was the greatest threat to that social stability and subordination whose maintenance was even more important for governments than to foster wealth. So in 1770, after a catastrophic harvest, and several lean years beforehand, Terray hurriedly reimposed controls on both external and internal export of grain, and they remained in operation throughout his ministry.[2] Terray believed that, however beneficial high prices were, it was wrong to allow them at any time to outstrip the pocket of the consumer; and therefore he returned to the system of building up reserves under royal control, with which to supplement markets where supplies were scarce and expensive.

Where did the parlement of Bordeaux stand in this debate? It wavered according to circumstance. In the 1760s it revealed itself extremely suspicious of free trade in grain.[3] Early in 1770 it ordered all grain in its jurisdiction to be sold only in authorized markets. Terray at first upheld this decision against the protests of the intendant of Limoges, Turgot, but the parlement itself was divided, and there was no apparent protest when, later, the council quashed its action.[4] Indeed, by the time Terray's renewed restrictions on the trade were laid before it, the parlement had changed its line completely and at first refused to register the new regulations.[5] Unlike their colleagues of Toulouse, who were mainly grain-growers and were consistently opposed to restrictions on the trade from the start,[6] the magistrates of Bordeaux had little personal stake in the great debate. It was, therefore, mainly an administrative problem to them. They were well aware that Guienne, through its general infertility and the lucrative competition of vines, was hardly self-sufficient in grain. But up river were the abundant Agenais and the plain of Toulouse, which could normally supply the province's deficiencies. It took a great crisis to force the parlement into defining its attitude more clearly.

In 1772 the harvest failed over much of southern France, after several mediocre years.[7] Despite the building-up of reserve stocks under the direction of the intendant, it was clear that the failure of normal sources of supply would push up the price of bread all along the Garonne valley in the spring of 1773. Rising prices brought the danger of speculation. Bread prices in Bordeaux were fixed from week to week by the *jurade*, and early in May, on receipt of a consignment of reserves, they abruptly lowered the price of bread by 4 *deniers*. It was clear to the bakers that this situation could hardly last in a time of such scarcity, and they therefore attempted to hold on to their supplies until the price of flour rose again. This it did within a week, and the *jurats* promptly raised the price by 5 *deniers*. The result was a riot against bakers' shops on 8 May, and an appeal by 400 women to Gascq, newly returned from Paris, to procure them bread.[8] Gascq was horrified at the situation he found, and over the next few days flung himself into a fury of activity. He induced the parlement to issue an *arrêt* revoking the new price and forbidding any further rise. The city was to make good any losses that the bakers thereby incurred.[9] On 12 May the parlement also forbade the merchants to sell their corn above a certain price, and ordered all those with corn in hand to bring it to market. Dudon in calling for this *arrêt* confirmed popular suspicions by declaring bluntly that the shortage was the work of hoarders and speculators.[10] Subsequently another *arrêt* was issued prescribing the usual popular remedy, visits of inspection to seek out suspected hoards.[11] Ships in the roadstead, already laden with flour for the Indies, were seized and unloaded.[12] Finally on 17 May the parlement voted an extraordinary contribution leviable on the rich according to resources, in order to help the poor buy bread, and itself donated 50,000 l. to start the fund.[13] By such measures the ferment in Bordeaux was somewhat calmed. But in the countryside the situation was worse. Market days all along the Garonne valley were scenes of riot, pillage, and popular price-fixing and convoys of grain destined for Bordeaux were attacked.[14] Panic-stricken peasants poured into the city in search of bread and only increased popular anxiety there. On 14

May the parlement forbade tumults on pain of death, but this *arrêt* remained without force until the arrival of troops during the third week in May[15] at the urgent request of Gascq. Only their presence kept the situation in hand until the arrival of new supplies from the north early in June. Gascq was convinced that his action alone had saved the city and the province from devastation and disaster. When the crisis was over the city owed the bakers and merchants 325,000 l. in subsidies for the price-fixing,[16] but this seemed a small price to pay for avoiding the worst excesses of violence and anarchy.

Gascq was deeply shocked at how near Bordeaux had come to being sacked by a hungry populace. Yet all he received from Versailles was censure, accusations that the parlement was trying to boost its own reputation,[17] and bland assurances that there was nothing to worry about. 'Le peuple n'a pas tort de se plaindre', he told Richelieu,

> il est hors d'etat de payer son pain, cela est demontré, . . . leur propos le plus ordinaire est de dire nous aimons mieux mourir sur un gibet que de mourir du faim, cela est plus court. qu'on reflechisse tout qu'il est impossible de calmer les progres d'une sedition. surtout lorsqu'elle a une cause aussi generale, aussi imperative que le sentiment de la faim ou seulement la crainte d'une famine le plus sage est de la faire cesser par des voyès de douceur et de charité. Si . . . le peuple eut pillé, brulé, saccagé la ville on dirait mais pourquoy s'obstiner a soutenir le prix du pain? pourquoy ne pas faire un sacrifice? a quel autre usage plus pressant, plus sacré, plus legitime, peut on employer les deniers publics? pour moy, je lavoue, il me semble que dans un païs ou les impots sont portez a l'excez, le souverain est tenu d'assurer a ses sujets le seul bien qui leur reste: la vie.[18]

The agonized tone of concern is unmistakable. Gascq clearly saw that in the last analysis public order was the central issue in the debate on the grain trade, and that in an emergency some authority had to fix prices at a level realistic for the consumer. Two weeks later, when the crisis was passing, he declared that:

> je crois que les principes de L'abbe Controleur sont les veritables en matiere de subsistances. Liberté indefinie dans les temps d'abondance, circulation libre dans le royaume quand les recoltes sont mediocres, tout tenir dans la main du gouvernement dans la disete . . . mais au dernier cas si lon disoit tous les mais on ne finiroit jamais et lorsqu'on prend ce dernier party il faut choisir les mains les plus pures et les plus attentives et meme les surveiller sans cesse sans quoy les sousordres se relachent et il y a dans les details des friponeries atroces qui plongent les sujets du roi dans la misère et la cupidité et ce genne fait de si cruels progrès qu'on finit par les faire mourir de faim.[19]

Whether these views were exactly those of Terray is open to debate. But many of Gascq's colleagues, though prepared to intervene willingly enough to overcome the crisis of May 1773, were convinced that it was the government and its agents who had caused the crisis initially by upsetting the free play of the market by intervention. On 31 August the parlement drew up and even had printed (against Maupeou's standing orders) a vigorous set of remonstrances on the grain trade.[20] Gascq wrote that although he disapproved of their printing and circulation he found their general argument undeniable.[21]

The crisis of May, these remonstrances roundly declared, had been artificial. It had begun suddenly, when corn throughout the province had disappeared all at once, as if by a prearranged signal. But when the mercantile community had been asked why it did not bring in supplies from other well-stocked areas, it had pointed out that most of the other ports of the kingdom were not open for free export of corn; the government had relied only on merchants commissioned by itself to bring in supplies; only to them were the ports open.

> Ils se sont trouvés seuls chargés de la subsistance publique, & ils en ont été les maîtres. La concurrence qui perce toujours contre la cupidité & qui malgré tous ses efforts tient toujours les grains à un prix modéré, n'existoit plus pour eux. Tous les Ports leur étoient ouverts, tous les obstacles disparoissoient dans leurs mains, en un mot, ils jouissoient seuls de la liberté du commerce.[22]

The effect had been to push the price of available corn far beyond the pockets of the consumers: 'Voilà, SIRE, les effets dangereux d'un commerce réuni dans des mains privilégiées'.[23] As a port, Bordeaux should never lack access to abundant supplies. But any closing of the inter-provincial corn trade must lead to hardship, especially for provinces whose own harvest fell short. This had happened in May. If the government had not given its own commissioners the monopoly of procuring emergency supplies, they would have been abundant, cheaper, and of better quality. Nor would the parlement have had to intervene in the crisis. The moral was clear:

> Daignez rétablir, SIRE, dans l'étendue de votre Royaume, & cette concurrence dans l'importation des grains étrangers, & cette circulation heureuse & libre de province à province, qui la féconde et les enrichit toutes les uns par les autres. Redonnez à notre commerce ce degré d'activité intérieure qu'il a perdu, & qui seul peut le faire fleurir.[24]

Faced with a crisis, the parlement had been forced to make up its mind, and had pronounced unequivocally in favour of free trade in corn.[25] In this attitude it remained consistent right up to the Revolution. When Turgot once more declared complete free internal trade, it raised no demur.[26] Necker's renewed restriction provoked no comment because, apart from that of 1777, harvests were good and there was no scarcity; and even in that year, and the dangerous spring which followed, the local policy of the intendant Dupré de Saint-Maur was to overcome the crisis by guaranteeing the maximum of freedom for the local market.[27] Subsequent good harvests throughout the 1780s pushed the question into the background. When it next occupied the attention of the parlement, the Revolution had begun and changed everything.[28]

Was, then, the parlement in the van of the advanced economic thought of the day? Did it subscribe more generally to the gospel of free trade? It would be misleading to think so. The magistrates in general[29] were not interested in economic arguments except insofar as they bore on the political problem of public order. Free trade in grain seemed to them the best way of assuring this. When it came to other economic questions, where public order was not at issue, their views were far less advanced.

The most obvious case is that of the wine trade. Here they could speak from close personal involvement. The parlement had had a clear policy on the wine trade for centuries, which was to maintain intact the whole elaborate apparatus of the wine privilege,[30] and to protect the wine of Bordeaux against competition, adulteration, and fraud. Thus the trade was subject to constant intervention from the court. In 1764 it forbade the blending of Bordeaux wines with others, after complaints from consuming countries.[31] The full price for pure Bordeaux wine, it was alleged, was being charged for blended wine, and this practice was slowing down the growth of trade. The merchants were incensed by the new measures, and in vigorous letters to the minister of the province, they protested against both the assumptions behind them and the provisions for enforcing them. Only blending, they claimed, ensured the sale of inferior wines. 'Si nos Magistrats étoient payés par nos rivaux, ils ne pourroient pas les servir plus à souhait'.[32] But the members of the parlement were mainly interested in the purity of the superior wines which many of them grew, and the government passively supported them. Foreign complaints were also responsible for the parlement's action in 1772–73 to standardize the *barrique bordelaise*. Ever since 1597 Bordeaux wines had been sold in vessels of a special size, to distinguish them from others.[33] By the mid-18th century this size was becoming vague, since the city had lost the prototype of the gauge, and buyers were beginning to complain of fraud. For this reason, the parlement now laid down precise dimensions for the *barrique bordelaise*, and heavy punishments for those not using vessels of this size, or using them without authorization.[34]

Whenever the parlement protested, as it did repeatedly, at the ever-increasing burden of taxation which the province bore, the effect of this burden on the wine trade was always strongly emphasized. The remonstrances of 1772 against Terray's financial policies emphasized the burden on the wine-grower not only of the twentieths and their surcharges, but also of the supplement to the municipal *octrois*, known as the 'free gift'. This supplement, leviable on foodstuffs and drinks entering cities, was imposed as a war emergency measure in 1758–59 for six years, but was repeatedly prolonged. It was bad enough in wartime, when export was impossible, declared the magistrates,[35] to tax the only market left to the producers—the city itself. But to prolong this emergency tax after a decade of peace, along with the twentieths, would ruin the wine-growers. Whereas the price of ordinary wine for domestic consumption had risen over the century by a third, the costs of cultivation and apparatus had doubled. When the new taxes imposed since 1749 were taken into account, this meant that the real revenue of the average wine-grower had fallen by two-thirds over the century. 'Des charges fixes et certaines absorberont insensiblement des revenus incertains . . . et la propriété se trouvera réduite à une vaine apparence . . . une progression perpetuelle dans l'augmentation des impôts ne peut s'appliquer à un produit toujours casuel, toujours incertain . . .'[36]

But the most serious threat lay not so much in the ever-increasing burden of taxation, as in governmental plans to abolish the wine privilege completely. The restrictions imposed by the privilege on the export of up-country wines from Quercy and Perigord were a long-standing complaint on the part of the inhabitants of these regions, a complaint not unheeded in governmental circles. The intendants of Bordeaux, while keeping a diplomatic silence within the city itself, since 'Les vins sont une matière si délicate dans cette province qu'on ne peut y toucher sans exciter une fermentation générale', privately took an unfavourable view of the privilege in their reports to the government.[37] But the problem was, as one minister put it in 1767, that:

> [le] . . . bien public . . . n'admet aucun privilège exclusif dans la vente des denrées nécessaires à la vie; l'abolition de ce vieux privilège serait très-désirable, mais en présence de l'attitude du Parlement, se déclarant protecteur surtout sur les vins, des privileges de toute nature . . . il faut laisser à l'avenir le soin de proclamer, en Guienne la liberté de commerce des vins . . . étant assez d'avoir fait la loi de la liberté du commerce des blés.[38]

And in 1773, when Richelieu broached this subject, perhaps on the government's behalf, with Gascq, the latter replied: 'Soyez sur que le parlemt se fera plustot aneantir que de souffrir la descente des vins de haut . . .'[39]

Nevertheless, on coming to power, Turgot was resolved to make the attempt to abolish this privilege and all like it. The first sign came in April 1775, when he lifted the normal prohibition on up-country wines in the port of Bordeaux after 8 September. This *arrêt*, temporary in effect, promised a general law to follow. Turgot instructed the intendant to tell him at once if the parlement made any attempt to impede the execution of this measure, and the intendant replied that the parlement was certain to protest against it.[40] However, throughout 1775 the magistrates were completely absorbed in persecuting one another, and no protest was made. Soon afterwards intendants were instructed to send in accounts of all existing wine privileges, and as many documents as they could collect.[41] Clugny at Bordeaux warned that any attempt to suspend or abolish the privilege in general would certainly antagonize the parlement without some previous propaganda designed to allay the fears of the magistracy,[42] but on 12 April 1776 an edict was finally published.[43]

A lengthy preamble gave an account of the various wine privileges existing in the kingdom, especially that of Bordeaux. The sale of up-country and up-river wines was hampered both by the regulations keeping them out of the port of Bordeaux in effect until all local wines were sold, and by disadvantageous rules on their storage and marketing even at times when they were allowed into the port. Such restrictions were condemned as unfair to unprivileged producers, exorbitant for consumers even within privileged towns, depressing to agriculture, and not even beneficial to those who enjoyed them:

> Partout où le privilège existe, il est nuisible au peuple consommateur, nuisible au commerçant; les propriétaires des vignes ne sont favorisés en apparence qu'aux dépens des autres propriétaires et de tous leurs concitoyens . . . Bordeaux . . . dont la prosperité s'accroît en raison de l'activité, de l'étendue de son commerce, et de l'affluence des denrées qui s'y réunissent de toutes parts, ne peut avoir de véritable intérêt à la conservation d'un privilège qui, pour l'avantage léger et douteux de quelques propriétaires de vignes, tend à restreindre et à diminuer son commerce.
>
> Ceux qui ont obtenu de nos prédécesseurs l'autorisation des prétendus privilèges de Bordeaux . . . n'ont point stipulé le véritable intérêt de ces villes, mais seulement l'intérêt de quelques-uns des plus riches habitants, au préjudice du plus grand nombre et de tous nos autres sujets.[44]

These plain words were followed by plain provisions, whose effect was to suppress the wine privilege entirely, in all its aspects, right down to the standard *barrique bordelaise* and the right of *bourgeoisie*, and declare the wine trade free throughout the king's dominions.

The parlement of Toulouse, as might be expected, registered the edict at once.[45] That of Bordeaux, equally predictably, decided to send remonstrances. But remonstrances took time to draw up, and in the meantime the intendant distributed 200 copies of the edict in the city, together with reports of its registration at Toulouse, Grenoble, and Perpignan.[46] In fact the parlement was so absorbed in its own internal bickerings, that it forgot these remonstrances, and was taken by surprise by a forced registration at the end of the session.[47] Only the very day of this registration, as the edict went into force, did it hurriedly protest and throw together its reflections in the form of the remonstrances of 31 August 1776.[48] They protested that the edict of April, though doubtless honestly motivated, destroyed a network of privileges hallowed by immemorial usage. Moreover,

> Detruire ces privileges, et ces Réglements, C'est renverser l'ordre public, C'est porter dans la Société le trouble et la dissension, sous le prétexte spécieux de réformer des Abus anciens, c'est tromper les espérances des propriétaires des fonds de cette Sénéchaussée, qui, sur la foi de ces Réglemens toujours en vigueur, se sont empressés a former des Vignobles, plus utiles à l'Etat qu'a leur interêt personnel . . . Pourquoy . . . faire fleurir le commerce de nos voisins en ruinant le nôtre, par une Concurrence aussi nouvelle que dangereuse?

The remonstrances went on to defend the principle of privilege on the grounds that it was part of the order of nature, and pour scorn on artificial attempts to introduce equality between men. The effect of the edict would be to ruin cultivators by flooding the market, to destroy the immemorial value of the right of *bourgeoisie*, to encourage fraud through the blending of wines, and to turn over good and valuable grain lands outside the Bordelais to vines. It was, in short, 'un Edit qui ne peut que ruiner cette Sénéchaussée'. Doubtless all this was an overstatement of the case. The best Bordeaux wines need hardly fear competition from the coarser vintages of Cahors and Bergerac. The lesser wines of Bordeaux, however, might well have been undercut; blending might well have increased, and above all a market freed of restrictions might later have made the glut of the 1780s even worse than it was. So Turgot's measures would undoubtedly have affected the magistrates adversely and in these remonstrances they spoke more obviously than usual in their own interests. Nevertheless, within days peasant producers were bringing their wine into the hitherto privileged city unimpeded.[49]

Unfortunately Turgot had fallen several months beforehand, and some of his reforms had already, even before the military session, been reversed. The wine edict soon followed. Letters patent of 30 November 1776 suspended its operation,[50] and the privilege came back into force. Subsequent years saw repeated requests from up-river areas for its abrogation, and in 1787 they were given some satisfaction in the form of the suspension of export duties.[51] But the wine privilege of Bordeaux only disappeared with the Revolution. Its survival had little to do with the parlement, however, which had protested too late and with a surprising lack of urgency considering how closely the edict affected the livelihood of its members. The magistrates could count themselves lucky that the intrigues and vendettas of Versailles had reversed what their own squabbles had nearly led them to see pass into law without protest.

One of the arguments of the belated remonstrances of 1776 was that freedom of export for non-Bordelais wines would upset the colonial wine market. 'En permettant la circulation, que de mélanges, que de fraudes pour tromper la bonne foi des colons qui croiront acheter des vins de Bordeaux dans toute leur pureté . . .'.[52] The magistrates well knew how lucrative was the market for the sturdy *palu* wines in the colonies. But their interest or involvement in the colonial trade did not end there. Many of them as proprietors in the colonies, who often experienced difficulty with the resident managers of their estates, were keenly interested in colonial questions.

The relationship between the French West Indian colonies and the merchants who supplied them with everyday necessities from the mother country was notoriously hostile.[53] The official colonial policy of the French government over most of the 18th century was firmly Colbertian; colonies were founded and existed for the exclusive benefit of the mother country, and therefore the colonial trade was subject to the most rigid controls. The colonies might only trade directly with France. This meant that the French merchants who supplied the colonies from such ports as Bordeaux, La Rochelle, and Nantes, could charge monopoly prices for all the essentials of life, such as flour, wine, and manufactures. In wartime, when British blockades and the financial risks to French merchants drastically diminished the flow of essential supplies, the choice lay between starvation and the suspension of the system, and the islands only survived by admitting neutral shipping in considerable numbers.[54] Each time an emergency forced a breach in the exclusive system, however, the French monopoly became harder to restore when it was over. The chambers of commerce of the Atlantic ports knew this well, and bitterly opposed all breaches in the system. Equally, the colonists campaigned persistently against the system, and the pressure for some modification of the Colbertian pattern grew. Economists too began to argue that the colonies were not so much dependencies of France as integral parts of it, and insofar as freedom of overseas trade was good for France, it was good for her colonies, too.[55] Such arguments, reinforced by the difficulty of expelling from colonial ports the neutral traders who had been allowed in during the Seven Years' War, led the government in the 1760s to make the first formal breach in its exclusive system. Free import was allowed, first of one commodity, then another, regardless of the protests of metropolitan merchants. The American war saw the French open their colonies to their American allies, and the colonists welcomed them with open arms. After the war ended, the French government was inclined positively to favour the inrush of American traders in pursuance of one of its major war aims—to swing the weight of American economic dependence from Britain to France. Finally, an *arrêt* of the council of 30 August 1784 opened the trade with the French colonies in foodstuffs and secondary products to all flags.[56]

All over France, the chambers of commerce raised a chorus of protest.[57] 'O COLBERT!', wailed that of Bordeaux melodramatically, 'toi le créateur des Arts & du commerce de la France, comment a-t-on pu outrager ton génie en lui supposant des erreurs?'[58] The trade of Bordeaux was declining, it warned, and the admission of American goods to the colonies at cheaper prices could only hasten that decline. The mercantile community was so alarmed that it sent a deputation to the parlement, asking it to take up the case.[59] The younger Dudon, procurator-general (whose family had colonial interests), at once called upon the parlement to remonstrate with the king.

The objective of states, Dudon declared, was economic self-sufficiency, and colonies were a means to this end.

> Il résulte nécessairement des Principes que nous venons d'établir, que le commerce des Colonies doit appartenir exclusivement à la métropole, et que l'accès doit en être interdit sans reserve à toute nation étrangère . . . Favoriser les rapports des Colonies avec l'étranger, c'est attaquer dans sa source le Lien essentiel qui les unit à la métropole, et qui leur en fait sentir la dépendance, non comme une servitude, mais comme la source de leur bien-être.[60]

All colonial commerce was undertaken on the assumption that the exclusive Colbertian system, the sole guarantee of worthwhile profits, would be maintained. Such safeguards as the *arrêt* left in existence would soon be circumvented by 'la Cupidité de Certains habitans des Colonies Jointe à l'ambition speculative des Etrangers'. The interests of absentee plantation-owners living in France were entirely against the new law, Dudon explained, doubtless to a sympathetic audience. For there was no way of preventing their managers on the spot from converting most of their primary sugar products, destined for France, into molasses and syrups for quick sales to the Americans. The colonies were privileged and rich; the United States could not have achieved nationhood without French help. Both should now be grateful for the status they enjoyed, and not clamour for further concessions. He concluded by calling for a letter of protest to be addressed to the king.

The parlement was quick to agree, and the letter was duly drawn up and dispatched on 29 January 1785.[61] The magistrates were expressing, they declared, the alarm of the mercantile community, whose prosperity was so essential to the state. They then repeated almost word for word Dudon's definition of the function of colonies. It was one thing, and a good one, to open the colonial trade to all French ports, as had been done by the *arrêt* of the council of 31 October 1784; it was quite another to open it to foreigners.[62]

> La faiblesse et la force sont relatives. Tout ce que nous perdons et que l'étranger gagne, devient une double perte pour notre force réele. Si les Nations voisines ou rivales, acquièrent par le droit ou par le fait, la faculté de féconder leurs échanges dans nos colonies, il ne restera plus à la France qu'un vain titre de souveraineté, chèrement payé par les sacrifices que leur population et leur defense nécessite en tems de Paix et pendant la guerre.

Proceeding to general principles, the parlement went on:

> La Liberté Géneralle du Commerce semble, surtout depuis quelques années, etre l'illusion favorite des Esprits élevés et des ames sensibles; mais le developemens dans la pratique, déconcertent trop tot ces conceptions

flateuses d'une théorie séduisante. Si la France, suivant l'exemple que lui donneroient d'autres Nations, ouvrit les Ports de ses Colonies, elle feroit sans doute un sacrifice inapréciable pour concourir avec tous les Peuples à une fraternité universele. Mais cette conduite plus que généreuse, restant sans imitateurs, ne sembleroit elle pas aux yeux clairvoyants des rivaux du Commerce français, un aveu de l'insuffisance des moyens de notre Marine Marchande, la derniere ressource de l'administration pour faire prospérer nos établissements dans le nouveau monde; enfin ne seroit elle pas un partage de notre propriété sans compensation?

The French merchant navy could already handle all the trade of the colonies, and indeed needed the stimulus of this trade after the setbacks of the recent war. The new *arrêt* would encourage fraud and smuggling since what restrictions were left in force might easily be circumvented; it would encourage the Americans, who had already left a trail of havoc in the French West Indies by paying for their wartime purchases in worthless paper money; above all—the parlement admitted it quite frankly—foreigners could supply the colonies more cheaply than the French merchants. To loosen the commercial bonds of the islands would therefore not only ruin French commerce, but also set the islands on the road to economic and perhaps even political independence of France, with all the disadvantages that that would entail.

The worst of it, declared the letter, was that the new law had been issued without adequate prior consultation of the commercial interests involved, and at the instance of 'small interests'.

Au reste ce n'est point ici le vice d'un département, C'est la suite d'un systême Général; le seul peut être qui ait été suivi constament dont le but est de voüer à une nullité absoluë tous les corps, meme ceux qui par leur nature sont les moins propres à faire ombrage. Suivant l'expression d'un Grand Magistrat[63] *il semble qu'on ait prononcé une interdiction générale contre la Nation* . . .

Qu'ils sembleroient heureusement Compensés les moments d'allarmes qui nous agitent; s'ils appelloient enfin ces assemblées antiques et solemnelles trop longtems suspendues, le plus Noble Triomphe des Rois, comme le plus beau Moment des Peuples!

. . . les etats Généraux n'ont jamais donné d'ombrage sur les prérogatives de la Couronne: ce seroit donc tromper la Confiance de Votre Majesté, que d'éloigner une Restauration importante, en semant autour du trone de vaines inquiétudes . . .

Nous ne pouvons plus longtems vous le dissimuler, Sire, les ressorts de la Monarchie sont dans un relachement Général, le dégout s'est emparé de tous les Corps et de toutes les professions; si l'on n'arrête par quelque grand moyen les progrès du mal on en viendroit bientôt à ne tenir à la Patrie que par le lien affligeant des tributs ou de la dette Nationale, qui ne commandent gueres aux individus, qu'un intérêt de sollicitude . . .

So the climax and conclusion of the parlement's protest was a call for the Estates-General, the first time this cry had been heard in Bordeaux since 1771. Coming on top of the *corvées* and the *alluvions* affairs, the *arrêt* on the colonial trade seemed just one more instance of the government, bowing to hidden but powerful interests, deliberately ignoring the common welfare. Interestingly enough the parlement made this call for the Estates-General in the name of the mercantile community. In previous times, the letter declared, 'la Commerce, dégradé par une opinion absurde, étoit loin de devenir ainsy qu'il le fut depuis la route d'un anoblissement honorable, et de participer Comme de nos jours à la Culture de l'esprit et à la Généralité des lumières'. Nowadays, it seemed, trade was respectable and its opinions should be heard in the formulation of national policy.

Not that this letter had any effect. It was simply one among many such protests not only from chambers of commerce, but from other sovereign courts, like the parlement of Rouen and the court of aids of Montauban, over the nine months following the publication of the *arrêt* in France in November 1784.[64] The British ambassador did indeed wonder in June 1785 whether the government would bow to the pressure and withdraw the *arrêt*,[65] but nothing was done, beyond the inauguration of an inquiry in October 1785 to see whether the gloomy predictions of the *arrêt*'s opponents had been borne out.[66] The new law did come at a time of recession for the colonial merchants of Bordeaux, but the volume of trade grew once more in 1786 and 1787. If the rate of growth was slower than before the American war, this was not so much the result of competition from emancipated foreigners, as a general slowing-down of the colonial boom as a whole.[67]

Merchants and magistrates sometimes found themselves at loggerheads, as over the blending of wine in 1764, or over the question of bankruptcy. As early as 1715 the chamber of commerce had angrily drawn attention to: 'La facilité que les officiers du Parlement trouvent de se faire payer à la faveur des décrets de prise de corps, ce qui leur est deu et à leurs amis, au préjudice des autres créanciers des faillis'.[68] In 1783 an *arrêt* of the parlement restricted the terms of definition of bankruptcy so much that the chamber of commerce was led to protest that many creditors might under the new rules lose all chance of securing repayment. The council of state, on the protests of the merchants, quashed the parlement's *arrêt*.[69] Nevertheless, far more often merchants invoked the help of the parlement when they had grievances, and they gratefully acknowledged this help.[70] When in 1770 the farmers-general demanded that thenceforth all duties on goods entering the port of Bordeaux should be paid in specie, the merchants, whose main wealth was represented by negotiable bills, persuaded the parlement to forbid the receivers to operate the order.[71] 'Notre parlement . . . a mis le commerce sous sa sauve-garde Contre les prétentions du fisc', wrote the chamber of commerce to that of Rheims in 1785,[72] when the parlement opposed by prohibitions the attempts of the domain to levy stamped paper duty on bills of exchange. These *arrêts* were quashed, but the parlement remained adamant, and at the Versailles session of 1786 the government conceded defeat.

The parlement's involvement in mercantile Bordeaux was in fact deep, and not confined to those magistrates with a personal stake in the colonial trade. It was after all the supreme court of appeal for commercial cases like any others. Besides, two most important members of the court of first instance in maritime cases and one of the busiest in the realm, the Admiralty, were also members of the parlement.[73] Merchants and magistrates alike realized from close everyday contact that their interests in the trade of Bordeaux coincided more often than they diverged.

The parlement's outlook on economic affairs was broadly conservative. It may seem odd that the magistrates should be partisans of free trade in grain, and yet support existing restrictions on the wine and colonial trades. But the issues were different. The grain trade was far more obviously of common importance than the other two, and had never been characterized by sectional privilege as the others were. Nobody had a vested interest in maintaining the restrictions, not even the growers; if they were maintained, it was because the authorities believed that they were the best means of assuring the subsistence of the population as a whole. Opponents equally believed that freedom was the best way of achieving the same end. No such common convictions underlay the positions of the two sides over the wine and colonial trades. These were fields in which the interests of the Bordelais, protected in both cases by special privileges, did not coincide except on the most remote general plane with those of other areas and groups. It was easy to conclude that, since the privileges had not restricted expansion in either trade over the century, this expansion must itself have resulted from the privileges. Their abolition therefore might mean ruin. Such a diagnosis was not without some truth.

Besides, the parlement was inclined on principle to uphold privileges, hallowed as they usually were by prescription and legal precedent. The colonial monopoly was in its way as much of a privilege as *bourgeoisie* of Bordeaux, or several of the other mercantile practices which the parlement defended. In all these cases, merchants and magistrates alike were shown what damage could be done by a government that could and did legislate without prior consultation. They were thus brought to see that the basic issue behind their altercations with the government was not so much economic as constitutional.

NOTES

1. For a convenient summary of these developments, see D. Dakin, *Turgot and the Ancien Régime in France* (London, 1938), ch. 7, *passim.*
2. See G. Weulersse, *La Physiocratie à la fin du règne de Louis XV, 1770–1774* (Paris, 1959), ch. 7, *passim*, and J. F. Bosher, 'The French Crisis of 1770', *History* (1971).
3. Dakin, op. cit., 97.
4. ibid., 106–7.
5. Weulersse, op. cit., 171.
6. Forster, *Nobility of Toulouse*, 66–76; Weulersse, op. cit., 171, 173–5. See also above, pp. 94–5.
7. The fullest account of the crisis is P. Caraman, 'La disette des grains et les émeutes populaires en 1773 dans la généralité de Bordeaux', *R. Hist. Bx.* (1910). The national debate is chronicled in Weulersse, op. cit., 176–85.
8. Caraman, op. cit., 300–2.
9. ibid., 303; Weulersse, op. cit., 182.
10. Caraman, op. cit., 313.
11. ibid., 316.
12. Weulersse, op. cit., 182–3.
13. Caraman, op. cit., 317.
14. ibid., 303–9.
15. ibid., 309–11.
16. ibid., 319.
17. ibid., 316.

18. BVC Richelieu XVII, f.187, Gascq to Richelieu, 22 May 1773. Several letters around this date give valuable information which supplements the other sources cited.
19. ibid., f.173, same to same, 4 June 1773. He repeated these opinions on 16 Aug. 1773, f.203.
20. Printed in *Journal historique*, V, 83–94, 14 Dec. 1773; extensively quoted also in Weulersse, op. cit., 179–81.
21. BVC Richelieu XVII, f.214, Gascq to Richelieu, 28 Sept. 1773, and f.216, same to same, 24 Oct. 1773. His absence at Bagnères meant that he was unable to prevent the printing.
22. *Journal historique*, V, 90.
23. ibid., 91.
24. ibid., 93.
25. There was talk at Versailles of quashing these remonstrances, and an objectionable *arrêt* of 7 Sept., probably against the sale of bad grain. But in the end the government took Gascq's advice and simply ignored them. BVC Richelieu XLI, no. 79, Gascq to Richelieu, undated (internal evidence suggests September 1773).
26. The Maupeou parlement registered this edict on 9 Jan. 1775. AM MS 225 (Mélanges 1759–89), copy of the edict with *arrêt* of registration.
27. E. Bourgouin, 'Une disette en Guyenne à la fin de l'ancien régime (1777–1778)', *R. Hist. Bx.* (1918–19), *passim*.
28. See below, p. 304.
29. We must except avowed disciples of the economists, like president de Verthamon; see above, p. 136.
30. For these privileges, see above, p. 92.
31. *Arrêts* of 18 July and 21 Sept. 1764; AAE MD France, 1587, ff.371, 421. For reactions to this measure, and its limited success, see Butel, 'La croissance', I, 455–7.
32. AAE MD France, 1587, f.420, anon. letter to Choiseul, 18 Sept. 1764.
33. Kehrig, *Le Privilège des vins à Bordeaux*, 27.
34. ibid., 32; AD C4265, chamber of commerce to Boutin, 20 Aug. 1784; letter concerning the *arrêts* of the parlement of 28 Aug. 1772 and 21 April 1773. The volume of the *barrique* prescribed under these *arrêts* was 235 litres. Brutails, *Recherches . . . mesures*.
35. AN K708, no. 53, remonstrances of 18 Jan. 1772.
36. ibid., no. 54, remonstrances of 19 Feb. 1772.
37. G. Martin, 'Les intendants de Guyenne au XVIIIe siècle et les privilèges des vins bordelais', *R. Hist. Bx.* (1908), 461–70. The quotation is from Tourny the younger in C1617, on p. 466.
38. AD C3260.
39. BVC Richelieu XLI, no. 79, Gascq to Richelieu, undated (but clearly Sept. 1773).
40. AD C3683, no. 53, Turgot to intendant, 25 April 1775; no. 54, Clugny to Turgot, 2 Sept. 1775.
41. AD C1613, no. 130, Trudaine to intendant, 17 May 1775.
42. ibid., no. 132, intendant to Trudaine, 30 May 1775.
43. G. Schelle, *Oeuvres de Turgot et documents le concernant* (Paris, 1913–23), 5 v., V, 369, Turgot to bishop of Cahors, 6 Feb. 1776; 370–84 for the preamble and text of the edict.
44. ibid., preamble, 380–1.
45. Dakin, *Turgot*, 252–3.
46. AD C3683, no. 59.
47. See above, pp. 171–2.
48. AN K708, no. 58. They appear to have been predated, for they were in fact sent on 3 Sept., the day of the forced registration.
49. BVBx MS 1201, V, 12 Sept. 1776.
50. Martin, loc. cit., 468. These letters gave force of law to the *arrêt* of the council of 24 Nov.
51. J. F. Bosher, *The Single Duty Project; a study of the movement for a French customs union in the eighteenth century* (London, 1964), 130.
52. loc. cit. above, n. 48.
53. G. Debien, *Les Colons de Saint-Domingue*, 49–53; R. Pares, *War and Trade in the West Indies*, 326–43. See also above, pp. 102–4.

54. ibid., 343–75.
55. G. Weulersse, *La Physiocratie sous les ministères de Turgot et de Necker (1774–1781)* (Paris, 1950), 294.
56. G. Charpentier, *Les Relations économiques entre Bordeaux et les Antilles au XVIIIe siècle* (Bordeaux, 1937), 79–88. There were some restrictions, but these were easily ignored. The *arrêt* is in Isambert, Jourdan, Crusy, *Recueil générale*, XXVII, 459.
57. AN Colonies F⁴24 contains a selection of these protests. See also Butel, 'La croissance', I, 98–103, where he argues that the colonial monopoly did indeed play a crucial role in the expansion of the Bordelais trade, especially in the earlier part of the century.
58. AN Colonies F²B 8, *Mémoire des directeurs du commerce de la province de Guienne sur l'arrêt du conseil du 30 août 1784* (1785), 6.
59. Bachaumont, XXVIII, 124, 17 Feb. 1785.
60. AN Colonies F⁴24 no. 22, Dudon's *réquisitoire* before the assembled chambers, 7 Jan. 1785.
61. ibid., no. 29.
62. Although the freeing of the ports had followed the opening of the colonies, as a natural and just corollary.
63. 'Mr. de Malesherbes', says a footnote.
64. AN Colonies F²B 8; Lescure, *Correspondance secrète*, I, 566, 1 June 1785.
65. O. Browning (ed.), *Despatches from Paris, 1784–1787* (Camden third series, vol. XVI, London, 1909), 59–60, Dorset to Carmarthen, 9 and 16 June 1785.
66. F. Crouzet, in *Bordeaux au XVIIIe siècle*, 318.
67. ibid., 316–21.
68. AD C4261, quoted in M. Lhéritier, *Histoire des rapports de la chambre de commerce de Guienne avec les intendants, le parlement, et les jurats de 1705 à 1791* (Bordeaux, 1913), 28.
69. AD C4476, *arrêt* of the parlement, 10 March 1783; *arrêt* of the council, 26 June 1783.
70. On these relations in general, see Lhéritier, op. cit., and the introduction by J. A. Brutails to vol. III of the *Inventaire-sommaire des archives départementales de la Gironde, série C*, although both are less than fair to the parlement.
71. AD C4264, *arrêt* of the parlement, 15 March 1770.
72. AD C4266, letter of 9 April 1785.
73. The lieutenant-general de Navarre and the king's procurator de Lascombes. Gouron, *L'Amirauté de Guienne*, 307–9.

CHAPTER 14

Intervention II: Constitutional Attitudes

The central constitutional problem of 18th-century France, at least until 1788, was that of governmental responsibility. How was a government which everybody agreed, however vaguely, to exist for the common good, to be kept to that purpose? Were there any effective guarantees? The theory of absolutism held that there were; the king was responsible to God for the exercise of his power, and in this exercise he had a duty to observe the laws. The king of France was a monarch, chancellor Lamoignon observed, to whom everything was possible but everything was not permitted.[1] This was what distinguished him from a despot. In the view of Montesquieu there was the further restriction of the 'intermediary bodies', repositories of the fundamental laws. The most important of such bodies were the parlements, with their rights of registration and remonstrance, through which they kept the king acquainted with the fundamental laws. Naturally the parlements themselves shared these views, and until 1771 at least, so did many of the political nation. It was no theorist, but Maupeou, who really demolished Montesquieu. He demonstrated the practical weakness of the intermediary bodies by showing how easily the government might override them, and it was from his time that men began to turn their thoughts towards more tangible and permanent checks on governmental power.[2] Nevertheless, attempts to restrict the effective power of the parlements were not confined to the experiments of Maupeou. The government sporadically sought to promote the power of rival yet more subservient authorities. Thus many constitutional conflicts took the form of clashes of jurisdiction.

There were, for example, clashes between various courts in the judicial hierarchy. The grand council was a court which claimed national as opposed to regional jurisdiction over appeals, on specific issues. During the mid-1750s the government had encouraged its pretensions, thereby provoking the fury of the parlements. They ultimately defeated the new policy; but not before the ominous doctrine that all the parlements were really one—the *union des classes*—had been launched to combat it.[3] The doctrine, and the upheaval which had given rise to it, continued to echo down the century. Maupeou suppressed the grand council in order to staff his new parlement of Paris with its members, but it was restored in 1774 in all the vagueness of its jurisdiction, with the additional function of serving as a reserve panel of magistrates to replace the parlement should remodelling ever prove necessary again.

This could be ignored; but it was not so easy to ignore the augmentation in the powers of the presidial courts, when the parlements were restored.[4] A *présidial* was a court of second instance, usually identical in personnel with a seneschalcy, although not all seneschalcies were presidial courts. In the jurisdiction of the parlement of Bordeaux there were no less than 15 of them, and their function was to judge cases on final appeal up to the value of 250 l., and subject to appeal, up to the value of 500 l.[5] In the event of disputes of jurisdiction between them and parlements, the cases were decided by the grand council. Any attempt to increase their powers, therefore, could be interpreted as a covert attempt to boost the grand council's jurisdiction, especially galling since the members of the grand council were now tainted with the stain of having served Maupeou. Moreover, the new law was explicitly designed to perpetuate the spirit of the superior councils, increasing business by raising the level of jurisdiction of inferior courts. On the surface the king could claim to be merely revising a scale of values reduced almost to nothing by centuries of price rises. So the value of cases cognizable in the last resort by the presidial courts was raised to 2,000 l., and, subject to appeal, to 4,000 l. As with the superior councils, this diminished the cost of justice to many litigants by obviating the need to travel to the seat of a parlement for a hearing; it also had the effect of limiting the parlements' jurisdiction. On such grounds the procurator-general reserved his opinion on the Bordeaux edict at the session of restoration in March 1775. Yet the remonstrances which he suggested were never sent owing to the internal quarrels which followed the restoration. Instead the court simply disrupted any attempt by the presidial courts to use their new powers by refusing to recognize them. This was in line with the conduct of all the other parlements. The result was that in 1777 the government was forced to modify its edict. The grand council's jurisdiction over disputes between parlements and presidial courts was now implicitly abolished by the abolition of that part of the powers of the lower courts which was subject to appeal in the parlements. More fatal still to the presidial courts themselves, litigants were now given the choice of using them or not, as they preferred.[6] This edict, insofar as it concerned the powers of the grand council, only confirmed that body's decline. The parlements smelled victory, and when that of Bordeaux refused in 1784 to recognize the evocation of a case from its own jurisdiction to that of the grand council, the latter's members were led to protest to the Keeper of the Seals that it would be better to suppress it than leave it prone to repeated insults and impotence.[7] It disappeared with the old régime, but it had lost all importance some time before 1789.

As regards the presidial courts themselves, the parlement remained unsatisfied. It simply refused to register the new edict, and royal declarations interpreting its meaning, of September 1778 and August 1779, were equally ignored.[8] In these uncertain circumstances, what business these courts had continued to handle came to a complete standstill. 'La Jurisd^on presidiale est comme abolie dans cette province', reported the intendant in August 1780.[9] 'Les appels ne sont plus portées aux Presidiaux, mais au Parlement, ce qui devient tres onereux au public et ruineux pour nombre de familles'.[10] Letters of *jussion* ordering registration of the new laws were unavailing. Matters were only settled at the military session of 21 September 1780, when the new rules were forcibly registered, along with the prolongation of the twentieths and measures concerning Dupaty and Dufaure de Lajarte. These personal questions were the ones which inflamed its passions most, and in concentrating on these, it let the rules on the presidial courts pass. In any case, its hostility had so effectively crippled the proposals of 1775 that only details were outstanding, and even these could be circumvented in everyday practice.

Military sessions were normally the last word in any constitutional conflict, as we have had occasion to see. Although parlements invariably protested that they were null and illegal, they seldom refused to implement what was registered at them, for they were conducted by governors or commandants bearing the orders of the king and invested with his personal authority. The middle years of the century had seen governors and commandants acquire new importance as the need to overbear provincial parlements became more frequent, and their powers gave rise to new jurisdictional conflicts in the 1780s.

In 1782, when rumours (erroneous, as it turned out) were circulating that Mouchy was about to resign his office of lieutenant-general in Guienne to become governor of Provence, the procurator-general Dudon sent some private reflections to the minister of the province on the role of these officers. To replace Mouchy with a mere military commander was not, he insisted, enough.[11]

> un officier général emploïé, présume trop ou trop peu de l'autorité qui luy est Confiée; dans le premier cas, il se fait des affaires cruelles avec le Parlement, et les autres Corps de la province; dans le second cas, toujours timide et chancelant, il n'ose rien entreprendre, et il finit par n'etre a rien dans l'ordre civil; ses fonctions sont bornées au militaire, et alors il est vrai dire [sic] que personne ne commande dans la province.
>
> Si le Roy, Monsieur le Comte, se determine a envoier un Commandant à Bordeaux, il faut qu'il soit sous tous les rapports d'une aussi grande place; il faut qu'a un grand nom, et a de grandes dignités, il joigne les vertus, et les talens nécessaires pour se faire aimer, craindre, et respecter. Sil ne s'agissoit que d'une Commission passagère, je ne me permettois pas ces observations; mais si on donnoit la grande patente a un homme qui ne fut pas aussi décoré, que l'ont été ceux qui ont commandé en Guyenne depuis deux ou trois siècles, je prevois qu'il auroit bien des desagrements à éprouver, a moins que pour les éviter il ne fit souvent le sacrifice de ses devoirs les plus essentiels ...
> La disposition des esprits est telle, qu'on ne scauroit prendre trop de mesures pour éviter de compromettre l'autorité, et pour la faire respecter ...

Richelieu had amply fulfilled all Dudon's criteria. The remodelling of the parlement in 1771 was, as Gascq never tired of emphasizing, peculiarly the governor's own work, and was the product of his good relations with the magistrates up to that time. These relations were built on mutual respect: 'La facon dont on menace tout le monde indiferement du parlement', the governor wrote in 1769,

> comme on fait aux enfans de la grande beste, est la chose du monde la plus plaisante. Je l'aime en gros, et en détail je le revere beaucoup, mais je ne le crains point quand j'aurai raison. Je dois dire même que hors pour de petit détaills, de misère, de ceremonial, sur quoi il est un peu deraisonnable, quellques fois, comme tous les corps, je l'ai toujours [trouvé] plein de raison et d'equité, dans toutes les affairs que j'ai eu a traiter avec lui.[12]

After 1775, of course, part at least of the parlement could never regard Richelieu in the same light again, and his memory was subjected to a number of indignities.[13] Yet although he never returned to Bordeaux, his influence was still felt there, as was shown in the case of the vicomte de Noé.[14]

Noé was mayor of Bordeaux, and among his prerogatives was the maintenance of the rights of the *jurade*. These included, so the *jurats* claimed, the supervision of the Bordeaux theatres; but Richelieu, who as governor had played a major part in promoting the construction of the new grand theatre, claimed that right as his own. In 1784 he demonstrated this by prohibiting all except the two noble *jurats* from sitting on the stage at performances, and sent a Swiss porter in royal livery to enforce this new rule. When the Swiss, however, attempted to implement his orders, Noé had him arrested. Richelieu's response was to take advantage of the fact that Noé held a military rank, and hale him up before the tribunal of the Marshals of France, of which he himself was president. Not unexpectedly this court found the mayor guilty of insulting the governor, condemned him to apologize in abject terms, and suspended him from his mayoral duties for a year. When Noé refused to accept a verdict which he regarded as incompetently rendered, and appealed to the parlement of Paris, Richelieu attempted to arrest him, and he fled to Spain.

The affair caused a sensation in Bordeaux, where it was claimed that the governor was infringing the rights of the city. There was talk of convoking the *cent trente*, the largest civic assembly, which only met in extreme emergencies.[15] In the meantime Dudon led certain magistrates in attempting to persuade the parlement to intervene.[16] Opinion was completely divided,[17] but before any action could be taken, Noé's case had been raised in the parlement of Paris by the redoubtable counsellor Duval d'Eprémesnil, who wrote a long memorandum in his favour.[18] Copies of this memorandum arrived in Bordeaux just before the chambers assembled for a second discussion of the case,[19] and its appearance convinced the magistrates that the affair would be more effectively handled in Paris. There, it developed into a jurisdictional wrangle between the tribunal of the marshals, the council of state, and the parlement. In September the latter presented the king with an outspoken set of remonstrances.[20] Mouchy reported late in August that the case would not be ventilated again in Bordeaux,[21] but early in September d'Eprémesnil himself arrived in the city, ostensibly to lecture on Mesmerism, probably to court Mme Thilorier,[22] but perhaps also to investigate the Noé case more deeply. His visit was followed by a vehement set of remonstrances from the parlement, in which it mentioned the Noé case as part of a more general indictment of governmental evocations to exceptional tribunals.[23] However, at the same time the magistrates declared themselves content to leave the case in the hands of their Parisian colleagues. What with the Dudon case, the *corvées* question, and the ever more ominous development of the *alluvions* issue, they had more pressing matters to occupy them.

Richelieu was characteristically unrepentant about the storm he had raised. 'Je ne suis nullement jaloux', he wrote to Vergennes,[24]

> d'une autorité dont je ne faise jamais usage, mais je suis ne avec l'amour de la regle de l'administration dont jai fait usage pendant quarante cinq ans, dans le languedoc et la guienne, et javoue que chaque delabrement que jy

aprens j'y suis aussi sensible que je le serois a celui de mes propres affaires. je les cognois aussi sufisament pour vous assurer, que les complaisance ne font que leur doner courage a en exiger jusqu'a l'abus et qu'une fermeté tres juste en ne seccartant jamais . . . les conduit doucement et agreablement come jause vous dire que j'ai toujours fait nayant jamais eu aucune contradiction que pour le bouleversement des parlemens, et encore fut il bien peu de patriotisme . . .

Noé did not return to France until after Richelieu's death in 1788. Had he done so before, the affair might have exploded afresh; and as it was, it only subsided locally because it was ventilated nationally.

The Bordelais in 1784 were particularly sensitive to abuses of power by governors and commandants, because the previous year Mouchy himself had been at the centre of a similar case. Early in 1783 the comte de Beaumont, commanding in Perigord, authorized the provost of the marshalcy to judge a case which had come to him on appeal, with the result that one of the parties had been committed to prison. The condemned man appealed to the parlement, and the grand chamber ordered his release.[25] Soon afterwards the *tournelle*, headed by Dupaty, ordered the release of three persons long before acquitted of criminal offences but since imprisoned on Mouchy's orders. It also issued and distributed printed copies of an *arrêt* which forbade all governors and military commanders, and Mouchy by name, to imprison people on their own authority. This resounding declaration of the primacy of civil justice infuriated Mouchy. 'Je me flatte, Monsieur le Comte', he wrote to Vergennes,

que vous aurés la bonté detre chocqué de l'incartade que M^r Du Paty vien de me faire. Je ne lui ai jamais fait que du bien, et il saisit la premiere occasion ou il peut me faire de la peine, et de la façon du monde la plus indecente; je reçois touts les jours des plaintes de ma trop grande douceur, ma plus longue prison est de 15 jours, et ce n'est que d'après les temoignages les plus authentiques; renouveller une affaire depuis 6 ans, ne pas m'en faire part, prononcer un arrest, et ordonner qu'on l'affiche est un procédé indigne d'un honneste magistrat; mais il a été toujours ennemi de l'autorité, a declamé contre quoiquil aye eu tant de besoin pour etre receu, il a suivi son humeur et son caractere: javoue que si je n'obtiens pas de la justice et de la tbonté d Roy . . . je suplierai tres humblement sa Majesté de me permetre de lui remettre mon commandement ou jai fait de mon mieux dans les neuf voyages que j'y ai fait . . .[26]

Most of the inhabitants of Bordeaux, and indeed the parlement itself, disapproved of the *tournelle*'s action, he declared; it was an insult to the king's authority.[27] He insisted that, if he were not to resign, the offending *arrêt* be quashed by the council of state.[28] Dupaty disclaimed responsibility,[29] but the council hastened to oblige Mouchy. By an *arrêt* of 25 April 1783 it quashed the order of the *tournelle*. But this shifted the ground of the conflict. The parlement, however much it might regret the precipitate action of the *tournelle*, could hardly accept the rejection of the principle upon which it had acted, since the grand chamber had acted in exactly the same way in the case of the comte de Beaumont. And so the *arrêt* led to remonstrances.[30] 'Les Gouverneurs et Commandants', they declared, 'n'ont cessé de former ces entreprises contre les jurisdictions ordinaires, ils ont toujours cherché à se créer un tribunal indépendant et absolu pour rendre leur autorité plus formidable'. The sole authority of governors was military; they could not

> exercer aucune fonction dans tout ce qui a rapport à l'ordre civil, ils ne peuvent avoir ni inspection, ni police. Le gouvernement françois n'est point militaire. C'est un gouvernement civil. Vos sujets sont régis par des loix. Ils ne peuvent reconnaitre d'autre autorité, que celle qui est verifiée par les tribunaux qui en sont les dépositaires.

Such principles were commonplaces in the rhetoric and ideas of the parlements, but their constant repetition shows how much they were felt to be threatened. To the magistrates, the government was always under suspicion of trying to undermine the liberties of Frenchmen, sectional, regional, and national. Nowhere did the danger seem more acute than in the field of taxation.

Taxation had always been a problem of deep concern to the parlements, but from the time of the introduction of the first twentieth in 1749, it had become peculiarly urgent. For within 11 years of its first introduction, the costs of war had trebled it and burdened it with a number of additional surtaxes. Taxpayers were naturally alarmed at such a sudden rise, and the parlements took a lead in calling for a speedy diminution of these new burdens as soon as the emergency was over. A sympathetic ministry in 1763 acceded to these demands, abandoning the third twentieth. It also acquiesced in two fundamental assertions of the parlements, led by that of Paris—that the second twentieth should not be levied beyond 1770, and that meanwhile the assessments should on no account be revised or raised. This implied that the twentieth was a once-for-all grant for an emergency, neither perpetual nor renewable. The parlements were invited at the same time to send in their own suggestions for the improvement of the finances.[31]

The parlement of Bordeaux set out its own position clearly in 1760 when, while registering the third twentieth in recognition of the needs of the king, it ordered remonstrances to point out that:

> . . . à tous les maux actuels qui accablent les sujets dudit Seigneur Roi, se joint la crainte de ne pouvoir presque point espérer de soulagement; . . . l'on a vû les charges de l'Etat, dont l'acquittement avoit été annoncé dès le commencement du regne dudit seigneur Roi, s'accroître de jour en jour, les impositions passagères devenir perpétuelles, les anciennes considérablement augmenter, & les généreux efforts du Peuple le plus soumis & le plus fidèle, devenir impuissant [sic] pour acquitter les dettes contractées au nom de l'Etat . . .[32]

Ever-increasing taxes, it declared, were the ruin of agriculture, and their effect was aggravated by enormous costs of collection, spending on purposes other than the original declared purpose, and governmental extravagance. These were themes that recurred regularly in the parlements' reactions to tax increases throughout the last decades of the old régime.

In 1763 the parlement joined the other sovereign courts in insisting that assessments for the twentieths should on no account be revised, and that the operation of the first twentieth should not extend for more than ten years after the peace.[33] It applauded the creation of a sinking fund, serviced by part of the yield from the twentieths; it had itself called for such a fund to pay off the king's debts in 1760. When in 1764 the magistrates sent in their advice on the improvement of the royal finances, they were even more radical. Recognizing that the nation was overtaxed, but that the royal revenues could not be cut without some cut in expenditure, they reviewed the possibilities without optimism. They rejected the physiocratic panacea of a single tax on land, as likely to depress agriculture. Instead they proposed a new tax on state *rentes*, comparable in weight to those borne by land. Its yield could be applied either to reducing the burden of other taxes or, more radically, to amortizing the very debt on which the *rentes* constituted interest. It was an ingenious plan, and taxing liquid assets was an idea with a future, but it seemed excessively optimistic to expect the debt to be completely liquidated by these means as early as 1793, and there is no evidence that the government took any more notice of this memorandum than it did of remonstrances.[34]

For all the suggestions of the parlements the finances did not improve, and by December 1768 the comptroller-general Maynon d'Invau saw no immediate alternative to the prolongation of the second twentieth until 1772. This provoked a storm of protest from the parlement of Paris, and the burden was taken up by the others. At Bordeaux, the prolongation had to be registered in a military session on 7 September 1769, a registration which the parlement impotently declared to be 'nulle, illégale, contraire aux Loix de l'Etat', and condemned, in repeated remonstrances.[35]

The accession to power of Terray was marked at first by a partial bankruptcy, to which the parlements objected either weakly or not at all, since they regarded the state's major creditors as irresponsible and immoral speculators, who for the most part got what they deserved. However, his tax increases of 1771 were a different matter, and as we have seen,[36] evoked vehement remonstrances from most of the parlements, but Bordeaux in particular. Those of 18 January 1772 were mainly concerned with the impact of the tax increases on the wine trade, but they based themselves squarely on the general principle that:

> Des subsides extraordinaires établies pour subvenir aux besoins de la guerre peuvent etre prorogés dans un tems de paix sans alarmer les peuples; ils peuvent croire que leur destination est de reparer les pertes et d'acquiter les dettes que l'Etat a pu contracter mais quand a la suite de plusieurs années de paix les mêmes impôts sont prorogés; que le terme de leur prorogation recoit chaque jour une nouvelle extention, qu'ils prennent enfin le caractère de la stabilité; alors les peuples étonnés ne peuvent s'empêcher de porter les yeux sur l'administration, et sans entendre en pénétrer les Secrets, ils sont forcés de s'appercevoir qu'il ne reste plus de proportion entre les besoins de l'Etat et les facultés des contribuables; ils voient disparoître tous les avantages que la paix sembloit devoir leur procurer, et ne prevoient plus le genre de secours qu'ils pourront suppléer dans les extrêmités les plus pressantes...

Recent times had seen the levy of the so-called 'free gift', and the prolongation of the two twentieths in such a way as to suggest their permanency:

> ... ainsi dans l'espace de moins de trente années trois espèces d'impositions inconnues à vos peuples deviennent permanentes, et nous sommes encore forcés de nous apercevoir par des opérations multipliées, que l'administration cherche sans se lasser des secours et des ressources; qu'après avoir frappé sur les principaux objets elle ne dédaigne pas ceux [que] leur modicité sembloit devoir epargner. Si l'avenir nous prépare une semblable progression dans les impots quelle esperance restera t'il aux peuples! et si par les suites d'une administration vicieuse le crédit de la Nation demeure toujours languissant, quelles ressources restera-t-il pour le rétablir?

If so many taxes were prolonged without opposition at one time, declared the remonstrances of 19 February, it was to be feared that future governments might come to regard them as permanent, and imagine that in times of need further taxes might be raised on an extraordinary basis without overwhelming the king's subjects. In fact they were overwhelmed already, and it was to be feared that if a new war necessitated further supplies, the government would find itself unable to raise them.

> Ce concours de subsides, la durée de leur Prorogation, tendent à détruire tout l'espoir de vos peuples, ces impositions Prorogées jusques ici avec une sorte de ménagement sembloient leur annoncer un desir constant de les soulager; mais le terme perpetuellement renvoyé et toujours des progressions plus reculées, cette multiplicité d'accessoires qui apésantissent de plus en plus le fardeau, répandent parmi vos sujets la Consternation et l'accablement.

The burden of the remonstrances of 18 March was similar, but the constant ignoring of their previous protests by the king injected a growing note of stridency. How could the parlement in all conscience freely register tax increases which would ruin the inhabitants of its province? How did it know that there would not be other such increases?

> Le terme indéfini du premier Vingtième est de la conséquence la plus allarmante Pour les peuples; un impôt prorogé sans borne se présente à leurs yeux comme stable et Permanent; le second Vingtième prendra successivement la nature du premier, de nouveaux besoins en ameneront un troisième; des estimations arbitraires en augmenteront successivement les Cottités, et vos sujets ne seront plus que les Colons Partiaire du Patrimoine de leurs ancêtres.

The point could hardly have been made more strongly, and it was these remonstrances which precipitated the governmental crisis which led to the military session and forced registration of 10 April.

The crisis of 1771–72 was followed by a lull of several years in discussion of the taxation issue. No more taxes were either introduced or prolonged until 1780. Necker's loans provoked little demur from the parlement of Paris, before which they were laid, and even less from provincial parlements, before which they were not. Controversy in the late 1770s mostly concerned the methods of levying taxes which were already in existence. Terray had not confined himself to prolonging and increasing the burden of taxes. He also put into operation for the first time a system of revising the assessments for the twentieths through regular inspections,[37] precisely the process which the parlements had ruled out by their provisos of 1763, which did not appear in the registrations of 1771 and 1772. Nor did the inspections end with Terray's fall and the restoration of the parlements. In 1776 new general instructions were issued to guide inspectors in making reassessments, and Necker confirmed them when he came to power in 1777.[38] Unable to prevent them, the parlement of Paris conducted an inquiry into malpractices in their conduct, on the results of which it partly based the conclusions of its great remonstrances on abuses in the twentieths of 1778.[39] That of Rouen went so far as to resign *en masse* on the issue of revising the rolls.[40] The government bowed to the furore somewhat when, by an *arrêt* of the council of 26 March 1778, it confirmed a declaration made by Necker the previous year, that all revised assessments were not to undergo further revision for at least 20 years; but it did not suspend the revisions themselves.[41] In the generality of Bordeaux, inspections were authorized by an *arrêt* of 2 September 1777, which was heatedly discussed in the parlement in April 1778.[42] However, there was little urgency in the situation, since the wine-growing disaster of the previous autumn forced the intendant to suspend revisions almost at once in the face of violent resistance from distressed communities. They were resumed in 1780, but coincided with the modification by the parlement of an edict further prolonging the twentieths, and they were again suspended until this measure was registered.[43]

Terray's edict of 1771 had only prolonged the second twentieth for ten years, but the war made it impractical to let it lapse when its term arrived. An edict of February 1780 therefore prolonged it for another ten years.[44] The reception among the parlements was mixed. Most were unwilling to appear to be obstructing the government in time of war, but some felt bound to insert provisos in their formulae of registration.[45] Bordeaux registered the edict on 2 May with the proviso, which echoed that of 1763, that the current assessments should on no account be raised.[46] The weather had largely disrupted the intendant's plans for inspection and revision, so that the parlement, preoccupied in any case with its own internal affairs, had not interfered in the process before this moment; but it had forced him to abandon a project for revising the capitation roll of the *bourgeois* of Bordeaux,[47] and now this renewed proviso forced the suspension of inspections.[48] The edict incorporated Necker's 1778 declaration that new assessments should not be subject to revision for 20 years, but the parlement's proviso was intended to prevent any new assessments at all, let alone after 20 years. The parlement ignored letters patent of 3 June ordering the registration of the edict purely and simply, without emendations. On 25 August sittings were prolonged into the vacation. The edict was finally registered, purely and simply, at the military session of 21 September 1780, along with Dupaty's provisions.[49] This was not before the parlement had sent remonstrances claiming that the level of the twentieths had risen alarmingly in the province since 1776, and that this rise had been accompanied by all sorts of administrative abuses.[50] But the government took no notice, and inspections and revisions were resumed.

The prolongation of the second twentieth was the first step in a new round of tax increases, given added momentum by the fall of Necker. In August 1781 a 10 per cent surcharge was imposed on most indirect taxes, along with even larger increases on certain items. As part of a bargain to end enforced vacation sittings[51] the parlement registered this edict at the end of September, but at the same time it suspended its operation pending the dispatch of remonstrances. Letters of *jussion* of 1 February 1782 ordered a pure and simple registration, but eventually this had to be carried out by the comte de Fumel at a military session on 27 May.[52] Such resistance makes it all the more curious, on the surface, that the third twentieth, introduced by an edict of July 1782, met with no resistance whatsoever and was peacefully registered on 29 August.[53] This new levy was to last until three years after the peace, and represented a theoretically heavy increase in taxation. The facts that it was a war tax, born of the emergency, that the government had kept its word and abandoned the previous third twentieth in 1763, and that Necker had recently shown the apparent state of the finances to be basically sound, were all perhaps reassuring. Above all, the government made a capital concession in the edict; it abandoned all its attempts of the previous decade to revise the assessments for the twentieths.[54] But the parlements of Grenoble, Besançon, and several others were hardly reassured and created far more trouble over this twentieth than the prolongation of the second.[55]

The third twentieth was the last tax increase which the parlement of Bordeaux was called upon to register before the financial and constitutional crisis of 1787. All the most controversial financial measures of the intervening years were loans, which only required the registration of the Paris parlement. Nevertheless, suspicion of the government's fiscal policies persisted, as the case of the *corvées* demonstrates.[56] Attempts to increase revenue without reference to the courts, the constant overriding of the parlement's interventions by the council of state, the final imposition of the royal will by unanswerable authority—these were complaints that constantly recurred. What remedies did the parlement propose?

One was a drastic reduction in the powers and activities of the council of state, most clearly expressed in the remonstrances of 17 November 1784.[57] Prepared in the course of the *alluvions* affair, they reflected a year of frustration through quashed *arrêts* over the younger Dudon and the *corvées* too. They directed their attack against 'le Despotisme clandestin . . . exercé sous le nom du Conseil'. Of course the king wished to rule well and in accordance with the laws, but despite these good intentions, arbitrariness was coming to characterize his government.

> Autant la confiance pour le Monarque est absolue, autant la France apprit à craindre les suites de ces émanations partielles de la Puissance Royale, que le Prince daigne confier pour un temps à quelques-uns de ses sujets. Les variations qu'on remarque dans les opérations de ceux qui se succedent dans cette carriere, doneroient à penser que leurs principes sont aussi mobiles que leurs places & leur pouvoir. C'est donc le plus inviolable & le plus important des devoirs du Magistrat de réclamer avec force & constance, pour les maximes du droit public, de ne point laisser intervenir, par l'arbitraire, l'ordre immuable des Jurisdictions, & de s'opposer à ce que le glaive de l'autorité tranche les difficultés que la loi seule a droit de résoudre. Si le choix de ceux que VOTRE MAJESTÉ rassemble autour d'elle rendoit le mal présent moins grave; qui rassurera la Nation allarmée sur l'abus que leurs successeurs pourroient faire de l'usage dangereux d'appeler tout à leur Tribunal par des Arrêts du Conseil?

The case was the eternal one deployed by the judge against the administrator, although obviously it was decked out with an apparatus of particular laws and precedents. However, declared the magistrates,

... nous insisterons moins sur nos titres que sur les abus, sur le maintien de nos prerogatives, que sur les droits de la nation & d'une province, qui, depuis quelques années, semble plus exposée que toute autre à cette subversion de l'ordre Judiciaire; c'est en leur servant d'organe que nous vous representerons que les evocations sont contraires au droit naturel, contraires au droit public de la France, à la forme de législation établie, contraires enfin aux privilèges de la Guienne.

The magistrates declared themselves solidly against 'les horreurs d'une aristocratie judiciaire', yet between that, represented by an absolute veto on legislation in the hands of the parlements, and a government which in the last analysis was always able to enforce its will, there was no obvious middle way. Nevertheless, the endless progression of new taxes and continued impunity with which the agents of the executive seemed to be extending their powers clearly demanded something more than the mere muzzling of the council of state. The magistrates also believed that Guienne should be turned into a *pays d'états*.

Like most of their ideas, it was not original. As far back as the late 1750s and early 1760s, the parlement of Rouen had repeatedly issued calls for provincial estates,[58] and several others had alluded to them. In 1775 the court of aids of Paris adopted remonstrances suggesting that estates be generally established throughout the kingdom; their text was made public in 1778.[59] In May 1776 the parlement of Grenoble called for the re-establishment of the estates of its own province.[60] By the late 1770s the idea of provincial representation in the administration was well developed, and the establishment by Necker of two 'provincial administrations' or assemblies in 1778 was both a witness to the popularity of the idea and a stimulus to further discussion of it. Necker's assemblies were not estates; they represented generalities, not provinces; they voted by head, not by order; their members were nominated, not elected; they existed to impose taxes, not grant them. Nevertheless, the principle was similar: the association of the governed in the processes of government. It was an appealing way out of the constitutional deadlock, and upon it the parlement of Bordeaux based its remonstrances of 26 August 1779.[61] These remonstrances were the first in the *corvée* affair,[62] and the proposal arose, like that of Grenoble, out of the *corvée* problem. Not all *pays d'états* were without *corvées*, but the roads of Languedoc at least were the wonder of travellers, and were financed out of taxes raised and granted by the estates. Nor were the advantages of estates confined to good roads.

La force d'un etat vient de l'attachement que chacun a pour l'etat, et cet attachement ne peut prendre naissance que dans la propriété. La propriété d'un citoyen dans un bon gouvernement s'etend et se modifie de mille manieres; ses loix, sa liberté, ses privileges, son Roi, sa religion, sa patrie, tout devient un objet de propriété, plus ils sont a lui, et plus ils lui sont chers.

Tout homme qui ne tient à l'etat que par son bien n'est point Citoyen, ainsi en changeant tous les païs d'Election en pays d'etats vous étendez en quelque sort l'existence et les biens de chaque individu, puisque vous étendez ses motifs d'affection, et vous le liez par cela meme plus entroitement à l'etat, cette administration interieure a laquelle il participe, ou croit participer, débarrasse le gouvernement des objets de detail et devient un gage assuré de sa fidelité, de son zèle, et de son amour. Sa liberté même est un bien de plus qui l'enchaine a sa patrie, et qui la lui rend encore plus sacrée.

Dela, Sire, que d'efforts les provinces d'etats ne font elles pas dans ces moments de crise ou les besoins sont plus presants et les ressources plus rares: que de secours extraordinaires et presque incomprehensibles, ne donnent elles pas au gouvernement dans les tems ou son Credit est entière- ment épuisé. C'est alors qu'on sent l'avantage des pays d'etats, leur Con- stitution fait leur force. Comment des païs d'Election pourroient ils dans des tems facheux fournir a l'etat en argent, en troupes, en vaisseaux, en muni- tions; qui s'engageroit au nom de la province dès qu'elle n'auroit point de representants? et qui pourroit accorder mille interets divers, qui tendent tous au bien public, il est vrai, mais qui ne sauroient y concourir puisqu'il n'y a point de centre auquel le voeu général puisse se réunir?

Only estates, the magistrates claimed, could know a province in sufficient detail to make the best of its capacities, respect its limitations, and prevent injustice. Obviously then, they would promote more harmonious and more efficient govern- ment. They would put the grant of taxes in the hands of the taxpayer, and although (a fact they did not mention) they would clearly rival the authority of the parle- ment, at least they would have more strength to restrain the abuses of arbitrary authorities.

Not that the parlement campaigned for them consistently. After these remon- strances, nothing more was heard of the proposal until an assembly of chambers of January 1785,[63] and then the speaker drew no distinction between estates and assemblies. A few days later the parlement moved to the altogether more ambi- tious proposal for the Estates-General.[64] Nevertheless, the appeal of provincial estates persisted, and in 1787 the parlement based its opposition to Brienne's provincial assemblies upon the position that estates were a preferable form of representation. Soon afterwards, the whole nobility of the province took up the cry, convinced that they would be the best guarantee possible against the arbitrariness and 'despotism' of the government and its local agents.

This, too, the parlement had predicted in 1779:

Mais ce qui est peut-être plus difficile encore cest de pouvoir contenir ou arrêter les subdélégués; Toujours occupés à augmenter leur autorité, ils flattent les grands, ils écrasent les petits et sont redoutés de tout le monde. Leur pouvoir est d'autant plus à craindre qu'ils croient être indépendants des Tribunaux de justice et ne relever que d'un Commissaire départi, interessé à maintenir leur autorité pour étayer la sienne . . .

Votre Parlement, Sire, a cru qu'à tous ces excès d'un pouvoir arbitraire portant essentiellement sur la Constitution de la Province il étoit de son devoir de chercher un remède proportionné au mal et digne d'être mis sous les yeux de Votre Majesté.

For estates were the solution to more problems than that of the *corvées*. Behind the debate over the roads lay the greater issue of the authority of the oldest and most persistent enemies of the provincial parlements, the intendants. A closer examination of the *corvées* conflict itself makes this clear.

NOTES

1. Grosclaude, *Malesherbes*, 279.
2. For a fuller discussion of these trends, see W. Doyle, 'The parlements of France and the breakdown of the old régime, 1771–1788', *French Historical Studies* (1970), *passim*.
3. Egret, *Louis XV et l'opposition parlementaire*, 72–6; J. H. Shennan, *The Parlement of Paris* (London, 1968), 311.
4. For the edict regarding the parlement of Paris, see Isambert, Jourdan, Crusy, *Recueil générale*, XXIII, 57–8; J. Flammermont, *Remontrances du parlement de Paris au XVIIIe siècle* (Paris, 1888–1908), III, 251–3.
5. M. Marion, *Dictionnaire des institutions de la France aux XVIIe et XVIIIe siècles* (Paris, 1923), 449–50.
6. ibid. The edict, of 7 Aug. 1777, is not in Isambert, and the whole question is poorly documented in secondary sources. For an informed contemporary opinion, however, see S. N. H. Linguet, *Annales politiques civiles et littéraires du XVIIIe siècle* (Paris, 1777–92), II, 277–317, which includes the text of the edict, 306–14.
7. Bachaumont, XXVI, 152–3, 19 Aug. 1784.
8. Neither of these texts is in Isambert, Jourdan, Crusy, op. cit.
9. AD C3452, intendant to Keeper of the Seals, 30 Aug. 1780; see also his previous letter of 26 Aug., printed in Marion, *Dictionnaire*, 451.
10. AD C3452, same to same, 4 Jan. 1780.
11. AAE MD France, 1589, ff.108–9, Dudon to Vergennes, 30 March 1782.
12. *AHDG*, II (1860), no. CCLXVI at p. 423, Richelieu to Tranchère, 9 March 1769.
13. See above, p. 175, n. 95.
14. H. Cole, *First Gentleman of the Bedchamber* (London and New York, 1965), 278–80, contains a convenient summary in English of this affair. The most convenient French source is Bachaumont, XXV, 231 (16 April 1784), 272 (4 May), 275 (6 May); and XXVI, 38–9 (11 June 1784), 86 (9 July), 113–15 (24 July), 158 (23 July).
15. AAE MD France, 1589, f.307, Mouchy to Vergennes, 9 April 1784.
16. ibid.
17. ibid., f.319, same to same, 3 July 1784.
18. *Récit de la conduite des maréchaux de France à l'égard du vicomte de Noë, maire de Bordeaux, fait au parlement, les chambres assemblées, le mardi 6 juillet 1784* (Paris, 1784). Duval raised the case in the parlement on 6 July.
19. AAE MD France, 1589, f.326, Mouchy to Vergennes, 24 July 1784.
20. Flammermont, *Remontrances*, III, 590–9, 5 Sept. 1784.
21. AAE MD France, 1589, f.327, same to same, 17 Aug. 1784.
22. ibid., f.343, same to same, 15 Sept. 1784.
23. BPR Le Paige 828, p. 34. See also below, pp. 226–7.
24. ibid., ff.305–6, Richelieu to Vergennes, 19 March 1784.
25. Bachaumont, XXII, 182, 31 March 1783, and 197, 8 April 1783.
26. AAE MD France, 1589, f.286, Mouchy to Vergennes, 21 [March] 1783.
27. ibid., f.110, same to same, 10 April 1783.
28. ibid., f.112, same to same, 15 April 1783.
29. In his request to be relieved in the autumn 1783; see above, p. 189.
30. BVBx MS 1696, IV, pièce 100, for these remonstrances; a copy of the *arrêt* of the council in AD C3630.
31. Marion, *Histoire financière*, I, 226–34.
32. AD C3044, printed copy of edict of Feb. 1760, and *arrêt* of registration, 14 April 1760.
33. AD C3159, mention of *arrêt* of 24 Dec. 1763.
34. BN Joly de Fleury 1432, ff.167–79, 'Mémoire sur la liberation de L'Etat et le soulagement des peuples, presenté par le Parlement de Bordeaux . . . [etc.]', 5 Sept. 1764. Marion, loc. cit., 233–4, gives rather a twisted and unfair account of this memorandum.
35. *Arrest de la Cour de Parlement . . . du Lundi 11 Decembre 1769*, publicly posted.
36. See above, pp. 150–4.
37. Marion, op. cit., 266–9, 271–2.
38. ibid., 314; also G. Lardé, *Une Enquête sur les vingtièmes au temps de Necker. Histoire des remontrances du parlement de Paris (1777–1778)* (Paris, 1920), 7, 18.
39. ibid., 56–70; remonstrances in Flammermont, *Remontrances*, III, 394–439.

40. Marion, op. cit., 315–16.
41. Lardé, op. cit., 20–1, 68.
42. AAE MD France, 1386, f.43, Loret to Vergennes, 18 April 1778.
43. Summary of G. Lassalle, 'L'administration financière de Dupré de Saint-Maur en Guyenne (1776–84)', *Positions des thèses de l'Ecole des Chartes* (1949).
44. Isambert, Jourdan, Crusy, op. cit., XXVI, 275, notes this edict without giving its text; analysis in Marion, op. cit., 317.
45. ibid.; Doyle, 'The parlements of France', 447–8.
46. Copy of this *arrêt* in AD C3044; Marion, loc. cit.
47. Lassalle, op. cit.
48. AD C3618, intendant to Necker, 7 Oct. 1780.
49. AD IB 56, f.115; see also above, p. 182.
50. I have been unable to find a copy of these remonstrances, but their existence is attested by the intendant's letter to Necker, cited above, n. 48. BN Albertas, VII, f.3542, 18 Oct. 1781, says they contained implicit praise of Necker. They were sent either on 13 Aug. or 20 Aug. 1780. BVBx MS 1201, IX, 31 Aug. 1780.
51. See above, p. 187.
52. AD IB 56, f.160 vo. If these remonstrances were ever sent, I have not been able to trace a copy of them. See Marion, op. cit., I, 338–9, and G. T. Matthews, *The Royal General Farms in Eighteenth-century France* (New York, 1958), 260.
53. Marion, op. cit., I, 339, implies that there was resistance. The edict is noted, but no text given, in Isambert, Jourdan, Crusy, op. cit., XXVII, 206; the record of the session is in AD IB 56, f.162 vo.
54. Marion, op. cit., I, 339.
55. ibid., 340.
56. See below, ch. 15.
57. Printed copy in BPR Le Paige 828. See also below, p. 253.
58. Egret, *Louis XV et l'opposition parlementaire*, 130; A. Cobban, *A History of Modern France* (London, 1957), I, 127.
59. Grosclaude, *Malesherbes*, 315; Marion, *Histoire financière*, I, 322.
60. Egret, *Parlement de Dauphiné*, II, 129.
61. Copy in AD C1989.
62. See below, pp. 234–5.
63. In a speech, subsequently printed, of 14 Jan. 1785. See below, pp. 241–2.
64. See above, p. 212.

CHAPTER 15

Intervention III: The Corvées

The magistrates of the parlements were in no way affected by the *corvée* system of road-building by forced labour. Some lords had had the right to compel their vassals to perform public works from time immemorial, and during the reign of Louis XIV the king himself began to require his subjects to build roads and bridges without payment. The convenience of such a system was obvious, and it spread. By 1740, except in certain *pays d'états* like Languedoc, it had become general throughout the kingdom, although its weight varied considerably from place to place. But nobles, ecclesiastics, and townsmen were all exempt. The *corvées* were one more burden borne by the peasantry alone.

Yet despite the exemption of their members, the parlements frequently pointed out abuses in the administration of the *corvées*. In the 1750s the parlements of Bordeaux, Toulouse, Grenoble, and Rouen all attacked the abuses and cruelties of the system in their own areas.[1] In the 1760s that of Rennes joined the chorus.[2] Admittedly these criticisms sprang less from compassion for the lot of the peasantry, than from suspicion of the arbitrary power of the governors, intendants, and their agents who ran the *corvées*. Abuses were important because they resulted from arbitrariness, and not because they were inherent in the whole system. Its value properly administered seemed undisputed. After all, it did produce the finest roads in Europe.

Nor were the economists who criticized the *corvées* particularly concerned, except in the most indirect way, with the plight of the peasantry. If they wished to make the peasant more comfortable, it was only by increasing the general level of wealth, and his share in it. They gave little thought to the peasants' immediate relief. Certainly the economists wished to abolish the *corvées*; but to substitute for them some kind of money payment destined to provide for the upkeep of the roads. This would have the double advantage of maintaining a good system of highways to promote the circulation of wealth, while not taking the peasants away from the land, that source of all wealth, as the *corvées* did. Such thinking took no account of any preference the peasant might have for a few days of forced labour over yet another money tax; after all, the *corvées* were obviously unpopular. The endless resistance of the peasantry to its demands showed that. The equally endless attention required in overcoming the resistance emphasized that the system was inefficient too.[3] Given the administrative convenience and economic

231

advantage of replacing the *corvée* by a money tax, the preferences of the peasants were taken for granted rather than consulted.

The obvious disadvantages of the system meant that almost as soon as it had become general, some intendants were introducing commutation. In the 1750s the intendant of Caen introduced a scheme under which communities might opt for commutation or labour.[4] Better known was the scheme introduced by Turgot, intendant of Limoges, in his generality during the 1760s, under which parishes performing the *corvées* obtained reductions in their *taille*, and peasants performing the work were paid for their services.[5] Such schemes passed without comment from the parlements so long as they involved no obvious increase in the level of taxation.[6] The parlement of Bordeaux did not obstruct Turgot's work in Limousin.[7] But they were deeply suspicious of anything that looked like a new tax, and any scheme that appeared to replace the *corvées*, from which many were exempt, with taxes from which none were exempt. Yet this was obviously the next step, and under Terray extensive inquiries were set in train to see how the *corvées* might be reformed.[8] Turgot's reputation as an economist led to a general expectation that he would attack them when he became comptroller-general. With Terray's information to work on, he did not disappoint these expectations, and in 1776 produced his famous edict to abolish the *corvées*, and replace them by a money tax payable by all landowners whether they had previously been subject to the *corvée* or not.[9]

This edict raised perhaps more storm in the parlement of Paris than any other part of his programme.[10] But like all Turgot's measures, it went through. Impassioned remonstrances[11] could not change the effect of a *lit de justice*. What prevented the full operation of the edict was its reversal, which followed the dismissal of Turgot. Within two months of his fall, it had been rescinded, and only four of the provincial parlements had even received it by that time. Bordeaux certainly had not, although it took the opportunity of its remonstrances on the wine trade to observe scornfully that the *corvée* edict would have meant 'un impôt de plus et des chemins de moins'.[12] Not all of those parlements which had received it had proved as hostile as Paris,[13] but none thought fit to protest when it was withdrawn. Perhaps they were satisfied with the dispensation which replaced it; for on 6 September new administrative regulations for the *corvée* allowed schemes of commutation to be introduced on the basis of an addition to the *taille* paid by each community.[14] This rule allowed a money tax to be substituted, as Turgot had intended, while exempting from its payment those who had not been liable to the *corvée* in kind. It thus yielded to the main principle enunciated in the remonstrances of the Paris parlement, that 'nul n'est corvéable s'il n'est taillable',[15] a principle Turgot had rejected. The new rule allowed commutation when circumstances required, but it did not prescribe it universally. Yet it opened the way to a gradual and piecemeal transformation of the *corvée*. This was the rule under which all roadworks were managed until 1787.[16]

One obvious virtue of the new rule was that it allowed the *corvée* to be managed according to local circumstances, which differed from area to area. The generality of Bordeaux had its peculiarities like any other. They were well summarized in a memorandum of 1770.[17]

Le peu d'avancement du travail des Corvées, pour la perfection des Routes et Chemins ouverts dans la Gen[eral] ité, doit etre attribué [en] partie au grand nombre de pretendus privilegiés, lesquels sous pretexte de places honorifiques ou lucratives qu'ils occupent, refusent journellement de contribuer a l'avancement des travaux et deffendent a leurs ouvriers et valets de se rendre sur les Chemins, d'ou il s'ensuit que les pauvres miserables habitans de la Campagne se trouvent seuls chargés d'un travail penible dont profitent presque seuls les plus Riches habitans de la province par l'augmentation de la valeur de leurs denrees.

The memorandum went on to cite examples of representative communities—Beautiran, Villenave, Barsac, Sauternes—in which only half the available wagon teams of oxen were liable for the *corvées* thanks to these privileges. They went back to an *arrêt* of the court of aids of 1762, which forbade the officers of bridges and roads to co-opt for the *corvée* either the employees or the animals of members of the court and their relatives. The parlement quickly followed this example, and soon the church, the nobility, the *bourgeois de Bordeaux*, and all privileged groups were claiming the same exemption for their people. The original *arrêt* of the court of aids was in fact quashed by the council of state in 1767, but for some reason the intendant never published the cassation, and it remained unknown. Thus in 1771 the intendant could still write to Trudaine that:

Il n'est pas possible qu'un sindic des corvées commande les gens ou les bestiaux d'un privilegié, quel qu'il soit quelques vaines que soient ses titres, sans s'exposer a être decreté, soit par la Cour des Aydes, soit par le parlement . . . Il y a a ce sujet un entetement qu'on ne peut point esperer de vaincre, même par les meilleurs raisons du monde, Il tient à l'interest ainsy qu'a la vanité, deux mobiles Toujours egalement puissans . . .

. . . je ne puis ordonner de corvees sans etre sur, que les trois quarts de ceux qui doivent se rendre a l'attelier, ne s'y trouveront pas, souvent meme personne ne s'y trouve. J'ay fait, pour l'Exemple, emprisonner quelques uns des defaillans, mais si J'eusse fait Tomber cet exemple sur les gens de quelques privilégiés, sur le champ, J'aurois eu un Tracasserie très vive, Vous en auriés été informé, et le remede que jaurois voulu employer contre ce mal, en auroit produit un beaucoup plus grand encore, celui de compromettre l'autorité, et de me compromettre moy-même.[18]

But when the intendant asked permission to operate a scheme of commutation identical to that operated by Turgot in Limousin, permission was refused.[19] This was the situation when Dupré de Saint-Maur became intendant in 1776.

Dupré's policy was to profit to the utmost from the dispensation of September 1776. Accordingly, in the spring of 1777 he issued orders allowing each community to opt between continuing to perform the *corvée* in kind, and paying for it by an addition to their *taille*. Unfortunately many payers of the *taille* were *de facto* exempt from the *corvée* as servants of privileged persons, and were therefore being asked to compound for nothing. The very principle, theoretically unexceptionable, that only *taillables* should bear the weight of the *corvée* or its commutation, was not applicable in these special circumstances. Moreover, the regulation of September 1776, under which Dupré's new policy was introduced, had not been submitted to the courts and therefore had not been registered by them. This provided a convenient pretext for intervention, and on 20 March 1778 the court of aids, exercising fiscal jurisdiction, forbade the collection of all funds in commutation of the *corvée*, and so brought Dupré's policy to a standstill.[20] Evidently its intention was to perpetuate the situation brought about by its own *arrêt* of 1762, and prevent the servants of the privileged from being forced to pay an addition to the *taille*. Such an addition, of course, could only be passed on ultimately to the employers, who often already paid the *taille* of their employees over their heads.[21] But if it was true, as some estimates suggested, that half the inhabitants of the generality performed no *corvée*,[22] then the court's action must have commanded widespread support at all levels of society.

The *arrêt* of 20 March was, inevitably, quashed by the council on 3 May; but the court of aids ignored this ruling and ordered the arrest of several collectors of the *taille* who were levying funds for *corvée* commutation. On 28 May the council once more intervened, revoked these orders, and instructed the court not to interfere with matters of administration. But the magistrates were adamant, and on 17 June they declared that the extra sums for commutation had 'no legal character', and that no new tax was legal until registered by the courts. Their collection was once more prohibited. Doubtless this intransigence was one more reason for the court's exile to Casteljaloux that summer.[23]

Arrêts of the council of 14 and 17 October 1778 overruled the new prohibitions, but not before the whole machinery of both the *taille* and the *corvée* in the generality had been thrown into confusion. Dupré had to circularize his subordinates in May 1779, ordering them to stand firm.[24] It was at this moment that the parlement decided to intervene. At an assembly of chambers of 2 July Dupré's policy was denounced. To give communities the alternative, one magistrate declared,[25] between performing the *corvée* and compounding for it was a system which, advantageous at first sight and dictated by humane considerations, was in fact full of serious drawbacks.

> la plupart des Communautés, épuisées par les impositions ordinaires, par le malheur des temps & la cherté des vivres, n'ayant que leurs bras à offrir à l'Etat, & craignant que la contribution qu'ils payeraient une année, ne devînt une contribution perpétuelle & arbitraire, ont préféré de faire leur tâche en nature, afin de faire avorter un plan qui leur presentoit l'idée effrayante d'un nouvel impôt.

Communities were not, the denouncer implied, being given a free choice; numerous specious inducements were being employed to make them opt to compound. The court, acting on this denunciation, promptly forbade all collection of monies in lieu of *corvées* until their levy should have been registered by the courts. Meanwhile it decided to remonstrate.

The quashing of this *arrêt* on 18 July did not prevent the dispatch of the remonstrances, which were ready on 26 August.[26] These were the famous remonstrances in which the parlement called for the transformation of Guienne into a *pays d'états*.[27] But they began by painting a black picture of the *corvée*, which,

> source de mille maux épuise, énerve, étouffe l'agriculture et dépeuple les champs . . . Un malheureux obligé de faire vivre de son travail une femme,

des enfants, une famille entière, doit-il être contraint de sacrifier son temps à réparer des chemins qui lui sont presque inutiles, et à les réparer sans salaire?

Turgot's proposals had been well intentioned but unworkable. Unfortunately 'l'état ne peut pas se passer de Corvées, et . . . ce mal reconnu tel par toute la nation est un mal quant à présent nécessaire'. The regulation of 6 September 1776 was designed to eliminate the abuses of the old system now restored, but the intendants were taking advantage of it to extend abuses. This charge was followed by pages of justificatory details. Peasants were being forced to work too far from home, arrears in *corvée* service were being allowed to mount up, and vague instructions were allowing the imposition of an excessive work load. All this seemed a deliberate attempt to make the *corvée* in kind particularly unpleasant, in order to persuade communities to agree to compound for it. And in the final analysis the matter at issue was nothing less than a new tax not registered by the courts, and levied on the arbitrary authority of the intendant. This in itself was enough to render it illegal. In conclusion, the parlement applied itself to thinking of adequate alternatives to the *corvées*; it was then that it came to the proposal for making Guienne a *pays d'états*. How much truth there was in the parlement's charges was difficult to ascertain,[28] but it is at least clear that many communities doubted the benefits of compounding. In one batch of 44 parishes of the Entre-deux-Mers in 1780, ten opted to compound, two were undecided, and 32 chose to continue with the *corvées*.[29] The parishes of Saint-Vincent de Paul d'Ambès and Bassens even carried this preference into their *cahiers* of 1789, and complained of governmental pressure of exactly the sort which the parlement alleged had been applied.[30]

The parlement's intervention certainly prolonged administrative confusion. On 22 November 1779 the court renewed its prohibitions on collecting sums in lieu of *corvées*, after Dupré had published printed instructions to various sub-delegates on how it should be done. The intendant was furious. 'Que le ministre s'arme de fermeté', he wrote to Necker,

> . . . et impose silence aux tribun[x] & il ne se passera pas 2 ou 3 ans sans que cette partie de l'administration ne soit bien montée. Les roles des tailles deviendront bientot pour tous les non privilegiés une regle de proport. qui ecartera les mauvaises difficultés. alors la corvée ne sera plus un fléau pr. les campagnes, la contribut. des petits cultivat. et celle des journaliers se trouvera reduit selon le degré de leurs facultes, tandis que la contribution des gens aisés formera une nouvelle ressource pour le pauvre qui aura un moien de plus de gagner sa vie en s'emploient aux travaux des chemins.[31]

The parlement's renewed *arrêt* was of course quashed, but work on the roads did not resume momentum. The reports of the chief engineer of bridges and roads for 1780, 1781, and 1782, showed that nothing was being accomplished. Some communities were opting to continue with the *corvée* and then refusing to perform it.[32] Subdelegates were confused over whether to obey the parlement or the intendant, and in 1782, two of them had to be constrained to obey the latter's orders on the *corvées* by an *arrêt* of the council. It is true that throughout the years 1780–82 most of the parlement's attention was absorbed by its own internal affairs. During this time Dupré's option scheme established itself as the normal régime for the *corvées* in the generality. Even so, the parlement found time later in 1780 to attack the subdelegate of Mont-de-Marsan, who had imprisoned two municipal officers of the parish of Bascons for failing to perform their *corvées*.[33] On the motion of a counsellor resident in the area,[34] the court on 22 November inaugurated a secret inquiry into the case; and although this decision was quashed on 13 July 1781, it was not before the subdelegate had been dismissed on orders from Versailles.[35]

And meanwhile there were new moves on Dupré's part to extend his system. The scheme he had attempted to operate since 1777 involved compounding for the *corvée* on a basis of the *taille*. Thus those who escaped the *taille* escaped the *corvée* too. However, the elections of Agen, Condom, and Dax were areas of *taille réele*, where the *taille* was payable according to the nature of land owned rather than personal status. In these areas it was possible for a person to be subject to the *taille* but not to the *corvée*, or vice-versa. As a result the *corvée* compounding from 1777 was assessed on the basis of the rural capitation, which noblemen did not pay, being taxed separately as an order. However, in 1780 certain communities petitioned the intendant to change the basis to one of the *taille*, which would be more just in that the poor would be liable to pay less, and the rich more. In 1782 Joly de Fleury authorized such a charge. As a result, on 3 March 1782 Dupré published new rules under which, in these areas, the assessment for the *corvée* was to be based upon the *taille*.[36]

The consequences were startling. The *taille* was a much heavier tax than the capitation, and in many places the result was to double or triple the assessments for compounding for the *corvée*. People with *taillable* land in more than one parish became theoretically liable for the *corvée*, or the tax compounding for it, in several places at once. Above all, nobles and ecclesiastics who owned *taillable* land in substantial amounts now became subject to a tax compounding for a burden to which they were not subject, thus raising the problem which the 1776 regulation had attempted to avoid.[37] Doubtless it was naturally unjust, as the petitioning communities pointed out in 1780, that the richest landowners should not contribute to such common burdens as the repairs of public highways, but to expect them to do so was inequitable under the law as it stood. And when such inequities proceeded from the apparently arbitrary decision of an intendant, the fault seemed all the greater. Soon the new rules were being denounced in the parlement by a magistrate with property in the region of Casteljaloux.[38]

This denunciation opened a new and more bitter phase in the conflict. When he heard that trouble was brewing, the intendant offered to meet the magistrates to discuss the matter, but they refused.[39] Soon afterwards Dupré left for Paris on routine business, and it was in his absence that the parlement took its next step. This consisted of an *arrêt* of 27 March 1784 which suspended the operation of the regulations for the *taille réele* elections. 'L'Ordonnance . . . du 3 Mars 1783', declared the parlement,

> établit le systême effrayant de l'arbitraire; elle substitue aux formes légales, une perception aussi contraire aux Loix de l'Etat, qu'aux vues bienfaisantes du Seigneur Roy; . . . le Commissaire départi s'y arroge le pouvoir d'augmenter à son gré les Impositions, de détruire les privileges, d'attaquer le droit sacré des propriétés.[40]

This time the parlement did not confine itself to protests. It established a commission of inquiry into the malpractices of Dupré's administration of the *corvées* since 1777.[41] The letter of the first president announcing the inquiry to subordinate jurisdictions, by a detailed recital of the rumours which had prompted it, gave clear notice of what abuses it was expected to uncover,[42] and the parlement showed how convinced it was of the fact of malpractices in other ways too, notably by decreeing the arrest of Chauveton, the intendant's first secretary, whom it held mainly responsible for his chief's policies. Chauveton only saved himself by flight.[43]

If these moves in his absence took the intendant by surprise, being in Paris he was at least able to press for a vigorous response, and on 17 April the council quashed the parlement's action in strong terms. The *arrêt* was signified to the chief-clerk of the parlement on 24 April 'by the king's very express command', that is to say, he could not refuse to accept it for the records of the court. At the same time copies were sent to all inferior jurisdictions. On 28 April, the first available moment, the chambers were assembled and the parlement issued a lengthy protest at this high-handed action.[44] To quash the inquiry, declared the magistrates, was to deprive them of one of their most important functions, that of conveying popular grievances to the king in their remonstrances. Only inquiries could ascertain what these grievances might be. The commissioners appointed in March had worked with great speed, heard many witnesses, and had already drawn up their main conclusions. The parlement therefore, while begging the king to withdraw the *arrêt* of the council, decided to ignore it, maintained the force of its own *arrêt* of 27 March, and proposed to send the king a set of remonstrances accompanied by the results of the inquiry.

These remonstrances were dispatched on 13 May 1784, and printed as soon as they appeared. The text of them ran to 30 pages, but after that came another 41 pages of *pièces justificatives* in the form of footnotes and extracts from the judicial inquiry.[45] The theme was that the province was already overtaxed, and that the fiscal officers of the government were always seeking new ways of increasing the burden. The plans of the domain for the *alluvions* were one example;[46] so were the proposals for the *corvée*, despite the humane motives which inspired attempts to reform it:

> Oui, SIRE, c'est en vain que V. M. daignoit aller au devant des inconvéniens dans une instruction adressée au Commissaire départi, & qui portoit tous les caracteres d'une bienfaisance aussi tendre qu'eclairée. C'est en vain que vous accordiez l'option de faire la Corvée en nature, ou de la racheter par une contribution pecuniaire. Il s'introduit un systême pour établir uniquement, & bientôt arbitrairement, une imposition dans la Généralité sans aucun enregistrement prealable.[47]

Most variations from the traditional *corvées* were declared more expensive, more oppressive, more inefficient, and more prone to abuse than the system they replaced. The system as operated by Dupré de Saint-Maur and Valframbert, his chief engineer, showed this. It had the additional defect of cutting across the traditional privileges of many groups:

> nous avons juré à vos pieds de maintenir les propriétés de tous vos sujets. Le lien seul du serment a donc pu, dans cette circonstance delicate, nous

arracher le mot de privilégiés. Il nous est interdit de disposer des droits du Citoyen favorisé par la Loi, qu'elle que soit cette faveur.[48]

These terms recalled those of the remonstrances of the Paris parlement on the *corveés* in 1776,[49] and the appearance of the results of the Bordeaux inquiry evoked much interest in Paris, where the parlement had been pursuing inquiries of its own ever since 1776.[50] On 10 May, d'Aligre, first president, sent a memoir to Vergennes on behalf of his colleagues, declaring that:

> Les Plaintes du Parlement de Bordeaux relativement aux corvées, sont Très fondées; il a toute raison: il est de la justice du Roy de mettre fin aux abus enormes qui se commettent dans cette partie. Le Premier Président et le Procureur Général du Parlement de Paris n'ont cessé, depuis huit ans, de remettre au Ministere des mémoires de plaintes, sur cette partie d'administration importante, et de demontrer les abus sans nombre qui sy Commettent; du tort que cela fait aux Interrêts du Roy, à ceux de ses peuples et même aux grands chemins. Jusqu'a present Leurs representations ont été inutiles.[51]

The newsheets were also beginning to take an interest in the case and fix public attention on abuses in the *corvées*.[52] But the parlement of Bordeaux on one side, and the council on the other, remained adamant.

On 17 May a new *arrêt* of the council quashed the parlement's persisting *arrêt* of 28 April, without waiting for the remonstrances. This new act of authority was brought to the palace by the comte de Fumel and compulsorily registered in a military session on 25 May.[53] The parlement, incensed, at once declared the transcription illegal and announced new remonstrances, which were dispatched on 7 June.[54] They constituted a bitter attack on the powers of the administration:

> Comment ne pas redouter de voir, aux extrémités d'un grand Royaume, le repos de toute une Généralité sous la garde d'un seul, quelquefois novice en administration; d'un homme que divers soins de son département, l'ambition, ou des interêts domestiques, appellent trop souvent du centre de ses devoirs; d'un homme, qui, le plus souvent juge & partie, mû par les impressions intéressées de ses subalternes, qu'il soutient par systême, est trop facilement induit à consacrer leurs torts, par l'exercice d'une autorité sourde & inflexible; d'un homme enfin qui peut être vicieux & injuste, par cela seul qu'il est homme . . .[55]
> . . . les oppresseurs d'un peuple que vous voulez rendre heureux, les exacteurs qui s'enrichissent de ses depouilles, les plus vils subalternes qui profanent votre nom sacré pour vexer vos sujets; tous les êtres enfin, qui forment les anneaux de cette chaine, qui pèse sur les campagnes, se couvrent du nom imposant d'administration; & des Magistrats dont les erreurs même auraient quelque droit de trouver grace aux yeux de *Votre Majesté*, si le zele qui les enflamme les porte trop loin; des Magistrats pour lesquels la confiance publique est un besoin; des Magistrats qui consacrent leur vie entiere à s'en rendre dignes & dont elle est l'unique recompense, sont dénoncés comme coupables à la nation entière, & l'on attire sur eux toutes les marques d'une disgrace, que la voix publique eut dirigé sur d'autres têtes.[56]

They ended with a plea to the king to establish a new and more just system of maintaining the public highways of the province. But they made no suggestions as to what this system should be.

Clearly the king must do something, and to send Dupré back to Bordeaux with a new brief offered no solution. The action of the parlement, Vergniaud noted, had utterly destroyed his reputation.[57] In these circumstances, the government decided to send a commission of inquiry to take evidence on the spot. Dupré's absence from Bordeaux made this convenient, and the commission was officially intended to administer the generality while he was away. In reality everybody knew that its main business was to look into the *corvées*.[58] Its two members were the councillor of state Boutin, a former intendant of Bordeaux who had got on well with the parlement,[59] and the master of requests Boisguibault. They were accompanied by the sub-engineer of bridges and roads of Périgueux, Brémontier,[60] for expert advice; and preceded to Bordeaux by Mouchy, whose mission was to pacify tempers and secure them the co-operation of the parlement. 'J'ai trouvé . . . le Parlement', he reported to Vergennes on arrival,

> dans la plus grande fermentation contre M. Dupré de St. Maur, ce qu'il y a de plus facheux pour cet Intendant cest que la Noblesse, le clergé, et le tiers etat sont touts egalement animés, ce qui me fait penser que quand même il seroit justifié, Il auroit bien de la peine a retablir la confiance que tout homme en place doit avoir pour operer bien.[61]

Nor was this all. The parlement proved extremely suspicious of the commission.

> Il regarde cette fonction comme une méfiance contre un corps qui croit meriter la confiance du Roy, pour mettre un peu d'eau sur le feu, j'ai bien assuré que l'intention de sa Majesté n'etoit que de constater par les commissaires de son Conseil les enquetes deja faites par son Parlement et qui avoit [sic] été mis sous ses yeux, et que son intention etoit de proteger ses sujets contre toute vexation, je ne peux en douter le Roy ayant eu la bonté de me le dire quand jai pris ses derniers ordres.

However, soothing words were unavailing. The parlement resolved not to receive courtesy visits from the commissioners, to demonstrate its mistrust. In private, relations were better, but nothing Mouchy could do could get the public resolution reversed. But it hardly hampered the commissioners in their work;[62] their arrival brought down a blanket of silence on the whole affair, while for four months they toured around the generality taking evidence.

Back in Paris, Dupré de Saint-Maur was naturally mortified by such developments, and sent a self-justifying memoir to the government. This document served as the basis for his public reply to the adverse publicity he had received ever since March, under the title of *Lettre d'un Subdélégué de la Généralité de Guienne à Monsieur le Duc de***relativement aux corvées*. Such an appeal to public opinion, which appeared in Paris early in December, and in Bordeaux in January 1785,[63] was an unprecedented step for a public official to take, even anonymously.[64] But it showed that Dupré realized that the whole affair turned upon the question of public confidence.

There was nothing very original about the argument. The charge that the debate over the *corvée* was a conflict of rich against poor had often been discussed in 1776.[65] Dupré now repeated, however, that the only opponents of *corvée* commutation were the rich; the poor, on the other hand, favoured it, for who would not prefer to pay a little more in taxes, in order not to lose 12 days of labour each year on his own lands?[66] Taking this dubious proposition as self-evident, he moved on to survey the history of the controversy since 1777, commenting adversely on the pronouncements of the parlement, and ending with an imaginary dialogue between a merchant and a president. The merchant accused the magistrate of throwing roadbuilding throughout the generality into confusion, and with obstructing a more equitable system in the lands of *taille réele*. 'Qu'appellez-vous . . . une mode de repartition plus equitable?' exploded the president.

> Comment! j'ai, en pays de Taille réele, une terre pour laquelle, en raison de mes fonds ruraux, je paie plus de 2,000 livres de Taille, et l'on m'assujetterait à 6 ou 700 livres de Corvées. Non, Monsieur, les Magistrats du Parlement donneront plutôt leur démission.[67]

Matters never reached that extreme stage; yet the operations of the commissioners by no means entirely satisfied the parlement. Their mission had three objectives: to inquire into alleged abuses, to make recommendations for the future, and to get the administration of the highways moving again in the interim. As far as the last objective was concerned, the commissioners saw no objection to the principle upon which Dupré had operated: to give each community the choice between performing the *corvée* and compounding.[68] The faults they uncovered in his administration were of implementation rather than principle. So on 19 October they issued an ordinance declaring that work should be resumed on the roads on the basis of choice.[69] They also issued a series of regulations designed to clear up cases left in suspension by the quarrels of the preceding years, and inevitably this involved some rough and ready decisions, including abandonment of outstanding claims on both sides. Some magistrates, ever suspicious, seized on these; and on 19 November, soon after the court had reassembled for the new judicial year, the regulations were denounced.[70] They contravened, so it was alleged, a promise made by the king in letters patent covering the *arrêt* of the council of 17 May, that he would notify the parlement in the usual manner of his eventual decisions on the question of roadworks. No new law had since been promulgated, yet here were the commissioners acting arbitrarily, like the unlamented intendant, to reimpose his unlamented system, when 'La seule manière légale de pourvoir à l'entretien des chemins étoit, sans doute, la corvée en nature'. The regulation of 1776, whatever the magistrates said, did permit the *corvées* to be compounded for. But in making such exaggerated claims, their mind was really on more worrying matters:

> Enfin cette Ordonnance parle d'une imposition pour le rachat des corvées. On ne peut lever aucun impôt dans le Royaume, que d'après une loi duement enregistrée, & il n'en existe aucune qui établisse une imposition sur les corvées.

Accordingly, the court voted to open a further inquiry, this time into the execution of the new ordinance, and any other relevant facts that might have come to light since the spring. Lower jurisdictions were to be circularized to gather information, and the results were to be presented when the court reassembled after Christmas, on 7 January 1785.[71]

In Paris meanwhile, Dupré de Saint-Maur was preparing yet another vindication for the press, in the form of his *Mémoire important sur l'administration des Corvées dans la Généralité de Guyenne et Observations sur les remontrances du Parlement de Bordeaux du 13 mai 1784*, which appeared in January under his own name.[72] By this time the two commissioners had returned to Paris to compile a report on their findings.[73] 'Je n'ai pu me dispenser d'établir', Dupré confided to Latapie, a Bordeaux correspondent,[74]

> et prouver que ces M^rs s'étoient trompés jusque d'un bout à l'autre dans l'objet de leur mission, et dans la manière dont ils l'avaient remplie. Ma réponse pourrait peut-être avoir quelque succès à l'impression . . .
>
> . . . Quand [sic] à moi je presse et je presserai pour qu'on me debarasse de l'Intendance de Bordeaux qui n'en va surement pas mieux en attendant.[75]

The *Mémoire* was certainly a monumental piece of work. It ran to 135 pages, of which 118 were given over to a detailed analysis of the *pièces justificatives* annexed to the parlement's remonstrances. If the commission of inquiry had not so clearly found against the intendant, after four months of investigations, it might be thought a conclusive refutation.[76] Dupré certainly believed passionately in his own rectitude. The *corvée* controversy, he repeated, was an 'espèce de guerre entre les riches et les pauvres',[77] and the parlement's aim was to re-establish the old *corvée* purely and simply. The only good likely to emerge from the whole contest was that the king might think again about introducing a completely new system for the maintenance of roads,[78] for the diversity which had crept into the system over the preceding 20 years only promoted chaos.[79] As to the parlement's inquiry: 'il n'est presque pas un seul témoignage qui ne soit marqué au coin de la fausseté ou de la passion'.[80] The magistrates, fair-minded as individuals, had been swamped by the force of collective prejudice when assembled together.

> lorsque je vois le Parlement se fabriquer des principes relativement à la corvée, & établir, par exemple, qu'on n'a pu, sans blesser sa nature et son essence, prendre, pour base de sa répartition, tel impôt au lieu de tel autre, je ne suis plus étonné qu'il en tire une multitude de fausses conséquences & que, confondant les causes qui ont toujours rendu la Corvée odieuse, il aille jusqu'à envenimer les moyens mêmes que le Ministère prenait pour y rémédier.[81]

And finally there was the perpetual cry of the administrator in the face of the lawyer:

> Mais quelles essais utiles l'Administration pourra-t-elle tenter, lorsquelle se verra perpétuellement contrariée par les Tribunaux? S'ils croyent en savoir plus qu'elle sur ce point, qu'ils s'en expliquent de manière à porter la conviction dans les esprits, & non le trouble dans les opérations.[82]

Judges are rightly unimpressed by such pleas, but the magistrates in this case were infuriated. On 14 January both the *Mémoire* and the *Lettre d'un Subdélégué* were denounced to the court and there was a discussion as to whether they should be burned. The *Mémoire* was preceded by an open letter to the king, which aroused fears that it had been published with royal approval. If that were the case, the parlement's whole position seemed threatened. For these reasons the parlement

decided that it was essential to publish the full substance and results of its
inquiries, so that any misapprehensions, public or royal, about the value of them
should be corrected.[83] In the urgency of this task, the court completely forgot
about its quarrel with the commissioners. All evidence it had collected was now
brought together into a massive 797-page volume, and rushed into print,[84] while
another was announced. Meanwhile, the court declared that it 'disdained' to
deliver Dupré's writings to the severity of the laws.[85]

Dupré, who had just given his own evidence to the commission of inquiry, took
this news in a confident mood. 'Le Parlement a donc avoué patemment, et par un
imprimé, son impuissance de répondre à mes mémoires. J'en suis presque fâché,
et j'aurois préferé qu'il eut voulu engager un grand combat . . .'[86] However, the
next month the commissioners at last presented their report, which gave a very
different picture of the matter.[87]

The commissioners had visited all the major roads in the generality, in all states
of repair. They had devoted four months to their inquiries, taken evidence in
public from all classes of the population, and examined all relevant documents.
Thus armed, they now surveyed the administration of the *corvées* in Guienne
since 1777. They did not come to this work without prejudices of their own; the
whole language of the report reveals them as legal purists, and they stated at one
point that, properly administered, the traditional *corvée* could produce roads
second to none.[88] Nevertheless, they also stated that in their view no system was
more just than that authorized in 1776,[89] so they could not be accused of prejudice
against Dupré's intentions. Nor indeed did they criticize the intendant for his
intentions. It was their execution which they found at fault. And here, most of
the evidence uncovered by the inquiries of the parlement was confirmed:

En resumant les faits qui viennent d'être exposés on voit evidemment
1⁰ que d'un coté, les contributions pour rachat de corvée etaient surchargées
de tout ce qui pouvait les rendre les plus odieuses au peuple—Excès de
l'impot dans un pays ou le numéraire est rare,—Exces de frais accessoires,
—Rigueur abusive dans le recouvrement,—clandestinité des adjudications,
—choix de certains adjudicataires,—précautions pour exclure leurs con-
currens,—défaut de publicité pour la réception de leurs ouvrages,—
versement des fonds de rachat entre des mains souvent suspectes, application
de ces fonds à d'autres parties de Route que celles pour lesquelles il avaient
été payés,—enfin défaut absolu d'ordre pour la comptabilité.
2⁰ d'un autre coté et dans le tems même ou l'on déférait, disoit-on, l'option,
en employant tous les moyens possibles pour forcer les peuples au rachat,
—mobilité continuelle des atteliers, excès de travail,—excès de la distance,
soit de la paroisse à l'attelier, soit de l'attelier aux carrières et gravières
indiquées, inexactitude des piqueurs destinés à conduire les corvéables,—
difficultés excessives pour la reception des taches,—ajoutons y encore tous les
moyens de detail que devait produire le concours de l'interêt des subalternes.
L'interêt des Conducteurs qui ordinairement etaient adjudicateurs,—
interet des subdélégués, a raison des droits de vérification,—interet de leurs
secrétaires (ordinairement trésoriers des Corvées) à raison de leur droit de
recette . . . enfin si les sous ingenieurs n'avaient aucun interet pecuniaire qui
les attachat au sistème du rachat, il est au moins certain qu'il leur etait

infiniment plus commode d'avoir quelques adjudicataires à surveiller qu'une infinité de corvéables à conduire.

De la tout le monde concluait; on ne rend le travail impossible que pour avoir de l'argent; L'intendant veut l'imposition par esprit de sisteme; et ses subalternes par esprit d'interêt.[90]

It followed that the major responsibility for the disorder in the system lay in the lower ranks of the hierarchy rather than at the top. Even so, the intendant had ultimate responsibility. The commissioners found that he delegated too readily, and trusted his subordinates too completely. He did not make enough tours of inspection, and was not willing enough to hear complaints.

But their true censure was reserved for the defaulting subordinates. Chauveton, the intendant's trusted first secretary, was probably responsible for keeping much important information from his master, and was an object of much public hatred. He had already fled the province to escape the hands of the parlement; it was now recommended that he should never hold office there again.[91] Five subdelegates were also censured, although one of these had already been dismissed, another had fled, and another was dead.[92] Above all, Valframbert, the chief engineer, who had died in 1784, was held responsible for the abuses. He was accused of 'dureté et . . . inconcevable négligence', and, declared the commissioners, should certainly have lost his post had he not died.[93] Dupré himself confessed in a private letter[94] that Valframbert's 'caractère dur et insociable' had done much to aggravate matters. When Dupré had been intendant in Berry, Valframbert had been chief engineer there, and a source of much trouble. The intendant had therefore had him promoted to Guienne, only to be moved there himself a few years later.

Tout le Berry attesterait, en effet, qu'en moins d'une année, il parvint, par son peu de liant, à démonter toute la machine des corvées qui allait le mieux du monde auparavant . . . Lorsque je suis arrivé en Guienne, j'ai prévu de reste les tracasseries que ce même homme m'attireraient, et Dieu sait à quel point j'ai toujours taché de lui inspirer de la douceur, mes lettres en feroient foi . . . il se plaignait souvent de ne pas trouver en moi tous les secours de l'autorité.

The report ended by emphasizing how much depended upon the intendant's vigilance, and although no recommendation was made regarding Dupré's future, clearly the question was raised by implication. Despite the intendant's own repeated wish, there was a party on the king's council which favoured his return to Bordeaux.[95] The convenient death of the councillor of state Le Pelletier de Beaupré left a place vacant into which he could honourably retire, however, and he was duly appointed to it. And despite some intransigent talk of sending him back to Bordeaux with this added distinction,[96] it was deemed in the end wisest not to risk provoking further trouble by such a step. He was replaced by Le Camus de Néville, intendant of Bayonne, who as director of bookshops between 1776 and 1783 had established a reputation as a stern administrator.[97]

Nevertheless, Guienne was delighted by the news. 'On nous annonce un nouvel intendant', noted Vergniaud,[98] 'M. Dupré de Saint-Maur a été fait Conseiller d'Etat . . . Le Parlement ne le reverra plus. Il est content'. It was a famous victory. The parlement had, by persistence and intransigence, broken an intendant and forced the government to withdraw him. It had vindicated its right to inquire into matters of administration, and had refurbished its reputation, somewhat eclipsed during the personal quarrels of the preceding years, as a defender of the oppressed against administrative tyranny. Having done this, it let matters drop. The second volume of its inquiry was never published, and the remainder of the judicial year 1784–85 was increasingly dominated by that other struggle against administrative 'despotism', the *alluvions* case. The final post-script came at the Versailles session of July 1786, when the proceedings against Chauveton, along with the loose ends of several other minor matters outstanding, were quashed.[99]

The popularity which the parlement acquired through its actions was beyond question. By disrupting the intendant's arrangements for the *corvées*, it brought roadworks throughout the generality to a standstill. The *corvée* ceased to be per-formed, nor was it compounded for. The exempt who had been threatened by it were grateful for a stay of execution; the *corvéables* were relieved of the burden of either work or commutation, so long as the conflict lasted. The real sufferers were the travellers. 'En entrant dans la généralité de Guienne', noted Guibert[100] in September 1785, 'on s'apercoit d'un autre régime pour les chemins. Ils sont en général mauvais et mal entretenus'. Nor was the damage made good in the years that followed. In 1792 Brémontier, Valframbert's successor, reported that 'Il n'y a pas une seule Route en bon Etat, et sur laqu'elle il ne se trouve des reparations tres importantes et urgentes à faire'. Nothing had been done between 1777 and 1790.[101] Before 1784, there had been the conflicts; after that date, national re-forms suspended everything.

For no sooner had the parlement triumphed over Dupré de Saint-Maur than the old *corvée* was suspended all over France. In June 1785 Dupré sent Latapie a pamphlet against the *corvée* by one of his friends. Most of the evidence used was from the parlement of Bordeaux's published inquiry, and the ministry promoted its publication in order to prepare public opinion for the policy changes that were imminent.[102] In April 1786 the intendants were instructed to suspend all *corvées*, and on 6 November an *arrêt* of the council formalized this experiment for three years. The *corvées* were to be replaced by a tax.[103] Calonne's great plan of reform of the next spring went even further and proposed their final suppression in favour of a tax for the upkeep of roads, and Brienne incorporated this proposal into his own programme.[104] It might be expected that these proposals would provoke an explosion from those courts which had shown themselves hostile to Turgot's and kindred schemes; especially the parlement of Bordeaux. And doubt-less this might have been the case if the reform had been promulgated in isolation. But it was not. It had hardly been announced before it became a minor feature of a much vaster plan of reform which raised a multitude of questions at least as important and controversial. The result was to change the perspective of the *corvées* question, and Brienne's edict was registered to general amazement by the parlement of Paris.[105] However, that court was preparing to take its stand else-where. At Bordeaux, the proposed reform was not even discussed when it was laid before the court in the spring of 1788, for the magistrates were refusing to discuss anything until the Libourne exile was revoked.[106] Eventually it was registered forcibly at the interminable military session of 8 May, when once again more pressing questions were at stake.

Besides, positions on both sides had evolved. Initially the parlement's stance had been that any compounding for the *corvée* should not fall upon those who were exempt, and that any tax levied by the government for whatever purpose, must first be registered in the courts. This seemed in effect to rule out anything but the traditional system. But in the course of the inquiries undertaken during the conflict, the parlement learned much about the drawbacks of the system as it operated; and by the end of the conflict it was calling for a complete 'Régime nouveau, pour la confection des chemins, marqué du sceau de la justice et de l'humanité, épuré dans le creuset d'un enregistrement libre, revêtu de la sanction de la loi'.[107] This is what Calonne and Brienne offered, and in their proposals the *corvée* was to be compounded for by a simple addition to the *taille*. There was no question, as there had been with Turgot, of extending the payment to groups which had been exempt from the labour. In these circumstances, when the old *corvée* was so manifestly inefficient, the new law could be welcomed. By 1789, only rural *cahiers* still questioned the assumption that the peasants would rather pay a new tax than work on the roads.

NOTES

1. J. Egret, *Louis XV et l'opposition parlementaire*, 112–13.
2. B. Pocquet, *Le Duc d'Aiguillon et La Chalotais* (Paris, 1900–01), I, 425.
3. For examples, see Dakin, *Turgot*, 54–5.
4. Egret, loc. cit., 113–14; Dakin, op. cit., 66–7; and above all E. J. M. Vignon, *Etudes historiques sur l'administration des voies publiques en France aux XVIIe et XVIIIe siècles* (Paris, 1862), III, 41–53.
5. Dakin, op. cit., 68–70; Vignon, op. cit., III, 53–63.
6. Although that of Rouen supported the local court of aids in criticizing the 'abusive' operation of the Caen scheme: Egret, op. cit.; Vignon, op. cit., III, 46–53.
7. AD C1989, Dupré de Saint-Maur to d'Ormesson, 10 June 1783.
8. Dakin, op. cit., 239.
9. ibid., 239–42.
10. See the Turgot–Miromesnil debate in Schelle, *Oeuvres de Turgot*, V, 163–200, summarized in Dakin, 244–6.
11. See Flammermont, *Remontrances*, III, 275–92.
12. AN K708. For a full analysis, see above, p. 209; see also especially C. Dartigue-Peyrou, *Dupré de Saint-Maur et le problème des corvées en Guienne* (Mont-de-Marsan, 1937), 20.
13. See Doyle, 'The parlements of France', 446–7; and Vignon, op. cit., III, 93–6.
14. Vignon, op. cit., III, 99–104.
15. Flammermont, loc. cit., 290.
16. On government policy in general in this period, see A. Lesort, 'La question de la corvée des grands chemins sous Louis XVI après la chute de Turgot, 1776–1786', in *Ministère de l'Instruction Publique et des Beaux Arts: comité des travaux historiques et scientifiques, section d'histoire moderne (depuis 1715) et d'histoire contemporaine*, t. VII, *Etudes et documents divers* (Paris, 1922), 51–95.
17. AD C3720, dated July 1770, anonymous.
18. ibid., intendant to Trudaine, 2 March 1771.
19. ibid., Trudaine to intendant, 17 March 1771.
20. Dartigue-Peyrou, op. cit., 38; this account seems to be based largely upon Dupré's own *Lettre d'un subdélégué de la généralité de Guienne à Monsieur le Duc de ****, *relativement aux corvées* (Bordeaux, 1784), 12ff., and Vignon, op. cit., III, 113ff.
21. Like counsellor Darche: Forster, 'Noble wine producers', 28.

22. Dartigue-Peyrou, op. cit., 19–24.
23. Vignon, op. cit., III, 113, 199–207; see also above, p. 172.
24. Dartigue-Peyrou, op. cit., 43–7.
25. AD C1989, *arrêt* of 2 July 1779. The magistrate is not identified. The *arrêt* is also printed in M. Marion, *Les Impôts directs sous l'ancien régime*, 389–90, and Vignon, op. cit., III, 207–9.
26. Copy in AD C1989, annotated by Dupré de Saint-Maur; extract in Vignon, op. cit., III, 212–14; see also Dartigue-Peyrou, op. cit., 55–9.
27. For an analysis of this proposal, see above, pp. 227–8.
28. But see below, pp. 242–3, for the findings of the commission of inquiry.
29. AD C3720.
30. AD Cahiers de Doléances, 1789, sénéchaussées de Bordeaux et de Libourne.
31. AD C1989, intendant to director-general, 26 Nov. 1779, draft.
32. Reports ibid.
33. The report of the 1785 commission of inquiry has the full details on this affair. AN K910, 'Mémoire sur l'administration des chemins de la Guienne', 34, and 'pièces à joindre', no. 17.
34. Perhaps Perez d'Artassan.
35. *Lettre d'un subdélégué*, 18–19; Vignon, op. cit., III, 115–16.
36. *Lettre d'un subdélégué*, 22–3; Vignon, loc. cit., III, 116; AN K910, 'Mémoire', 35–7, and 'pièces à joindre', nos. 6–10; Dartigue-Peyrou, op. cit., 84, is misleading on this point.
37. The details of the scheme, and its results, are from AN K910, 'Mémoire', 37–40.
38. *Lettre d'un subdélégué*, 23. This person is not identified.
39. ibid.; Vignon, loc. cit.
40. *Lettre d'un subdélégué*, 24–5.
41. Marion, *Les Impôts*, 117; Vignon, op. cit., III, 117, 233; Dartigue-Peyrou, op. cit., 90.
42. *Lettre d'un subdélégué*, 37–8, for Le Berthon's letter of 31 March 1784.
43. AAE MD France, 1589, f.308, Mouchy to Vergennes, 16 April 1784; Bachaumont, XXV, 271, 16 April 1784.
44. Marion, op. cit., 93. Copy of the *arrêt* in BPR Le Paige 580, p. 138.
45. Copy ibid., BPR Le Paige 828; see also Bachaumont, XXVI, 105, 20 July 1784.
46. Remonstrances, BPR Le Paige 828, 14. See below, ch. 16.
47. ibid., 16.
48. ibid., 30.
49. cf. Flammermont, *Remontrances*, III, 287–8: 'Quoique tous soient également fidèles et soumis, leurs conditions diverses n'ont jamais été confondues et la nature de leurs services tient essentiellement à celle de leur état . . . Ces institutions ne sont pas de celles que le hasard a formées et que le temps puisse changer.
    Pour les abolir, il faudrait renverser toute la constitution française . . .'
50. Lesort, loc. cit., 57–61.
51. AAE MD France, 1398, ff.126–7, d'Aligre to Vergennes, 10 May 1784.
52. Bachaumont, XXVI, 36–7, 11 Jan. 1784.
53. AD IB 56, f.175; Bachaumont, XXVI, 39, 12 June 1784; Vignon, op. cit., III, 117, 234–40.
54. BPR Le Paige 828, p. 15. Summarized in Bachaumont, XXVI, 87, 10 July 1784; printed in Vignon, op. cit., III, 240–3.
55. BPR Le Paige 828, pp. 7–8.
56. ibid., 21–2.
57. Vatel, Vergniaud, I, 98–9, Vergniaud to Allaud (undated, but clearly spring or summer 1784).
58. Bachaumont, XXVI, 61–2, 21 June 1784; Vignon, op. cit., III, 118.
59. See above, p. 51, n. 54. His popularity persisted. AAE MD France, 1589, f.321, Mouchy to Vergennes, 20 July 1784.
60. See above, p. 83, n. 63.
61. AAE MD France, 1589, f.313, Mouchy to Vergennes, 12 June 1784.
62. Bachaumont, XXVI, 64, 22 June 1784; AAE MD France, 1589, f.313, 12 June; f.316, 22 June; f.317, 26 June; f.321, 20 July 1784; also the commissioners' own account in AN K910, 'Mémoire', p. 1.

63. Mention of its appearance in Bachaumont, XXVII, 46–8, 2 Dec. 1784; and Vatel, op. cit., I, 99, Vergniaud to Allaud, 29 Jan. 1785.
64. P. Ardascheff, *Les Intendants de province sous Louis XVI* (Paris, 1909), 189–90.
65. e.g., Flammermont, *Remonstrances*, III, 290.
66. *Lettre d'un subdélégué*, 8–9.
67. ibid., 30–1.
68. AN K910, p. 49.
69. Bachaumont, XXVIII, 65, 27 Jan. 1785.
70. BPR Le Paige 828, p. 17, 'Extrait des registres du parlement', 19 Nov. 1784. The denouncer is not identified. See also Vignon, op. cit., III, 119, 243–5.
71. BPR Le Paige 828; AAE MD France, 1589, f.346, Mouchy to Vergennes, 4 Dec. 1784; Dartigue-Peyrou, op. cit., 105.
72. Bachaumont, XXVIII, 74, 30 Jan. 1785.
73. ibid., XXVII, 46, 2 Dec. 1784.
74. François de Paul Latapie (1739–1823). Academician, inspector of manufactures of the province of Guienne. See *AHDG*, LIII and LIV (1919–22) for his notes on a tour of the province in 1782.
75. BVBx MS 1666 (copies of the Dupré–Latapie correspondence), pièce 10, Dupré to Latapie, 3 Jan. 1785 (dated 1784, but on internal evidence this must be wrong).
76. See below, pp. 242–3. Dartigue-Peyrou, author of the only secondary work devoted entirely to this affair, was clearly convinced; indeed most of the book is based upon Dupré's two pamphlets. But although the author mentions the report of the commissioners, 130, he does not appear to have used it.
77. *Mémoire important*, 133.
78. ibid., 131.
79. ibid., 4.
80. ibid., 2.
81. ibid., 3.
82. ibid., 5.
83. Bachaumont, XXVIII, 74, 30 Jan. 1785; Vignon, op. cit., III, 120, 247–8.
84. *Enquête sur le fait des corvées dans la généralité de Guienne, ordonnée par les arrêts du 17 mars & 28 avril 1784, rendus toutes les chambres assemblées: lesdites enquêtes imprimées en exécution de l'arrêté pris toutes les chambres assemblées le 14 janvier 1785. Tome premier* (Bordeaux, 1785).
85. ibid., introduction, p. x.
86. BVBx MS 1666, pièce 17, Dupré to Latapie, 29 Jan. 1785.
87. AN K910, fully cited above, n. 33; a few short extracts in Vignon, op. cit., III, 248–50.
88. AN K910, p. 29, n.
89. ibid., p. 49.
90. ibid., pp. 32–3.
91. ibid., pp. 46–7.
92. ibid., p. 47.
93. ibid., pp. 33, 47–8.
94. BVBx MS 1666, pièce 12, Dupré to Latapie, 6 July 1784 (or 1785?).
95. ibid., pièce 25, same to same, 26 Feb. 1785.
96. ibid.; see also Lescure, *Correspondance secrète*, II, 548, 19 March 1785.
97. Bachaumont, XIV, 147, 13 Aug. 1779.
98. Vatel, op. cit., I, Vergniaud to Allaud, 7 May 1785.
99. See below, p. 259.
100. *Voyages*, 261, 26 Sept. 1785.
101. AD C3713, 'Mémoire sur la situation des grandes routes et communications du département de la Guienne'; see also Dartigue-Peyrou, op. cit., 132.
102. BVBx MS 1666, pièce 28, Dupré to Latapie, 10 June 1785. Calonne had set up a commission to study the reform of the system in March 1784. Vignon, op. cit., III, 122–4 says the pamphlet was written by one of this body, made up mainly of intendants, and Lesort, loc. cit., 82, confirms this, attributing it to de la Galaisière, councillor of state and intendant of Alsace. Lesort, 68–95, is the best guide to the evolution

of government policy at this time, but see also R. Lacour-Gayet, *Calonne: financier, réformateur, contre-révolutionnaire, 1734–1802* (Paris, 1963), p. 153.

103. ibid.; Marion, *Les Impôts directs*, 118; Vignon, op. cit., III, 124–6, 251–63; Lesort, loc. cit., 82–93.

104. Decree of 27 June 1787; Egret, *La Pré-Révolution Française* (Paris, 1962), 98; Vignon. op. cit., III, 270–2.

105. Egret, op. cit., 161.

106. See below, p. 275.

107. Remonstrances of 7 June 1784, loc. cit. above, n. 54.

CHAPTER 16

Vindication: The Alluvions

In the opinion of magistrates, if the king's duty was still to live of his own and only levy extraordinary taxes for extraordinary purposes, then the royal domain should be one of his most important sources of regular income. He had, therefore, a special duty to maintain its extent and so its revenues. The parlements consequently regarded the domain, as the advocate-general Saige put it in 1764,[1] 'moins comme le Patrimoine du Prince, que comme celui de l'Etat; destiné moins à soutenir la splendeur & la dignité du Trone, qu'à pourvoir aux besoins publics, & à épargner aux Peuples, le poids des secours extraordinaires'. Yet the domain had been decimated by alienations, and its revenues run down through neglect:

> vous serez étonnés de l'état de dégradation, où, malgré votre vigilance, l'ont successivement jetté, ou les malheurs des tems, ou les surprises faites à la générosité de nos Rois, ou l'administration infidèle des mains auxquelles il fut livré.
>
> Vous gémirez en voyant que cette ressource qui devroit être si abondante ne peut offrir dans cet instant qu'un foible secours; & que le deperissement de ce Domaine doit être regardé lui-meme comme une des causes du fardeau qui s'est appesanti sur les Peuples . . .

The established view of the parlements was that the domain should be inalienable, and in principle the government agreed. In practice, only economizing ministers like Terray insisted on this and attempted to implement its corollary, the resumption of alienated domains. The trouble with such policies was that the domain usually insisted on being judge in its own cause, as it showed in the reconstruction of the royal terrier, in progress from the middle of the century onwards. It was authorized for Guienne by letters patent of 15 August 1752. However, these letters occasioned a bitter conflict with the parlement lasting several years, for the revision was to be made by a special commission composed of treasurers of France, with no right of appeal to the parlement.[2] In 1781 a similar case arose when an *arrêt* of the council of 15 November authorized a general survey of all walls, fortifications, and ramparts, which it claimed belonged to the royal domain; the whole process was to be supervised, without right of further appeal, by the treasurers of France. By this *arrêt*, protested the procurator-general, 'le Parlement, qui est essentiellement la Cour féodale du Roi, est dépouillé de la Jurisdiction qui lui appartient sur le Domaine Royal'.[3] This was the nub of the matter. The parlement held that nothing but good could come of the resumption and turning to profit of the royal domains, but only if it were done legally, and subject to judicial appeal, so that the rights of legitimate proprietors might be protected. The parlement regarded itself as the natural court of appeal on such matters. 'Les Gens du Fisc', Dudon declared, 'ont été de tous les temps les ennemis des formes, & ils n'ont que trop souvent réussi à se procurer des titres, dont l'exécution prompte et facile a dérobé leurs manoeuvres à l'inspection sévère & religieuse des Tribunaux'. Such an attitude distracted the magistrates from their desire to see the domain turned to the maximum profit, into what they regarded as an even more grave concern—the protection of property against arbitrary governments. This was clearly demonstrated in the great test-case of the 1780s, the affair of the *alluvions*.

Ostensibly it began with an *arrêt* of an council of 5 July 1781, which declared that:

> tous les atterrissements, alluvions et relais dans les rivières de Gironde et de Dordogne, et sur la côte du Médoc depuis la pointe de la Grange jusqu'à Soulac paraissent être usurpés; il est d'une nécessité absolue pour les intérêts de Sa Majesté de connaître d'une manière irrévocable la véritable consistance de ces objets, et le nombre d'usurpations, afin de réunir au domaine tout ce qui porroit cn dépendre ou de confirmer, s'il y a lieu, les possesseurs actuels qui feraient leur soumission à cet effet.[4]

Proprietors were ordered to present their titles, on demand, to the grand master of waters and forests of Guienne, who was authorized to judge all contests arising out of the survey, subject to appeal to the council of state.

This *arrêt* was not unprecedented. It followed in the tradition of Terray's public search for lands to resume. Terray had turned his particular attention to *alluvions* and islands in navigable rivers, much to the alarm of proprietors in such areas. The publicity with which this policy was pursued encouraged a host of informers and speculators to bombard the government with projects for exploiting lands taken from proprietors whose rights they alleged to be usurped from the domain. Nor was the government blind to the new fields of patronage which such resumptions opened up. 'Ce n'est pas', commented the abbé de Véri, who reports these policies,[5] 'toujours un zèle pur pour le trésor royal qui fait défendre ses droits avec tant de constance. Des faveurs accordées par les membres du gouvernement en sont souvent la cause'. The affair of the *alluvions* of the Gironde began in just such circumstances.

Not that the lands over which the issues first arose were *alluvions*; it was the greedy attempts of speculators to secure the concession of the marshes of Ambès, Montferrand, and Ambarès which first alarmed proprietors. As early as 1761 counsellor Leblanc de Mauvezin of the parlement had astonished his colleagues by alleging that these marshes were vacant and part of the royal domain.[6] His attempt to gain the concession of them failed, but Mauvezin was not alone in coveting the marsh. In 1775 an engineer named Courregeoles, alleging that the marsh was alluvial and therefore part of the royal domain, requested it as a concession, and in January 1779 the intendant ordered a survey to facilitate further inquiries. His subdelegate, for one, believed that it was domainial territory which the king might dispose of as he saw fit,[7] but the communities around the marsh loudly disputed this suggestion. Among the leaders of these protests was P. de Richon, counsellor at the parlement and syndic of the parish of Montferrand. Perhaps it was he who first aroused his colleagues' suspicions that the true object of the *alluvions* survey was to clear the way towards obliging concession-seekers.

For projects concerning the marshes of the Bec d'Ambès continued to flow in, at both regional and central level. Notable among these proposals, first submitted in 1780 and again in 1781, was that of one chevalier de Pestels, who petitioned for a perpetual lease (*bail emphytéotique*) of no less than 275,565 *journaux* in the area, including the marshes and all islands in the Garonne and Dordogne which were unclaimed. These land, he alleged, were usurped from the domain, and if the king would resume them and grant them to him, he was prepared to offer a rent of one livre per *journal* per year for the first ten years of the concession, rising to 30 *sols* after that.[8] The scale of the request was certainly breathtaking, but so of course was the potential revenue to the treasury; and not only the power of Pestels's arguments prompted the government into action. Far more important people than he saw opportunities for profit in such a massive resumption by the domain. The baron de Bourg, who was Pestels's partner, wrote to Vergennes that they had first presented their plans to him on the recommendation of the duchesse de Villeroi.[9] In 1781 and again in 1782 the comptroller-general wrote to the intendant of a rival scheme proposed by a member of the influential Dillon family; the proposals had been handed to him by the queen and highly recommended by the comte d'Artois.[10] Such details certainly make more credible the widespread rumour that the Polignacs were involved in the *alluvions* affair.[11] In any case, Pestels and his partner received every encouragement from the government's suggestion that they advertise shares in a company to exploit any concession that might be made.[12] Whatever the government's later intentions, therefore, the original idea of an inquiry into lapsed domainial rights along the Gironde probably came from the repeated proposals of speculators like Pestels, supported by influential persons at Court. The government confined itself in the first instance to launching a broad official survey, making no mention of specific areas such as the marshes of the Bec d'Ambès; hoping no doubt to discover what the possibilities were. But the prolonged public controversy over the marshes cast suspicion on any such moves from the start.

Naturally then, the news of the 1781 *arrêt* filled the riverside proprietors of Guienne, many of whom sat in the parlement, with alarm. 'Dès que cet Arrêt fut connu', Dudon later recalled,[13]

> la consternation fut générale. Les propriétaires des fons riverains se virent au moment dêtre dépouillés, par voye de fait, du patrimoine de leurs pères; les Seigneurs voyaient échapper de leurs mains les droits les plus utiles de leurs seigneuries, & ceux qui ne se trouvoient pas personnellement intéressés, n'en furent pas moins alarmés, par la crainte de se voir un jour exposés à la même dépossession, sous le même prétexte, ou par quelqu'autre moyen aussi violent et aussi mal-fondé.

Nobody disputed that the beds of navigable rivers, or that part of the seashore which lay between high and low tide, were part of the royal domain.[14] The ambiguity lay in the fact that the Gironde and parts of the rivers emptying into it were tidal, and in them there were islands made up of alluvial material, whose dimensions were constantly changing with the shifting of sandbanks. The domain apparently considered these islands, as well as all recent alluvial deposits north along the shore of the Médoc from just north of Bordeaux,[15] to be usurped from the king. It was not clear whether it held the same opinion of the ever-lengthening Bec d'Ambès too. It was certain, however, that all riverside proprietors and lords in the Médoc, and all owners or lords of islands in the Gironde, would be required to present their titles, and that those whose only title was immemorial or prescriptive were threatened with dispossession by the crown. What was more, contests arising out of the survey were to be referred directly to the council of state. The parlement, supreme court of the province, was thus deprived of any chance to protect the rights of those over whom it was set. No wonder proprietors were worried.

The duchesse de Lesparre, whose husband owned extensive lands in the Médoc, wrote from Paris that although it would be imprudent for him to show any overt interest in the matter, let alone to lobby against the *arrêt*, opposition was

> la cause publique et générale des propriétaires vexés ou exposés à l'être, par la cupidité de quelques particuliers entreprenants qui font icy mouvoir le domaine et jetter l'allarme dans toutes les familles d'une Province entière, sans intérêt réel pour le Roy, dans le seule vue de s'enrichir eux mêmes des dépouilles d'autruy . . .[16]

Mouchy himself wrote to Vergennes that the *arrêt* 'paroit depouiller les particuliers de leurs possessions'.[17] The magistrates of the parlement were deeply affected personally, although the best vineyards in their hands were not directly threatened, as was sometimes alleged. Some owned islands in the rivers.[18] Even more had property or seignorial rights in the fertile *palus*, the best all-round land in the province precisely because they were made up of alluvium. Among the shoreline proprietors in the Médoc, for instance, were the Basterot, Verthamon, Castelnau, Sauvat de Pommiers, and several other families. And all the numerous magistrates with territories in the Bec d'Ambès parishes of Ambès, Ambarès, and Montferrand, which the confluence of the Garonne and Dordogne extended almost daily, could also consider themselves in danger. As long before as 1755 counsellor Darche de Lassalle had been accused of constructing breakwaters out into the river from his meadow in the area, in order artificially to extend them with alluvium and so impinge on the royal domain.[19] Such incidents underlined the dangerous vagueness of the *arrêt*. However, far more people than the members of the parlement stood to lose if the *arrêt* did have a broad meaning, and there seems little doubt that the parlement's decision to intervene enjoyed universal support among the propertied classes of the province.

The intervention came on 3 May 1782 when the parlement ordered the operation of the *arrêt* to be suspended while it sent remonstrances to the king.[20] The intervention came at a time of some ministerial instability, and this doubtless was the reason why the government dealt with such defiance in a leisurely way. At any rate, it was not until 31 October 1783 that the council of state quashed the parlement's suspension of action, and reiterated its orders to the grand master of waters and forests to proceed with the survey.[21] In a covering note, the Keeper of the Seals conceded that 'les détenteurs de bonne foi . . . pourraient être maintenus sans inconvenients', and that in any concessions which might follow the survey, those in possession would be given preference. If appeal lay to the council of state rather than to the parlement, that was merely to ensure swifter justice.[22] This argument was hardly likely to impress the magistrates.

In these exchanges, the most awkward position was occupied by the hapless grand master of waters and forests. Unsure of what to do next, although the parlement's prohibition had been quashed, he wrote for advice early in 1784 to the procurator-general. Dudon's reply was clear:

> Il n'est point de résistance que le Parlement ne soit déterminé à employer pour s'opposer à l'execution des arrêts du Conseil . . . Je n'ai point voulu dissimuler . . . la resolution que le parlement a prise, et la volonté bien décidée ou je suis d'employer les forces qui me restent pour m'opposer autant qu'il sera en moi à l'execution d'un plan, ou d'un projet aussi contraire au droit de propriété, et à la liberté civile de chaque citoyen.[23]

What this meant became clear on 24 April, when he went before the assembled chambers to declare that:

> L'arrêt du conseil du 31 octobre 1783 ne contient aucune reponse aux remonstrances du parlement. C'est un acte d'autorité absolue, qui n'indique aucun principe, qui ne résout aucunes difficultés; on n'y trouve aucun raisonnement dans le droit, aucun éclaircissement sur le fait; pour tout dire en un mot, il porte tous les caractères de la surprise. Tout annonce qu'il a été obtenu par l'importunité, que le crédit et l'intrigue se sont reunis pour faire illusion au ministre et tromper la religion du souverain . . .[24]

The parlement was the natural defender of the domain, but it was also the natural defender of the liberties of the subject, and it was these that were in the greater danger. On Dudon's recommendation, the parlement decided to renew its remonstrances, and meanwhile it once more prohibited the grand master from proceeding with the survey. These decisions, and Dudon's speech, were printed and publicly distributed. So the matter was laid before a wider audience, obviously a deliberate escalation of the affair. Dudon's speech was inflammatory, with its hints of unsavoury intrigues at Versailles. To print it was to spread these rumours. Moreover, the parlement took equal care to print its new remonstrances, dispatched in November, as the next judicial year began.[25] In these, the magistrates continued to broaden the attack, to take in not only the rights claimed by the domain, but the whole principle of evoking cases to the council of state: 'Votre Parlement de Bordeaux a joui depuis son institution de la prérogative de juger en dernier ressort de toutes les affaires du Domaine; l'en dépouiller, c'est donner atteinte aux loix de l'Etat . . .' The magistrates clearly felt that if they could once have appeals over the *alluvions* attributed to them, and not to the council, then the survey would be subject to adequate supervision.

The government could hardly be expected to make such a concession, and a new *arrêt* of the council of 16 October 1785 once again quashed the parlement's prohibitions and condemned both the violence of Dudon's language and the decision to print his speech. The king's object, it said, besides the conservation of the domain, was to reassure those proprietors with titles, and to substitute for the rigour of the law as applied in the ordinary courts such as the parlement, a wide degree of administrative discretion so as to allow the king the maximum opportunity for exercising his benevolence. This *arrêt* reiterated all the previous orders to the grand master, and empowered him to accept declarations of obligation from those in occupation of the lands in question, upon which he might confirm their property rights. It also reiterated that any appeals lay only to the council of state, and Dudon was forbidden to interfere further. However, such further intervention became inevitable with the reappearance of the chevalier de Pestels.

What he had been doing since 1781 is obscure, but shortly after this latest *arrêt* of the council, he arrived in the Bordelais armed with a royal authorization to make his own investigations into the extent of the royal domain in the area.[26] The government never disavowed this authorization even though later it revoked it. Perhaps private pressure had once more been brought to bear at Versailles. In any case, Pestels' appearance could only aggravate the magistrates' hostility. They would have been even more incensed had they known how long he had been involved in the affair, and what his original suggestions had been. Nevertheless, Pestels began his investigations in the parishes of Soussans, Cantenac, and Parempuyre, in upper Médoc, where there were considerable stretches of marsh and *palu*, some 30,000 *journaux*. By interrogation and inducements offered to the peasants exploiting these marshes, he succeeded in extracting legal declarations from several of them, made before a notary public at Cantenac, that they had never recognized any lord but the king, except that a few had paid the *cens* to members of the parlement.[27] These declarations, made by men without formal titles, ended with requests to the king to confirm rights of ownership, and offered recognition of his overlordship in return. Clearly this was an attempt to insinuate that the parlement was only acting in the personal interests of its members—as of course it was, but far from exclusively. At the same time the declarations could be used as proof of the original royal assertion that there were usurped domain lands along the Gironde.

The magistrates recognized at once the danger of such proceedings, as both a slur on themselves and a threat to their whole case against the government's policy. The investigation also seemed to confirm that the domain's intention was indeed to take over all the *palus* indiscriminately as had been feared from the first. So on 11 January 1786 the procurator-general came yet again before the assembled chambers and demanded the arrest of Pestels, the notary, and all those makers of declarations who could be identified, pending investigations into what they had done, and proceedings against them. All this was done in pursuance of the parlement's earlier prohibitions against implementing the government's policies, although these prohibitions had twice been quashed. Pestels and his confederates were duly taken and deposited in the prisons of the palace.

This took the matter beyond the civilized exchange of injunctions. Both sides had shown in practical terms that they meant to have their way. It was now a question of the government's ability to impose its authority, and the need for such a demonstration dictated the next step. On 19 May *lettres de cachet* were issued to all members of the parlement, which ordered them to attend at the palace on the 30th, in the presence of the comte de Fumel, newly-appointed commander-in-chief, for a military session. On 29 May the parlement issued an *arrêt* condemning in advance all that it might be forced to accept, and sure enough, on the 30th, Fumel brought new letters patent from the king, dated 14 May, which reinforced the repeated quashings by the council of state of the parlement's prohibitions. These letters, while they attempted to clarify the government's intentions by pointing out that the only mainland mentioned in the 1781 *arrêt* was the strip of shore between the pointe de la Grange and Soulac, changed nothing of what had already been ordered. Dudon, ignoring his technical duty to conclude for registration regardless of his personal convictions, refused to say anything; Fumel therefore merely signed the registers to the effect that he had had been heard, but had not delivered conclusions! His substitute was enjoined to distribute the letters patent to lower jurisdictions.[28] At the same time a further set of letters patent, dated 14 May 1786, were registered to quash the arrest of Pestels and his collaborators, and all proceedings connected with it. The gaolers were ordered to release their prisoners forthwith. Admittedly these letters also contained a concession: the commission of Pestels was revoked. It had only been, the letters explained, 'pour prendre sur les lieux des renseignements préliminaires', and the implication was that he had exceeded his authorization. But the effect of the military session was only to increase the magistrates' bitterness without allaying any of their suspicions.

The result was the *arrêt* issued and printed by the court later that day, by which it declared the forced transcription to be null, void, and illegal, and reiterated all its previous prohibitions. The royal domain, the court declared, was confined exclusively to terrain over which water actually flowed; everything else was private property. This included the *alluvions* properly so-called, which formed along the banks of rivers, since the material which formed them came not from the river bed, but from other private properties further upstream. These principles were enshrined in Roman law and the general laws of the kingdom, and the whole province was expressing its alarm to see such hallowed laws thus ignored.

> . . . cette atteinte portée à la liberté publique & à la propriété, intéresse tous les Citoyens . . . si on commence à dépouiller les Propriétaires dans l'étendue de vingt-deux lieus de côte, on a tout à craindre pour les héritages de même nature qui bordent toutes les rivières navigables & flottables; . . . si ce premier essai de la destruction des propriétés réussit, on n'aura aucune digue à opposer à ses progrès; . . . il n'y aura plus rien d'assuré; . . . le découragement universel s'emparera des esprits et des coeurs . . . le tableau qui s'offre à l'imagination est trop allarmant pour qu'on puisse le suivre dans tous ses apperçus.[29]

Evocations usually implied, 'sinon une injustice à couronner, du moins une faveur que la Loi ne peut avouer'. In these terms the magistrates publicly hinted once more that backstairs intrigue at Versailles was the true motivating force of government policy. If that was the case

> l'obéissance que [la Cour] doit aux volontés du . . . Seigneur Roy, ne doit pas etre une obeissance aveugle et impassible; . . . la Cour ne doit point se preter à tollerer le mal lorsqu'elle le connoit, . . . dans ce cas, son obeissance elle même deviendroit un Crime et la rendroit complice des malheurs publics . . .

On such grounds, the court reaffirmed its previous intransigence, and announced new remonstrances.

By this time, however, echoes of the dispute were being heard far beyond the province of Guienne and the corridors of Versailles. In June, the parlement of Toulouse publicly associated itself with that of Bordeaux by denouncing in advance any pretensions that the domain might have on the upper Garonne.[30] Even more sensational was the resignation of Mouchy as commander-in-chief in Guienne in the middle of May, in obvious protest against the government's persistence in its policy, and to avoid the position of having to force that policy upon the parlement in the military session planned for the 30th.[31] It was rumoured that only with great reluctance had Fumel consented to deputize for him in coercing the parlement.[32] The very fact that around this time the affair began to be mentioned in public chronicles and the despatches of ambassadors, shows the degree of public interest it was provoking. The parlement had brought this situation about by openly defying the government. Everybody was now waiting to see what the ministry would do.

Vergennes, as minister of the province, had contacted Miromesnil with a view to working out a policy the moment he had news of the defiant resolution of 30 May:[33]

> Cest à votre sagesse à nous tracer la marche qu'il convient de faire. La plus promtc et la plus vigoureuse semble préférable. Une deputation ne suffiroit pas pour la lecon, si necessaire à tous; vous penserez sans doute que cest le cas de mander tout [sic] la Compagnie et de les faire longuement s'ennuier dans des villages pour apprendre [à] ces Messieurs ce quils doivent a leur maitre. la suspension de la justice ne fera pas un grand mal, car ils ne la font ni ne la rendent.

Before anything could be done, however, the parlement's *arrêt* had been printed, and by late June, copies were circulating at Paris and Versailles, where they were selling for a *louis* a time,[34] and the government felt obliged to defend itself by having the letters patent printed in official journals.[35] This did nothing to reassure opinion. On the contrary, speculation went so far as to suggest that the choice now lay between the destruction of the parlement or the disgrace of a minister.[36] In these circumstances the king decided to adopt the course proposed by Vergennes, and on 4 July the parlement was ordered to come in a body to Versailles and there await his pleasure on the 20th.[37] The magistrates were ordered to bring all registers containing minutes of the successive acts in the *alluvions* affair, and several others still unfinished too. Obviously the parlement was to be subjected to a *lit de justice* in the presence of the king himself, as the parlement of Besançon had been in 1783, on the issue of the third twentieth.

Short of exile, to be convoked in a body to Versailles was the most serious punishment a parlement could undergo, yet the news was not received with complete gloom in Bordeaux.[38] The magistrates departed with the fire of martyrdom in their eyes, emphasizing their seriousness of purpose by voting to abstain from visiting Paris until their business was over.[39] It was rumoured that, before leaving, they had drawn up a whole series of contingency plans for unanimous action, depending on the line taken by the king—among them mass resignation. In any case, they took with them, in addition to the registers which the king had

demanded, a new set of remonstrances, dated 30 June. Unrepentant, they added
to their old protestations the new grievances of the release of Pestels and the
forced transcriptions of 30 May.[40] By 14 July they had all set out, travelling in
three large groups, having first raised a loan of 200,000 l. to cover the costs of a
journey in due style.[41] By the 20th they had all arrived in Versailles and taken up
quarters allotted to them by the Keeper of the Seals. There were 93 in all,[42]
including several aged and infirm, not to mention a number of women and
children; and it was noted that on this occasion Dupaty made a point of journey-
ing from Paris to join those who were still technically his colleagues.[43] On the
morning of the 21st they marched in a double column, fully robed, to wait upon
the pleasure of the king.[44] They were watched by huge silent crowds of courtiers
—the silence directed more towards the ministry than these defiant champions of
the rights of property. It was rumoured that they brought with them a list of the
projectors who had solicited the *arrêt* of 1781 from a too-complaisant government, that they had come prepared to resign rather than submit, that they were
the spearhead of a concerted campaign by all the parlements against the enter-
prises of the domain. The Polignacs hurriedly and stridently denied all hand in
the government's policy, but were not readily believed.[45] The whole Court
seemed to be on the parlement's side against the ministry.

At a quarter past twelve Vergennes, as minister of the province, led the magistrates to the king. He received them civilly, seated amid a crowd of ministers and
great noblemen including Richelieu, and ordered them to surrender their registers for examination. He had, he declared, deputed Vidaud de la Tour and
Bertier de Sauvigny, councillors of state, to examine the whole case of the
alluvions, in company with the first president and the procurator-general, under
the supervision of the Keeper of the Seals. He then consented to receive the
remonstrances of 30 June, and dismissed the parlement, ordering it to await his
further instructions.

The magistrates were pleased with their reception.[46] Much worse had been
predicted and expected. The idea of calling the court in a body to Versailles may
have originated with Vergennes, but the implementation of such an extreme
course seems to have resulted from the king's own anger at the repeated defiance
of the parlement.[47] However, the council of despatches met immediately before
the audience, and there it appears that the king was made aware that the parlement perhaps had a case against the domain. Certainly a party at Court, led by
Mouchy, had been busy lobbying in the parlement's favour ever since the summons to Versailles had been made public,[48] and the ministry was far from united
on the question.[49] Perhaps the matter had not come before the council before, for
the king to appreciate the complexity of the problem. At any rate, his civility
surprised everybody, and suggested a sudden change of opinion. This impression
was confirmed by a remark which he allegedly made after the audience was over:
'on m'a induit en erreur; mais je m'en souviendrai long temps'.[50]

The magistrates had to wait over a week before hearing the results of the
examination of the registers. The king insisted on being minutely informed of the
details of this examination.[51] Such a close interest on Louis's part again suggests
that he felt himself to have been ill-informed during the early stages of the affair
and did not wish to repeat his mistake. At any rate, the commissioners worked
long hours on the registers, several ministers were consulted in the process, and

weight was given to the opinions of Le Berthon and Dudon. Such care was essential, Miromesnil explained to the king, 'pour que les magistrats de votre Parlement voient que cet Examen nest pas de pur Céremonial, et que votre majesté veut connoitre a fond ce qui interesse le bien de ses Sujets, et le maintien de son autorité'.[52] What resulted from the examination was a compromise on the *alluvions* which left all sides satisfied. It emerged at the second royal audience, which took place on 29 July.

This time the assembled parlement waited upon the king at 11 in the morning, and was subjected to a forced transcription in his presence which lasted several hours. He even cancelled his afternoon's hunting, and allowed aged magistrates, standing in his presence, to leave the room at intervals to rest themselves. His tone, in fact, was one of good-humoured indulgence, a sign that the apparent imposition of the royal will upon the parlement involved in reality a substantial concession. He would, he said, never permit a parlement to forbid the execution of his orders, and he ordered the erasing of all the parlement's prohibitions in the *alluvions* and several other cases from the registers.[53] New letters patent were then registered,[54] dated 28 July, which declared that the parlement had interpreted the letters patent of 14 May in a sense absolutely contrary to that intended, and its zeal had led it into misunderstandings which the king now felt obliged to dispel once and for all. So, while all the previous acts of the government were upheld, and the parlement's interventions overridden, the royal intentions were clarified. The survey was to proceed,

> sans néamoins que l'on puisse en induire que les alluvions, atterissements et relais formés sur les bords des . . . rivières ni d'aucune rivière navigable puissent appartenir à d'autres qu'aux propriétaires des fonds adjacents à la rive des . . . rivières et à nous, lorsque la rive des . . . rivières sera adjacente a de fonds de terre faisant partie de notre domaine. N'entendons que sous prétexte de rechercher et de vérifier les terrains dépendants de notre domaine on trouble les propriétaires dans la possession et jouissance de fiefs, terre, seigneuries et autres propriétés qu'ils possèdent d'ancienneté par eux ou par leurs auteurs, et que rien n'annonce faire partie de notre domaine.[55]

If this was not clear enough, the king added verbally after the transcription that:

> Le domaine est un des patrimoines de la couronne, qui lui est le plus ingérant. Je dois etre attentif à veiller à la conservation de ses droits; mais je ne souffrirai jamais qu'on en porte les prétentions jusqu'à vouloir dépouiller de leurs biens les possesseurs légitimes.[56]

The magistrates were delighted. It was not indeed a complete surrender to their position; the survey was to go ahead and contests were still to be cognizable only by the council of state. Nevertheless, the greatest ambiguity in government policy was cleared up. The domain was to confine its researches to the beds of navigable rivers, and alluvial deposits were recognized as the property of those on whose land they were left. The threat to lords and proprietors in the *palus* disappeared. 'Thus', noted the British envoy, 'by a just and reasonable concession on the part of the Court, an affair is terminated, which, had it been persisted in, might have raised a ferment in the Kingdom, which, in all probability, it would not have been easy to compose'.[57]

The government also took the occasion to clear up a whole series of minor issues outstanding between it and the parlement. The case against Pestels was terminated by a rule of silence. So was that against Chauveton, secretary to Dupré de Saint-Maur.[58] The king promised to examine afresh the whole question of the *corvées*.[59] The court was ordered to carry the name of the younger Dudon purely and simply, without qualification, on its membership list.[60] Various prohibitions concerning indirect taxes were also overridden, but that of 1785 against stamped-paper duty on bills of exchange[61] was upheld and the king withdrew the law. The session proved the occasion for clearing up much unfinished business, for psychologically it was the right moment; major concessions softened the impact of minor intransigencies. After the formalities were over, the king exchanged politenesses with the magistrates, and hinted that perhaps he would soon visit Guienne as he recently had Normandy.[62] Meanwhile he recommended them to cease their internal divisions, and return to their duties as soon as possible so as to catch up on arrears in judicial business, but he gave them permission to visit Paris, and they were allowed until 21 August to return to Bordeaux. These were the ultimate signs of royal goodwill, and it was in such an atmosphere that the session ended. The magistrates left Versailles stronger than ever in the conviction that it was not the king, but his ministers, who troubled his subjects. The monarch himself, correctly informed, was good and just and could not fail to act benevolently. 'Les officiers de votre Parlement de Bordeaux', Miromesnil informed him on 1 August,

> sont presque touts partis, quoique vous ne leur avés pas deffendu d'aller a Paris. Il n'y en a que très peu qui y aient été. M. le premier President doit partir demain ou peut etre ce soir; son intention ainsi que celle de la plus grande partie de Mrs du parlement, est de tacher d'etre a Bordeaux asses tost pour pouvoir ouvrir les sceances le neuf aoust. touts m'ont paru pénétrez des sentiments que doivent leur imprimer votre Justice et la bonté avec laquelle vous avés bien voulu les traitter. Jen ai vu avoir les larmes aux iëux en me parlant de Votre Majesté . . .
>
> au surplus, quelque favorables que soient les apparences, il faut pour les bien juger attendre la conduitte qu'ils tiendront à leur arrivée a Bordeaux, et dans la suitte . . .[63]

The results of the confrontation at Versailles had been eagerly awaited in Bordeaux, though not without trepidation. There was some discontent at the suspension of justice during the court's absence,[64] but men of property in general felt that it was worth the delay if the threat to their rights were finally to be averted. When the news finally came through, the town went wild with delight. 'Vous pouvez aisément vous faire une idée de la joie que cette heureuse nouvelle a causé [sic] ici', wrote Vergniaud to his father.[65] 'On étoit toujours dans les allarmes'. The magistrates arrived back in the city in small groups over the first two weeks of August, and although it was rumoured that the government had given them plenty of time to return home in the hope that by the time they did, the first enthusiasm of their fellow-citizens would have passed,[66] they all received hero's welcomes. There were laurel crowns for each of them, flowers strewn in their paths, and public ovations.[67] The celebrations did not attain the scale of those of 1775, but they were large enough to recall them to several commentators.

Nor did the magistrates repeat their mistakes of that year, and revel too openly in their triumph. They were rumoured to have refused 100,000 l. offered by the government to defray the costs of their journey, on the grounds that this would be a burden for the taxpayers.[68] Le Berthon declined an invitation from the *musée* to attend an assembly in his honour, and the whole parlement followed his example when the chamber of commerce proposed a festive reception.[69] By 12 August Le Berthon could write to the Keeper of the Seals that the grand chamber would hold its first sitting on the 14th, and that he was delighted to report an unprecedented zeal and determination, on the part of his colleagues, for the king's service.[70] On 29 August they put these sentiments into words in a flattering letter to the king:

> Sire! Les Bons Rois sont trop peu connus de leurs sujets; leurs noms trop souvent profanés des fiscaux . . . Combien chacun de vos sujets est assuré contre les Surprises qui pourroient etre faites à Votre Majesté par le témoignage Eclattant que vous venés de leur donner de votre amour pour la justice et la vérité et de votre Patience infatiguable dans sa recherche, toutes les fois qu'il s'agit du bonheur de vos Peuples.[71]

The whole province, the magistrates declared, was rejoicing and calling down benedictions on the name of the king. They begged him to crown these demonstrations of loyalty and gratitude by paying a visit to Guienne, where his other subjects might be vouchsafed the privilege, which they themselves had so recently enjoyed, of seeing him. And so the judicial year ended in harmony, zeal, and an effusion of loyalty unprecedented since 1775.

But September 1786 marked more than the end of a judicial year. It marked the end of a distinct phase in the life of the parlement. There is a dramatic satisfaction for the historian in the events of 1786: they constitute a climax and conclusion to the history of the parlement since the restoration. The royal session at Versailles saw not only the successful termination of the *alluvions* dispute, but the last echo of the *corvées* affair, the final resolution of the last dispute arising from the Maupeou parlement concerning the younger Dudon, and even the last act of the Dupaty affair, although accounts vary concerning the impression made by Dupaty's impulsive gesture in coming to Versailles.[72] So the loose ends of a decade were tied up, and the parlement could look forward to a new start and perhaps more harmonious times.

The events of 1786, however much they were enveloped in the language of royal authority, were a triumph for the parlement. The magistrates knew it, and so did the world at large. 'Notwithstanding the good grace with which the court has yielded on this occasion', commented the British envoy, 'there still remains the painful impression of a failure in a measure precipitately undertaken, and in which the will of the sovereign has been successfully opposed'.[73] It was an astonishing achievement for the parlement after so many bitter and confused years, even though the cause which brought the magistrates into unity was the most powerful possible—a threat to property—and even though it was a case in which they spoke as genuine representatives of a whole class, and a whole province. For once, the parlement really was playing the role to which it repeatedly laid claim. It triumphed, however, only because the government gave it the opportunity. A clearer statement of intentions at the outset, and a less rigid persistence in clinging to a policy so open to suspicion, would have saved the government much trouble and loss of face, and left the parlement absorbed in those lesser matters to which it was only too willing to turn its attention, despite the damage they did to its reputation.

As it was, the parlement went into the pre-revolutionary crisis without any unfinished business to absorb its attention, with the recent memory of 'ministerial despotism' only narrowly defeated by a firm stand on principles, and with the reputation of a defender of rights and privileges far wider than its own—those of a whole province and indeed the whole propertied nation.[74]

NOTES

1. AD 8J 67 (Fonds Bigot), 'parlement,' speech of 5 Dec. 1764.
2. On this affair, see *Recueil de mémoires, arrêts remonstrances et autres pièces concernant l'affaire présente du parlement de Bordeaux* (Bordeaux, 1756), and Lhéritier, *Tourny*, II, 427–8, 447–9.
3. AD C1989, speech of 27 May 1782.
4. Quoted in A. Plantey, 'Un exemple de continuité des principes du droit public français: l'affaire des alluvions (Bordeaux, 1781–6)', *Revue de Droit Public et de Science Politique*, LXXI (1955), 558. An older account of the affair in general is in Boscheron des Portes, op. cit., II, 345–55.
5. J. de Witte (ed.), *Journal de l'Abbé de Véri* (Paris, 1928–30), I, 135–7.
6. Members of the parlement were as active as anybody in this field; see above, pp. 71–3.
7. AD C3675, memorandum of 1778.
8. AN K1164 for the 1781 proposal; also printed in *AHDG*, XIX (1879), 382.
9. AN Q I 264, baron de Bourg to Vergennes, 18 May 1783.
10. AD C3675, comptroller-general to intendant, 11 July 1781 and 3 June 1782.
11. The British envoy had heard these rumours and believed them. Browning, *Despatches from Paris*, I, Hailes to Carmarthen, 3 Aug. 1786. The Swedish ambassador also reported that the intrigues of courtiers lay behind the government's action. L. Léouzon Le Duc (ed.), *Correspondance diplomatique du Baron de Staël-Holstein . . . (1783–1799)* (Paris, 1881), 32, 13 July 1786. See also Lescure, *Correspondance secrète*, II, 61, 26 July 1786; Bachaumont, XXXII, 127, 24 June 1786; and BN MSS Fr. n.a. 6685 (S. P. Hardy, 'Mes Loisirs'), p. 397, 29 July 1786.
12. AN Q I 264, Pestels to 'M. de St. R.', 13 May 1782.
13. Speech of 24 April 1784; see below, p. 253.
14. Here I follow the interpretation of a lucid but anonymous brief on the case drawn up by a government lawyer in 1786. AN K708, no. 68.
15. The pointe de la Grange is formed by a bend in the Garonne about half-way between the city and the Bec d'Ambès.
16. BVBx MS 1696, XXII, no. 49, Noailles duchesse de Lesparre to an unknown lady (clearly connected with the parlement), 10 May 1782.
17. AAE MD France, 1589, f.119, Mouchy to Vergennes, 21 May 1782.
18. See, for example, above, pp. 72–3.
19. AD C2352, anon. memorandum of 1755 sent to Pereyre de Moras, councillor of state and intendant of finances.
20. I have been unable to find a copy of these remonstrances.
21. Plantey, op. cit., 540–1; Boscheron des Portes, op. cit., II, 346.
22. AN K708, Calonne to Miromesnil, 25 May 1784.
23. ibid., Dudon to Bastard, 15 April 1784, copy sent by Calonne to Miromesnil.
24. Plantey, loc. cit., 541.
25. BPR Le Paige 828, printed copy of the remonstrances of 17 Nov. 1784. For a fuller analysis, see above, pp. 226–7.

26. Boscheron des Portes, op. cit., II, 348–9, and Plantey, op. cit., 548.
27. Among parlementaire families with property in Parempuyre were those of Lamouroux, Montsec de Reignac, Basterot, and Lalande; in Cantenac, the families of Castelnaun d'Essenault, Guyonnet, and Casaux. In 1778 and 1779 president de Casaux had been involved in negotiations for draining the marshes of Cantenac by the digging of drainage channels across his property. AD C302.
28. AD IB 56, ff.193–4, for this transcription.
29. Copy in AN K708.
30. Bachaumont, XXXII, 131–2, 26 June 1786; Browning, *Despatches*, I, 122, Hailes to Carmarthen, 6 July 1786.
31. Bachaumont, XXXII, 123, 22 June 1786; Léouzon Le Duc, *Correspondance diplomatique*, 31, 13 July 1786; BN MSS Fr. n.a. 6685, p. 389, 4 July 1786; Lescure, *Correspondance secrète*, II, I, 15 June 1786. See also M. Lhéritier, *La Révolution à Bordeaux dans l'histoire de la Révolution française: la fin de l'Ancien Régime et la préparation des Etats Généraux (1787–1789)* (Paris, 1942), 51.
32. BN loc. cit. above, n. 31.
33. AN K708, no. 64, Vergennes to Miromesnil, 9 June 1786.
34. Bachaumont, XXXII, 126, 24 June 1786.
35. ibid., 161, 7 July 1786; BN MSS Fr. n.a. 6685, p. 389, 4 July 1786.
36. Lescure, op. cit., II, 48, 21 June 1786.
37. AAE MD France, 1589, ff.357–9, circular from Miromesnil giving dates and arrangements.
38. Vatel, *Vergniaud*, I, 107, Vergniaud to Allaud, 14 July 1786.
39. AAE MD France, 1589, f.358.
40. AN K708, no. 67, copy annotated by Miromesnil; some quotations in Plantey, op. cit., 549–50.
41. Bachaumont, XXXII, 196, 24 July 1786.
42. Estimates varied, but in AN O¹ 352, no. 466, there is a list giving the names of all those who came to Versailles on this occasion.
43. Bachaumont, XXXII, 176, 14 July 1786.
44. There are many accounts of the parlement's reception at Versailles. The fullest, apart from those in Bachaumont, Lescure, and Hardy's 'Loisirs', is in Vatel, *Vergniaud*, I, 108ff., Vergniaud to Allaud, 29 July 1786. It seems to have been copied by Vergniaud from some eyewitness account.
45. Lescure, op. cit., II, 55 (10 July), 58–9 (20 July), and 61 (26 July).
46. Bachaumont, XXXII, 193–4, 22 July 1786; BN MSS Fr. n.a. 6685, p. 398, 21 July 1786.
47. Léouzon Le Duc, op. cit., 32, 30 July 1786.
48. BN MSS Fr. n.a. 6685, p. 397, 20 July 1786.
49. Browning, op. cit., I, 120, Hailes to Carmarthen, 29 June 1786.
50. Hardy's version, BN MSS Fr. n.a. 6685, p. 398. According to Lescure, op. cit., II, 61, it was 'Je crains qu'on ne m'ait induit en erreur, mais qu'on y prenne garde, je m'en souviendrai'.
51. AN K163, Miromesnil to Louis XVI, 23 and 25 July 1786.
52. ibid., same to same, 25 July 1786; AN K708, no. 72 for the *procès-verbal* of these meetings.
53. ibid., no. 73, the king's speech, in the hand of Miromesnil.
54. AD IB 56, ff.196ff., for this transcription.
55. ibid., partially quoted in Boscheron des Portes, op. cit., II, 353, and Plantey, op. cit., 546.
56. AN K708, no. 73; Boscheron des Portes, loc. cit.
57. Browning, op. cit., I, 128, Hailes to Carmarthen, 3 Aug. 1786.
58. See above, p. 237.
59. Bachaumont, XXXII, 214, 1 Aug. 1786.
60. See above, pp. 196–7.
61. See above, p. 213.
62. BN MSS Fr. n.a. 6685, p. 402, 29 July 1786.
63. AN K163, Miromesnil to Louis XVI, 1 Aug. 1786.
64. Bachaumont, XXXII, 196, 24 July 1786.

65. Vatel, op. cit., I, 113, undated, but clearly August 1786.
66. Bachaumont, XXXII, 217, 2 Aug. 1786.
67. ibid., 258, 20 Aug. 1786.
68. Boscheron des Portes, op. cit., II, 354.
69. AD 2E 1213[5] (tit. fam. Filhot de Chimbaud), Boudin to Filhot, 19 Aug. 1786.
70. AN K163, Miromesnil to Louis XVI, 16 Aug. 1786.
71. AAE MD France, 1400, ff.299–301.
72. Hardy, BN MSS Fr. n.a. 6685, p. 402, 29 July 1786, reports that Dupaty's presence at Versailles completed his reconciliation with his colleagues; but Lescure, op. cit., II, 66, 19 Aug. 1786, reports continued hostility in the parlement, and Bachaumont, XXXII, 235, 11 Aug. 1786, says he was treated coldly and ignored by his colleagues at Versailles.
73. Browning, op. cit., I, 128, Hailes to Carmarthen, 3 Aug. 1786.
74. The *alluvions* affair echoed long after 1786. Several of the *cahiers* of 1789 discussed the question, and called for a new general law on the public domain, e.g., *Archives Parlementaires*, V, 772, Noblesse de Saumur.

CHAPTER 17

Revolution I: The Constitutional Crisis

The months between July 1786 and the spring of 1787 were the calmest the parlement of Bordeaux had enjoyed since the days of Maupeou. No major controversy agitated it, and, relieved of the burden of greater matters, it turned its attention to the renovation of the neglected affairs of Bordeaux.[1] But this was only possible because the legislative activity of the state was at a standstill for most of 1786. Calonne spent much of that year preparing his great plans for the regeneration of the monarchy. Then throughout the first half of 1787 public attention all over France was fixed on the Assembly of Notables before which he had chosen to lay these plans. No provincial parlement could be expected to make news when such momentous events were taking place on the national stage. Besides, the first presidents and procurators-general of the parlements were all among the notables summoned to Versailles. Far from depriving the magistracy of the chance to comment on Calonne's proposals, the Assembly of Notables brought its leaders together in an unprecedented way and positively invited their comments.

The interests of Guienne were represented in the Assembly of Notables by Mouchy, vicomte Duhamel, deputy mayor of the city, the intendant Le Camus de Néville, the first president Le Berthon, and the procurator-general Dudon the elder. The two representatives of the parlement were deemed opponents of Calonne, on the strength of their stand over the *alluvions*, although Dudon was at first viewed with some suspicion by 'patriots', on account of his earlier co-operation with Maupeou.[2] He was assigned in the assembly to the bureau of the intransigent prince de Conti, where he was very active.[3] Le Berthon, a member of the bureau of the comte d'Artois, which proved the most amenable to Calonne, played a lesser role than Dudon,[4] perhaps because of differences with Artois. Artois was a strong believer in subordinating Calonne's proposed provincial assemblies to the intendants,[5] a position which the parlement of Bordeaux later underlined as the crucial flaw in the programme of reform.[6] Cardinal Loménie de Brienne was also a member of this bureau. Le Berthon was thus able to acquaint himself with the first minister against whom the parlement was to take its stand. At any rate, he and Dudon were able to give their colleagues a full account of the proposals considered by the notables, and the arguments then voiced both for and against them. So the parlement was not taken by surprise when the first of Brienne's reforming edicts arrived that summer.

The two magistrates arrived back in Bordeaux on 22 June. None of the new measures arrived for registration before the installation of the comte de Brienne, brother of the new first minister,[7] as lieutenant-general and commander-in-chief in succession to Mouchy.[8] On 19 July there was a glittering session at the parlement, attended by the cream of the province's nobility, for the registration of his letters of provision.[9] On this occasion all seemed harmonious. However, by now the government had begun to publish its programme. At the hub of it was the creation of provincial assemblies to assist with administration and preside over a reformed tax structure. The edict of June 1787, which implemented this part of the plan, was the first to be received for registration by the parlement of Bordeaux.[10]

The provisions of the edict were not the same in every detail as those envisaged by Calonne. Calonne's assemblies would not have guaranteed representation for all three orders, in this departing from the two assemblies set up by Necker in 1778. Brienne conceded that the assemblies should sit by order, with double representation for the third estate, as Necker's had. Doubtless this concession was intended to allay the fears of the clergy and nobility as expressed by the notables. But the edict did nothing to dispel the far greater fears regarding the powers and procedure of the assemblies. Calonne had proposed a hierarchy of assemblies, each category electing the one above it, from parish up to provincial level. The 'province' was to be the old generality. But nothing clear was stipulated either by him or by Brienne about the franchise for the elections and their procedure. Such things were to be controlled by special complementary regulations for each province, to be issued in subsequent months. The same applied to the vital question of the precise powers and competence of the assemblies. They were to advise and co-operate with the intendant and his subordinates in the levy of taxes and in local government, but their share of executive power was left vague. This had worried the notables. It seemed to them that if these assemblies were to be mere advisory bodies with no power of their own, then they were worse than useless; far from diminishing 'ministerial despotism', they would only extend its power.[11] None of this uncertainty was clarified by Brienne's edict.

As a result, several provincial parlements insisted on qualifying their registrations of the edict, either to reserve their own powers of registering legislation, or to call for the speedy issue of the complementary regulations.[12] In Bordeaux such precautions were deemed inadequate. The Bordelais magistrates refused to register the edict until they saw the regulations. 'Je me fais un devoir', wrote Le Berthon to Lamoignon, new Keeper of the Seals, on 26 July,

> de vous informer que ma Compagnie arrêta mercredy derniere d'une voix presque unanime d'adresser au Roi une lettre très respectueuse pour supplier S.M. de vouloir bien faire remettre au Parlement, préalablement à toute délibération sur l'enregistrement de l'Edit portant établissement des assemblées Provinciales, tous les reglemens annoncés par l'art. 6 de cet edit. Ce préalable a paru indispensablement necessaire pour être invariablement fixé sur les motifs de la Crainte vraye ou mal fondée qu'a fait naitre a peu près dans tous les esprits la formation peut etre trop vague de cet Edit . . .[13]

A day later, the parlement sent a formal letter to this effect to the king:

> L'Edit portant création des Assemblées Provinciales donne un grand espoir
> à la Nation. Votre Majesté n'a conçu cet Etablissement que pour le Bonheur
> de ses sujets. Mais le bien qui peut en résulter dépend des fonctions, des
> pouvoirs de ces Corps, et de leur organisation. Ces objets ont une telle
> connexité avec l'établissement même, que l'on ne peut être fixé sur ses
> avantages qu'en les considerant ensemble.[14]

The Keeper of the Seals replied that there was no cause for alarm, and ordered
the immediate registration of the edict.[15] He did not appear at this stage to
anticipate trouble.

But were the magistrates' fears groundless? The complementary regulations
for the 'provincial assembly of Aquitaine', alias the generality of Bordeaux, were
already in existence, although they did not know it.[16] They envisaged an assembly
of 48 members, of whom 24 would represent the third estate. The first assembly
would sit at Bordeaux, its successors at Libourne, and last for three years. The
members of the first one would be nominated directly or indirectly by the king
and meet at Bordeaux on 28 August. They would have to supervise the establishment of machinery for the election of their successors through a series of subordinate assemblies. This would surely have been unexceptionable, since the
details of the franchise at every level were clearly set out. But on the central question of the powers of the assembly, nothing was clarified. The king reserved the
right to regulate as he saw fit the functions of the assemblies, and their relationship to the intendant (Art. 14). The magistrates' suspicions were therefore amply
grounded.

Everything that subsequently happened only increased their mistrust of the
government. The regulations for the provincial assembly of Limousin, a distant
part of the parlement's jurisdiction, had been published on 12 July, and its first
meeting was set for 11 August on the assumption that the general edict would
encounter no trouble. This assumption proved unwise, for on 4 August, Dudon
wrote a warning letter to the lieutenant-general of the seneschalcy of Limoges.
Sure as he was that 'rumours' circulating in Bordeaux that an assembly was about
to meet in Limoges, were false, he felt obliged to remind the officer that no such
assembly would be legal until the parlement had registered the edict. He enclosed
a copy of the parlement's deferment of registration, and demanded immediate
information on the situation in Limoges.[17] The 'rumours' were of course quite
accurate; the duc d'Ayen arrived in Limoges on 5 August to make active preparations for the assembly. He told the government that he expected everything to be
ready by the 12th or 13th.[18] In the meantime, however, on the 8th the parlement
intervened more publicly and decisively, and issued an *arrêt* which forbade any
assembly to meet in its jurisdiction until it had registered the edict.

The authorities were taken by surprise. The duc d'Ayen suspended all operations pending further instructions from Versailles.[19] From Bordeaux, where he
had begun preparations for the assembly of Aquitaine, archbishop Champion de
Cicé advised that it be deferred into September or beyond if possible; clearly the
parlement was not disposed to register anything freely, and if he divulged his
orders at this juncture, he feared 'de nouvelles vivacités' and perhaps a prohibition.[20] Meulan d'Ablois, intendant of Limoges, agreed, although he suggested
that once an assembly had met, it might be possible to keep it sitting, despite all

prohibitions.[21] This bold advice found some favour with the ministry; on 12 August d'Ayen was instructed to continue his preparations, though in secret.[22] The government, in fact, was preparing to set aside the legal formalities with a spectacular act of authority. By an *arrêt* of the council of 12 August it condemned the position taken up by the parlement. Any assembly convoked by the king was *ipso facto* lawful, it declared, and no parlement had the right to decide otherwise. The *arrêt* of 8 August was quashed, and the comte de Brienne was ordered to lend all force necessary to see that this cassation was duly signified to the parlement. But this was not all. 'Sa majesté a jugé', Brienne was told,[23]

> que sa Justice ne sera pas satisfaite si elle s'en tenait à la cassation de cet arrêt. Elle a reconnu que dans une occasion si importante, ou il s'agit d'un etabliss[t] pr. lequel Elle a reçu le voeu général de la nation, il importait au maintien de son autorité et à l'intérêt de la portion de ses peuples dont le pt de Bordeaux a voulu éloigner la jouissance Rélativ[t] au bienfait qui leur est promis, de témoigner d'une maière éclatante que cette Compagnie a encouru sa disgrace. Sa majesté a donc résolu d'en exiler tous les membres à Libourne . . .

The speed, severity, and contempt for forms of this response were all remarkable. There was no formal reply to the parlement's letter of 27 July, and no recourse to letters of *jussion* ordering registration, although both were normal procedures. There was no warning either of imminent severity. Most striking of all, the government simply ignored the fact that the edict creating assemblies was unregistered, and ordered d'Ayen and the archbishop to proceed with their respective preparations.[24] Perhaps the parlement was exiled not only to punish it and break its resistance, but also to get it out of the city while the assembly of Aquitaine was meeting. In any event, the court was certain to be more antagonized than intimidated, and the likelihood of an agreeable reception for the other measures in the government's plan, the stamp tax and the territorial subvention, was much diminished.

The magistrates were exiled by individual *lettres de cachet*, dated 12 August, and conveyed to them by soldiers of the garrison during the night of 17/18 August.[25] However, they were given two days to make the journey, and this left time for a session of the court on the 18th. The magistrates only dispersed at length at 10 in the evening; but the result was an *arrêt*, subsequently printed and publicly posted, in which the parlement renewed its prohibitions on the meeting of any assembly, and persisted in its refusal to register the edict until the complementary regulations were sent.[26] The court was not, it declared, hostile to representative institutions, and it recalled its remonstrances of 1779 requesting provincial estates. But in times when all governmental projects, even those most characterized by apparent benevolence, seemed to be aimed primarily at increasing the weight of taxation, the court felt justified in the exercise of extreme circumspection in registering new edicts. In any case, it declared, only the Estates-General could avert the ever-increasing threat to property. Until they met, the parlement was the people's only shield against despotism. The recent case of the *alluvions* proved as much. So the court declared that until the regulations were sent, the government's intentions must remain subject to suspicion. On this defiant, well-publicized note the magistrates made the move to Libourne.

Doubtless they were comforted to learn a few days later that the parlement of Paris had been similarly exiled to Troyes, for its opposition to the new taxes.[27] But meanwhile d'Ayen, ignoring the renewed prohibitions, held the first session of the Limousin assembly on 20 August, overriding a protest on the parlement's behalf by the lieutenant-general of the seneschalcy as he did so.[28] Yet the sittings were a token gesture rather than a serious move, and on the 23rd they were adjourned until November. In Bordeaux, the archbishop repeatedly postponed the meeting of the Aquitaine assembly on the grounds that circumstances were not yet favourable, and late in August he was formally warned by the king's procurator at the seneschalcy that he should take no steps to hold any assembly until the parlement had registered the edict.[29] It never did convene. Clearly the parlement's authority and influence were in no way diminished by its exile.

All indications meanwhile suggested that a speedy return to Bordeaux was not to be expected. On 27 August the court at last received *lettres de jussion* ordering it to register the edict, letters in which the king also took the opportunity to disclaim any attempt to levy arbitrary taxation, and cited the remonstrances of 1779, when the parlement itself had called for representative institutions for the province.[30] But there was of course all the difference in the world between the estates the parlement had suggested then and the vaguely constituted assemblies which were now proposed. The government repeatedly missed, or ignored, this point; the parlement was accordingly unimpressed. Nor were the efforts of the crown's agents in the province any more availing. On 31 August Brienne went to Libourne apparently to deliver new *lettres de cachet* instructing the magistrates to hold their sessions there until further notice.[31] Any negotiations he may have attempted were certainly fruitless. Two days later the archbishop, who apparently wished to negotiate about the projected assembly, was coldly received and snubbed by Le Berthon. When he attended a deliberation of the court to observe its mood, he was forced to confine his remarks to lofty platitudes about peace and harmony.[32] On 3 September the court emphasized its intransigence by publishing an extract from its registers in which it protested at being transferred to Libourne, on the grounds that the transfer was illegal under the capitulation of 1451, and harmful to justice in that the records of the court had not also been transferred, without which work was impossible. Finally the court declared that in future it would register no tax not approved by the Estates-General. So it joined in chorusing what was becoming the dominant theme throughout France in the protests against the government's policies.

But the government had not exhausted its armoury. In the first days of September the magistrates received new *lettres de cachet* by which they were ordered to be present at the town hall of Libourne, the court's temporary quarters, on the 5th in the presence of Brienne. They had time to protest a day in advance against all that might then be done,[33] but what was done was legally dubious for other reasons too. Brienne came on the 5th to force registration of letters patent dated 12 August, which formally transferred the parlement to Libourne; even though these letters had not been submitted first for free registration by the court. The next day a protesting *arrêt* from the parlement tore the legality of the government's proceedings to shreds, and declared them null and void. Then on the 7th it turned its attentions to the letters of *jussion* of 28 August, which it refused to obey until the complementary regulations were sent.[34] This *arrêté* was particularly noteworthy for the clarity with which it expressed the case against the government's policy. The edict was

> moins une loi que le projet d'une loi; . . . on y voit, à la vérité, le voeu d'un Roi bienfaisant, qui désire le bonheur de ses Peuples; mais . . . ce n'est que par la connaissance approfondie de l'organisation des Assemblées Provinciales, que le Parlement peut juger de l'utilité, ou du désavantage de ces Etablissements inconnus jusqu'à nos jours . . .
>   . . . la bonne ou mauvaise organisation de ces Assemblées dépend des Réglements que le Gouvernement leur donnera . . .
>   . . . ces Reglements sont de l'essence des Assemblées Provinciales, puisque, sans eux, elles ne sauroient exister.
>   . . . l'Edit envoyé à l'enregistrement, & les Réglements que le Parlement demande, ne doivent former que la même loi, sont les parties intégrantes & individuelles du même corps.

The conduct of the government had justified suspicion, especially since the idea of the assemblies came from the proposals of 'un Ministre déprédateur, qui cherchoit les moyens de rétablir les finances de l'Etat, que ses dissipations avoient epuisées'—so much for Calonne. The significant fact about the registration of the edict by other parlements was that most had qualified their registrations in some way; this proved that the edict was defective. The *arrêt* concluded in explicit terms:

> . . . le Parlement reconnoît combien les Assemblées Provinciales, bien réglées, seroient preferables à l'administration souvent arbitraire d'un Commissaire départi; mais . . . cependant en 1779, en désirant cette forme d'administration, il developpait des vues bien différentes de celles que le gouvernement propose . . . le plan qu'il traçoit alors, concilioit le Soulagement des peuples, la gloire & la puissance du Souverain, mais . . . il etoit bien éloigné de demander, pour son Ressort, plusieurs petites Assemblées Provinciales, amorcelées, incohérentes, étrangères les uns aux autres, qui, sous un Ministre imperieux, n'auroient d'autre volonté que celle de quelques Commissaires, choisis par l'administration, & qui pourroient servir à favoriser l'oppression, loin d'en garantir les Peuples . . .

In short, 'le projet proposé par le Parlement, à cette epoque, avoit pour objet de faire de la Guienne, un Pays d'Etat'.

It is easy to see flaws in the parlement's argument. Many complementary regulations had already been published in various parts of France, without arousing demur. The magistrates could easily have inferred how the assemblies of the south-west would be regulated. On the other hand, the regulations they knew about still seemed suspiciously vague. There seemed no good reason why the government should not choose to dispel their suspicions and end the crisis simply by sending the regulations, especially since this *arrêté* of 7 September clearly shows the magistrates to have been under the mistaken impression that the proposed assemblies for their area were to be numerous and small. In fact a general assembly for the whole of the south-west was envisaged, far nearer in size and jurisdiction to their beloved estates than they suspected.[35] Yet the government could hardly be expected to accord the parlement of Bordeaux special treatment in this matter when all the other parlements had freely registered the edict in one way or another; even if to yield to the parlement might end its resistance. In any case, this course might not work; the regulations were full of evasive ambiguities. Both sides were trapped in the positions they had taken up, with no alternative left but to proclaim them to each other and see who would weaken first.

Throughout September, the government increased the pressure. No sooner was the military session of 5 September over than the magistrates received new *lettres de cachet*, dated 4 September, which ordered them to be present for a further session on the 10th. On this occasion Brienne registered a new set of letters patent prolonging the sittings of the parlement into the vacation, and distributed yet more *lettres de cachet* which forbade the magistrates to leave Libourne until further notice.[36] Denunciations naturally followed; by this time the parlement was mustering its allies to swell the protest. On 4 September the *jurade* addressed a long letter to the king, in which it declared that the exile of the parlement was unconstitutional and destructive of public confidence in the government. It hinted that if there was no change of policy, the *jurats* might press for that extreme emergency recourse, the assembly of the *cent-trente*.[37] On 7 September the court of aids registered its own protest, attributing the ills of the state to the dismissal of Necker and the appointment of Calonne. The courts, it declared, must persuade the king that authoritarian acts were unconstitutional and against his own interests. This proposition created some stir in Bordeaux, more it seemed for the source from which it came, than for its intrinsic novelty.[38] Other parlements, too, saw the exile of that of Bordeaux as yet another example of the government's 'despotism'. There were protests and letters of sympathy from Toulouse and Pau, and of course the parlement of Paris, itself in exile, was especially sympathetic.

However, from this quarter a rude blow was in preparation. The government offered to abandon the stamp tax and the territorial subvention, if the parlement of Paris would agree to register a further prolongation of the twentieths, but on a new set of assessments. To the exiled magistrates this seemed a fair compromise. As a result, on 20 September the exile to Troyes was revoked, and the parlement returned to Paris with the glory of having forced the government to abandon its proposals.[39] Admittedly one of its first acts on its return was to petition the government in favour of its Bordeaux colleagues, and it renewed these appeals in October. The transfer of sittings to Libourne, it declared, was authorized by no law, justified by no circumstances, and contrary to the capitulation of 1451— clearly the Parisians were well informed on the regional arguments. Moreover, the exile deprived a whole province of justice, and a great city of judicial supervision.[40] But these representations failed to impress the government and did little to console the magistrates of Bordeaux either. They regarded the bargain struck by their Parisian colleagues as a surrender and a betrayal, and late in October sent off a bitter letter castigating this action.[41]

Meanwhile judicial business was at a complete standstill. In the absence of their records, the magistrates refused to consider cases. This caused particular alarm in the mercantile community, who feared that it would result in bad debtors and false bankrupts going unpunished. The merchants begged the commander-in-chief to advise the government to recall the parlement to Bordeaux.[42] The advocates too were naturally worried at an exile which imperilled

their very livelihood. Nevertheless, they were more inclined to blame the government than the parlement,[43] and indeed, most people of consequence seemed to
take this view. 'The Language of every Aret', reported the U.S. consul,

> indicates a new and entire Change of Sentiments. Royalty is no longer the
> main spring. The People appear ripe to Espouse a new Doctrine, the eager-
> ness of every Individual to purchase the Antiministerial publications as they
> appear are not less, if not more than ever appeared in America. The Assembly
> of the States are the General conclusions, but it is not pointed out the special
> Business to which they are to attend.[44]

Above all, the parlement found itself obeyed on the original point at issue. The
provincial assembly of Bordeaux, or Aquitaine, never met. That of Limousin
never reassembled after its preliminary meeting in August. That of Gascony,
most of which lay in the jurisdiction of the parlement of Toulouse, met but without representatives from those districts which lay in the jurisdiction of Bordeaux.[45] Despite its exile, despite its isolation now that Paris had compromised,
the Bordeaux parlement clearly remained a power in its province and the
leader of 'patriotic' aspirations. The magistrates affected nonchalance meanwhile, and escaped the boredom of inactivity by a round of balls and theatrical
performances.[46]

Nevertheless, the government's firmness seemed to be having some effect.
Already late in September it was rumoured that counsellor de Marbotin was at
the head of a small band of 'false brethren'[47] who were prepared to negotiate.
Half-way through the same month Brienne left for Paris to take up the post of
secretary for war. He was replaced as commander-in-chief by the comte de
Fumel, a local nobleman who was always personally popular with the parlement.
Perhaps the government hoped that his personal intimacy with the magistrates
might enable him to achieve some accommodation. At any rate, he went to
Libourne in the last days of October followed by the archbishop.[48] There does
not, despite rumours,[49] seem to have been any sort of military session on this
occasion, and Fumel was well received personally.[50] But he came away with no
concessions. All that resulted from his visit on a public level was a new set of
intransigent remonstrances.[51]

Fumel's mission was to deliver the edict of October, prolonging the second
twentieth and its surcharges until 1792. The remonstrances of 31 October did not
confine themselves to the question, hitherto paramount, of the provincial assemblies; they also surveyed and condemned the whole of the government's financial
policy and this latest development in particular. In 30 pages of invective they
attacked government waste and projects for increased taxation. Since Calonne's
proposed taxes had now been abandoned, they plausibly suggested, why not
abandon his provincial assemblies too? They were mere devices to give the
appearance of a fairer distribution of taxes, while maintaining all the reality of
arbitrary imposition. They defended, in legalistic detail, their own refusal to
register the June edict without seeing the complementary regulations, but capped
this with a new assertion: only the Estates-General had the authority to make
such a radical change in the constitution. Accordingly the parlement called for
the assembly of the Estates, and meanwhile declared that it would register nothing while it was in exile and its members bound by *lettres de cachet*.

It was a brave but dangerous course, for at this stage in affairs the parlement was very much alone. To refuse to register yet another law which the parlement of Paris had earlier agreed to, only isolated the Bordeaux magistrates still further. It was hard to see where this intransigence could lead, when matters seemed to be arranging themselves in Paris. Even in other provinces, where the edict was received with hostility, few parlements went so far as a blank refusal to register it.[52] What brought the position of the parlement back into the mainstream of events was the new quarrel between the government and the parlement of Paris which broke out in the royal session of 19 November. The forced registration of loans, and the arbitrary measures employed on those who had protested against them, swung Paris back into the ranks of the opposition, and reflected glory onto Bordeaux as the only parlement which had refused consistently to compromise with so feckless a government. The importance now assumed by the stand of the Bordeaux magistrates was attested by the unprecedented publicity which the government gave to its reply to the remonstrances of 31 October.

This reply was in the form of a letter from the Keeper of the Seals to the parlement, dated 29 November,[53] which was printed, widely distributed, and sold in the streets of Paris in December.[54] It was a good example of the techniques to which all sides in the constitutional disputes increasingly resorted during these months. Quite obviously it was written to be widely read, yet its tone towards the parlement could only reinforce the despotic impression the government had created. The finances were the king's affair and nobody else's; the parlement should not therefore pry into them. It was common knowledge that certain rich men of property in Bordeaux were taxed on a separate, privileged roll, and as a result, bore an unequal burden; this could not go on much longer. The Keeper of the Seals could have been referring to the separate capitation roll of the parlement,[55] and obviously the intention was to arouse popular suspicion. It was hypocrisy, the minister went on, to call so loudly for the Estates, since the king had already promised that they would meet by 1791 at the latest; and even more hypocritical was to blame the government for judicial inactivity, since the magistrates themselves had deliberately refused to judge. Only a return to their duties would end their exile and restore the king's benevolence.

The advocate Bernadau, whose political attitudes at least faithfully followed the mass, took a sour view of this reply: '*Timeo Danaos et dona ferentes*', he mused.

> S'ils ne connaissent pas l'état des finances, ils ont néanmoins le droit d'y regarder, comme citoyens et comme réprésentants du peuple. A la Cour, les connait-on bien? S'ils ont refusé d'enregistrer l'établissement des assemblées provinciales, que les autres parlements ont admis, l'expérience du passé et les reclamations actuelles des Cours trop obéissantes prouvent qu'ils ont eu raison.[56]

The letter in fact marked a renewal of governmental pressure on the parlement, now that the policy of allowing it to isolate itself had failed. In mid-November Fumel, acting perhaps on information he had received in Libourne at the beginning of the month, suggested to the government that new letters of *jussion* on the provincial assemblies might be fruitful. By the first week in December the ministry had accepted his suggestion.[57] He could have wished, he declared, that they had been more imperative in tone,[58] perhaps in order to give waverers more excuse for obedience. 'Il est certain', he added,

> que plusieurs Magistrats commencent à ressentir le désagrément de leur position et s'attiedisent dans leur resistance; l'union n'est plus entiere mais elle n'assure pas encore la pluralité des suffrages.

> Je connois deux opinions dans cette Compagnie. le plus grand nombre se tient rigoureusement à la lettre de leurs arrêtés, Ils y trouvent un obstacle invincible pour enregistrer quoi ce que soit [sic] à Libourne.

> Les autres croiroient donner au Roi une preuve de leur Soumission en enregistrant l'Edit des assemblées Provinciales d'après les promesses réitérées de leur adresser en son tems le Reglement définitif à quoi l'on ajouteroit quelques autres modifications qu'on massure etre peu importantes ... Cette derniere opinion pouvant etre agreable au Gouvernement, Je vais donner tous mes soins pour le faire adopter.

With this intention, on 17 December Fumel made his way to Libourne with the letters of *jussion*, and they were presented at an assembly of the chambers on the 21st. Attended by 80 magistrates, it lasted from 4 in the afternoon to 11 at night, and was marked by a lively debate in which the divisions within the company came to the surface. At the first round of opinion, 19 or 20 magistrates, led by the procurator-general, pronounced themselves for obedience[59]—registration of the edict subject to certain modifications. However, at the second round a number of them[60] lost their nerve and joined the majority for intransigence. The next day Fumel reported 'with the greatest pain' that he had not been able to secure obedience, despite the strenuous efforts and co-operation of the procurator-general.[61] An anonymous observer, however, declared that part of the failure was attributable to the fact that too much reliance had been placed on Dudon, whom his colleagues viewed with suspicion. Any attempt at conciliation either through his agency or that of the archbishop would achieve nothing. In any case, all approaches would be fruitless while the court remained at Libourne.[62] The court confirmed this by resolving once more not to register the edict of June without the accompanying regulations: 'Le parlement désire l'établissement des assemblées provinciales, et . . . il les désire dans les mêmes vuës qui animent le . . . Seigneur Roi, pour le bonheur des peuples; mais . . . les réglements, qui doivent former ces assemblées, peuvent seuls garantir que cet objet sera rempli'. A copy of this *arrêté*, together with a new set of remonstrances to refute the Keeper of the Seals's recent letter, was sent by Le Berthon to the government on Christmas Day.[63]

So the stalemate continued. The parlement ensured that its latest remonstrances were printed, and they were even widely distributed in Paris, in order to offset the effect of Lamoignon's letter.[64] It also subsidized the printing of a favourable pamphlet on its own presses,[65] and Le Berthon the younger even defended his company's honour in a duel with an officer of the Franche Comté cavalry regiment who had criticized the parlement.[66] Above all, the court made renewed efforts to induce the other local authorities to petition the government in its favour, and it took the opportunity of their New Year visits to make plain its views. The courts of aids at least had never ceased to press the case; it followed up its September protest with yet another in November, in which it proclaimed its intention to remonstrate in the parlement's favour.[67] These remonstrances appeared in print late in December.[68] On the strength of such professions, the parlement decided now to use the court of aids as its agent in Bordeaux to procure its recall. Remonstrances and legislative intransigence having failed to move the government, it seemed that the stalemate could only be broken by calling in new forces. Apart from the Estates-General, the only new force that might make any difference to the parlement's position was the *cent-trente*, which only met in times of emergency, and was convoked by the *jurats*. If it could once be assembled, it could declare that the exile of the parlement was contrary to the capitulation of 1451 and so to the privileges of the city. However, the *jurats'* initiative in such matters was limited. In their September letter of protest at the exile of the parlement, they had already hinted that there might be a case for convoking this assembly,[69] but they had not carried the matter further, since the minister of the province had forbidden them to do so.[70] Pressed by the advocates early in December to consider the idea, they wrote once more to the minister, but his response was the same.[71] The *jurats* in service at that time already had the reputation of tools of the ministry, having been arbitrarily continued in office without the election of new candidates in August 1787.[72] Such arguments, therefore, failed to impress the parlement. When the *jurats*, in full robes, came to Libourne to greet the parlement on the occasion of the New Year, their compliment was cut short by Le Berthon, who asked what they had done to bring the assembly of the *cent-trente* nearer. When they replied that they had done all in their power, and that their conscience was clear, he shortly suggested that they should consult their conscience again, and come back when they had something to report. All the other bodies paying their compliments were politely received.[73]

This was the signal for the court of aids to go into action, and throughout January it encouraged and welcomed deputations from the various courts, corporations, and companies of the city, pressing it to intercede with the government to allow the convocation of the *cent-trente*.[74] Among them were the seneschalcy, the money tribunal, the judges and consuls of the *bourse*, the university, and the corps of advocates. Thus fortified with a show of public demand, it invited the *jurats* of 21 January to come and discuss matters, at length officially ordering them to convoke the assembly.[75] The next day, the *jurats* formally decided, in view of the pressure from all sides, to assemble the city notables with a view to convoking the *cent-trente*. This looked like victory for the parlement and its protagonists, but of course it was unlikely that the government, to whom the *jurats* were legally responsible, would allow any such decision to take effect. Sure enough, on 26 January Fumel summoned the hapless city fathers and expressly forbade them to convoke either assembly.[76] The syndics of the advocates, who had done much to organize the movement for the *cent-trente*, were at the same time exiled from Bordeaux by *lettre de cachet*. It was even rumoured that if the court of aids attempted to ignore the clear manifestation of the government's intentions, Fumel had orders to dissolve it by force. All this stopped the new movement dead in its tracks.

Protests were unavailing. The end of January and the first days of February saw calls for the *cent-trente* from the cathedral chapter and the office of finances, and a bitter new set of remonstrances from the court of aids (30 January), in which it castigated the government for ignoring a patently popular demand.[77]

When, later in February, the Keeper of the Seals sent a haughty reply reminding the court that as a fiscal tribunal it had no business interfering in public affairs let alone inciting the city to revolt, the court simply published the letter and allowed it to speak for itself.[78] Such defiant gestures were small comfort either to the parlement or its supporters. The government was plainly in control, and plainly resolved not to concede anything until the parlement became more co-operative. The parlements of Pau, Grenoble, and Rennes, who interceded for their Gascon colleagues in remonstrances, were either ignored or told to mind their own business.[79] The parlement of Bordeaux itself, its strategy in ruins, had no alternative but to return to its remonstrances, swelling the stream that was now pouring in from all the courts of the kingdom.

Thus on 4 March it took up the theme of the *lettres de cachet*; not a new one, but one of peculiar relevance to current circumstances, when not only Fréteau, Sabatier, and the duc d'Orléans in Paris were suffering under them, but also the syndics of the Bordeaux advocates, and of course the magistrates themselves at Libourne.[80] The arguments against such arbitrary orders were familiar, but the parlement also took the opportunity to blame the government once again for all the ills of the province, from the cessation of justice to the refusal of the *cent-trente*. The court of aids added its voice to the chorus, rebutting the Keeper of the Seals's arguments regarding its competence.[81] Nothing, however, could disguise the complete stalemate to which matters had returned.

The degree of interest aroused by these events in Bordeaux is hard to assess,[82] but the prevalence of wild rumours is certain. An imminent *coup* against the parlement like Maupeou's was always being predicted; in mid-February Bernadau heard[83] that the government had planned to replace it with a commission of councillors of state and masters of requests, a plan only abandoned because the treasury could not afford the wages. Events were to prove this rumour at least prophetic. Meanwhile the government, aware of the divisions within the parlement and suspecting that the failure to secure a meeting of the *cent-trente* had aggravated them, made another attempt to win the court's submission. Early in March it submitted new reforming edicts, popular ones, which it would do the court's reputation no good to refuse to register. They included those for the redemption of the *corvées* and the grant of civil status to protestants. The gambit almost succeeded; the court refused registration, but by the narrow majority of 7 votes.[84] This division underlay the apparent firmness of an *arrêté* of 15 March, which declared that in future the court would not even discuss new laws sent to it, until it had had replies to its two latest sets of remonstrances.[85] Still, on 15 April it returned to the charge with yet another set of remonstrances, this time against the imprisonment of Catellan, advocate-general of the parlement of Toulouse, who had acted to forbid the collection of the prolonged twentieth after its forcible registration.[86] Arbitrary arrest was once more attacked, and crown lawyers declared to be the instruments not so much of arbitrary power as of the fundamental laws. They ended by declaring that only the Estates-General could remedy the accumulated grievances under which France was labouring. But by the time the government received the remonstrances it was planning another way out, recalling 1771 rather than 1614.

Rumours that a new *coup d'état* was in preparation had been common throughout the spring, and by the last week in April the government had firmly decided

on such a course.[87] Drastic measures were most effective when they came suddenly; but the example of 1771 had equally shown that some preparation was desirable, and in Bordeaux the archbishop was charged with sounding out possible
collaborators in any reform. He was particularly active among the advocates,
who he doubtless hoped would blame the parlement rather than the ministry for
the cessation of justice. In early May he was said to have a tentative list of members for a council to replace the parlement, even though most of the lawyers had
indignantly spurned his proposals.[88] By the end of the first week in May it was
clear that a national reform was in the offing. In Paris, the result had been the
ringing declaration of the fundamental laws of the kingdom on 3 May, followed
on the 6th by the arrest of its prime movers, d'Eprémesnil and Goislard.[89] In the
south-west a full realization of what was about to happen dawned in Toulouse
before Bordeaux, and the first alarm was given when the parlement of Toulouse
wrote to its colleagues of Bordeaux and Pau with news of its latest measures and
an implicit suggestion that they concert their action in the face of the imminent
threat.[90] On 5 May came confirmation that something extraordinary was about to
happen; Fumel was closeted all day with the intendants of Bordeaux, Limoges,
and Montauban. The government intended, so ran the rumour, to create four
superior councils in place of the parlement, to dissolve the court of aids and the
office of finances, and replace the *jurade* with a police lieutenant.[91] When this
news reached the parlement at Libourne the next day, it assembled at once and
passed an *arrêté* protesting in advance against any steps which might be taken
against it:[92]

> L'opposition des cours au systéme fiscal est le seul crime des magistrats, ...
> leurs representations respectueuses sont restées sans réponses, ... leur con-
> duite prescrite par l'honneur et le devoir, a été calomnié aux yeux de la
> nation . . .

Now, it seemed, even their right of registration was in danger; however,

> ... l'enregistrement dans les Cours represente le consentement de la nation
> ... si le souverain disposoit de l'enregistrement qui represente le consentem^t
> des peuples, il concentreroit en lui seul tous les pouvoirs; et rendroit illusoire
> le concours de la nation essentiel par la constitution de la monarchie . . .

These high functions could never be fulfilled if the magistrates were dismissed
and replaced by 'des hommes peu delicats, dévoués servilement au pouvoir
ministeriel, et . . . peu touchés de la gloire du Sgr Roi'. In any case, the court
finally declared, if its members were dispersed and not allowed to reassemble,
they would not cease to enjoy the status of magistrates, of which they could only
be deprived by due process of law. Obviously they were determined not to be
overcome as they had been 17 years before hand. Nor was this the only echo of
Maupeou. The preceding months had shown that some among them were prepared to compromise with authority, as in 1771. Therefore this *arrêté* also declared that:

> tous les magistrats composant lad. cour, ne p[euvent] sans violer leur ser-
> ment, se départir de ses engagemens pris unanimement, ni consentir sans
> prevarication, a aucune reduction de ses fonctions, ou remplacement quel-
> conque, sous quelque formation ou denomination que ce soit.

There had, of course, been a similar unanimous disclaimer in 1771, which half the magistrates subsequently ignored.[93] This one was couched in more careful terms and publicly printed too, to prevent similar defections this time.

On this same 6 May, the first presidents both of the parlement and the court of aids received orders to assemble their respective courts for military sessions on the 8th, the day fixed for the *coup* all over France. The court of aids spent the whole of the 7th in secret session to fix its attitude,[94] and the next day, when the marquis de Caupenne and the intendant of Limoges arrived at 8 in the morning, they found only the first president and the procurator-general there, all their colleagues having decided that they were under no specific orders to attend. The session began at 4 in the afternoon, after each magistrate had been summoned by a hurriedly drafted *lettre de cachet*.[95] Even then matters only got under way after the reading of an *arrêté* of the previous day which protested at the illegality of all that was about to happen. The sitting thus begun only ended at 5 in the afternoon of the next day. Meanwhile, Fumel and the intendant of Bordeaux had made their way to Libourne, where polite exhanges could not obscure the true nature of the occasion. The commandant and the intendant had to endure the reading of the *arrêté* of the 6th, since they had no orders to stop it, before they could begin. Then the procurator-general challenged the form of their commission, and after the registration of each edict they had to sit by while the court declared it illegal. The session, which saw the forced registration of 13 pieces of legislation,[96] began at 8 in the morning of the 8th and ended at 11 on the morning of the 9th. By that time the whole ground of the constitutional debate had been completely transformed.

The edicts fell into two groups. One was a collection of unfinished business, outstanding in some cases since June 1787. This included edicts for the freeing of the grain trade, the redemption of the *corvées*, the suppression of various customs duties, civil status for protestants, the prolongation of the second twentieth, and the establishment of provincial assemblies. All these measures had been casualties of the parlement's refusal to transact business during its exile. The other group, all dated May 1788, together constituted a radical reform of the judicial system, far more thoroughgoing than anything Maupeou had ever dreamed of. The plenary court, first announced at the restoration in 1774–75, was for the first time activated. As originally conceived,[97] its object was to try cases of strikes or mass resignations by the parlements. Now, however, it was accorded the sole right of registering or remonstrating upon laws of general effect; this meant all fiscal measures and the establishment of such institutions as the provincial assemblies. Parlements retained these rights in the case of measures applying solely to their own jurisdictions; this obviously was intended to diminish their power and prestige considerably. Of similar effect was the creation of the grand *baillages*, four of which were set up in the jurisdiction at Bordeaux, Condom, Dax, and Périgueux. They were to be a third-instance jurisdiction, with final cognizance of appeals up to the value of 30,000 l., thus depriving the parlement of the right to hear all but the most expensive cases. The corollary was that the parlement as stood was overstaffed; another edict therefore suppressed (although with compensation) all but 48 of the offices in the court, abolishing in the process the second chamber of inquests, that of requests, and even the presidencies in the remaining chamber of inquests.[98] The combined effect of these reforms would not have been to abolish the parlements, but their powers would have been so drastically pruned in both the political and judicial spheres that they would be no serious obstacle to the government in anything it might choose to do. There was no disguising these implications; the registration at the same time of a long-overdue edict reforming and humanizing criminal procedure failed to distract critical attention. At last 'despotism' stood unmasked; if it were not defeated now it never would be.

All over France, 'patriots' rallied behind the stricken parlements. All the military sessions throughout the kingdom had concluded with letters patent putting the parlements into vacation until the judicial reorganization was complete; at Bordeaux the same letter patent at last revoked the exile to Libourne. Such measures did not, however, prevent most of the parlements from protesting at the *coup*,[99] and in these protests they were supported by popular demonstrations whose sincerity and spontaneity was not open to doubt. On 9 May the parlement issued an *arrêt* protesting at all that had been done the previous day, pronouncing it null, illegal, and incapable of effect; but to this usual formula of protest it added a formal injunction to subordinate courts not to co-operate in the reforms, or recognize anything that had been forcibly registered on the 8th.[100] The court of aids protested the same day at the illegal registration of the same laws. The royal commissioners who had conducted this transcription were jeered as they left the palace, while the first president and procurator-general were acclaimed. The commissioners were disturbed all night by the noise of street demonstrations.[101] And these were nothing to the scenes which greeted Le Berthon on his return from Libourne on 10 June.

They would doubtless have equalled those of 1775 if the town had been warned. Even so, the news of his return spread rapidly and that evening large and festive crowds converged on his house in the rue du Mirail despite bad weather. The merchants of the Chartrons and the legal fraternity lit up their windows in celebration, and the rest of the town soon followed. The next day Le Berthon received visits, and in the evening several merchants arranged a popular festival in the rue du Mirail, with fireworks and fountains flowing with wine. Such receptions were the popular way of showing hostility to the ministry.[102] Behind the festivity lay a genuine concern lest the government's projects succeed, and the normal round of life was disrupted by cancellations as well as rejoicing. The *musée* expressed its concern by postponing its meetings during the crisis; the *basoche*, that large and sinister world of lawyers' clerks, cheer-leaders for the parlement, abandoned its annual Maytime festivities for 1788 in view of the serious turn of affairs.[103] Mob violence was feared. On 12 June, when the town lit up its windows in the parlement's honour for the second night in a week, gangs of 'patriotic' youths, hundreds strong, roamed the streets breaking windows which showed no lights.[104] The architect Laclotte warned Fumel in July that his workmen were declaring themselves ready to fight for the parlement and that this could bring thousands onto the streets.[105] The troops of the garrison were on the alert for weeks after the military sessions, as rumours of revolt and anarchy filled the air.[106] Public fears were not calmed by the complete cessation of justice throughout the judicial hierarchy, which produced dangerous overcrowding in the prisons, and encouraged rural brigandage.[107] A storm of pamphlets, some against but most vehemently for the parlement, gave further stimulus to public excitement, and the commandant's clumsy efforts to restrict publishing only incensed the 'patriots'.[108] The nobility itself was beginning to talk of meeting together to concert its action,[109] and in July the magistrates of the parlement were noticed holding secret assemblies under cover of night.[110] Most ominous of all, rumours began to circulate that officers in the army were talking of refusing to act for the government.[111] The edicts of May seemed abruptly to turn a constitutional crisis into a revolutionary situation, and in Guienne the parlement was the rallying-point for all the opponents of the government.

In the event, the May reforms never established themselves, as fear of later reprisals, inter-tribunal jealousy, and patriotic conviction all played their part in persuading the legal profession not to co-operate in them.[112] The lawyers of Bordeaux were very prominent in this movement. In Paris Dupaty, still technically a president in the parlement of Bordeaux, resigned from Lamoignon's commission for law reform in protest at the new measures.[113] In Bordeaux, the 48 magistrates to serve in the parlement were never designated, and the advocates also refused to have anything to do with the new order.[114] The law students of the university followed this example and wrote a letter to the Keeper of the Seals to inform him of their decision.[115] Attempts to set up the grand *baillage* of Bordeaux likewise foundered upon the refusal of lawyers to co-operate. The seneschalcy court, scheduled itself to be promoted to this new status, refused to register the May edicts; on 29 May the intendant conducted a forced registration; and after the session was over the court passed a formal protestation against all that had happened.[116] It had already, on 15 May, unanimously declared that none of its members would serve in a grand *baillage*. Soon afterwards the lieutenant-general Laroze, who clearly led his company in its militancy, was deprived of the royal pensions which he enjoyed.[117] The intendant subsequently made a month's tour of the generality to raise support for the reforms and recruit personnel, but spent much of his time conducting forced registrations.[118] Not all the lower courts were recalcitrant, especially those which thought they stood to gain prestige over old local rivals by promotion to the status of grand *baillage*, like the seneschalcies of Périgueux, Condom, and Dax.[119] That majority which were not so promoted showed far less enthusiasm, and some, like the *présidial* of Brive, put up a lively resistance.[120] So long as the future was uncertain there could be no confidence in the permanency of the new order; and men were accordingly reluctant to commit themselves to it, even if they believed in its intrinsic merits, as large numbers clearly did not.

Comparisons with Maupeou were obvious, and Dudon agreed that the new reforms dealt the parlement a far more severe blow than Maupeou's.[121] But as in 1771 what happened in the Bordelais was of little importance in dictating events. For all the rumours of mob violence and talk of mutiny among the nobility and the garrison, it was not local pressure which brought about the withdrawal of the reforms. It was the fall of Brienne and Lamoignon, and the return to power of Necker. Already early in August the ministry attempted to reanimate the state's collapsing credit by suspending the newly-created plenary court until the meeting of the Estates-General, now definitely fixed for 1 May 1789.[122] But credit did not revive, and by the middle of August the payment of the state's debts in money had to be abandoned. There was nothing left but to recall the one man whose personal credit remained boundless—Necker. Brienne was forced to resign, and his fall was inevitably followed by that of Lamoignon. The fall of ministers meant nothing if it did not also entail the abandonment of their policies, and Necker considered a reversal essential if order and stability were to be restored. Thus the declaration of 23 September, which brought forward the meeting of the Estates-General, also announced the abandonment of the May reforms and the complete reintegration of the parlements.[123]

The news of Necker's recall and the fall of Brienne arrived in Bordeaux on 29 August, and that night the mercantile community lit up its windows in celebration.[124] The next night, illumination was general and there were celebrations throughout the city.[125] It was not, however, until 12 October that the declaration of 6 October which re-established the parlement reached Bordeaux and was delivered to the procurator-general.[126] The session for its registration was deferred several times owing to the reappearance, now the emergency was over, of the old factious spirit among the magistrates. At preliminary unofficial meetings there was talk of excluding Dudon and several other known friends to authority from the honours which the magistrates felt sure of receiving when sessions were resumed. Pichard, Bernadau improbably heard, was attempting to postpone the session so that Le Berthon and Dudon would have left for the second Assembly of Notables, leaving him to preside at the triumph.[127] However, all these manoeuvres came to nothing, and on 20 October the court's triumphal return eventually took place.

It was the parlement's last great public ovation, comparable in scale to that of 1775.[128] The news became known only on the 19th, which precluded elaborate preparations, but there were fireworks on that evening and the *jurats* offered those magistrates who were returning from the country for the occasion the use of the *maison navale*—the civic state barge, used only for monarchs, princes, and governors—for crossing the Garonne. On the morning of the 20th Le Berthon awoke to find his house decorated with laurels, and a great crowd in the street outside. His coach, too, had been decorated, and it trundled slowly towards the palace through festooned streets lined with cheering crowds, preceded by a military band. The whole procession was repeatedly stopped by deputations, and arrived late at the palace, where an immense crowd had already watched each magistrate arrive to the sound of cheering and church bells. Inside, the galleries were filled by eminent personages from the city and farther afield. What they witnessed was a largely ceremonial occasion, as one after another the courts and companies of the city came to pay their compliments to the restored 'senate'. After the sitting was over, jubilant crowds unhitched the horses from Le Berthon's coach, and dragged the tearful first president back to his house in triumph.

> Illustre LEBERTHON, quel Français mieux que toi,
> A constamment servi sa Patrie et son Roi?
> Accepte de nos coeurs la Couronne civique,
> Tribut que nous devons à ton âme heroïque.

So ran a poem commemorating the occasion.[129] That night there were fireworks, citizens danced in the streets till dawn, and the late ministers and those who had collaborated with them were burned in effigy. The next day there were similar scenes, and in the evening Le Berthon's name was written across the sky in fireworks. At the theatre, there was patriotic applause as the company gave *Henri IV aux Champs Elysées.* The 22nd was marked by a celebratory sitting of the restored court of aids and a *Te deum* at the cathedral. And on 24 October a week of festivities was rounded off with a solemn session of the parlement's vacation chamber, at which the magistrates proudly declared that they had no need of being reestablished, since in law they had never been dismissed. All legal proceedings and all oaths taken since the May edicts were declared null. Then, having established its own position, the parlement formally promulgated the royal declaration to convoke the Estates-General.[130]

It was appropriate that the two should be linked. Ever since the summer of 1787 the parlements had increasingly attached their own fate to that of the proposal for the Estates-General. And, just as the *coup d'état* of May 1788 had been intended to avoid the Estates by eliminating the opposition of the parlements, so its reversal brought not only the return of the parlements, but the promise of an early meeting of the Estates. In the euphoria of their restoration, the magistrates hardly thought of the host of new questions which these dispositions raised. They only knew that despotism had been checked, that the parlements, symbols of constitutional government, had survived, and that they and everything else were now to be guaranteed by the Estates-General. But they seem to have had no more idea at this stage than a year beforehand what exactly the Estates were to do. These questions were to dominate the months to come.

Meanwhile, it looked like the end of the crisis, one in which the parlement of Bordeaux had been distinguished for its seemingly inflexible opposition to the machinations of 'despotism'. In this cause it had suffered harassment and exile, and won the sympathy and support of more than its fellow-provincials in doing so. Nevertheless, its concrete achievement remained limited; it prevented the functioning of the provincial assemblies in its jurisdiction, and it deterred a certain number of subordinate lawyers from co-operating in the Lamoignon reforms. It did not, unlike the parlement of Grenoble, achieve its goal of provincial estates for Guienne; and it never, on its own, forced the withdrawal or modification of a single law. Nor was there anything distinctive about its fate in May 1788. It was a parlement, so it was remodelled. Nothing suggested that it had caused the government extraordinary trouble or forced it to modify its policies. Despite the national prominence gained by the exile to Libourne, therefore, the parlement's only distinctive contribution to the crisis was a local one.

But here there can be little doubt of its importance. In Bordeaux, it was a symbol and rallying-point for 'patriotic' convictions, and there was little to suggest that future patriots were already making reservations about the mettle of their champions. Undoubtedly the conduct of the parlement sharpened political consciousness in the city and throughout the province, and its treatment at the hands of the government brought national problems into local focus. In this sense, Bordeaux and Guienne were led into the Revolution by their parlement, and in the celebrations of October 1788 they paid homage to this leadership. But the end of the constitutional crisis raised more problems and more passions than it settled. In the deeper crisis which followed, the parlement was to find itself rapidly eclipsed.

NOTES

1. See Bernadau, *Annales de Bordeaux*, 255, 21 June 1786 for measures against prostitutes; BVBx MS 713 (V), 'Tablettes' of Bernadau, 28–31, 18 April 1787, for a lengthy entry on the parlement's new-found civic zeal; AD C3730 contains an *arrêt* of 21 March against smallpox inoculation; see also *Jefferson Papers*, XI, 491–500, for the affair of Thomas Barclay, an American imprisoned for debt.
2. Bachaumont, XXXIV, 172, 21 Feb. 1787.
3. Bernadau, 'Tablettes' (henceforth to be referred to simply as 'Bernadau'), 50, 22 June 1787. See also P. Chevallier (ed.), *Journal de l'Assemblée des Notables de 1787* (Paris, 1960), 96.
4. ibid., 45, for an intervention by Le Berthon.
5. Egret, *La Pré-Révolution*, 23.
6. See below, pp. 265–9.
7. Louis-Marie-Athanase de Loménie, comte de Brienne (1730–94), younger brother of cardinal Loménie de Brienne. Colonel, regiment d'Artois, 1747; camp-marshal, 1762; commander-in-chief in Guienne, Aug.–Oct. 1787; secretary for war, 1787–88; executed during the Terror.
8. The comte de Fumel had performed the functions of this office in the interim, but he had never been formally invested with it.
9. Bernadau, 56–7, 60, 19 and 29 July 1787.
10. On the provincial assemblies, see Léonce de Lavergne, *Les Assemblées provinciales sous Louis XVI* (Paris, 1879), and P. Renouvin, *Les Assemblées provinciales de 1787* (Paris, 1921); also Egret, *La Pré-Révolution*, 108–22.
11. Egret, op. cit., 23; A. Goodwin, 'Calonne, the assembly of French Notables and the "révolte nobiliaire" of 1788', *English Historical Review*, LXI (1946), 343–4.
12. Egret, op. cit., 215.
13. Copy of this letter in AN H1596.
14. ibid.; see Lhéritier, *La Révolution à Bordeaux*, I, 70–1.
15. AN H1596, Lamoignon to Villedeuil, 2 Aug. 1787; Lhéritier, loc. cit., I, 71.
16. AN H1605, pp. 134ff., dated 18 July 1787; article 14 is on p. 142.
17. AN H1596, Dudon to de Roulhac, 4 Aug. 1787 (copy).
18. ibid., duc d'Ayen to Villedeuil, 6 Aug. 1787.
19. ibid., same to same, 10 Aug. 1787.
20. ibid., Champion de Cicé to Villedeuil, 10 Aug. 1787.
21. ibid., Meulan d'Ablois to Villedeuil, 10 Aug. 1787.
22. ibid., Villedeuil to d'Ayen, 12 Aug. 1787 (draft).
23. ibid., Villedeuil to Brienne, 12 Aug. 1787 (draft).
24. ibid., Villedeuil to Champion de Cicé, 16 Aug. 1787; Bachaumont, XXXV, 399, 24 Aug. 1787; Lhéritier, op. cit., 72.
25. AM MS 135³ no. 75, Fauquier's *lettre de cachet*; Lhéritier, loc. cit., 72–3; Boscheron des Portes, op. cit., II, 359–60.
26. Bachaumont, XXXIV, 434–5, 2 Sept. 1787; Bernadau, 68, 19 Aug. 1787; copy in AM Fonds Delpit 167.
27. Egret, op. cit., 173.
28. J. Plantadis, *L'Agitation autonomiste de Guienne et le mouvement fédéraliste des Girondins en Limousin, 1787–1793* (Brive, 1910) (originally a series of articles in *Bulletin de la société des lettres, sciences et arts de la Corrèze*, 1908–10), 11.
29. Bernadau, 74, 2 Sept. 1787.
30. Lhéritier, op. cit., 74.
31. Bernadau, 73, 31 Aug. 1787; AM MS 135³, no. 76, Fauquier's *lettre de cachet*, 28 Aug. 1787.
32. Bernadau, 73–5, 2 and 3 Sept. 1787.
33. Lhéritier, op. cit., 76.
34. AD 8J 136 (Fonds Bigot); Lhéritier, loc. cit., 76–7.
35. See above, pp. 227–8.
36. AM MS 135³, nos. 77 and 78; AD IB 56.
37. Lhéritier, op. cit., 75.

38. ibid.; see also abbé O'Reilly, *Histoire complète de Bordeaux* (2nd ed., Paris, 1863), III, 432–7, and Bernadau, 76, 15 Sept. 1787.
39. Egret, op. cit., 178–81.
40. *Arrêtés* of 24 Sept. and 25 Oct. 1787; Lhéritier, loc. cit., 75; Egret, op. cit., 239.
41. Bernadau, 96, 27 Oct. 1787.
42. AD C4259, registers of the chamber of commerce, 22 Nov. 1787.
43. Lhéritier, op. cit., 83–4.
44. *Jefferson Papers*, XII, 117, Bondfield to Jefferson, 11 Sept. 1787.
45. AN H1605, report of the *procureurs-syndics* of the province, 1788.
46. Bernadau, 94–5, 24 Oct. 1787.
47. ibid., 84, 25 Sept. 1787.
48. ibid., 97, 31 Oct. 1787.
49. Bernadau, 99, 4 Nov. 1787, speaks of a *lit de justice* and a packet of orders from Versailles, but there is nothing on the registers of the court around this date under Fumel's signature. Clearly his mission was provoking enough, however, to give rise to the remonstrances of 31 Oct.
50. Bernadau, loc. cit.
51. Widely printed and distributed: copies in AN H1596 and K708, no. 83. Heads in BVBx MS 1696, IV, pièce 105. See also Lhéritier, op. cit., 77–8. The author of these remonstrances was the eloquent counsellor Bouquier, who was often called upon to draft the court's declarations in times of crisis. Bernadau, 100, 6 Nov. 1787.
52. Egret, op. cit., 223–36.
53. The most accessible text is in L. Gallois (ed.), *Réimpression de l'ancien Moniteur, . . . Mai 1789–Novembre 1799* (Paris, 1840–45), I, 355.
54. Lhéritier, op. cit., 79, n. 2.
55. See above, p. 59.
56. Bernadau, 118, 15 Dec. 1787.
57. Lhéritier, op. cit., 80, n. 1.
58. AN H1596, Fumel to Breteuil, 14 Dec. 1787.
59. There are several accounts of this session: AN H1596, Fumel to Breteuil, 22 Dec. 1787; AN 4 AP 189 (Loménie de Brienne papers), no. 123, an anon. account, seemingly addressed to the comte de Brienne, 25 Dec. 1787; Bernadau, 123, 24 Dec. 1787. The anon. account gives 20 for obedience; Bernadau gives 16. The figure 19 comes from Boscheron des Portes, op. cit., II, 362, where no source is cited.
60. Six, says the anon. account, which would leave 14. Bernadau's 16 may refer to the second rather than the first round.
61. AN H1596.
62. Anon. account, cited above, n. 59.
63. AN H1596, letter of Le Berthon, with enclosures, 25 Dec. 1787; ibid., for the original MS of the remonstrances, 21 Dec. 1787. Other copies in AN K708, no. 77 and AD 8J 136 (Fonds Bigot).
64. Lhéritier, op. cit., 80.
65. Bernadau, 142, 9 Jan. 1788. The pamphlet, entitled *Entretien d'un militaire et d'un simple citoyen, sur les remontrances du parlement de Bordeaux, du 31 Octobre 1787*, is analysed in Lhéritier, op. cit., 81–3.
66. Bernadau, 123, 24 Dec. 1787.
67. ibid., 105, 19 Nov. 1787.
68. ibid., 128–9, 29 Dec. 1787.
69. See above, p. 270.
70. Lhéritier, op. cit., 84.
71. ibid.
72. ibid., 150–3.
73. Bernadau, 135, 3–5 Jan. 1788.
74. ibid., 21 Jan. 1788.
75. Lhéritier, op. cit., 86.
76. ibid., 87. He also gave them a *lettre de cachet*, dated 25 Jan., to the same effect.
77. Quoted ibid., 88–9.
78. Bernadau, 180–1, 2 March 1788.

79. ibid., 144, 13 Jan. 1788, and 130, 31 Dec. 1787; Lhéritier, op. cit., 89; Egret, *Parlement de Dauphiné*, II, 194.
80. Copies in AN K708 and AD 8J 136.
81. Lhéritier, loc. cit., 89.
82. Egret, *La Pré-Révolution*, 222, 224, suggests that the exile of the parlement caused little stir because Bordeaux was a commercial town. Quite apart from the *non sequitur* here, the statement is supported by no positive evidence, and undermined at least by the report of Bondfield, cited above, p. 271, the registers of the chamber of commerce, and much evidence from Bernadau.
83. Bernadau, 14 Feb. 1788.
84. ibid., 187, 13 March 1788.
85. ibid., 189, 21 March 1788; copy of the *arrêté* in AN K708.
86. Egret, *La Pré-Révolution*, 235, 239 n. 2; copies of the remonstrances in AN K708 and AD 8J 136; comment in Bernadau, 207, 22 April 1788, where authorship is attributed to counsellor de Raignac.
87. Egret, op. cit., 246-7.
88. Bernadau, 209-10, 29 April and 2 May 1788.
89. Egret, op. cit., 251.
90. Bernadau, 213, 5 May 1788.
91. ibid., 213, 6 May 1788.
92. MS copy in BPR Le Paige 923; partially quoted in Lhéritier, op. cit., 90-1.
93. See above, p. 145.
94. Bernadau, 214, 8 May 1788.
95. ibid.
96. These transcriptions are to be found in AD IB 56 and 58; the fullest account of the session is in Bernadau, 216, 9 May 1788. The reforming edicts, registered everywhere, are to be found in Isambert, Jourdan, Crusy, *Recueil générale*, XXIX, 534-53, 560-7.
97. See above, p. 163.
98. Presidents *à mortier* were to perform these functions in the future.
99. Egret, *La Pré-Révolution*, 257-60. Technically, the parlement's protest seemed to imply that the ending of the exile was illegal too. However, the magistrates took the line that since the exile itself was illegal, any measure revoking it was simply superfluous. BPR Le Paige 923, no. 74, MS note by Le Paige.
100. Lhéritier, op. cit., 93-4.
101. Bernadau, 218, 9 May 1788.
102. ibid., 231-4, 10-14 June 1788; 244, 1 July; 246, 2 July 1788; 214, 7 May 1788; also Vatel, *Vergniaud*, I, 126, Vergniaud to Allaud, 14 May 1788.
103. ibid., 246, 4 July 1788.
104. ibid., 233, 12 June 1788; Vatel, loc. cit. above, n. 102.
105. Bernaudau, 251, 10 July 1788.
106. ibid., 234, 14 June 1788.
107. ibid., 249, 8 July, and 251, 9 July 1788.
108. ibid., 239, 23 June 1788.
109. ibid., 254, 13 July 1788.
110. ibid., 267, 24 July 1788.
111. ibid., 272, 31 July 1788; Egret, op. cit., 263-5.
112. ibid., 281-90.
113. Lescure, *Correspondance secrète*, II, 258, 22 May 1788.
114. Vatel, loc. cit. above, no. 102; Egret, loc. cit., 282.
115. Bernadau, 228, 4 June 1788; copy of this letter, dated 22 July 1788, in BPR Le Paige 923, no. 76.
116. Bernadau, 226, 29 May 1788.
117. AN B III 34, p. 987, Laroze to Keeper of the Seals, 14 April 1789; Lhéritier, op. cit., 95.
118. Bernadau, 243, 30 June 1788.
119. Egret, op. cit., 289.
120. Bernadau, 271, 30 July 1788.
121. ibid., 287, 16 Aug. 1788.

122. Egret, op. cit., 313.
123. ibid., 319–20.
124. Bernadau, 300, 29 Aug. 1788.
125. ibid., 303, 31 Aug. 1788; Lhéritier, op. cit., 99.
126. Bernadau, 352, 13 Oct. 1788.
127. Bernadau, 358–9, 19 Oct. 1788.
128. ibid., 359–64, 20 Oct. 1788, is one account; see also AD 8J 136 (Fonds Bigot), *Lettre secrète sur ce qui s'est passé à Bordeaux à la rentrée du parlement, les 19, 20, 21, 22, & 25 octobre 1788*; also *Récit de ce qui s'est passé à Bordeaux lors de la reprise des fonctions du parlement et de la cour des aides des 20, 21, 22, et 23 octobre 1788*, analysed and paraphrased in Lhéritier, op. cit., 100–3.
129. M. J. Berliquet, *La Nation à ses magistrats, sur la révolution du 8 mai 1788: ... et sur la rentrée des cours souveraines dans le cours du mois d'octobre suivant* (Bordeaux, 1788). These lines are also reproduced on a portrait of Le Berthon, specially printed to commemorate the occasion.
130. Bernadau, 370, 24 Oct. 1788.

CHAPTER 18

Revolution II:
The Eclipse of the Parlement

Although 'despotism' seemed in the autumn of 1788 to be in retreat on most fronts, there was one on which it seemed as aggressive as ever. This was municipal government. The *jurade* of Bordeaux had been the tool of the government for most of the century; but the Bordelais, even though they had lost the substance of control over their own city, cherished its remaining appearances. The most obvious of these was the annual August ceremony of election by the 24 city notables of nine candidates for the three vacant places in the *jurade*. There was an outcry whenever these procedures were ignored, as for instance in 1781 when the younger Dudon was prolonged in office;[1] we may guess therefore that, if the fate of the parlement had not absorbed everybody's attention, the protests would have been even louder when in August 1787 the government ignored the election and simply prolonged the term of office of all the serving *jurats*.[2] Their subservience was only emphasized by the ease with which the government crushed the campaign for the convocation of the *cent-trente* the following winter;[3] and the next summer it did not even allow the elections. It filled vacancies caused by death, replaced one *jurat* and continued two others, by simple act of authority.[4] When two of those nominated excused themselves, the government attempted in September to re-model the *jurade* yet again, but encountered another set of refusals. It was a clear sign of the popular discredit into which municipal office had fallen during the crisis. Necker authorized new elections, but these could not take place until the parlement reassembled to depute its customary two commissioners to observe the elections.[5] So for the moment the old *jurats* remained in office, and it was they who brought the compliments of the city to the restored parlement in the ceremony of 20 October. Their appearance alone drew no applause: but Le Berthon's frigid reception of them received a great ovation. They hoped by their conduct, they declared, to deserve the future protection and benevolence of the court. Le Berthon retorted that the parlement was the surest guardian of the city's rights, and would only accord its protection and benevolence to those who shared the same concern. Clearly the court had not forgiven the city fathers for their subservience to the ministry over the previous year. The parlement, never reluctant to interfere in municipal affairs, was now prepared to continue the struggle against despotism at that level.

Aggrieved members of the municipal hierarchy were quick to respond to the first president's declaration. On 23 October the notables, representing the three orders of the city (nobles, advocates, and merchants), led by the brother of president de Lancre, lodged a formal protest against the appointment over the previous year of certain executive officers by *lettre de cachet*, notably the town clerk, Lamontaigne, brother of the counsellor.[6] The parlement's response was to make new elections impossible by refusing to send commissioners to observe them until their freedom was guaranteed; and to order the *jurats* to submit their registers to the court for examination.[7] The *jurats* retorted that they were not obliged to show their registers to anybody; and soon afterwards Lamontaigne left Bordeaux in great secrecy to put their case to the ministry.[8] The result of his mission was new orders to the *jurats* not to produce their registers, variously rumoured to be an *arrêt* of the council which the *jurade* could not notify to the parlement for lack of a willing process-server,[9] or a simple ministerial letter.[10] Either way, it was not easy to demonstrate the orders to the parlement, and the magistrates remained convinced that the *jurats* were prevaricating. No representatives of the municipality appeared at the Martinmas commencement,[11] and while the parlement meditated its next step, its more extreme members stirred up public debate by irregular methods. Le Berthon the younger went so far as to produce, with the help of an amanuensis, a pamphlet attacking the city fathers;[12] and it is certain that such attacks were well received by a public which had lost all faith in the *jurade* as a representative of its interests. Equally, however, the parlement would have to show itself effective in the measures it took to coerce the *jurade*, if it was not itself to lose public confidence as a defender of local interests. Already on 10 November the notables had remonstrated with the king, rather than renew their complaint to the parlement, at the continued paralysis in municipal life.[13] The only remedy, they declared, lay in a return to the ancient constitution of the city through the convocation of the *cent-trente*.

The *cent-trente* was an assembly for emergencies. Made up of deputies from most of the companies and corporate bodies of the city, it existed to be convoked only when the rights and privileges of the city were in peril; thus the call for it had only arisen in recent times during the persecution of the mayor by Richelieu,[14] and during the exile of the parlement. The subordination of the *jurats* to the government was obviously a comparable crisis; the problem was that the *cent-trente* could only meet on the summons of the *jurade*. The only body outside the government which felt itself to have the authority to force the *jurats* to act was the parlement. Thus on 15 November, tacitly abandoning its demand to inspect the registers, the court changed tack completely and issued an *arrêt* ordering the *jurade* within three days to assemble the notables with a view to convoking the *cent-trente*.[15] This *arrêt* was issued on the conclusions of Dudon the younger, himself an ex-*jurat*, who observed that there was no part of the city constitution over which the parlement did not have the right and duty of surveillance. It was a legalistic point, concerned with the limits of jurisdictions. As such it showed that the parlement's idea of the *cent-trente* was very much the traditional one, of an emergency assembly whose functions ceased with the emergency. The point at issue remained the freedom of elections to the *jurade*. There is no evidence that the magistrates saw in the *cent-trente* the embryo or forerunner of a permanent representative government for the city. But in the new atmosphere of the autumn of 1788, this was precisely the prospect which appealed increasingly to the third estate who would dominate it, and in placing itself at the head of the campaign for the *cent-trente*, the parlement was unwittingly contributing to the emergence of forces which would exclude it from much of its influence in municipal affairs.

To the *arrêt* of 15 November the *jurats* at once responded that a *lettre de cachet* of 25 January[16] forbade them to convoke the *cent-trente* without ministerial orders. However, they wrote at the same time to Versailles to plead for just such orders to end their misery.[17] On 21 November the parlement declared the *lettre de cachet* of 25 January illegal, and renewed its orders of the 15th.[18] Soon afterwards the ministerial reply to the *jurats'* request, dated 19 November, ordered them to submit their registers to the scrutiny of the parlement whenever the court required it—an apparent change of policy humiliating for the *jurats*. More important still, the minister authorized them to convoke the *cent-trente*.[19] This authorization, although granted in response to their request, was also humiliating in its way, since any convocation would appear to be in obedience to the parlement's orders, even though it was not. There followed, accordingly, an elaborate series of manoeuvres by the *jurats* to convoke the assembly without formally notifying the parlement and so avoiding the appearance of compliance with its orders. A formal meeting of the 24 notables took place on 25 November, and it convoked the *cent-trente* for 2 December. On 30 November the *jurats* received *lettres de cachet* dated the 23rd, revoking those of 25 January which had forbidden them to convoke the *cent-trente*. On 2 December, the day of the assembly itself, the parlement seized the last word by promulgating a hurried *arrêt* to authorize the assembly, and the session only opened with the arrival of the court's two commissioners.[20]

It was a victory like most of the others claimed by the parlement—not the result, except in the most indirect way, of any of its initiatives. It is not clear why the government suddenly decided to authorize the *cent-trente* to meet, but without this authorization, the parlement certainly could not have forced the *jurats'* hand. Perhaps the government saw in this apparent concession an opportunity to rob the parlement of public attention. Whatever the intention, that was certainly the result. The parlement was poorly represented on the *cent-trente*, an assembly dominated by merchants and lawyers of the third estate.[21] Yet the *cent-trente* at once set about inquiring into the conduct of the city government and the policies of the *jurade* over the preceding years, matters hitherto the prerogative of the parlement alone. When in January and February 1789 the shortage of food came to the parlement's attention, it no longer as formerly summoned the *jurats* and ordered them to take the matter in hand; the procurator-general went before the *cent-trente* and offered his co-operation.[22] The coincidence of the first sittings of the new assembly with the usual midwinter lull in the business of the parlement also helped to distract public attention from the court which had so recently been its focus. And when in February 1789, after almost three months of investigations and inquiries, the *cent-trente* proceeded without authorization to elect new candidates for the *jurade*, and had their action quashed by the government, the parlement did not intervene and was not asked to do so. The government's action at one blow nullified most of the gains made since October 1788, but by this time those with grievances could afford to wait. The elections to the Estates-General were under way and they, it was expected, would provide a universal remedy.[23]

Faith in the Estates-General had not always been as absolute or all-embracing as it was in the spring of 1789. Nowhere was it less than in the ranks of the parlement. The problems which most preoccupied it were local ones and so were the first remedies to occur to it. Thus it had propounded the suggestion of provincial estates in 1779, and had based its resistance to Brienne's provincial assemblies upon the argument that estates were a far more desirable form of representative government at provincial level. Even though these events were eclipsed in the public mind by the *coup* of May 1788, the nature of this climax only underlined the need for a new form of government.

The obvious innovation at the local level remained provincial estates, and the nobility of Bordeaux took over this idea from the parlement to make it one of the key points of its protest against the May *coup*. This protest originated soon after the *coup* itself, and was ready by 25 June to be circulated for signatures.[24] After two months it was eventually sent, on 27 August 1788, to various members of the government and the royal family. Even though events had already rendered much of it out of date by the time it arrived, it was a clear expression of the distaste and suspicion felt by the nobility of Guienne towards the government; and more important, it propounded the nobility's solution to the state's problems in three main points. First came the restoration of the parlements:

> Ces Corps *dont les racines touchent au fondement de la Monarchie* sont par leur masse, par leur rang, la fortune et la consistance des Magistrats qui les composent à l'abri de toute séduction, de toute impression étrangère à la Justice . . .

Second came the meeting of the Estates-General. Even so, their power was not to be unlimited. They were to share the government of France with provincial estates, the third proposal. No doubt this idea was given added point at the last minute by the arrival of the news, on 23 June,[25] of the assembling of deputies in Dauphiné to deliberate on the rights of the province, who subsequently transformed themselves into estates. But it had its local roots in the public pronouncements of the parlement, and it is surely less than fanciful to see the encouragement of the parlement behind the protest and its proposals, even though it was drafted, according to Bernadau, by the advocate Lumière.[26] Of course the parlement's hand would be hidden; a protest in the court's favour needed to look spontaneous, and out of its 390 signatures only 15 can be attributed certainly to members of the parlement, with a handful more uncertain. But the Bordelais nobility was small and very closely knit. Amongst the signatories were a host of fathers, brothers, sons, and distant relatives of magistrates. In any case the sentiments could only flatter the court. The Lamoignon *coup*, therefore, had united the local nobility behind one of the parlement's most long-cherished projects.

Nor did this movement lose momentum with the collapse and reversal of the reforms. Throughout the autumn various pamphleteers attempted to show that Guienne had once enjoyed estates, and ought to again. Lumière's *Mémoire*, with all its signatures, was printed and published. The same author produced, in three instalments over the winter, an erudite-sounding series of *Recherches sur le Droit*

Public et les Privilèges de la Province et des principales villes de la Guienne,[27] in which he attempted to show that the province had had its own estates before French rule, and that since the capitulation of 1451 had assured the province the enjoyment of all its rights, privileges, and franchises, the estates must be included and should be restored. Of course these 'researches', if not spurious, were at least tendentious and based on scanty and ambiguous evidence. The real arguments for local estates were more practical, and were set out by the noble journalist Gaufreteau in his *Projet de Restauration des Etats de Guienne*.[28] This project envisaged an 'estates-general of Guienne' representing the seneschalcies of Bordeaux, Libourne, Bazas, Castelmoron, Casteljaloux, Agen, Condom, Nérac, Mont-de-Marsan, Périgueux, Bergerac, Sarlat, St-Séver, Bayonne and Labourt, Dax, Tartas, Limoges, Tulle, Brive, Uzerche, St-Yrieux, Martel, Angoumois, and Saintonge. This, with the exception of the Angoumois, was an area curiously coterminous with the jurisdiction of the parlement. It was supposed to represent the area of the old English-ruled duchy of Guienne, but obviously the mere size of the area was the most important thing—size equalled strength in the face of the government. The estates were to meet annually and be composed of land-owners. They were to be made up of 80 deputies of the clergy, 160 deputies of the nobility, and 240 deputies of the third estate, deliberating and voting by order. Only residents of the province, not employed by the government, and not holding office at Court, were to be eligible. The estates would not grant taxes; that pre-rogative was reserved to the Estates-General. However, they would have some right to bargain over them, and complete control over their distribution and collection. Indeed, they were to supervise all local administration and public works, and they might remonstrate with the government to safeguard the 'maintien des droits & privilèges de la Guienne, de chaque Ordre, de chaque ville, de chaque Citoyen en particulier & principalement aux prérogatives & privilèges des tribunaux'.

The project, whose author admitted openly to inspiration by the example of Dauphiné, was similar to many mooted throughout the *pays d'élections* in the later months of 1788. They were usually sponsored by the nobility; and they usually skated over the question of the proportions in which the three orders were to be represented in order to emphasize that the estates' first purpose must be to present a strong face to the government. Their effect would have been to make France into a federation of large, semi-autonomous provinces, each governed, as *pays d'états* like Languedoc already were governed, by estates under the domina-tion of local landowners and above all noblemen.

As schemes for curbing 'despotism', such proposals had much to commend them and they were exhaustively discussed during these months. By the end of August, despite prohibitions, the nobility of Bordeaux was meeting together at night to discuss the promotion of such a scheme.[29] On 11 September they resolved to make contact with the nobility of the various districts which they believed constituted the ancient duchy of Guienne, with a view to concerting action on public affairs.[30] These attempts met with some success, and on 10 October the nobility of 'Guienne, Gascogne & Périgord' dispatched a joint letter to Necker, congratulating him on his return to office, and expressing the hope that he would permit the 're-establishment of their ancient estates'.[31] Through-out October the correspondence continued, and notable among those active in its conduct was J. de Gombault de Rasac, knight of honour at the parlement, friend and neighbour of Le Berthon.[32] His participation suggests once again that the parlement was more closely involved in the movement than might at first appear, and on 13 November, the day after the Martinmas commencement, the magistrates came into the open by admitting the nobility to sit alongside them in a formal joint session. On this occasion, the younger brother of president de Casaux, in the name of his brother nobles, asked the court to take note and custody of all the order's deliberations since May.[33] Pichard, presiding, replied that the court would be delighted to do so. Since most of these deliberations had been in favour of provincial estates, the parlement thus threw its authority solidly behind the nobility's campaign, and the next day it emphasized its support by hearing a memorandum in favour of them.[34] A few days later Gaufreteau's project appeared and the nobility, secure in the parlement's backing, invited the other two orders to meet with them in the Church of the Jacobins to discuss it.

This meeting took place on 20 November, and the other orders showed enough interest to be willing to designate deputies to attend further meetings.[35] However, when the deputies of the various corporations and companies assembled again on the 29th, many of the third estate declared that it was far more important to discuss the form of their own representation at the forthcoming Estates-General, and they withdrew to deliberate separately on this subject.[36] Some of them also were openly suspicious of the nobility and its motives. They did not like the scheme's ambiguities regarding tax-exemption and voting by order.[37] In any event the solution offered was the same: settle the question of the Estates-General and they in turn would soon settle all other questions including that of provincial estates. Even the clergy took this line, complaining at the same time of its poor representation under the project. By January it had dissociated itself completely from the plan.[38] And the same story was soon coming in from outlying districts. Despite the efforts of Gombault de Rasac and counsellor Voisin de Gartempe[39] the nobles of La Marche Limousine felt that nothing should be done until after the Estates-General met.[40] In any case, they doubted whether La Marche had ever been part of Guienne, and feared that their local interests would be swamped in the deliberations of some general body of dubious title and authenticity for the whole south-west.[41] In vain did Gombault stress that size was one of the scheme's main merits; many of the replies coming in from up-country repeated the argument and some districts, like the Agenais, called for the restoration of their own estates, long defunct but at least historically well-established.[42] In Limousin, the indefatigable Poissac spent the Christmas holiday of 1788 publicizing the ideas of the Bordeaux nobility and distributing copies of Gaufreteau's project for signature by the local nobles. He generated enough support to bring together a meeting of the orders at Tulle,[43] but as at Bordeaux, the result was simply a call from the third estate for adequate representation in the Estates-General. It was the same in Limoges.[44] And even when estates were considered, many were more attracted by the idea of particular estates for Limousin, an idea carried over into the *cahiers* of spring 1789.[45] By February of that year the campaign for the estates-general of Guienne had collapsed in Limousin, and Poissac was plunging into electioneering for the national Estates-General.[46]

The whole campaign for local estates proved one more stage in the parlement's fall from prominence. It began at a time when the magistrates were dispersed and powerless; indeed, it was chiefly attractive as a remedy for that powerlessness. However, linked as it was to a petition for the recall of the parlement, the magistrates could not appear to associate with it too openly. Thus the non-robe nobility was able to seize the initiative and leadership in the struggle for local autonomy. When it did reconvene, the parlement as a body could do no more than give its belated blessing to a movement that was already approaching its climax, and public attention was caught more by the awkward and comical behaviour of the nobility at the palace than the purpose and result of the session.[47] But the ordinary nobility retained the initiative. At least one pamphleteer, hostile to the project for estates, believed that the relative silence of the parlement on this question was a result of embarrassment at the excessive success of its campaign against assemblies, and a realization that estates with real power would inevitably destroy its own position.[48] Nevertheless, he also believed that the nobility and the parlement had formed a 'coalition' to promote the scheme, and a number of individual magistrates favoured it strongly, in 1788 as much as in 1779. Some devoted most of their time to it, and of course this was made easier by the habitual inactivity of the parlement between November and late January. This inactivity also meant, however, that most of the discussion took place while the parlement was not in session, and by the time sittings resumed, matters were settled and the third estate had rejected the nobility's proposals.[49] They had gained momentum too late: in December, the government had conceded double representation to the third in the Estates-General, and the third were now concerned with winning vote by head too. The Guienne scheme had followed that of Dauphiné in offering the doubling of the third in the provincial estates, but not vote by head. It was thus open to the same objections as the new rule for the Estates-General, and its discredit accordingly continued to grow, even after its rejection. 'Les gentilhommes', Bernadau had recorded on 20 November, 'en qualité de restaurateurs de l'antique constitution provinciale, espèrent conserver une partie de leurs privilèges, tout en feignant de les sacrifier'.[50] By the spring, this was the harsh opinion of the whole third estate. They mistrusted all that emanated from the nobility; and the parlement, a body of aristocrats which had openly commended the noble proposals, naturally became the object of similar mistrust. By spring 1789 the parlement was therefore falling into the background of Bordelais politics; it had already lost forever the leadership of the 'patriotic' cause, as members of the third estate, in the *cent-trente* and the assembly which had first met to consider the noble proposals, made that cause peculiarly their own.

By the spring the attention of all orders was primarily absorbed by the preparation for the Estates-General, now decreed for 1 May. Everybody was entitled to propose an opinion on their composition since the government had professed itself uncommitted and asked for advice when it had proclaimed them in July 1788.[51] Necker, when he returned to power, was no more definite and recalled the notables to deliberate upon it. But meanwhile, his declaration convoking the estates for 1 January had been registered by the parlement of Paris on 25 September, with the famous proviso that they should meet 'according to the form observed in 1614'. Few events in the Revolution are more surrounded by legend. The parlement's intention was to put the estates beyond ministerial meddling by invoking the superior authority of precedent.[52] Its well-founded mistrust of the government's 'despotic' tendencies made such restrictions seem entirely reasonable, for in fact the government was under pressure from some quarters to impose its own pattern on the estates.[53] To the 'patriotic' party, however, despotism had already been defeated, and the debate over the form of the Estates-General offered opportunities to extend the campaign into the new field of opening power to the third estate. For the estates to meet according to the forms of 1614 would perpetuate the old power structure in which nobility and clergy were predominant. Patriotic publicists therefore at once turned on the parlement, by then in vacation and unable to reply, to label it the enemy of the third estate; and this label apparently stuck.

News of this storm reached Bordeaux before the parlement was restored there, sounding a warning note. 'Les bons citoyens', observed Bernadau on 18 October,[54]

> redoutent de voir les parlements ternir leurs lauriers en se montrant trop personnels dans une affaire nationale. Celui de Paris s'est déjà aliéné partie du public, en disant dans son enregistrement que le roi serait supplié de convoquer les Etats généraux dans la forme qu'ils se tinrent en 1614. Or on sait que le Tiers Etat y fut malmené et presque compté pour rien. L'opinion publique qui avait soutenu les parlements, tant qu'ils ont paru soutenir les intérêts de la Nation, pourrait bien les abandonner, si elle voit qu'ils abusent de l'autorité pour s'eriger en tyrans du peuple.

Not surprisingly, the Bordeaux parlement was more circumspect. When, at the first session of the vacation chamber on 24 October, the declaration convoking the Estates-General was solemnly published, the court only declared that the king should be begged to assemble them 'in a legal way' and compose them of 'freely elected' representatives. To Bernadau, these provisos appeared 'plus sages que celles arrêtées par les autres Cours'.[55] No doubt the parlement shared the continuing belief of its Paris counterpart that 'despotism' was still the main problem. So did the nobility of Bordeaux, which declared, in its deliberation of 11 September, that the constitution required 'la fixation des Etats-Generaux, non selon une organisation ministérielle, mais suivant les formes anciennes'.[56] But in October nothing was as yet decided, and the parlement felt that its registration was adequate to apply to all eventualities, while at the same time studiously avoiding the unwise commitment of the Paris formula. It made no more pronouncements before dispersing for the Christmas holiday. When it returned to regular duties in January this like all other questions in which the magistrates were interested had been settled for them. The parlement of Paris had hurriedly withdrawn from its exposed position of September;[57] the notables had, by large majorities, pronounced against any concessions to the third estate except equality of taxation;[58] Necker had gone over their heads and declared that the third estate was to have double representation in the Estates-General;[59] the third estate, wanting the logical corollary of vote in common and by head, remained unsatisfied. The position of all sides had polarized, and the orders went into the spring elections embattled. The parlement of Bordeaux had played no part in the polarization, but it could not avoid its effects.

On 9 January 1789 the nobility of Guienne severed its links with the third estate by declaring itself against vote by head and in common.[60] The third estate, it vainly proclaimed, had been seduced by the agents of despotism to oppose, against their own interests, noble pretensions:

> L'on sentira pourquoi la Magistrature et la Noblesse, qui ont opposé la première résistance à la funeste revolution tentée par le précedent ministère, sont, dans ce moment, les pouvoirs redoutables que l'on voudrait anéantir, pour ôter toute barrière aux attentats du despotisme . . . [61]

The parlement, too, expressed reservations about meddling with the form of the Estates, in a letter sent to the king in January on a quite extraneous judicial matter.[62] The third estate reacted accordingly with suspicion, if not hostility. There was no welcome for the magistrates returning from the notables: 'il faut rendre les lauriers', said a notice pinned to Dudon's door.[63]

Nevertheless, the parlement was determined to play a role in the elections. On 20 February it sought to ingratiate itself with public opinion by permitting, for the first time since 1785, the performance of that anti-noble piece *Le Mariage de Figaro*[64] and perhaps this was a minor reason why, when the electoral process began, the magistrates found some of their brother nobles hostile. Early in February, the preliminary assemblies of the various orders held their first meetings, and at that of the nobility on 10 February a document was adopted laying down guidelines for the *cahier* of the nobility of the seneschalcy. This document appears to have been drafted in the parlement, and have had the support of the magistrates and their relatives.[65] Its proposals echoed many that were notoriously dear to the parlement—an end to *lettres de cachet*, the safeguarding of the rights of registration and remonstrance, the restoration of provincial estates. They also entered, in some detail, into the composition and powers of the Estates-General. Above all they stressed that the deputies elected should be strictly bound by a precise mandate to pursue the objectives enunciated in the *cahier*. This proviso was contrary to the royal regulation that mandates should be general;[66] it was a clear indication that the nobility of Guienne, with the parlement at its head, wished to circumscribe the freedom of action of the Estates. The proposals were approved by a large majority of those present, and they formed the basis of the *cahier* which the nobility subsequently drew up. But 27 noblemen refused to sign the project, and a few days later produced a rival draft of their own. The main apparent objection of the dissidents was to the project's strict line on mandates, but the real objection was to its authors rather than its content, to the role of the parlement in drafting the proposal. The leaders of this group were the duc de Duras and M. A. Dupérier de Larsan, grand seneschal of Bordeaux. Thus, even before the elections began, the nobility was divided, and beneath the apparent principles professed by the opposed sides, lay the more real issue of the political role of the parlement. The traditional hostility between robe and sword, long since without significance socially, was reawakened by the opening of access to wider political power; as it was elsewhere at the same time, notably in Franche Comté.[67]

The schism in Bordeaux assumed special importance because it was led by Dupérier de Larsan, the grand seneschal. This office was in normal times a dignified sinecure; theoretically its holder was the head of the seneschalcy court, but in practice these functions were always exercised by a lieutenant-general. Dupérier was thus a country gentleman scarcely known in Bordeaux. However, the one function which only the grand seneschal could perform was the supervision of elections to the Estates-General; and Dupérier hastened to Bordeaux in order to bask in the unexpected glory. On 18 February he arrived at the seneschalcy court to register the proclamation and writs of election, brushing aside a number of regular formalities, and ignoring the lieutenant-general, who was of course J. S. de Laroze, honorary counsellor at the parlement.[68] Laroze at once protested to higher authority; the antagonism between the two men only underlined the schism in the nobility.

At the first step in the elections, a general assembly of the three orders on 9 March, there were more acrimonious exchanges. Laroze insisted on appearing in his red robe at the head of the deputies of the third estate. Dupérier regarded this as an insult to his presidency, but his orders to Laroze to leave, and to take off his robe, were unavailing. After an hour the murmurings of the third estate induced Dupérier to desist, and Laroze, though a member of the nobility and the parlement, made good his official right to lead and preside over the third estate.[69] Further wranglings absorbed so much time that the assembly only proceeded to business on the 10th. Even then, discussions soon became bogged down in disputes over procedure and the verification of powers, and on 14 March matters were further complicated by the arrival of a letter from the Keeper of the Seals to Laroze, informing him that the grand seneschal had purely honorary duties, and that the business of presiding was the sphere of the lieutenant-general.[70] Naturally Dupérier refused to accept this, since the letter was not addressed to him, and Laroze was reduced to further protests. It was not until the third week in March that all powers were eventually verified, functions clarified, and oaths taken. Now the orders separated to elect their own deputies to the Estates-General and prepare their own *cahiers*. 'Selon toutes les apparences', complained Dupérier, alluding to Laroze,[71]

> cette Robe par son influence avec toutes les autres Robes feront nommer les Députés qu'elles auront choisi.
> Je ne dois pas vous taire que le Parlement a cessé ses fonctions, pendant tout le temps qu'a duré l'Assemblée Générale des trois ordres, et que tous les Membres de ce Corps, à la reserve d'un très petit Nombre, n'ont pas manqué une Assemblée . . .
> . . . tout le . . . désordre qui s'en est suivi et qui dure encore n'a pour premier motif que l'influence qu'a mon Lieutenant Général tenant au Parlement lui-meme, dans toutes les Assemblées particulieres qui continuent de se tenir pour la rédaction des Cahiers.
> Je suis instruit que le Parlement y préside, si ce n'est pas publiquement c'est du moins en secret, et mon Lieutenant a l'attention de porter chaque jour chez Mr. le President de Pichard les Cahiers du Tiers Etat. plusieurs Membres de cet ordre m'en ont porté verbalement leur plaintes . . .

How far the presence of Laroze alone dictated the drawing-up of the third estate's *cahier* or the election of its deputies is, however, dubious. He was not among the commissioners appointed for the *cahier*, nor was he elected a deputy.[72] Indeed, when matters were completed, he sent some scathing comments on the *cahier* to the Keeper of the Seals:

Cet ouvrage s'est ressenti et de la precipitation qu'on a mis à le composer et du caractère d'inquiétude de jalousie et peut-être du peu d'aptitude des Rédacteurs. On a voulu se mêler de tout, reformer tout. Le Cahier est incohérent, mal écrit et souvent contradictoire. On demande des suppressions d'offices et on ne parle seulement pas du Remboursement des Titulaires ni de la Conservation des prerogatives et privilegès attachés à leurs offices et achetés sur la foi publique . . .[73]

'Ce sont sans doute', he later added,[74] 'de beaux rêves platoniques'.

The influence of the parlement is equally hard to discern in the order of the clergy, whose discussions were completely dominated by the archbishop.[75] Apparently the clergy received printed circulars advising them to elect the abbé de la Boissière, clerical counsellor at the parlement, to the Estates, but this never became a formal proposal.[76] It was only within the order of the nobility, in fact, that the parlement played an obviously effective role in the elections.

The order was presided over by Dupérier in person. 476 nobles attended the meetings or sent accredited representatives.[77] Among these were 73 members of the parlement, of whom only four did not appear in person. Over 40 magistrates apparently neither appeared nor sent representatives (although some participated in other seneschalcies)[78] but in addition to the 73, there were at least 110 relatives of members of the parlement. On the face of it therefore, Dupérier had some grounds for his sour observation that the deputies 'sont déjà désignés dans le public sous le nom de Députés du Parlement'.[79] However, even on the rash assumption that the magistrates and their relatives would vote unanimously, they still did not constitute an absolute majority. They were merely the largest obvious group in the assembly, a group skilled in assembly politics, and experienced in public affairs; naturally therefore they took a lead. They were also in relatively comfortable circumstances, and lived in Bordeaux; this was important because many of the country gentlemen attending the assembly, as Dupérier pointed out to the government, were not rich and could ill afford a long stay in the city, especially during that expensive spring of 1789.

Of the 12 commissioners elected on 23 March to draw up the *cahier*, two were members of the parlement, three were younger brothers or sons of magistrates, and at least two others had close family links with the court.[80] None of them had signed the minority protest of February, much to Dupérier's fury. They took over two weeks to produce a *cahier* owing to the recurrence of the question of the mandates to be given to the deputies in the assembly at large. Nevertheless, in the final vote on this question, the dissidents of February were crushingly defeated. The *cahier*, at last finished on 6 April, and agreed to by 213 votes to 24, bound the deputies by strict mandates. The election of the four deputies of the order then proceeded.[81] On 7 April Le Berthon, although he had played no part in the assembly, secured 226 out of 374 votes, to be elected first deputy. The second, elected next day, was a soldier, the vicomte de Ségur-Cabanac, who received 254 out of 375. On the third vote nobody secured an adequate majority, but on the fourth F. M. de Verthamon, son and brother of presidents, was elected by 234 votes out of 343. The fifth vote was again indecisive, but on the sixth, president de Lavie received 178 of the 320 votes cast, and was duly elected.

It was easy to infer from these results that these were the deputies of the parlement. An anonymous note of 10 April, probably by Dupérier,[82] analysed the deputies as follows:

> 1º M le Berthon p. p^{dt}. qui ne pouvait plus decemment ni rester ni revenir. C'est pour le tirer d'embarras qu'on la nomme [sic]. il ne fera ni bien ni mal. 2º M le Vte de Segur fort borné, gendre de magistrat.[83] 3º M de Verthamon fils et frere de magistrat, fort borné. 4º M le p^{dt} Lavie. C'est celui qui a le plus d'esprit et des principes plus sains, mais avec des idées extraordinaires, beaucoup de gout pour l'angleterre, de la singularité. mal avec le Berthon.

Yet this last observation raises doubts as to the solidarity of the parlementaire caucus. Pichard hastened to point out to the government, in his comments on the elections, that their appearance was deceptive. Lavie

> n'a été considéré que comme Gentilhomme et quoiqu'il soit encore Président à Mortier, il a toujours mis sa charge en vente. Il y a plus de dix ans qu'il n'entre pas au Palais.[84] Il n'a pas accompagné le Parlement lorsqu'il fut mandé à Versailles pour les alluvions, et il a crû pouvoir se dispenser de le suivre à Libourne lorsqu'il y a été exilé.
>
> Aussi on ne doit pas être surpris lorsqu'on saura ce détail qu'on ait choisi deux Magistrats dans l'ordre de la Noblesse, tandis que dans le fait il n'y a que le premier Président qui le soit à juste titre, M^r delavie ne pouvant être consideré que comme un Gentilhomme qui ne demeure pas même à Bordeaux et qui a toujours passé sa vie dans ses Terres.
>
> J'ai cru devoir vous faire ce détail pour eviter ce que des Mechants esprits pourroient dire sur l'influence qu'avoit le parlement dans les assemblées il n'y avoit guerre plus de 40 à 50 magistrats qui les ayent suivies et le jour que le premier président fût nommé, Il y eut 374 suffrages en comptant les procurations.[85]

Pichard was perhaps as over-indulgent towards his colleagues as Dupérier was harsh. He could not deny either their experience in this sort of assembly and in public affairs, or the prestige enjoyed by certain of them outside the court, which made the election of noble deputies and the noble *cahier* of 1789 in a sense the parlement's last substantial achievements in public affairs. Equally, the machiavellianism attributed to the parlement by Dupérier was almost certainly overdrawn, but the influence of the 'robes' was a clever accusation for the dissident minority to throw at the majority, appealing as it did to certain deep-seated noble prejudices. No doubt it helped in their own minds to explain why their proposal for mandates that were not binding was repeatedly rejected. At any rate, a minority of 20 nobles, led by Dupérier and the duc de Duras, remained completely unreconciled to the deliberations of the majority, proceeded to draw up a dissenting *cahier* of their own, and even to elect a rival set of deputies to the Estates-General. But the opinions and representatives of such a small minority failed to secure acceptance at Versailles.[86]

The activities of serving or honorary members of the parlement in the elections were not confined to the seneschalcy of Bordeaux. In that of Bazas, where 86 nobles were assembled, there were nine past or present members of the parlement represented, although only three came in person. There were also at least 12 close relatives of magistrates. The secretary elected by the order was counsellor

Castelnau d'Auros, and the first deputy to be elected, by 59 votes out of 86, was the grand seneschal, C. A. de Piis, honorary and former counsellor at the parlement.[87] In the seneschalcy of Tulle, counsellor Lafagerdie de Saint-Germain was elected secretary of an order containing several of his relatives, and Poissac reaped the benefit of his earlier activities by being elected deputy for the nobility against the opposition of the duc d'Ayen.[88] Most surprising of all, in Mont-de-Marsan counsellor F. Perez d'Artassan emerged as one of the two deputies for the third estate.[89] Probably elections in outlying districts owed little to the prestige of the parlement. Nevertheless, they meant that the parlement of Bordeaux was better represented in the Estates-General than most others. Apart from Paris, which had eight members elected, only Rouen had as many as four.[90] Even so, the magistracy as a whole was poorly represented, and unable, when the moment came, to put up a convincing resistance to its own destruction.

What were the public opinions of the parlement of Bordeaux as the old régime drew to its close? They can presumably be found most conveniently in the *cahier* of the noble majority,[91] with which it was so solidly identified.

First came a commitment to the Estates-General as a regular part of the French constitution, existing primarily so that the citizens of France might consent to their own taxes, and their own laws. The parlement had made a similar commitment in 1771, and 1785, and continuously from 1787. Previously, the Estates had been regarded as an emergency recourse, in desperate situations. The *cahier* now called for them to meet regularly. However, it insisted that the Estates as of old should vote by order, and that deputies should be closely bound by the mandates they received from their electors. Clearly its authors were against any domination of political life by the third estate.

Beyond this, however, the *cahier* was full of reforming ideas, many of them according with old grievances of the parlement. It pronounced firmly against *lettres de cachet* and all arbitrary orders. It condemned the evocation of judicial cases to Paris on the grounds of the expense and inconvenience to litigants as well as the prejudice to the jurisdiction of their natural, local, judges. More surprisingly, it condemned the privilege of *committimus*, whereby a nobleman might have his case evoked directly to a parlement, bypassing lower jurisdictions. The implication was that the chamber of requests should be abolished. Yet in general the *cahier* supported a strong position for the parlements. It ignored the idea of a permanent intermediate commission while the Estates-General were not in session, on the grounds that the rights of registration and remonstrance of the sovereign courts were a perfectly adequate safeguard of national rights. Thus the magistrates envisaged for themselves a continued association in the governmental and legislative process.

In administration the aim should be to establish the responsibility of government; ministers should be answerable to the Estates-General for their conduct of affairs. The responsible expenditure of public funds at local level was best assured, however, by putting it in the hands of provincial estates. This mention in the *cahier* was all that came of the nobility's sustained campaign in favour of estates over the preceding winter. At municipal level the *cahier* was in favour of the restoration of civic liberties for Bordeaux, and an end to the tutelage of the executive power; this again reflected the events of the previous months.

The *cahier* also called for general reforms: freedom of the press, a new criminal code, abolition of internal customs duties, simplification of the system of taxation and its establishment on a fairer basis. Under this last heading the *cahier* called for a tax on moneyed men, or 'capitalists', as well as on those whose wealth lay in land; it also suggested that poor noblemen be allowed to trade. Above all, it proclaimed a complete willingness on the part of the nobility to surrender its fiscal privileges. This willingness was doubtless a product of the crisis since 1787; the question had not been prominent before then. But the ever-growing weight of taxation had preoccupied the parlement a great deal since mid-century and many of the remedies proposed, such as the tax on 'capitalists', had been repeatedly suggested by parlements throughout that time. In short, the framers of the *cahier* did not expect or want a social revolution, but rather radical constitutional reform, which would clear up the multifarious ambiguities of French public life and eliminate forever the danger of despotism. The history of the parlements had made this danger apparent; it is no wonder therefore that so many of the antidotes followed suggestions first made by these same sovereign courts.

An examination of the general *cahiers* of its jurisdiction also indicates what the public at large thought of the parlement.[92] The parlement of Bordeaux is only mentioned specifically in one noble *cahier* (Agen) and two third-estate ones (Bordeaux, Labourt). But since it was the only parlement of which these 19 seneschalcies had any direct experience, it seems permissible to take their remarks on the parlements in general as reflecting their view of the one under which they were set.

None of the *cahiers* called for the abolition of the parlements, and one, from the third estate of Nérac, specifically demanded their continued existence. Some called for a reduction in the size of their jurisdictions, although this was not as widespread a source of grievance as might be expected. It was most often voiced by the third estate, and so was the complementary call for augmenting the competence of lower jurisdictions—a move the parlement had always resisted. Nearly all the third-estate *cahiers* recommended the abolition of the privilege of *committimus*, although only five noble *cahiers* joined that of Bordeaux in condemning it. Some *cahiers* also attacked age dispensations, some attacked ennoblement by office, and nearly half the *cahiers* of the third estate attacked provisions requiring nobility for entry into a parlement. There were condemnations of the whole system of venality from all three estates, although the strongest and most frequent came from the third. But the matter upon which grievance was most evenly spread was the registration of laws. No *cahier* which mentioned it (although not all did) expressed satisfaction with the existing system, for they all feared that a delaying power which had been used to obstruct the king might also be used to obstruct the Estates-General. Five clerical *cahiers*, eight noble, and ten third-estate called for immediate pure and simple registration by all parlements, without delay, remonstrance, or modification. Four noble and five third-estate *cahiers* were prepared to allow the parlements more freedom with royal edicts between meetings of the Estates, but only then. On the other hand, many *cahiers* took up the cry of the parlements themselves against the power of intendants, against evocations, against justice dispensed by commissions, and in favour of security of tenure for magistrates. It seems therefore that the parlement was not viewed with deep hostility. It required reform rather than abolition. What is surprising is how little mention there was of the endless quarrels and vendettas which had so held up the course both of justice and public affairs in the preceding years. One or two *cahiers* asked that justice should not suffer interruption on any pretext whatsoever, but the demand was neither widespread nor persistent. We can only conclude that the parlement, by its 'patriotic' activities in resisting despotism since 1786, had expunged or at least compensated for the memory of its factious and irresponsible behaviour since the king's accession.

Yet if there was no deep hostility, there was undoubtedly suspicion, as the remarks on registration show. The parlement, in 1788 the focus of a fairly general opposition to despotism, had by the spring of 1789 become much more narrowly identified with the aspirations of the nobility, and not the most liberal segment of the nobility at that. It had avoided directly alienating third-estate opinion, unlike its Parisian counterpart; but by encouraging the third estate to political action on its own account, in the *cent-trente*, and in the assembly originally convoked to discuss provincial estates, the parlement had unwittingly sponsored powerful rivals for public attention and esteem. As the national debate moved from the question of despotism to that of the relative position of the orders, these bodies were able, during the Christmas dispersal of the parlement, to wrest from it the leadership of the 'patriotic' cause. The magistrates had incurred the suspicions of the third estate by their support of the nobility in its campaign for provincial estates dominated by the privileged orders. By the time of the elections the parlement's eclipse in other matters had restricted its effective field of action to the order of the nobility, thus emphasizing further its links with the privileged orders whose pretensions it was now the third's central preoccupation to crush. And here the parlement threw itself behind a programme which, for all its liberal trimmings, would have left the noble power in the Estates-General intact. The months preceding the meeting of the Estates were remarkable in Bordeaux for the relative lack of rancour between the orders, but this was not because the positions they each assumed were less extreme than in other places: it was rather because of differences within each order. These resolved themselves: more fundamental disagreements did not. There could be little doubt by May 1789 that when the patriots of Bordeaux did declare open war on aristocracy, the parlement would be the most obvious and immediate target.

NOTES

1. See above, p. 191.
2. Lhéritier, *La Révolution à Bordeaux*, I, 152–3.
3. See above, pp. 274–5.
4. Lhéritier, op. cit., 154–5.
5. ibid., 158–9.
6. Bernadau 368, 23 Oct., and 388, 2 Nov. 1788; see also Lhéritier, loc. cit., 155.
7. ibid., 160; Bernadau, 373, 25 Oct. 1788; see also O'Reilly, *Histoire complète de Bordeaux*, III, 573.
8. Lhéritier, loc. cit.
9. Bernadau, 404, 15 Nov. 1788.
10. ibid., 406, 18 Nov. 1788.
11. ibid., 399, 12 Nov. 1788.
12. *Requête présentée à MM les Jurats par le brave Guillot: de l'Imprimerie de Jean sans-peur.* Bernadau, 389, 2 Nov. 1788.

13. Lhéritier, op. cit., 161; Bernadau, 417, 29 Nov. 1788.
14. See above, pp. 220–1.
15. Bernadau, loc. cit. above, n. 11; Lhéritier, loc. cit., 161.
16. See above, p. 274.
17. Lhéritier, op. cit., 162.
18. Bernadau, 411, 21 Nov. 1788.
19. loc. cit. above, n. 11.
20. Lhéritier, op. cit., 163–4; Bernadau, 420–1, 3 Dec. 1788; O'Reilly, op. cit., III, 570.
21. Lhéritier, op. cit., 165.
22. Bernadau, 474, 4 Jan. 1789; 506, 7 Feb. 1789.
23. On the *cent-trente* in general between December 1788 and March 1789, see Lhéritier, op. cit., 164–77.
24. AM MS 225 (Mélanges, 1759–89) for a copy of this *Mémoire adressé au Roi par la noblesse de la province de Guienne, Gascogne et Périgort, au sujet des opérations ministérielles, du 8 Mai 1788*. See also Lhéritier, op. cit., 105–7.
25. ibid., 105; see Egret, *Parlement de Dauphiné*, II, 254–9.
26. Bernadau, 319, 12 Sept. 1788.
27. BVBx MS 713, série II, no. 34; see also Lhéritier, op. cit., 110.
28. BVBx MS 713, série II, no. 4; the attribution comes from a MS note by Bernadau.
29. Bernadau, 301, 30 Aug. 1788.
30. Abbé Dardy, 'Documents sur le projet d'union de la Marche à la Guienne, 1788–9', *Mémoires de la société des sciences naturelles et archéologiques de la Creuze* (1893–94), 478–9, Gombault de Rasac to marquis de la Celle, 2 Oct. 1788.
31. BPR Le Paige 79 for a copy of this letter, which had appeared in the *Gazette d'Amsterdam*.
32. He wrote the letters from Bordeaux printed by Dardy, loc. cit.
33. Bernadau, 402, 13 Nov. 1788.
34. Lhéritier, op. cit., 111.
35. Bernadau, 409–11, 20 Nov. 1788; Lhéritier, op. cit., 111–12.
36. ibid., 113–14.
37. ibid., 119, 121.
38. ibid., 122–4.
39. Dardy, op. cit., 488, Gombault to de la Celle, 6 Dec. 1788.
40. ibid., 481–2, de la Celle to Gombault, 18 Oct. 1788.
41. ibid.
42. Lhéritier, op. cit., 124.
43. AN B III 73, pp. 11–17, 'Extrait d'une lettre écrite par un citoyen de Tulle à M. l'intendant de Limoges'; also printed in J. Plantadis, *L'Agitation autonomiste*, 30–5.
44. ibid., 32–3.
45. ibid., 40–6; see also Bernadau, 513, 13 Feb. 1789.
46. ibid., 35.
47. Bernadau, 402, 13 Nov. 1788.
48. BVBx MS 713 (sér. II), no. 23, *Seconde lettre d'un amateur du bien public, au sujet du rétablissement des états particuliers en Guyenne, 1789*. According to a MS note by Bernadau, the author was the advocate Thomas Marie de Saint-Georges.
49. A final attempt to win the support of the third failed in February. Lhéritier, op. cit., 138–9.
50. Bernadau, 409, 20 Nov. 1788.
51. Egret, *La Pré-Révolution*, 325.
52. ibid., 338.
53. ibid., 321–3.
54. Bernadau, 357, 18 Oct. 1788.
55. ibid., 371, 24 Oct. 1788.
56. Dardy, 'Documents', 478.
57. H. Carré, *La Fin des Parlements, 1788–90*, 66–8; Egret, *La Pré-Révolution*, 374–51.
58. ibid., 339–46.
59. ibid., 360–7.
60. Dardy, op. cit., 494–9; see also Lhéritier, op. cit., 204.
61. Dardy, loc. cit., 499, nobility of Guienne to nobility of Guéret, 16 Feb. 1789.

62. Bernadau, 496–7, 27 Jan. 1789; Lhéritier, op. cit., 206, n. 2.
63. Bernadau, 502, 1 Feb. 1789.
64. ibid., 520, 20 Feb. 1789.
65. Lhéritier, op. cit., 205–9.
66. See B. F. Hyslop, *A Guide to the general cahiers of 1789* (2nd ed., New York, 1968), 38–9.
67. Carré, op. cit., 94–5.
68. Lhéritier, op. cit., 209–10; Bernadau, 518, 18 Feb. 1789; A. Brette, *Recueil de documents relatifs à la convocation des Etats-Généraux de 1789* (Paris, 1915), IV, 234–5.
69. Lhéritier, op. cit., 223–4; Brette, op. cit., IV, 243.
70. Lhéritier, op. cit., 230–1; Brette, op. cit., IV, 235.
71. AN Bª 22, Dupérier to Villedeuil, 28 March 1789; another copy in AN B III 34, pp. 844–6; partially printed in Brette, op. cit., IV, 244, and in Lhéritier, op. cit., 233. Much of Lhéritier is based upon documents in these items of the archives and his use of them seems perfectly reliable. Hence the multiplicity of references to him alone.
72. On this process, see Lhéritier, op. cit., 255–67, and Brette, op. cit., IV, 241–2.
73. AN Bª 22, Laroze to Keeper of the Seals, 4 April 1789; also in AN B III 34, pp. 871–4, and partially printed in Brette, op. cit., IV, 244.
74. ibid., Laroze to Keeper of the Seals, 14 April 1789; also in AN B III 34, p. 983.
75. See Lhéritier, op. cit., 236–42; Brette, op. cit., IV, 236–7.
76. Bernadau, 620, 21 May 1789.
77. These figures, and others in the paragraph, are calculated from the official printed lists of nobles attending the electoral assemblies, in AD *Etats-Généraux*, liasse B.
78. See above, pp. 297–8.
79. loc. cit. above, n. 71.
80. The names in AN B III 34, p. 423; also Lhéritier, op. cit., 243.
81. Details from AN B III 34, pp. 423–52; Brette, op. cit., IV, 237–8.
82. In AN Bª 22; attributed to Dupérier by Lhéritier, op. cit., 246.
83. I have been unable to discover to whom this refers.
84. Something of an exaggeration; he had last appeared in 1780 or 1781.
85. AN B III 34, pp. 924–5, Pichard to Keeper of the Seals, 11 April 1789.
86. Lhéritier, op. cit., 289–97.
87. AD *Etats-Généraux*, liasse B, sénéchaussée de Bazas; see also Doyle, 'Deux parlementaires bazadais au XVIIIᵉ siècle', 25, 28; and Brette, op. cit., IV, 298.
88. AN B III 73, pp. 151–7; Brette, op. cit., III, 576.
89. AN B III 91, pp. 278–99; Brette, op. cit., IV, 319.
90. Carré, *La Fin des Parlements*, 95–9.
91. Original in AD *Etats-Généraux*, liasse B. Printed in *Archives parlementaires*, II, 394–7; analysed in Lhéritier, op. cit., 251–5.
92. *Archives parlementaires*, scattered throughout vols. I–V, and supplemented by information and texts from Hyslop, *Guide to the general cahiers*, 368–74, 429–40. The seneschalcies concerned were those of Agen, Bayonne, Bazas, Bordeaux, Cahors, Castelmoron, Condom, Dax, Libourne, Limoges, Mont-de-Marsan, Nérac, Périgueux, Rochefort, Saint-Jean d'Angely, Saintes, Tartas, Tulle, Ustaritz.

CHAPTER 19

Conclusion

Qui l'auroit cru? Ces Parlemens qui se disoient les Pères du Peuple, qui furent réclamés par la Nation en 1788 sont, un an après, rejettés par le voeu général.

Leur anéantissement est résolu: personne ne les plaint; & une aussi étrange différence dans l'opinion, n'est pas même l'effet d'une contradiction.

En 1788, on vit avec douleur le despotisme s'efforcer de détruire les seuls Corps qui pussent lui résister. En 1789, on prévoit l'arbitraire dangereux, dont ces Corps, devenus inexpugnables, portoient les principes . . .

Jusques à ces jours les Parlements s'étoient annoncés comme un quatrième Ordre, ou comme les protecteurs des trois distinctions qui constituoient la Nation: tout-à-coup, dans un moment de délire, ils se sont liées avec les Nobles; & l'on a vu avec effroi, (pouvait-il en arriver autrement?) l'autorité de la Justice s'unir avec la redoutable Aristocratie . . .

Magistrats des Parlemens, terribles Robinocrates, Despotes, Aristocrates, vous avez mérité ce qui vous arrive.[1]

In these words a pamphlet summarized Bordelais opinion on the parlements in the autumn of 1789. For if by the time the Estates-General met in May, the parlement had already suffered an eclipse in local politics, subsequently it went into almost total oblivion, and would no doubt have perished with hardly a murmur had it not been for the determination of its enemies to make its last few months humiliating.

Nothing in May 1789 indicated that the end of the parlements was imminent, and they were little noticed throughout that summer as public attention was absorbed by the third estate's struggle for mastery of the kingdom. And often when they did attract attention—as when late in July the parlement of Paris was censured by the deputies for sending an address to the king and not to themselves —it was inadvertently.[2] Certainly in Paris, Rouen, and Besançon, there was popular suspicion of the magistrates,[3] but this was more on account of their past than anything they were doing in 1789. Indeed, rather than incur popular hostility, most parlements preferred to abdicate many of the public responsibilities that were still technically theirs.

Members of the sovereign courts were not indeed inactive in the National

Assembly. D'Eprémesnil, Duport, d'André, Fréteau, and Le Peletier all took prominent roles, and not all on the aristocratic side. But very little was heard from the Bordeaux deputies. Lavie, for all his liberal reputation, kept silence. Le Berthon, in his few interventions, showed himself still fighting the battles of 1788. When a Besançon magistrate came under suspicion of blowing up a number of peasants in July,[4] Le Berthon declared, through sobs, that it was harsh for magistrates to lose public confidence, but was so overcome with emotion that he was unable to finish his speech.[5] Later in the year, he opined against giving the executive the power to interpret laws,[6] and against the title of King of France; a King of the French, he declared, would never be seduced by the old legend that the kingdom was his property.[7] In the euphoria of renunciation following the night of 4 August, Le Berthon also abandoned a river toll.[8] Nothing, however, was heard from Poissac, Piis, or Perez d'Artassan; indeed by 1790 all three had withdrawn from the Assembly on one pretext or another.[9]

Back in Bordeaux the parlement quietly returned to its judicial work and waited to see what would happen on the national stage. However, the ever-deepening food crisis of that spring could not escape its attention, and it was repeatedly called upon to use what authority it still had to preserve calm. On 7 May it forbade the manufacture of flour-barrels until further notice, so as to prevent export, and ordered all flour to be put at once on the market. It even ordered searches to be made, much to the indignation of a number of merchants.[10] Doubtless such interventions further diminished the parlement's standing among certain important elements of the third estate. On 20 May it forbade all armed gatherings, after two days of rioting in the Entre-deux-Mers and the Blayais.[11] Without the parlement's vigilance, commented Bernadau at the end of June, the danger of famine would be real.[12] All this was done in co-operation with the municipal authorities, although where ultimate municipal authority now lay was none too clear. The *jurats* and the *cent-trente* stood side by side at the head of affairs, but disputed sovereignty. When, early in July, the *jurats* tried to cancel a meeting of the *cent-trente*, the parlement intervened to prevent them doing so, thus ranging itself on the popular side of local politics.[13] Up to this time it had behaved impeccably in uncertain circumstances, and none but a few aggrieved merchants could criticize the quality of its 'patriotism' since the Nation had been assembled.

The events of July were to shake this reputation. The first news of the Parisian revolution of 14 July reached Bordeaux in a letter which arrived on 17 July, and it was immediately proposed to print and publish it. The procurator-general Dudon forbade it, whereupon a group of 'patriotic' young men appealed to the comte de Fumel, who authorized its publication despite the prohibition.[14] The parlement did not protest. A few days later a young enthusiast slammed a church door in Dudon's face, and although he was forced to apologize, it was a sign of the licence 'patriots' felt justified in using towards those with whom they disagreed.[15] On 18 July the 90 electors of the third estate of Bordeaux followed the example of those of Paris, and seized municipal power, thus at one blow superseding the *cent-trente* and eclipsing the *jurats*. They immediately set up a 'patriotic army' of citizens under their control, which took on the main responsibility for public order and so pushed the parlement yet further into the background. Before July ended, Dudon had declared before the electors that the parlement had lost public confidence and therefore all power to help maintain public order,[16] although in August it was still trying to control the grain supply in co-operation with the electors, as the Great Fear spread to Bordeaux.[17] By the middle of that month, however, news from Paris was becoming ominous.

The abolition of the parlements had already been proposed on 5 August,[18] and in the decree of 11 August formalizing the renunciations of the 4th, venality of offices and judicial fees were suppressed.[19] Then on 17 August, Bergasse presented a report on behalf of the constitutional committee recommending a complete reform of the judicial system along new lines.[20] The committee had decided, with regret, that in the new order there was no place for the parlements, for all their record of resistance to despotism. Now that despotism was no more, any power to resist the properly constituted authorities was dangerous, and must be destroyed. This reform could not be effected at once, and Bergasse's speech ended with an appeal to the magistracy to continue their work until the new order was set up. Nevertheless, his recommendations were the death-sentence of the parlements. All that remained uncertain was when it would take effect.

In Bordeaux, the news was received with indifference. The zeal of the magistrates was already flagging by mid-August, and few of them attended public ceremonies.[21] The last few days of the judical session were marked by an unprecedented flow of candidates to be received advocates, since the new proposals required that all candidates for judicial office should be thus qualified.[22] All this could only fill the magistrates with a sense of the fruitlessness of continuing, and they debated at length whether the chamber of vacations should sit through until Martinmas, as president Daugeard proposed. It was decided that it should not. As Bernadau noted:[23]

> Il tarde a chacun de ces Messieurs de se dérober aux humiliations qui les accablent depuis 8 mois, sans qu'ils y aient donné lieu. De toutes les Cours, c'est celle qui s'est le moins mêlée d'affaires publiques. Mais il est de mode de crier au *Robinocrate*.

This was perhaps somewhat generous. The parlement had been deeply involved in public affairs that year. Nevertheless, its involvement had been by no means so great as that of Rennes, or Grenoble, or Besançon, and since the meeting of the Estates it had behaved with great circumspection. Its control over the grain trade had made a distinctive contribution to public order. But a governing assembly which approved nothing but the total freedom of the grain trade was hardly likely to show gratitude for this.

The 15 members[24] of the vacation chamber did not prolong their sittings. Despite enough business pending to justify another month's work, they held their last session at the beginning of the fourth week in September.[25] Nobody protested; as usual the vintage took advocates and litigants alike off to the country. The magistrates who also took their leave at this time could hardly have suspected that they would never reassemble; but this was the intention of the 'patriots' in the Assembly. Half-way through the judicial vacation, the events of the October days emphasized how precarious the 'patriotic' victory still was, and they made it seem imperative to destroy as soon as possible all rallying-points for aristocrats. The parlements were obviously that, and, although their ultimate

destruction was now decided upon, its date was not, and it would be possible for
them to make trouble in the meantime. Already those of Rouen, Metz, and
Rennes were restive. On the other hand, the judicial system would be thrown
into confusion if they were instantly dissolved. This dilemma was resolved by the
proposal to leave them in vacation.

On 3 November 1789 Alexandre de Lameth laid it before the Assembly. In
view of the tutelage which certain parlements had exercised over municipal life,
he declared, it was important to muzzle them to prevent the obstruction of the
new administrative system which the Assembly was about to impose on France.[26]
They had once served a useful purpose, but now they were incompatible with the
constitution, and rivals of the Assembly. All doubts about the capacity of vacation
chambers to handle a full burden of business were overridden; the same day a
decree was almost unanimously passed which put the parlements into permanent
vacation until their replacement. They were thus, as Lameth put it, 'buried
alive',[27] for this decree robbed them of the opportunity to assemble the chambers,
that essential prerequisite for action on public affairs. A few weeks beforehand
another decree had ordained that all parlements should register and publish the
decrees of the Assembly without demur within ten days of their arrival.[28]

Naturally there were protests from the parlements, even though some, like that
of Paris, made them secretly. Rouen and Metz were openly hostile, and suffered
different degrees of reprimand or censure from the king and the Assembly. The
resistance of Rennes and Dijon was considered so flagrant that they were completely replaced by interim judicial commissions.[29] But at Bordeaux the parlement obeyed without demur. For the vast majority of the magistracy, it meant
that their career was already at an end, and perhaps not a few greeted the news
with relief, in times when their labours had become so thankless. Nevertheless,
the parlement was still to attract national attention with one last convulsion.

It happened when the vacation chamber resumed full business in February
1790. On the 20th of that month Dudon came before it to denounce the disorder
rampant in the parlement's jurisdiction. Nor did he scruple to imply that the
blame lay with the Revolution:[30]

> Tout ce que le roi avait préparé pour le bonheur de ses sujets; cette réunion
> des députés de chaque baillage, que vous avez sollicitée vous-mêmes pour
> être les représentants de la nation, pour travailler à la réformation des abus,
> et pour assurer le bonheur de l'Etat; tous ces moyens, si heureusement
> conçus et si sagement combinés, n'ont produit jusqu'à présent que des maux
> qu'il serait difficile d'énumérer . . . Voilà, Messieurs, les premiers fruits
> d'une liberté avant la loi qui devait en prescrire les bornes, et dont la mesure
> a été livrée à l'arbitraire de ceux qui avaient tant d'intérêt à n'en connaître
> aucune. Donnez aux juges de votre ressort l'exemple de ce courage qui ne
> connaît que le devoir; inspirez leur la force de poursuivre ces brigandages
> avec toute la sévérité des ordonnances.
>
> Les destructeurs de la magistrature, inquiets ou jaloux de l'arrêt que vous
> allez rendre, se hâteraient vainement d'en publier l'insuffisance pour en
> atténuer les effets; ils ne nous accuseront pas d'avoir vu tant de maux avec
> indifférence; ils n'abuseront plus la crédulité des peuples; et dût cet acte de
> votre justice souveraine être le dernier, ce peuple y reconnaîtra peut-être

encore ceux dont il a pleuré la captivité, ceux qu'il a si souvent et si juste-
ment appelés ses défenseurs et ses pères . . .

But local 'patriots', far from approving such vigorous action, were incensed at
what they regarded as an attack on the Revolution. Boyer-Fonfrède of the
Bordeaux 'patriotic army', later to achieve fame on a wider scale,[31] denounced
the *arrêt* of the parlement to his colleagues. It ought, he said, to find as many
denouncers as there were citizens. It was derogatory for Dudon to refer to the
National Assembly as the 'deputies of each *baillage*'; it seemed that there was an
aristocratic conspiracy to deny the Assembly its title—'c'est ainsi, je pense, qu'un
athée doit frémir en prononçant le nom sacré de la Divinité'.[32] He proposed that
all members of the vacation chamber holding posts in the patriotic army should
lose them, and that the *arrêt* should be denounced to the municipal authorities.
This was duly done, and the authorities passed the denunciation on to the
Assembly, where it was good for several days of impassioned debate. A report on
the event was read on 4 March. There was much debate on whether or not there
had been enough disorder in the court's jurisdiction to warrant the action it had
taken, and there were wild calls from the left for the instant suppression of all the
vacation chambers.[33] Eventually it was decided that Dudon, in view of his age,
might defend himself by letter, but that the president of the vacation chamber,
Daugeard, should be called before the Assembly to explain himself and receive a
reprimand.

Daugeard made his appearance on 8 April, at a session marked by uproar
created by the right. He showed himself polite but unrepentant:

> La chambre des vacations a exercé toute la plénitude du pouvoir judiciaire
> qui était entre ses mains; elle a rendu un arrêt que les malheurs du temps
> sollicitaient de son patriotisme, et elle n'a eu d'autres regrets que d'avoir
> différé trop longtemps cet acte de justice. Des hordes de brigands dévastaient
> les campagnes et violaient les propriétés le fer et la flambeau à la main . . .
> La chambre des vacations voulait consoler un roi si bienfaisant, dont les
> malheurs présentaient à l'Europe étonné un si étrange contraste avec ses
> vertus. Des motifs aussi pressants auraient-ils pu égarer des magistrats
> impassibles comme la loi dont ils sont les garants? La chambre a ordonné la
> publication de son arrêt pour annoncer sa résistance aux ennemis de l'état.
> J'ai honoré mon nom en souscrivant à cet arrêt. Voilà les considérations qui
> ont déterminé notre conduite. Si vous nous demandez nos motifs, vous les
> découvrirez tous dans le désir du bien public et dans l'amour de nos
> devoirs.[34]

Applause from the right and loud protests from the left greeted this stand, and
when Daugeard withdrew, the Assembly had still not decided its reaction. Not
until 28 April did it pass a decree to announce its disapproval of Dudon's remarks
of 20 February, and have it formally read to Daugeard. It was noted that neither
Le Berthon nor Lavie made any contribution to the debate on their colleagues'
action.[35] But it was obvious that nothing they could have said would temper the
Assembly's action more than the clamours of the right had already done, and it
might have had a contrary effect. Besides, Le Berthon had in effect ceased to be a
member of the parlement since the decree of perpetual vacation and Lavie's

connection had become purely nominal years before that. They were well out of the bitter, undignified squabble caused by the parlement's last defiant gesture.

Although the decree abolishing the parlements was not passed until 6 September 1790, and the vacation chambers did not cease to function until 30 September,[36] the Dudon episode finally destroyed the zeal even of the magistrates who remained in Bordeaux. Dudon himself made no further appearances in court; his son confined his public activities to the patriotic army; the advocates-general claimed that they had no right to plead before a vacation chamber. In these circumstances, criminal justice came to a standstill. On 19 July the advocate and publicist Marie de Saint-Georges even offered his own services to Daugeard as temporary procurator-general in order to relieve the pressure on the prisons, but the offer was ignored, not surprisingly coming as it did from an open enemy of the old judicial order.[37] The parlement therefore ended its life with the same sort of backlog in its business which had characterized so many of its last years.

The end, when it came, was unremarkable. The decree of 6 September was registered at Bordeaux on the 28th, and in conformity with it, the municipal officers locked and sealed the empty palace on the 30th. Some parlements, like Toulouse, went protesting loudly to their end; some, like Paris and Besançon, consigned secret protestations to their registers; others succumbed without a murmur.[38] The magistrates of Bordeaux contented themselves with a letter to the king, dated 28 September, ostentatiously ignoring the Assembly which was the instrument of their destruction.[39] 'Sire', they declared,

> Votre Parlement descend du tribunal avec la sécurité qu'inspire une conscience pure. Il ose se flatter que son roi, que la France entière rendent justice à ses sentiments. Plein de confiance en vos vertus, Sire, votre Parlement dépose dans les mains de Votre Majesté le Glaive et la Balance qu'elle lui avait confiés. Daigne le Ciel protéger ce royaume, accorder à Votre Majesté, à votre auguste épouse, aux princes de votre illustre sang, des jours heureux et sereins, ramener parmi nous la concorde et la paix et y rétablir pour toujours l'empire et la religion des moeurs et des lois!

The final paradox was that this letter was not sent. The magistrates, afraid of the public effect of such declarations, consigned it to the safe-keeping of counsellor Bouquier, one of their most intransigent colleagues, to deliver when times improved.[40] But this happy day did not come until 1814, and by then the parlement and its protestation were little more than historical curiosities.

So ended the 339-year history of the parlement of Bordeaux.[41] Its last acts were proud, defiant, but unavailing—curiously echoing much of its previous history in that it was unable, alone, to resist the will of a determined government. This had been the clearest lesson of the years since 1771.

Parlements were passive bodies; it was their reaction to events, rather than their own initiatives, which formed their public history. Thus between 1771 and 1790 the most important feature in the history of the parlement of Bordeaux had been government policy. Such policy was seldom tailored to the particular susceptibilities of parlements or their provinces, and so the greatest landmarks for the parlement of Bordeaux in this period were also landmarks for the other parlements, and for France as a whole—the remodelling of 1771, the restoration of

1774–75, the attempted reforms of 1787–88, and the dissolution of 1790. These events fell in the provinces like random thunderbolts, unforeseen and (directly at least) unprovoked. Only in their reactions to them did individual parlements distinguish themselves, and only then was the government compelled, as in the exile to Libourne, to take account of the individuality of each parlement. In reacting to policies emanating from the centre, each provincial parlement admittedly drew on a common fund of parlementaire ideas and rhetoric, and a uniform challenge provoked a certain uniformity of response. New taxation, and the exercise of arbitrary power by chancellors, governors, or intendants, were attacked in language readily comprehensible everywhere. During its last years, the parlement of Bordeaux helped to swell the chorus of protest against the ever-increasing pretensions of the central government, and helped in so doing to restrain the government, by fear of what people might think. Public opinion was one of the keys to the power of the parlements. 'Cette monarchie', observed the Swedish ambassador, 'ne diffère du despotisme que par l'influence de l'opinion publique. Elle est la seule sauvegarde du citoyen'.[42] The remonstrances of parlements were the most obvious way of stimulating this opinion. Nevertheless, though a safeguard, the appeal to public opinion was not a strong one, and the extreme language of many protesting *arrêts* and remonstrances reflects the increasing desperation of parlements in the face of governmental power. The plenitude of that power was most graphically demonstrated in 1771. The memory of that experience, and fears of its recurrence, haunted the last years of all the parlements and made many of them unwilling, even in the rare cases where they were able, to push matters to extremes of opposition on national issues. Provincial parlements knew, and the tax increases of the early 1780s re-emphasized the fact, that they were in the last analysis powerless to stop the government from instituting national policies. All they could hope for were local adjustments, and even these were rare. Only on purely local issues could parlements hope for success in opposition. Matters like the *corvées* and the *alluvions* were only coincidentally of national interest. Even the opposition to provincial assemblies in 1787 sprang from a conviction that the parlement's own idea of local estates was preferable. The parlement's influence on national policy and the debate on national issues, and its contribution to arresting the growth of despotism was, therefore, worthy, important, but neither remarkable nor original.

The most distinctive public role of the parlement was defender of the province. Its most original ideas, and those in which it ran against national currents, were all evolved in the provincial crucible. Its liberal attitude to the gain trade, its restrictive attitude to the wine and colonial trades, its stand on the *corvées*, its fury over the *alluvions*, and its opposition to provincial assemblies—all these reflected the peculiar experience of the province of Guienne. The parlement was the only voice of the province at the foot of the throne, and the only substantial defender of its customs and privileges. All social groups under its jurisdiction benefited from its interest and protection from time to time. It is not only crude and unsubtle to see the parlement as the narrow defender of the interests of one social group; it does not fit the facts either. There can be no doubt that all the inhabitants of Guienne, in their different ways, saw the parlement as their defender, and applauded its triumphs accordingly. For the magistrates themselves, personal involvement only lent added passion to causes intrinsically worth espousing.

Undoubtedly then, the magistrates deserved the expressions of gratitude muttered at them by grudging patriots in the summer of 1789. Yet they also deserved the reservations, for the parlement was a very slipshod champion. Divided within itself, it seldom presented a united face to power. In 1771 and 1787 those who preferred to co-operate with 'despotism' nearly equalled those who stood firm. On practically no issue were the magistrates unanimous, and there were few in which dissidents were prepared to accept a majority decision as final. Thus at the moments of greatest constitutional crisis—September 1771 and December 1787 —the government was able to win over enough magistrates, or nearly enough, to gets its policies accepted. On both occasions the contrast between professions of high principles and a subsequent willingness to abandon them was glaring. Nor did those who stood firm on these occasions show a greater sense of public responsibility at other times. The martyrs of 1771 were the vindictive returners of 1775, and the opponents of Dupaty in 1780, who showed complete indifference to the breakdown of public and judicial business occasioned by their vendetta. If the greatest landmarks in the history of the parlement were acts of government, the most constant preoccupation of the magistrates was their quarrels with their colleagues, and their utter indifference to public responsibilities and outside opinion in the pursuit of them. Disgust among those over whom the parlement was set is easily understandable therefore, as is their lack of interest when the parlement was destroyed on the promise of a better order. The people who applauded the return of the parlement in the autumn of 1788 were fickle friends; but then the parlement had been, ever since 1771, an equally fickle hero.

Much, though not all, of the public conduct of the parlement reflected the private circumstances of its members. They took their position in the world, with all its privileges and prerogatives, completely for granted. Undoubtedly this assurance sprang from social confidence, which in its turn rested upon wealth, nobility, and the esteem of others for the same attributes. There is little evidence that these criteria were in danger until the collapse of the government brought a weakening of the social structure. Much of the behaviour of the magistrates, both the duties they fulfilled and those they neglected, must be seen against this background of an assured social and economic position. The provincialism which characterized so many of the parlement's public attitudes was equally obviously a reflection of the magistrates' circumstances. They were a highly distinctive group, dominating the weak local nobility in numbers, wealth, and prestige to a degree unusual elsewhere. Their recruitment and their family relationships were overwhelmingly local; their fortunes were of a type quite peculiar to the Bordelais. All this makes clear the reasons for their leadership of provincial causes.

Similarly, the dominance of personal quarrels in the daily life of the magistrates must reflect to some extent the limited opportunities offered to men of talent by a career in a provincial parlement. The willingness of some to co-operate with the government, as well as the activity of others in opposition to it, both certainly owed something to the frustrations of the career of magistrate. They were simply different ways of reacting to it. These circumstances were not new, but they were particularly important in the last 20 years of the parlement's life. The experience of the Maupeou schism, by dividing colleague against colleague, made professional questions particularly explosive.

The Maupeou schism was only marginally a social or economic question. It was primarily a political affair, and so were the quarrels which followed from it. The spirit of party which is the parlement's most obvious characteristic throughout the reign of Louis XVI had a momentum and justification all its own. Pursuing their internal quarrels, the magistrates often faltered in their vigilance for threats to their personal interests, and their attention was only fitful at best. When the paths of politics and vested interest crossed, politics usually claimed the right of way. But most of the issues upon which the magistrates were vocal had little to do with their personal, private lives. If they had had a clearer idea of where their own interests lay, they would surely have behaved less recklessly after 1775, and would have greeted the collapse of authority in 1788 with far less enthusiasm. That collapse brought political victory. Nobody in the parlement imagined that it could so rapidly lead to social hostility, political uncertainty, and institutional annihilation.

Part of the fascination of the French Revolution lies in the extraordinary impact it had on the humdrum lives of individuals. For the magistrates of Bordeaux, it cut short a career. What did it substitute?

Some ex-members of the parlement remained in the law. Ex-counsellor de Chalup, for example, was almost constantly employed as a judge, even during the Terror.[43] Ex-counsellor de Loménie was found in 1792 presiding over the local law court at Marmande (Lot-et-Garonne).[44] Probably several more, with their legal experience, attained judicial office. Others, no longer judges, still made figures in public life during the Revolution. Ex-counsellor Voisin de Gartempe sat in the Legislative Assembly; ex-president de Lavie went on to be elected to the Council of Five Hundred.[45] Most notorious of all, Saige, ex-advocate-general, became mayor of Bordeaux in 1791 and directed its participation in the Federalist revolt of 1793, a role which brought him that autumn to the scaffold.

Not all of the aristocratic magistrates remained in Bordeaux or even in France to see these dark days. The boldest estimate[46] is that no less than 42 ex-members of the parlement emigrated, and the most conservative concedes over 20.[47] Some supposed émigrés must surely have been mere absentees, such as Pichard or Le Berthon, who both moved to Paris and died there. The very scattering of estates which typified so many parlementaire fortunes must have made false presumptions of emigration common, and indeed they could be turned to malicious advantage. The goods of Pichard at Salles were confiscated by the mayor and commune, on the grounds of their owner's presumed emigration. But the mayor who conducted this operation was none other than Giraudeau, that same unthrifty steward whom Pichard had persecuted years before.[48] Perhaps the settling of similar old scores put other ex-magistrates on the emigration lists. Nevertheless, many emigrations are confirmed. There was ex-counsellor de Basterot, who went to Ireland in 1791 to pursue his creditors, but understandably did not return.[49] There was ex-counsellor Castelnau d'Auros, who ended up in Russia, serving his fellow-émigré the duc de Richelieu (grandson of the notorious marshal), and Tsar Paul I.[50] Others went to Spain or Italy. The younger abbé de Meslon was deported, for refusing the clerical oath of November 1790.[51] But when an attempt was made to constitute a parlement in exile at Mannheim after the outbreak of war, only one ex-magistrate from Bordeaux, Poissac, turned up.[52] Some doubtless preferred to make a more positive contribution to the counter-revolutionary cause: ex-counsellor Gauthier de Latouche was one of the 13 *émigrés* captured with arms in their hands in October 1792, and one of the nine to suffer execution for it; he was also found in possession of pious objects which could hardly, by this time, redound to his credit.[53]

Gauthier was the first victim of the Revolution who had served in the parlement; he was followed to the guillotine by a number of others. In Paris, Pichard perished in 1794, under suspicion of having helped his daughter and her husband to emigrate. But most ex-members of the parlement, 25 out of 28, were executed in Bordeaux in the aftermath of the Federalist revolt of 1793,[54] when a military commission was set up to purge the city of its disloyal elements. Saige was the first to go, within two days of the establishment of the commission in Bordeaux. Then on 22 Messidor, Year II, a batch of nine ex-members of the parlement appeared before the commission, all to be condemned. Former magistrates, the representative on mission Lacombe told one of them, had to prove that they would have been torn apart in the event of a restoration of aristocracy, if they now wished to avoid the scaffold.[55] Among those who died were the ex-procurator-general Dudon the younger, the ex-advocates-general Dufaure de Lajarte and Lalande, ex-presidents de Rolland and de Filhot, and ex-deputy de Piis. Of those who were arraigned, only ex-president de Lavie was acquitted.[56] The Terror, in fact, saw the execution of more ex-members of the parlement of Bordeaux than any other except those of Toulouse and Paris; proportionally, only the parlementaires of Toulouse suffered more.[57] In addition to those who were condemned, at least 27 more suffered imprisonment as suspects in the course of Year II.[58] So only a few of them passed through the most violent phase of the Revolution untouched by its political justice. These facts in themselves are surely a retrospective measure of the importance of the magistrates in the society of pre-revolutionary Bordeaux.

Many of the *émigrés*, however, had returned by the later years of Napoleon's rule, and they benefited from his increasing taste for employing former dignitaries and noblemen of the old régime. In 1811, he decided upon a widespread reform of the judicial structure and personnel of the higher courts in France, with the apparent object of giving them more continuity with pre-revolutionary institutions. An obvious way of doing this was to recruit as many former members of the sovereign courts as could be found. Prefects were instructed to seek out such men, and prepare reports on their age, their current occupations, the state of their fortunes, and their likely capacity as judges. The list drawn up by the prefect of the Gironde survives, and gives fascinating details on what had happened to the ex-magistrates in the 21 years since their dispersal.[59] In 1811 there were records of ten ex-members of the court of aids and 31 former parlementaires. At least six more certainly survived.[60] Many were now old men, and hardly any were under 50. Three were described as rich, 13 had fortunes termed 'honnête', but the rest were in poor or mediocre circumstances. Ex-president de Casaux had squandered an immense fortune on dubious business ventures, and by 1816 he was in litigation against 47 of his creditors.[61] Ex-counsellors Chauvet and Dubergier de Favars had also become merchants, but both now lived in Paris. Most ex-magistrates were gentlemen of leisure. Ex-counsellors Duluc, de

Marbotin, and de Filhot de Marans were members of the general council of the department. The abbé de Meslon had survived his deportation and was now a canon of the cathedral of Saint-André. Ex-counsellor Lajaunye was mayor of Langoiran, while ex-president Lynch had been mayor of Bordeaux itself since 1809 and was a count of the Empire. Ex-counsellors de Malet and de Marbotin also held imperial titles. The object of the inquiry was to find likely magistrates, and it revealed that ex-counsellors de Chalup and Lafagerdie de Saint-Germain already were members of courts of appeal. So was Voisin de Gartempe, had the prefect known it. The former abbé de Poulouzat was practising as an advocate in Limoges. As a result of the inquiry, at least 11 more former magistrates were now considered for office in the new imperial courts. Of these, Domenge and Boucaud declined the offer to join the new court at Bordeaux, but Marbotin, Chalup, and Malet accepted. Voisin de Gartempe became first president at Metz; Lajaunye was appointed to Angers. Between 1811 and 1814 ex-president de Spens and ex-counsellor Maurice de Sentout the younger also joined the court at Bordeaux.[62]

This unexpected return to power and prestige was threatened by Napoleon's fall and the Bourbon restoration. As in 1771, the choice could not be evaded, but once again loyalties were divided. Lynch made a substantial contribution to the Bourbon cause in 1814 when he delivered Bordeaux into the hands of the English armies advancing from Spain. Napoleon swore never to forgive him, but Louis XVIII rewarded him with a peerage.[63] None of the others could be so sure of automatic Bourbon gratitude when the position of all holding judicial office came under review in the light of their political record during the Hundred Days. At Bordeaux, 16 of the 30 counsellors of the Royal Court (formerly the Imperial Court) were dismissed by the new government, including the ex-parlementaire Lajaunye. All the others, however, kept their offices, and Marbotin became first president. Among the new members replacing the dismissed 16 were the ex-parlementaires de Lamouroux and Bouquier.[64]

Others, too, won subsequent social and professional preferment. Chalup in 1818 became first president of the court at Angers. Voisin de Gartempe in 1819 became a counsellor at the Court of Cassation in Paris. He also served as a deputy between 1815 and 1824, and 1827 and 1834, when he joined Lynch as a peer of France. Filhot de Marans also served as a deputy in the year 1815–16. When Castelnau d'Auros returned from Russia, he was rewarded for his loyalty there to the duc de Richelieu with a marquisate.

The government of Louis XVIII was therefore very generous to the survivors of his brother's parlement of Bordeaux. In spite of the Revolution, those ex-magistrates who survived long enough usually ended their careers as much men of social consequence as when they had begun them, under the old régime. Most were still financially comfortable. Those who remained in the Bordelais still occupied prominent positions of public trust. Genealogies even show that intermarriage among former parlementaire families remained common. Nevertheless, the families which survived the Revolution were a small proportion. Many had been destroyed and others scattered. And the number of those who could remember the days of the parlement diminished all the time. When Lajaunye approached the government in 1831,[65] still pathetically seeking judicial office after yet another revolution, he was already 80 years old. But at least none of his former colleagues were likely to testify against him. Most of them were long dead.

NOTES

1. BVBx MS 713, série II, no. 39, *Les Parlements à tous les diables* (Bordeaux, 1789). According to a MS note written on it by Bernadau, 'Ce pamphlet est ce qu'a fait de mieux l'avocat Saint-George'. His 'Tablettes', 716, 6 Sept. 1789, record its appearance on that day.
2. L. Gallois (ed.), *Réimpression de l'Ancien Moniteur*, I, 16 July 1789; Carré, *La Fin des Parlements*, 113–14.
3. ibid., 112, 117–22.
4. ibid., 118–22.
5. J. Marchand (ed.), J.-A. Creuzé-Latouche, *Journal des états-généraux et du début de l'Assemblée Nationale, 18 mai–29 Juillet 1789* (Paris, 1946), 278, 25 July 1789.
6. *Ancien Moniteur*, I, 538, 30 Sept. 1789.
7. *Archives parlementaires*, IX, 385, 8 Oct. 1789.
8. *Ancien Moniteur*, I, 296, 6 Aug. 1789.
9. See the entries in A. Robert, G. Cougny, and E. Bourloton, *Dictionnaire des parlementaires français* (Paris, 1891), 5 v.; also AN B III 91, pp. 451–2, Perez d'Artassan to assembly of the communes of Marsan, 6 Dec. 1789.
10. Bernadau, 610, 7 May 1789.
11. ibid., 619, 20 May 1789.
12. M. Lhéritier (ed.), *Les Débuts de la Révolution à Bordeaux d'après les Tablettes manuscrites de Pierre Bernadau* (Paris, 1919), 69, 30 June 1789.
13. ibid., 70, 9 July 1789.
14. ibid., 73–4, 17–18 July 1789.
15. ibid., 75, 21 July 1789.
16. O'Reilly, *Histoire complète*, III, 60; Boscheron des Portes, *Histoire du Parlement de Bordeaux*, II, 399.
17. Lhéritier, *Débuts*, 83, 8 Aug. 1789.
18. *Ancien Moniteur*, I, 292, 5 Aug. 1789.
19. ibid., 332, 11 Aug. 1789.
20. ibid., 340–7, 17 Aug. 1789.
21. Bernadau, 696, 15 Aug. 1789.
22. ibid., 718, 7 Sept. 1789.
23. ibid., 721, 11 Sept. 1789.
24. *Etrennes bordeloises* for 1790 lists them as follows:

President	J. C. Daugeard
Counsellors	M. A. Geneste de Malromé, cleric
	L. de Loyac
	A. J. de Minvielle
	P. F. Duval
	F. A. de Ruat
	J. de Baritault de Soulignac
	G. Bouquier
	G. R. de Filhot de Marans
	P. J. Laboyrie
	N. M. Moreau de Montcheuil
	H. M. S. de Labat de Savignac
	A. M. F. Montsec de Reignac
	J. L. J. Duval
	A. F. Durand, cleric

Plus all the crown lawyers.

25. Bernadau, 729, 20 Sept. 1789.
26. *Ancien Moniteur*, II, 131, 3 Nov. 1789.
27. Carré, op. cit., 136; E. Seligman, *La Justice en France pendant la Révolution (1789–1792)* (Paris, 1901), 221.
28. Carré, op. cit., 135, 10 Oct. 1789.
29. ibid., 138–54; Seligman, op. cit., 221–6.
30. The text of his speech in *Ancien Moniteur*, III, 526–7, 4 March 1790. Accounts of the incident in Boscheron des Portes, op. cit., II, 401–11, and Carré, op. cit., 185–97.

31. Jean-Baptiste Boyer-Fonfrède (1765–93). Son of a rich colonial merchant; aide-major-general, armée patriotique de Bordeaux, 1790; deputy from Bordeaux to the Convention, 1792; follower of Vergniaud; purged June 1793; executed 31 Oct. 1793.
32. *Ancien Moniteur*, III, 528.
33. ibid., 529.
34. ibid., IV, 76.
35. Carré, op. cit., 196–7.
36. *Ancien Moniteur*, V, 579, 6 Sept. 1790.
37. BVBx MS 713, série II, no. 23, T. Marie, *La Prompte Expédition des prisonniers ou réclamation adressée à M. le Président de la Chambre des Vacations de Bordeaux . . . le 31 Juillet 1790*.
38. For details of other places, see Carré, op. cit., 229–42.
39. The text is in Boscheron des Portes, op. cit., II, 413.
40. AN BB⁵ 74, Bouquier to Keeper of the Seals, 27 Nov. 1820, confirms the account of Boscheron des Portes, loc. cit., II, 413–14.
41. I take its origins to lie, as the magistrates themselves did, in the capitulation of 1451, although of course I am fully aware that this is a point for scholarly disagreement. See above, pp. 5–6.
42. Léouzon Le Duc, *Correspondance diplomatique*, 32, 30 July 1786; see also the remarks of Bernis, *Mémoires*, I, 338, and more generally Doyle, 'The parlements of France and the breakdown of the ancien régime, 1771–88', *French Historical Studies* (1970).
43. AN BB⁶ 56.
44. AD 4L 110, tax request of 1792.
45. Robert, Cougny, Bourloton, *Dictionnaire des parlementaires*.
46. D. Greer, *The Incidence of the Emigration during the French Revolution* (Cambridge, Mass., 1951), 85, n. 2.
47. Carré, op. cit., 274.
48. AN W 40 (927), Tribunal révolutionnaire: Pichard. See above, pp. 97–8.
49. See above, p. 58.
50. See Doyle, 'Deux parlementaires bazadais', 28–9, and E. Féret, *Statistique générale du département de la Gironde* (Bordeaux, 1874–89), III, 125.
51. AD Q930, inventory after deportation of Meslon's goods.
52. Carré, op. cit., 269, n. 1.
53. *Ancien Moniteur*, XIV, 250, 21 Oct. 1792, and 279, 23 Oct. 1792; see also E. Biré, *Journal d'un bourgeois de Paris pendant la terreur* (Paris, 1895), I, 160–2.
54. Boscheron des Portes, op. cit., II, 451–7; A. Vivie, *Histoire de la terreur à Bordeaux* (Bordeaux, 1877), II, 339. D. Greer, *The Incidence of the Terror during the French Revolution* (Cambridge, Mass., 1935), 162, lists 31 victims of the Terror from the 'robe nobility' of the Gironde department; Carré, op. cit., 277, gives 26 victims of the Terror from the parlement of Bordeaux. I have been able to raise this number to 28.
55. Vivie, loc. cit.
56. See above, p. 69.
57. Carré, loc. cit., 277–8.
58. AM MS 350–7, 'Dictionnaire des arrestations' by Aurélien Vivie.
59. AN BB⁵ 73, 'Etat des anciens membres du Parlement, de la Cour des Aides de Bordeaux', dated 24 Feb. 1811. There are some errors and omissions.
60. 33 were listed, but three of those named were in fact brothers or sons of former magistrates.
61. AM factums, $\dfrac{IX}{107}$.
62. AN BB⁶ 56.
63. On Lynch's role, see P. Bécamps in *Bordeaux au XVIIIᵉ siècle*, 470, 473–7.
64. AN BB⁶ 56.
65. ibid., Lajaunye to minister of justice, 18 April 1831.

Appendix I

Alphabetical List of Members of the Parlement of Bordeaux 1775-1790

This list gives surnames, Christian names, and details (where necessary) of the career of each magistrate within the parlement. Each name is followed by four dates, which are, respectively, those of birth, entry into the parlement, end of career in the parlement, and (where this is known) death. Honorary (i.e., former) members of the parlement are not included.

Barbeguière, Hyacinthe-Louis	
clerical counsellor	1730–1759–1788–18
Baritault, Jean-Joseph-François-Godefroy de	
counsellor	1706–1730–1779–1779
Baritault, Jean de	
counsellor, son of above	1747–1767–1790–1794
Barret, Jean-Baptiste-Luc	
chief-clerk	1709–1743–1780–1780
Barret, Pierre-Jean-Baptiste-Marie	
counsellor, son of above	1747–1767–1790–18
Basquiat de Mugriet, Joseph de	
counsellor	1728–1762–1785–
Basquiat de Mugriet, Alexis-Marie-Joseph	
counsellor, son of above	1764–1785–1790–18
Basterot, Barthélemy de	
counsellor	1743–1771–1790–1822
Bergeron, François-Jacques-Marie de	
counsellor	1760–1780–1790–18
Bienassis, Jean-Etienne de	
president requests	1731–1766–1790
Biré, Jean-Joseph de	
counsellor requests, 1768; inquests, 1775	1747–1768–1790–18
Boucaud, Jacques-Joseph de	
counsellor	1744–1765–1790–1814
Bouquier, Gabriel	
counsellor requests, 1769; inquests, 1776	1741–1769–1790–1828

Brach, Pierre-François de
    knight of honour   1738–1768–1789–1789
Brane, Joseph-Hector de
    counsellor   1746–1780–1790–18
Brivazac, Jean-Baptiste-Guillaume-Léonard de
    counsellor   1729–1755–1790–1791
Cajus, Pierre-Nicolas
    counsellor requests   1739–1766–1790–
Carrière, Jean-Antoine-Elisabeth-Pic de
    counsellor requests   1750–1778–1790–18
Casaux, Pierre-Emmanuel de
    counsellor, 1740; president *à mortier*, 1775   1716–1740–1778–1778
Casaux, Guillaume-Joseph de
    counsellor, 1784; president *à mortier*, 1785;
    son of above   1758–1784–1790–18
Castelnau d'Essenault, Léonard-Antoine de
    counsellor   1742–1763–1790–
Castelnau d'Auros, Gabriel de
    counsellor   1757–1780–1790–1826
Chalup, Joachim de
    counsellor   1757–1783–1790–1825
Chanceaulme de Fonroze, Elie-Jean
    counsellor   1739–1767–1790–1794
Chaperon de Terrefort, François-Joseph de
    counsellor   1734–1759–1790–1794
Chauvet, Jean-Baptiste
    counsellor   1755–1779–1790–18
Conilh, Jean-Antoine-François de
    counsellor   1704–1730–1775–1775
Conilh, Pierre-Guillaume de
    counsellor, son of above   1743–1769–1788–1788
Cursol, Joseph-Antoine de
    counsellor   1713–1734–1785–1785
Dalon, Romain
    counsellor   1739–1760–1776–
Dalphonse, Jean-Baptiste
    counsellor   1709–1754–1777–1779
Darblade de Séailles, Auguste-Jean-Bertrand
    counsellor   1757–1784–1790–
Darche, Jean-Luc
    counsellor   1731–1751–1790–
Darche de la Salle, François-Benoît
    counsellor   1723–1744–1790–1792
Daugeard, Jean-Charles
    president *à mortier*   1725–1768–1790–
Daugeard de Virazel, Jacques-Armand-Henri
    president *à mortier*, brother of above   1736–1769–1790–179

Degères de Loupes, Pierre
counsellor   1737–1762–1790–18
Delpech, André
chief-clerk   1751–1783–1790–18
Delpy de la Roche, Jean-Louis-Henri
counsellor   1734–1757–1786–
Demons de Saint-Pauly, Léonard-Joseph
counsellor   1736–1758–1776–178
Desmoulins de Maspérier, René
counsellor   1763–1783–1790–
Desnanots, Jean-Baptiste-Daniel
counsellor   1725–1749–1779–
Domenge de Pic de Blais, Claude-Ange
counsellor   1703–1749–1788–1788
Domenge de Pic de Blais, Pierre-Joseph
counsellor, son of above   1748–1780–1790–18
Doudinot de la Boissière, François
clerical counsellor   1746–1776–1790–
Drouilhet de Sigalas, Charles-Ignace
counsellor   1709–1737–1780–1780
Dubarry, Jean-Baptiste
counsellor   1730–1762–1790–179
Dubergier de Favars, Jean-Clément
counsellor   1717–1737–1780–1780
Dubergier de Favars, Raymond-Jean-Antoine
counsellor, son of above   1763–1784–1790–18
Dudon, Pierre-Jules
advocate-general, 1739; procurator-general, 1764   1718–1739–1790–1800
Dudon, Jean-Baptiste-Pierre-Jules
procurator-general *en survivance avec exercice*,
son of above   1750–1783–1790–1793
Dufaure de Lajarte, Elie-Louis
counsellor, 1778; advocate-general, 1779   1754–1778–1790–1794
Duluc, Laurent
counsellor   1729–1755–1790–18
Dumas de Fonbrauge, Jacques-François-Joseph
counsellor   1734–1765–1790–1794
Dumas de Laroque, Pierre-Henri
counsellor   1736–1766–1790–1794
Dupaty, Charles-Marguerite-Jean-Baptiste-Mercier
advocate-general, 1768; president *à mortier*, 1780   1746–1768–1788–1788
Durand, Aubin-Félix
clerical counsellor   1743–1788–1790–18
Durand de Naujac, Pierre-André
counsellor requests, 1753; inquests, 1758   1722–1753–1780–1780
Duroy, Jean
counsellor   1723–1746–1778–1788

Dussault, Jean
  counsellor; dean   1700–1721–1780–1781
Dussault, Jean-Maurice
  counsellor, son of above   1729–1756–1790–1794
Duval, Pierre-François
  counsellor   1746–1768–1790–
Duval, Jean-Luc-Joseph
  counsellor   1764–1786–1790–1794
Fauquier, Jean-Baptiste de
  counsellor   1714–1738–1790–1793
Féger, Joseph
  clerical counsellor   1725–1755–1789–1789
Féger, Jean-Baptiste
  chief-clerk, nephew of above   1740–1768–1777–1777
Filhot de Chimbaud, Jean-François de
  counsellor requests, 1758; inquests, 1761   1719–1758–1775–1775
Filhot de Chimbaud, Joseph de
  counsellor, son of above   1763–1783–1789–1789
Filhot, Gabriel-Barthélemy-Romain de
  counsellor, 1769; president inquests, 1789   1746–1769–1790–1794
Filhot de Marans, Gabriel-Romain de
  counsellor, brother of above   1753–1779–1790–18
Fonteneil, Jean de
  counsellor   1717–1749–1778–1782
Garat, Jean de
  counsellor   1719–1764–1785–1785
Gascq, Antoine-Alexandre de
  counsellor, 1730; president *à mortier*, 1739   1712–1730–1779–1781
Gaufreteau, Guillaume de
  counsellor   1761–1785–1790–
Geneste de Malromé, Marc-Alexandre
  clerical counsellor   1721–1743–1790–1802
Gobineau, Thibaud-Joseph de
  counsellor   1722–1768–1790–1796
Gombault de Rasac, Joseph de
  knight of honour   1723–1748–1790–
Gourgue, Laurent-Marc-Antoine de
  counsellor, 1738; president *à mortier*, 1753   1717–1738–1779–1779
Gourgue, Michel-Joseph de
  counsellor, 1739; president inquests, 1760,
  brother of above   1718–1739–1790–18
Guillaume, Louis-Joseph de
  counsellor   1764–1787–1790–
Jaucen de Poissac, Etienne-François-Charles de
  counsellor   1733–1760–1790–
Labat de Savignac, Pierre-François-Ignace de
  counsellor   1713–1736–1781–1781

Labat de Savignac, Hyacinthe-Marie-Servidie de
  counsellor, son of above   1750–1776–1790–18

Laboyrie, Pierre-Joseph de
  counsellor   1753–1777–1790–

La Colonie, Jean-François-Aymard-Martin de
  counsellor; dean, 1781–90   1706–1733–1790–17

Lafagerdie de Saint-Germain, Antoine de
  counsellor   1757–1781–1790–18

Lafargue de Laroque, Jean-Armand
  chief-clerk   1742–1777–1783–1783

Lafargue, Louis-Armand
  chief-clerk, brother of above   1732–1787–1790–1820

Lagubat, Thomas-Martiens de
  counsellor   1742–1776–1790–

Lajaunye, Antoine
  counsellor   1751–1782–1790–18

Lalande, Pierre de Raymond de
  counsellor   1727–1747–1778–

Lalande, Jean de Raymond de
  counsellor, 1779; advocate-general, 1780; son
  of above   1756–1779–1790–1794

Laliman, Jean-Joseph de
  counsellor requests, 1763; inquests, 1768   1740–1763–1790–1794

Lamolère, Jean-Baptiste de
  counsellor   1734–1759–1783–1808

Lamontaigne, François de
  counsellor   1724–1746–1784–1812

Lamouroux de Parempuyre, Joseph de
  counsellor   1753–1776–1790–18

Laporte-Paulliac, Armand-Yves-Jean-Baptiste de
  counsellor   1754–1776–1790–1794

Laroze, Joseph-Sébastien de
  counsellor   1715–1756–1784–179

Laroze de Fonbrune, Gabriel-Marie-Anne-Joseph de
  counsellor, son of above   1757–1784–1790–18

Lasalle, Jean-Martin de
  counsellor   1730–1768–1790–

Lascombes, Jean-François de
  counsellor   1735–1763–1783(?)–

Lassime, Louis-Jacques
  counsellor requests   1751–1785–1790–1794

Latouche-Gautier, Etienne-Hyacinthe de
  counsellor requests   1747–1777–1790–1792

Lavie, Paul-Marie-Arnaud de
  counsellor, 1768; president à mortier, 1768 1747–1768–1790–1801

Le Berthon, André-Jacques-Hyacinthe
  counsellor, 1733; president inquests, 1736;
  president à mortier, 1748; first president, 1766 1713–1733–1790–1800

Le Berthon, André-François-Benoît-Elisabeth
  counsellor, 1777; president *à mortier*, 1779; son
  of above   1751–1777–1790–1792
Leblanc de Mauvezin, Jean-Antoine
  counsellor   1706–1731–1779–1779
Leblanc de Mauvezin, Jean-Joseph-Timothée
  counsellor, son of above   1756–1777–1790–
Leblanc de Mauvezin, Jean-Louis-Alexandre
  counsellor, brother of above   1760–1783–1790–
Leydet, Joseph-François-Hubert
  counsellor requests   1733–1764–1785–
Loménie, Martial de
  counsellor requests   1747–1777–1790–
Loret, Jean-Paul de
  counsellor, 1728; president inquests, 1738   1708–1728–1790–1791
Lorman, Jean-Baptiste-Valentin
  counsellor requests   1724–1760–1782–
Lorman, Jean-Gérard
  counsellor requests, son of above   1756–1783–1790–
Loyac, Laurent de
  counsellor   1734–1757–1790–1794
Lynch, Pierre-Jean-Baptiste
  counsellor, 1771; president inquests, 1783   1749–1771–1790–1835
Maignol, Etienne
  counsellor   1723–1752–1775–179
Maignol, René
  counsellor, nephew of above   1763–1786–1790–1800
Malet, Jean de
  counsellor   1753–1788–1790–1849
Marbotin de Conteneuil, Jean-François-Laurent-Amédée de
  counsellor   1748–1768–1790–1824
Marbotin, Jean-François de
  counsellor   1728–1749–1790–1794(?)
Maurice de Sentout, Jean-Jacques
  counsellor requests, 1759; president requests,
  1764   1725–1759–1790–179
Maurice de Sentout, Jacques-Léger-François-Magdeleine-Marie-Joseph
  counsellor, son of above   1767–1789–1790–18
Meslon, Antoine de
  clerical counsellor   1720–1755–1775–1778
Meslon, Eléazar de
  clerical counsellor, nephew of above   1750–1776–1790–18
Meslon, Jean-André de
  counsellor, brother of above   1748–1768–1790–1794
Minvielle, André-Joseph de
  counsellor   1744–1765–1790–18
Montalier de Grissac, Joseph-Marie de
  counsellor   1739–1768–1790–18

Montforton, Guillaume de
  clerical counsellor   1699–1750–1775–1780
Montsec de Reignac, Arnaud-François-Bernard-Martin de
  counsellor   1747–1776–1790–1794
Moreau de Montcheuil, Nicolas-Martin
  counsellor   1744–1770–1790–18
Mothes, Louis-Josph de
  counsellor   1743–1779–1790–
Navarre, Jean-Baptiste-Raymond de
  counsellor   1732–1752–1790–
Paty du Rayet, Léonard de
  counsellor   1732–1757–1790–1794
Pelet, Jean-Jacques
  counsellor   1717–1740–1788–1788
Pelet d'Anglade, Jacques
  counsellor, brother of above   1723–1743–1790–1793
Perez d'Artassan, François
  counsellor   1722–1764–1790–1798
Peyronnet, Louis-Elie
  counsellor   1760–1782–1790–1792
Pichard, Nicolas-Pierre de
  advocate-general, 1755; president à mortier, 1760   1734–1755–1790–1794
Pichard, François-Nicolas-Pierre de
  counsellor, son of above   1764–1786–1790–
Piis, Charles-Antoine de
  counsellor   1742–1763–1776–1794
Pocquet de Lillette de Puilhéry, Louis-Claude
  counsellor   1721–1757–1776–1800
Prunes Duvivier, Alexis-Jacques-Mathieu
  counsellor   1742–1763–1790–179
Ragueneau, Pierre de
  counsellor   1717–1748–1778–1778
Raignac, Gaston-Jean-Baptiste-Joseph de
  counsellor   1750–1770–1790–1794
Raymond de Sallegourde, Gabriel de
  counsellor   1711–1737–1786–1786
Raymond, Pierre-Louis de
  counsellor   1754–1786–1790–
Reculès de Poulouzat, Pierre-Martial
  clerical counsellor   1746–1776–1790–18
Richon, Philippe de
  counsellor   1723–1753–1782–1794
Roche de Lamothe, Bernard
  counsellor requests   1722–1768–1790–
Rolland, Jean-François de
  counsellor, 1763; president inquests, 1766   1725–1763–1783–1794
Ruat, François-Amanieu de
  counsellor   1742–1763–1790–1803

Saige, François-Armand
   advocate-general   1734–1760–1778–1793
Sauvat de Pommiers, Charles
   counsellor   1755–1787–1790–18
Souc de Plancher, Annet-François de
   clerical counsellor   1716–1759–1775–
Spens d'Estignols de Lancre, Pierre-François-Joseph de
   counsellor, 1742; president *à mortier*, 1755   1721–1742–1777–1777
Spens d'Estignols de Lancre, Pierre-François-Mathieu de
   counsellor, 1777; president *à mortier*, 1778, son
   of above   1757–1777–1790–1818
Taffard, Jean-Baptiste
   counsellor   1743–1764–1777–1786
Thilorier, Jacques
   counsellor   1742–1765–1776–1783
Verthamon d'Ambloy, Martial-François de
   counsellor, 1739; president inquests, 1761   1719–1739–1787–1787
Verthamon d'Ambloy, Jean-Baptiste-Maurice de
   president *à mortier*, son of above   1746–1770–1790–1809
Voisin de Gartempe, Jean-Baptiste
   counsellor   1759–1785–1790–1840

Appendix II

The Parlement Maupeou

(Italicized names indicate intruders, not previously serving in the parlement)

First president	A. A. de Gascq
Presidents	N. P. de Pichard
	J. Duroy
	J. de Bacalan[1]
	J. M. Dussault
Counsellor-presidents	J. P. de Loret
	J. F. de Rolland[2]
Clerical counsellors	M. A. Geneste de Malromé
	G. de Montforton
	A. de Meslon[3]
	H. L. Barbeguière
	J. de Laborde de Pachère[4]
Counsellors	J. J. F. G. de Baritault
	J. de Baritault
	P. J. B. M. Barret
	J. J. de Boucaud
	P. N. Cajus
	L. A. de Castelnau[5]
	E. J. Chanceaulme de Fonroze
	F. J. Chaperon de Terrefort
	J. A. de Cursol[6]
	F. J. Dalbessard[7]
	J. B. Dalphonse
	J. L. H. Delpy de la Roche
	C. A. Domenge de Pic de Blais
	C. J. Drouilhet de Sigalas
	A. J. Drouilhet de Sigalas[8]
	J. B. Dubarry

J. C. Dubergier de Favars
J. F. J. Dumas de Fonbrauge
J. Dussault, dean
P. A. Durand de Naujac
J. Filhot de Chimbaud
J. de Fauquier
J. de Fonteneil
J. de Garat
B. J. C. A. de Gascq[9]
J. B. de Gascq[10]
G. A. C. de Goyon d'Arzac[11]
J. J. de Laliman
J. S. de Laroze
P. M. de Laroze[12]
F. de Lamontaigne
J. F. de Lascombes[13]
J. B. V. Lorman
A. E. Maignol[14]
E. Maignol
J. F. de Marbotin
A. J. de Minvielle
J. M. de Montalier de Grissac[15]
N. M. Moreau de Montcheuil
J. B. R. de Navarre
J. J. Pelet
P. J. Peynaud[16]
F. A. Ruat
J. B. Taffard

Procurator-general   P. J. Dudon

Advocates-general   F. A. Saige
J. B. P. J. Dudon

NOTES

1. Joseph de Bacalan (1701–1750–1772–1772). Professor of French Law at the University of Bordeaux, 1748; counsellor at the parlement, 1750; president in the Maupeou parlement, 1771; died in office; succeeded by J. F. de Rolland.
2. Succeeded J. de Bacalan as full president in 1773; succeeded as counsellor-president by J. F. de Lascombes; returned in the restored parlement of 1775 to his old office of president in the inquests.
3. Resigned 1773; succeeded by J. de Laborde de Pachère; returned in the restored parlement of 1775 to his old office of clerical counsellor.
4. Jean de Laborde de Pachère (1741–1774–1775–   ). Priest, advocate; succeeded A. de Meslon, who resigned in 1773.
5. Resigned, 1772 (see above, p. 150); succeeded by B. J. C. A. de Gascq; returned in the restored parlement of 1775 to his old office of counsellor.

6. Resigned 1773; succeeded by G. H. C. de Goyon d'Arzac; returned in the restored parlement of 1775 to his old office of counsellor.

7. François-Jacques Dalbessard (1731–1757–17 –   ). Son of F. J. Dalbessard, president in the inquests, lieutenant-general at the seneschalcy until 1748, and professor of law at the University of Bordeaux; the precise career of this son is not clear; it is possible that he was in the parlement after 1775, although he is not listed in Appendix I, for his office was certainly not sold until 1782, when it was purchased by A. Lajaunye.

8. André-Joseph Drouilhet de Sigalas (1741–1772–1775–   ). Son of C. I. Drouilhet de Sigalas, counsellor; succeeded A. E. Maignol, who died in 1772; object of quarrels after 1775 (see above, pp. 166, 171).

9. Blaise-Jean-Charles-Alexandre de Gascq (1747–1772–1775–   ). Son of Charles de Gascq, a distant cousin of the first president of the Maupeou parlement; succeeded L. A. de Castelnau who had resigned in 1772.

10. Jean-Baptiste de Gascq (1752–1773–1775–   ). Brother of above; succeeded J. F. de Lascombes, on the latter's promotion to president, 1773.

11. Guillaume-Henri-Charles de Goyon d'Arzac (1740–1773–1775–   ). Advocate, son of C. de Goyon d'Arzac; succeeded J. A. de Cursol, who resigned in 1773.

12. Philippe-Marie de Laroze (1746–1771–1775–1799). Eldest son of counsellor J. S. de Laroze; object of quarrels in 1775 (see above, pp. 13, 26, 197); became president in the court of aids, 1779.

13. Succeeded J. F. de Rolland as counsellor-president on the latter's promotion to full president, 1773; succeeded by J. B. de Gascq; returned in the restored parlement of 1775 to his old office of counsellor.

14. Alexis-Etienne Maignol de Mataplane (1725–1764–1772–1772). Elder brother of counsellor E. Maignol, who later became procurator-general of the court of aids; died in office; succeeded by A. J. Drouilhet de Sigalas.

15. Dismissed 1772 (see above, p. 154); succeeded by P. J. Peynaud; returned in the restored parlement of 1775 to his old office of counsellor.

16. Pierre-Jacques Peynaud (1714–1773–1775–   ). King's procurator in the tribunal of waters and forests of Bordeaux, 1757–72; succeeded J. M. de Montalier de Grissac, who had been dismissed in 1772.

BIBLIOGRAPHY

(A) Manuscript Sources

(1) Archives Départementales de la Gironde

Apart from those referred to in the footnotes, the value of recording here every single item consulted seems limited. Several hundred items were consulted in series C alone; a mere list of numbers would be unhelpful, and a detailed description of each would be overwhelming in a work of this size. I shall, therefore, confine myself to indicating only the major items or series. The researcher wishing to follow up these references must, in any case, use the catalogues and repertories in the various depositories.

Series B (cours et juridictions), for the most part unclassified. The *arrêts* of the parlement for this period are, however, easily available, and the following sub-series have been classified:
1 B (registres du parlement)
7 B (fonds des négociants).

Series C (administration), mainly administrative correspondence and fiscal records, a mine of essential though random information on the most diverse topics.

Series E (seigneuries, communes, familles).
E (notaires, terriers)
2 E (titres de famille)
3 E (minutes notariales), the source of marriage contracts, wills, and numerous other documents. Items 3E 12675–12694, records of sales of offices collected during the Revolution, have been conveniently inventoried and summarized in the archives' typewritten *répertoire numérique* no. 100.

Series H (clergé régulier), unclassified, but certain items are accessible.

Series J (dons et acquisitions), another collection of random but often extremely useful information.

Series L (Révolution)
4L (contributions).

Series Q (domaines), for stamp tax records, etc.

Series Z (cartes et plans).

Etats-Généraux 1789 (2 dossiers).

(2) *Archives Municipales de Bordeaux*
Much the same remarks apply here as to the departmental archives.

Fonds Ancien
  DD (travaux publics)
  FF (justice)
  GG (instruction publique; état civil), including registers of births, marriages, and deaths
  HH (commerce)
Fonds Révolutionnaire
  G (contributions; administrations financières)
Fonds Baurein (inventaire de la jurade)
Fonds Albert Mengeot (la restauration à Bordeaux)
Fonds Alain D'Anglade (généalogie)
Fonds Jules Delpit (mélanges historiques), containing much diverse but very useful information
Manuscrits (the best items from various *fonds*, catalogued by X. Védère in 1938)
  135, 225, 350–57, 641, 650–56, 637–8, 709, 715, 732, 204, 806–9 (the last volumes of the 52-volume Verthamon collection of the secret registers of the parlement), 816–21, 826
Factums
  Barret *v.* Boubée, sucession Delpy, succession Lavie, Loyac *v.* Jaucen de Poissac.

(3) *Bibliothèque de la Ville de Bordeaux*
Manuscrits
  380
  383
  713 (fonds Bernadau)
    série I (V) 'Tablettes', 1787–89
    série II, 'Spicilège', vols. 3, 4, 6, 8, 15, 23, 26, 39
  828 (fonds de l'Académie)
  829 (fonds du Musée)
  847, 849–54 (lists of confiscated libraries)
  1201 (correspondance Duplessy)
  1666 (correspondance de Dupré de Saint-Maur)
  1696 (fonds Lamontaigne).

(4) *Archives Nationales*
Section Ancienne

E (conseil du Roi)	3701
F (contrôle générale)	F¹ 1955, 1956, 1961, not publicly classified
H (administrations locales)	91, 92, 93 bis, 1503, 1596
K ('monuments' historiques)	163–4, 708, 874, 910, 1164, 1237
KK 9 (*idem*, registres)	1326–7

M (mélanges, généalogie)   260, 391, 412, 427
O¹ (maison du Roi)   265–70, 352, 353, 484
Q (titres domainiaux)   264
Section Moderne
  B (élections et votes)   B III 25, 34, 73², 91, 163
  C (procés-verbaux des assemblées) 16
  W (tribunaux révolutionnaires) 400
  BB (ministère de la justice)   BB⁶ 56, 62, 80, 86, 504
                                  BB²⁰ 58

Fonds Spéciaux
  AD (archives imprimées)   I XIV 13
Fonds des Colonies
  E (personnel individuel)   18
  F³ (collection Moreau de Saint-Méry) 224
  F⁴ (bureau de contentieux)   24
  F 5 B (passagers)   39–42
Archives Privées
  AP 109 (Gourgue)
  AP 141 (Beaumont de Brivazac)
  AP 158 (d'Eprémesnil)
  AP 189 (Loménie de Brienne)
Minutier Central
  Etude CXLIII (Maupetit), 27 Oct. 1766.

(5) *Bibliothèque Nationale*
Manuscrits Français
  13733–13735   ('Histoire des événements arrivés en France . . . 1770–
                       1775', by Régnaud)
  n. a. 4386–4392   ('Journal de Nouvelles' of marquis d'Albertas)
  n. a. 6686   ('Mes Loisirs', by S. P. Hardy, vol. 6)
  n. a. 22295
Fonds FM (Franc-Maçonnerie)
  FM¹ 110
  FM² 170–78
Fonds Joly de Fleury
  1051
  1432.

(6) *Archives des Affaires Etrangères*
Mémoires et Documents, *France*
  1371, 1375, 1383, 1386, 1388, 1392, 1395, 1398, 1399, 1400, 1403, 1587, 1588,
  1589.
(7) *Archives de la France d'Outre-Mer*
Fonds de l'Indemnité (not officially classified)
Papiers Hulot de Collart (familles de la Martinique).

(8) Bibliothèque Victor Cousin, Sorbonne
Papiers de la famille de Richelieu, deuxième section: papiers du Maréchal de Richelieu

    XVI 'Languedoc, Guienne, Gascogne', lettres diverses
    XVII 'Languedoc, Guienne, Gascogne', correspondance du président de Gascq
    XVIII 'Languedoc, Guienne, Gascogne', correspondance du président de Gascq
    XXXVIII 'Languedoc, Guienne, Gascogne', correspondance du président de Gascq
    XLI, lettres diverses et pièces détachées.

(9) Bibliothèque de Port Royal
Collection Le Paige
    570, 573, 580, 820, 828, 922, 923.

(10) Bibliothèque du Lycée Louis-le-Grand
Fichier Dupont-Ferrier (élèves, 1563–1804)
    5 boxes.

(11) Bibliothèque de La Rochelle
Manuscrits
    355–8 (biographie Rochelaise)
    362 (mélanges)
    682–3 (mélanges)
    629 (lettres concernant la famille Dupaty)
    784 (lettres diverses)
    1903 (correspondance Dupaty–de Sèze).

(12) Bibliothèque Royale Albert Ier, Brussels
Manuscrits
    6862 (papiers et correspondance de Linguet concernant l'administration de la France)

(13) Private Papers
Papers of the marquis Du Paty de Clam

Archives of the notary Chalu, Bordeaux, in the keeping of Me. Jondrau, cours de Verdun.

(B) Unpublished Secondary Sources

D'Anglade, A., 'Recherches sur la compagnie des conseillers secrétaires du roi maison et couronne de France à Bordeaux (XVIIᵉ et XVIIIᵉ siècles)' (this is a manuscript *fichier* in the possession of the author)
Larboust, P. de Péguilhan de, 'Les magistrats du parlement de Toulouse à la fin

de l'ancien régime, 1775–90' (*diplôme* of the Faculty of Letters of Toulouse, 1965)

Crébassol, G., 'Le parlement Maupeou à Toulouse, 1771–1775' (*diplôme* of the Faculty of Letters of Toulouse, 1949)

Butel, P., 'La croissance commerciale bordelaise dans la seconde moitié du XVIIIᵉ siècle (doctoral thesis of the University of Paris, I, 1973), 2 v.

(C) Printed Primary Sources

Almanach historique de La Guienne (Bordeaux, 1775–90, appearing annually)

Almanach royale (Paris, 1775–90, appearing annually)

Archives historiques du département de la Gironde (Bordeaux, 1859–1932), a periodical whose object was to print historical documents

Asse, E. (ed.), *Lettres de l'abbé Galiani à Mme d'Epinay* (Paris, 1882), 2 v.

Augeard, J. M., *Mémoires secrets* (Paris, 1866)

Automne, B., *Commentaire sur les coustumes générales de la ville de Bourdeaus et pays bourdelois* (Bordeaux, 1621, 1666, 1728)

[Bachaumont], *Mémoires secrètes pour servir à l'histoire de la république des lettres en France depuis MDCCLXI jusqu'à nos jours* (Londres, 1784–89), 36 v.

Baurein, J., *Les variétés bordeloises ou essai historique et sur la topographie ancienne et moderne du diocèse de Bordeaux* (Bordeaux, 1784–86), 6 v. Another edition was published in 4 vols. in 1876

Bernadau, P., *Annales politiques, littéraires et statistiques de Bordeaux* (Bordeaux, 1803)

Besterman, T. (ed.), *Voltaire's Correspondence* (Geneva, 1953–)

Boyd, J. P. (ed.), *The Papers of Thomas Jefferson* (Princeton, 1950–), publication still in progress

Brette, A., *Recueil de documents relatifs à la convocation des états-généraux de 1789* (Paris, 1894–1915), 4 v.

Breval, J., *Remarks on several parts of Europe* (London, 1738), 2 v.

Browning, O. (ed.), *Despatches from Paris, 1784–90*, I (London, Camden third series, XVI, 1909)

Butterfield, L. H. (ed.), *The Adams Papers, series I—diaries* (Cambridge, Mass., 1961), 4 v.

Chevallier, P. (ed.), *Journal de l'assemblée de notables de 1787* (Paris, 1960)

Courteault, P. (ed.), *Chronique bordelaise, 1757–1784, de François de Lamontaigne* (Bordeaux, 1926)

Dardy, Abbé, 'Documents sur le projet d'union de la Marche à la Guyenne, 1788–89', *Mémoires de la société des sciences naturelles et archéologiques de la Creuze* (1893–94)

Denisart, J. B., *Collection de décisions nouvelles et de notions relatives à la jurisprudence actuelle* (7e ed., Paris, 1771), 4 v.

Dupaty, C. J. B. M. M., *Mémoire justificative pour trois hommes condamnés à la roue* (Paris, 1786)

——, *Lettres sur la procédure criminelle de France* (Paris, 1786)

——, *Lettres sur l'Italie* (Paris, 1788)

Encyclopédie méthodique: Jurisprudence (Paris, 1782–91), 10 v.

Essai sur la dernière révolution de l'ordre civil en France (Londres, 1782), 3 v.

Etat nominatif des pensions sur le trésor royal, imprimé par ordre de l'Assemblée Nationale (Paris, 1789–90), 5 v.

Etrennes bordeloises ou calendrier raisonné du palais (Bordeaux, 1775–90), appearing annually

Expilly, Abbé, *Dictionnaire géographique, historique et politque des Gaules et de la France* (Paris, 1762), I

Flammermont, J., *Remontrances du parlement de Paris au XVIIIe siècle* (Paris, 1888–1908), 3 v.

Grosclaude, P., *Malesherbes: nouveaux documents inédits* (Paris, 1964)

Guibert, *Voyages de Guibert, dans diverses parties de la France et en Suisse, faits en 1775,1778,1784, et 1785 . . . ouvage posthume, publié par sa veuve* (Paris, 1806)

Guyot, P. J. J. G. (*et al.*), *Répertoire universel et raisonné de jurisprudence civile, criminelle, canonique et bénéficale* (Paris, 1775–83), 64 v.

Isambert, Jourdan, and Crusy, *Recueil générale des anciennes lois françaises depuis l'an 420 jusqu'à la Révolution de 1789* (Paris, 1822–33), 31 v.

Journal de Guienne (*dédié à M. le Maréchal duc de Mouchy*) (Bordeaux, 1784–93, appearing daily), 18 v.

Lamothe, A. and D., *Coûtumes du ressort du parlement de Guienne* (Bordeaux, 1768), 2 v.

La Rochefoucauld, F. de, *Voyages en France en 1784* (Paris, 1938), 2 v.

Léouzon Le Duc, L. (ed.), *Correspondance diplomatique du baron de Staël-Holstein (1783–1799)* (Paris, 1881)

Lescure, A. de (ed.), *Correspondance secrète inédite sur Louis XVI, Marie-Antoinette, la cour et la ville de 1777 à 1792* (Paris, 1866), 2 v.

Lhéritier, M., *Les Débuts de la Révolution à Bordeaux d'après les tablettes manuscrites de Pierre Bernadau* (Paris, 1919)

Linguet, S. N. H., *Annales politiques, civiles, et littéraires du XVIIIe siècle* (Paris, 1777–92), 19v.

Marchand, J. (ed.), *Journal des états-généraux de 1789 par J. A. Creuzé-Latouche* (Paris, 1946)

Marion, M., Bencazar, J., and Caudrillier, J., *Documents relatifs à la vente des biens nationaux: département de la Gironde* (Bordeaux, 1911), 2 v.

Masson, F. (ed.), *Mémoires et lettres de François Joachim de Pierre Cardinal de Bernis (1715–1758)* (Paris, 1878), 2 v.

Ministère des Finances, *Etat détaillé des liquidations opérées par la commission chargée de répartir l'indemnité attribuée aux anciens colons de Saint-Domingue— en exécution de la loi du 30 avril 1826 et conformément aux dispositions du 9 mai suivant* (Paris, 1828–33), 6 v.

Moreau, J. N., *Mes Souvenirs* (Paris, 1898–1901), 2 v.

Nicoullaud, C. (ed.), *Récits d'une tante—mémoires de la comtesse de Boigne, née d'Osmond, publiés d'après le manuscrit original* (Paris, 1907–08), 2 v.

[Palmer], *A Four Months Tour through France* (Dublin, 1776)

Puraye, J. (ed.), *Les Mémoires du comte Louis de Gobineau* (Bruxelles, 1955)

Réimpression de l'Ancien Moniteur, Mai 1789–Novembre 1799, avec introduction historique et notes explicatives par Léon Gallois (Paris, 1840–45), 29 v.

Roton, A. de, *Les Arrêts du Grand Conseil portant dispense du marc d'or de noblesse* (Paris, 1951)

Salviat, L. F. de, *La Jurisprudence du parlement de Bordeaux, avec un recueil de questions importantes agitées en cette cour et les arrêts qui les ont décidées* (Paris, 1787)

Schelle, G. (ed.), *Oeuvres de Turgot et documents le concernant* (Paris, 1913–23), 5 v.

Soulavie, J. L., *Mémoirs historiques et politiques du règne de Louis XVI* (Paris, 1801), 6 v.

Vatel, C., *Vergniaud—manuscrits, lettres et papiers—pièces pour la plupart inédites, classées et annotées* (Paris, 1873), 2 v.

de Witte, J., *Journal de l'Abbé de Véri* (Paris, 1928–30), 2 v.

Young, A., *Travels in France, 1787–90* (ed. C. Maxwell, Cambridge, 1926)

(D) Printed Secondary Sources I: works on Bordeaux and its area

Audubert, E., *Le Régime dotal d'après la coûtume et la jurisprudence du parlement de Bordeaux* (Paris, 1918)

Bachelier, L., *Histoire du commerce de Bordeaux depuis les temps les plus reculés jusqu'à nos jours* (Bordeaux, 1861)

Baillenx, L. de, *Notice généalogique sur la famille de Marbotin du parlement de Bordeaux avec des notes sur les familles alliées* (Bordeaux, 1960)

Barckhausen, H., 'Essai sur l'administration municipal de Bordeaux sous l'ancien régime', introduction to *Inventaire-sommaire des archives municipales de Bordeaux, II, Livre des privilèges* (Bordeaux, 1878)

Barrière, P., *L'Académie de Bordeaux—centre de culture internationale au XVIIIe siècle (1712–1792)* (Bordeaux, 1951)

Basterot, Cte de, *Souvenirs d'enfance et de jeunesse—notes biographiques et ethnographiques* (Paris, 1896)

Baulny, O., 'Miranda à Bordeaux', *R. Hist. Bx.* (1966)

Bencazar, J., 'La disette à Bordeaux, 1747–8', *R. Philomat. Bx.* (1904)

——, 'Les jeux de hasard à Bordeaux, 1701–1789', ibid. (1905)

——, 'Dom Devienne historiographe de Guienne', ibid. (1906)

——, 'Fondements de la politique des vins dans la sénéchaussée de Bordeaux (XVIIIe siècle)', ibid. (1907)

——, 'Eclaircissements sur les finances de Bordeaux (XVIIIe siècle, 1701–1791)', *R. Hist. Bx.* (1916–17)

Bernadau, P., *Histoire de Bordeaux* (Bordeaux, 1837)

Betgé-Brezetz, A., 'Les archives départementales de la Gironde', *R. Hist. Bx.* (1953)

Bonnaffé, E., *Bordeaux il y a cent ans—un armateur bordelais, sa famille, et son entourage (1740–1809)* (Paris, 1887)

Boscheron des Portes, C. B. F., 'Les registres secrets du parlement de Bordeaux: essais historiques et critiques sur ce corps judiciaire depuis sa création jusqu'à sa suppression', *Revue historique de droit français et étranger*, XIII (1867)

——, *Histoire du parlement de Bordeaux depuis sa création jusqu'à sa suppression (1451–1790)* (Bordeaux, 1878), 2 v.

Boulangé, R., *Les Seigneurs de Benauges des origines à la Révolution* (Lyon, 1954)

Bourgouin, E., 'Une disette en Guienne à la fin de l'ancien régime (1777–8)', *R. Hist. Bx.* (1918–19)

Boutruche, R., 'Bordeaux et le commerce des Antilles' in S. Denis (ed.), *Nos Antilles* (Orléans, 1935)

——, *Une Société provinciale en lutte contre le régime féodal. L'alleu en Bordelais et en Bazadais du Xe au XVIIIe siècle* (Rodez, 1947)

—— (ed.), *Bordeaux de 1453 à 1715* (Bordeaux, 1966)

Brace, R. M., *Bordeaux and the Gironde* (New York, 1948)

Brives-Cazes, E., 'Le parlement de Bordeaux bureau de la grande police, 1763–7' *Actes de l'académie des sciences, belles-lettres et arts de Bordeaux* (1874)

——, *De la police des livres en Guyenne, 1713–85* (Bordeaux, 1883)

——, *Les Origines du parlement de Bordeaux* (Bordeaux, 1887)

Brouillard, R., *Des impositions extraordinaires sur le revenu pendant la Révolution (contribution patriotique—emprunts forcés) et de leur application dans la commune de Bordeaux* (Bordeaux, 1910)

——, 'Le pillage de l'hôtel Saige', *R. Philomat. Bx.* (1937)

Brun, Abbé, *L'Abbé J. P. Lapauze, Vén ∴ de la L ∴ Ang ∴ O ∴ de Bordeaux, curé de Bonzac et de Galgon, archiprêtre de Fronsac, au diocèse de Bordeaux 1750–1792* (Bordeaux, 1903)

Brutails, J. A., *Inventaire-sommaire des archives départementales de la Gironde série E* (Bordeaux, 1908)

——, *Recherches sur l'équivalence des anciennes mesures de la Gironde* (Bordeaux, 1912)

——, *Inventaire-sommaire des archives départementales de la Gironde: série 1B, 1 à 58* (Bordeaux, 1925)

Butel, P., 'Grands propriétaires et production des vins de Médoc au XVIIIe siècle', *R. Hist. Bx.* (1963)

——, 'Défrichements en Guyenne au XVIIIe siècle', *Annales du Midi* (1965)

——, 'Le trafic européen de Bordeaux de la guerre d'Amérique à la Révolution' ibid. (1966)

Campagne, M., *Une Famille bordelaise—Des Mesures de Rauzan, XVIIe et XVIIIe siècles* (Bergerac, 1904)

——, *Histoire de Bacalan* (Bergerac, 1905)

Caraman, P., 'La disette des grains et les émeutes populaires en 1773 dans la généralité de Bordeaux', *R. Hist. Bx.* (1910)

Carré, H., 'Dupaty et la correspondance de Vergniaud', *Revue universitaire* (1893)

Cavignac, J., *Jean Pellet, commerçant de gros, 1694–1772. Contribution à l'étude du négoce bordelais au XVIIIe siècle* (Paris, 1967)

——, 'Le compagnonnage dans les luttes ouvrières du XVIIIe siècle: l'exemple de Bordeaux', *Bibliothèque de l'Ecole des Chartes* (1968)

Céleste, R., 'La société philomatique de Bordeaux de 1783 à 1802', *R. Philomat. Bx.* (1897–98)

Chaperon—généalogie (Brest, 1876)

Charpentier, G., *Les Relations économiques entre Bordeaux et les Antilles au XVIIIe siècle* (Bordeaux, 1937)

Chauvot, H., *Histoire du barreau de Bordeaux, 1775–1815* (Paris, 1856)

Chavreau, P., 'La formation topographique du quartier des Chartrons', *R. Hist. Bx.* (1928–29)

Cocks, C., and Féret, E., *Bordeaux et ses vins* (Bordeaux, 1849)

Communay, A., *Le Parlement de Bordeaux, notices biographiques sur ses principaux officiers* (Bordeaux, 1887)

——, *Esquisses biographiques—les grands négociants bordelais au XVIIIe siècle* (Bordeaux, 1888)

Couderc, C., *Catalogue général des manuscrits des bibliothèques publiques de la France: départements XXIII—Bordeaux* (Paris, 1894)

Courteault, P., 'Les impressions d'une Anglaise à Bordeaux en 1785', *R. Hist. Bx.* (1911)

——, 'Autour de la Maison Gobineau', ibid. (1915)

——, *La Place Royale de Bordeaux* (Paris and Bordeaux, 1923)

——, *La Révolution et les théâtres de Bordeaux d'après des documents inédits* (Paris, 1926)

Damas, P., *Histoire de la juridiction consulaire de Bordeaux* (Bordeaux, 1947)

Dartigue-Peyrou, C., *Dupré de Saint-Maur et le problème des corvées en Guienne* (Mont-de-Marsan, 1937)

De Gères, J., *Tableau historique et méthodique des travaux et publications de l'académie de Bordeaux (depuis 1712 jusqu'en 1875)* (Bordeaux, 1877)

Delayant, L., 'Les Dupaty', *Bulletin de l'académie de La Rochelle* (1856)

Desgraves, L., 'L'intendant Claude Boucher, 1720–1743', *R. Hist. Bx.* (1952)

——, 'Les subdélégations et les subdélégués de la généralité de Bordeaux au XVIIIe siècle', *Annales du Midi* (1954)

——, *Evocation du vieux Bordeaux* (Paris, 1960)

Devienne, J. B. d'A., *Histoire de la ville de Bordeaux* (Bordeaux, 1771)

Doyle, W., 'Le prix des charges anoblissantes à Bordeaux au XVIIIe siècle', *Annales du Midi* (1968)

——, 'Aux origines de l'affaire Dupaty', *R. Hist. Bx.* (1968)

——, 'Deux parlementaires bazadais du XVIIIe siècle', *Les cahiers du Bazadais* (1969)

Dravasa, E., 'Les classes sociales au XVIIIe siècle à Bordeaux d'après les contrats de mariage', *Annales de la Faculté de Droit de Bordeaux, série economique* (1963)

Drouyn, L., *Essai généalogique sur la famille de Meslon* (Bordeaux, 1879)

Ducannès-Duval, G., *Inventaire-sommaire des archives municipales—période révolutionnaire (1789—An VIII)*, IV, (Bordeaux, 1929)

——, 'L'hôtel de Ragueneau', *R. Hist. Bx.* (1939)

Ducorneau, A., *Essai sur l'histoire de Bordeaux* (Bordeaux, 1844)

Féret, E., *Statistique générale du département de la Gironde, III, Biographie* (Bordeaux, 1889)

Ferradou, A., *Mémoire sur la propriété des dunes de La Teste* (Bordeaux, 1930)

——, *Le Rachat des droits féodaux en Gironde* (Bordeaux, 1928)

Flottes, P., 'Le club des Jacobins de Bordeaux', *La Révolution Française* (1916)

Forster, R., 'The noble wine-producers of the Bordelais in the eighteenth century', *Economic History Review*, second series, XIV (1961–62)

Fortier-Maire, C., *Le Président Dupaty* (Bordeaux, 1874)

Froment, T., 'Un salon parlementaire à Bordeaux au XVIIIe siècle', *R. Philomat. Bx.* (1898)

Fuchs, M., 'Le théâtre à Bordeaux de 1772 à 1790, d'après le "manuscrit Lecouvreur" ', *R. Hist. Bx.* (1940)

Garrett, C. W., 'The Moniteur of 1788', *French Historical Studies* (1968)

Gaston, J., *La Communauté des notaires à Bordeaux, 1520–1791* (Bordeaux, 1913)

Gaubran, O., *Histoire de La Réole* (La Réole, 1873)

Gaullieur, E., *Histoire du College de Guyenne* (Bordeaux, 1874)

Gouron, M., *L'Amirauté de Guienne, depuis le premier amiral anglais en Guienne jusqu'à la Révolution* (Paris, 1938)

Gradis, H., *Histoire de Bordeaux* (Paris, 1838)

Gras, M. and Gouget, A., *Archives départementales de la Gironde: inventaire des archives civiles, série C, nos. 1–3132 (Intendance et bureau des finances)* (Paris, 1877)

Grellet-Dumazeau, A., *La Société bordelaise sous Louis XV et le salon de Mme Duplessy* (Bordeaux and Paris, 1897)

Guignard, F., *Histoire de Castillon-sur-Dordogne (l'une des filleules de Bordeaux) et de la région Castillonaise depuis les origines jusqu'à 1870* (Paris and Laval, 1912)

Guillaumin, T. A., *Le Parlement de Bordeaux sous Louis XV* (Bordeaux, 1878)

Guillon, E., *Les Châteaux historiques et vinicoles de la Gironde, avec la description des communes, la nature de leurs vins et la désignation des principaux crus* (Bordeaux, 1866–69), 4 v.

Hubrecht, G., 'Les colonies et le port de Bordeaux au XVIIIe siècle', *Annales de droit et de sciences sociales* (1934–36)

——, 'Notes pour servir à l'histoire de la franc–maçonnerie à Bordeaux', *R. Hist. Bx.* (1954)

Joinville, P. de, *Le Commerce de Bordeaux au XVIIIe siècle* (Paris, 1908)

Jullian, C., *Histoire de Bordeaux depuis les origines jusqu'en 1895* (Bordeaux, 1895)

Kehrig, H., *Le Privilège des vins à Bordeaux jusqu'en 1789* (Paris and Bordeaux, 1886)

Labadie, E., 'Les almanachs bordelais du XVIe au XIXᵉ siècles', *R. Hist. Bx.* (1916)

Labat, G., 'Beaumarchais à Bordeaux: octobre, novembre et décembre 1782', *Actes de l'académie des sciences belles-lettres et arts de Bordeaux* (1904)

Labraque-Bordenave, M. V., 'Histoire des députés de Bordeaux au conseil du commerce, au comité national, et à l'agence commercial de Paris, 1700–1793', ibid. (1889)

Lacave Laplange Barris, *Dictionnaire de l'émigration gasconne* (Auch, 1919)

Lanoire, E., 'Cagliostro à Bordeaux', *R. Philomat. Bx.* (1932)

Larouverade, de, *Les dernières années du parlement de Bordeaux (1771–90)* (Bordeaux, 1867)

Lassalle, G., 'L'administration financière de Dupré de Saint-Maur en Guyenne (1776–1784)', *Positions des thèses de l'Ecole des Chartes* (1949)

Leroux, A., *Les Religionnaires de Bordeaux de 1685 à 1802* (Bordeaux, 1920)

——, *Etude critique sur le XVIIIe siècle à Bordeaux* (Bordeaux, 1921)

Lévy-Schneider, L., *L'Application du concordat par un prélat d'ancien régime. Mgr Champion de Cicé* (Paris, 1921)

Lewden, L., 'Villegouge', *R. Hist. Bx.* (1933)

Lhéritier, M., *Histoire des rapports de la chamber de commerce de Guienne avec les intendants, le parlement, et les jurats de 1705 à 1791* (Bordeaux, 1913)

——, 'La Révolution à Bordeaux de 1789 à 1791—la transition de l'ancien au nouveau régime', *R. Hist. Bx.* (1915–17)

——, *Tourny* (Paris, 1920), 2 v.

——, *La Révolution à Bordeaux dans l'histoire de la Révolution française: La fin de l'ancien régime et la préparation des états-généraux (1787–89)* (Paris, 1942)

Malvezin, C. T., *Histoire du commerce de Bordeaux des origines à nos jours* (Bordeaux, 1892), 4 v.

Marion, M., *L'Impôt sur le revenu au XVIIIe siècle, principalement en Guyenne* (Toulouse and Paris, 1901)

——, 'Une épisode du mouvement de 1789 à Bordeaux', *Revue d'histoire moderne et contemporaine* (1901–02)

——, 'Etat des classes rurales au XVIIIe siècle dans la généralité de Bordeaux' *Revue des études historiques* (1902)

Marionneau, C., *Victor Louis—sa vie, ses travaux* (Bordeaux, 1881)

——, *Les Salons bordelais ou expositions des beaux-arts à Bordeaux au XVIIIe siècle (1771–1787)* (Bordeaux, 1883)

Martin, G., 'Les intendants de Guyenne, au XVIIIe siècle, et les privilèges des vins bordelais', *R. Hist. Bx.* (1908)

Maupassant, J. de, 'Un grand armateur de Bordeaux: Abraham Gradis (1699–1780)', *R. Hist. Bx.* (1913–14)

Meaudre de Lapouyade, *Un Maître flamand à Bordeaux—Lonsing (1739–1799)* (Paris, 1911)

——, 'Impressions d'une Allemande à Bordeaux en 1785', *R. Hist. Bx.* (1911)

Meller, P., *Les Anciennes Familles de la Gironde* (Bordeaux, 1895–96), 2 v.

——, *Les Gentilshommes de la sénéchaussée de Libourne en 1789* (Libourne, 1901)

——, *Armorial du Bordelais, sénéchausées de Bordeaux Bazas et Libourne* (Paris, 1906), 3 v.

——, *Etat civil des familles bordelaises avant la Révolution—mariages* (Bordeaux, 1909)

——, *Généalogie de Paty* (Bordeaux, n.d.)—a work completed by comte de Saint-Saud, of which only five copies were ever produced

——, *Essais généalogiques* (familles de Baritault, Brivazac, Dudon, Duroy, Peyronnet) (undated phamphlets)

Mesuret, R., 'Antoni Ponz à Bordeaux en 1783', *R. Hist. Bx.* (1959)

Nicolaï, A., *Histoire de l'organisation judiciaire à Bordeaux et en Guyenne, et du barreau de Bordeaux du XVIIIe siècle au XIXe siècle* (Bordeaux, 1892)

——, 'Etude des moeurs bordelaises au XVIIe siècle et au XVIIIe siècle—la passion des cartes', *R. Philomat. Bx.* (1905)

——, *Au bon vieux temps: chronique économique du XVIIIe siècle pour Bordeaux et la Guienne* (Bordeaux, 1906)

——, *Essai statistique sur le clergé, les communautés religieuses, la noblesse, la magistrature, la bourgeoisie, les corporations et les mouvements de la population à Bordeaux au XVIIIe siècle, 1700–1800* (Paris and Bordeaux, 1909)

O'Gilvy, G., *Nobiliaire de Guienne et Gascogne* (Bordeaux, 1856–83), 3 v., but a later vol. was added by P. J. Bourrousse de Laffore

O'Reilly, Abbé, *Histoire complète de Bordeaux* (Paris, 1863), 6 v. (2nd ed.)

Pariset, F. G. (ed.), *Bordeaux au XVIIIe siècle* (Bordeaux, 1968)

Petit, D., *La Capatalat de Buch pendant la Révolution française (1789–1804)* (Bordeaux, 1909)

Petit, D. and D'Anglade, A., *La Seigneurie de Castres, Portets, et Arbanats* (Hossegor, 1934)

Plantadis, J., *L'Agitation autonomiste de Guienne et le mouvement fédéraliste des Girondins en Limousin (1787–93)* (Brive, 1910), originally published as a series of articles in *Bulletin de la société des lettres, sciences et arts de la Corrèze* (1908–10)

Plantey, A., 'Un exemple de continuité des principes du droit public français: l'affaire des alluvions (Bordeaux, 1781–6)', *Revue de droit public et de science politique*, LXXI (1955)

Poussou, J. P., 'Expérience aquitaine et méthodologie des contrats de mariage au XVIIIe siècle', *Annales du Midi* (1964)

——, 'Les structures foncières et sociales des vignobles de Caudéran et du Bouscat en 1771', in *Vignobles et vins d'Aquitaine, histoire, économie, art* (Bordeaux, 1970)

Quet, S., *L'Élection de Guienne au XVIIIe siècle* (Bordeaux, 1937)

——, 'La cour des aides de Guyenne: ses rapports avec le parlement de Bordeaux', *R. Hist. Bx.* (1939–40)

Rebsomen, A., 'Passage à Bordeaux des comtes d'Artois et de Provence (1777–1782)', *R. Hist. Bx.* (1923)

Renouard, Y. (ed.), *Bordeaux sous les rois d'Angleterre* (Bordeaux, 1965)

Ribadieu, H., *Histoire de Bordeaux pendant le règne de Louis XVI* (Bordeaux, 1853)

Richard, G., 'La noblesse commerçante à Bordeaux et à Nantes au XVIIIe siècle', *L'Information historique* (1958)

Roche, D., 'Milieux académiques provinciaux et société des lumières. Trois académies provinciales au XVIIIe siècle: Bordeaux, Dijon, Châlons-sur-Marne', in G. Bollème *et al.*, *Livre et société dans la France du XVIIIe siècle*, I (Paris—La Haye, 1965)

Rouxel, M., *La Compétence de la cour des jurats de Bordeaux* (Bordeaux, 1949)

Saint-Saud, J. M. H. A. d'A. de, *Essais généalogiques périgourdines* (Paris, 1934)

Shackleton, R., *Montesquieu, a Critical Biography* (Oxford, 1960)

Védère, X., 'Les allées de Tourny', *R. Hist. Bx.* (1930–31)

——, *Archives municipales de Bordeaux: catalogue des manuscrits* (Bordeaux, 1938)

Vivie, A., *Histoire de la Terreur à Bordeaux* (Bordeaux, 1877), 2 v.

Wheaton, R. B., 'Notes critiques sur "Les classes sociales au XVIIIe siècle à Bordeaux d'après les contrats de mariage",' *Revue Historique* (1969)

(D) Printed Secondary Sources II: works on the parlements and judicial history

Amiable, L., *La Franc-maçonnerie et la magistrature en France à la veille de la Révolution* (Aix, 1894)

Antoine, M., *Le Conseil du roi sous le règne de Louis XV* (Paris—Genève, 1970)

Bastard d'Estang, H. de, *Les Parlements de France* (Paris, 1857), 2 v.

Bickart, R., *Les Parlements et la notion de souveraineté nationale au XVIIIe siècle* (Paris, 1932)

Bien, D. D., *The Calas Affair: persecution, toleration and heresy in eighteenth-century Toulouse* (Princeton, 1961)

Bisson, P., *L'Activité d'un procureur-général au parlement de Paris à la fin de l'ancien régime: les Joly de Fleury* (Paris, 1961)

Bluche, F., *Les Magistrats du parlement de Paris au XVIIIe siècle, 1715–1771* (Paris, 1960)

——, '*L'Origine des magistrats du parlement de Paris au XVIIIe siècle (1715–1771)—dictionnaire généalogique* (Paris, 1956)

E. Carcassonne, *Montesquieu et le problème de la constitution française au XVIIIe siècle* (Paris, 1927)

Carré, H., 'Les fêtes d'une réaction parlementaire, 1774–1775', *La Révolution française*, XXIII (1892)

——, 'Turgot et le rappel des parlements', ibid., XLIII (1902)

——, 'La "mise en vacances" des parlements', *Revue d'histoire moderne*, IX (1908)

——, *La Fin des parlements, 1788–90* (Paris, 1912)

Cobban, A., 'The *parlements* of France in the eighteenth century', *History*, n.s. XXXV (1950), reprinted in his *Aspects of the French Revolution* (London, 1969)

Colombet, A., *Les Parlementaires Bourguignons à la fin du XVIIIe siècle* (Dijon, 1937)

Curzon, A. de, *L'Enseignement du droit français dans les universités de France aux XVIIe et XVIIIe siècles* (Paris, 1920)

Delbeke, F., *L'Action politique et sociale des avocats au XVIIIe siècle* (Louvain, 1927)

Doyle, W., 'The parlements of France and the breakdown of the ancien régime, 1771–88', *French Historical Studies* (1970)

Dubédat, J. B., *Histoire du parlement de Toulouse* (Toulouse, 1885), 2 v.

Duboul, A., *La Fin du parlement de Toulouse* (Toulouse, 1890)

Egret, J., *Le Parlement de Dauphiné et les affaires publiques dans la deuxième moitié du XVIIIe siècle* (Grenoble, 1942), 2 v.

——, 'L'opposition aristocratique en France au XVIIIe siècle', *L'Information Historique* (1949)

——, 'L'aristocratie parlementaire française à la fin de l'ancien régime', *Revue Historique* (1952)

——, *La Pré-Révolution française, 1787–88* (Paris, 1962)

——, *Louis XV et l'opposition parlementaire, 1715–1774* (Paris, 1970)

Esmein, A., *Cours élémentaire d'histoire du droit français* (Paris, 1895), 2nd ed.

Esmonin, E., *Etudes sur la France des XVIIe et XVIIIe siècles* (Paris, 1964)

Estignard, A., *Le Parlement de Franche-Comté, 1674–90* (Paris, 1892), 2 v.

Flammermont, J., *Le Chancelier Maupeou et les parlements* (Paris, 1883)

Floquet, P. A., *Histoire du parlement de Normandie* (Rouen, 1840–43), 7 v.

Foisset, T., *Le Président de Brosses: histoire des lettres et des parlements au XVIIIe siècle* (Paris, 1842)

Ford, F. L., *Robe and Sword: the regrouping of the French aristocracy after Louis XIV* (Cambridge, Mass., 1953)

Frondeville, H. de, *Les Présidents du parlement de Normandie* (Rouen, 1953)

Glasson, E., 'Les examens d'entrée dans l'ancienne magistrature', *Revue du Palais*, I (1897)

——, *Le Parlement de Paris* (Paris, 1901), 2 v.

Gruder, V., *The Royal Provincial Intendants: a governing élite in eighteenth century France* (Ithaca, New York, 1968)

Hardy, J. D., Jr, *Judicial Politics in the Old Régime: the parlement of Paris during the regency* (Baton Rouge, La., 1967)

Hayot, E., 'Les officiers du conseil souverain de la Martinique et leurs successeurs les conseillers de la cour d'appel, 1675–1830', *Mémoires de la société d'histoire de la Martinique*, I (1964)

Hudson, D. C., 'The parlementary crisis of 1763 in France and its consequences', *Canadian Journal of History* (1972)

——, 'In defense of reform: French government propaganda during the Maupeou crisis', *French Historical Studies* (1973)

Jacomet, P., *Vicissitudes et chutes du parlement de Paris* (Paris, 1954)

Krug-Basse, J., *Histoire du parlement de Lorraine et Barrois* (Paris, 1899)

Lacombe, B. de, *La Résistance janséniste et parlementaire au temps de Louis XV: l'Abbé Nigon de Berty (1702–1774)* (Paris, 1948)

La Cuisine, E. F. de, *Le Parlement de Bourgogne depuis son origine jusqu'à sa chute* (Paris, 1864), 3 v.

Lardé, G., *Une Enquête sur les vingtièmes au temps de Necker. Histoire des remontrances du parlement de Paris (1777–1778)* (Paris, 1920)

Le Moy, A., *Le Parlement de Bretagne et le pouvoir royal au XVIIIᵉ siècle* (Paris—Angers, 1909)

——, *Remontrances du parlement de Bretagne au XVIIIᵉ siècle* (Paris—Angers, 1909)

Léonce de Lavergne, *Les Assemblées provinciales sous Louis XVI* (Paris, 1879), 2nd ed.

Ligou, D., 'La cour des aides de Montauban à la fin du XVIIIᵉ siècle', *Annales du Midi* (1952)

Mahuet, H. de, *La Cour souveraine de Lorraine et Barrois (1641–1790)* (Nancy, 1959)

Marion, M., *La Bretagne et le duc d'Aiguillon, 1753–70* (Paris, 1898)

——, *Le Garde des sceaux Lamoignon et la réforme judiciaire de 1788* (Paris, 1905)

——, *Les Impôts directs sous l'ancien régime, principalement au XVIIIᵉ siècle* (Paris, 1909)

Maupeou, J. de, *Le Chancelier Maupeou* (Paris, 1942)

Metzger, P., *Contribution à l'étude de deux réformes judiciaires du XVIIIᵉ siècle. Le conseil supérieur et le grand baillage de Lyon (1771–1774–1788)* (Lyon, 1913)

Paulhet, J. C., 'Les parlementaires Toulousains à la fin du XVIIᵉ siècle', *Annales du Midi* (1964)

Piétri, F., *La Réforme de l'état au XVIIIᵉ siècle* (Paris, 1935)

Pillot, G. M. L., *Histoire du parlement de Flandres* (Douai, 1849), 2 v.

Pocquet, B., *Le Duc d'Aiguillon et La Chalotais* (Paris, 1900–01), 3 v.

Raynal, J., *Histoire des institutions judiciaires* (Paris, 1964)

Robinne, P., 'Les magistrats du parlement de Normandie à la fin du XVIIIᵉ siècle (1774–1790)', thesis of the *Ecole des Chartes*, summarized in *Annales de Normandie* (1967)

Rogister, J. M. J., 'New light on the fall of Chauvelin', *EHR* (1967)

Rothney, J., *The Brittany Affair and the Crisis of the Ancien Régime* (New York, 1969)

Rousselet, M., *Histoire de la magistrature française des origines à nos jours* (Paris, 1957), 2 v.

Seligman, E., *La Justice en France pendant la Révolution* (Paris, 1901)

Semichon, E., *Les Réformes sous Louis XVI: assemblées provinciales et parlements* (Paris, 1876)

Shennan, J. H., 'The political role of the parlement of Paris, 1715–23', *Historical Journal* (1965)

——, 'The political role of the parlement of Paris under Fleury', *EHR* (1966)

——, *The Parlement of Paris* (1968)

Villers, R., *L'Organisation du parlement de Paris et des conseils supérieurs d'après la réforme de Maupeou, 1771–74* (Paris, 1937)

Wattine, A., *L'Affaire des Trois Roués* (Paris, 1921)

——, *Magistrats célèbres du XVIIIᵉ siècle* (Paris, 1941)

Wolff, L., *Le Parlement de Provence au XVIIIᵉ siècle* (Paris, 1920)

(E) *Printed Secondary Sources III: general works*

Ambrosi, G., 'Aperçus sur la répartition et la perception de la taille au XVIIIᵉ siècle', *Revue d'histoire moderne et contemporaine* (1961)

Ardascheff, P., *Les Intendants de province sous Louis XVI* (Paris, 1909)

Barber, E., *The Bourgeoisie in Eighteenth century France* (Princeton, N.J., 1956)

Behrens, C. B. A., 'Nobles, privileges and taxes in France at the end of the Ancien Régime', *Economic History Review* (1963)

——, *The Ancien Régime* (London, 1967)

Biré, E., *Journal d'un bourgeois de Paris pendant la Terreur* (Paris, 1895), 5 v.

Bloch, M., 'La lutte pour l'individualisme agraire dans la France du XVIIIᵉ siècle', *Annales d'histoire économique et sociale* (1930)

——, *Les Caractères originaux de l'histoire rurale française* (2nd ed., Paris, 1964), 2 v.

Bluche, F. and Durye, P., *L'anoblissement par les charges avant 1789* (Paris, 1962), 2 v.

Bordes, M., *D'Etigny et l'administration de l'intendance d'Auch* (Auch, 1957), 2 v.

——, 'Les intendants sous Louis XV', *Revue historique* (1960)

——, 'Les intendants éclairés de la fin de l'Ancien Régime', *Revue d'histoire économique et sociale* (1961)

——, *La Réforme municipale du contrôleur-général de Laverdy et son application, 1764–1771* (Toulouse, 1967)

Bosher, J. F., *The Single Duty Project: a study of the movement for a French customs union in the eighteenth century* (London, 1964)

Braesch, F., *1789: l'année cruciale* (Paris, 1940)

Carré, H., *La Noblesse de France et l'opinion publique au XVIIIᵉ siècle* (Paris, 1920)

Chaix d'Est Ange, G., *Dictionnaire des familles francaises, anciennes ou notables à la fin du XIXᵉ siècle* (Evreux, 1903–   ), up to letter F

Champion, E., *La France d'après les cahiers de 1789* (Paris, 1897)

Chapuisat, E., *Necker, 1732–1804* (Paris, 1938)

Chérest, A., *La Chute de l'Ancien Régime, 1787–9* (Paris, 1884–86), 3 v.

Cobban, A., *A History of Modern France* (London, 1957), v. I

——, *The Social Interpretation of the French Revolution* (Cambridge, 1965)

——, *Aspects of the French Revolution* (London, 1969)

Cole, H., *First Gentleman of the Bedchamber: the life of the Duc de Richelieu, 1696–1788* (London and New York, 1965)

    Dakin, D., *Turgot and the Ancien Régime in France* (London, 1938)

Darnton, R., *Mesmerism and the End of the Enlightenment in France* (Cambridge, Mass., 1968)

——, 'Le lieutenant de police J.-P. Lenoir, la guerre des farines et l'approvisionnement de Paris à la veille de la Révolution', *Revue d'histoire moderne et contemporaine* (1969)

——, 'The memoirs of Lenoir, Lieutenant de Police of Paris, 1774–1785', *EHR* (1970)

Daumard, A. and Furet, F., *Structures et relations sociales à Paris au milieu du XVIIIᵉ siècle* (Paris, 1961)

Davies, A., 'The origins of the French peasant revolution of 1789', *History* (1964)

Dawson, P., 'The bourgeoisie de robe in 1789', *French Historical Studies* (1965)

Debien, G., *La Société coloniale aux XVIIᵉ et XVIIIᵉ siècles—les colons de Saint-Domingue et la Révolution—essai sur le club Massiac (août 1789–août 1792)* (Paris, 1953)

D'Estrée, P., *La Vieillesse de Richelieu (1758–1788)* (Paris, 1921)

Dienne, Cte de, *Histoire du dessêchement des lacs et marais en France avant 1789* (Paris, 1891)

Dion, R., *Histoire de la vigne et du vin de France des origines au XIVᵉ siècle* (Paris, 1959)

Doyle, W., 'Was there an aristocratic reaction in pre-revolutionary France?', *Past and Present*, 57 (1972)

Droz, J., *Histoire du règne de Louis XVI* (Paris, 1839), 3 v.

Du Puy de Clinchamps, P., *La Noblesse* (Paris, 1959)

Faure, E., *12 mai 1776: la disgrâce de Turgot* (Paris, 1961)

Faÿ, B., *Louis XVI ou la fin d'un monde* (Paris, 1955)

Forster, R., *The Nobility of Toulouse in the Eighteenth century: a social and economic study* (Baltimore, 1960)

——, 'The provincial noble: a reappraisal', *American Historical Review* (1963)

——, 'The nobility during the French Revolution', *Past and Present*, 37 (1967)

Gay, P., *Voltaire's Politics: the poet as realist* (Princeton, 1958)

Godechot, J., *Les Institutions de la France sous la Révolution et l'Empire* (Paris, 1968), 2nd ed.

Goodwin, A., 'Calonne, the assembly of French Notables, and the "révolte nobiliaire" of 1788', *EHR* (1946)

——, 'The social origins and privileged status of the French eighteenth-century nobility', *Bulletin of the John Rylands Library* (1964–65)

Goubert, P., *Beauvais et le Beauvaisis de 1600 à 1730: contribution à l'histoire sociale de la France du XVIIᵉ siècle* (Paris, 1960)

——, *L'Ancien Régime*, (Paris, 1969–73), 2 v.

Grassby, R. B., 'Social status and commercial enterprise under Louis XIV', *Economic History Review* (1960)

Greer, D., *The Incidence of the Terror during the French Revolution* (Cambridge, Mass., 1935)

——, *The Incidence of the Emigration during the French Revolution* (Cambridge, Mass., 1951)

Grosclaude, P., *Malesherbes, témoin et interprètre de son siècle* (Paris, 1961)

Hufton, O. H., *Bayeux in the late Eighteenth Century: a social study* (Oxford, 1967)

Hyslop, B. F., *A Guide to the General Cahiers of 1789* (New York, 1936)

Labrousse, C. E., *La Crise de l'économie française à la fin de l'Ancien Régime et au début de la Révolution* (Paris, 1944)

La Chenaye Desbois and Badier, *Dictionnaire de la noblesse* (Paris, 1863–76)

Lacour-Gayet, R., *Calonne: financier, réformateur, contre-révolutionnaire, 1734–1802* (Paris, 1963)

Lavaquery, E., *Necker, fourrier de la Révolution, 1732–1804* (Paris, 1933)

Lefebvre, G., *The Coming of the French Revolution* (Princeton, N.J., 1947)

——, *Etudes Orléanaises, I: contribution à l'étude des structures sociales à la fin du XVIIIᵉ siècle* (Paris, 1962)

Leroy Ladurie, E., *Les Paysans de Languedoc* (Paris, 1966), 2 v.

Lesort, A., 'La question de la corvée des grands chemins sous Louis XVI après la chute de Turgot, 1776–1786', in *Ministère de l'instruction publique et des beaux arts, comité des travaux historiques et scientifiques, section d'histoire moderne (depuis 1715) et d'histoire contemporaine, VII, études et documents divers* (1922)

Lough, J., *An Introduction to Eighteenth-century France* (London, 1960)

Lousse, E., *La Société d'Ancien Régime: organisation et représentation corporatives,* I (Louvain, 1962)

Mackrell, J. Q. C., *The Attack on 'Feudalism' in Eighteenth-century France* (London, 1973)

McManners, J., *French Ecclesiastical Society under the Ancien Regime: a study of Angers in the eighteenth century* (Manchester, 1960)

——, 'France' in A. Goodwin (ed.), *The European Nobility in the Eighteenth Century* (London, 1953)

Macloy, S. T., *The Humanitarian Movement in Eighteenth century France* (Lexington, Ky., 1957)

Mandrou, R., *La France aux XVIIᵉ et XVIIIᵉ siècles* (Paris, 1967)

Marion, M., *Machault d'Arnouville: étude sur l'histoire du contrôle-général des finances de 1749 à 1754* (Paris, 1891)

——, *La Vente des biens nationaux pendant la Révolution* (Paris, 1908)

——, *Histoire financière de la France depuis 1715: I, 1715–1789* (Paris, 1914)

——, *Dictionnaire des institutions de la France aux XVIIᵉ et XVIIIᵉ siècles* (Paris, 1923)

Matthews, G. T., *The Royal General Farms in Eighteenth century France* (New York, 1958)

Méthivier, H., *L'Ancien Régime* (Paris, 1961)

——, *Le Siècle de Louis XV* (Paris, 1965)

——, *La Fin de l'Ancien Régime* (Paris, 1970)

Meyer, J., *La Noblesse bretonne au XVIIIᵉ siècle* (Paris, 1966), 2 v.

Mornet, D., 'Les enseignements des bibliothèques privées au XVIIIᵉ siècle', *Revue d'histoire littéraire de la France* (1910)

——, *Les Origines intellectuelles de la Révolution française (1715–1787)* (Paris, 1933)

Namier, L. B., *The Structure of Politics at the Accession of George III* (London, 1929)

Olivier-Martin, F., *L'Organisation corporative de la France d'Ancien Régime* (Paris, 1938)

Pares, R., *War and Trade in the West Indies* (Oxford, 1936)

Reinhard, M., 'Elite et noblesse dans la seconde moitié du XVIIIᵉ siècle', *Revue d'histoire moderne et contemporaine* (1956)

Renouvin, P., *Les Assemblées provinciales de 1787* (Paris, 1921)

Robert, A., Cougny, G., and Bourloton, E., *Dictionnaire des parlementaires français* (Paris, 1891), 5 v.

Robin, P., *La Compagnie des secrétaires du Roi (1351–1751)* (Paris, 1933)

Rocquain, F., *L'Esprit révolutionnaire avant la Révolution, 1715–87* (Paris,) 1878

Roupnel, G., *La Ville et la campagne au XVIIᵉ siècle: étude svr les populations du pays dijonnais* (Paris, 1955), 2nd ed.

Sagnac, P., *La Formation de la société française moderne* (Paris, 1946), 2 v.

Sée, H., *La France économique et sociale au XVIIIᵉ siècle* (Paris, 1933)

Sentou, J., 'Impôts et citoyens actifs à Toulouse au début de la Révolution', *Annales du Midi* (1948)

——, *Fortunes et groupes sociaux à Toulouse sous la Révolution: essai d'histoire statistique* (Toulouse, 1969)

——, *La Fortune immobilière des Toulousains et la Révolution* (Paris, 1970)

Sevin, A., *Le Défenseur du roi: Raymond de Sèze, 1748–1828* (Paris, 1936)

Soboul, A., *La France à la veille de la Révolution* (Paris, 1966)

——, 'La Révolution française et la féodalité', *Annales historiques de la Révolution française* (1968)

——, 'La Révolution française et la féodalité: notes sur le prélèvement féodal', *Revue historique* (1968)

Taylor, G. V., 'Noncapitalist wealth and the origins of the French Revolution', *American Historical Review* (1967)

Tocqueville, A. de, *L'Ancien Régime et la Revolution* (ed. J. P. Mayer, Paris, 1953), 2 v.

Vignon, E. J. M., *Etudes historiques sur l'administration des voies publiques en France aux XVIIᵉ et XVIIIᵉ siècles* (Paris, 1826), 3 v.

Weulersse, G., *Le Mouvement physiocratique en France de 1756 à 1770* (Paris, 1910)

——, *La Physiocratie sous les ministères de Turgot et de Necker (1774–1781)* (Paris, 1950)

——, *La Physiocratie à la fin du règne de Louis XV (1770–1774)* (Paris, 1959)

Zeller, G., *Aspects de la politique française sous l'Ancien Régime* (Paris, 1964)

INDEX

absenteeism, 37, 104, 311
absolutism, 217
academy (of Bordeaux), 2, 96, 132, 133, 136
account books, 96–7
Acul (Saint-Domingue), 102
Adams, 2–3, 130, 165, 174n.
admiralty (court of), 25, 31, 47, 50n.
Adour (river), 74
advocates, 6, 14, 24, 38, 133, 134, 147–8, 160, 162, 164, 166, 186, 187, 189, 270–1, 274, 275, 276, 279, 305, 313
advocates-general, 6, 27, 43, 44, 45, 148, 161, 180, 190, 194, 287, 288, 305, 308
Agassac, 75, 88, 129
age (of magistrates), 24–5, 31, 37, 38, 44; (at marriage), 117
Agen, 12, 61, 236, 290, 299
Agenais, 6, 19, 61, 66, 68, 78, 128, 204, 291
agencement, 119, 120
agricultural society, 96, 132
agrières, 78, 80, 81
aids, court of: of Bordeaux, 5, 14, 16, 25, 28, 29, 43, 47, 48, 59, 61, 122, 124, 127, 134, 154, 166, 172, 190, 233, 234, 270, 273, 274, 275, 276, 277, 278, 281, 312; of Montauban, 213; of Paris, 145, 160, 227
Aiguesmortes, 87
Aiguilhe, 75, 76, 150
Aiguillon: family, 16; duc d', 144, 153, 159, 173
Aix, parlement of, 18, 151
Albret, 12, 15; cours d', 111
Alembert, 138
Alesme: family, 16, 23; Honorine Etiennette, 68
Aligre, 238
alluvions, 3, 81, 130, 188, 197, 198, 212, 220, 226, 237, 244, 250–60, 263n., 268, 297, 309
Ambarès, 70, 250, 252
ambassadors, 256; British, 213, 258, 260; Swedish, 216n., 309
Ambès, 71, 88, 128, 235, 250, 252; bec d', 87, 251, 252
Ambloy, 68

American society (resident at Bordeaux), 102
Americans, 211, 212, 271
Angers, 313
Angoumois, 290
annuities, 58, 105, 106; see also *rentes*
Aoudat, 71
Arbanats, 87, 94
Arcachon (bassin d'), 73, 74
archbishop: of Bordeaux, 4, 46, 70, 79; *see also* Rohan; Champion de Cicé
Arcins, 71, 88
Argenson, 8
arrêts de règlement, 7
Arsac, 88
Artois: comte d', 251, 264
assemblies of chambers: general, 26, 38, 43, 163, 172, 178, 184, 186, 306; (10 Apr. 1772), 152; (10 Mar. 1775), 164; (3 Aug. 1775), 169; (12 Aug. 1775), 169; (12 July 1779), 234; (13 Nov. 1779), 176; (16 Feb. 1780), 179–80; (23 Feb. 1780), 180; (3 Mar. 1780), 181; (7 Mar. 1781), 184, 200n.; (9 Mar. 1781), 184, 200n.; (20 July 1781), 185; (20 Feb. 1782), 187; (6 Aug. 1783), 193; (8 Aug. 1783), 193; (13 Aug. 1783), 193; (24 Apr. 1784), 253; (28 Apr. 1784), 237; (23 July 1784), 195–6; (Jan. 1785), 228; (8 Apr. 1785), 196; (11 Jan. 1786), 254; (18 Aug. 1787), 267; (21 Dec. 1787), 272; (6 May 1788) 276; (20 Nov. 1788), 280, 286
assignats, 54
Atlantic, 103
Ayen, 266, 267, 268, 298

Bacalan: family, 14, 48; J., 47
Bacon, 137
Bagnères, 129
banalités, 77
bankruptcy, 3, 58, 104, 105, 106, 124, 213, 223
Barbeguière: family, 66; counsellor, 150, 152
Bardineau, 131

345